The Second Creek War

INDIANS OF THE SOUTHEAST
Series Editors

Michael D. Green
University of North Carolina

Theda Perdue
University of North Carolina

Advisory Editors

Leland Ferguson
University of South Carolina

Mary Young
University of Rochester

"Ellisor's book should appeal to all those interested in Alabama history, for it provides a revealing new look at the complexity of the antebellum society and of Indian removal."
—Christina Snyder, *Alabama Review*

"With lucid prose and convincing arguments, Ellisor recovers the difficulties that troubled both Creeks and white Americans only twenty years prior to the American Civil War. . . . *The Second Creek War*'s substantive contribution to the evolving field of southern Native American history joins those of Claudio Saunt, Robbie Ethridge, Andrew Frank, and Cynthia Cumfer, among others. Like theirs, Ellisor's work deserves high praise."
—Thomas Chase Hagood, *Florida Historical Quarterly*

"*The Second Creek War* throws new light on Creek and Seminole removal and on the development of class in the early to mid-nineteenth-century South."
—Steven J. Peach, H-AmIndian

"Ellisor's book sheds new light on a very misunderstood period of our nation's history, an era that has been unfairly forgotten in many American textbooks."
—Al Hemingway, *Military Heritage*

"Ellisor's complex approach offers historians of the early American Republic much to consider as they look to expand their understanding of the United States within the larger global processes of the nineteenth century."
—Daniel Flaherty, *Historian*

The Second Creek War

Interethnic Conflict and Collusion on a Collapsing Frontier

John T. Ellisor

UNIVERSITY OF NEBRASKA PRESS | LINCOLN

© 2010 by the Board of Regents
of the University of Nebraska

Portions of chapters 1, 5, 7, and 8 were previously published in "'Like So Many Wolves': Creek Removal in the Cherokee Country, 1835–1838," *Journal of East Tennessee History* 71 (1999): 1–24.

All rights reserved
∞
Library of Congress
Cataloging-in-Publication Data
Ellisor, John T.
The Second Creek War: interethnic conflict
and collusion on a collapsing frontier /
John T. Ellisor.
p. cm.—(Indians of the southeast)
Includes bibliographical references
and index.
ISBN 978-0-8032-2548-0 (cloth : alk. paper)
ISBN 978-1-4962-1708-0 (paper : alk. paper)
1. Creek War, 1836. I. Title.
E83.836.E44   2010
973.5'6—dc22
2010009967

Set in Quadraat by Bob Reitz.
Designed by Ray Boeche.

Contents

List of Maps	vi
Introduction: *The Second Creek War?*	1
1. Creek Politics and Confinement in New Alabama	9
2. The Cusseta Treaty of 1832	47
3. Commodifying the Creek Domain	97
4. Resistance	140
5. Rebellion	182
6. The Federal Response	228
7. Flight through Southern Georgia	264
8. Recriminations	297
9. The War Revives in New Alabama	335
10. Seeking Refuge in West Florida	371
Epilogue: *The Legacy of the Second Creek War*	417
Notes	433
Bibliography	479
Index	491

Maps

1. Alabama, 1832–36   19
2. New Alabama   20
3. Resistance and war in New Alabama   141
4. War in southern Georgia   265
5. Cherokee Nation, 1835–38   274
6. New Alabama, 1837   341
7. War in West Florida   373

The Second Creek War

Introduction
The Second Creek War?

Whoever heard of the Second Creek War? Certainly the event never appears in history textbooks, though one may occasionally encounter the term Creek War of 1836, but without any meaningful description of what that conflict actually entailed. Other accounts, monographs on Creek history or Indian removal, say a bit more, but even here the Creek War of 1836 appears as a rather insignificant police action, lasting only a matter of a few weeks. Often we see the term Creek War of 1836 written in quotation marks to downplay its significance as a real war. Other times historians refer to the conflict as the so-called Creek War of 1836. Several historians have devoted a few paragraphs of their books to the war, but they mention it only in passing as they move on to other destinations. Scholars interested in Creek history or Indian-white relations consider the war as a mere sidelight to the more important story of Creek removal.[1] Military historians, for their part, pass over the Creek conflict and set their sights on the two other removal-era wars, the Black Hawk conflict in the Old Northwest and the long and costly Seminole War in Florida.[2] Consequently, for a century and a half, no historian has explored the Creek War of 1836 in any detail. Throughout the years, this war has remained largely ignored and unappreciated, which would have pleased many of the Alabamians, Georgians, and Floridians who fought in it. Indeed, they were not proud of the event and wanted the memory of it expunged. For far too long, they have had their way.[3]

INTRODUCTION

This book proposes to drag the Creek War of 1836 out of the dustbin of history and to explore what has been ignored or even purposefully concealed. In the process, it will show that the Creek conflict was a real war, one that should be called the Second Creek War (the Creek War of 1813–14 being the first) for a number of important reasons. First, contrary to popular belief, the war was more than a sudden, desperate affair. It was the culmination of a long contest between Georgians and Creeks for land and resources. Second, the Lower Creek rebels planned the war. They executed a definite strategy for sweeping whites out of New Alabama (the Old Creek Nation), and with a little more luck, they might have drawn many other southern Indians into the struggle. Third, the Creek war was more extensive than we have been led to believe. The Creek insurgents fought engagements with whites in Alabama, Georgia, and Florida. Fourth, the war was not really short-lived. The federal and state military response to the Creek uprising, while massive, was not as successful as it appeared. The war did not actually end in July 1836, when federal commanders declared victory and as a national defense measure sent most of the Creeks off to the West. Many Indians escaped federal and state troops and continued fighting for years. In fact, Creeks took the lead in Native resistance efforts during the last stage of the Second Seminole War in Florida. Fifth, some of the Creeks avoided removal and never left their ancient homeland. For them, the war was a victory of sorts. Sixth and finally, the Second Creek War had a significant impact on Native, white, and black southerners for the remainder of the antebellum era.

More importantly, however, this book attempts to place the Second Creek War within a larger and more meaningful historical context. The Spanish philosopher José Ortega y Gasset once wrote that "History is a song that can only be sung as a whole," and this statement certainly applies to our understanding of the Second Creek War, for that event does not stand apart from a long series of other episodes and causal factors preceding it. Moreover, the war was not an ending point in and of itself. It was most certainly a climax, because it led to the forced removal of the Creeks from the Southeast, but the struggle that the war represented has continued on to the present day. The Creeks, along with all other native communities, have faced a constant process of adaptation and survival, having to choose between accommodation and resistance, or some strategy in between, to live satisfactorily in a country dominated by non-Indians and a constantly expanding and demanding world economic system, which they did not create and which contradicts so many important aspects of traditional Indian religion and culture. The Second Creek War is important in this context because it was a rebellion against the process of a people's final incorporation into the world system, not only as a depressed class of workers, but as actual merchandise themselves. Indeed, one of the most devastating features of world capitalism is its inexorable drive to commodify everything, including people, and turn it all to account.[4]

But we should not suppose that Native Americans or other colonized people have been alone in dealing with the demands of the system. During the decade of the 1830s, Native land cessions and a booming cotton market propelled a rush of settlers into the Old Southwest. Many of these newcomers moved into country still occupied by the Cherokee, Creek, Choctaw, and Chickasaw nations and built their cabins and mansions by Native villages and fields. For a few years prior to the Indian removals, these white immigrants, their black slaves, and the Native inhabitants of the land lived as neighbors. In fact, the decade of the 1830s was unique in the history of southern ethnic relations, because at no other time in the antebellum era did so many Native, white, and black southerners live in such proximity. A study of the Second Creek War and the events leading to it reveals that non-Indians, too, had to accommodate themselves to or resist the economic order on the southern frontier, and this fact forced them into varying degrees of conflict and collusion with their Indian neighbors in a grinding competition to survive, if not to prosper. The war grew out of this situation and consequently we must view it as a multiethnic phenomenon. Indeed, just as we cannot fully appreciate the war apart from its long-term causes and consequences, we cannot properly comprehend its overall importance through the perspective of either the Creeks or colonizers alone. The war was above all a human event that tells us something very interesting about all of southern society during the antebellum era.

Beyond that, it illuminates the fact that the expanding world system grinds all societies before it, remaking families and communities and challenging traditional beliefs by "subordinating all relationships to the calculus of the bottom line." Indeed, Ortega y Gasset surely knew that just as the song of history must be sung as a whole, it must be sung by many voices at once. A single section of the human choir cannot do the piece justice.[5]

A grassroots, multiethnic approach to the study of the Second Creek War and the Creek removal is also important in another respect. Lacking such a perspective, most previous studies of Indian removal in the South, as well as more general studies of federal removal policy and U.S. expansionism in the Old Southwest, present us with the traditional and rather monolithic view of white versus red, of U.S. oppression and Native victimization. Certainly we see interaction between leaders and policy makers, both Native and white, but we see or hear little from all the other people. Consequently, we are left with the overall impression of a mass of white southerners, united in their hatred and mistrust of Indians and propelled by their incessant desire to conquer new land, driving the Natives from their homes. We also see the Indians as completely different creatures, forced to retreat, leaving very little trace of themselves behind. We do not see Native, white, and black people living together as neighbors with all the complexity and diversity of human motives and emotions that always exist in such situations. We also do not see a complete account of what part this interaction between peoples on the local level played in the whole removal-era story. Therefore, our image of that time is incomplete. Certainly there is much truth in the traditional view of the removal era in southern history, but in the end it is too simplistic.[6]

The picture that emerges from this particular exploration of the Second Creek War, and the pluralistic society that produced it, is one of more complexity. This study reveals that neither whites nor Indians were united in their goals and purposes. The settlers who entered New Alabama in 1832 were divided by class, politics, and economic interests. They competed with one another and exploited one another even as they sought to extract land and resources from the Creeks.

INTRODUCTION

Furthermore, rather than uniting behind the federal government's Indian removal plan, New Alabama's whites actually stymied the process. The competitive economy they created, based as it was on the complete dispossession of the Creeks, actually tended to hold the Natives in place, draining them of their resources. This exploitation, in turn, impoverished the Indians, who were already torn by ethnic competition as well as political factionalism. Divided against themselves, the factions of Creeks did not respond to the white challenge in the same way. Some Natives destroyed themselves; others sought accommodation with whites and exploited their fellow tribe members; still more took up arms to liberate themselves from New Alabama's grinding economy and to escape removal to the West. This armed revolt was the Second Creek War, and it lasted many years, owing both to the determination of the Creek resistance fighters and the divided and competitive nature of white society. The whites, often working at cross purposes, simply could not bring the hostile Indians to bay. Finally, the conflict simply wore itself out.

Thus, it seems that the Second Creek War resulted not from the meeting of culturally homogenous and diametrically opposed societies but from the intermingling of fractious, incohesive ones. In New Alabama, this lack of unity on all sides created volatility and increased social fragmentation, which set the stage for increasing acts of violence, leading to a war of surprisingly long duration. Indeed, this fact is the great lesson of the conflict and forms the central thesis around which this exploration of the previously neglected contest unfolds.

Seen in this light, the Second Creek War fits more readily into larger historiographical contexts as well. Obviously, scholars interested in frontier studies and/or the U.S. West may find familiar patterns here. Indeed, the New Alabama situation is common to other frontier situations throughout the world, a frontier being a "territory or zone of interpretation between two distinct societies," one society indigenous and the other intrusive. The two societies almost invariably compete for control of natural resources, but just as consistently, since no one society is monolithic, rival segments develop within both groups, while at the same time members reach across the ethnic divide to form ties and alliances. Furthermore, frontiers close when one political authority finally establishes its hegemony over the zone of interaction. In the New Alabama case, some Indians reacted to the closing of their frontier, their final incorporation into the capitalist system, and their complete subjugation to white authority in just the same way other Native people around the world have done. They rose in armed rebellion.[7]

Students of Native American history will see in the social aspects of this account much that relates to the "New World" and "Middle Ground" works so popular in that field. In essence, these works contend that Native Americans were not simply passive victims of white expansionism. On the contrary, Indians often adapted themselves to the ways of their neighbors, white and black, while at the same time holding fast to the elements of their traditional culture that gave their societies coherency and strength. Similarly, non-Indians learned skills from the aboriginal inhabitants of the land that helped them survive and prosper on the frontier, which was a challenging environment, a "New World," for all, regardless of ethnicity.[8]

Hopefully, this book will also tie the Second Creek War more firmly into mainstream studies of southern history as well as pique the curiosity of all those southern historians who still see Indian affairs as much less important than other themes and events that for them define the real meaning of the South. Indeed, the historian John H. Peterson Jr. once warned historians and anthropologists not to view Indians in the Old South as cultural isolates removed from the mainstream of the region's history. He contended that Native, white, and black people influenced one another in various ways in the antebellum South, and he called for scholars to adopt a "conceptual framework capable of dealing with the totality of human social relations in the Southeast as they changed through time."[9] This book offers the world-system approach as that conceptual framework and even suggests that far from being relatively unimportant in southern history, Indians, and Indian removal as an event, may have done much to form that elusive worldview we call the southern personality or mentality. Beyond this, historians and scholars of all sorts should see the Second Creek War as an important episode in the removal story and in U.S. history in general, deserving of serious mention in textbooks, right alongside its close kin, the Second Seminole War.

But the Second Creek War also has its place in world history. After all, the spread of the cotton plantation regime into the Old Southwest and the drive to remove Indians and take their lands were all part of the final stage of integrating the entire South into the capitalist world system as a mature resource-producing peripheral area. This process of incorporation, in turn, helped fuel the European economy and gave a major impetus to the Market Revolution in the United States as a whole. But the prosperity of the whites of the Western world came at a cost to the Native peoples they colonized, and in the end, the Second Creek War was only one of a number of revolts by these colonized peoples against an economic system that tightened its grip on much of the planet in the nineteenth century. In this regard, the Second Creek War should be of some interest to scholars other than historians, namely those sociologists and anthropologists who study ethnic resource competition, colonial resistance movements, dependency theory, and even peasant revolts around the world.

But regardless of its historiographical import, any study of the Second Creek War demands care. The principal sources—state and federal records, newspapers, letters and county histories—often contradict one another. Local newspapers were party organs, and political considerations often colored the reporting of events. Similarly, the individuals who wrote letters to the War Department often had political and financial interests, or military careers, to protect. The authors of Senate and House reports also had their own agendas. Early county histories, while providing invaluable details about the war and local society, give us little meaningful analysis, tending to view the sweep of events as evidence of the triumph of Christian civilization over Native primitiveness. In short, the great majority of our resource materials come from the points of view of the white males who won the struggle. We hear little from the authors of the hidden transcripts, the largely illiterate Creeks, blacks, and poor whites of the southern frontier. Moreover, the perspectives of women are lacking in the available documents about the war. Consequently, any meaningful social

INTRODUCTION

history of the war and Creek removal, which this book aspires to be, takes a great deal of time and tedious work to put together. Fortunately, there is an abundance of research material, and a very careful analysis of this material, employing the techniques of deconstruction and ethnohistory, along with the application of common sense in reading between the lines, can give us a meaningful interpretation of events, if not a completely full and accurate picture of what happened during this important period in U.S. history. In the end, that is about all we can expect from most historical studies.

A book of this sort also requires input from many individuals, all of whom deserve thanks for their help in producing the final product. Special mention should go to the staffs of the Alabama Department of Archives and History, the Georgia Department of Archives and History, the University of Tennessee Library and Special Collections, the University of Georgia Library and Special Collections, Auburn University Library and Special Collections, the Cobb Memorial Library, the Dothan Public Library, and the National Archives in Washington as well as the Southeastern Regional Branch of the National Archives in Atlanta. Beyond this, thanks extend to Dr. John B. Finger and Dr. Paul Bergeron of the University of Tennessee at Knoxville for their help on the dissertation that stands behind this book. And finally, sincere appreciation goes to Vassie Ellisor, Dr. Jennifer Brooks, Dr. Michael Green, and Dr. Theda Perdue for their continuing encouragement and help in bringing this work to life.

1. Creek Politics and Confinement in New Alabama

In September 1810 Tecumseh appeared on the square of Tuckabatchee with an entourage of northern warriors. They were an impressive sight: handsome men sporting eagle feathers in their hair, buffalo tails hanging from their arms and waists, faces painted solid black to signal the seriousness of their business. They marched around the square several times to show themselves off to the many spectators, increasing the curiosity and tension in the crowd. Finally, Tecumseh stood before all the Creek chiefs gathered at one end of the square and gave them gifts of tobacco as symbols of his goodwill. He did not, however, speak of his mission. He waited, biding his time for more than a week until the government's agent, Benjamin Hawkins, left Tuckabatchee along with others who should not hear what he had to say. Only then did Tecumseh deliver his long and animated address to his fellow Native Americans.[1]

We have no transcript of his remarks, but we know something of what he said. Hawkins had his informants in the crowd. Moreover, Tecumseh preached to many Indian nations during that time and his message was much the same wherever he traveled in the heartland. Undoubtedly, he echoed the words of his brother, the Shawnee prophet Tenskswatawa, calling for the Creeks and all other Natives to throw off the corrupting white ways and goods so they might reclaim their ancient spiritual power, unite as one people, and rise up in armed resistance to stop U.S. expansionism in the trans-Appalachian West. It also seems likely that Tecumseh promised the Creeks that the British in Canada, themselves no friends of the European Americans, would support and assist the great Native alliance once it was formed. But Tecumseh may have promised even more, for Tenskswatawa, like so many other revolutionary prophets trapped in world colonialism, foretold a coming apocalypse, a time when the Master of Breath would restore justice to the land. In Tenskswatawa's version of the sermon, that time would see all sinful Indians and whites buried, and the whole country given back to virtuous Indians, those who rejected white ways and returned to their traditional economy, taking from the land only what they needed to live.[2]

These bold declarations resonated among the Creeks. Tecumseh's mother was a Creek, and they considered the Shawnee leader a fellow tribe member, one of their own. But more importantly, the Creeks had been facing the aggressive expansionism of whites since the sixteenth century, and in that year of 1810, they felt truly threatened by the burgeoning young U.S. Republic. Just to their west, the Creeks saw settlers moving into the Mississippi Territory; not far to the north, the people of Tennessee perched over them like so many hungry vultures; and to the east, stood the greatest threat of all, the state of Georgia. For nearly one hundred years, the Georgians had pushed steadily against the Creeks, overrunning their best hunting grounds, then demanding that the Creeks cede those lands. In fact, the Georgians claimed the Chattahoochee River as the western boundary of their state and made no secret of the fact that they intended, with the help of the federal government, to clear Georgia of its Native population. Moreover, Agent Hawkins, just before he left Tuckabatchee, announced to the Creeks that the government would cut roads through the heart of their nation so the European Americans in the surrounding states and territories could communicate and trade with one another.[3]

However, Tecumseh may have stirred the passions of the Creeks most when he raised the specter of Indian dependence within the world economy. His brother constantly railed against the fur trade, deploring the fact that Indians destroyed animals solely for their skins, leaving their bodies to rot in the woods, and all to meet the demands of the whites for more leather and fur. Tecumseh surely passed this message to the Creeks, which must have reminded them that during the eighteenth century, at the height of the fur trade, they had, along with many other Native groups, become a "forest proletariat," scouring their territory for deer hides for the markets of Europe. In the process, they became addicted to foreign manufactured goods, as well as to alcohol, and so indebted to white traders and merchants that they had to sign away large chunks of land to pay what they owed.[4]

But Tecumseh had an even more painful reminder in store for the Creeks and all the other southern Indians he addressed during those fateful days. He spoke of slavery. In one speech, Tecumseh claimed that day by day whites stripped Indians of their ancient liberty and even dared to kick and strike them as they did "their black faces." At another time, he said of the European Americans, "They have seized our country, and our fathers in their graves reproach us as slaves and cowards." Then he addressed his Creek kin specifically: "Oh, Muscogees! Brethren of my mother! Brush from your eyelids the sleep of slavery, and strike for vengeance and your country!"[5]

Such a statement must have stung the Creeks. They knew all about slavery. One hundred years before, they had been slave catchers, destroying the Spanish mission system in Florida and selling the mission Indians to Carolina traders, who then sent them as slaves throughout the English empire. Then the Creeks, again owing to their participation in the world economy, became slave owners, buying, selling, and working black men and women in their fields. Beyond that, the Creeks saw how important slaves were to the southern plantation system, indeed to the whole economic structure threatening to finally engulf them, take their remaining lands, and possibly even reduce them to abject slavery, not just the weak dependency of which Tecumseh spoke.[6]

In the end, though, Tecumseh did not succeed in enlisting all the Creeks in his cause. The Creeks after all were not a single tribe but a collection of tribal peoples. The Muscogees were the most numerous group, and sometimes lent their name to the nation as a whole, but even they did not all think alike. Indeed, the Creeks were a particularist people; they each owed primary allegiance not to a tribe or the Creek Nation but to their individual towns and clans. Faced with all the disease, colonial warfare, and cutthroat economic competition brought to America by the Europeans and their U.S. descendants, the Creeks had come together to form a confederacy for mutual defense, but seldom did they unite behind any single plan of action. Furthermore, the Creeks suffered from a schism between nativists and accommodationists common to many Native American peoples. Big Warrior of Tuckabatchee represented the accommodationists. As the wealthy leader of the Upper Creeks, he owed much of what he had to his ability to get along with Agent Hawkins and fit himself into the whites' economic system. Ultimately, he rejected Tecumseh's plea and kept his townspeople out of the Shawnee's camp. Tecumseh did, however, raise a large nativist party in the towns surrounding Tuckabatchee, and the members of that party, called Red Sticks, soon found themselves locked in armed conflict with both Creek accommodationists and the Americans as part of the larger War of 1812 between Great Britain and the United States.[7]

Armies subsequently converged on the Creek country from three sides. The Tennesseans under Maj. Gen. Andrew Jackson took the lead in the fighting, defeating the Red Sticks at the battles of Tallushatchee and Talladega in the fall of 1813, before delivering what appeared to be the death blow to the Creek uprising in March 1814 at the famed Battle of Horseshoe Bend. Following close on the heels of this victory, Jackson assumed command of the Seventh Military District of the U.S. Army, extracted a punitive land cession from the Creeks (the Fort Jackson Treaty) that amounted to about half of all the lands they owned, and brought a decisive end to the War of 1812 by defeating the British at the Battle of New Orleans. The more recalcitrant Red Stick warriors, those who managed to escape death or capture, fled to the Seminole country in Spanish Florida.[8]

But Red Stick resistance did not end with the flight. The escaped Creeks merely united with disaffected Seminoles, escaped slaves, and British adventurers in continued opposition to the will of the United States. In doing so, they posed a threat to the settlement of the Creek cession lands bordering Florida, as well as to Georgia's cotton planters' use of the lower Chattahoochee and Apalachicola rivers as outlets to the Gulf of Mexico. So Jackson took to the war trail once again. In 1818 he illegally invaded Spanish Florida, burned a number of Indian villages, seized the Spanish fort at St. Marks, and even occupied the town of Pensacola, claiming that the Spaniards had given aid and comfort to the enemies of the United States. This bold stroke ended the so-called First Seminole War, which was in essence merely a continuation of the colonial revolt called the First Creek War.[9]

In fact, the First Creek War was only one of a number of such revolts staged by Native peoples around the world against the effects of colonialism, an integral part of the constantly spreading world economy. However, these revolts tended to be unsuccessful and even aided the expanding system by giving the colonizers an excuse to militarily crush Natives and appropriate their lands as punishment for their uprisings. In fact, the survival of the world economy meant that traditionalists must always lose out to one degree or another. And in the United States, fighting and defeating Indians came with some added benefits for whites. Coupled with westward expansion, Indian warfare contributed greatly to U.S. nationalism. But most importantly, the acquisition of more and more Indian land between the years 1815 and 1845 initiated a real Market Revolution in the country. It was, after all, the natural resource wealth of the West that proved the key factor in attracting capital and labor to the United States in these years, laying the foundation for the eventual urbanization and industrialization of the country. Furthermore, the Old Southwest was particularly important in the process. There the famed Cotton Kingdom took hold, which may have been the single most important event in building the national economy in the antebellum era. Cotton was the largest single U.S. export in the decades after the War of 1812. Cotton prices spiraled owing to a growing demand in Europe, and cotton purchases provided the nation as a whole with a huge source of income, which went a long way toward financing its overall economic development.[10]

But more immediately, the close of the War of 1812, along with the Creek and Seminole conflicts, put European Americans on the move, pushing onto the lands of the Creek cession in southern Alabama and Georgia. Spain, realizing the futility of trying to hold Florida in the face of the expansion-minded settlers, ceded that colony to the United States. Meanwhile, Georgia's politicians urged the federal government to finally honor the Compact of 1802, by which Georgia ceded all the land it claimed beyond the Chattahoochee River to the United States in return for a pledge by the government to extinguish Indian claims to Georgia's territory east of the river as soon as possible. With Georgia's population still increasing, and the Chattahoochee and Apalachicola rivers now clear for the transportation of cotton, the demand of Georgia politicians for the government to get the Creeks out of the state grew more and more insistent. Consequently, government officials began to ask the Creeks to consider moving west beyond the Mississippi River, or at the very least, relinquish their lands in Georgia and confine themselves to their holdings in the new state of Alabama, which entered the Union in 1819.[11]

Over the next few years the urging grew more intense, and by the mid-1820s the Creeks faced real pressure to get out of Georgia. Furthermore, a former Georgia governor, David B. Mitchell, replaced Hawkins as the Creek agent and used his position to bend the Creeks to his state's will. But he faced stiff opposition from the principal Upper Creek town, Tuckabatchee. Led first by Big Warrior, and after his death by Opothle Yahola, the speaker of the Upper Creeks, the Tuckabatchee headmen responded to U.S. demands by uniting against any more land cessions and most certainly against a complete removal from their ancient southern homeland. In this response they had the support of a party of educated Cherokees led by John Ridge, who wanted all the Cherokee and Creek people to present a firm front against the aggressive whites. But unfortunately for the Upper Creeks, the Georgians found an influential friend among the Coweta town of Creeks, most notably William McIntosh, speaker of the Lower towns, who, along with a few low-grade chiefs, representing only eight of the fifty-six towns of the Creek Confederacy, signed the Indian Springs Treaty in January 1825. Shockingly, this treaty, obtained through bribery and promises of federal protection for McIntosh's party, delivered not only all Creek lands in Georgia to the United States, but most of the Creek country in Alabama as well.[12]

McIntosh was a bicultural product of the fur and skin trade. His father was a Scottish trader, his mother one of the Wind People, the Creeks' most prestigious clan. McIntosh became a planter and innkeeper as well as a Lower Creek leader. Then, when faced with U.S. expansionism and the demands of the world system, he capitulated. In fact, his path sat directly opposite the one taken by the Red Sticks. Whereas they revolted, McIntosh not only sought accommodation with the European Americans, he actually placed his material well-being above the interests of his people. During the Red Stick War, he led an army of Lower Creek warriors against the nativists in Alabama. Then he assisted in Jackson's invasion of the Seminole country in Florida in 1818, just so he could profit from capturing blacks among the Seminoles and returning them to slavery in the states. And just for good measure, McIntosh and his warriors took a few Seminole women and children back to Georgia as well, selling them to the expanding cotton plantations. Simultaneously, the Creek headman partnered with the new Creek agent, David Mitchell, in criminal activity, including embezzlement of Creek annuity funds. Mitchell even used his share of the money to buy African slaves and smuggle them into the United States through the Creek Nation, all in violation of the federal law that declared the foreign slave trade illegal. But worse still, as far as the Creeks were concerned, McIntosh and Mitchell sought to demolish the traditional cohesiveness of Creek culture by pushing the Creek Council to approve, also in 1818, a written law code designed primarily to protect private property. These laws increased the policing power of the Creek constabulary, the "law menders," and legalized patrimony by allowing children to inherit from their fathers, both of which tended to break the traditional matrilineal structure of the ancient clans and pointed the Creeks toward the building of nuclear families headed by males with property concentrated in their hands—just the sort of family structure the world system dictated.[13]

McIntosh justified himself by saying that he did what he did for the good of his people, who had to change to survive. They had to learn to do business as the whites did, he claimed, and must relinquish their lands and move west to save themselves from utter ruin. However, his contention that he could serve his people while enriching himself was only a rationalization employed by many proponents of the system before and since. It was simply another way of saying that greed is good, that the aggressive pursuit of one's individual economic interests is also the best way to promote the greater good of society. But once implanted in the minds of McIntosh and those like him, this rationalization posed a great danger to the aspirations of Native peoples who wished to preserve a traditional community. Indeed, the system and its ideology always beguiled a segment of the indigenous population, who then tied their political and economic interests to those of the colonizers, thereby subverting the efforts of traditionalists to defend their territory and culture from encroachment. Furthermore, colonizers from Australia to Georgia understood the process. They knew full well how to exploit the accommodationists in Native communities, using them to achieve their desired ends. But they also knew ordinary individuals would not do; they needed to win over persons of authority. Thus, George M. Troup, Georgia's governor and chief advocate of planter interests, as well as the most vociferous proponent of Creek removal in his state, spared no effort in seducing McIntosh and bringing him to the treaty table at Indian Springs. However, Troup had an ally in the racial miscegenation that had accompanied, and in many cases aided, the entry of the world system into the southern woodlands. McIntosh, as it turned out, was Troup's first cousin through the old Scottish line.[14]

But more importantly, Troup and other proponents of the system were able to co-opt, incorporate, and corrupt Native economic practices for their own ends. Traditionally, Creek chiefs maintained their influence only insofar as they promoted the general welfare of their communities by encouraging sharing and reciprocity among the people. Creek leaders acted as intermediaries in the transfer of resources to the needy and gave from their personal stores in times of want. In return, the people gave these leaders their allegiance and helped them maintain their privileged economic and political positions. But in McIntosh's case, his source of supply came by way of his collusion with the Georgians, and by redistributing money, cattle, and slaves to the Lower Creeks he gained the firm loyalty of several villages. He then used the status derived from that support to do the bidding of his white allies. Worst still, this corrupt bargain repeated itself throughout Native America, and in the process an ancient redistribution system actually became a tool for the conquest of the country for the market.[15]

But the larger body of Creeks still had their defenses, including the adaptation of U.S. concepts of law and punitive justice in the protection of Native interests. While the Creek Nation never became a truly centralized political body, the pressure to cede more and more land to the United States did force the Creeks' council of headmen to solidify their hold on the tribal domain. They and the Cherokee chiefs made a pact that neither group would cede any more land to the whites. More importantly, the council chiefs secured an agreement from all the Creek towns of both the Upper and Lower divisions that no land claimed by them could be sold without unanimous agreement from the council members. Furthermore, the council passed a law several years before the Indian Springs Treaty, making the cession of land without the council's approval a capital offense. As a consequence, a party of Upper Creek warriors executed McIntosh and a few of his followers in April 1825. Others of the offending party, including McIntosh's family, fled east to towns in Georgia, seeking protection from Governor Troup, who called on the federal government to enforce the Indian Springs Treaty and punish McIntosh's murderers.[16]

But again, the Creeks had their defenses. President John Quincy Adams realized that the treaty was a fraud and declined to uphold it. Although the president favored Indian land cessions and removal, he believed the process should be conducted honorably and even threatened to use federal force if Georgians persisted in surveying and settling the Creek cession. Furthermore, the president, a New Englander, had little sympathy for southern slaveholders or their plans to extend their plantations across the entire South on lands swindled out of the hands of Native inhabitants. Northerners and southerners, generally speaking, had taken different paths into the world economic system:

the Northeast chose to follow Britain in the development of commerce, manufacturing, and banking, and the South turned away from becoming a core capitalist region to pursue commercial agriculture, developing into what might be termed a mature periphery area in the world system. Increasingly, these differing economic choices would bring North and South into political conflict and finally war. The dispute between Adams and Troup over the disposition of Creek lands was but one incident in a chain of North-South disputes leading to the great schism, and the Creek Council took advantage of it to defy Troup and remain on their lands.[17]

That victory was short-lived, however. While Adams may have found the southern point of view personally distasteful, he was, nevertheless, committed to the expansion of the United States. So when the pugnacious Governor Troup roused Georgians with the banner of states' rights and mobilized his state troops to fight for the Creek cession, the president backed down, unwilling to begin a U.S. civil war for the benefit of Indians. Perhaps Adams realized at that point that fighting his fellow compatriots was foolish when they all believed essentially the same in regard to Indians: U.S. civilization was superior to their culture and must overcome it in the end. Consequently, the president supported the creation of an "honorable" treaty with the Creeks, which would mollify the ill feeling between Georgia and the federal government by giving the Georgians what they wanted, more Creek land. However, government negotiators still used coercion and bribery to secure new, more "legitimate" treaties with the Creeks. Accordingly, the Creek headmen signed a series of accords with the United States, by which they agreed to give up all their lands in Georgia. They did, however, keep their territory in Alabama and gain an increased annual annuity payment from the government. This was certainly a great disappointment to the Georgia Creeks, but as most of the nation's towns sat along the banks of rivers in Alabama, the Creek core remained intact. Moreover, by retaining their Alabama land base, the Creeks were able to avoid a complete removal from their ancient southern homeland.[18]

However, life in Alabama would not be a happy one for the now-

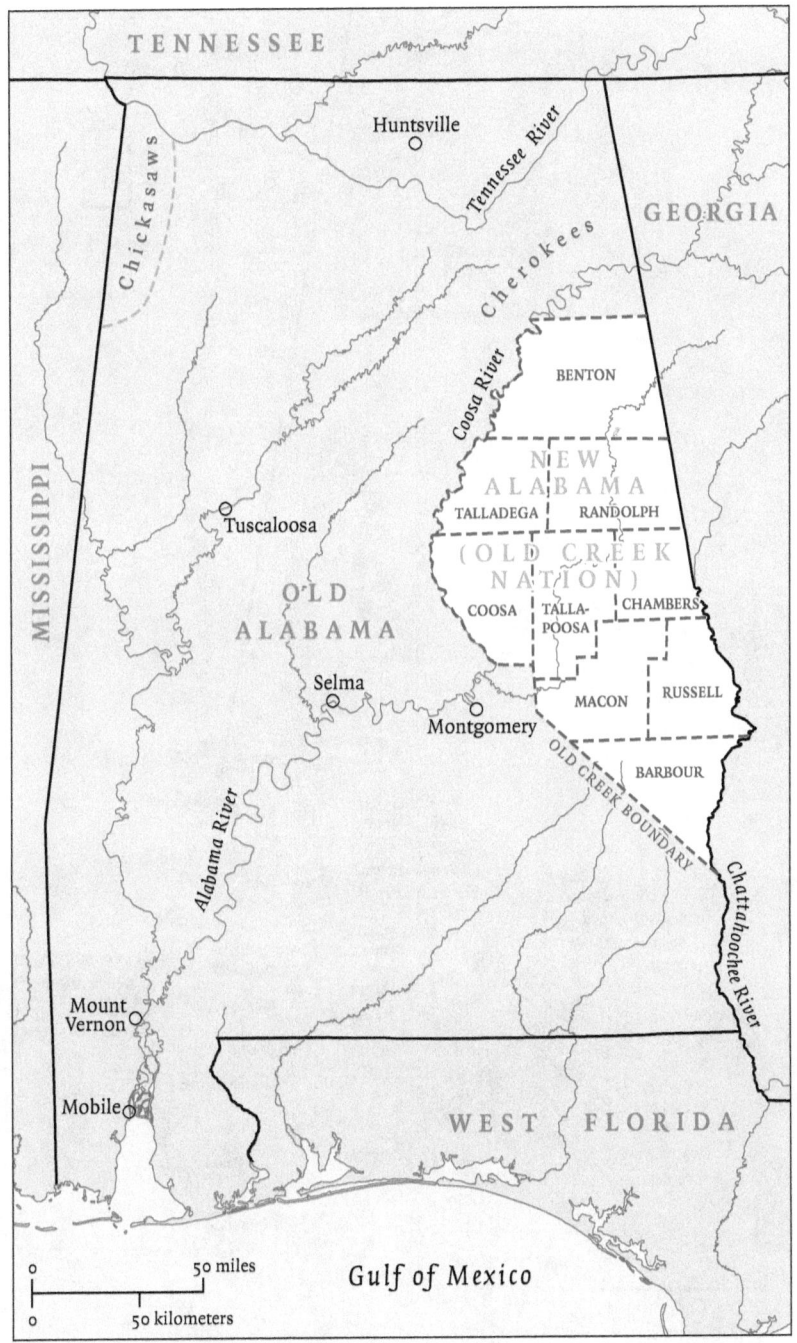

1. Alabama, 1832–36

2. New Alabama

concentrated Creeks. The movement of Lower tribespeople from Georgia across the Chattahoochee River into Alabama was the beginning of the end of the Creek Nation in the Old South. The Washington Treaty of 1826 obligated the Georgia Creeks to move en masse in a relatively short period of time, forcing them to give up their fields along the east bank of the Chattahoochee and its tributary streams, as well as those along the course of the Flint. Thus, many Lower Creeks came into Alabama rather suddenly, settling for the most part on the lands of their kin in the tribal town territories running down the west bank of the Chattahoochee. In descending order these territories were Cusseta, Coweta, Euchee, Hitchitee, Ositchee, Chehaw, Sawokli, Apalachicola, and Eufaula. But, unfortunately, many Georgia Creeks entered these tribal lands without the means to subsist themselves. Therefore, starvation would be a perpetual problem for the Lower Creeks in Alabama.

Lack of social cohesion posed another difficulty. Having for so long lived near the Georgia and Florida frontiers, the Lower Creeks had extensive contacts with whites and blacks and their genetic makeup showed visual evidence. In fact, Lower Creek towns "reflected the social mosaic of the Southern frontier," and one historian has claimed that the Lower Creeks were becoming "a distinctive, almost hybrid society ... genetically and culturally mixed." Moreover, those Lower Creeks consisted of people of "all complexions shading through white, red, and black."[19]

More significantly, the Lower Creeks had lost their hunting grounds sooner than the Upper Creeks and had been exposed to the economic practices and competitive values driven by the world system for a longer period of time. As a result, the Lower townspeople had lost a good deal of their traditional commonality. Like the whites, the Lower Creeks now had their own economic classes and social gradations. Some of the immigrants from Georgia were wealthy planters and/or ranchers, others were small farmers, many clung to village life and communal agriculture as best they could, and many more were simply poor and demoralized, unable to cope with the injustice done to them by white Georgians, the rise of market competition among them, and the decline of the traditional Creek communalism. This last group produced numerous young Indians who extended ancient Creek hunting and gathering practices to include the pillaging of Georgia farms and the butchery of Georgia livestock. These youths also engaged in one of the major industries of the southern frontier, horse stealing, and they often worked with white gangs in moving horses out of Georgia and across the Creek country to markets farther west. The Georgians called these young Creeks outlaws, and some undoubtedly were, even among their own people, but others might more appropriately be called social bandits. As such, they resisted the system and fed their starving families in the only way they could, a way that fit with the traditional roles of Creek men as hunters of animals and warriors against tribal enemies. But whatever we call them, this group of men contributed to the growing turmoil and lack of order in Lower Creek life.[20]

The movement of more Creeks into Alabama also increased political tensions in the confederacy. This resulted in part from more Indians living in closer proximity to one another but mostly because the Creeks faced steadily increasing pressure to give up even their Alabama lands and move beyond the Mississippi River. In fact, federal officials, led by Thomas L. McKenney, head of the War Department's Indian office, launched a successful effort to induce some of the detached and dispirited Lower Creeks, including both poor people and the highly acculturated followers of William McIntosh, into emigrating. But worse still as far as the Creeks were concerned, Andrew Jackson, a southerner used to excoriating the Creeks, became president in 1829, and rammed his Indian Removal Act through Congress in 1830. And while Jackson claimed to represent the best interests of both Indians and whites, his strongest support for removal came from planters, politicians, and land speculators who saw the large Indian groups in the South as an obstacle in the way of expanding the southern export economy. More precisely, the Indians impeded white southerners from supplying the world economy's enormous demand for raw cotton and cotton goods, a demand created by the Industrial Revolution. Thus, the Creeks discovered that besides the stress of more people living on less land, they would have to face renewed competition for that land from whites. Consequently, Creek leaders would have to weigh continually the advantages and disadvantages of staying in Alabama as opposed to giving up their ancient homeland entirely and seeking a fresh start in Indian Territory. But all this pressure only intensified existing political differences among the Creeks.[21]

The pressure tended to widen the divide between Upper and Lower towns, all of which worked against any attempt the Creeks may have made to unite behind a program to preserve traditional culture and the nation's common land base. Furthermore, the strain and tendency toward social fragmentation and political factionalism may have been even more pronounced among a group of people who gave loyalty first to family and their *talwa* (hometown). Thus, the Creeks splintered into parties centered on competing leaders and representing different ways of dealing with both intruders on the Creek domain and the government pressure to emigrate. And while factions had always existed in the Creek Confederacy, a polity that once took strength from incorporating diverse peoples and therefore different points of view, the movement of Georgia Creeks into Alabama forced these factions into closer contact and heightened disagreements and hostility between them. Thus, a former strength turned to weakness as far as dealing with the whites was concerned. Indeed, this tendency of the Creeks and their Seminole cousins to splinter into antagonistic factions perhaps as much as anything explains why they engaged in armed conflicts among themselves on two occasions in the early 1800s, something no other southern Indians did, even though those Natives faced similar challenges from the colonizers.[22]

The largest and most effective party in the nation was the Tuckabatchees, consisting not only of most of the inhabitants of Tuckabatchee town but of a half-dozen surrounding and related Upper Creek towns on or near the lower Tallapoosa River, some of which had been Red Stick towns during the late war. The council chiefs of Tuckabatchee led the party, and Opothle Yahola, the principal speaker and power broker of the Upper Creeks, sat at their head.[23]

Opothle Yahola rose to power during the treaty ordeals of the 1820s, standing in firm opposition to the McIntosh party, and by some accounts he was a traditionalist who early on flirted with the Red Stick cause.

In the 1830s Opothle Yahola still refused to wear white men's clothes or to speak English. He also played an important role in the religious ceremonies of his town, as any headman would, but his name Yahola indicates that he had been a singer in the Black Drink ceremony, which preceded the councils of Creek leaders. But Opothle Yahola was also a practical man who fought the Red Sticks in the end and learned to live within the economic system that engulfed his people. For his part, Opothle Yahola surely knew that a man must accumulate a measure of wealth to maintain his status as an important tribal leader, and in a traditional sense, have the resources necessary to provide for needy followers in times of crisis and want. Consequently, Opothle Yahola acquired a cattle herd and a plantation worked on by slaves. He may have had an interest in a trading store at Tuckabatchee, operated by merchants out of Montgomery, Alabama. Certainly the man earned a reputation as a shrewd trader, known to his people as "Old Gouge," and some of his descendants would use Gouge as their surname in later years. But Opothle Yahola and the other Tuckabatchee headmen provided sound leadership and endeavored to help the Upper Creeks follow in their footsteps, negotiating the difficult path between Native traditionalism and changes demanded by the irresistible forces of the marketplace and white society in general.[24]

In this respect the Tuckabatchees and most other Upper Creeks seemed to have learned some valuable lessons from the Red Stick War. Indeed, that destructive conflict had leveled their towns and society, forcing the Upper Creeks to make a choice and either give up their existence as a distinct Native community or come together to save themselves from extinction and move forward to a better day. To their credit, they found a way to bind their wounds, reconcile their differences, and reconstitute their society. They rebuilt their towns along the Coosa and Tallapoosa rivers and their tributary streams and down along Federal Road near where that thoroughfare passed out of the Creek country and into the state of Alabama. Then, many Upper Creeks actually returned to these towns to engage in communal life and cooperative agriculture, reversing their former, disintegrating trend of moving out of their core settlements to occupy family farms and ranches.

In part this return to town life may have been a conscious effort to tie their fractured society back together through cooperative effort, but in practical terms, the Upper Creeks had little choice. They had lost so much property during the war that few individuals or families had the means to support themselves; they needed the help of others just to survive from season to season.[25]

And along with this lesson came others. First of all, the Upper Creeks learned that a too hasty adoption of white ways had disintegrating and debilitating effects on Indians. Second, they learned that a complete rejection of foreign culture, particularly in the economic sphere, was impossible and could also place a Native people at a dangerous disadvantage in an environment increasingly controlled by outsiders. Consequently, the Upper Creeks chose a middle path, clinging to traditional ways and core values while adopting skills from European Americans that could help them survive and then prosper in the face of advancing white settlement and the growth of the market economy. This middle path became an integrating principle that appealed both to conservative former Red Sticks and the more integrated Creeks, those who grew cotton and corn for the market; ran ferries, roadhouses, and trading stores; and sent their children to mission schools. And again, Opothle Yahola stood forth as the principal spokesperson of this middle path.[26]

But Tuckabatchee's leaders had a serious problem beyond that of rebuilding and holding together Upper Creek society. They had to find a way to hold on to as much of their land as possible and to avoid removal to the West. In this regard, Opothle Yahola may have sought to consolidate Creek government to make it a more efficient tool for resisting the European Americans and disciplining the Lower towns. The Tuckabatchees certainly resented the fact that on more than one occasion Lower Creek headmen had ceded land to the United States without the assent of the Upper towns. Indeed, Opothle Yahola had played a major role in McIntosh's execution. There is also evidence to suggest that Opothle Yahola and the Tuckabatchees wanted to move beyond the localized, nondifferentiated religious-political structure of Creek government to create a Cherokee-Creek coalition with a large national treasury to help both nations better deal with their common problems vis-à-vis the United States. However, the Tuckabatchee party knew that armed resistance to the settlers was not an option here; they had seen firsthand its failure and the consequent destruction of many Upper Creek towns in 1813 and 1814. Consequently, the Tuckabatchees wanted to work with the Cherokee leaders in appealing to the conscience of the U.S. nation, meaning, in practical terms, convincing northerners to keep their southern brethren from Native lands. But, again, the Tuckabatchee chiefs, like other Creek leaders before them, failed to overcome Creek particularism. The Lower Creek chiefs, along with Agt. John Crowell and commissioner of Indian Affairs, Thomas McKenney, resented the collusion between Upper Creeks and Cherokees and moved to break it up. Thus, Creek factionalism and the Creeks' continued reliance on a town-centered governmental structure made it difficult for them to unite among themselves or with other Native nations in the South to nonviolently resist white aggression.[27]

Furthermore, Opothle Yahola had to fend off a serious rival for leadership in his own Tuckabatchee town. Big Warrior died in the mid-1820s, and at some point thereafter his son, Tuskenea, also known as Big Fellow, took over his position as headman of the Upper Creeks. Such a succession was improper according to Creek tradition. In a matrilineal society, the chiefdomship should have passed to a male member of Big Warrior's mother's clan. Tuskenea was not a member of that clan. He belonged to his own mother's clan. Consequently, Tuskenea's rise to office prompts questions. Did U.S. agents and/or businesspeople, thinking Tuskenea would serve their interests, have something to do with his appointment? Or had Big Warrior simply come to favor his son, and determined to pass along to him his public office and considerable property? It might be that Tuskenea's ascent was just one more example of the Creeks becoming more patrilineal, increasingly mirroring the property relations of white society. In any event, Tuskenea was unpopular, and the Upper Creek Council deposed him as principal chief in 1827, citing his improper appointment.[28]

But breaking tradition was not Tuskenea's biggest problem, for the Creek Council reinstated him as headman after a relatively short period of time. No, Tuskenea's main fault lay in his disposition. Like his father, he made enemies easily. He had a temper and was given to rash actions. Showing his displeasure at the government's efforts to remove Creeks in 1830, Tuskenea attempted to kill William Walker, the Creek subagent and his own brother-in-law. He also stopped a stagecoach passing through the Creek country, holding the passengers hostage and railing against the removal policy. For this offense, federal marshals arrested Tuskenea and the district court fined him one hundred dollars. The Upper Creek Council, undoubtedly at Opothle Yahola's instigation, then broke him as head chief for a second time, only to reinstate him yet again in 1831. Tuskenea continued to trouble the Tuckabatchees, however, largely because they did not trust his handling of the annuity payment. Consequently, they deposed Tuskenea and put in his place two other men who could share the growing responsibilities of the Upper Creek headman and who would be more amenable to Opothle Yahola's less foolhardy approach in dealing with the settlers and their removal agents. But Tuskenea's seethed under the affront and continued to pursue his claim as headman of the Upper Creeks. Worse, he had supporters. Indeed, the most notable Lower Creek chiefs supported Tuskenea as the legitimate leader of Upper Creeks, probably because they distrusted the powerful Tuckabatchee group and the potential it had to dominate the nation's affairs in the face of the disheveled state of the Lower towns. But even more ominous for the Tuckabatchee party and the peace of the nation, Tuskenea gained the support of some of the Tallassee people, whose main settlement sat just across the Tallapoosa River from Tuckabatchee.[29]

In fact, Tallassee had a history of conflict with Tuckabatchee, dating back to the late 1700s and possibly well before. Hoboithle Micco of Tallassee, also called Tame King in some quarters, served as headman of the Upper Creeks in the early 1800s. He opposed Benjamin Hawkins's civilization program for the Creeks, as well as the agent's plan to build roads across the Creek country for the benefit of the European Americans. Probably for those reasons, he lost the head chieftainship to Big Warrior of Tuckabatchee, who received the federal government's backing and largesse. Seething with resentment, Hoboithle Micco actually appealed to the British in the Bahamas for support, then welcomed their ally, Tecumseh, with open arms when he came among the Creeks to spread his evangelical nativism and call for all Indians to unite with the British in a last stand against the land-hungry settlers. Thereafter Tame King became the titular head of the Red Stick party, and once the Creek civil war began, he and Tallassee's war chief, Peter McQueen, attacked Tuckabatchee with gusto, hoping to dispose of Big Warrior and his ring of accommodationists. But William McIntosh marched from Coweta to save the Tuckabatchees; then a combined force of European Americans and allied Creeks smashed the Red Stick uprising altogether, killing the aged Tame King in the process. Yet his defiant spirit did not die; it lived on in some of his Tallassee people. Peter McQueen led hundreds of them on a flight into Spanish Florida, where they joined the Seminoles and continued their opposition to U.S. expansionism and Creek accommodation to whites. In fact, Andrew Jackson and William McIntosh invaded Florida in 1818 in part to discipline the Tallassees and hang McQueen. Subsequently, McIntosh fell in with the Tallassee camp, killed a number of warriors, and then rounded up the women and children and returned them to the Creek Nation. McQueen fled across the peninsula and died in lonely exile, while some of his followers made their way back to Alabama on their own. But other Tallassees remained in Florida, retaining their Red Stick nativism. One of these Tallassees was just a babe when Tame King died, but he became, in time, a nationally famous representative of Tallassee's spirit of opposition to U.S. authority. His name was Assi Yahola (Osceola).[30]

But why, given the conservatism and obstinacy of the Tallassees, would they support Tuskenea, a wealthy, slave-owning member of Tuckabatchee's economic elite, the very son of Big Warrior, whom they had detested as a U.S. toady? Most probably, the dissident Tallassees in Alabama needed a leader as their town chief, Tustenuggee Chopco, obviously did not share their level of anger and disaffection. However, Tuskenea, despite his wealth and town affiliation, resented U.S. domination, had actually befriended Tecumseh, sharply opposed removal, and harbored a grudge against the ruling Tuckabatchee party to which he once belonged. On those points he and the Tallassees found common ground. But it would not be fair to say that a majority of Tallassees gravitated to Tuskenea, nor does it appear his supporters lived in Tallassee town proper. More likely, they lived in two of Tallassee's *taliwas*, or daughter towns, Sougahatchee and Loachapoka, located on tributary streams of the Tallapoosa River. It is also possible that these people were part of the contingent of Red Sticks who fled to Florida in 1814 but returned to the Creek country sometime later. They may have kept in contact with Osceola and their Tallassee kin in Florida, however, and continued to nurse bitter memories of the Red Stick War and Jackson's subsequent invasion of Florida to root them out. Moreover, the Tallassees of Sougahatchee and Loachapoka, although officially classed as Upper Creeks, actually occupied a sort of middle ground geographically and politically between the Upper and Lower towns. In fact, they lived just to the west of the Lower Creek Coweta and Cusseta people and had once claimed hunting grounds far into Georgia in the vicinity of the Okefenokee Swamp. Accordingly, they would have interacted with Lower Creeks more than with other inhabitants of the Upper towns. Perhaps because of this, they tended to join the Lower Creeks in their opposition to Upper Creek leaders.[31]

The third party in the confederacy might be called the Lower Creek, or Cusseta, party; Cusseta and Coweta were the two largest Lower towns. Indeed, both these towns had numerous outlying villages up and down the Chattahoochee basin. These towns also housed the majority of the Muscogee element of the Lower Creek population, and as a general rule, the headman of the Lower towns came from one of the two towns. In the early 1830s, that headman was Neah Micco of Cusseta. He and the councilors on whom he depended, including his brother, Efau Emathla, lived well, carrying on profitable relations with the Creek agent, John Crowell, whose plantation sat in the heart of the Lower Creek territory, near an army post called Fort Mitchell. Indeed, Neah Micco got on well with whites in general and profited from his associations with them. He did, however, oppose removal. Furthermore, Neah Micco supported Tuskenea as head chief of the Upper Creeks and protested to Crowell when the Tuckabatchee party removed the man from that office. In fact, Tuskenea and Neah Micco made natural allies in their resentment of Tuckabatchee's power, and their alliance had the weight of history behind it. When the famed Alexander McGillivray rose to prominence among the Upper Creeks during the American Revolution, his two major political opponents were Tame King of Tallassee and the first Neah Micco (Fat King) of Cusseta, possibly the aforementioned Neah Micco's uncle. By the 1830s, Opothle Yahola held the seat of power in the Upper Creek country, and Tuskenea stepped into the rival's role once played by Tame King of Tallassee. Neah Micco simply picked up the challenger's mantle left to him by his relative of the same name, thereby standing for Lower Creek interests in the face of Tuckabatchee and the Upper Creeks in general. Unfortunately, though, just as the alliance between Fat King and Tame King had caused the Creeks problems in an earlier time, so the association between Tuskenea and Neah Micco would plague them during their days of confinement in New Alabama.[32]

But why was there a contest between the Tuckabatchee and Cusseta parties? In part it stemmed from the fact that Upper Creeks and Lower Creeks simply did not trust each other, especially when it came to the matter of land cessions to the United States. The Lower Creeks, largely because the system had reduced them to poverty, tended to support land cessions, while the Upper towns opposed them. But mostly, the contest for power between the Tuckabatchees and the Cusseta party had to do with control of annuity funds, the annual disbursements the federal government made to the Creek Confederacy as payment for past land cessions. The world system made it necessary for even Native peoples to have money, especially perpetual debtors like the Creeks, and neither the Upper nor Lower chiefs trusted the other side to handle and distribute these funds fairly without graft or corruption. In truth, the Tuckabatchees and Cussetas had little reason to trust each other as both sides had been guilty of wrongdoing, trying to claim too much of the annuity for themselves and accepting stipends and bribes to do the bidding of the government, traders, or other whites seeking to manipulate Creek policy or capture portions of the annuity. In 1826, for example, when the Creeks ceded all their remaining lands in Georgia,

70 percent of the treaty money went to just twenty-four headmen. And Neah Micco, being elderly and easily influenced by traders, reputedly lived well off the annuity while many of his followers suffered in poverty. Indeed, Neah Micco seemed to be a man who wanted only to live out his days in Alabama in peace and comfort, and had no plan for leading the Lower towns, much less the whole Creek Nation, through a time of great travail. Certainly Opothle Yahola resented Neah Micco for his lack of strong leadership, particularly his inability to control his confused people and keep them from committing acts of violence that could escalate into another war.[33]

While most of the Muscogee tribespeople in the Lower towns followed Neah Micco, many Lower Creek members of the non-Muscogee tribes or towns formed what might be termed the Seminole party in the Creek Nation. This party consisted of the Hitchitee-speaking Chehaws, Sawoklis, Apalachicolas, Ositchees, and Hitchitees proper, as well as the Euchees, who were ancient inhabitants of the Southeast and who spoke a tongue unrelated to that of the Muscogees or Hitchitees. All of these people had relatives and friends among the Florida Seminoles, were distinguished by their poverty, and kept up a mutually predatory resource competition with the frontier settlers of Georgia.[34]

The Euchees, in particular, maintained a particularly bad reputation as thieves and liars among the whites and Muscogee Creeks. Their customs differed from those of the Hitchitees and Muscogees, and many Euchees refused to mix with the Muscogees or speak the Muscogee tongue. When the famed naturalist William Bartram visited Euchee town in 1778, he proclaimed it the largest and most compact Indian town he ever saw, filled with large, neatly built houses. Later, Benjamin Hawkins, also impressed with the looks of the town, praised the Euchees as more orderly and industrious than the other tribes of the Creek Confederacy. But the Euchees began to leave their town to settle elsewhere; some drifted into Florida, and others, displaying the cultural conservatism of their tribe, joined the nativist party during the Red Stick War. Consequently, Euchee town fell into ruin and its people became one of the poorest and most unkempt of the Creek communities. At that point, like many other poor people, they acquired an unfortunate reputation. They recognized the elderly chief, or *micco*, of High Log town, a man called Blind King, as their senior headman, but as part of the Seminole party, the Euchees would also look to the headman of Hitchitee town, Neah Emathla, for leadership.[35]

Neah Emathla had a long history of opposing the will of the settlers, making him all the more attractive to restless young warriors and all the poor and disaffected inhabitants of the Lower Creek towns. This chief had supported the British in the War of 1812 and had helped precipitate the First Seminole War when he refused to vacate his village, Fowltown, in southwestern Georgia as per the Fort Jackson Treaty. Coming under U.S. attack, he moved into Florida and established a new village in the vicinity of a later U.S. settlement called Tallahassee. At that time, he became an ally of Peter McQueen of Tallassee and the refugee Red Sticks, many of whom took up residence with him. But the settlers also coveted Middle Florida for its rich agricultural lands and, with the Moultrie Creek Treaty, the U.S. government pressured the Indians into vacating the area in 1823. During the treaty meeting, the Florida Indians, a mixed lot of old-time Seminoles and more recently arrived Red Stick and non–Red Stick Creek refugees from Georgia and Alabama, came together as a body to elect Neah Emathla as their principal chief, which may have been the birth of the Seminole Nation. But Neah Emathla would not hold this position for very long. The treaty obligated the Florida Indians to move south onto a reservation in the peninsula, and while Neah Emathla could have stayed in Middle Florida on his own private reserve, he could not bear to see European Americans settling in around him. Consequently, he moved north to the Lower Creek country, built his new town there, joined the Creek Council, and approved the execution of William McIntosh for his violation of Creek law in taking it upon himself to cede Creek land. From that point on, Neah Emathla became the leader of many people like himself who had ties both to the Creeks and Seminoles and who visited back and forth between Alabama and Florida, sometimes conflicting with settlers along the way. In fact, of all the members of the Creek Confederacy, these Seminole-Creeks tended to be the most hostile to whites, and they gravitated to Neah Emathla because of his warrior reputation and strong presence, which displayed both courage and integrity and impressed even his enemies.[36]

On the opposite end of the political spectrum from the Seminole party stood the McIntosh crowd. By 1830 most of the members of this Lower Creek faction, including numerous prosperous planters, had emigrated and set up the western branch of the Creek Nation in the Indian Territory. In fact, the headmen of the McIntosh faction who signed the Indian Springs Treaty in 1825 expressed their willingness to emigrate in the very preamble of the accord. They also claimed to speak for the entire Creek Nation in this regard, although they excepted the Tuckabatchees, whom the McIntosh people tried to picture as a troublesome minority resisting removal. But the Tuckabatchees, and indeed the majority of Creeks, who certainly did not want to cede their entire country to the United States, got their revenge when the Creek Council ordered not only McIntosh's execution but the deaths of his chief associates as well. These associates included McIntosh's son, Chilly, along with Joseph Marshall, Samuel Hawkins, James Islands, Etomme Tustenuggee, and one Colonel Miller. Samuel Hawkins and Etomme Tustenuggee fell with McIntosh, but Chilly survived to become a leader of the Creek emigrants to the West. Joseph Marshall and James Islands also lived but did not move beyond the Mississippi. They stayed in Alabama and headed the McIntosh faction there along with Benjamin Marshall and Paddy Carr. These leaders, all owing allegiance to McIntosh's Coweta town, represented a number of bicultural Creeks who remained in Alabama either because they loved it or, more likely, because they had substantial cattle herds and other property that they could not transport easily or afford to leave. Indeed, one factor that distinguished the McIntosh Creeks was their ability to prosper, by fair means and foul, under the new economic regime steadily engrossing the Creek Nation. In this regard, they may have stayed in Alabama because they saw more economic opportunities opening for themselves as whites drew closer and closer in on the Creek heartland.[37]

And indeed, some whites had long since infiltrated the Creek Confederacy, forming yet another political faction pulling at the fabric of Creek unity. For want of a better name, we might call this faction the U.S. party. Undoubtedly, this party had numerous members, but existing documents mention only a portion of them: John Crowell, the Creek agent, and his brother Thomas; William Walker, son-in-law of the late Big Warrior of Tuckabatchee; the combative and colorful Thomas S. Woodward and his friend Nimrod Doyle; Charles McLemore; Drury Spain; John Scott; Luther Blake; and the redoubtable John H. Brodnax, next to Crowell the white man who exercised the most influence over the Creeks. Some writers have called these men Indian countrymen, but that term is not entirely accurate. The real Indian countrymen were those white residents of the Creek Nation who fully understood and identified with Native ways of thinking and acting, those who the Indians accepted as members of their nation. The U.S. party members, however, were self-conscious European Americans who, though they may have lived with the Creeks for years and spoke the Muscogee tongue, really had little knowledge of, or regard for, the Native worldview. In this respect the Creek willingness to welcome foreigners, white and black, into their confederacy, which had once made the Creeks so numerically strong, now served to weaken them, for the U.S. party men came into the Creek country not to escape the conformity of U.S. civilization, including the grinding demands of its competitive economic system, but to seek profit, to find yet another avenue to wealth. These whites came as traders, government agents, or farmers trying to gain rights to the rich river bottom lands by befriending Creek leaders or marrying into important Creek clans. More ominously, some of these men came to spy out and speculate in Indian lands, a long-standing business tradition in the South.[38]

In truth, the southern concept of states' rights actually began in the assertion that states had rights to Indian land lying within their claimed boundaries and that the central government should not interfere with those rights. Federal law said otherwise, that Indians held all rights to their lands, that only the central government could secure land cessions from the Natives, and that all squatting and land speculation in the tribal domain by state citizens was patently illegal. This did not stop speculators, however, and the U.S. party men meant to play key roles in opening the Creek country to economic development. They knew whites would eventually supplant the Creeks there, building roads, settlements, cotton plantations, and the rest. Knowing the terrain and the Indians as they did, the Creek countrymen realized they could be invaluable to the process of transferring the land out of Native hands and making it a part of the regional, national, and world economies. The opportunity for profit would be immense, so the countrymen attached themselves to various Creek chiefs, hoping to use those leaders in their schemes. Meanwhile, other speculators worked at both the state and federal levels in support of treaty after treaty designed to acquire Creek land cessions.[39]

The Indians knew the score, however. They had always been discriminating in their relationship with whites, and by the 1820s they were well aware of the dire consequences of allowing so many of them into their country. Indeed, they had started a move to purge their nation of outsiders, and race had become much more important to them in determining who was a Creek and who was not. Actually, they had learned the concept of race from the whites and imbibed it through their contact with the world system, which tended to divide the world's population along color lines and used color as a justification for the economic exploitation of one people by another. Consequently, the Creeks adopted only some white men, others they expelled from their midst, and many more they merely tolerated so they could use them for their own purposes. Some McIntosh party men, for example, enriched themselves by working with the speculators, and even those Creek leaders who opposed the speculators in principle found ways to benefit from their presence in the Indian country. Opothle Yahola, Neah Micco, and Tuskenea used various U.S. party men to help them make money or to act as advisers, even secretaries, in their dealings with the government. The large number of well-crafted letters sent by otherwise illiterate Creek chiefs to Washington attests to this fact. In truth, Creek leaders played the white men off against one another, just as these whites did to the Native chiefs, for while a common political goal united the various members of each political faction in the Creek country, the economic system made each individual responsible for his or her own material well-being in the end. This fact engendered both conflict and collusion among the members of all parties and ethnic groups in the Creek Nation, as individuals grasped and clawed for wealth or mere survival in an increasingly competitive environment. So, despite the existence of definable political boundaries in the nation, these boundaries existed on top of a complicated pattern of fractures and fissures, often economically determined, which broke across all other lines and even blurred the borders between natural friends and enemies. Indeed, this emphasis on individual economic competition proved to be the system's greatest source of strength. It undermined all political parties standing in its way; it divided and conquered all ethnic groups alike.[40]

But despite all the turmoil and pressure, the Creek Council managed to unite in the late 1820s on one important principle at least: the Creek people would not leave the last vestige of their ancient homeland in Alabama. Opothle Yahola expressed the majority opinion: "We feel an affection for the land in which we were born, we wish our bones to rest by the sides of our fathers." The whites who heard this may have appreciated the rhetorical flourish, but they certainly failed to comprehend the full import of the statement. The Creeks and other Native Americans believed that the buried bones of ancestors gave a people a direct physical claim to a country. More importantly, the bones gave them a spiritual attachment to the ground beyond anything the whites were able to understand. European Americans, after all, sprang from a vastly different economic and religious tradition. The Old Testament told them that God had separated them from Nature and given them the earth to rule over and use for their benefit, and their world economy taught them exactly how to commodify the land and its resources and turn all to full account, how to move relentlessly over the face of the earth extracting profit. Being essentially rootless, many whites, Andrew Jackson included, could not understand why Indians would not want to move west to find new land and a better life for themselves, precisely as settlers were doing every day. But the Creek Council members dug in their heels. They notified the secretary of war that they would cede no more land and had "determined to discourage and discontinue the practice as unprofitable to our people and as not being the correct mode of ensuring our national peace and prosperity." Then the council chiefs endeavored to bind up the largest Creek clans against any more land cessions and removal to the West. Finally, they turned to coercion and even violence to keep the Creeks together to defend the last piece of their once extensive territory. Armed warriors, acting under the council's authority, went out to threaten, whip, and occasionally murder tribespeople who signed up for removal with the Creek agent, John Crowell, or his minions. In fact, Neah Emathla, the militant of the Hitchitees, rigidly enforced the council's decrees. In one particularly ghastly incident, he and his young warriors beat and cut off the ears of some erstwhile Creek emigrants to the West. Warriors also burned storage buildings and other structures set up to facilitate removal but ultimately did stop numbers of people from going off to join the two thousand McIntosh Creeks who had emigrated earlier as per the Indian Springs Treaty.[41]

Simultaneously, Creek leaders began to harass Christian missionaries in their country. They had allowed those missionaries onto their Alabama lands in the 1820s to teach their children reading, writing, sewing, blacksmithing, and other skills needed to survive in a modernizing world. More to the point, Opothle Yahola contended that if young Creeks were "taught in the ways of the white man," they and their people could "stand unmoved in the flood of the white man." However, Creek leaders had no interest in an agricultural education for their children, in part because they thought the missionaries had especially designed that sort of training to fit the children for eventual slavery. Nor did the headmen care for Christianity, and they prohibited the missionaries from proselytizing it among the Creeks or Creek slaves. In part, the headmen saw Christianity as a false doctrine, Opothle Yahola once contending that he was more likely to get to heaven by worshipping the ceremonial brass plates buried under Tuckabatchee's square than bowing down to the whites' Jesus. But more importantly, Creek leaders saw in Christianity a threat to their traditional religion and thus a threat to the cohesion and coherency of Creek culture as a whole. And if their culture broke, the leaders probably reasoned, so would their hold on the land. Indeed, some evidence suggests that

Creeks attempted to revive old customs and cement their hold on the land during this time by shifting back from private family farms to communal fields. This turn back to tradition flew in the face of the missionaries, who taught that Indian families should live like white ones. However, the Creeks did not care. They must have realized on some level that Christianity, both in the ethics it taught and the way it was used against Native peoples by Europeans and their U.S. progeny, had become simply a handmaiden of the world system, allowing whites to take Indian land and work it with black slaves while proclaiming that blacks and Indians were the real sinners in need of moral uplift and salvation. Furthermore, when the Creek Council chiefs discovered that the missionaries supported the government's removal plan, they reacted violently. They began to break up Christian worship services, even beating and otherwise humiliating the blacks who made up the majority of Christian congregations in Creek Alabama. Eventually, the missions, one among the Upper Creeks and one among the Lower Creeks, simply withered away through lack of support.[42]

But in all honesty, there may have been another reason for the harsh reaction to the missions. Leaders like Opothle Yahola, Tuskenea, and Yargee—Tuskenea's industrious brother—were all strong opponents of the missionaries and undoubtedly advocates of traditional Creek religion. However, they were also well-to-do slaveholders, and they harassed the missionaries partly out of fear that their slaves would discover a message of deliverance and freedom from bondage in Christianity, as many people oppressed by the world system have done. Even Agent Crowell, a white man, opposed the missionaries for this very reason, fearing that their preaching would incite a slave insurrection in the Creek country, where he maintained an expansive plantation worked by numerous slaves. Actually, Crowell seems to have believed that the missionaries were abolitionists who planned to cause trouble in the Creek country. Thus, he declared that their "preaching to Indians was a fudge." And Crowell did have some reason for concern. Creek slaves had been showing signs of restlessness for some time, perhaps because of the Christian message, but more likely because they realized numbers of their Native owners had adopted the white view of blacks as something less than human, as mere commodities in the market.[43]

That sort of racism was a relatively new development in the Creek Nation. However, this evil did not rear its ugly head just because some Creeks wanted to practice commercial agriculture and needed a hard-working, disciplined labor force to do so. More likely, racism grew because some Creeks found it necessary to distinguish themselves from blacks in the eyes of the whites pressing in on the Indian country. Having a long-standing fear of enslavement themselves, these Creeks, along with many other southern Indians, felt they had to assert their superiority over blacks or be considered as one with them by whites and therefore as potential slaves. Consequently, some Creeks turned away from their former practice of kinship slavery, a benign form of bondage whereby slaves were treated more like family members and their offspring were born free. Creek Council members, namely McIntosh party men, also wrote the new attitude toward blacks into law. In 1818 they decreed that if a black person killed an Indian, he or she would be executed, but if an Indian killed a black person, a fine would suffice as restitution. Then in 1825 the council passed a law aimed at discouraging marriage between blacks and Indians, stating that "It is a disgrace to our nation for our people to marry a Negro." But a good deal of miscegenation between blacks and Indians had already occurred in the Creek Nation, and the rising racism caused some Creek families to divide against themselves along racial lines. At that point, even free black Creeks began to fear enslavement by their own tribespeople. Moreover, whites became more aggressive in invading Creek country to steal slaves, which more than likely meant any black person they could find. Little wonder then that some Creek slaves grew disaffected, and while none rose in armed revolt against the new racism, more than a few did leave the Creek Nation. They stole away south to the Seminole country, where they could enjoy more freedom and better treatment from Native leaders less tied to the world of commercial agriculture.[44]

Here we see more irony: Creek leaders fighting the system for their land and freedom, while at the same time adopting the values of their oppressors and denying freedom and equality to others. But that should come as no surprise. It was the way the system operated. It corrupted even those who fought it. It was insidious in that way and in the end all-powerful. However, it would not be fair to leave the impression that all Creeks oppressed their slaves at that time. At the very heart of Creek society, many people clung to traditional beliefs. These people were not so much affected by the marketplace and felt no need to impress whites with their level of acculturation. Among this group of Creeks, blacks still found acceptance and respect and, indeed, even more so as the system drew near and conservative Creeks retreated from it, using their slaves, and blacks in general, as buffers or intermediaries between themselves and the world of whites. Furthermore, slaves in the Creek country, even those facing more racism from Creek headmen and planters, still had better lives and lighter workloads than those blacks in bondage on white plantations in Georgia or Alabama.[45]

In fact, those states, not slaves, posed the real threats to the Creek Nation. Of course, Georgia had always been troublesome, but in 1827 Alabama began to exercise its young muscles by bullying and intimidating the Creeks. Alabamians, like many other colonizers, knew that "the commodification of land requires severing the powerful connection between indigenous peoples and their ancestral homes, followed by public policies that circumvent their legal rights to compete with new settlers for the soil." Consequently, the Alabama Assembly extended the legal limits of one of its existing counties over all the Creek land in Alabama that McIntosh had ceded to the United States by way of the fraudulent Indian Springs Treaty. At the same, the Alabama Assembly moved to restrict the Creeks' use of that land by passing legislation that prohibited Indians from hunting, trapping, or fishing "within the settled limits of the State, or upon any lands in this State, to which the Indian title has been extinguished." The following year the Alabama legislature extended the jurisdiction of two more counties over the Indian Springs cession, thus easing the judicial burden of the first county, making it easier for Alabama to impose its court system on the Creeks. Then, in January 1829, as if sensing they would have the support of the newly elected president Andrew Jackson, Alabama's lawmakers drew all the remaining Creek land in Alabama, which no Creek had ever ceded to anyone, into its county jurisdictions. Thus, the state of Alabama attempted to take administrative control of the whole remaining Creek Nation to pressure the Indians into removing west.[46]

Yet Alabamians, and indeed many other southerners, had another reason for exerting authority over Indians living within their state boundaries. They had to stand up for an increasingly important political principle in the South: states' rights. Having chosen their distinctive path in the world system, that of a mature agricultural periphery rather than an industrializing aspirant to the core capitalist communities, southern politicians had caught themselves in a time warp and sentenced themselves to perpetual economic dependency in a sense, and this caused political insecurity. This insecurity became really acute in 1828 when the U.S. Congress passed a bill imposing fairly high tariffs on imports as part of Senator Henry Clay's American System. Clay, of course, wanted to encourage all Americans to buy U.S. products by increasing the prices of foreign imports through the tariff mechanism. The people of New England, where manufacturing had replaced agriculture as the economic base, loved the plan, but southerners hated it because they were used to selling their cotton in Europe and using the proceeds to purchase high quality but reasonably priced European goods. Southerners simply did not want to be forced to subsidize the northern economy and tended to see the tariff as a federal imposition on their states' rights. And, increasingly, these southerners would erect states' rights as a shield to protect their economic interests against any threat, real or imagined, from the commercial centers of the North. Moreover, southerners used the states' rights doctrine to protect their access to a good supply of fresh farmland. Thus, Alabama proclaimed its right of political authority over the Creeks as a first step in pushing them off their rich river land.[47]

But the South's agricultural production also depended on slavery, and the congressional representative Dixon H. Lewis, a major proponent of the extension of Alabama law over the Creeks, made clear the real purpose of said legislation. He explained to his fellow politicians that if the federal government continued to claim jurisdiction over Indians in Alabama and to insist that Indians could not be subject to state authority, what would prevent the government "by a similar exercise of municipal power" from saying "that Negroes shall not be slaves." Lewis surely knew, although he may have been loath to admit, that Indian land and black labor were the keys to southern economic prosperity within the world system and that Alabama must secure and protect access to both commodities by continually raising the battle cry of states' rights. Ironically, though, southerners held more than their fair share of power in the federal government and were not above imposing centralized authority on the rights of other Americans if it served southern economic interests. The fugitive slave laws and the push for Indian removal stand as prominent examples.[48]

However, it should be noted that not all white southerners were virulent supporters of states' right and bent on abusing Indians. In truth not all whites acted alike in regard to the Natives, and Alabamians, as a general rule, were not as aggressively anti-Indian as Georgians were, for a few very good reasons. First of all, Georgia had a considerably larger white population than Alabama, and consequently Georgians pressed much harder against the Indian boundaries, ever desirous of invading and pushing the Natives out. Furthermore, Georgia, as one of the original colonies and states, held a charter claim to its lands. Consequently, Georgians tended to believe they held legal title to all the Indian lands in their state, and the Natives should quit those lands willingly. When the Indians refused, angry Georgians pictured themselves as the aggrieved parties. But most Alabamians did not have this sense of entitlement. Alabama was a new state, a public land state, a creation of the federal government. Alabamians knew that the title to all Indian territory within Alabama rested with the federal government and most did not see Native occupancy of that territory as an infringement of white property rights. In fact, Alabamians, as a general rule, did not approve of Governor Troup's radical tactics in driving the Creeks out of Georgia, and a good number of Alabama assembly members actually opposed the extension of their own state law over the Creek country, believing that only federal law should apply there. In truth, only the representatives of Alabama counties bordering the Creek Nation and the more boisterous states' righters really pushed the extension. Other assembly members fell into line and voted for the extension because, like Andrew Jackson, they believed, or had convinced themselves, that that would be best for the Creeks. These legislators contended that most Creeks wanted to emigrate beyond the Mississippi, but the Creek Council was holding them in place. The only remedy then was for Alabama to impose true justice in the Creek country and use its power to free the common Indians from the tyrannical and arbitrary rule of the chiefs.[49]

Nevertheless, the extension of Alabama law and the county court system over the Creek lands proved a great tragedy for the Indians. It acted as an open invitation to settlers to invade the Indian country, and this they did, claiming Creek cornfields and cattle herds as well as notching trees to mark the acreage they now called their own. However, most of these squatters were Georgians, not Alabamians, and they even set up small villages for themselves in direct violation of federal laws that protected Native lands from white intrusion. Before, the Creeks always had a frontier between themselves and white settlers, and while the line may have been fluid, the Creeks always held to a protected heartland they could call their own and live on as they pleased without fear of molestation. But now the state of Alabama had broken down the frontier buffer zone and begun a process of incorporating the Creeks into a pluralistic society where they would soon be a minority ethnic group with all the problems that status entailed. Neah Micco, headman of the Lower Creeks, believed that he and his people would soon be driven from their homes, and in January 1832 the state of Alabama seemed to move in that direction. The lawmakers in Tuscaloosa passed a bill striking directly at the power of the Creek Council, seeking to eliminate it as a rival governmental entity within the state and to disable it as a body that could resist removal or protect its people. The 1832 bill stated that "all laws, usages, and customs of the Creeks and Cherokees that violated the constitution and laws of this state" were prohibited. Furthermore, the bill forbade "any Indian or Indians [to] meet in any council, assembly, or convention, and there make any law for said tribe, contrary to the laws and constitution of the state." However, the Alabama legislators did allow Creek councilors to meet with government officials to negotiate removal: "it shall, at all times, be lawful for the chiefs and head-men, or any portion of any of the Indian tribes within this state, to meet any agent or commissioners of the United States, or this state, for any purpose whatsoever." Thus, the Alabamians attempted to incapacitate the Creek Council. However, another section of the law did even greater damage to Creek efforts to hold on to their remaining lands, even though the wording of the section appeared harmless, even kind. It stated that Indians were to enjoy the privileges of white people in their various counties of residence and could record their official documents in county courts, but, and here was the rub, Indians could testify in courts only in cases involving other Indians. In other words, Creeks were subject to the penalties of Alabama law, but they could not defend themselves against whites in court with their testimony or that of their Native witnesses. Needless to say, another rush of intruders entered into the Creek country on the heels of this last piece of state legislation.[50]

At that point, the Creeks really began to suffer. Whites settled on their lands and dared the Indians to do anything about it. Murders occurred on both sides, but the intruders went unpunished as Indians could not testify against them. Worse still, famine struck the Lower Creek towns along with the dreaded smallpox. In Columbus, Georgia, just across the Chattahoochee River from the Creek country, Indians staggered about the streets "haggard and naked," begging door-to-door for food. Other Creeks made do eating berries, roots, and tree bark. Seeing all this, a reporter wrote back to his newspaper, "To see a whole people destitute of food, the incessant cry of the emaciated creatures being bread! bread! is beyond description distressing."[51]

Now the Creek Council members realized their complete inability to resist Alabama's authority. They must have been disappointed when the Cherokees tried and failed to have the Supreme Court stop the Georgians from extending their laws over the part of the Cherokee Nation lying within Georgia. Indeed, the *Cherokee Nation v. Georgia* case must have shown the Creeks that they would be equally unsuccessful if they attempted a federal lawsuit against Alabama. Furthermore, the whole idea of Indian tribes being sovereign polities seemed uniformly unpopular in Washington, the lawmakers there being fond of quoting that part of the Constitution that declared "no new States shall be formed or erected within the jurisdiction of any State without the consent of the Legislature." And even a northerner such as former president John Quincy Adams seemed surprised that Indians had responded to the introduction of civilization and Christianity (and the world system) by "claiming to be independent and rivals of sovereignty with the territories of the members of our Union."[52]

Of course, all this ignored the historical fact that Indian communities predated the United States, but facts and logic did the Creeks no good, especially when the Alabama Supreme Court showed its abject hostility toward the notion of Creek sovereignty with its decision in the *Caldwell v. Alabama* case. James Caldwell, a white intruder on Creek lands, murdered an Indian on those lands in 1831, and the state convicted him of that crime. But he appealed to the state's highest court, claiming that only federal law applied in the Indian country, and Alabama's extension of authority there, along with his conviction, should be invalidated. Ironically, this appeal served the interest of the Creek Council. Even though they had no love for Caldwell, they surely supported his effort to exclude Alabama's authority in the Creek country. However, the court upheld Caldwell's conviction, and in the process, went to great lengths to justify the extension of state law over the Creeks. Worse still, the Indians saw that President Jackson encouraged the extension of state authority over all the southern Indian territory as a means of pressing the Natives into vacating their country and moving beyond the Mississippi River.[53]

And so the Creeks knew they had reached a critical stage in their history. Since the coming of the first Europeans, Creek land and resources had been under duress. But the world system had not yet won, not completely. It had not detached the whole body of Creeks from a spiritual attachment to their land, from the belief that the land and themselves were one. Under pressure they had given up most of their territory, but still they did not view the land as a marketable commodity. They had not lost the traditional view common to most Native communities that to lose the land was to lose oneself. And perhaps this common belief was the one factor that really held the otherwise diverse Creek Nation together through all the changes over the years, that gave them a sense of identity and common purpose despite their other differences and the outside forces working to rip and homogenize them into the mass. Incredibly, the Creeks had not disintegrated as a nation long before. Indeed, the world system had not turned them into a collection of competing individuals detached from nature and clan, nor had it enslaved them, although the pauperism they were beginning to suffer may have been taken as a precursor to complete enslavement.

At that point the leaders of the various Creek factions realized they must save the nation. They must come together to represent the general will and best interests of their people. Thus, they came together in council at Cusseta town in early 1832, determined to settle on an agreement, which they would propose to the War Department. Hopefully, this agreement would allow the Creeks to avoid removal from their ancient homeland and at the same time protect at least a portion of that homeland from white encroachment. Indeed, the council members knew that just staying in Alabama would not be enough. Their people also needed a protected space, a place for themselves where they would have the freedom to be Creeks. They must retain some semblance of a frontier between themselves and others. They could not allow more whites to intrude on them or all would be lost, their land and freedom. With all this in mind, the council members did, indeed, decide on a plan and then move to implement it. They picked a mixed delegation of Upper and Lower Creeks, along with white advisers, and sent them off to Washington, paper in hand, to negotiate yet another treaty with the government. They hoped against hope it would be the last.[54]

2. The Cusseta Treaty of 1832

On March 24, 1832, the delegation of Upper and Lower Creek headmen, advised by the Creek agent, John Crowell, and an Indian country trader and planter, John Brodnax, met with War Department officials in Washington and put their marks and signatures to a document known to Alabamians and Georgians as the Cusseta Treaty of 1832. Under the terms of the agreement, the Creeks ceded all 5,200,000 acres of their tribal lands in Alabama to the United States. The federal government then promised to survey the cession and allot approximately 2,187,000 acres of it to individual chiefs and heads of Creek households in severalty. The remaining acres of the Creek country would be open to settlement by whites. The treaty also gave the individual Creek landholders an option: they could sell their allotments to whites and move west to land reserved for them in the Western Territory or they could hold on to their property and remain in Alabama as independent freeholders and state citizens. Once the allotments were made, the Creeks had a five-year period to make their decisions. Finally, the government promised to protect the Indians' tribal domain from encroachment by whites from the time of the cession to the end of the decision period.[1]

On the face of it, the Cusseta Treaty seemed like a clever bargain for the Creek delegates. They meant for their tribespeople to take their individual land allotments in blocks, clustered about their old town sites, and thus maintain some semblance of communal life and town integrity despite a much-reduced land base. Furthermore, the federal government would protect the allotments until the individual chiefs and heads of families gained deeds to their holdings. These Creek landowners then could use those deeds to guarantee their property rights under Alabama law and in the Alabama courts. In short, it appeared that the Creek delegates, at the price of giving up half of their national territory, could use the Cusseta Treaty to manipulate federal power and state law to their own best advantage in protecting the rest of their domain.[2]

However, the whites had other ideas. During 1832 many citizens of the southern states were hard at work shifting the center of cotton production from the Atlantic Coast region into the Old Southwest. These people saw the Cusseta Treaty as a great boon, for it would open three million acres of new public land to white settlement and agricultural production. Moreover, the treaty would free the other two million acres of Creek allotment land from the control of a tribal government. That fact would allow aggressive whites to purchase the finest lands in the Old Creek Nation directly from relatively unsophisticated Native landholders. In fact, President Jackson counted on this happening. He and his colleagues in the War Department saw the Cusseta accord merely as a market-based removal treaty. They believed that once the government sold all the land surrounding the Creek allotments to settlers, Alabama's white population would press the Natives to sell their landholdings. Then the Creeks would realize they lacked both the means and the desire to compete economically with their white neighbors. Consequently, the Indians would sell their allotments for substantial sums and use the money to finance new starts for themselves in the West. Thus, Jackson hoped to bring the forces of the marketplace to bear on the Creeks and finally compel their removal, something government negotiators had been unable to do for years.[3]

Ultimately, both Jackson and the Creeks would be disappointed with the Cusseta Treaty. Turning the Creeks over to the tender mercies of the marketplace during the flush times of the 1830s cotton boom was a mistake. Rather than restricting white intrusion and protecting their land, the Creeks would see the Cusseta Treaty become an entering wedge for whites into the last stronghold of the Creek Nation. These whites found ways not only to strip the Creeks of their land allotments but to dispossess them of all their money and disposable property as well. This was not what Jackson wanted. While he meant to exert enough economic pressure to compel removal, he never sought to impoverish the Creeks. Furthermore, Creek land and Creek possessions fell into the hands of speculators, not the respectable independent farmers and planters the president said he wanted to serve. Even worse, the Cusseta Treaty actually retarded Creek removal rather than stimulated it. Speculators and other whites would not let the Creeks leave Alabama until they extracted the last measure of land and disposable wealth from them. Furthermore, speculators stymied federal removal agents so they could take charge of the removal themselves and profit from government contracts. Thus, the treaty failed on all accounts, and by creating a dispossessed Indian population that could neither stay in Alabama nor leave without being further exploited, the Cusseta accord became the immediate cause of the Second Creek War.

Certainly, it did not take long for the flaws of the treaty to reveal themselves. In the wake of the agreement, the Alabama Assembly divided the Creek Nation—now called New Alabama—into nine counties for administrative purposes, and another wave of settlers penetrated the Creek country intent on marking homesteads, building roads, establishing towns, and erecting local governments and court systems well in advance of the government's survey and sale of the public-lands portion of the Creek cession. Unfortunately, many of these intruders claimed property already occupied by Creeks, land the Indians meant to include in their allotments when the time came. Indeed, the Cusseta accord set up a classic case of resource competition among the old residents and recent settlers of New Alabama. Beyond that, the treaty created competition between the whites themselves and also turned Indians against Indians in a combustible blend of interethnic conflict and collusion. As the Native-white frontier collapsed, this tragic yet interesting mix finally burst into flames in a conflagration that, while having its local peculiarities, was not entirely unique. After all, colonialism was part and parcel of the spread of the world system, and resource competition and sometimes outright warfare had and would continue to occur all over the globe between Native populations and the colonizers. Knowingly or unknowingly, colonizers sought to integrate frontier regions into international capitalism by disarticulating preexisting economies and societies and putting together, usually with violence, new ones more suitable for supplying the world market and creating surplus value. In the case of New Alabama, and many other places, this process meant expropriating land and other resources from the Natives, turning the land over to commodity production, using the landless Natives as a cheap or even free labor supply, forcefully expelling Natives who resisted incorporation, importing slave labor, and increasing the amount of capital and circulating money in the region by engaging in unsound banking practices and promising exorbitant profits to outside investors. Unfortunately for Creeks and colonizers, such an exploitive, even immoral, process, while beneficial to the world market and distant core capitalist regions, as well as to a relative few local elites, created blighted, relatively poor, and economically underdeveloped peripheral areas within the world system. That, it can be argued, is what Alabama became, and the black, white, and Indian people of the state can thank the Cusseta Treaty for helping make such deplorable conditions possible.[4]

Two of the first men to note problems with the treaty were Thomas J. Abbott and Maj. Benjamin S. Parsons, both two respectable Alabama citizens and members of President Jackson's political party. In May 1832, Lewis Cass, the secretary of war, commissioned these men to take a census of the Creeks in anticipation of the allotment of their lands in severalty to chiefs and heads of households. Article 2 of the treaty stipulated that ninety Creek chiefs would receive full sections of land each and all other Creek heads of households could claim a half section for themselves and their families. Secretary Cass's initial instructions to the commissioners defined these household heads as every married man or every unmarried man or unmarried woman who maintained a separate residence and had "inmates or dependents living with them." However, Abbott and Parsons found that while these directions might have worked well enough in a typical white community, they wholly failed to comprehend the cultural complexity and diverse living arrangements of people in the Creek Nation.[5]

Traditionally, the Creeks maintained a matrilineal society, and this had much to do with the way they conceived of heads of households. It also influenced the way they divided and used their land. Individual Creeks traced their descent through their mothers; they belonged to their mother's clan; they grew up in clan compounds or neighborhoods in close association with their mothers and her sisters and other female relatives. In Creek society, the women headed the households, controlling the children and managing domestic property. Fathers, still members of their own clans, acted the part of invited guests in the wife's household, and she and her clan did not even consider him blood kin to his own children. Creek women also did the farming. The clans divided the bottomlands contiguous to a Creek town and the female clan members worked together to produce the Indian staples of beans, corn, and squash, as well as a wide variety of other fruits and vegetables. Traditional Creeks believed that because women produced children, they brought special talents and indeed a strong reservoir of spiritual power to the production of crops and naturally should control and manage the use of agricultural land. However, the census commissioners, coming as they did from a patrilineal society where men tended to control farmland, first sought out males to list as head of Creek households and consequently as potential owners of half sections of land. And while this plan appealed to nontraditional Creeks, those who had adapted to white ways, adopted patriarchy, and farmed cotton and corn for the market economy, many Indian women found it objectionable. Parsons, in fact, found it astonishing that females seemed the most interested in the final division of the Creek estate and hounded him with questions about his job.[6]

Creek women also moved to protect their interests in the budding resource competition in very clever ways, which the commissioners, owing again to their ignorance of Native culture, termed census fraud. Article 2 of the treaty also said that the land issued to a household head should include land that person had already improved and was using. Consequently, many Creek women, married and single, left the extended households in which they were living, at least temporarily, and ventured out to erect a simple cabin or make some other small improvement to a valuable piece of property so they could enroll as a family head and claim ownership of that property when the time came. Realizing this, the census commissioners cried foul. First, they believed that an Indian could claim only the property on which he or she lived at the time of the treaty. Second, they did not think any married woman could enroll and claim land as a household head. Even if a man had several wives, they would all be included in his family for census purposes and would have to make do with his single half section of land. According to the commissioners, only single women with dependents could register for land, but not necessarily that land they tried to improve since the treaty. This seemingly unfair decision, which failed to conform to the realities of traditional Creek social life and would leave many deserving female household heads and their children without land, surely upset women all over the Creek country. Nevertheless, some of these women found ways to stay one step ahead of the commissioners in claiming their traditional rights to the land. Creek girls living in the households of relatives occasionally told the commissioners they were married to white men living in Georgia to establish themselves as household heads entitled to property. And some of these girls may have had Creek husbands but could not say so and receive allotments in their own names. In either case, these ingenious females knew it would be difficult for the commissioners to disprove the existence of a husband living outside the Creek country.[7]

But a number of Creek women did have white husbands living with them in New Alabama, and this posed more difficulties for the census takers. Some of these husbands were real Indian countrymen who had been cohabiting with the Creeks long before the Cusseta Treaty, had fathered numerous children, and were considered regular members of Creek society. Naturally, they expected to receive land reserves along with all other household heads. For a time, officials at the War Department agreed. But the government's position changed when numbers of other white men entered the Creek Nation after the Cusseta Treaty and married Indian women for the sole purpose of establishing themselves as heads of Creek families and laying their grasping hands on land reserves. The Creek chiefs complained loudly and often that these men would leave their wives as soon as they received title to the land. Realizing the truth of these complaints, and wanting to keep the list of Creek landholders as short as possible, Secretary Cass eventually informed the census commissioners that no white man should receive land as a head of household. Presumably, the wives of the Indian countrymen received land allotments and these men acquired the title or financial benefit from the land through these women.[8]

But the commissioners' rigid ideas of race and what an Indian was continued to cause them problems in taking a census in an inclusive and ethnically diverse body like the Creek Nation. In their travels through New Alabama they came upon Indian men living with black slaves, free blacks living with Indian women, and Indian men living with white women, and they immediately sent off missives to the War Department asking if these were legitimate Creek families for census purposes and, if so, who should be listed as household head. But most perplexing to the commissioners were the cases where generations of miscegenation had produced Creeks who did not look like Indians at all. In fact, numbers of Creeks probably seemed racially indistinguishable from the commissioners themselves. One Samuel Brashears stands as a good example. A descendant of the famed Alexander McGillivray, Brashears had only a trace of Indian blood, but Tuskenea, a chief of the Tuckabatchee town where Brashears lived, recognized his Creek citizenship and vouched for him before Parsons. Yet the commissioner could not get beyond the fact that Brashears looked white. Furthermore, Samuel had a white wife and white children, and Parsons could not grasp the fact that being Creek was not necessarily a matter of race. Consequently, he refused to enroll Brashears as a head of a Creek household entitled to a land reserve, even though he did enroll the man's brothers, who may have looked a bit more Indian and did have Indian wives. In the end, Parsons merely advised Brashears to take his case directly to the War Department. In his letter of appeal, Brashears ironically highlighted the amount of racial toleration and basic humanity still existing among the Creeks, as opposed to a corresponding intolerance in white society:

"I was born and principally brought up in it [the Creek Nation], and if I am not so very red, perhaps my ancestors were; and if they had a right to the soil, I have also, for the Indians like their children too well to cast them off on account of their color."[9]

The commissioners also discovered that the Creek Nation was not only more ethnically varied than they at first thought, but also more geographically widespread. Creeks did not live in New Alabama alone, and this contributed to the difficulty of taking an accurate census of them. Creeks inhabited villages along the Apalachicola River in Florida and lived in Seminole villages farther south in the Florida peninsula. Creeks also made their homes farther north in the Cherokee country, an extensive body of land extending over portions of Tennessee, North Carolina, Georgia, and Alabama, and farther west with the Chickasaws in Mississippi. Some continued to live in Old Alabama, working on cattle ranches and farms; others owned considerable plantations by the Alabama and Tensaw rivers toward Mobile, the state's port on the Gulf of Mexico. An uncertain number of Creeks also remained in Georgia despite the treaties by which they gave up all of their land there and agreed to leave the state. Some of these Creeks intermarried with whites or blacks and tried to assimilate themselves into Georgia's society, while others simply roamed the wild piney woods in the southwestern portion of the state, hunting and preying off the livestock of the sparse white settlements there. And then, of course, there were the western Creeks, the people who had moved beyond the Mississippi to the Arkansas country, following the Georgia treaties. These people, mostly Lower Creeks of the acculturated McIntosh Party, were supposed to be the founders of the new Creek Nation in the West, and the president and his minions at the War Department, not to mention a large majority of the white population of the southern states, hoped the rest of the Creeks would soon leave Alabama and join the McIntosh crowd. However, the census takers discovered that the reverse was somewhat happening. The lure of valuable land allotments tended to cause consolidation of the disparate Creeks in New Alabama, just when whites were hoping they would leave. Creeks returned from the West, from Florida, from Old Alabama, Mississippi, and Georgia to get their names on the census roll and to stake out half sections for themselves. Again, the overwhelmed commissioners begged the secretary of war for help, asking whom they should include in the census and whom they should leave off.[10]

The influx of Indians from other parts certainly made the work of the census commissioners more difficult, but worse, it created competition and conflict among the Creeks themselves. An Upper Creek headman, Selochta, more famously known as General Chinubbee, and two other Indian leaders gave evidence of this clash in a statement sent to the War Department. They represented the interests of established residents of the Creek Nation and complained that one William H. Moore, a land speculator, had actually brought in Creeks from the Cherokee Nation to claim allotments, which Moore intended to buy from them, presumably at a cut rate. Furthermore, Chinubbee and company declared that Moore's Creeks had no intention of emigrating west once they sold their land; they meant to return to live with the Cherokees. Obviously, the Upper Creek chiefs believed this was wrong, but what irritated them most was the fact that many of the returning Indians were not responsible members of the Creek Nation. They had left their hometowns years before and had not supported the communities—where they now wanted land—by engaging in traditional public works projects such as cultivating communal town fields or tending the crops of the chiefs. Moreover, Chinubbee, one of General Jackson's former allies, contended that the Creeks coming in from the Cherokee country were bad people, actually old-time Red Sticks, who had fled their homes to escape Jackson's wrath at the close of the First Creek War, then refused the peaceful overtures of both Jackson and the Creek Council, who together had assured all the Red Stick refugees wherever they were that if they returned to their hometowns they would be welcomed and could reclaim all their rights and privileges as members of the Creek Nation. Their refusal and absence from the Creek towns for more than twenty years, said Chinubbee, meant that the Cherokee Creeks had forfeited those rights, including the right to claim land reserves under the Cusseta Treaty. Consequently, Chinubbee and his fellows urged the secretary of war not to allow any of the

Creeks returning from the Cherokee, Choctaw, or Chickasaw lands to receive allotments in the country they previously abandoned. But in the case of the Cherokee Creeks he had no need to worry. The residents of Upper Creek Tallushatchee town settled the matter by beating them up and running them back north to the Cherokee Nation.[11]

However, while many Creeks competed to get their names on the census rolls, some seemed indifferent or even resisted inclusion, making the commissioners' work even more tiresome and time consuming. Indeed, the more traditional Creeks strongly opposed the whole notion of individual property ownership and thus opposed the census. Other Creeks, while willing to enroll themselves on the census, showed reluctance to enumerate their slaves, perhaps fearing the whites would take them. But by far the greatest difficulty was simply collecting or hunting the Creeks, many of whom lived widely dispersed up and down New Alabama river and creek valleys. Moreover, these people belonged to more than seventy different communities. In former times, the Creek towns had been fairly compact, but by the 1830s, owing to increased cattle ranching and the construction of individual family farms on the American pattern, numbers of these towns had become more nominal than real. The town proper consisted of only a council ground, possibly a stickball field, and a few houses and storage sheds. The homes of all the people claiming allegiance to the town then straggled prodigiously out in all directions. One town, the commissioners discovered, extended by fits and starts for a distance of forty miles. Thus, the commissioners had to ride great distances in pursuit of household heads, and rains, creeks, and swamps often delayed their journeys. Then, just when the commissioners thought they had finished their task, they would discover more impositions and frauds, as they called them. At one point Abbott complained that the census had been inflated by as many as 2,000 illegitimate household heads. At another time, Commissioner Parsons went back and retook the census in nine whole towns. As a result, the commissioners spent a whole year at their task. Parsons completed the census of the Upper Creek towns on May 1, 1833, listing a total of 14,142 people, including 445 slaves, living in forty-five settlements. Nearly two weeks later, Abbott certified a roll for the Lower Creek towns, showing a population of 8,552 people, including 457 slaves, living in thirty-two towns and villages. Out of the total Creek population of 22,694 individuals, the commissioners designated 6,557 as heads of families entitled to allotments. The addition of chiefs and orphans eligible for allotments brought the total number of Creeks to receive either half or full sections to 6,696 individuals. The land these people were to receive would amount to 2,187,200 acres. But even then, the Creek chiefs complained of the inaccuracy of the census, contending that numbers of eligible tribespeople had been excluded.[12]

The chiefs were probably correct about the census, but it soon became evident that the Cusseta Treaty would cause them an even greater problem. On April 5, 1832, the secretary of war moved to honor Article 5 of the accord, which obligated the government to remove intruders from the Creek counties of Alabama, excluding temporarily only those people who had planted crops and had not infringed on Indian farmland or expelled Creeks from their homes. The treaty granted these settlers permission to stay where they were through the summer, but then, after the fall harvest, they too must leave the ceded territory until the Creeks received their reserves. At that point, the settlers could return to New Alabama and occupy parcels of land not claimed by Indian families. Unfortunately for the Creeks, this seemingly fair treaty exemption would have disastrous consequences on their ability to hold their land reserves.[13]

Secretary Cass assigned the task of intruder removal to Robert L. Crawford, U.S. marshal for the Southern District of Alabama, headquartered in Mobile. Cass instructed Crawford to repair to the Creek country and notify all intruders, except those claiming the temporary exemption, to vacate the district by such date as the marshal should designate. Surprisingly, the secretary expressed the belief that these people would readily obey Crawford's order and honor the government's treaty pledge to the Indians. But at the same time, Cass told the marshal that those intruders who did not obey the removal order must be expelled, forcefully if necessary. Consequently, he ordered the commanding officer at Fort Mitchell, an army post located near the Creek agency in Russell County, to provide Crawford with troops should he require them. Finally, Cass asked Crawford to begin the removals as soon as possible, during the planting season, so the intruders would not keep the Indians from cultivating enough land to feed themselves in the fall and winter.[14]

But Marshal Crawford seemed to lack enthusiasm for his task and was in no hurry to carry it out. He informed Cass that he had to attend the spring session of the district court and could not leave Mobile for the Creek country before June 1. He then published notices in three Alabama newspapers informing the intruders that they did not have to vacate New Alabama until July 15. Furthermore, he sought assurances from Cass that the government would reimburse him for the necessarily heavy expense of intruder removal.[15]

In fact, the marshal did not start work until July 1, when he entered the Creek counties near Montgomery. From there he traveled in a southeasterly direction to the village of Irwinton, about forty-five miles south of the Creek agency and Fort Mitchell. The Alabama legislature had incorporated Irwinton just the year before, appointing commissioners to mark off one square mile of land by the Chattahoochee River. The town was supposed to serve as a cotton port, receiving the produce of southeastern Alabama and southwestern Georgia for shipment downriver to the Gulf of Mexico. But Irwinton's founders had located their settlement on the site of Eufaula, a Lower Creek town. In the process, these intruders drove the Indians away from the place and burned or removed their houses. In fact, some of the dispossessed Natives fled for a distance of forty or fifty miles back into the Creek country, and there, deprived of their corn and livestock, they had to live by eating roots. But with the Indians out of the way, the whites made Irwinton a prime entry point for a stream of intruders coming over the river from Georgia, as well as a beachhead for the expansion of the nation's market economy into southern Alabama. Indeed, though whites entered all nine counties of the Creek country, their intrusion was especially aggressive and harsh in the Lower counties near the Chattahoochee River. These counties—Chambers, Macon, Russell, and Barbour—contained the best cotton lands in the Creek Nation and naturally attracted a host of Georgians, who found it an easy matter to cross the river and take up residence on the fertile bottoms of the Chattahoochee and its tributary streams. These Georgians had a long tradition of territorial expansion at the expense of the Creeks, and they tended to view the Natives with more hostility than did the Alabamians or other white southerners. Little wonder then that the federal marshal chose to begin the task of intruder removal at the log town of Irwinton in Barbour County.[16]

When reaching the community, Crawford discovered that the settlers also had encroached on the farmlands of the Eufaula Creeks who still lived near Irwinton. These Indians had enclosed their fields within a town fence to protect them from grazing livestock, but Crawford noted that the Eufaulas left borders of woodland between their cultivated patches of corn, potatoes, beans, and peas. Consequently, some of Irwinton's clever intruders had moved inside the Indian fence to clear away the woodland borders for their own fields and had incorporated even some of the Indians' plowed land into their new farms. These intruders then proclaimed to Crawford that because they had planted lands not in use by the Eufaulas, they fell under the exemption clause given in Article 5 of the treaty and should not be removed from New Alabama. Crawford also found that some intruders, who might have been entitled to the exemption because they took land outside the Indian fence, actually had stolen Indian cabins and moved them to their new homesteads, thus depriving the Eufaulas of shelter if not farmland. Other intruders appropriated Indian fields outright but lived in Irwinton, two miles distant from their farms, and thereby sought to escape Crawford's notice and his removal order. Beyond these injustices, numerous whites ran their cattle and horses onto pastureland already occupied by the Indians' livestock.[17]

Seeing all this, Crawford determined that among the Irwinton intruders "were some of the most lawless and uncouth men I have ever seen; some of them refugees from the State of Georgia, and for whom rewards are offered." He also decided that "rough men require rough treatment," and so he enlisted the aid of a detachment of troops from Fort Mitchell and expelled the worst offenders from Irwinton, packing them back across the Chattahoochee. He also returned the Eufaulas' land to them and even gave them the fields the intruders had cleared outside the Indian fence. And finally, at the Indians' request, he burned all the cabins the intruders had stolen from them to prevent whites from reoccupying them in the future.[18]

Although he had made an impressive start, Crawford still lacked the stomach for intruder removal, as his subsequent actions demonstrated. From Irwinton, he proceeded north up the Chattahoochee to Fort Mitchell. Yet he reported to the War Department that he found few intruders along the way, and those he did not remove because he claimed they "lived in harmony with the Creeks." Leaving Fort Mitchell, the marshal moved farther north to the Coosa and Tallapoosa rivers, in the Upper Creek country. But there he discovered the same situation: numbers of settlers, but very few abusing the Indians or taking Indian land. In light of the fact that the Creeks had been complaining of intruders for years and had devised the Cusseta Treaty to put an end to white encroachment on their land, Crawford's findings seem fantastic. In the end, he removed only a handful of intruders from New Alabama in the summer of 1832, and this was a crucial mistake. Furthermore, even those few culprits Crawford did expel returned to the Creek counties as soon as he went back to Mobile. At Irwinton they came back fully armed, with reinforcements, and threatened to defend themselves against anyone seeking to displace them again. They also brought in the county sheriff to serve writs of trespass on the marshal, the commanding officer of troops, and any Indians occupying the homesteads Crawford had forced the intruders to vacate. But as the marshal and troops were nowhere to be found, the angry intruders simply ran the Indians off and took back possession of their farms. The principal chief of the Eufaula Creeks, Fushatchee Emathla, informed the Creek agent that most of his people had fled into the woods, without subsistence, to hide from the settlers. The Eufaula chiefs also complained to Abbott when he came to their district to take the census in October 1832. One of these men, Yelker Harjo, reported that the aggressive whites were gathering all the corn from Indian fields, and if the government did not act, the whole Eufaula tribe would face starvation and death in the near future.[19]

Furthermore, the intruders began to acquire the backing of powerful men interested in New Alabama's economic development. Dixon Lewis, a U.S. representative and states' rights advocate, and William Irwin, a state legislator and the largest landowner in southeastern Alabama, both protested to Secretary Cass that Marshal Crawford had not only removed some of the county's "best citizens" from Irwinton but burned all their improvements as well, including a large warehouse frame. Then, when the poor residents of the town tried to stop this outrage by having the sheriff serve a civil warrant on one of the army officers assisting Crawford, that officer ordered one of his men to bayonet the sheriff, severely wounding him. However, William Irwin became infamous for his propensity to exaggerate events in the Creek country, and it seems likely the bayonet incident never happened as he described. Certainly, Crawford denied it in one of his reports to Cass. Nevertheless, this and future protests claimed the secretary's attention and may have made him more cautious about enforcing intruder removal in New Alabama against the interests of powerful politicians and their constituents.[20]

By summer's end the real problem with the Cusseta Treaty had revealed itself, and the Creek Council, led by Neah Micco and Tuskenea, made the situation known to the War Department. By holding out the possibility of choice homesteads to both whites and Indians in the same locale, the treaty had set up an intense resource competition between the two peoples. The chiefs lamented to the secretary that far from intruders being removed, their numbers had greatly increased since the signing of the treaty. They went on to say that "instead of our situation being relieved, as was anticipated, we are distressed in a tenfold manner—we are surrounded by the whites with their fields and fences, our lives are in jeopardy—we are daily threatened for fear we should make choices of their improvements—we are prevented from building new houses, or clearing new fields—we have for the last six months lived in fire, yet we have borne it with patience, believing our father, the President, would comply on his part what he pledged himself to do."[21]

Enoch Parsons, Benjamin's brother and assistant, agreed that New Alabama had become "thickly settled with white people" following the

Cusseta Treaty and the extension of state law over the region. Parsons also confirmed the fact that the whites came for land. However, he went on to note another attraction drawing intruders to the Creek country. Article 9 of the treaty obligated the United States to pay one hundred thousand dollars to the Creeks so that they might settle all their debts acquired prior to the treaty and become financially solvent. But Parsons saw that many whites had come to New Alabama to put the Indians in more debt, hoping that they could then get a share of the government payment, which amounted to a considerable sum for a cash-poor frontier section of the country. Parsons observed that the Creek counties were "full of traders and merchandise" and worse, "ardent spirits." In fact, the intruders used liquor, sold on credit, as the key to drawing the Indians into debt and dependency, the chief means of depriving them of land, money, and, indeed, liberty. Furthermore, Parsons suspected that not one of the trading posts in New Alabama had a license as required by Alabama law. Consequently, he suggested to the War Department that the traders be either prosecuted by the state or removed from the Creek country by the federal government. Then Parsons went on to make a surprisingly accurate prophecy. He declared that the trading houses would retard the removal of the Creeks to the West and thereby thwart the government's ultimate goal. He rightly foresaw that if the Indians remained in Alabama two or three more years under the influence of the whiskey dealers, they would not be "worth in morals or property much." And when the Creeks finally decided to leave Alabama, said Parsons, the traders would produce bail writs for debt against them and have them thrown in jail until they surrendered all of their remaining property. To prevent this sad state of affairs, Parsons asked that Cass petition Alabama's legislature to repeal its extension of law over the Creek country and turn back the region to complete federal control. Then the central government would be able to stop all liquor sales to the Indians, remove intruders without interference from state politicians, prevent Indian indebtedness to whites, and remove the Indians more quickly and efficiently. However, Parsons failed to mention in his otherwise insightful appeal that the Creeks might take matters into their own hands at some point and use an armed rebellion to break free of oppression. He did not foresee the fact that the Indians might actually fight to rid themselves of poverty, indebtedness, and moral decay, not to mention the government's constant demand that they leave their ancient homeland and move west.[22]

But in the final analysis, intruding farmers and trading-store operators were not the greatest threats to the Creeks and their resources. The greatest danger came out of Columbus, Georgia, a brand new town situated on the east bank of the Chattahoochee just across from the Creek counties of New Alabama. Columbus was the only commercial emporium of any consequence in the Lower river valley, and its merchants and bankers meant to control the trade and commerce of all the land drained by the Chattahoochee and its tributaries. This expanse of land included not only most of western Georgia but the best part of New Alabama as well. Hence, Columbus businesspeople did much to encourage the intrusive settlement of the Creek country by whites. Moreover, they made plans to acquire and profit from the resale of as many of the Creek land reserves as possible. On April 5, 1832, only a few days after the Creek delegation signed the Cusseta Treaty, twenty wealthy townspeople formed the Columbus Land Company for that purpose. They sent agents into New Alabama to set up stores filled with trade goods and whiskey. They instructed these agents to sell to the Creeks on credit, luring them into debt to the company, and then to demand as payment bonds for title to the rich lands the individual debtors would claim for their allotments. The members of the company also sent black interpreters called "strikers" into New Alabama to hound and pressure potential allottees into selling their land claims to the company for a fraction of what the property would be worth on the open market. In the end, the Columbus land buyers and speculators proved to be the real bane of Creek existence.[23]

However, Indians were not the only ones to complain of the resource competition set in motion by the Cusseta Treaty. Independent farmers and planters also protested the situation. They believed that the treaty had turned New Alabama into public domain. Furthermore, they saw the extension of Alabama law over the area as an open invitation to settle that public domain. But now, after investing time, money, and hard work to create homesteads for themselves, the government threatened to ruin them by removing them from the land. Some of these people complained that they would have great difficulty leaving the Creek counties, even if they wanted to, because they had sold their wagons to get money to live on until their first harvest. But this set of intruders felt most threatened by the government's plan to let Indians select land reserves for themselves, rather than the government choosing allotments for the Creeks. In their letters to Secretary Cass, numbers of New Alabama whites contended that they had taken up farms as much as fifteen miles away from any Indian town, to avoid land conflicts with the Natives, but the Creeks were leaving the used-up land around their old settlements and coming out to them. The Indians were moving out into the countryside to claim the improvements of newly arrived settlers as parts of the reserves they would receive under the treaty. Moreover, the intruders told the secretary that government functionaries, most notably Agent Crowell, encouraged the Creeks to do this, and they may have been right. Certainly Crowell meant to acquire a considerable body of Indian land for himself, and he may have wanted his Creek charges to spread out and hold off whites that might try to settle land he and his cohorts already coveted.[24]

Indeed, one should not suppose that the competition for land reserves was a simple one pitting Indians against settlers. The treaty also set up a contest for land among three different groups of whites—Columbus land speculators, respectable farmers and planters, and frontier roughs. The conflict between respectables and roughs was bitter. The respectables, as they always did, tried to bring civilization to the frontiers by reestablishing the same institutions and value systems they left behind. However, the lower orders, called roughs, gravitated toward frontier regions to escape the constraints of so-called civilized society and to establish "contraculture" communities more amenable to their own desires. Accordingly, roughs moved over from Georgia to take Indian wives in hopes of setting themselves up as the heads of Indian families eligible for land reserves. Many of these men ran grog shops as another means of despoiling the Indians of their land claims. In fact, grog-shop owners often directed the Indians where to settle their land allotments, then lured them deeper into debt so they could take those choice reserves as payment when the time came. Respectable settlers became the most vociferous critics of the liquor stores, and not simply because they feared drunken Indians as a threat to their security. They saw the grog-shop owners as having an unfair economic advantage in the general competition for New Alabama's resources. Not only did the whiskey dealers have better access to Indian lands, but they also competed with the farmers and planters in purchasing Creek livestock and produce. Moreover, the farmers complained that if the government insisted on removing respectable citizens from the country, they too would have to sell their animals and other possessions to the liquor stores. However, the farmers and planters reserved their greatest spite for the land speculators. They knew full well that the Columbus Land Company meant to monopolize the Indian reserves by any means possible for the sole purpose of reselling the land at a high rate of return to good, hard-working settlers like themselves. One such settler, Lewis Watkins, crafted a protest and appeal to Washington he knew would catch the attention of President Jackson, the spokesperson for mass democracy and the champion of the commoner. In self-serving fashion, Watkins pictured the New Alabama farmers as the honest poor, who rather than remain as tenants on the property of oppressive landlords in their former states had come to the Creek country seeking asylum. Watkins contended that if the government allowed such people to remain in New Alabama and protected them from Indians and land speculators, they would become prosperous citizens and, by implication, Jacksonian Democrats. However, should the government remove them, the speculators and moneyed elites would hold sway and the Indians would stay in the country much longer.[25]

Nevertheless, the War Department was obligated to uphold the provisions of the Cusseta accord, and as the fall harvest began, Secretary Cass took steps to remove intruders from the Creek country. He instructed John Elliott, district attorney for the Southern District of Alabama, to defend the Eufaula Creeks in the circuit court of Pike County against suits of trespass brought against them by the Irwinton intruders—the people who took Indian land and property, then used the legal system against the Indians when they tried to take it back. That much done, Cass ordered Marshal Crawford to proceed with another round of intruder removals. Crawford, in turn, dispatched the deputy marshal Jeremiah Austill to the Creek country to do the job. Finally, Cass ordered two additional companies of federal troops to Fort Mitchell "for the purpose of expelling and keeping off intruders."[26]

Unfortunately for the Creeks, the fall ejection of intruders turned into a fiasco. When Deputy Austill appeared at Fort Mitchell to get the troops he would need to help him remove all the intruders from the Creek counties, he found that the soldiers had not yet arrived. Then, Marshal Crawford, still lacking enthusiasm for the whole venture, ordered Austill back to Mobile. By way of explaining himself to the War Department, Crawford reported that he had no money to devote to intruder removal and had not yet received reimbursement from the government for his work in the summer. Furthermore, he said he would need two hundred troops to effectively remove settlers from New Alabama, for the intruders would resist violently should any fewer number of men be sent against them. Yet when the two companies of troops finally arrived at Fort Mitchell in December 1832, neither Crawford nor Austill was around to direct them. Consequently, they left New Alabama and returned to their former stations. Seeing this, the Creek chiefs, writing from their fall council ground at Wetumpka town in Russell County, informed Cass that because the intruders had not been removed, they were now bragging about their final victory over the Creeks. Moreover, they were preparing for another season of planting, "making large fields and building new houses." The chiefs proclaimed that the Creeks were being "surrounded by enemies," who prevented them from plowing new fields of their own. "In many instances we are entirely fenced up," lamented the Creek leaders.[27]

But now Creek pleas fell on deaf ears in the War Department. Secretary Cass had changed his approach to intruder removal based on advice from President Jackson's political allies in Alabama, namely William Rufus King, Clement C. Clay, and Samuel W. Mardis, all members of the state's congressional delegation. These men convinced Cass that he should not worry about expelling any intruders from the Creek country until after the Indians received their land allotments. And then the government should remove only those settlers seated on actual Creek reserve lands. Undoubtedly, Cass saw this plan as his salvation. It allowed him to honor the Cusseta accord in principle without the trouble, time, and expense—not to mention the political damage—of removing hundreds, if not thousands, of potential voters from New Alabama before the Creeks declared exactly which lands they would be living on when they took title to their individual family allotments. So Cass changed his intruder removal policy and announced the change in December 1832. Simultaneously, he closed the Creek agency in New Alabama, making it known to all that the federal government intended to withdraw from the business of Indian affairs in Alabama as soon as possible. Thereafter, Cass's chief concern would be Creek removal, not settler removal.[28]

But as often happened in New Alabama, Cass's new scheme ran into problems. The secretary obviously thought that the process of taking the Creek census and issuing allotments would not take very long. Yet three months into the year 1833, Abbott, the Parsons brothers, and John J. Abert, an assistant, were still traveling over the Creek counties filling out their rolls. Meanwhile, more intruders poured into those counties, and the secretary found himself bombarded with reports of their offenses against the Indians. Most alarmingly, the intruders, particularly the land speculators, had discovered a way to more firmly root themselves in the country and stake legal claims to the most desirable tracts of Indian land. They placed potential Creek allottees under bond by giving those Indians down payments, usually five or ten dollars each, for the purchase of the land reserves those Indians would receive. The Creeks then signed contracts obligating them to complete the sales at the time of allotment. These contracts also stipulated that the buyers could occupy for use the lands in question until such time as the president approved the final sales of those lands. However, the contracts allowed the Indians to remain on the land as well, in places designated by the buyers, until those final sales took place. These contracts consequently set up a system of joint ownership and occupancy of the best tracts of real estate in New Alabama. Moreover, the contracts gave the intruders a legal document they could take before state courts to delay, if not completely forestall, any efforts the federal government might make to remove them from the Creek country. To Cass's chagrin, the intruders were proving to be as clever as they were tenacious and greedy. They had found a way to exploit the basic contradiction of the Cusseta Treaty, which claimed police powers for the federal government in an area where state law already operated. Nevertheless, War Department officials contended that no person could attempt to make a contract for the purchase of Creek land prior to the allotments without the president's consent. And since the president had not consented, all such contracts were illegal in any court. Furthermore, the efforts of whites to imbed themselves in the Creek country so infuriated these officials that Elbert Herring, acting as secretary of war in Cass's absence from Washington, ordered Marshal Crawford to undertake yet another round of intruder removals, despite Cass's earlier decision to wait until the allotment process was complete.[29]

At the same time, War Department operatives realized the land allotment practice, as outlined in the Cusseta accord, was not working as planned. As the census commissioners moved through the Creek towns, they saw the detrimental impact the procedure was having on the Indians. They reported that the system had speeded up the process of decentralization of tribal existence, even the complete breakup of town and community life, as tribespeople moved even farther away from their community centers to settle new tracts of land. In illustration of this fact, the commissioners pointed out that prior to the implementation of the Cusseta Treaty, one section of land (640 acres) in a Creek town contained the houses and fields of a number of Indian families; since the treaty, however, that same tract, having been claimed as a chief's reserve, contained only his family. The rest of his townspeople had moved far away from the chief's reserve to claim their own half section, or 320-acre, allotments. But once there, these families often conflicted with white intruders seeking to occupy the same tracts of land. The commissioners went on to report that the Creek towns, now largely deserted, had become "dilapidated" and, even worse, the Indians, having moved from their old fields, suffered from want of food.

Many who wished to plant crops had to compete with intruders for places to do so. Other Creeks, expecting to sell their allotments and move west rather quickly, had stopped planting altogether and lived off either the small amounts settlers paid them to lease their fields or credit from the grog shops. In this unsettled state of affairs, the grog shops flourished, and one commissioner complained that some Indians carried everything they had, "even their ration of meal," to the shops to trade for liquor." Thus, starvation loomed on the horizon for some Creeks as the allotment process dragged on into the year 1833. Other Creeks simply became browbeaten and cowed as they could not live under or enforce their own tribal laws for fear of punishment by the state. Yet the state would not, or could not, protect the Creeks with its own law as intruders moved in to exploit them and take their land. Given this situation, Indian society, not unlike other societies falling under the pall of colonial occupation, tended to implode and eat away at itself. The Creeks turned more and more to alcohol consumption and self-destructive behavior—fighting, suicide, and the like. And because the Creek Council had no policing powers to enforce law, the Creeks fell back on their clan vengeance system, meaning the relatives of a murder victim, failing to come up with the murderer, could seek out and kill one of his or her innocent relatives in retribution. But given the conditions of the time, this ancient clan justice system led only to more killings, causing a pitying John J. Abert to lament of the Indians that "more murders of each other have been committed in the last six months than for as many previous years," and whites, he declared, would not bring the murderers to justice because they saw Creeks killing Creeks as beneficial for their side in the competition for land. Consequently, Abert and the other commissioners urged Cass to seek some alternative to the Cusseta Treaty and its technique of chopping up the tribal land domain. These men were learning the hard way that the Creek sense of self-worth was related to the integrity of their tribal community, not individual land ownership or the accumulation of personal wealth, as was the case in a white society already well versed in the ways of the world system.[30]

Hearing all this, Secretary Cass decided to seek a new treaty with the Creeks in the summer of 1833, one which would allow the Indians to sell their land reserves to the government, not individual buyers in New Alabama. Obviously, Cass hoped this would enable the Indians to dispose of their property more quickly and avoid being cheated out of it by unscrupulous speculators. The Indians could also avoid legal entanglements in the Alabama courts by selling to the government and more easily pull free from the corruption whites had brought them. The new treaty would provide the Creeks with more annuities, payment for removal expenses, blacksmiths, farm implements, educational costs, and other considerations. In sum, a new treaty would enable the Creeks to gain the money, materials, and tribal integrity necessary to make new starts for themselves in their western territory, a body of land consisting of some twelve million acres. Undeniably, Cass wanted, above all else, a new treaty that would encourage the Indians to emigrate, thus saving the president from the embarrassment caused by his failure to enforce the protection clause of the Cusseta accord.[31]

Following Cass's instructions, Abert, now a treaty commissioner, sent out a call to the Creek head chiefs for a grand council meeting to be held at the Creek Agency on June 19, 1833. In essence, he proposed that the government purchase each individual land reserve at an average price per acre, which would be paid directly to the land owner. If any owner had already taken money from a purchaser in New Alabama, the government would refund that amount to said purchaser and then deduct that sum from the total amount paid the land owner. Furthermore, the government would pay interest on the down payments already made by those purchasers of Indian reserves. In this way, Cass hoped to assuage the powerful speculators who might otherwise stand in the way of the treaty to protect their investments in Creek property. Furthermore, the secretary and his agents in New Alabama hoped that the prospect of soon clearing the district of Indians would unite all the whites there behind the new treaty.[32]

But again Cass failed to see that the Creeks would not be managed. They had their own point of view and they meant, as much as possible, to shape their own destiny. The Creek Council refused to make a new treaty. The chiefs contended that they, as a body, had no lands left to sell and did not need a new treaty. They needed for the government to enforce the old one as promised. In fact, they demanded that the War Department remove intruders and locate the individual land reserves as soon as possible. And this reply must have frustrated the government agents for it revealed yet another flaw in the Cusseta Treaty. President Jackson and Lewis Cass had always believed that only the Creek chiefs stood in the way of removal, so if they could wrest the tribal domain from these leaders and place it in the hands of the common Indians, those people would quickly dispose of the property and flee to the West. But now that the tribespeople did, in fact, have rights to that property, the chiefs claimed they were powerless to sell it and thereby speed up emigration. Moreover, the Creek headmen complained that they had never received money promised them in the old Fort Jackson Treaty of 1814, suggesting that the government needed to live up to its long-standing obligations before making more demands on the Creeks. But most strikingly, the chiefs declared that neither they nor their people were ready to emigrate, illustrating the fundamental difference between Cass's interpretation of the treaty and that of the Creeks. Cass saw the Cusseta accord as an Indian removal treaty; the Creeks saw it as an instrument that would enable them to stay in Alabama, on protected land holdings, for as long as they wished. Abert himself had once observed that the Creeks clung dearly to their old homeland and looked for any bit of hope to delay removal from it. In fact, the Creek Council had informed the War Department even before the Cusseta Treaty that "Our aged men and women beseech us to remain upon the land of their birth. They view a removal as the worst calamity that can befall them. Under these circumstances we as their Representatives feel not authorized . . . to enter into any definite arrangement with your government here to change their situation." Indeed, the aged and all other Creeks of a traditional nature absolutely feared removal, and not only because they held a deep spiritual attachment to their ancient homeland. In the Creek cosmos, the West was where the spirits of the dead went to dwell. It was a region of despair and woe for living beings, a place they dare not go. Moreover, the reports of earlier Creek emigrants to the West seemed to bear out this awful truth. Only disease, misfortune, trouble, and death awaited any Indian foolish enough to leave Alabama. But beyond this, the chiefs had a more secular reason for resisting removal. They knew that even in the West it would only be a matter of time before their people were "reduced to subservience to the odious trammels of laws, and government of the white men." The chiefs simply had no more confidence in the War Department's promises, for, as one observer stated, "a melancholy experience of the past has instilled into them the gloom of despair for the future."[33]

But, in reality, the Creek Council members never had any intention of signing a removal treaty, and shortly after the Cusseta accord, closed ranks to expel those among them who would not resist emigration. The Lower Creek councilors deposed John Oponee of Chehaw, Col. John Stedham of Sawokli (Raccoon town), and Toma Micco of Thlakateka (Broken Arrow) as chiefs. Meanwhile, the Upper Creek chiefs broke four of their number—Autosee Micco, Efau Tustenuggee, Tuckabatchee Fixico, and Colome Tustenuggee—and filled their seats on the council with four new chiefs from Tuckabatchee town. Autosee Micco found this reduction in status particularly appalling as he had been a chief for forty years. Consequently, he wrote to the War Department criticizing the leaders of Tuckabatchee not only for trying to consolidate their power over the Upper towns but of raising up more of their warriors to chiefly status so they could secure larger land allotments under the Cusseta Treaty. He might have added that in the disorderly and economically competitive environment of New Alabama, Opothle Yahola and his followers felt it absolutely necessary to exert some kind of strong authority over the Upper towns to prevent their fellow Creeks from losing their land to acquisitive whites, to ward off removal, and to generally keep the peace. Unfortunately, the Lower Creek Council members had no leader of Opothle Yahola's stature and foresight, and by deposing Oponee, Stedham, and Toma Micco, they may have removed a stabilizing influence in those Lower towns, where young warriors tended to join the Seminole party. Indeed, Chehaw, Sawokli, and Broken Arrow soon became centers of hostility toward the whites.[34]

The treaty commissioners, however, saw little of this in the summer of 1833. Still not wanting to admit the flawed nature of the treaty, or give the Creeks credit for controlling their own destiny, Abert and the Parsons blamed the land speculators for the unwillingness of the chiefs to sign yet another treaty. In fact, Parsons and Abert claimed that had the treaty council not been held so close to Columbus, the seat of speculation, the land buyers would not have been able to attend the meeting in such large numbers and influence the chiefs against the treaty. And indeed, the speculators were active in this regard. Even before the council began, they announced to the War Department that because the state of Alabama no longer recognized the authority of the Creek chiefs, they would oppose any attempt these chiefs made to sell land allotted to individual tribal members. And they made no apologies for the fact that they would oppose the treaty to protect the investments they had made in those allotments. Unfortunately, their opposition included threatening the Creeks with their debts and even violence should they support the new treaty. The speculators also exploited the natural mistrust the Indians had for the government. John Scott, an Indian countryman and principal purchasing agent for the Columbus Land Company, told the Creeks that the government lacked the necessary funds to pay them for their land, but the wealthy citizens of Columbus did have the money. Scott even promised to take the Indians to the town banks to show them all the piles of silver set aside for those land purchases. He also promised that if they sold their holdings to the Columbus speculators and moved west, he would go with them and build schools for them so their young people would have a better chance of prospering in their new homeland. Then Scott made perhaps his most persuasive appeal. He told the Creeks that even after selling their land to him, they could stay on that land for five more years, protected by the Columbus buyers. He may also have pointed out to them something they knew from their own experience: the government could not, or would not, give them such protection. In any event, the speculators undoubtedly did convince numerous Creeks to oppose the proposed treaty, and Scott purchased the rights to Creek allotments for relatively small amounts.[35]

However, the census commissioners were wrong in placing principal blame on the speculators for the failure of the new treaty. In reality, the internal state of Creek society at the time had much more to do with the treaty's demise. Some Creeks resented their chiefs for making the Cusseta Treaty in the first place and did not trust them to make another, possibly even more foolish, pact with the government. Indeed, a fear of retaliation undoubtedly accounts for some of the reluctance of the council chiefs to sign a new accord with Cass's commissioners. But more to the point, individual tribespeople wanted the ability to receive and sell their land reserves without interference from government or chiefs. A simple need for ready cash to operate in the whites' market-oriented world accounts for some of the opposition to the new treaty. This need for money also tore at the fabric of tribal unity, making some Indians more individualistic, competitive, and less trusting of their leaders. In these respects, they were acting more like their white neighbors. But, in the end, the principal reason for the new treaty's failure was its clause requiring the Creeks to sell their reserves and emigrate immediately. While government officials in the Creek country had been saying for years that the majority of tribespeople wanted to move west, this was simply not the case. Certainly many Creeks suffered and wanted to emigrate, but others, particularly Upper Creeks, managed to hold their own and reach a middle ground of accommodation with the whites. In short, the so-called Creek Nation was not a homogenous entity, and this fact prohibited a concerted, unified action in any direction, particularly in the move westward. In fact, the commissioners stated as much in their treaty report. They claimed that "there is not the bond of common feeling among them which would be an inducement to such a plan [emigration]. Entire towns might be prevailed upon to move at once, or one or two adjacent towns having habits of intercourse. But generally the several towns are strangers to each other, with different customs, and in some cases different languages."[36]

And here lay the key point. The heterogeneous Creek Confederacy had once been a powerful body because of its ability to attract diverse peoples and tribes, but under the stress of white intrusion and the coming of the market economy, Creek diversity became a liability. The Creeks owed first allegiance to clan and town, not to any Creek

Nation, and in times of hardship this sense of localism encouraged internal fragmentation, political factionalism, and bickering among Creek groups rather than a united effort to either emigrate or resist intrusive threats from the white world. And yet the treaty commissioners failed to note, perhaps because they were looking for another excuse to justify their failure, that many Creeks did, despite their differences, take strength from a common belief system dating back to the age of the Mississippian mound builders, if not before. They also had a common language, Muscogee. And, even more importantly, they unified around the common desire to hold on to their native soil, even if they could not agree on the best way do it. Furthermore, the Creek Nation had formed in the first place as a response to outside pressure, and some Creeks continued to hold together, indeed were forced together as a people, in the face of even more intense pressure from the encroaching whites and their economic system. All this gave the Creeks a sort of unity and coherency the treaty commissioners could not understand because they had never been a part of an oppressed minority.[37]

Meanwhile, yet another problem with the Cusseta Treaty revealed itself. While the Creek chiefs had signed that accord primarily to secure title to their land base and stave off removal, they also had another motive: money. The chiefs needed money to get themselves and their people out of debt. Otherwise, they would never be able to establish an independent existence for themselves in New Alabama and would in time lose their land to creditors. Moreover, the Creek debt had grown substantially since the Georgia Creeks moved into Alabama following the Washington Treaty of 1826. As the heads of a traditional communal society, the chiefs had to borrow money to feed, clothe, and house these people. Furthermore, individual Creek families often bought on credit against the annuity fund, and the chiefs thus became responsible for paying these debts as well. Consequently, the Creek delegates to the treaty negotiations in Washington asked that the government provide them with one hundred thousand dollars for a debt payment fund as part of the Cusseta pact. The president granted the request and Article 9 of the accord guaranteed the Creeks that fund. However, the chiefs made it clear, and the administration agreed, that the money would apply to only those tribal debts acquired before the Cusseta agreement. Reflecting a realization of the new economic order, the chiefs did not want to be personally responsible for all the individual debts their people would accrue as the whites established themselves in New Alabama. This, of course, was a break in Creek tradition brought on by the realities of the market economy and the ability of whites to use it to their advantage. Now Creek headmen had to look out for their own financial security and by extension they would force all tribal members to do the same. But many Creeks were not prepared for the change. For them, it meant only more debt and poverty and perhaps loss of faith in their leaders. This was a dangerous situation. A tragedy stood in the offing.[38]

The chiefs thought they would get the hundred thousand dollars fairly quickly after the treaty went into effect. They also thought they would have complete control over the money. They were mistaken. In June 1832, Secretary Cass announced that a board of commissioners would collect a list of financial claims against the Creeks and recommend to the government which ones should be paid out of the debt fund. This decision upset the chiefs, who saw it as yet another government effort to undermine their authority. Already President Jackson had recommended to the War Department that the government pay the Creeks their annuity to individual families instead of in the traditional manner of giving a lump sum to the two head chiefs of the nation. Befitting his image as savior of the commoner, Jackson claimed that by the old method of paying the annuity "the wealthy chiefs receive the whole, and the poor receive nothing." And while there may have been a bit of truth to this statement, Jackson's observation reflected primarily his bias against the elite commercial interests in his own society. Moreover, the president used his concern for the welfare of poor Indians as a cover for his real motive in changing the annuity payment plan. More than anything, he wanted to facilitate Creek removal. He knew that if he broke the financial power of the chiefs, they would not be able to oppose removal as well as they had done in the past.[39]

However, the chiefs did not stand idly by and let Jackson dictate his desires. They protested to the War Department that, rather than seek riches, they had gone into debt to supply the needs of their people and thereby did "that which would reward them before the Great Spirit." They had set up blacksmith shops for their people, bought them iron and steel, cotton cards, spinning wheels, crosscut saws and whipsaws, and other necessary items. Furthermore, the whites presented unjust debts for which the chiefs were liable. Therefore, it would be unjust to take the annuity out of their hands and parcel it out to individual Creeks. Indeed, the chiefs feared "ruination" if the government instituted such a policy, and they concluded their protest with a telling point. They reminded Secretary Cass that government officials had always accepted the fact that Indians held land in common and individual tribespeople could not sell land without consent of the tribal council. Consequently, those government officials had always paid the money for land purchases to the chiefs as representatives of the tribal body. The annuities were merely installments on land the government had bought over the years and could not with justice be paid to individual Creeks by family. This made sense. However, the chiefs did not note that they themselves wanted to break with tradition by making individual Creeks responsible for their own debts.[40]

In the end, the chiefs' argument prevailed. At the Wetumpka town council meeting in September 1832 the government paid the annuity in two equal parts to the head chiefs of the Upper and Lower Creeks. Tuskenea and Neah Micco each received $29,960 to distribute to their respective town chiefs. The Creek Council members were not entirely happy, however. They complained that they had not yet received the $100,000 debt fund, and the delay had caused serious problems for them. The lure of so much money had drawn even more intruders into the Creek country, all of them seeking to seduce the Indians into more debt. In fact, New Alabama filled to overflowing with traders and their "ardent spirits." Worse still, many tribespeople, suffering from poverty and the excesses of the intruders, continued to cry out against the chiefs for signing the Cusseta Treaty in the first place. The chiefs, in turn, begged for the immediate delivery of the debt fund and complained again that government commissioners should not decide how it would be expended. They also pointed out, quite skillfully, that any decision those commissioners might make would not be final in the eyes of disappointed creditors. Those angry white men would surely file suits and the Alabama courts would step in to decide debts against the Creeks. In the meantime, poor Indians would continue to suffer. But the secretary of war did not relent. He informed the chiefs that government supervision of fund expenditures was entirely necessary because of all the false debt claims against the Creeks and the fact that Indians had accumulated many new debts since the Cusseta Treaty, debts that should not be paid out of the fund. Furthermore, the secretary told the chiefs that they should meet in council with the debt fund commissioners in January 1833 to go over the list of debt claims against their people. The chiefs should then decide which claims were valid and of those which ones were national in nature—debts contracted by the chiefs for the good of the Creek Nation as a whole. The commissioners would then review this list of national debts and decide which ones would be paid out of the hundred thousand dollars. Then, if any money remained in the fund after the payment of these national claims, the government would deliver it to the chiefs so that they could pay their local or individual town debts.[41]

The chiefs certainly did not welcome this news from Washington, but in the end, the fact that the government wanted to manage their financial affairs proved to be one of their smaller concerns. In truth, the whole debt fund, rather than allowing the Creeks to achieve financial stability, merely exacerbated both their financial woes and their internal political struggles. Delegates from the Upper and Lower towns met in council with the debt fund commissioners for three full weeks and emerged from the process even more divided. As expected, the commissioners discovered numerous false claims, often backed by forged papers. Moreover, merchants often charged the Creeks much more than their goods were worth. Worse still, the existence of the debt fund increased the intruder problem, as whites rushed into the Indian country to set up shop and peddle their spirits, anything to pile more debt on the Creeks. But some of the chiefs were willing to sign off on almost any claim, legitimate or bogus, simply because Tuskenea and Neah Micco did so. All this hinted at a lack of diligence or even outright complicity to rob the nation on the part of these two principal chiefs. Moreover, these headmen approved claims submitted by Agent Crowell and John Brodnax that Commissioner Parsons thought were not really national debts but ones the Lower towns alone should pay. In fact, the more impoverished Lower Creeks had run up numerous bills that both the commissioners and the Upper Creek chiefs disavowed. Moreover, Paddy Carr and Benjamin Marshall, two acculturated Lower Creek planters with personal interests in the debt claims, served as interpreters for the council. Seeing all this, Opothle Yahola and the Upper chiefs present in council demanded that the commissioners divide the debt fund evenly between the two divisions of the nation. Otherwise, they feared the lion's share of Lower Creek debt would be imposed as national in nature and would eat up most of the fund. And, indeed, this is exactly what happened. On a day when not all the Upper chiefs attended the meeting, the Lower chiefs, along with two Upper chiefs who may have accepted bribes, voted to approve a list of national debts weighted in favor of the Lower towns. Consequently, Opothle Yahola and the angry Tuckabatchee chiefs petitioned the War Department, asking that the government set aside the vote of the debt fund council and simply allow the commissioner Enoch Parsons to divide the money as he saw fit. These chiefs accused their Lower town brethren of collusion with white speculators and expressed confidence in Parsons's ability to ferret out and cancel all the unjust national claims the Lower chiefs wanted to pay with money that should go to the Upper towns. The Tuckabatchee party also asked that no money be paid out to the Creeks at the agency, because the white residents of Fort Mitchell and its environs were so "good at getting their hands on it."[42]

The commissioners reviewed the council's schedule of debts and Parsons submitted a report to Washington recommending that some of the national claims favored by the Lower Creeks be dismissed. Agent Crowell, however, submitted a dissenting report complaining that those creditors holding dismissed claims did not know that they would have to prove their claims to the government. In this, he suggested that the word of the council should be good enough for creditors to get their money. Tuskenea and Neah Micco also took offense at the

Parsons brothers' report as well as the criticisms leveled at them by the Tuckabatchee party. They fired off a missive to Washington accusing General Parsons of trying to subvert the decision of the council because of his own designs on Creek money. Then the two headmen vowed that if the government refused to pay all the national claims submitted by them, they would make good on those claims out of any residual funds allotted to the individual Creek towns. In the end, the government used about three-quarters of the hundred thousand dollars to pay the Creeks' national debt. Brodnax, Crowell, Carr, Marshall, and other Lower Creek creditors living near the agency received considerable portions of the fund. The Upper and Lower towns divided the remaining quarter of the fund among themselves, but most probably, that money soon found its way into the pockets of creditors as well.[43]

Unfortunately, the proper use of the debt fund was not the only issue that divided the Creek political factions during the early months of 1833. Some members of the acculturated and ever-opportunistic McIntosh party of western Creeks moved to claim a share of the land reserves and money coming to their eastern cousins by way of the Cusseta Treaty. Consequently, Chilly McIntosh and Benjamin Hawkins made their way back from the West and presented themselves at the debt fund council meeting to negotiate a treaty of peace between their portion of the nation and the eastern Creeks. And, indeed, these men appeared to be the very models of magnanimity, as both had lost their fathers in the conflict between the McIntosh faction and the Creek Council. Chilly and Benjamin were the sons respectively of William McIntosh and Samuel Hawkins, two Lower Creek leaders the council executed for their unauthorized sale of the whole Creek domain to Georgia in 1825. So it must have appeared to all present that if these two young western Creeks were resolved to make peace, so were the rest of their people. Certainly the government commissioners welcomed the emissaries with open arms and encouraged a treaty between the eastern and western parts of the nation as a way to facilitate Creek removal from New Alabama. They reasoned that if peaceful relations could be established, the eastern people would be much more willing than they had been to move out among the westerners. The Lower Creek chiefs in council also favored an understanding with McIntosh and Hawkins, because most of the western Creeks belonged originally to Lower Creek towns. Both Benjamin Marshall and Paddy Carr, for example, owed allegiance to Coweta town, the same old Creek mother town that spawned the McIntosh family. They, like most of the Lower Creek leaders, undoubtedly had relatives and friends among the westerners. Consequently, it did not take long for the Lower chiefs to strike a deal with McIntosh and Hawkins. Both sides agreed to peace and cancelled all old debt claims against one another. Then, for good measure, the council delegates gave the western Creeks five sections of the twenty-nine sections of land allotted to the Creeks for their general use by the Cusseta Treaty. But there was a problem. Very few Upper chiefs, and none of the Tuckabatchee party members, signed the agreement, indicating a general reluctance on their part to either forgive the McIntosh crowd or trust them to forget the past. Certainly, Opothle Yahola remembered his part in bringing William McIntosh to justice. Likewise, Menawa, another Upper Creek chief who served on the delegation meeting to consider the debt claims, could not have felt kindly toward the western Creeks. After all, he had led the Red Sticks and fought against William McIntosh and Andrew Jackson at Horseshoe Bend. Then, years later, he actually led the execution party that shot McIntosh to pieces and made Sam Hawkins "eat fire."[44]

Whatever their reasons, the Upper Creeks were right not to rush into an agreement with the western emissaries. Hawkins and McIntosh soon sold the rights to the five sections of Creek reserves to John Milton, one of the Columbus land speculators, for two thousand dollars. Then, as part of the contract, they signed a bond obligating the western Creek Council to pay Milton the extravagant sum of twenty thousand dollars in compensation should the government fail to recognize the sale. In other words, this stipulation was designed to force the Indians to turn the land over to Milton regardless of what the government thought of the deal. Worse still, McIntosh convinced the War Department to hire him as a removal agent, claiming he could get a significant number of Creeks to return west with him if the government would pay him per head. He then used his share of the land-sale money to begin to finance his removal operation. However, Parsons complained that McIntosh's emigration plan was selective in nature. He meant to remove only his relatives from Alabama or poor Indians whose land he could then claim for his own. In the end, the government would finance the scheme. On hearing this, the western Creek Council promptly revoked the power of attorney given to McIntosh and Hawkins, and the War Department did, indeed, deny the legality of their land sale to John Milton. Opothle Yahola and the Upper chiefs could only look on and shake their heads knowingly. They had to have thought that Chilly McIntosh was proving to be as materialistic and tricky as his father, and the Lower chiefs continued to display the same bad judgment as always.[45]

With his new removal treaty in ruins, the Creek leaders squabbling among themselves, and his commissioners not yet ready to issue the Indians their land allotments, Secretary Cass had little choice but to honor the Cusseta accord and initiate yet another round of intruder removals. This time, however, the government's attempt to expel settlers from New Alabama would bring into glaring relief a third major flaw in the treaty. By authorizing the use of a federal police force within the boundaries of a sovereign state, most especially a southern state, the treaty set up an inevitable confrontation between Alabama's governor and the War Department.

Deputy Marshal Austill arrived at Fort Mitchell on July 1, 1833, to begin his work. He reported that most of the intruders in the vicinity of the fort were "civil enough to the Indians," but they disturbed the Creeks by bringing in "large stocks of cattle, horses, and hogs," which led the Indians' herds astray and caused the Creeks to lose them. Austill also discovered that the local tribespeople lived in a "deplorable condition" and had been exploited by a local gang of intruders. This gang consisted of six men: John and Little Sims, John Grace, the previously mentioned John Scott, and two men named Gormand and Pugh. Scott and Grace had obtained bonds for most of the valuable lands south of Fort Mitchell, and according to Austill, half the Indians did not know the bonds were for their allotments. Meanwhile, Pugh, Gormand, and Grace drove Indian families off the valuable river bluff east of the fort and installed a Native stand-in on it so he could claim it as his reserve under the Cusseta Treaty. At that point, the man would sign over the title to the three intruders. But Austill found himself powerless to do much about the intruder gang. They held the Indians in debt and used that power to keep themselves in place, threatening to sue the Creeks if the government removed them from New Alabama. Grace even told a local chief that he would kill him if Austill removed the stand-in from his valuable riverfront property. Moreover, the intruder gang threatened the deputy marshal himself with a lawsuit if he persisted in his assigned mission. Moving south into Barbour County, Austill found that intruders in the vicinity of Irwinton had forced the Eufaula Creeks to rent their land, and the Indians had no redress for these and other abuses except in the state courts. But the courts worked against them. Officers of the courts, operating on false warrants and claims, seized the Creeks, put them in jail, and thereby forced them to surrender everything they had, including their land claims, to the intruders. In the end, Austill expelled only a half-dozen intruders from the Lower counties of New Alabama, but these were not men of much consequence. The intruder gang stayed in place. Furthermore, Austill reported to the War Department that it would be impossible for him to remove more intruders and keep them out of the Creek country unless he had a significant number of mounted troops under his command. He could not patrol the five million acres of the Creek counties by himself or with a few foot soldiers. Indeed, the fact that Secretary Cass had not already sent a large body of mounted troops to New Alabama showed his lack of real commitment to the whole idea of intruder removal.[46]

Leaving Fort Mitchell, Austill marched north along the Chattahoochee, past Columbus to the village of West Point, Alabama, situated in Chambers County by the Georgia line. This settlement was a popular entry point for intruders coming out of Georgia into the northern counties of New Alabama, and Austill discovered that many had offended the local Indians, most of whom lived in the branch villages of Cusseta and Coweta. The deputy promptly expelled several of the more notorious intruders for threatening Indians off valuable farmlands and preventing others from moving into Chambers County to settle on land reserves there. Austill also burned the homes of these offending intruders and turned their crops over to the Indians as compensation for their losses to the whites. But at the same time the deputy began to face serious resistance from the settlers. In fact, the Chambers County intruders attempted to raise a force of their own, strong enough to drive off Austill and his small contingent of soldiers. The deputy, however, thwarted their design by calling them together and promising to burn all of their farms if they did not desist. Austill also brokered an agreement between the intruders and Indians, whereby the Creeks allowed the settlers to stay in place until after the fall harvest, provided all those trespassing on Creek claims either moved off the land or paid compensation for occupying it. But Austill knew that the settlers would increase in number, and they would become bolder in their resistance to his authority. Consequently, he asked that Cass give him the power to arrest settlers who defied his removal orders. Moreover, he wanted permission to transport his prisoners to Mobile for trial in federal court. But again, Cass failed to give the deputy the tools necessary to effectively enforce the stipulations of the Cusseta accord.[47]

After establishing a measure of order in Chambers County, Austill returned to the Fort Mitchell neighborhood for a fateful encounter that would bring national attention to the intruder problem in the Creek country and precipitate a portentous states' rights debate between Alabama and the federal government. The controversy began when several Creek chiefs complained to the deputy about Hardiman Owens, an intruder living in Russell County some twenty miles from the fort. Austill went to the man's home on July 29 and informed him of the charges brought against him: appropriating Indian fields for his own use, selling the hogs and horses of his Creek neighbors, breaking a young girl's arm, and otherwise beating and abusing the Native inhabitants of the county "in a most cruel manner." Moreover, some said Owens robbed Creek graves for valuable artifacts and sold them in his little store. So Austill informed the man that as both Indians and whites had witnessed and testified to these events, he must leave the Creek country forthwith and not return. Owens, however, would not go, proclaiming, quite truthfully, that he would die before leaving his home. Subsequently, Austill arrested the man to escort him out of the county, but Owens escaped and then set a trap for the deputy and his squad of soldiers. Feigning friendship and a change of heart, Owens attempted to lure the deputy and his men into his powder-charged house so he could blow them up. Then, when some Creek bystanders warned Austill and foiled his plan, Owens escaped again. But the deputy persisted. He and his troops caught up to the intruder a third time and attempted yet another arrest. This time Owens resisted with force, and one of the soldiers shot him in the head. But if Austill believed that settled the matter, he was sadly mistaken. The killing prompted a loud states' rights response from Alabama's governor, John Gayle. He accused Marshal Crawford of introducing an armed force into the midst of a "civil and peaceable society" to enforce the claims of Indians, who, according to Gayle, did not have any greater rights in New Alabama than white citizens. Furthermore, he declared that the whole federal attempt to remove settlers from the district was unconstitutional and a violation of Alabama law. He also reiterated his belief that disputes between Indians and whites over land had to be adjudicated in Alabama courts, not by a single federal marshal. Then Gayle demanded that Marshal Crawford hold Austill in check and stop his harassment of New Alabama settlers until he informed the president of his complaints.[48]

At that point, the *Alabama Journal*, a states' rights newspaper published in Montgomery, joined in the fray. The paper's editor supported Gayle's position but went further, upholding Owens as a victim and fallen hero, murdered by imperious federal authorities while standing up for the legal rights of Alabama citizens. The paper also supported the right of Creek country settlers to raise an armed force to resist federal oppression. In all, the *Journal*'s editorials made Austill's job much more difficult. When he visited the Creek towns on the lower Tallapoosa River in Macon County, he found intruders farming inside the fences of all those Native settlements, including in Tuckabatchee, the principal Upper Creek town. These intruders had forced the Indians to accept renters on their fields, even though all the local chiefs forbade the practice of renting land to settlers. Furthermore, this income did the

Creeks little good, for as Austill noted, the number of New Alabama grog shops had grown to four hundred, and these establishments soaked up rent money as fast as the Indians received it. Most disturbingly, the deputy found it difficult to remove the Macon County settlers because they did pay rent and because they had the backing of the *Alabama Journal* and a local judge who urged them to defy federal authority. Some of the intruders even threatened the Tuckabatchee chiefs with death if they or any of their people complained to Austill about their activities. The irritated deputy responded by asking Secretary Cass for permission to post notices prohibiting the sale of liquor to Indians or paying them rent. Austill also accused the *Journal* of espousing the Doctrine of Nullification and declared that he would like to expel all the New Alabama settlers just to spite the paper's editor and all those like him. However, Austill knew that the government's ultimate goal was Creek emigration, and he saw that the pressing intruders were making the Indians more amenable to the idea of leaving Alabama. Consequently, he informed Cass that he would continue to expel only the most obnoxious intruders from the Creek country.[49]

Col. John Abert also came to believe that Creek removal, not intruder removal, should be the sole focus of government policy. In fact, he contended that the government had been too lax, had waited too long to remove any significant number of intruders, and now it would not be possible. The intruders had grown too numerous and firmly entrenched. They had also established a regimen of economic exploitation that was reducing the Creeks to poverty and improvidence. Consequently, said Abert, the government should no longer be chiefly concerned with protecting Indian land rights in Alabama. The real danger now was that the demoralized Creeks would become content with their diminished and dependent status and remain in the state until they were entirely ruined as a people. Thus, Abert thought that Creek salvation lay in removing them away from their white neighbors. Indeed, he contended that left to themselves the Creeks adhered to their own positive moral codes, religion, and governmental practices. But placed under Alabama law and besieged by intruders, Creek society had disintegrated: "The whites are the chief causes of the corruption and debaucheries of the Indian, and are the instructors in most of the arts of knavery and fraud with which they are reproached. From these therefore they must be separated or their improvement is hopeless." Yet when Abert talked of improvement, he meant "common schools" and other "advances in the arts of civilization." In short, he wanted to make the Creeks more like whites, the very people who introduced the Indians to corruption and debauchery in the first place. Unfortunately for the Creeks, this contradiction never occurred to Abert or any of the other Jacksonian humanitarians who wanted to send the Indians west for their own good.[50]

Enoch Parsons also lost confidence in intruder removal and came up with his own plan for getting the Indians out of Alabama. Essentially, he wanted to bribe the chiefs into signing a new treaty giving up all their lands. Furthermore, this treaty would pay off the speculators with even more money for the lands they had purchased from the Creeks. But just as Parsons and the War Department's other field operatives began to temporize on intruder removal, President Jackson and Secretary Cass decided to pursue a hard-line on the subject. Obviously stung by intruder defiance, not to mention Governor Gayle's long letters accusing him of unconstitutional behavior, Cass chastised Marshal Crawford for granting the New Alabama settlers so many indulgences. He informed the marshal that because the intruders had been allowed to harvest one season of crops in the Creek country, they now believed they had a legal right to stay as long as they pleased. He wanted Crawford to disabuse them of that notion. And President Jackson was even more irate, for while he wanted to serve the interests of his citizens, his personality was such that he could not tolerate any hint of disobedience or defiance of his authority. He declared that he would not consent to paying bribes to chiefs or speculators and he did not care if the Indians destroyed the improvements of New Alabama settlers. They had intruded on the Creeks at their own risk and should leave. Consequently, Crawford announced that after the next harvest all settlers, without exception, must vacate the Creek counties until the Indians received their land reserves. Only then could the settlers return and attempt to buy the reserves or take up homesteads on public land in New Alabama. Cass also informed Crawford that after consulting with the attorney general he had determined that by an act of Congress dated March 3, 1807, the marshal had the authority to arrest for trial all settlers who refused his order to vacate the Creek counties. Then Cass directed the marshal to post the War Department's latest instructions in Alabama newspapers for all to see. However, Cass concluded that he could not grant Crawford the power to shut down grog shops or prohibit in any manner the sale of liquor to the Creeks as that would violate the legal jurisdiction of the state. Once again, Cass tried to walk the impossibly fine line between state and federal authority in New Alabama.[51]

When Crawford announced January 15, 1834, as the date for the final removal of all intruders from the Creek country, he set off a storm of pleas and protests. Governor Gayle sent off more states' rights missives to Washington. The rich planters living in the fertile river bends of the Chattahoochee between Columbus and Fort Mitchell also complained to the War Department. They explained that they had cleared extensive fields to plant cotton and corn, and when they found it necessary to use Indian fields, they paid sometimes extravagant rents for the privilege. They also said that they had not been included in any previous removal orders, the Indians had never protested their presence, and they could not understand why the government wanted them to move now. Similar protests came in from Talladega and Tallapoosa counties in the far northwest portion of the Creek country. Those counties contained the most dense intruder population, but those settlers claimed, and Deputy Austill agreed, that they had cleared all their own fields and had never encroached on Indian farm land. Therefore, they did not think any general removal order should apply to them. One of these settlers, a man named P. Parsons, even went so far as to describe what must have been a common living arrangement between settlers and Creeks in Talladega County. He did so to make sure Cass could fully understand the impact of his blanket removal order on the respectable class of intruders. According to Parsons, he came to New Alabama from Tennessee and settled on a plot of land that would be part of a 320-acre allotment claimed by a Creek man called Pinehill. In fact, he erected a cabin only a few hundred yards from where the Indian lived. He then agreed not to bother Pinehill's fields and instead cleared his own, there being enough land on the reserve for both families. Of course, Parsons meant to purchase the entire allotment from his Creek host when the time came, but he insisted that he had not, and would not, make a down payment on the land without the government's permission to do so. Furthermore, he stated that he maintained nothing but the friendliest relations with Pinehill and all the other inhabitants of Conjada (Econchattee), the local Creek town. Yet he realized that he and the other settlers existed as mere tenants at the sufferance of the government, and he knew that if the War Department ordered it, he must abandon his farm. But he asked that Cass have mercy and allow him to stay in New Alabama until the Indians received title to their reserves and gained the ability to sell them legally to settlers.[52]

Meanwhile, the controversy over the killing of Hardiman Owens reached a boiling point, and it appeared that the state of Alabama and the federal government might actually go to war over the issue of states' rights. During the October term of the circuit court in Russell County, a grand jury indicted trooper James Emmerson for murder in the shooting death of Owens. In addition, the jury indicted Deputy Austill and all the other solders of Emmerson's squad as coconspirators in the crime. Then, when Maj. James S. McIntosh, the commanding officer at Fort Mitchell, refused to surrender his men to the county sheriff, the court indicted him for contempt and ordered his arrest. Gayle supported the indictments, and a frightened Marshal Crawford reported that the governor was organizing militias in the New Alabama counties for a possible fight with federal troops. For his part, Major McIntosh prepared for combat by ordering a fresh supply of arms and ammunition from the federal arsenal at Augusta, Georgia. Indeed, the controversy became so heated that Maj. Gen. Winfield Scott, as head of the army, submitted a plan to the War Department for the armed subjugation of Alabama. This plan included a naval blockade of the state's cotton ports, which undoubtedly served as a model for the Union's blockade of southern ports thirty years later.[53]

In the wake of all this, Marshal Crawford grew so alarmed that he completely withdrew from the intruder removal business, despite the War Department's orders. He now proclaimed, quite incredibly, that very few intruders, only about eighteen or twenty, had taken forcible possession of Indian land, whereas several thousand had settled peaceably among the Creeks. Therefore, he concluded that no removal should take place, as poor settlers would be hurt and would join Gayle's militia movement. Then Crawford went even further. He informed Cass that the intruders had not injured the Indians as much as previously reported and that a few designing whites, namely land speculators and Indian countrymen, had caused the Creeks to complain to the government so federal troops would drive out the honest, respectable settlers who dared compete with the speculators and Indian countrymen for good tracts of property. Furthermore, declared Crawford, the government could not expel all the intruders from New Alabama because it simply did not have enough troops in the entire army to do so. And if the government attempted any wholesale expulsion of settlers, armed resistance and bloodshed would result. That much said, Crawford concluded his report to the secretary with his real reason for abdicating his responsibilities. He said he feared for his own life.[54]

At this point, President Jackson and his minions at the War Department must have realized the nature of their political blunder. Jackson had taken over the presidency in 1829, intent on realizing his Indian removal policy. He had promptly urged the states to extend their laws over tribal lands as a means of reducing the resistance of tribal governments and pressuring the Indians into moving west. Then, despite significant opposition, he pushed his Indian Removal Act through Congress in 1830. But he also sanctioned the Cusseta Treaty of 1832, an agreement that allowed Creeks to remain in Alabama and promised federal protection of their property for a period of five years, at which time they might become state citizens. In effect, Jackson worked at cross purposes, advocating the establishment of state law and white settlement in the Creek country on one hand but using federal marshals and troops to remove settlers and protect Native property owners on the other hand. Governor Gayle persuasively impaled the president on the contradiction, and at the worst of all possible times. The sectionalism that would eventually lead to the Civil War was starting to take firm hold in the 1830s. The heady expansion of cotton and slavery, the Nullification Controversy between South Carolina and the federal government, the rise of a serious antislavery movement in the North, and the ancient conflict between Georgia and the central government over the conduct of that state's Indian affairs all contributed to the creation of a loud southern states' rights party standing in opposition to Jackson's Unionism. Now the intruder removal fiasco in Alabama, which promised to burst into armed conflict, spurred the growth of a states' rights party in that state. Consequently, Jackson had two problems: first, living up to his obligations to the Creeks; and second, maintaining the power of his own Union Democratic Party in his native southland, in Alabama in particular.

Jackson attacked the problems by moving vigorously to avoid a collision between the federal government and the state of Alabama. He sent Francis Scott Key as a special envoy to the state to work out a compromise that would accommodate the interests of the white citizens but uphold the "just rights" of the Creeks and the "plighted faith" of the government. On his arrival in Alabama, Key set out to talk to as many important people as possible and gather as much information as he could about the situation in the Creek country. First, he consulted with Governor Gayle and the members of the state legislature. Then he went to New Alabama to visit with the settlers and Creeks. He found the Indians, at least in the Lower counties, "in a deplorable condition." They were starving, having made very little corn during the year. Reflecting their dire need of subsistence, almost all of them had sold their prospective land reserves two or three times over for "any trifle that had been offered them." Key, in fact, met crowds of Creeks "going to Columbus with bundles of fodder on their heads to sell, and saw numbers of them in the streets where they exchange every thing they carry for whiskey." After talking with the Indians, Key concluded, as government officials always did, that nine-tenths of them were ready to emigrate and awaited only the final acquisition and sale of their reserves. He did note, however, that the Creeks wanted to handle the land sales themselves and did not trust their chiefs to sell their property for them. Yet Key saw that the Indians were not free people. Land speculators kept their agents constantly among the Creeks, controlling them. In this regard, he remarked on the prominence and power of the Columbus Land Company, now headed by two bank presidents, Seaborn Jones and Judge Eli S. Shorter. These speculators and their associates, said Key, had already bought up the property rights from three or four thousand Indians for a mere pittance of a down payment. Furthermore, he warned that the speculators would rely on these leases to give them possession of Indian land until such time as they could demand deeds for the property from the government. Key also concluded that the speculators would never pay the balance of the amounts they promised for the property; they would merely produce fraudulent accounts for whiskey and other items against the Indians and exchange the debts for land.[55]

As far as the intruder problem was concerned, Key downplayed the issue. He concluded, quite erroneously, that the situation was not quite as bad as previously reported. In the first place, he said, a recent census revealed only about ten thousand settlers in the nine counties of New Alabama, and most of these settlers were single men without families. However, it seems certain this census was incomplete, and Governor Gayle was more accurate in using the estimate twenty-five thousand to thirty-five thousand to lend weight to his argument that the government should leave the settlers alone. Second, and more truthfully, Key saw for himself that not all the intruders abused the Indians. He confirmed earlier observations that settlers in the northern counties were generally respectable and treated the Creeks fairly well. He also believed that if allowed to stay in New Alabama, the settlers in Talladega County would actually help the government expel the frontier roughs who exploited and corrupted the Indians. But Key did distrust the intruders in the Lower counties of the Creek country, particularly those in Russell County. He believed that had they been able to lay hands on the soldiers accused of killing Hardiman Owens, they would have executed them. He also contended that if government troops had to remove all the intruders from New Alabama, Russell County should be the last county they entered. The settlers there would surely fight.

Moreover, Governor Gayle could not be trusted. According to Key, he was looking for an excuse to call out the state militia to defend the intruders against expulsion. However, Gayle would not have the full support of Alabama's leading citizens should he attempt to defy the government with force. Referring to Mobile, Key concluded that "all the respectable part of the community there are warmly in our favor and loud in condemning the Governor." Moreover, he thought that a majority of the state legislature felt the same way. However, Key did finally admit that the government's inability to show firm resolve against the intruders in the first place had led them to believe that they could get away with anything.[56]

Most heartening for the Jackson administration, Key found that Gayle had not organized militias in New Alabama to resist the dictates of Washington. Furthermore, many Alabamians did not support the governor's states' rights stance, at least not completely. In fact, a fair number of state legislators had opposed extending state law over the Creek country in the first place. These legislators either had little interest in promoting white settlement there or simply believed, quite rightly, that the state could not, or should not, try to govern Indians on Indian land. And many of those Alabama politicians who had supported the extension of state law over the Creek country still believed in Andrew Jackson and shared his view that the federal government had to honor its treaties with the Indians. This last group of politicians made up the solid center of Alabama's moderate Union Democrats, and U.S. Senator Clement C. Clay of Huntsville shone as one of their leading lights. During the height of the intruder controversy, he came forward to express what was most certainly the sentiment of the majority of citizens of Old Alabama. Clay said that he feared the forced removal of what he believed were thirty-five thousand New Alabama settlers. He thought an armed conflict would result. Consequently, he wanted the government to seek a compromise to the problem. However, Clay made it clear that he opposed the radical states' rights nullifiers in Alabama who helped stir up the intruder controversy just to strengthen their political standing. Moreover, Clay expressed the desire that the government and the state treat the Creeks honorably; he wanted the

Indians to emigrate, but he did not want them swept out of Alabama without regard to their rights.[57]

New Alabama settlers themselves held differing political views and were not at all united in opposition to the government's intruder removal policy. Writing to the *Columbus Enquirer* from his home in the Fort Mitchell neighborhood, a "Friend of the Union" proclaimed that he was an intruder and had not always been a supporter of President Jackson. However, he believed in the Union, and the president had won him over with his strong stand against Nullification and the National Bank. Now, this man proclaimed, the nullifiers were at it again. They were exploiting the intruder removal issue for political gain, and Jackson, as he did in South Carolina, should stand strong and put them down by expelling all settlers from the Creek country. The writer then vowed that he was ready to leave himself for the good of the Union. Similarly, another correspondent blamed radical states' rights supporters for the intruder furor, particularly focusing on one Thomas Woodward, a well-known Indian countryman living in Macon County. He called Woodward a "sworn nullifier" and accused him of raising a force to resist the "federal bayonet." But Woodward denied the charges and instead placed all the blame for the intruder controversy on government operatives in New Alabama, particularly John Crowell, the former Creek agent, and fellow Indian countryman John Brodnax, chief legal adviser to the Creek Council. Woodward claimed that these men vilified the settlers in hopes of getting government troops to remove them. That would leave the way clear for Crowell, Brodnax, and their friends to acquire the best Creek land reserves without fear of competition from the settlers. Woodward was especially angry at Brodnax, a much-neglected historical figure, who had begun his long association with the Creek leaders at his first trading post on Flint River in Georgia and had become a chief confidant and scribe for some of the leading Creek chiefs, Opothle Yahola in particular. But all the while Brodnax worked in service to the Creeks, he also looked out for himself and would become, in time, one of the more successful land developers in New Alabama. Indeed, Brodnax would not have seen his own best interests and those of the Creeks as being at all incompatible, and he may have played a major role in fashioning the Cusseta Treaty, which he undoubtedly saw as the best way to mediate the conflict between the whites and Creeks over land in New Alabama and also secure for himself, through his association with the chiefs, some of the best town sites in the country once the Indians claimed their allotments. Having designs on Creek land himself, Woodward envied Brodnax's talent and influence in Creek councils more than he detested the man's criticism of intruders. Indeed, both these Indian countrymen had much in common. Whether they supported President Jackson and his intruder removal policy or not, their ultimate goals were the same. They both wanted land, and neither one of them ever proclaimed that the Creeks, just as a matter of common justice, should stay in the place they had lived for untold generations.[58]

In the end, the New Alabama intruder controversy produced more smoke than fire. There was never much chance of a civil war between Alabama and the federal government because, like Woodward and Brodnax, both sides really wanted the same outcome: the transfer of Creek land to U.S. hands and the removal of the Indians from the state. The arguments stemmed from disagreements on methods, legal jurisdictions, and, of course, the larger principle of states' rights versus federal authority. Had there been any real danger of armed conflict, it quickly passed when John Abert and William Bright, the government commissioners in charge of issuing the Creeks their land allotments, announced that they would be able to locate the Indians on their reserves by January 15, 1834, the deadline for intruder removal. Consequently, Key informed the Alabamians that a wholesale expulsion of settlers from the Creek counties would not be necessary. Only those settlers squatting on the reserves without proof of purchase from the Indian allottees would have to move away. But even these people would not have to leave New Alabama entirely. They could simply move a short distance onto public land and make their homesteads. This announcement satisfied Governor Gayle and the citizens of Old and New Alabama, although Gayle would remain estranged from the state's Union Democrats and, along with other states' righters, would form a Whig opposition party in the state. In Russell County, court officials dropped their attempts to prosecute Deputy Austill and the Fort Mitchell troopers for the murder of Hardiman Owens. And in Tuscaloosa the state legislature resolved to pass laws protecting the Creeks on their reserves. This promise pleased the Jackson administration, although Key admitted that the government had capitulated on the intruder removal issue. Simply put, Jackson had solved the problems presented by the flawed Cusseta Treaty by abandoning the Creeks to the intruders and their county courts during a crucial transitional period. The end result would be devastating for the Indians.[59]

Meanwhile, the completed Creek census allowed the government to move on to the next stage in the Cusseta Treaty process: the assignment of land reserves to individual Creek families. In the late months of 1833, surveyors went to work in earnest dividing off the Old Creek Nation into ranges, townships, sections, and half sections. Then, a special commission, employing white men familiar with the Creek country as locating agents, began to help the Indians select their individual allotments. Wherever possible, these allotment selections were supposed to include the land and dwellings the allottees already occupied. However, some of the locating agents conspired with the land speculators and "floated" some Creeks off valuable pieces of property, fixing their names instead to poor land in the pine woods. The Indians did not know until later that they had been hoodwinked. By that time, speculators had claimed their valuable land because government record books showed that no Indians owned it. The property had become part of the public domain open to white settlement and purchase. But honest or not, the locating agents completed their work during the first month of 1834, concluding for the Creeks their first two years of life under the Cusseta Treaty. Owing to intruder pressure and the lack of government resolve to enforce the accord, the treaty had not worked well for the Indians thus far. In fact, it had broken down the final frontier protecting the Creek Nation and set in motion a resource competition that threatened to reduce the Creeks to abject dependency within the world system. This was a terrible turn of events, but as bad as the years 1832 and 1833 had been, the worst was yet to come.[60]

3. Commodifying the Creek Domain

Officials in Washington expected that most of the Creeks would sell their allotments as soon as they received them and move to the Western Territory. Consequently, the secretary of war appointed four officials to oversee the process of Creek land sales, instructing each to witness every transaction and see to it that the Natives received fair prices for their land. Leonard Tarrant and James Bright assumed the task of certifying sales among the Upper Creeks in the northern portion of New Alabama, including the counties of Coosa, Tallapoosa, Talladega, Randolph, and Benton. Robert McHenry became certifying agent for the middle portion of New Alabama—Chambers and Macon counties. Both Upper and Lower Creeks lived in these middle counties, which contained some of the most fertile lands in the state. And some of these tracts were all the more valuable because they bordered on Federal Road, the main thoroughfare through New Alabama. Finally, John W. A. Sanford, a prominent Georgia politician and militia commander, took charge of the supervision of Creek land sales in Russell and Barbour counties at the southern end of New Alabama. These counties also contained an abundance of good farmland, as well as the majority of the Lower Creek population and the very worst of the intruders from Georgia. The secretary of war sent out a few regulations regarding the land sales but, for the most part, allowed each agent to devise his own procedures for assuring fair transactions. Cass did, however, order each man to send his certified contracts along to Washington for review and final approval by the president. In addition, Cass assigned John Abert, one of the commissioners charged with issuing the Creeks their reserves, the task of reviewing all contracts for Creek land made before the government sales offices actually opened. Once these old contracts were approved, along with the new, the government would send deeds to all the legitimate purchasers, and the Indians, their money in hand, could set out for their new homes in the West.[1]

Looking back on that time, it is almost impossible to believe that Cass's agents did not know they were about to jump into a cesspool of fraud and corruption. After all, Cass did not send them in from Washington; they were not naive foreigners; they were residents of Alabama and Georgia who had firsthand knowledge of the nasty resource competition set off by the Cusseta Treaty and the government's failure to keep intruders out of the Creek Nation. They should have known that the process of stealing Creek land allotments had already begun and the business would only get worse now that the government had officially thrown open all the Indian reserves for sale to all comers. Surely the certifying agents knew Indian landowners would be assailed and cheated by land speculators, traitorous Creeks, and the same rough and lawless element who first intruded on the Creek domain. How could they not know they would be asked to preside over one of the dirtiest land grabs in U.S. history? Or, perhaps they did know. Perhaps they were not at all naive. Perhaps they understood on some level that the system required dirty land grabs from time to time and they would simply do what they could to tidy up around the edges. Unfortunately, though, turning the land into a marketable commodity rather than a living, breathing part of themselves as most Creeks believed was only part of the problem. Following close on the land grab, the colonizers would seek to commodify every other resource in the Creek domain, including the Natives themselves. And therein lay the worst crime, as well as the key reason for the Second Creek War.

Naive or not, McHenry began certifying the sale of Indian reserves in his district in January 1834, setting up headquarters at old Fort Hull in Macon County. Not surprisingly, his office, located as it was in the heart of the richest part of the Creek land domain, did the most business. But McHenry immediately noted a problem. Along with several other regulations designed to ensure fair sales, the War Department required that if at all possible purchasers of Indian land pay for that property in the presence of the certifying agent. But McHenry observed that local store owners brought in numerous Creeks, one after another, and paid them with the same new bills, time after time. When he asked the purchasers why this was the case, they merely produced their ledgers to show that the Indian landholders owed them money for goods previously sold on credit. Thus, they took back the bills from the Creeks in payment of those debts. McHenry obviously believed that this sort of exchange had been rigged to the Indians' disadvantage, but under existing regulations he could do little about it. He also discovered another shady transaction at work. At least one land company, made up in part of Nimrod Doyle, a noted Indian countryman, and James Islands, an opportunistic Creek chief of Coweta town, paid out money for land purchases and then took it back from the Indians as loans. These two crafty speculators promised to repay the money with interest as soon as they resold the land to incoming settlers and after the Creeks had emigrated west. Yet McHenry knew they would never make good on their promises. In the end, they would simply deprive the Creeks of land and money and probably delay removal in the process.[2]

McHenry's insight revealed evidence of another basic mistake in the Cusseta Treaty process. Jackson and Cass hoped that the market system would facilitate Indian removal; they failed to realize that placing Creek land on the market might have the very opposite effect. In fact, McHenry was discovering that without a fair payment for their land, Creeks could not afford the move west. In hopes of remedying the situation, McHenry told Secretary Cass that the government should place one-third to a half of the money from Creek allotment sales in the bank for the Indians' future use. Cass received McHenry's suggestion at the same time Sanford began to report frauds in his district, so the secretary knew he had to act. He suspended land sales as well as the approval of old contracts, then sent Return J. Meigs, a Tennessee lawyer, to investigate the situation and recommend regulation changes to alleviate the problem.[3]

Meigs issued a report quite critical of the negligence of the land-sales agents and recommended that the government sell the Creek reserves at public auction and use half the proceeds to pay the debts of the owners and give the other half to the owners once they reached their new homes in the West. But Cass did not accept this recommendation. He believed the Cusseta Treaty gave the Indians the right to sell their own property and handle their own money, and government officials could not auction off any land unless they purchased it from the Indians first. Like many European Americans, Cass was addicted to the notion of private property rights. The secretary also became convinced, as a result of his correspondence with Sanford and his conversations with Abert, that it would not be possible to eliminate all fraud from the sale of Indian property and that the government had to be very careful not to deny certification of contracts on mere suspicion of fraud. Abert, in fact, feared that aggrieved buyers might actually sue Sanford, McHenry, and the other land agents. Consequently, Cass merely warned these men to be vigilant and allowed the certification of contracts to continue. Thus, the speculators and their kind won out, but in doing so, led New Alabama farther down the path to war.[4]

But the fault lay not with the speculators alone. In fact, the guiding ethos of the United States' market revolution bore responsibility. Abert, after being offered a bribe by the Columbus Land Company, proclaimed this ethos in one of his letters to Sanford: "The desire to grow rich, and to grow rich rapidly, are the besetting sins of our country.... In a government or community which bestows no mark of distinction, but such as are awarded by the common consent of the community, these become the prize for which ambition seeks, and with a commercial people, that distinction is wealth.... If one is only successful, the means of acquiring it are not looked into, and if not too glaringly dishonest are rarely condemned. Look around you in the world and see what a crime it is to be poor." Thus, Abert saw greed and corruption evident not only in the actions of the New Alabama land buyers but in the nation as a whole. But then, in good U.S. fashion, he quickly moved to temper his criticisms by stating that in the end the quest for wealth was good, for it led the individual and the nation to a higher stage of civilization and morality. He claimed this was already happening in some of the older areas of the United States and strongly implied that what was transpiring on the Alabama frontier was a natural occurrence as it were, a necessary evil that no one could stop and that in time would result in a more prosperous and moral community by generating wealth and from that a higher stage of human development. It was the classic argument of ends justifying the means, the same one Jackson and his followers used to support Indian removal and probably the same one that led William McIntosh to his death. But be that as it may, Abert concluded his missive by cautioning Sanford not to sacrifice himself in a fight to correct all the Creek land frauds, because "the fault is in society, and until more correct notions of morality prevail the evil is not to be corrected." What a provocative rationalization that was, and in the end a real indictment of what the world system had done to its most favored children, the economically aggressive U.S. people.[5]

Of course, Abert found his argument easy to make because he was not the one who would really have to suffer as his nation clawed its way to a higher plane. That painful task fell to the Creeks and all the other Native Americans. However, these people had an ethos of their own, and they were not yet ready to sacrifice themselves so speculators and others could accumulate the capital necessary to realize the white person's dream of turning Alabama into a better place. For the remainder of the year 1834 land sales slowed considerably, because many Creeks, no doubt at the urging of the chiefs, refused to sell their reserves and move west. This delay, of course, did not suit the War Department, and government agents moved to speed up the Indian removal process. They appeared at the Creeks' fall council meeting at Fish Pond town asking, once again, that the chiefs sell all remaining land reserves to the United States and take their people out of Alabama as soon as possible.[6]

Always before, the chiefs had met this request with a firm refusal, but now they started to equivocate a bit. A new road connecting Columbus to the New Alabama settlement of Tuskegee had recently opened, bringing in a flood of people, numbers of whom took up homesteads along the thoroughfare. Simultaneously, settlers continued to pour into the Creek country by way of Federal Road to the south and Georgia Road out of West Point to the north. All this press of new settlement may have caused some chiefs to reconsider the removal question. Opothle Yahola, for example, informed the agents that he was taking a trip west in the spring, and on his return he might be able to give the government a positive reply on the land deal. On further inquiry, the agents and land speculators, who also attended the Fish Pond conference in numbers, discovered that Opothle Yahola had been at work developing his own alternative removal plan for the Upper Creeks. Although he had always been a staunch opponent of emigration, by the end of 1834, the chief had come to realize that the future welfare of the Tuckabatchees, as well as the people of related towns on the Tallapoosa, depended on separation from the white residents of Alabama as well as from the poor and disorderly Lower Creeks, whom he had come to regard as almost a separate and distinct Indian people. Indeed, Opothle Yahola's actions and subsequent events revealed that the Creek Nation was starting to splinter and break apart under the stress of a collapsing frontier. Further evidence of this comes from the fact that Opothle Yahola, after leading his people out of Alabama, had no intention of going to the land of the western Creeks. He had received negative reports about the soil and climate there from Samuel Grayson, an earlier Upper Creek émigré who had returned to Alabama to live. But most troubling to Opothle Yahola was the fact that his most despised political enemies, the McIntosh faction of Lower Creeks, lived in and ruled over that portion of the Indian Territory assigned to the Creek Nation. Furthermore, Opothle Yahola, as he had already informed government agents, did not believe Cass's promise, made at the time of the Cusseta Treaty, that Creek lands in the West would be theirs "as long as the grass grows and the rivers run." On the contrary, Opothle Yahola believed that U.S. settlers would soon come among the Creeks residing on lands in the West, forcing them to face all the same problems they were having in Alabama. Consequently, the chief had decided to take his followers to the Mexican state the settlers called Texas. Moreover, a Montgomery land company, Weir, Billingslea, and Cowles, was more than happy to assist him in getting there if they could profit in the bargain. This firm advanced Opothle Yahola the twenty-three thousand dollars needed to make a down payment on a tract of land 150 square miles northwest of Nacogdoches. In return, the company's speculating partners hoped to claim the valuable full sections of land allotted to Opothle Yahola and each of the Upper Creek Council chiefs by the Cusseta Treaty. In fact, on observing these tracts, one government agent proclaimed them "the finest body of land I have seen in Alabama." Apparently, the headman of Tuckabatchee was now willing to give up these tracts and sell the remaining Upper Creek lands to the government once he secured a new home for his people in Texas.[7]

The white men attending the Fish Pond Council also discovered another plan afoot. A delegation of proremoval Cherokee leaders arrived at the meeting to propose that the Creek and Cherokee peoples raise a large joint national fund of money for their mutual use in establishing themselves in the West. Opothle Yahola, who had long sought the advice of educated Cherokees in his dealings with the government, may have sponsored this proposal, possibly wishing to ally his people with the more solid and progressive Cherokee Nation while he detached them from the disheveled Lower Creeks. Whether or not this was the case, the joint national fund proposal certainly sent shock waves through the land speculator community. Eli Shorter, for one, believed that Opothle Yahola meant to sell the Creek reserves to the government to raise money for the fund, which meant the speculators would lose the opportunity to buy said reserves themselves directly from unsophisticated tribespeople.[8]

At that point, the members of Shorter's Columbus Land Company devised a scheme of their own, one that would allow them to grab up the best of the Creek reserves before Opothle Yahola or the War Department could stop the whole process of private sales to individuals. This scheme was called "personation." The speculators simply paid one Indian a small fee to go to the land office and pretend he was another Creek, the owner of a desirable allotment. The speculator then purchased that allotment from the impostor in the presence of the certifying agent, left the office, took back the money from the impostor, and claimed a valuable property without the real owner knowing anything about the sale. Seeing the success of personation, other groups of speculators joined in the game so as not to lose out on acquiring the best pieces of real estate. And not only did personation allow all these speculators to steal valuable properties, it also scared legitimate Indian landholders into selling their reserves before a chief or some unknown Indian came along to sell the property out from under them. One speculator even admitted that "the plan of stealing had been adopted to bring about a reaction, and cause the true owners to sell their lands." Thus, with one simple yet devious tactic, the Columbus Land Company stimulated a New Alabama land boom in the early months of 1835. And in doing so, the company also laid waste to any plans Opothle Yahola or the government might have had for getting the Creeks out of Alabama quickly and without bloodshed.[9]

Not surprisingly, Shorter's crowd first put their new scheme into effect in Columbus itself, where their fellow Georgian, John W. A. Sanford, maintained an office to certify land sales for his district of the Creek Nation. Using personation as their tool, the Columbus speculators quickly gobbled up the better lands in nearby Russell and Barbour counties. The allotments of deceased Indians proved especially easy targets for the practice, and some Creeks may have been murdered to get at their valuable reserves. Milton S. Booth, a Barbour County settler well-acquainted with the Indians of Eufaula town, recalled to federal agents an incident in which a reservee was killed on a Thursday evening and his allotment stolen by personation before General Sanford the following Monday. All the fertile lands acquired in this way belonged to Cussetas, Euchees, Hitchitees, Sawoklis, Ositchees, Cowetas, or Eufaulas, and it is not surprising that these people, being the first Creeks to lose their lands to theft, were also the ones who became the most angry and rebellious as the year wore on. However, the greedy land thieves never stopped to consider this possibility. They merely moved north into Chambers County to continue their nefarious operations in front of McHenry, who had moved from Macon County to establish an office for certifying land sales in the village of Cusseta. But once in Chambers County, the Columbus crew encountered stiff competition from other companies of speculators determined to cash in on the personation craze. These men drove mobs of Indians, four hundred to one thousand in number, into the county and camped them in the woods just out of sight of McHenry's office. Then they led these Creeks in a few at the time to appear before the certifying agent and sell land that did not belong to them. One enthusiastic speculator explained his company's activities at McHenry's agency: "There is nothing going on at this time but the stealing of land with about fifty Indians. Pay them $10 or $5 when certified and get all the balance back, and 400 or 500 contracts certified with fifty Indians is all the game. . . . Now is the time or never! Hurrah, boys! Here goes it! Let's steal all we can. I shall go for it, or get no lands! Now or never!"[10]

But this was not to say that the flurry of land stealing was all a joyous lark. The village of Cusseta also seethed with tension, anger, and resentment as speculators competed for the best tracts in the county. In fact, one of the more bellicose land thieves, Dr. Columbus Mills, stood on the steps of McHenry's office and proclaimed that if anyone interfered with his business, he would "cut his throat from ear to ear." Judge Eli Shorter, a successful planter and banker as well as land speculator, also found the level of competition in Chambers County very upsetting. Expressing the class consciousness and sense of noblesse oblige of a southern aristocrat, he lamented, "When I see such men, with so few advantages, getting so much valuable land at $10 per tract, and see how much money we have paid out, the *power* we have had, and see the *quantity* and *quality* of land we have received, and particularly when I think of the reason why these things are so, I can almost tear my hair from my head." But Shorter did not back away from the challenge. In fact, it appears that he swung the pendulum of advantage back in his company's favor by buying off McHenry. On March 1, 1835, he wrote a letter to his colleagues, telling them that he had the agent's promise to meet them at any place of their choosing to certify contracts. Furthermore, he acquired McHenry's record book, from which he took a list of Indian reserves not yet purchased. Then he informed his partners, quite mysteriously, that he had to give "another man" an interest in the Columbus company to ensure their success. But he would never say who the man was, allowing only that "it is unnecessary to mention names: the thing was necessary, and was therefore done."[11]

And so the drive to dispossess the Creeks continued. Having cleaned out the best reserves in McHenry's district by mid-March, the speculators prepared to move west across the Tallapoosa River to invade Leonard Tarrant's district, which lay in the very heart of the Upper Creek country. By that time, however, news of the massive land fraud had reached Washington. And interestingly enough, whites, not Indians, sent in the first reports. In fact, the respectable settlers in Chambers County hoisted the red flag, complaining to the War Department out of "due respect for ourselves and the character of our community." Furthermore, these citizens knew, and declared, that because so much of their county's land had been procured by fraud, they would see nothing but turmoil and endless litigation over titles and boundaries for years to come. They feared, quite rightly, that their community would never grow and develop properly with such a corrupt foundation. But most importantly, the Chambers County settlers knew that the land frauds would cause serious problems with their Indian neighbors. They proclaimed that the land stealing had delayed Creek emigration, for the Indians had "declared their settled determination to remain [in Alabama] until their father, the President, restored them to their homes." Moreover, the settlers warned that if Washington did not act to rectify the frauds, the Indians, losing confidence in the government, might be driven into a state of desperation "fatal to the peace and safety of the community in which we live." Arnold Seale, who operated a store at McHenry's agency in Cusseta, even informed the speculators themselves that their land stealing would cause the deaths of innocent farmers, for "the Indians were declaring daily that they would kill any white man who would come and settle their lands, as they had never sold." Unfortunately, all these statements proved true in the end, but some of the Chambers County petitioners had another reason for complaining to the War Department. Charles McLemore, John J. Williams, and other community leaders bought Indian lands themselves, and they certainly resented the competition for those lands by outside speculators. Moreover, Arnold Seale not only made a living by selling goods to the speculators and their Indian personators but also hoped to purchase Creeks lands himself.[12]

The Upper Creek chiefs also protested the fraud. Opothle Yahola was especially upset, having returned from an unsuccessful buying trip in Texas to find his people in distress. He and his fellow leaders informed agents Tarrant and McHenry, as well as the War Department, that the Lower Creeks, having lost or disposed of their land, now came into the Upper Creek country with the speculators to claim Upper Creek names and sell reserves they did not own. In fact, the Upper Creek headmen claimed that by the last week in March, the speculators had stolen, through personation, one-third of the land reserves in the related Tallapoosa River towns of Tuckabatchee, Thlobthlocco, Chewalla, Tallassee, and Autosee. This situation could only have deepened Opothle Yahola's urge to separate his people from the irresponsible Lower Creeks. Worse still, the injured Upper Creek landholders could do nothing about the thefts. The chiefs complained that their people could not discuss the problem with McHenry through fear of the "merciless horde" of speculators that surrounded his office. And those supplicants who did reach McHenry found that he placed the full burden of proof on them to show fraud had occurred. Furthermore, the frauds actually placed Creek lives in danger, threatening them with starvation. As the chiefs explained, "While we have been at home preparing something for our dependent children to subsist on, other Indians have sold our homes, our all, the only means of our support." Then, by way of a remedy, the Upper Creek leaders recommended that the War Department investigate the frauds and give legitimate Creek landholders a chance to speak. Moreover, Opothle Yahola asked the president to conduct an investigation of the land sales and not to permit the certification of future contracts except in the presence of responsible chiefs. Finally, the Upper Creek headman and his cohorts exerted a bit of leverage to make sure the president would act favorably on their requests. They informed agent Tarrant that they were willing to send a delegation to Washington to discuss emigration arrangements.[13]

Of course, neither Opothle Yahola nor his fellow council members actually wrote down the clear, well-reasoned argument they sent to the War Department. That task fell to their white friend and ally, John Brodnax, the man who had helped them craft the Cusseta Treaty. In truth, Brodnax, and a few men like him, were the key figures in the transfer of the entire southern country from Native to white hands during the Indian removal era. They stood firmly in the middle ground between the two societies, wielding the skills and knowledge necessary to mediate relations between Indians and the government and at the same time take advantage of all economic opportunities that might come their way. But these men did not gain this enviable position overnight. They had set themselves up for it through years of calculating effort, no doubt understanding all the while that they could one day be wealthy leaders in a prosperous white society by first ingratiating themselves in the Native one. Brodnax, for example, had operated a trading store on the Georgia-Creek frontier for a number of years. Then, after the Washington Treaty of 1826, he followed the Lower Creeks migrating into Alabama and set up another store for them in West Point, Georgia, just across the Chattahoochee River from several Indian towns. All the while, Brodnax won the trust of the Creek chiefs, and in the Cusseta Treaty he helped them craft something that suited their interests as well as his own. Certainly he knew that a treaty that allowed individual tribespeople the right to own and sell their land would benefit someone in his situation. After all, he knew many Creeks personally. He spoke their language. He held them in debt. He also opened a school serving both Indian and white students, and its popularity became such that Creek chiefs asked that their children be sent home from government boarding schools to attend Brodnax's little institution. Thus, this industrious Indian countryman occupied the best position possible to acquire some of the better tracts of Creek land when they came up for sale, and he set out to do so with a definite goal in mind. He moved west to Tallapoosa County, worked to gain the confidence of Opothle Yahola, and managed to buy some choice real estate along the Tallapoosa River, one of Alabama's central waterways. Then, using his skills as a land surveyor—in fact, he had helped survey the Creek country and break it up into individual reserves—he laid out new town sites and sold lots to incoming merchants and professional people, who, along with the cotton planters, would be the very people needed to integrate New Alabama into the regional and national market economy. Indeed, he may have helped the Upper Creek chiefs write their land-fraud protests because unscrupulous speculators threatened the realization of his dream.[14]

But all this does not mean that Brodnax duped the Creeks, especially not Opothle Yahola. The chief was a relatively wealthy man himself and certainly understood the market forces driving white society. He was also an astute politician and surely knew that Brodnax, Barent Dubois, and other white advisers had their own economic concerns in mind when they sat in council and helped him and his fellow headmen compose their letters to Washington. But Opothle Yahola knew he needed such men and could put their knowledge and talents to good use for the benefit of his people. And if he must pay a certain price for such services, so be it. In fact, the coming of the market system to New Alabama meant that not only would there be competition and conflict cutting across the now mixed society of Indians, whites, and blacks but there would be collusion between sometimes diverse individuals and groups who needed one another to survive if not prosper in the free-for-all struggle the system engendered.

But whatever their motives, the New Alabama protesters, Native and white, made their point in Washington. By the spring of 1835 it was clear that "every prudential restraint was set at defiance, and acts which should make men cover their faces and shun sunlight, came to be the boast of the spoilers of Indian property." Consequently, the secretary of war suspended the certification of land-sale contracts altogether and ordered his agents to investigate the accusations of fraud in their respective districts of the Creek Nation. The agents did not object. By that time, even McHenry was admitting that itinerant Creeks were roaming all over the country selling land they did not own, and "a number of land purchasers think it rather an honor than a dishonor to defraud an Indian out of his land." This was somewhat of an understatement. Soon McHenry allowed that nineteen out of twenty contracts he certified were fraudulent and that he had even certified blind contracts, sales not made in his presence. Indeed, one Henry C.

Bird, a justice of the peace, signed blank affidavits and sold them to speculators, who then filled in the terms of fraudulent purchases and took them to McHenry for official certification. John W. A. Sanford, elected to Congress in the spring of 1835, also admitted that there was "not a shadow of doubt of the existence of fraud, of very great fraud" in his district. In fact, only Leonard Tarrant was able to say that he had certified only a few fraudulent contracts. He neglected to mention, however, that fraud of another sort occurred in his district. Speculators there persuaded nearly all the Indians to sell their lands without resorting to personation. But then, according to Opothle Yahola, the buyers later took back the money they paid out in Tarrant's presence, telling the Indians that President Jackson did not want them to receive the funds until they got to Arkansas.[15]

The Columbus speculators and their immediate rivals in the land business then did all they could to interfere with the government's land-fraud investigations. Taking ill, Opothle Yahola could not attend the investigation at McHenry's office, so he sent several trusted chiefs to help McHenry conduct a clear review. However, these men discovered that their old nemesis Tuskenea was already there, "hiding about in the bushes," telling all those Indians who intended to complain to the agent of fraudulent sales that the investigation was merely a government ploy. As soon as they appeared before McHenry, said Tuskenea, they would be arrested and sent off immediately to Arkansas. Opothle Yahola claimed that the Indian countrymen, Thomas Woodward and William Walker, put Tuskenea up to this to prevent discovery of their land thefts. He also claimed that the two men issued papers to all the would-be complainants, assuring them that they, not the government, would secure the return of their stolen property. In a move to counteract the influence of these speculators, Opothle Yahola sought a meeting with the ever-obstinate Tallassees, whom Tuskenea had wooed as allies after his fall from grace with the Tuckabatchees. But on riding into Tallassee, Opothle Yahola found Tuskenea there before him and "up to his old tricks." Opothle Yahola remonstrated with him about "the evil course he had been pursuing." He also accused Tuskenea of being the dupe of the speculators and warned him, as he had once warned William McIntosh, that if he did not come to his senses the "consequences would be ruinous." But Tuskenea remained unbowed, for he had a plan of his own. He meant to resist removal, and because he had no trust in the government's promises to rectify the land frauds, he looked to Woodward and Walker for assistance in keeping his people in Alabama. In return, he was willing to help them get what they wanted, some valuable tracts of land. Indeed, Walker was a kin of sorts, married to one of Tuskenea's sisters, showing again that collusion as well as conflict was an important aspect of ethnic relations in New Alabama.[16]

But land-thieving speculators fostered more conflict than anything else. In fact, they began to agitate the poorer Creeks against their chiefs, telling them that Opothle Yahola and the government agents were attempting, through the investigations, to take all the land away from the common Indians to use for their own benefit. The speculators also began to tell the poorer Creeks that they should defend their land by rising in armed rebellion against the chiefs. They even sold the Indians pistols, powder, knives, and lead for that purpose, never realizing that those instruments of death might be used against the whites. However, the incensed Opothle Yahola knew that the speculators had lit a flame that would burst into an open war.[17]

But not all speculators opposed the government inquiry. In fact, Cass's investigation order opened up a new vista of opportunity for those businesspeople who missed out on the initial Creek land grab. On May 19, 1835, Alabama speculators formed a company for the repurchase of all the contracts that the government's certifying agents would overturn. Robert J. Ware, Thomas M. Cowles, and Clement Billingslea, all of Montgomery and business associates of Opothle Yahola, were the leading lights of this company, and they soon brought into their fold a few independent Georgia speculators, as well as some prominent Indian countrymen. Similarly, the members of another partnership, Ware, Dougherty, and Company, allied themselves with some of the respectable planters in the southern counties of New Alabama and worked with these men in protesting the frauds committed by the Columbus speculators. In addition, the Alabama speculators probably encouraged the Creeks to claim fraud even when they sold their lands legitimately. The company's major objective was to convince the president that he should annul all Creek land purchases made after January 10, 1835. That way the Alabama speculators could move in and buy up all the voided contracts, thus getting a chance to cheat the Indians themselves. Witnessing this scene, Agent McHenry noted that the contest for the Creek lands had changed dramatically. It was no longer a struggle between red and white, he claimed, but one between white and white, with "the interest of the Indian not much at heart."[18]

And with that realization, both McHenry and Sanford seemed to lose interest in completing their assigned tasks. Consequently, they did not seek to rectify the land frauds by properly investigating and reversing bad contracts. McHenry did overturn some three hundred contracts, but he let many more stand. Moreover, he promptly recertified the overturned contracts to new buyers, who may not have been any more honest than the first purchasers. And the soon-to-be congressional representative Sanford turned in an even poorer performance. He returned to Columbus to conduct his investigations and sent word out to the Creeks in his district that they should come into town to make their complaints. But Columbus was the seat of the speculators, and the Indians balked at going there to accuse them of wrongdoing. Furthermore, the speculators hired "linquisters" to visit the Creek towns and tell the inhabitants that Sanford had no intention of restoring their stolen lands to them. He only wanted to lure them to Columbus so he could arrest them for old debts and send them to the West under guard. Hearing this, Neah Micco went to Sanford and asked him to meet with the Indians across the Chattahoochee in their own country. But the agent refused. Worse still, he soon abandoned his task and took off for his new job in Washington, leaving many wronged Creeks in the lurch. In fact, Sanford left the scene before the Indians living far down the Chattahoochee could even learn of the investigations, much less make the journey all the way up to Columbus. Then, on reaching the nation's capital, the agent covered over his negligence by simply proclaiming that no Indians had complained to him and therefore he could do nothing to rectify the frauds in his district. That much said, he concluded his written report to the War Department with the remarkable recommendation that the president approve all the contracts he had certified, fraudulent or not. At that point, close observers of the situation in New Alabama must have wondered if Eli Shorter had not bought off Sanford as well as McHenry. More likely, Sanford, as a good Georgian politician, simply decided to take Abert's earlier advice and go with the flow of the system, to accept the inevitable fact that whites would supplant Creeks in New Alabama and the process would never be a purely clean one.[19]

But government agents facilitating land sales was only one part of the process of fully incorporating New Alabama into the U.S. political and economic order. The other part involved actually enrolling Indians for removal and getting them out of the state. This task presented more problems. From the time of the signing of the Cusseta Treaty in the spring of 1832 until the spring of 1835, only one party of Creeks emigrated. However, both President Jackson and Secretary Cass believed that the Indians would soon move west en masse following the rush of land sales earlier in the winter. Consequently, they appointed John B. Hogan as superintendent of Creek removal, for they believed that Hogan, a Mobile resident and staunch Jacksonian, could handle the important tasks of enrolling large parties of Creeks for emigration, seeing to it that they had supplies and then sending them off to the West under the direction of army officers. Hogan too was optimistic, although he knew he would have to counteract the influence of all the interested speculators, planters, grog shop owners, jackleg lawyers, county sheriffs, frontier roughs, and others who sought to hold the Creeks in place for profit. On entering New Alabama, he set up his headquarters at Fort Mitchell and hired four removal assistants to help him tour the Creek towns, sign up willing Natives, and ferret out the "evil designs" of his white and Indian opponents. Hogan concentrated his efforts among the Upper Creeks, who were more numerous than the Lower Creeks and showed more interest in leaving Alabama. He began to court Opothle Yahola, the Upper Creeks' most influential leader, believing that he was the key to a rapid emigration. If Opothle Yahola could be convinced to go quickly, Hogan contended, the rest of the Upper Creeks would follow. And once the Upper Creeks were off, the Lower Creeks would certainly find their isolation in a sea of settlers intolerable and choose to hurry after the Upper Creeks. Unfortunately, Hogan found that Opothle Yahola, and the white men who advised him, had other ideas about how the Creek removal should proceed.[20]

And that was not the only alternative removal plan Hogan would have to face. Indeed, given the sorry state of affairs with settler intrusion and land frauds, numerous Creeks had decided to leave New Alabama, but they had no intention of going where Hogan wanted them to go. Twelve to fifteen hundred Creeks fled to the northern counties of Alabama and Georgia to live on Cherokee land. Several hundred more moved to the Chickasaw country in Mississippi. These movements caused widespread alarm among whites, particularly the citizens of north Georgia who believed refugee Creeks meant to form an armed alliance with the Cherokees there to resist removal. Then Tuskenea, Opothle Yahola's chief rival for leadership of the Upper Creeks, and also a major opponent of emigration, announced his plans to move his followers out of their villages along the Tallapoosa River to settle on a tract of land farther south in the Black Belt prairie below Federal Road, the main highway through New Alabama. William Walker, Tuskenea's brother-in-law, owned this tract and intended to let Tuskenea's people live on it in exchange for their allotment lands. The advantage for Tuskenea was that the prairie land would remain in Walker's name. Consequently, the chief and his followers could stay in Alabama as invited guests, living on land owned by a state citizen who had the legal right to use his personal property as he saw fit. The advantage for Walker, and the speculators associated with him, was that the Indian allotment lands he would receive were much more valuable than acreage on the prairie.[21]

These alternative removal schemes, and the continued resistance of the Lower Creek chiefs to emigration, doomed Hogan's hopes of sending any Indians west in the spring of 1835. Irritated, Hogan sent a request to the War Department, which if granted he believed would eliminate the Lower chiefs as obstacles to removal. Hogan knew these chiefs were making a good living off Creek annuity money and as long as they had access to those funds, they would not feel the need to leave Alabama. Furthermore, the removal superintendent complained that Neah Micco was the worst offender. He gave as evidence the fact that at the last annuity payment, Leonard Tarrant, the Creek subagent, had divided the money in two parts, giving one half to Opothle Yahola of the Upper Creeks and the other to Neah Micco of the Lower Creeks. Then, Neah Micco, as he was supposed to do, called a meeting to pay claims against the Lower Creeks and to distribute the balance of the money to the various Lower towns. However, the elderly chief paid only some of the claims against his people and did not give any money to the towns. He and the speculators he associated with kept most of the annuity money for their own use. Thus, according to Hogan, Neah Micco opposed emigration because he found no difficulty living in Alabama and did not want to kill his golden goose. He was comfortable, not destitute and starving like many of his people, about whom he seemed to care little, if Hogan is to be believed. Consequently, the superintendent asked that the government facilitate removal by taking the annuity out of the hands of Neah Micco and all the other headmen and giving it directly to the common Indians instead. Without exorbitant income from the government, he said, the chiefs would not be so anxious to stay in Alabama.[22]

The War Department did not grant Hogan's request. Nevertheless, with the coming of summer, events seemed to turn in his favor. Opothle Yahola's Texas land deal fell through, a deal he thought he had negotiated successfully with Sam Houston, who represented the Galveston Bay and Texas Land Company, a New York corporation that had obtained a large grant of lands from the Mexican provinces of Texas and Coahuila. But the Mexican government disavowed the cession and thus negated Opothle Yahola's purchase of a portion of the tract. Moreover, the Mexican-American Treaty of 1831 obliged both parties to prevent the movement of Indians from one nation to the other, and so the U.S. government could not give its consent to the Creeks moving to Texas. Consequently, Opothle Yahola lost prestige—not to mention his down payment on the Texas tract—and some important chiefs became disillusioned with his leadership and began to support Hogan. Among the Upper Creeks, Governor Bruner and William McGillivray of the Hickory Ground town proclaimed that they would work with Hogan in getting their people ready to move to Arkansas. Similarly, one of the more hostile opponents of removal, Old Dog Warrior of Alabama town, capitulated and informed Hogan that he and Mad Tiger of Coosada would prepare their people to emigrate. Next Sampson Grayson, a former émigré, announced that he would stop talking against removal and prepare to return to the Creek lands in the West.[23]

But the failure of the Texas deal and Opothle Yahola's loss of face were not the sole reasons more Creek leaders decided to accept Hogan's removal plan. The arguments over emigration, along with the economic pressure exerted on them by whites, were causing Indians to turn on one another and even kill each other as never before. Worse still, the murderers had lost all regard for the sacred places in Creek towns. Killings on council ground, for example, had become so common that bystanders ceased to be alarmed by them. In one incident, witnessed by Hogan himself, one Creek man stabbed another to death; then the "relations of the dead Indian immediately took the murderer, tied him to a tree, and stabbed him to death, and left his body hanging to the tree." And, according to the superintendent, "there were a great many white persons on the ground, but neither of them, or the chiefs, took any notice of the affair." Moreover, the violence touched Opothle Yahola's own family, making him much more amenable to the idea of emigrating to the Western Territory. He saw his son, Dick Johnson, stab another Indian to death in a fight, then fly away west to avoid clan vengeance. Johnson was later murdered in Texas, which had to have saddened Opothle Yahola. But for the time being, his son's criminal behavior surely convinced the chief that a rapid departure from Alabama was necessary to keep his oppressed people from completely self-destructing.[24]

Even more heartening for Hogan, the leading chiefs of the Cusseta party—representing the Muscogee towns of Cusseta, Coweta, and Broken Arrow—were ready to admit that they could no longer live in Alabama. They addressed a letter to the War Department in August 1835, stating that many of their people wanted to emigrate, but they needed money to do so, and they could get that money only by selling their land. But they could not sell the land because so many of them had lost it to theft, while other Creeks, still holding land, could not get money for it because the War Department had suspended all land sales. Furthermore, the chiefs complained that John W. A. Sanford had not conducted a proper investigation of the frauds in their district and had not returned any stolen property to them. Therefore, the chiefs requested that the president send a trusted man to reinvestigate the land frauds, but this time in the Indian towns, among the wronged people themselves. This agent, said the chiefs, should have the authority to certify land contracts for all those Indians who wished to sell their reserves for the first time, as well as those who would have stolen lands returned to them by said agent. Then, the chiefs implied, the Indians would be off to the West in a flash.[25]

The letter made sense, but Neah Micco, the letter's principal signatory, was playing a double game. Actually, he had no intention of emigrating and could not have wanted his people to do so. He pretended to go along with removal only to appease Hogan and force Secretary Cass to open a real investigation of the frauds and return Creek lands to their rightful owners. Beyond that, Neah Micco could not have wanted his people to resell those lands, for then they would have to emigrate. Therefore, he feigned interest in renewed land sales to gain the assistance of the Alabama speculators in realizing a goal both he and they held in common: overturning fraudulent land contracts made by the Georgia crowd. In the end, Neah Micco found it in his best interest to collude with some colonizers while he conflicted with others. But all the while, he pursued his own plans, hidden from both. That was the way many Native leaders around the world responded to the demands of colonization and the economic system driving it. Deception and intrigue, playing whites off against one other, was the way those leaders tried to cope, to resist, to shape their own destinies. Ultimately, though, the system prevailed.

In the short term, however, Neah Micco had some success. Once President Jackson and Secretary Cass realized that the land frauds were obstructing Creek emigration, they followed the chief's advice and appointed a trusted man to reinvestigate all the questionable contracts. And, as it turned out, that trusted man was already stationed in New Alabama. Cass notified John B. Hogan in early September 1835 that he should take charge of a new land-fraud investigation as part of his duties as removal superintendent. Then, acting on suggestions made by both Opothle Yahola and Neah Micco, Cass instructed Hogan to visit all the Creek towns and conduct hearings on cases of alleged fraud on the town council grounds, making sure to give advance notice to all parties, Indians and land buyers, so that they could prepare and present their evidence. However, the secretary did not grant Hogan the power to overturn fraudulent contracts. Those contracts, along with all incriminating evidence, must be sent to the president for a final decision. Only Jackson could void contracts and return land to Creek allottees. Finally, Cass sent word to the certifying agents, Tarrant and McHenry, that they could resume the certification of contracts on all the unsold Creek lands.[26]

With hopes renewed, Hogan informed the War Department that large parties of Creeks would emigrate in the fall of 1835. Unfortunately, he had underestimated the creativity of the local capitalists and the propensity of Jackson and Cass to make unwise decisions. A group of Columbus land speculators now moved to take charge of the removal themselves as a new source of profit, to make Creek emigration yet another part of New Alabama's exploitive "Indian business." This group consisted of S. C. Benton, Luther Blake, John D. Howell, Dr. S. M. Ingersoll, and Col. Alfred Iverson, one of the editors of the *Columbus Sentinel* newspaper. Benton soon resigned and two other men took his place in the company: J. Beattie, a land and slave thief, and Benjamin Marshall, the Creek planter and McIntosh party member, who only joined the company so he could move his family and slaves out of Alabama without being assailed by greedy whites like his associates. Some, if not most of these men, were states' righters, but hoping to make their company more appealing to the War Department, they set up none other than Representative Sanford, a leader of Georgia's pro-Jackson Union political party, as their head and petitioned the War Department for a contract to remove the Creeks. At the same time the company sent secret agents to the Creek towns to delay Hogan's removal until they could get their contract approved. According to the terms of this contract, members of Sanford and Company promised to enroll the Indians for emigration, set up removal camps, and supply the wagons, boats, tents, food, guides, and all other necessary items for transporting the Indians to the West at a cost of a mere twenty dollars per Indian, twenty dollars less than the amount the government would spend conducting its own removal. Jackson and Cass were impressed and decided to give private enterprise a chance. They notified Hogan of the change to contract removal and ordered him to dismiss his own agents. They retained Hogan as removal superintendent, however, and ordered him to see to it that Sanford and Company complied with the terms of their contract and treated the Creeks properly. For his part, Sanford actually resigned his seat in Congress and returned to Georgia to act as a respectable figurehead for his company, while his more sullied partners did the dirty work behind the scenes.[27]

Hogan and the Creek chiefs were aghast. The members of Sanford and Company were some of the more infamous speculators in Creek lands. How could the president turn the removal process over to them? The Indians' enthusiasm for a fall removal—the enthusiasm Hogan had worked so hard to cultivate—died away all over the Creek country. Rumors spread among the Natives that the contractors meant to collect their money from the government and then take the Creeks only as far west as Mississippi, where they would be enslaved and put to work on cotton plantations. Tuskenea complained loudly that his people would not be led away by speculating contractors "like a parcel of pigs to market." Many other Indians "swore that they would never move under those Georgians." Hogan protested the government's decision, claiming that he had been very close to removing thousands of Creeks from Alabama. He also claimed that the contractors were not dealing with the government in good faith. They could not profit from moving Indians at twenty dollars a head, he said. They were using their contract only as a means of tightening their hold on the Creeks so they could extract more Native land. Hogan was probably correct, and more than likely, the emigration company hoped to extract more money from the government than the modest amount they first proposed. Company members certainly meant to make a great deal of money somewhere. Why else would otherwise wealthy men engage in the enterprise? And why would Sanford resign his newly won seat in Congress to head the operation and engage in what one observer called the "pin-hook" business of Indian removal?[28]

Unlike Hogan, the new contractors were confident that they could get the Creeks to move West. They expected to remove five thousand by July 1836, when their contract expired. Having done that, they expected the government would extend their contract for another year, allowing them to remove the remainder of the tribespeople. In anticipation of a fall removal of a couple of thousand Coweta, Cusseta, and Tuckabatchee Creeks, the contractors made large purchases of beef, corn, wagons, and other supplies. They expected a firm commitment to emigration by the Creek chiefs at their fall council meeting at Dudley's store, a popular trading post for Creeks and settlers in Chambers County. And, indeed, their optimism seemed more than justified by the actions of the council chiefs. These leaders began to clear the way for a move west by arranging for the sale of the twenty-nine sections of land given in common to the members of the Creek Nation by the Cusseta accord. This sale took place at Tallassee on October 28, and Superintendent Hogan took charge of the money to keep it out of the hands of all the whites who preyed on the Natives. During their meeting at Dudley's, the Creek Council members also dismissed Tuskenea, for the third and final time, as principal chief of the Upper towns, thus reducing his influence against removal among the Upper Creeks and defeating his plan to establish a Creek colony on the Alabama prairie. Neah Micco, Tuskenea's ally and still an opponent of removal, protested Tuskenea's demotion along with the high-handedness of the Tuckabatchee party, but to no avail. Tuskenea was left to his own devices, licking his wounds, and free to cause even more trouble behind the scenes.[29]

By the end of October, however, the contractors began to see that Creek removal would be more difficult than they imagined. Despite the actions of the chiefs, individual Creeks were reluctant to enroll for emigration with men they knew as speculators. At the same time, rival speculators worked to hold the Indians in place until Hogan finished his investigation and returned lands to the Creeks for resale. Whiskey shop owners continued to oppose removal no matter who carried it out, and respectable planters and farmers criticized the company because they believed it could never remove the Creeks successfully. Furthermore, the company members became convinced that Hogan was working against them among the Indians, trying to defeat their contract so he could take back control of the removal process. Through their connections in Washington, the company members gained access to Hogan's correspondence to the War Department and read for themselves all the complaints the superintendent made about them.[30]

However, Creek culture, coupled with widespread poverty, posed the greatest obstacle to removal. According to one government agent, the Indians "cherished a passionate attachment to the land where they were born, and where their ancestors lay," a "love of country" lying in "a vivid recollection of all those endearing associations with which mankind become familiar in their advance from youth to manhood, and from manhood to old age." Indeed, many Creeks "regarded their eternal separation from the country of their nativity with a kind of superstitious horror," and when an agent arrived in any town to enroll its inhabitants for emigration, runners dispatched the news to all the other towns, exciting "universal alarm." In truth, the thought of removal, and perhaps the realization of its inevitability, totally demoralized some Indians. In Coosa County, for example, a Creek warrior murdered a storekeeper, went to trial, and received the death penalty. Standing on the gallows in Wetumpka, he spied another Indian in the crowd of spectators and in jest asked the man to take his place on the scaffold, offering him two ponies to do so. When the man refused, the condemned warrior simply shrugged and said that it was just as well; he would just as soon hang as go to Arkansas.[31]

The fact that the Creeks lived in dispersed settlements also made it difficult for government agents or removal contractors to consolidate them for shipment out of Alabama. And even when some members of the towns sold their lands fairly and wanted to emigrate, they would not do so as long as their less fortunate friends and relatives waited on fair payments for their properties. Indeed, most Creeks simply did not have enough money to pay their debts and finance the trip west. Superintendent Hogan tried to rectify the problem by beginning his land-fraud investigation in the vicinity of Tuckabatchee, where the Natives expressed the most interest in emigrating. He quickly overturned many fraudulent land contracts—most because the land buyers failed to appear at the hearings—but he lacked the power to recertify the retrieved lands for sale. Consequently, the prospective Creek emigrants still could not get their money out of the land. Furthermore, the superintendent found that the tribal roll did not contain numbers of eligible household heads. These poor people had never received allotments to sell and now lacked any means of paying their debts. Moreover, Creek heirs could not get access to the land left by deceased allottees. The Cusseta Treaty made no provision for inheritance, and Alabama law did not permit Indians to inherit property directly. County judges took charge of land owned by deceased Creeks and turned it over to white administrators. These administrators then did as they pleased with the property, including selling it to speculators or cutting all the timber from it. The Creek heirs received little or nothing. And without money, these heirs and other oppressed Indians had little choice but to remain in Alabama. But the longer they stayed, the more debt-ridden and impoverished they became. They lived by borrowing and buying on credit, writing orders on their principal chiefs to be paid out of the annuity fund. However, this fact placed the chiefs in an ever-tightening economic bind. Opothle Yahola and the other chiefs of the Tuckabatchee Creeks informed Hogan that they could not emigrate because creditors held them personally responsible for their people's debt. Should they try to leave Alabama, those creditors would step forward to seize all their slaves, horses, and other property. The move west would mean their economic ruin.[32]

As a result of all these problems, Sanford and Company removed a party of only about five hundred Creeks in November 1835. Company members Ingersoll and Marshall escorted this party west along with Lt. Edward Deas of the U.S. Army. Sanford lost heart, and once again showed his propensity to run from a difficult task. Believing that his company could not fulfill its commitment to remove five thousand Indians by July 1, 1836, he resigned from the organization. He cited Hogan's investigation and the government's failure to certify Creek land sales as the reason for the failure. Hogan disagreed. He claimed the company failed because it was unpopular both with the Indians and New Alabama's white "gentry." He also stated that the Indians' inability to resell their lands had not delayed removal. That notion was only an excuse contrived by land speculators to force the government to put Creek property back on the market. Again Hogan asked the War Department to cancel the removal contract, claiming that Sanford had been the only respectable and efficient man in the organization and without him the company would never be able to remove the Creeks satisfactorily. In this regard, Hogan pointed out that following Sanford's resignation, the emigration company had taken Thomas Woodward and William Walker, two of the more notorious New Alabama Indian countrymen and land speculators, into their fold as members. In so doing, the company further alienated the Creeks. However, the superintendent knew it would be difficult for the government to rescind the removal contract with "so many Georgians" seeking to "make their fortunes from it." He was correct. Ingersoll boasted that he would put two or three members of Congress to work on Secretary Cass to see to it that his company stayed in business. Consequently, the War Department stuck to the contract, leaving both Hogan and the removal company to set the spring of 1836 as the new target date for a mass emigration of Creeks.[33]

Hogan was not being entirely honest when he said that the Creeks' inability to resell their stolen lands did not delay removal. He knew more than anyone else that the Natives were caught in an economic trap and needed money to leave Alabama. In fact, he took decisive steps to help the Indians buy their way out of the state and move west in the spring. Whereas before he had informed the Upper Creek chiefs that the government would pay their 1836 annuity in the West, he now promised the leaders that he would have the government make the payment in April in Alabama, provided they agreed to assemble their people in removal camps as soon as they received the money. He intended that the encamped Indians should pay their debts promptly and then depart for their new homes immediately. Then to assist the Creeks further in establishing financial solvency, Hogan and the Creek subagent, Leonard Tarrant, helped the chiefs make arrangements to sell twenty sections of land set aside for Creek orphans by the Cusseta Treaty. Hogan believed that the money from these sales, along with their annuity payment, would be enough to get the Creeks on their way. However, he continued to use his land-fraud investigation to hasten emigration. He finished his inquiries in McHenry's district and, in the process, overturned 656 contracts, involving more than one hundred square miles of land. Then Hogan submitted a report to the War Department in which he recommended that all the land involved in the cancelled contracts be returned to the Indians for resale. That done, he breathed a little sigh of relief. As a consequence of all his efforts, prospects looked good for a spring removal. The four leading chiefs of the Tuckabatchee Creeks sold their individual sections of allotment lands for a total of thirty-nine thousand dollars and began to prepare their people for the journey west.[34]

At that point Hogan moved his headquarters to Fort Mitchell to investigate the frauds among the Lower Creeks in Sanford's district. He knew that these poor people needed financial relief even more than the Upper Creeks. Unfortunately, Hogan arrived at the post in January 1836 only to find the speculators well prepared to block his investigation. He attempted to hold hearings at the fort, but the Columbus land pirates came over the Chattahoochee en masse to disrupt the proceedings. Working through their Creek interpreter, Paddy Carr—a shareholder in the Columbus Land Company—as well as a group of "smart and active" Creek blacks, the speculators bribed, intimidated, and intoxicated the assembled Indians to get them to deny the existence of any land frauds. Finally, the superintendent admitted that there was simply "too much chicanery to hold hearings at Ft. Mitchell" and moved on to the individual Lower Creek towns to conduct his investigation. He went to Hatchechubbee, High Log, Cowiggee, Opelika, Ositchee, Chocolowocklo, and Totalugulnar. This last village, Totalugulnar, also called Watoolahawka (Whooping Crane), was an important place. Situated at the west end of Russell County near the new road connecting Columbus and Tuskegee, the village received numerous visitors. Also, Chapman's store, a popular trading station and community center for blacks, whites, and Indians, sat close to Totalugulnar. But most significantly, this village was Neah Micco's home, the place he held court surrounded by grasping petitioners. In fact, wherever Hogan went, "gangs of from twenty to forty speculators" followed him, trying to interfere with his work primarily by buying off local chiefs so that they would keep their people away from the investigation. The Cusseta chiefs, Oakfuskee Yahola and Cusseta Micco, both living in the village of Secharlechar, succumbed to the bribes of speculators. Moreover, Daniel McDougald of the Columbus Land Company broke up Hogan's investigation at Chapman's store by taking several hundred dollars in silver from his own saddlebags and throwing it on the ground at the agent's feet. Then, as a display of speculator power he ordered the Indians to pick it up. And, indeed, hard money was the key to speculator success, for in a country filled with poverty, false promises, and annuities paid with deflated bank notes, silver was the only currency the Creeks trusted. In the end, the Columbus Company had coins to display and Hogan did not.[35]

Nevertheless, Hogan had some success. He found numerous Creeks willing to step forward and tell the truth, many of them women. In fact, women had always managed much of the property in the Creek Nation, and by late 1835 they also held a considerable number of the land allotments, owing no doubt to the frequency of divorce among the Creeks, which created more households headed by single women than in the average white community in that time. Also, Creek women gained more access to property of various sorts during this time because the male population was in decline because of self-destructive behavior—murder, suicide, and alcoholism. And perhaps because so much of the economic burden rested on their shoulders, women, since the days of Benjamin Hawkins if not before, seemed more interested than their men in understanding and becoming proficient in the skills necessary for survival in the whites' system. One of these skills was the ability to speak English, and Hogan noted that numbers of Creek women not only spoke the tongue but used it to condemn the land frauds. As he visited their communities, these women stepped up to him "and uttered their complaints." Hogan also contended that the women did so with "greater freedom [than their men] because they could do so with impunity." By this he probably meant that the speculators were less likely to kill women, but he might also have been referring to the fact that the Alabama legislature purposely defied those who would prey on the property of Indian women by passing a law protecting them from the sorts of court actions that threatened Creek males. One would like to think that this noble act of the lawmakers resulted from their recognition of the important role women played in Creek life, and that may have been the case, but more likely the move to protect Creek females and their property stemmed from southern paternalism and the code of chivalry southerners used to distract themselves from all the negative consequences of their participation as an increasingly backward agricultural periphery in the world system. Creek women had no choice but to confront those negative consequences, and according to Hogan, were "active and clamorous, and appealed for redress to their chiefs, as well as the agents of the United States, with persevering importunity."[36]

However, Hogan also received support from armed groups of Alabama speculators, who attended his proceedings to purchase the contracts taken away from the Columbus men. Thus, Hogan was able, despite the efforts of the Georgians, to overturn numerous contracts and discovered the true extent of land fraud among the Lower Creeks. The situation was worse than he imagined. The speculators had stolen about three-fourths of the Lower Creek land. The members of the Euchee town lost virtually all of their property to theft, as did the Creeks of Cusseta town. Hogan also uncovered a number of ingenious schemes the speculators used to get the Indians' land. At Cusseta, Paddy Carr bought the land of his tribespeople, then took back all the purchase money with a false promise. He told his fellow Creeks that he would use the money to send a delegation to Washington to get the president to reverse all the land sales and return all the allotments to the Creek Nation. At Eufaula town (Irwinton) in Barbour County, Hogan found that two speculators, Alexander J. Robinson and Gen. William Wellborn, had bought 113 half sections of land for only five or ten dollars per tract. Robinson and Wellborn made these cheap purchases with the understanding that they would give the Indian allottees more money when the land titles were perfected. Then the men turned around and sold the rich land to planters and farmers for three thousand dollars for each tract. The Eufaula Creeks had yet to receive another cent. Worse, some speculators bought Creek land with the understanding that the Indians could continue to live on the property as long as they pleased. This specious arrangement made the Indians beholden to their landlords and reluctant to talk to Hogan about the land frauds. It also made the Natives less willing to abandon their homes and move west. After examining fourteen towns in the Lower Creek district, a disgusted Hogan concluded that "a greater mass of corruption perhaps has never been congregated in any part of the world than has been engendered by the Creek treaty."[37]

Having failed to stop Hogan's investigation in Sanford's district, the speculators now sought to lessen the impact of his report. They launched a public relations campaign in the newspapers and brought pressure to bear on the War Department. Eli Shorter, one of the founding members of the Columbus Land Company, headed this campaign. He and his associates swamped the War Department with letters, testimonials from New Alabama planters, and forged statements from Indian interpreters and Lower Creek chiefs. All these missives said much the same: the land frauds were a myth; allegations of frauds came from jealous speculators who wanted to repurchase Creek contracts; Superintendent Hogan, seeking profit, had allied himself with these speculators; Hogan was trying to overturn good contracts as well as bad ones; and the superintendent's investigation was blocking Creek removal. Then the Columbus gang claimed that the federal government actually lacked the power to cancel land contracts, which could be done only through judicial proceedings in state courts. The gang also warned Secretary Cass that if the government returned all the supposedly stolen land to the Creeks, thousands of respectable white settlers would be displaced. Consequently, the speculators asked the secretary to stop the investigation and to remove the Creeks from Alabama, by force if necessary. Without land, the Natives were now the real intruders, they reasoned, and had no right to stay. And what a hypocritical twist of logic that was. When whites were the intruders, Shorter and the other states' rights supporters had proclaimed that the federal government had no right to touch them. In those days, they claimed trespass on land within a state was a state matter. But now, being Georgians, they had no faith in the state of Alabama to protect their interests and they called on the federal government to do it. However, the Columbus men did make one point President Jackson should have taken to heart. They raised the ominous threat that if allowed to stay in Alabama, the poor Creeks would have to steal from their white neighbors to survive. The settlers would resist this theft and an armed conflict would result. Therefore, said Shorter, the government must act to remove the Indians or risk war. Despite his selfishness, the man could not have been more correct.[38]

Cass refused to call off the investigation, but the speculator campaign, as well as the complaints of the removal contractors against Hogan, did influence him. First, the secretary warned Hogan to keep his investigation within workable bounds and to tailor it to the larger goal of removal. Then he decided to strip Hogan of his removal duties. He assigned those duties to Capt. John Page at Fort Mitchell, a man more friendly to the contractors and speculators. Next, bowing to the will of the Georgia delegation in Congress, Cass appointed J. W. Burney and George W. Anderson as commissioners to assist Hogan in his investigation. Cass made these appointments both to speed the investigative process and to assure that Hogan would not be in sole charge of overturning land contracts. Then in March 1836 the secretary further astonished Hogan by ordering him and his fellow investigators to go back and hold new hearings on all the contracts Hogan and agents McHenry and Tarrant had overturned. Obviously the large number of specious contracts had staggered the secretary and president, and they were reluctant to disappoint so many land buyers and investors by returning so much property to the Indians. The secretary was especially concerned that the investigators had overturned so many contracts simply because the land buyers had not turned up at the investigation sites to defend their purchases. Indeed, in their appeals to the War Department, the speculators constantly bemoaned the fact that Hogan conducted ex parte investigations, disapproving contracts on the mere word of an Indian. This situation allowed the land buyers to claim that the government favored the interests of the Creeks over its own citizens, and they threatened to bring suits in the Alabama courts to uphold the validity of their land deals. Given the timing of their protests and Cass's order to start the investigation all over again, it seems obvious that the speculators convinced the secretary that he should not declare any land contracts invalid without more solid documentation of fraud. Or it may have been that Cass had another motive. Some historians have claimed that the secretary always believed that an exploitative relationship existed between Indians and whites on the U.S. frontier, and he decided to pursue a course deliberately designed to aid the speculators in the Creek imbroglio. In any event, the secretary instructed Hogan and his two associates from Georgia to collect the documentation.[39]

Cass's decision to do the investigation all over again stopped removal cold. Without the money from the resale of their stolen lands, the Creeks could not free themselves from New Alabama's grinding economy and depart in the spring of 1836. Worse, the administration failed to alter the treaty to allow Indian heirs to claim the lands of their deceased relatives. Those Natives who had sold off their possessions in anticipation of leaving began to starve; others began to prepare their fields for another crop, signaling that they would stay in their old homes through the fall, waiting for an end to the land-fraud investigation. Seeing this reluctance to emigrate, particularly on the part of the Lower Creeks, Captain Page, the new removal superintendent, resorted to threats. He turned up at the Creeks' spring council meeting at Loachapoka town and informed the assembled chiefs that 1836 would be the last year the Creeks could remove at government expense. Thereafter, the settlers, who now owned the land, would forcibly expel them from Alabama. But Page's declaration was a terrible mistake. He should have saved his threats for the acquisitive and economically competitive whites. The emigration contractors were not ready to remove a mass of Creeks in the spring. They were afraid to venture among the angry and aggrieved Lower Creeks, and both Hogan and more objective observers accused the contractors of delaying removal until they could get an extension and an increase in their pay. Furthermore, the whiskey dealers and speculators continued to hold the Lower Creeks in place and refused to turn the Natives over to the removal contractors until they could get their hands on the annuity payment that Hogan had requested from the government. In fact, it began to appear that devious whites would never let the Creeks leave Alabama. Some of them had put the economically dependent Indians to work clearing land for plantations and "performing other labor for white men." In fact, one observer reported that the Lower Creeks were being used as a "substitute for slaves and avarice will make them such." This whole situation alarmed the members of the Alabama Assembly, especially the realization that self-interested whites were actually holding the Indians in place, blocking their emigration to the West. Consequently, the legislators passed a law stating that "if any person dissuaded the Indians from meeting a commissioner of the United States [for purposes of removal], he should be liable to be indicted, and, on conviction, should be imprisoned for three months."[40]

Indeed, by failing to stop the intrusion into Creek country or to adequately supervise Creek land sales, the federal government had allowed a highly exploitive and competitive economy to take root and flourish in New Alabama. Unfortunately, the complete dispossession of the Creeks formed the foundation of this economy. The acquisition of Creek lands was the most important aspect of this dispossession, but taking those lands was not enough. Land alone was just land. To develop it, make it productive and yield surplus value, and integrate it into the world system, the colonizers needed two additional means: capital and labor. And, as it turned out, the Creeks could supply those commodities as well. After all, they had money from their annuity payments as well as currency gained from legitimate land sales. They also had livestock, slaves, and various other valuable possessions. But beyond these sources of capital, the Creeks had their own bodies, meaning their labor. From the time of the signing of the Cusseta Treaty in 1832 to the outbreak of the Creek War of 1836, a multifaceted and highly exploitive Indian business became New Alabama's leading economic endeavor. Simply said, the new residents of the Old Creek Nation set out to take not only Creek land but everything else the Indians owned, including their most highly prized possession, their freedom. Should we wonder that a war occurred?

New Alabama's county seats and market towns—Tuskegee, Tallassee, Talladega, Irwinton, LaFayette, and Wetumpka—became bustling centers of the Indian business, along with the Georgia towns of Columbus and West Point, both situated just across the state line from several Creek settlements. In these commercial emporiums the land speculators concocted some of their more outrageous schemes, such as getting control of the estates of deceased Indians. Under Alabama law, Indians were not competent to represent themselves in court or to inherit land directly. Thus, an Indian heir had to have a white person serve as his or her executor, the person who would take charge of the estate and manage it for the Creek client. Speculators took full advantage of the situation. Normally a clique of them went in on a court bond to manage an estate. They then declared to the judge that the dead person's debts exceeded his or her disposable property and asked the court's permission to sell the individual's land reserve to get the money necessary to settle the debts. Once that was done, they promised to give any leftover money to the heir or heirs of the deceased. But as soon as the judge agreed to the proposal, the speculators sold the land to themselves at a low price, probably just enough to cover the debts of the deceased if there really were any. The heirs got little or nothing from the deal, but the speculators turned around and sold the land reserve to an incoming farmer or planter at a healthy profit. Such scams went on in endless variety, so attorneys and interpreters set up shop in the market towns and found constant employment as the Creeks came to seek redress from the speculators or to defend themselves in concocted lawsuits or to stand trial for various offenses against the state laws. Indeed, Indians with property soon learned that they needed lawyers and official documents to protect their interests.

Neah Micco, for example, knew that white men could claim his slaves in payment of both his personal debts and those of his tribespeople. Consequently, he made sure to transfer ownership of those slaves to his children while he was alive and have those transfers duly recorded by the Russell County court clerk. Some of these children were much too young to supervise slaves themselves so the chief undoubtedly continued to use them for his own purposes. And this was a wise move, for all the early New Alabama court records show that Indians made up a majority of defendants in both property and criminal cases. In fact, almost without exception the first people tried for murder and sentenced to death in the county courts were Creeks accused of killing other Creeks. Having outlawed the traditional Creek justice system, state authorities obviously felt the need to discipline the Indians quickly with their own laws to preserve order as the country passed from Native to white ownership. But beyond that, Indian executions became an economic activity. Crowds gathered for the spectacle and the delighted town merchants welcomed them to their stores, selling merchandise to Creeks and settlers alike.[41]

But the county seats were not the only places used to exploit the Creeks. Trading stores located on the county roads and in the Creek towns did a booming business. Even those Indians who sold their land fairly and received a decent price soon found that they had to spend their money to survive in New Alabama. Without land they had no place to plant crops, and consequently they bought food from white merchants and farmers. The proprietors of the country stores also encouraged the Creeks to take merchandise on credit so they could present their bills to the government for payment out of the Creeks' annuity fund. This fund amounted to thirty thousand dollars, the largest single cash pool in New Alabama. The indebted Natives also had to surrender their land to some of the country merchants, who also used their economic position to gain political influence with the Creek chiefs. Members of the Montgomery group of speculators operated stores in Tuckabatchee, the leading Upper Creek town and the home of Opothle Yahola. The proprietors of these stores loaned the Creek leader money and no doubt supplied him with merchandise to win his favor and keep his support in their land war with the Columbus men. Similarly, the Columbus land dealers operated stores in the Lower Creek country, using them as beachheads for their assault on the Creek land base.[42]

But the grog shops, called *sneezers* by the Indians, represented one of the darkest parts of the Indian business. Hundreds of them lay scattered about the Old Creek Nation, and they became more profitable as the Creeks grew more demoralized, even though the state of Alabama had made it illegal to retail spirituous liquors to Indians. The Creeks referred to the larger of these shops as a *sneezer chupco* (long sneezer); the shop's owner they designated *sneezer chupco micco* (long sneezer chief). Such a person exercised great influence over the Indians, because they had become dependent on his product. Simply put, the Indians used strong drink to escape the hunger and hardship of their lives. And this fact, coupled with a possible genetic predisposition, caused many of them to become hopelessly addicted. But in all fairness, we should not suppose that the Creeks were much different than their white neighbors in the use of alcohol. Over consumption of strong drink was common on the southern frontier among all parties, and respectable whites lamented that some of their own communities were destroyed by alcohol use and other frontier vices such as gambling and fighting for sport. We also should not forget what Andrew Jackson and others certainly knew: that Natives took most of their bad habits from whites. Indeed, that was one of his justifications for Indian removal, to separate Natives from their corruptors. Nevertheless, many Creeks had an alcohol problem in those days, and some turned up at the grog shops to trade everything they had, including their food, for liquor. Whiskey sales to Indians also boosted the economy of Columbus. Each day Creeks trudged across the bridge from New Alabama with bundles of firewood on their backs to sell or trade for alcohol. Oftentimes, the streets of Columbus teemed with parties of drunken Indians, each one watched over and directed by a sober, well-dressed black slave. But each night the Creeks recrossed the bridge to their homes, for while the Columbus merchants welcomed Indian shoppers during the day, a town ordnance prohibited them from staying in Columbus overnight.[43]

The grog shops also became centers of another reprehensible aspect of the Indian business, the sexual exploitation of Creek females. It appears that most shop operators, particularly the sneezer chupco miccos, sought out Indian wives, both to get at their land holdings and enjoy their sexual favors. In some cases this involved wife stealing, whereby the liquor dealers used whiskey or their influence and economic power either to seduce married women or outright coerce them into leaving their husbands. By the end of 1835, this wife stealing excited a good deal of commotion among the Creeks, and a council of chiefs held in the Tallassee neighborhood decried the practice. In fact, some Indians thought wife stealing had become almost as extensive as land stealing. Respectable whites also disapproved. After a Russell County jury convicted a young Creek man of killing his wife and sentenced him to death, the sheriff and judge both petitioned the governor for a pardon. They explained that the man killed his wife because he found her with a white man conducting herself in "a lewd and lascevious [sic] manner." Furthermore, come dark the woman and the white man "retired together." The petitioners also promised that if freed, the prisoner would depart for Arkansas immediately and cause no further harm. But in the end, the young man lost both his wife and his life. The governor refused him clemency and he was executed—another casualty of New Alabama's exploitive Indian business.[44]

The traditional gatherings of the Creeks were also good places to conduct the Indian business. Land and liquor dealers went to all the major council meetings to sway the decisions of the chiefs. Lawyers and merchants stalked about the grounds, their pockets full of accounts against the Indians. Similarly, the Native stickball matches attracted acquisitive whites in droves. The Indians referred to the game of stickball as the "little brother of war" because it held a social significance beyond mere recreation. In fact, tribespeople used the game to settle disputes among the towns and give their young men practice for real warfare. Played on a vast field with one hundred men on each side, the game had few rules and often degenerated into a brutal slugfest as the contestants, each armed with two hardwood hurls, competed for the honor of driving a small buckskin ball through the opponent's goal.

The spectators bet heavily on the outcome of these matches; winning towns increased in wealth, and losing ones went away much poorer. Some Indians even risked whole cattle herds on the contest. Moreover, the games seemed to increase in number and ferocity as the Creeks became more impoverished and demoralized. Whites recognized this, and in a frontier region starved for entertainment and opportunities for profit, the stickball matches proved a great draw. To quote one local historian, "Everybody in 100 miles who happened to learn of the game crossed mountains, swam rivers, and fought wild beasts to be present." Liquor dealers filled their coffers at the matches, and other opportunistic visitors found numerous ways to profit from the action surrounding this ancient Native American game. As one observer explained, "A huge crowd of drunkards, thieves, speculators, gamblers, horse racers, bums of every type, and crooks from swamp and glade hung on the flanks" of the assembled Creeks "ready to steal anything from a section of land to a red hot stove. The Indian was a dead game sport, he'd bet everything he had, including his wife, pony, dog, and hope of salvation, on the game."[45]

Individual farms and plantations also became points of exploitation. Over the centuries the Creeks cleared extensive fields; the settlers used those same fields to produce their first corn and cotton crops. Whites also appropriated the Creeks' expansive apple and peach orchards and used the fruit to make a fiery brandy for local use and sale elsewhere. Then the settlers ran their huge herds of livestock into the Creek woodlands, which the Natives had maintained as deer parks by burning off the undergrowth each year. Now the whites' cattle, horses, and hogs ate all the rich mast and tender young shoots the Creeks had produced for their deer. Worse, farmers cut down the forests to grow crops because they knew that the centuries of brush fires had deposited layers of rich potash over the soil. More ominously, the planters exploited the labor of the Creeks, many of whom, having lost or sold their own lands, desperately needed employment, shelter, and protection from other whites. A traveler in New Alabama in the late months of 1835 would have seen gangs of Indians, treated almost as slaves, clearing new corn and cotton lands. This traveler also would have seen Creek field hands picking cotton on the extensive plantations that had grown up along the Chattahoochee River and its tributaries.⁴⁶

President Jackson and Secretary Cass did not mean for this to happen. They wanted to make life in Alabama uncomfortable for the Creeks so they would leave, but they did not want to destroy them as a people. Furthermore, these leaders discovered that despite the sorry state of affairs, Alabama's Natives were not enrolling for emigration with the government's removal agents. In fact, an unanticipated and decidedly ironic situation had developed out of the Cusseta Treaty. Like many other European Americans, President Jackson saw the eastern Indians as an obstacle to the nation's economic development and wanted them removed to the West. He had agreed to the Cusseta Treaty as a means of applying economic pressure on the Creeks, anticipating that they would chose to flee this pressure and seek solace on the land set aside for them in the Western Territory. However, by exposing the Creeks to the marketplace without adequate protections, Jackson actually created the opposite effect. In New Alabama some opportunistic whites discovered that the Creeks were a "natural resource" they could use to facilitate economic development, and consequently they worked against the government's efforts to remove them. As one removal agent explained, "while the government continues to pay the annuities in Alabama, or the Indians have lands to sell, or negro property, these speculators will not let them go." Another agent lamented that there were "a great number of whiskey shops in the nation, the owners of which are universally opposed to the Indians removing until they can get the last cent they have." But that was not the full extent of the problem. Other whites tried to take over the removal process itself as a source of profit. In doing so, they delayed removal. During the delay, the Creeks became even more impoverished and indebted to New Alabama's whites and found it increasingly impossible to emigrate. Thus, many Creeks were being assimilated into the larger society as a permanent underclass of thieves, beggars, and debt-bound peons working the land they lost to the whites. Left to its own devices, the Indian business that the Cusseta Treaty helped create would not have driven the Creeks west. It would have ground them to pulp and even reduced them to abject slavery right where they were. The Indians must have seen this end in sight. After all, the world system was built on the backs of enslaved laborers, and the Creeks had feared such bondage since the seventeenth century, the days of the Indian slave trade. Now the horror was coming true, and one can only imagine how much anger and anxiety this realization caused the Natives.[47]

But one of the most destructive effects of the Cusseta Treaty and the exploitive economy it engendered was to turn Creeks against Creeks in the struggle to survive. The rise of the market economy in New Alabama meant that all the diverse Creek tribespeople, more than twenty thousand in number, had individual decisions to make as to how they would deal not only with the settlers and speculators but with each other in a new and highly competitive commercial environment. In some cases, this was not an insurmountable problem. We know from studies in other areas of the world that Native communities experiencing occupation and subjugation do not always burst apart under the pressure. Those communities with strong leaders and firmly implanted communal values can more or less hold their own in the storm; the people help each other survive. However, some communities do come apart, setting their people free to look out for themselves and experience the angst and ennui of individual economic competition. But, of course, these feelings of alienation and insecurity are not exclusive to Natives suddenly torn from traditional supports; they are common to all societies where the world capitalist system has taken hold. However, one can reasonably conclude that the disintegration of communities, and the attendant psychological and physical harm to individuals, was more pronounced among the Lower Creeks than the Upper Creeks. Early settlers noted, for example, that social distinctions had taken hold among the Lower Creeks. The "better class lived in snug, hewed log houses, with the logs notched down very close, and with narrow sheds on each side," while the "poorer class lived in camps of pine bark." These poorer Creeks maintained a marginal existence, trying to make a living by hiring themselves out as laborers or peddling firewood, wild strawberries, and fish to their white neighbors. Some Creek girls even ventured onto the streets of Columbus to join poor white girls in the prostitution trade. But, unfortunately, some Creeks became as acquisitive and predatory as the land speculators and grog-shop operators. In fact, New Alabama's economic exploitation often cut across racial lines, and this made it all the more destructive to Creek society. Some Creek headmen lived comfortably on the annuity fund while their townspeople drifted further into poverty; some Creeks, most notably Benjamin Marshall and Paddy Carr of Coweta town, worked with the land speculators to defraud less sophisticated Indians; some astute Creeks rented their land out to white farmers and lived off the proceeds; a goodly number of Lower Creeks posed as Upper Creeks and sold land that did not belong to them; some young women undoubtedly took white husbands to better protect their property as well as gain additional wealth and status; and not a few older Creek women set up tables along the busy Federal Road and sold liquor to their demoralized tribespeople. On seeing these Native liquor dealers, an English traveler remarked that the Creeks, in imitation of the whites, "were doing their best to prey upon each other." No other statement better illustrates how fragmented and competitive life in New Alabama had become as a result of the Cusseta Treaty.[48]

Unfortunately, many Creeks could not cope with white oppression and economic competition with their own tribespeople. In the wake of growing poverty, alcohol abuse became all the more destructive to Creek society. Levels of tension and anger rose, and as with most subjugated groups, the Creeks entered a period of self-destruction before turning their anger and frustration outward in armed rebellion against their real oppressors. The Creeks fought and murdered one another at an alarming rate and suicides increased, particularly among the males. Sometimes distressed warriors simply walked into the woods and hanged themselves with grape vines. An army officer at Fort Mitchell on the Chattahoochee River, writing to Washington in 1836, reported that the adult male population of the Creeks had declined by approximately three thousand individuals in only three years. The most noticeable effect of the economic situation, however, was the widespread hunger. Deprived of their lands, the Creeks turned back to hunting, but this resource soon failed because of the competition from all the settlers. The whites often hunted in large parties, killing off many deer and scaring the rest into "inaccessible swamps and morasses." Settlers also set traps for the game and shot hungry Indians they found pulling animals from the snares. In fact, according to a law passed by the Alabama Assembly in 1830, Indians could not legally hunt at all within the state limits. Thus denied their ancient means of subsistence and increasingly lacking the moral and material supports of old clan and town affiliations, many Creeks roamed the countryside, living in tents and huts and fishing, stealing food, or begging morsels at the doors of New Alabama's settlers. Indeed, the women and children often asked permission of the settlers to glean up small potatoes left in the fields after harvest, and "regarded this permission as an inestimable favor." Worse still, the desperate Creeks often found themselves reduced to stripping off the inner bark of trees, boiling it in water, and drinking "the decoction as a substitute for food." And even those fortunate Indians who had money to purchase food sometimes had difficulty doing so, because all the white people moving into the country bought up the available supplies of corn and meat at exorbitant prices. Some of the whites felt sympathy for the Creeks, but any inclination they had to be charitable was tempered by their belief that helping the Indians would only allow them to linger in the state, which would be the worst situation for Creeks and whites alike. In the end, simple starvation resulting from all the exploitation may have been the spark that set off the Second Creek War.[49]

4. Resistance

While some Creeks reached an accommodation with the new economic order and others found themselves overwhelmed by it, still more resisted all the exploitation from the start. This resistance, in turn, set the stage for the outright armed rebellion to come. Not surprisingly, resistance was strongest among the disheveled Lower Creeks, who had always lived on the eastern border of the Creek Nation and as a consequence had, for one hundred years, borne the brunt of contact with the expansion-minded Georgians. These Lower Creeks left homes and valuable property behind when they moved across the Chattahoochee into Alabama in 1828, and they had not begun to recover from that ordeal when the Cusseta accord brought the Georgians rushing right into their midst. Worse, the Georgia speculators lusted after the land along the west bank of the Chattahoochee and its tributary streams, the best cotton land in New Alabama and the very soil on which the Lower Creek villages stood. Consequently, the Lower Creeks were the first members of their nation drawn into the commercial web cast by Columbus, and the first Creeks to face complete dispossession and starvation. Similarly, they were the first to see planters, farmers, and slave gangs settling in around them, and the first Creeks to realize that they were losing their very freedom along with the last little portion of their ancient homeland. But these Natives were not the only people to face this sort of dispossession, nor was their resistance unique. In fact,

3. Resistance and war in New Alabama

the forms of Creek resistance resembled those employed by colonized and oppressed people in many other countries. Angry Creeks sometimes stole chickens and other possessions from the whites; shot down hogs, dogs, and mules for spite; burned barns; poisoned wells; destroyed plows and other agricultural tools; and even killed settlers in retaliation for crimes committed against them.[1]

Numbers of Lower Creeks, mostly of the Hitchitee- and Eucheespeaking Seminole party towns, also returned to Georgia to plague their old enemies. In fact, these Natives incorporated the resources of the Georgians into their normal hunting and gathering activities. In February 1834, Georgia's governor, Wilson Lumpkin, reported to the War Department that "a large number of strolling vagabond Indians" had taken up residence in the thinly settled southern part of the state and had done "immense damage" to the local population by "killing their cattle and hogs, and stealing and consuming their corn, potatoes, &c." Later in the year, the governor informed Washington that another group of Creeks had moved into the northern part of the state to live on lands still held by the Cherokees. Lumpkin also accused these Indians of "continually robbing and plundering our citizens," and he feared they would turn the Cherokees hostile. He asked that the War Department use its influence with the Creek chiefs or its own troops to return the offending Natives to Alabama. If not, he warned, Georgia would have no choice but "exterminating the evil in the only practicable way."[2]

But the problem only grew worse. Owing to the strangely cold winter of 1835, when snow covered Columbus for weeks and ice blocked the Chattahoochee north of the town, Creeks became even more destitute and desperate to find food. A hungry band of Hitchitees crossed the river into Georgia in search of sustenance and fought a brief battle with the citizens of Stewart and Sumter counties. Then an unknown group of Indians, perhaps Seminoles traveling from Florida to visit kin in Alabama, their "mother country," slew two militiamen in a skirmish in Baker County, castrating and cutting out the eyes of one man. In another grizzly incident, Indians cut the throat of a Dooly County school teacher. Meanwhile, numerous settlers in southwestern Georgia reported heavy losses in livestock, furniture, and other property, owing to Indian depredations. Furthermore, the disorganized, undisciplined county militias seemed powerless to stop them, especially since the Indians carried rifles—deadly at long range—while the state sent the local militiamen only muskets. Thus, the Georgians felt vulnerable, and their Indian problems continued right through the spring of 1836, in part because the state of Alabama could not keep the Creeks at home or police the Georgia border. This, of course, was another negative consequence of the short-sighted states' rights position that removed federal authority from the Creek country in the first place, and both Governor Lumpkin and his successor William Schley realized the problem. Tired of seeing Creek and Seminole marauders cross back into Alabama to escape punishment, almost as if they were fleeing from the United States into Mexico, these men petitioned Washington for even more assistance. This time the War Department sent two companies of troops down from the Cherokee country to Fort Mitchell to assist state officials in containing the Lower Creeks. But Eli Shorter wanted more. He and the other Columbus land speculators made the most of the situation by proclaiming that all land-fraud investigations should end, and the government should send the Creeks west or the attacks on whites and their property would reach disastrous proportions in both Georgia and Alabama.[3]

Insofar as he predicted disaster, Shorter was correct. The Lower Creeks were demonstrating that they were not completely powerless in the face of oppression. Furthermore, the Creek resistance proved especially terrifying to local whites because it exposed certain weaknesses in their own society. First and foremost, theirs was a transitional society, one without firm roots and established institutions. Hundreds of migrants and their slaves passed daily down the deeply rutted Federal Road toward Old Alabama, Mississippi, Louisiana, and beyond. Some of these people stopped off in the Creek country for good, many only for a time. These temporary residents lived on a plot of ground year by year, making it yield as much cotton or corn as possible, but always ready to sell out and move to more fertile land to the west. These farmers, along with cattlemen, tradesmen, transients, and outlaws, lived in perpetual motion, unwilling to lay out money to improve roads, build churches and schools, or establish any towns of consequence. Thus, New Alabama supported a white population made up largely of independent, competitive, restless, and insecure people, who exploited one another in the course of exploiting the Creeks and their land. Seeing these people, Thomas Hamilton, an Englishman, concluded that they were a worried and unhappy lot, with "furrowed and haggard countenances" and eyes "almost uniformly expressive of care and cunning." In the end, such people found it difficult to unite in suppressing the Creek resistance because they lacked a sense of community among themselves. Ironically, the expansion of the U.S. people and their market economy that so shattered the Creek Nation also fragmented white society, dividing its members socially, politically, and economically. As the Second Creek War approached, this fact became more and more evident.[4]

In truth, white society on the frontier was something more than just divided. It was almost at war with itself: the respectable upper and middle levels on one side and the poorer whites and roughs on the other. Class conflict was a constant. The roughs formed outlaw gangs to win their way; respectables formed vigilance committees to fight the gangs. This intraethnic clash alone would have made New Alabama a fairly violent place, but adding Creek resistance to the mix made for an especially dangerous environment. The respectables had the most to fear from the situation, however, because Creeks, as an exploited group of poor people, naturally became part of the underclass of a now pluralistic society. It should not be all that shocking, then, that angry Creeks formed an interethnic alliance with white roughs to prey on respectable settlers, the people who came to colonize the Creek country. Nor should we be amazed the Creeks and their allies were following a tradition of lower-class resistance to the injustices of the spreading world capitalist economy.[5]

Of course, the roughs and Indians were not exactly friends, only people who found common cause over time. In fact, New Alabama's roughs—also called "minions of the moon"—had been some of the first intruders in the Creek country, and they discovered unlimited opportunities for themselves in the Indian business. Besides driving Indians off their land, they robbed Native graves and stole horses, cattle, and slaves from the Creeks. They also married Indian women to get their property. But these roughs were inveterate opportunists; they also stole livestock and slaves from prosperous whites. Indeed, they often saw respectable farmers and planters, not Indians, as their worst enemies. After all, these farmers and planters, as part of their quest for respectability, drove roughs off the land on which they squatted, then sought to civilize the frontier and stamp out the sinful way of life roughs loved. Little wonder then that roughs, once respectable settlers established themselves in the country, joined the Creek resistors in crimes and acts of rebellion against those settlers. When, for example, the sheriff of Russell County imprisoned a group of Creeks for killing William Fannin, the younger brother of a despised land speculator, roughs broke the Indians out of the county's flimsy jail and set them free. Roughs also formed notorious subversive communities, such as Sodom, just across the river from Columbus, where they lived side by side with Natives and blacks and formed a democratic yet violent and boisterous union respectables found appalling. Furthermore, the roughs ran faro banks and grog shops, where they gave the Creeks whiskey in exchange for money, goods, and horses stolen from settlers and travelers. In fact, the Hitchitees and Sawoklis living at the mouth of Cowikee Creek often stole herds of horses in Georgia, swam them across the Chattahoochee to their village, and sold them to whites, who, in turn, protected the horse thieves by apprising them of any movements sheriffs or aggrieved planters might make against them. Some white men even accompanied Creek marauders on their forays into southwestern Georgia and engaged in what would become a southern tradition: poor whites torching the property of their social superiors. In October 1834, one John Howard was found guilty of arson and ordered out of Chambers County for inciting the Indians. Then when an act of arson destroyed the church in the little Chattahoochee River community of Fort Gaines, Georgia, in January 1836, local residents did not know if it was the work of "an incendiary white man or some skulking Indians." But it is clear that roughs formed a criminal underworld in New Alabama, brought disaffected Creeks into their orbit, plotted with them against the authorities, and urged the Indians to resist removal. Not only did this alliance of Indians and roughs terrify respectable whites, it may also explain why Alabama and Mississippi, the southern states with the largest Indian populations, led the nation in vigilante justice during the period 1800 to 1835. Indeed, one plantation owner in Barbour County, illustrating the deep cultural division between respectables and roughs, lamented that one of the most unfortunate problems about having Creek neighbors was that they associated with lower-class whites.[6]

Governor Gayle did not care for the association either. In the late spring of 1835, he tried to do something about the criminal collusion between Indians and roughs, but his solution did not involve much action on his part. Despite all his earlier grandiloquent protests that Secretary Cass and the federal government stood in violation of Alabama's state rights, he now asked Cass to deal with what he considered to be New Alabama's main criminal concern: "The grog shops, which I understand are the most common establishments throughout the country, should receive your prompt and decided reprehension. They are generally established as I learn, for the accommodation of the Indians, and can any one doubt that to these fountains of crime and immorality are to be ascribed many of the difficulties which our citizens have to encounter." A true statement in part, but why would Gayle write it? Only the year before he had declared that Alabama, not the federal government, should and could impose law and order in the Creek country. And indeed, the Alabama Assembly had passed a law making it illegal for anyone to sell spirituous liquor to Indians. So why did Gayle ask Cass to deal with the grog shops? Why not close them himself? Obviously, he thought he could not. The task was too big. There were too many shops and too many people profiting from them. Furthermore, not all of these people were roughs. The land companies, backed by wealthy and otherwise respectable men, established some of the stores. Probably Gayle was reluctant to march against these people and risk the sort of political criticism he himself had leveled against the central government when federal marshals tried to evict intruders from the Creek country. Beyond this, Gayle must have known on some level that the grog shops were the foundation of New Alabama's whole Indian business, and in reality, the entire state benefited from that economic enterprise. It was generating wealth and bringing the old Creek country into the market; as governor, Gayle could not challenge the economic system, even though he deplored some of its negative consequences. But Gayle's dilemma was not a new one or unique to Alabama; it was central to the capitalist world economy. At some point in every society the line between large profits and outright theft blurred, leaving politicians like Gayle to focus on the "crime and immorality" of the underclasses while leaving the system free to generate untold riches for those above. And in this regard, it is not surprising that Gayle targeted New Alabama's grog shops as the fountains of disorder. Within the larger world system, pubs and grog shops often become sources of subversive activity for the underclasses of all societies. The upper classes then feared them as threats to the system as well as simple seedbeds of common vice.[7]

But the collusion between Creek resistors and white roughs was not the most fearful aspect of life in New Alabama for respectable whites. Large-scale agricultural production depended on slave labor, and settlers could not make the lands of the Old Creek Nation productive without placing large numbers of blacks in close proximity to the Indians. However, all these blacks became potential allies of the Creeks and a source of dread to their owners. The problem was especially great in the southern counties of New Alabama near Columbus. There the Lower Creeks lived near numerous large plantations owned by absentee planters. Many of these planters resided in Columbus or on estates on the Georgia side of the Chattahoochee. Large groups of slaves farmed their Alabama holdings and lived much to themselves, supervised only by a single overseer for each plantation. Naturally enough, some of these slaves gravitated toward local Indian communities, where the inhabitants often treated them as equals. A Russell County slave named Henry would explain later that he spent his free time among the Creeks, participated in their ceremonies and games, and even won the heart of a beautiful Creek girl. Henry also reported that one of his good friends, a Creek resistor, actively sought his aid and support against the settlers. This association of Creeks and blacks so disturbed one of the white inhabitants of Russell County in the summer of 1835 that he swore out a complaint and had the county sheriff arrest Neah Micco for harboring blacks in his town on Big Euchee Creek. Interestingly, though, other settlers came to the elderly chief's defense, petitioning Governor Gayle to pardon him as he was not personally responsible for what they called the widespread and deplorable tendency of Creeks to welcome slaves into their settlements.[8]

But whites also had to be suspicious of all the free blacks and slaves who lived permanently in the Indian communities. As a general rule, these people made industrious farmers and lived well, despite the fact that some Creek planters had adopted the racist attitudes and postures white society and the economic system demanded. One traveler in the Creek country described the blacks there as alert, sleek, and happy, as opposed to the dull and morose-looking slaves owned by whites. Certainly Creek slaves did not have to work as hard as plantation slaves, nor did they suffer as many beatings, and their children often grew up on terms of equality with the Indian youngsters. Moreover, black Creeks were well equipped to deal with the white intrusion. Unlike many Indians, these blacks spoke both English and Creek tongues, and they understood how both Native and white societies worked. Consequently, they were much less likely to be hoodwinked by whites, and the Creeks depended on them to serve as intermediaries and counselors (cultural brokers) in their dealings with whites. One observer reported that on the streets of Columbus he saw numerous parties of drunken Indians, each group led by "a negro-man, the slave of some one present, but commonly well dressed in the European manner, having an air of superior intelligence to his masters, and evidently exercising over them the power and influence derived from superior knowledge: the negroes, in fact, appeared the masters, and the red-men the slaves." The observer did not seem to understand that Indians often required one of their party to serve as a sober caretaker when they went off to drink, but he was correct in noting that black Creeks knew how to take care of themselves in those rough-and-tumble times. Indeed, they could be experts of economic opportunity, colluding with the Natives on one hand, while they served as "strikers" and interpreters (linksters) for the land companies on the other. For these reasons, New Alabama's respectable settlers could not have been happy about the influence of blacks in the Creek country. Furthermore, these settlers certainly knew that blacks had inspired some of the Seminoles' resistance to white expansionism in the Florida Territory to the south, and they surely suspected black Creeks of doing the same in Alabama.[9]

The acts of Creek resistance, as well as the possibility of an alliance between Natives, blacks, and white roughs, were especially troublesome to respectable settlers because county officials lacked the ability to punish these crimes effectively in some areas. In their desire to exert their state's rights and to keep the federal government from interfering with their acquisition of the Creek country, the Alabama Assembly had extended state law over New Alabama. But in the process, the legislature created a law-and-order vacuum in parts of the region. By stopping federal marshals and troops from acting independently in regulating the contact between Creeks and whites and by prohibiting the Creek chiefs from enforcing their own laws over unruly tribespeople, the state of Alabama eliminated important forces for keeping the peace at the same time the Indian business ran rampant, creating more and more hostility and disorder. In place of federal and tribal controls, Governor Gayle and the Alabama Assembly substituted a puny county court system that lacked the will to prosecute whites fully for murdering Indians or even for selling liquor to the Creeks. The Chambers County solicitor, for example, refused to prosecute a number of indicted liquor dealers in October 1834, including a county commissioner and a Christian minister. Moreover, the sheriffs lacked the staff to bring Native criminals to justice in areas where Creeks still outnumbered settlers. In Macon County, for example, 2,000 Creek warriors lived among only 150 white men capable of bearing arms. In such counties farmers and planters thought that they lived under Creek rule, and they could not rest easy in their beds at night. At Irwinton, in Barbour County, one plantation mistress complained of constantly seeing "savage faces peeping and prying around the premises," and so feared the Indian women who came to her door that she readily gave them all her red dresses and other items they desired. On those occasions that county officials did manage to capture, try, convict, and hang Creek murderers, they did so at their peril, as witnessed by the actions of the white residents of Talladega in the months preceding the outbreak of the Second Creek War. Having executed a Creek man on the gallows in the center of town, the townspeople retreated to the courthouse, where they spent the night armed and huddled together in fear of the reaction of the local Indian community. In fact, George W. Featherstonhaugh, an English traveler on Federal Road in January 1835, noted that as he advanced into the Creek country everything he saw "announced the total dissolution of order." He may have been lucky to have survived his journey, for the editor of the *Columbus Enquirer* observed that the Creeks murdered other travelers on the road nearly every month. This editor, who once favored the extension of state law over Indians, both in Georgia and Alabama, now criticized the state of Alabama for the "weak and murderous policy" of claiming an authority it could not exercise.[10]

Now John Gayle grew desperate. He had declaimed against the use of federal troops to keep illegal intruders out of the Creek country, and in doing so, he helped the land speculators and others who would exploit the Indians gain a foothold. But now, in the spring of 1835, faced with mounting evidence of Native resistance, he wrote the War Department condemning the speculators and begging for federal troops to defend the good citizens of New Alabama from angry Creeks who consistently "placed the laws and civil magistrates at defiance." But what Gayle failed to see was that Creeks often committed acts of violence and defied the Alabama justice system in an effort to enforce their own laws and maintain some semblance of order in their communities. Indeed, the Creek view of the cosmos demanded that they continue to practice their traditional justice system. Gayle simply did not understand that the Indians saw the world about them as a complex whole consisting of various contending parts and forces that had to be balanced against one another to ensure the maintenance of order throughout. Spiritual power infused the whole, and any imbalance caused by humans led to a loss of power, permitting the onset of various misfortunes. Thus, a person might kill an animal, but he or she had to perform certain rituals to appease the spirit of the dead animal so harmony between humans and animals could be maintained. Otherwise, the offended animal realm might unleash disease on the person. Similarly, the crying spirit of a murdered person had to be appeased by the death of the murderer or a representative of the murderer, which would allow the offended spirit to fly away to the west. This would restore the proper balance and order to the cosmos and free the community of harm from a lingering unsatisfied ghost. Consequently, when one Billy-John, a Creek resident of Macon County, killed another Indian in a drunken fight, he realized, on sobering up, what he must do. The next morning "he drew his blanket around him and quietly laid himself down on the floor of his cabin to meet his fate." Shortly thereafter, Davy Harjo and two other warriors walked in and without saying a word shot Billy-John to death. Indeed, this sort of stoic resolve to meet the death penalty was common among the Creeks, tied as it was to their larger view of life in the community and cosmos. One observer noted, in fact, that "a heroic submission to the penalty of Indian law" was one of the "marked characteristics" of the Creeks. As a result, some local whites gained a certain admiration for Indian justice, including acts of violent retribution. The fact that a grand jury indicted Davy Harjo and the others for Billy-John's murder, but a jury of whites then failed to convict the men, may give evidence of the settlers' respect for the efficacy of Creek tradition. Unfortunately, Governor Gayle, believing the Indians lawless, saw all their acts of violence as crimes and called for federal troops to help stamp them out.[11]

However, the Native sense of justice also ensured continued resistance to oppression, and this resistance only increased throughout the remainder of 1835. While traveling through the Lower Creek country in May, Superintendent Hogan reported that the "Indians have become quite hostile in this part of the nation; they shot a man and woman in Chambers County, and some in this [Russell], and people are afraid to ride alone among them." Then, in December of that year, events occurred that made the Second Creek War inevitable, by giving inspiration to Creek resistors and throwing whites into a panic all over the Chattahoochee River Valley. The Seminoles, close kin to the Lower Creeks, took up arms to resist removal from the Florida Territory. They assassinated their agent, Wiley Thompson; ambushed and wiped out a company of more than one hundred U.S. troops under Maj. Francis L. Dade; and launched widespread attacks on the plantations west of St. Augustine. Reports also spread that large numbers of slaves were joining the Seminoles, and the newspapers declared that Cuban fishermen were running guns to the Natives from the West Indies. But that was not the worst of the news as far as settlers on the Chattahoochee River were concerned. They reported seeing Creeks going down the stream in canoes to join the Seminoles, and army officers in Florida claimed that Creek warriors were indeed reinforcing the Seminoles, marching in "with packs on their backs, like travelers." Already terrified by escalating acts of Creek resistance, whites in Alabama and Georgia began to suspect a Seminole-Creek conspiracy and feared that they would be the next targets of a mass Indian uprising. And then, as if to give credence to their wildest fears, some person or persons—either Creeks, disaffected white workers, or both—began to set fire to the buildings in Columbus at night, trying to burn the town to the ground.[12]

At that point, the whites took steps to defend themselves from assault. Men living outside those areas of Alabama and Georgia threatened by the Creeks rushed to volunteer to fight the Seminoles in Florida. Meanwhile, the citizens of Columbus instituted nightly patrols to watch for hostile Indians and asked their governor, William Schley, to call up enough state troops to station five hundred men every thirty miles along Georgia's southwestern frontier. In Russell County, Alabama, just across the river from Columbus, settlers began to form volunteer companies, erected their own fort, and asked the state for arms and ammunition. They also requested that their fellow citizens abstain from selling ardent spirits and gunpowder to the Creeks, something that should have been done long before. John Hogan, the government's chief adviser in the region, must have looked on with some amusement. He doubted the Creeks intended to attack the whites in concert with the Seminoles, yet he did note that there was little in the Lower Creek country to prevent such an assault. Fort Mitchell, the only federal military post, was merely an open camp run by a young lieutenant and only thirty troops.[13]

But again, the independent, competitive nature of Chattahoochee Valley residents prevented them from working together to establish much security for themselves. One Wiley Williams, for example, employed some seventy or eighty Euchees as workers on his plantation in Marion County, Georgia. Some of these people he held as slaves, having raised them from childhood. Wiley's neighbors, however, knew the Euchees had frequent interaction with their tribespeople in Alabama and feared that they would become a hostile force endangering the county. Consequently, county officials asked Williams to disband his Indian workforce, but he refused. Then, when they suggested they might raise a company of volunteers to remove his Indians from Georgia, the indignant plantation owner threatened to arm the Euchees so they could defend themselves and his estate against all comers.[14]

Incidents such as this only increased the Georgians' hostility toward Indians, a hostility conditioned by generations of conflict with the Creeks, Seminoles, and Cherokees. Invariably, this hostility led them to excess. To keep Creeks from coming into Georgia to hunt deer and prey on livestock—something the Natives did every winter—the state legislature passed an act on December 24, 1835, making it illegal for Creeks to enter Georgia unless they came to attend to legal matters accompanied by a respectable white person. The act also prohibited Georgians from continuing the practice of employing Creeks on their cotton plantations. Furthermore, the act made trading with Indians illegal in Georgia, a proscription obviously aimed at the grog shops lining the eastern bank of the Chattahoochee. Following their incursions into the Georgia interior, Creeks stopped at these shops to trade property taken from farmers for liquor. In fact, the roughs who ran these shops encouraged the Natives to commit robberies and even warned them of the movements of county sheriffs and their posses, the same practice that was happening on the Alabama side of the line. Although the new law would not go into effect until February 1, 1836, some hotheaded Georgians took it upon themselves to keep the Creeks out of Georgia as soon as the act passed. As part of their effort, they began to shoot Indians on sight, on both banks of the Chattahoochee. Most of their victims, however, were industrious, peaceful Eufaula Creeks, who earned much-needed money by picking cotton for planters. In one instance, eight or nine Georgians marched an elderly Indian out of a cotton field south of Irwinton and brutally executed him. This act incensed Creek resistors and made them more vengeful. After all, the traditional clan justice system of the Creeks mandated eye-for-an-eye retribution to appease the spirit of the man and all other murder victims like him. Respectable farmers up and down the Chattahoochee shuddered. They knew that for every Indian killed, some white person, probably an innocent one like themselves, would perish at the hands of Native warriors.[15]

Indeed, those warriors did not take the attacks on the cotton pickers lying down, especially in light of Seminole successes in Florida. After a river patrol fired on a small party of Chehaw Creeks sleeping beside a campfire in Georgia, a band of fifty warriors armed themselves and crossed into Georgia to claim the bodies of their slain tribespeople. By the time news of the crossing reached Columbus, frightened whites were saying that a war party of five hundred warriors had come over the river to ravage Georgia's farms and plantations. Consequently, twenty-two men led by John H. Watson descended the river fifteen miles to Bryant's Ferry to observe the Indian host. They found the Creeks, far fewer than they expected, about to cross back into Alabama. The Indians hoisted a white flag but Watson's men fired anyway. Thereupon the warriors took shelter in a ravine, returned fire, killed two Georgians, and ran the remainder back to Columbus. Though the Georgians did not know it at the time, this tendency to launch a precipitative attack on Creek warriors, followed by an equally precipitative, even cowardly, retreat, would become a pattern for them. In fact, the battle at Bryant's Ferry, fought on January 26, 1836, was only the first of several such engagements. It was also the opening salvo in a growing conflict about to blossom into the Second Creek War.[16]

The Bryant's Ferry fight also revealed how differently whites at the local level viewed the Creek resistance. More importantly, their reaction to the fight showed once again how difficult it would be for them to unite in suppressing that resistance. While the Georgians blamed the Natives for the outbreak of violence, federal officials on the scene thought the Georgians were even more responsible. Fearing that war would soon engulf the whole Creek Nation, 2nd Lt. John W. McCrabb, the officer in command at Fort Mitchell, wrote to Washington that the "Georgians have thus set fire to the match which the Indians have been some time preparing." John Hogan, who had just begun his land-fraud investigation among the Lower Creeks when the battle occurred, was even more critical. Locked in his own conflict with land thieves and removal contractors, Hogan believed that the Georgians, led by the Columbus speculators, were deliberately trying to goad the Creeks into war to stop his investigations in the Lower Creek towns. Furthermore, Hogan learned that General McDougald, Columbus's speculating military commander, in concert with General Bailey, commanding Georgia's Tenth Militia Division, intended to order up one thousand militiamen, then march them into Alabama to attack the Creeks. Hogan promptly notified Alabama's new governor, Clement C. Clay, of this outrage and told him that the citizens of Alabama had nothing to fear from the Creeks unless the Georgians invaded. Then, he warned, the Indians would surely go to war.[17]

Fortunately, the New Alabama settlers living near Fort Mitchell—the very people who would suffer most in an Indian war—managed to stave off such a conflict. A delegation hurried to Columbus, remonstrated against the planned invasion of their neighborhood, and arranged a meeting between generals McDougald and Bailey and the Lower Creek chiefs. This meeting took place at Fort Mitchell on February 1. McDougald and Bailey, as well as Superintendent Hogan, addressed the chiefs and informed them that the president was calling up troops from many states to crush the Seminoles. They went on to warn the chiefs that the same fate would befall the Creeks if they did not stop committing depredations in Georgia. The chiefs assured the white men that they wanted to keep the peace and signed a pledge that in the future they would turn over any tribespeople guilty of crimes in Georgia to the commanding officer at Fort Mitchell. They also promised to retrieve stolen property and take it to the fort. However, they made it clear that Creeks were not the only ones committing border depredations. Georgians often crossed the Chattahoochee to steal from the Creeks, and some warriors went to Georgia only to retrieve horses and other property taken from them and their families by whites. Nevertheless, the chiefs vowed that their people would no longer do this. Instead, they would make complaints of theft to Lieutenant McCrabb, who would forward them to General McDougald and the Georgia authorities for action. Fortunately for all concerned, these promises soothed the Georgians and prevented them from invading Alabama. That, however, only delayed the inevitable clash of arms.[18]

The action of the respectable settlers living in the Fort Mitchell neighborhood revealed that New Alabama did contain a solid core of people who understood the problems the Indians faced and were capable of coexisting with them. These settlers shared their friendship with the Alabama Natives and remarked on the general kindness, honesty, tolerance, and deep-seated spirituality of most Creeks. Despite their land speculation activities, whites admired prosperous Creek planters and farmers such as Benjamin Marshall, Paddy Carr, and James Islands. They saw too that numbers of Creeks could actually fit themselves into the new society being created in eastern Alabama. Yargee, Tuskenea's brother, for example, had discarded the dress and habits of his tribe and adopted those of the whites and had fashioned himself into a farmer, slave-owner, and well-to-do businessperson. But some settlers also appreciated the traditional Creek way of life. One Alabamian would remember his childhood in Russell County quite fondly because of his association with Indian neighbors. Having no white children to play with, and no church or Sunday school to go to on the Sabbath, he spent his Sundays in the Indian towns, where he passed the time "playing ball, eating potatoes or ground-peas, or drinking sofky," a gruel made of ground corn and hickory nuts mixed with water or milk, some molasses, and possibly a little good whiskey. Other settlers loved to attend Creek dances and religious ceremonies, particularly the annual Busk, a yearly renewal ceremony lasting eight days. During this time the Creeks returned to their *talwas* (hometowns) to celebrate the first corn harvest, purify themselves, and renew their spiritual power through fasting, dancing, and participating in other religious rites. John Howard Payne, actor, author, and national celebrity, witnessed the Tuckabatchee Busk in 1835 and proclaimed that he "never beheld more intense devotion." He also said admiringly that it was strange to see the religion and people of an "untraceable past" existing in the very "heart of the most recent portion of the most recent people upon earth." Then he concluded with the pensive observation that on "comparing the majority of the white and red assemblages there, the barbarian should be so infinitely the more civilized and the more interesting of the two."[19]

No matter how much well-meaning New Alabama settlers appreciated Creek culture, they proclaimed uniformly, as did President Jackson, that a close association with white society corrupted the Indians and destroyed by degrees their ancient nobility. They also saw that a growing sense of hostility was overcoming the Indians' natural kindness and hospitality. These facts mitigated against the possibility of any meaningful coexistence. Thus, the Fort Mitchell conference brought no lasting peace. While the Seminoles and Creeks never engaged in a widespread conspiracy to attack the whites, and few Creeks actually joined the Seminoles in the early months of the war in Florida, many whites believed such a conspiracy existed and they treated the Creeks accordingly. Their actions then pushed the Creeks toward more violence. Furthermore, the Seminole victories in Florida undoubtedly led some Natives to believe that they might seek a violent escape from the trap created for them by the Cusseta Treaty of 1832 and the operation of New Alabama's insidious Indian business. Indeed, by the spring of 1836 almost all the Lower Creeks had lost or sold their land. Many were starving. Yet like the Seminoles they did not wish to emigrate west to live in an inhospitable land already occupied and ruled over by the McIntosh Creeks. Furthermore, they were too poor to undertake such a relocation. Finally, they were reluctant to move while the government's investigation held out the promise to them of getting their lands back. And so they stayed in place, starving all the more, divided against themselves, exploited further by the Indian business, and suffering abuse from the Georgians. And yet it seemed the government, quite arbitrarily, had set the spring of 1836 as the deadline for their removal. Government agents and removal contractors alike were telling them that the grace period provided by the Cusseta Treaty was drawing to a close, that all Creeks without land must leave Alabama soon or face forcible removal by their white neighbors. The newspapers constantly proclaimed that now the Creeks, not the settlers, were the intruders in New Alabama. Little wonder that the Lower Creeks, faced with such a dilemma and seeing how successfully their Seminole cousins fought the whites, would chose war as a means of resisting removal, reclaiming their country, reestablishing their identity as an independent people, binding together their torn and impoverished society, and most importantly, feeding themselves.[20]

No one knows exactly when the Natives began to plan for war, but the settlers in the Lower Creek counties of Alabama noticed a significant change in the demeanor of their Creek neighbors just after the Fort Mitchell conference. Now denied access to their Georgia hunting grounds, as well as to the property of Georgia farmers, hungry Lower Creeks increased their depredations against the whites in New Alabama. At the same time, Superintendent Hogan noted that in his talks with the Indians every warrior arrived prepared for battle, armed with "rifle, knife, pouch, horn, &c." Furthermore, the warriors knew all the latest news from Florida, possibly because they received messengers from the Seminoles, but more likely because literate Creeks kept them informed from the newspapers. An anxious citizens' committee representing Montgomery County, just outside the Creek boundary, notified Governor Clay that the Indians were purchasing all the guns and ammunition they could get, and they obviously meant to follow the lead of the Seminoles and "push a war against the whites to the last extremity." The committee then went on to ask Clay to send "five hundred stand of muskets and accouterments, three hundred yaugers, and two hundred pistols and sabers" to the city of Montgomery so the citizens could defend themselves. Simultaneously, settlers living in the Lower Creek counties began to plead with the governor not to call out any of their men for service in the Seminole War. They contended that Indian warriors far outnumbered white men capable of bearing arms in their counties and to take any of these men from the state would compromise the ability of communities to defend themselves should the Creeks declare war. In fact, the settlers would probably have to flee their homes. This was a legitimate fear, but the settlers could have mentioned another one. At the time they wrote, Georgia volunteers were mustering at Columbus and setting off by steamboat for Tampa Bay to fight the Seminoles. The Creek resistors saw this and may have taken it as more encouraging evidence of Seminole success. They may also have thought that they now faced an enemy seriously weakened in numbers on the Georgia side of the Chattahoochee. They may have believed that the Seminoles had created a distraction for them, one they should take advantage of by moving beyond scattered acts of murder, property destruction, and theft to full-armed revolt.[21]

As governor, Clay had to take all requests for aid seriously, but in an economically competitive society like the one in New Alabama, he did not always know whom to believe. One petitioner, Thomas Woodward, an Indian countryman, land speculator, and avowed states' rights nullifier, not only asked Clay not to draft troops from Macon County but even went on to blame Clay, a Union Democrat, for the circumstances that made keeping the county's fighting men at home necessary. According to Woodward, the governor had exerted such little effort in apprehending Creek murderers that all the Indians had grown "quite impudent and troublesome." But Woodward should have blamed himself as well. He was a member of the U.S. party of Indian countrymen. He had been one of William McIntosh's associates and no friend of Opothle Yahola. He had also opposed federal attempts to keep intruders out of the Creek country or to regulate relations between settlers and Creeks. Then he used Tuskenea to scare Indians away from the government land offices when they came to complain about stolen reserves. And while Woodward may have possessed a drop or two of Indian blood and dressed the part in 1818 when he helped McIntosh invade Florida to snatch blacks from the Seminoles, he was at heart an U.S. opportunist, always on the lookout for the next best chance in the

Indian business. His sort helped create the conditions that nurtured Creek resistance and violence, the outbreaks he now blamed Clay for failing to stop. Clay knew this, and he must have found it difficult to tell if settlers actually needed help or if the requests came from interested land speculators and others who wanted only to protect their ill-gotten gains.[22]

However, settlers in the Upper Creek country also noted disturbing changes in the behavior of their Indian neighbors. One O. K. Truman wrote to Clay that he had heard an elderly Indian of the noted McGillivray family declare that the Creeks intended to go to war in the spring when "the trees put out their leaves." Determined to test the truth of this statement, Truman took a tour of the Upper Creek country in late February 1836 to observe the Natives and talk to settlers. He reported to Clay that he had seen many disturbing signs. First of all, the Creeks were in "a great commotion among themselves." Their towns in the middle and southern parts of the nation were "determinately sullen, and hostile," and some of the inhabitants of these towns were mingling with the friendly Creeks to the north on the Coosa River, agitating them. Furthermore, the Creeks, in an obvious attempt to move about unnoticed by whites, were using all their old trails, which "have been entirely disused for many years." In addition, the warriors had bought a great number of rifles at different settlements, particularly Wetumpka, and some of the chiefs had purchased powder by the keg. Curiously, the Indians also bought small brass kettles, pistols, and even a previously unwanted commodity, Mackintosh blankets. Like Hogan, Truman noted that he never passed an unarmed warrior, which was most disturbing because the Upper Creeks living north of Federal Road did not hunt and had seldom carried weapons in the past. In Truman's opinion, whites should be cautious, and he recommended to Clay that the governor assemble a military force to overawe the chiefs at the Creeks' spring council meeting at Loachapoka town.[23]

Governor Clay also received alarming reports from DeKalb and Cherokee counties in the northeastern corner of the state. These counties, inhabited by settlers and Cherokee Indians, stood outside the old Creek boundary. However, in December 1835, Creeks began to move up the Coosa River into these counties to escape the turmoil in their own country, as well as to avoid removal to the West. Most of these Creeks belonged to the Upper Creek towns of Sockapartoy, Econchattee, Tallushatchee, and Talladega, and by February 1836, approximately 2,500 of them had made camp in the Cherokee country. The largest number lived in a colony on the east side of the Coosa within six miles of Turkey Town, an old Cherokee community now occupied by white settlers. But at the same time the Creeks were putting down roots, DeKalb and Cherokee counties received a wave of Cherokee settlers, with some additional Creek refugees, moving in from northern Georgia, where the ever-aggressive Georgians had taken over their homes. At that point, the whites living among all these Indians began to bombard Clay with complaints. They told him that the Creeks were destitute and hostile. Their men stayed out of sight all day but came out at night to dance and hold council. Furthermore, they had commenced a system of plunder, breaking into corn houses and smokehouses to steal grain and bacon. They also threatened whites and had shot and killed a traveler, and their very presence had begun to inhibit white settlement in the area. Worst of all, the settlers told Clay that an old Cherokee had informed them that the Creeks meant to begin a war "when the trees budded out"—the same bit of information Truman had discovered. Furthermore, the settlers believed the Creeks were agitating hostility among all those Cherokees disaffected by the recent New Echota Treaty, which obligated them to give up all their territory in the East and move west. This treaty, which did not represent the will of the majority of Cherokees, had been rammed down their throats by federal commissioners, and the settlers who petitioned Clay believed that if the Senate ratified the treaty, those Cherokees opposed to removal, including their principal chief, John Ross, might very well join the Creeks in their war. Should this happen, Clay's informants pointed out, the outnumbered whites in northeastern Alabama would be annihilated. Consequently, they asked Clay to raise a large force of militiamen to remove the Creek intruders among them and send these people off to the land set aside for them beyond the Mississippi.[24]

However, these petitioners also pointed out that the selfishness of speculators lay at the heart of the Indian problem in northeastern Alabama. In fact, speculators had lured many of the Creeks to the Cherokee country. In some cases, these men actually transported the Indians there in wagons. Probably these speculators, including a wealthy Cherokee named James Vann, got the Creeks' land allotments from them by promising them new land in the Cherokee country, where they would be safe from removal. Then, after the Creeks arrived in Cherokee and DeKalb counties, these speculators established stores among them and sold them liquor. The Creeks, of course, paid for this liquor with the money the same speculators had given them for their land. With this scheme, the speculators managed to secure valuable land for a relative few barrels of cheap whiskey. They left the Indians destitute and angry, with no way to survive but to prey on white farmers. Participants in the Indian business were guilty of this sort of tactic throughout the Indian country, and their activities demonstrated again how difficult it would be for a white society, socially and economically divided, to prevent an armed insurrection by a portion of the even more fragmented and economically exploited Creek population.[25]

All this news from the Cherokee country must have upset Governor Clay, especially since it came with a new load of criticisms and provocative actions from the ever-troublesome Georgians. Once again they chided Clay for his inactivity in disciplining his Indian population, and the Georgia legislature showed him how it should be done. They responded to the feared combination of hostile Creeks and disaffected Cherokees by forming a special cavalry unit called the Georgia Guards to watch these Indians and keep the peace in northern Georgia. Unfortunately for the Cherokees, these guards took it upon themselves to intimidate even friendly Creeks and Cherokees and bully anyone they suspected of standing in the way of Cherokee emigration. At one point the guard even invaded Tennessee to arrest Chief John Ross so he would not go off to Washington to oppose the sort of removal treaty the guard wanted. The guard also arrested the chief's house guest, the traveling journalist John Howard Payne, a man known to have made complimentary statements about both Cherokees and Creeks. But still the Georgians were not done. To head off a possible black-

Indian alliance in its state, the Georgia legislature tightened restrictions on slaves and free persons of color to severely limit their contact with Natives. At the same time, state newspapers cautioned against the purchase of slaves from Indians, as those blacks had suffered few restrictions from their Native owners and had imbibed dangerous notions of freedom and insurrection. Finally, the Georgians moved to improve their militia system both to intimidate Natives and to be prepared for another Indian war.[26]

The Georgians also began to call for reparations for all the depredations committed by the Creeks in Georgia during the year 1835. They reminded the War Department that according to section 17 of the Indian Trade and Intercourse Act of 1834, the citizens of any state could receive restitution payments from the federal government if Natives, living in Indian country, passed into that state and committed depredations on people or property. The restitution money, the act said, would be drawn from the annuity of the offending tribe. On that basis, the Georgians appealed to the government for money to pay for property stolen or destroyed by marauding Creeks from Alabama. However, Secretary Cass informed the Georgians that the Trade and Intercourse Act no longer applied to the Creeks because the state of Alabama had extended its laws over the Creek territory. That territory was no longer an Indian country regulated by the federal government; it was simply a part of Alabama and the Creeks were state citizens. Thus, the Alabamians infuriated the Georgians in two ways: first, they failed to keep the Creeks from committing depredations in Georgia; second, they prohibited the Georgians from getting Creek annuity money as compensation for those acts. That being the case, the Georgia press began to float the idea that the state of Alabama, being unable to control its Indians, should be liable for the crimes of those Indians and compensate Georgia accordingly.[27]

The anguished cries of his fellow citizens, combined with the complaints and threats of the aggressive Georgians, aroused Governor Clay, and he attempted to act to prevent further trouble by sending state troops into New Alabama to establish order and prevent any union between Creeks and Seminoles. However, Clay found that his own fellow politicians, not the Indians, became the chief obstacles to his plans. The state constitution allowed the governor to call up militia forces only to suppress an actual insurrection or to repel an invasion. Neither of these situations existed in February and March 1836. Consequently, Clay asked the state legislature to give special permission to raise militia companies to range over the Creek counties and keep the peace. He also asked them to appropriate the money necessary to pay for this military operation. A majority of the legislators refused on both counts, revealing that many of Old Alabama's inhabitants either believed that the settlers in New Alabama, many of them Georgians, were exaggerating the dangers or that they deserved what was happening because they had injured the Creeks and stolen their land. Undoubtedly, some of the legislators who refused Clay's request were the same men who had opposed the extension of Alabama law over the Creek country in the first place.[28]

Clay's only alternative then was to request a federal authorization to call up state troops, in which case the War Department would arm, equip, and pay the militiamen he intended to send into the Creek counties. He finally secured this authorization through Maj. Gen. Winfield Scott, the officer in charge of the Seminole War effort. Scott had assembled a substantial army of federal and state troops to fight the Natives in Florida, but he was concerned that the Creeks would turn hostile and join forces with the Seminoles, making his task much more difficult. Therefore, he gave Clay permission to raise a regiment of troops both to prevent a linkup of Creek and Seminole warriors and "to restrain the Creeks from hostilities against the white settlers" in New Alabama. The governor then called up this regiment from the state's Seventh Militia Division, made up of several north Alabama counties, and ordered the men to rendezvous at the federal arsenal at Mount Vernon, Alabama, by March 10. Finally, Clay sent word to the arsenal's commanding officer, Capt. E. Harding, that he should muster the thousand-man force into the federal service and equip the soldiers before they marched east into New Alabama.[29]

Clay's regiment might have prevented the outbreak of the Second Creek War, but the troops never reached the Creek country. When Clay's force arrived at Mount Vernon, Captain Harding was not there to receive them into the service and provide them with arms. Mystified, the troops waited around the arsenal for a few days and then went home. Then, before Clay could organize another regiment, he received word from the secretary of war that President Jackson was withdrawing Scott's authorization for a militia force, and if Clay already had such a force in the field, he should disband it. In Jackson's view, actual hostilities had not broken out in Alabama, nor did they seem imminent. Therefore, the president claimed he lacked the necessary constitutional grounds for calling up militia troops. In explaining this position to Clay, Secretary Cass stated that he would like to send federal troops to Alabama, which he had authority to do, but no soldiers were available for that purpose. They had all been assigned to Florida, the western frontier, or other important posts. Thus, at that crucial point in the late winter and early spring of 1836, the federal government failed once again to take the necessary steps to establish order in New Alabama.[30]

The only other means of preventing war would have been a removal of the Lower Creeks during this period, but even here European Americans worked at cross-purposes and stymied the process. As early as February, Governor Clay asked the War Department to remove the Creeks from Alabama forcibly in the spring if the Natives would not emigrate on their own. But Cass denied the request, stating that the Cusseta Treaty gave the Creeks the right "to go or stay as they please," and the government could not make them leave Alabama before their land questions were settled. But no one was settling these questions because the removal contractors, and the speculators associated with them, were purposefully interfering with Colonel Hogan's land-fraud investigation and delaying Creek emigration in the process. In fact, Hogan discovered that Major General McDougald, Luther Blake, Dr. Columbus Mills, Capt. William Walker and other land speculators had called a secret council with Neah Micco, Efau Emathla, Tuskenea, and other antiremoval chiefs at Watoolahawka (Neah Micco's town) in early March to put in place a scheme that would satisfy all present. Working through their interpreter and agent provocateur, Paddy Carr, the speculators warned the chiefs to keep away from Hogan and his investigation. They claimed he was a government removal agent sent to fool the Indians. He was only pretending to take down their complaints about land frauds so he could get their names on an emigration list. That done, he would force them off to the Western Territory. Then the speculators delivered the coup de grâce. They informed the chiefs that General McDougald owned ten sections of land in the Lower Creek country, and if the chiefs promised to keep their people away from Hogan and his investigation, they could stay in Alabama and live on those ten sections as long as they pleased. This deal, sweetened with liberal bribes to the individual chiefs, turned the trick. When Hogan appeared at Watoolahawka, the Creek headmen said that they and their people had sold their land legitimately and had no complaints. Consequently, the speculators were able to prevent Hogan from both retrieving Creek lands and removing the Indians to the West. But this does not mean they fooled the chiefs. By that point in time, the Creek headmen certainly distrusted both Hogan and the speculators and took McDougald's deal only because it looked like the best way to delay the threatened forced removal from New Alabama.[31]

McDougald and his cohorts knew, of course, that any delay in Creek removal would be very unpopular among the white citizenry, so these speculators, and the Columbus crowd in general, had to cover over their culpability in causing that delay. Aided by the various presses owned by the states' rights party in Alabama and Georgia, the speculators simply blamed Colonel Hogan and President Jackson for the whole problem. They claimed that the government's land-fraud investigation held out a false promise to the Indians, leading them to believe that they could get their reserves back and live in Alabama as long as they wished. This false promise caused the Natives to stay where they were and make trouble for all the respectable settlers around them. The speculators and states' rights editors called on the government to end its overly long and useless investigation and just remove the Creek intruders from the land they no longer owned. Of course the government's critics never mentioned the fact that the activities of the speculators made Hogan's investigation necessary in the first place. In fact, the standard line of the states' rights presses and many Georgians like McDougald was that no frauds had occurred in the Lower Creek country, and that Hogan, as a tool of rival Alabama speculators, was simply inducing the Indians to make false claims and stay in Alabama, where they would continue to transgress against their white neighbors until such time as Hogan and his associates could get their land.[32]

The speculators were wrong in accusing Hogan of having designs on the Creek reserves, but given the highly competitive economic environment in which these people lived, they may have actually believed their accusations. Certainly it would have been difficult for them to believe that any person was not looking for profit somewhere along the line. In fact, some of the speculators, in their more reflective moments, claimed that they stole Creek land only because others were doing it and they could not afford to let those people have all the economic advantage. These speculators even claimed they would give up their questionable acquisitions if their competitors would do the same. But no one was willing to be the first to do the right thing. Nevertheless, the speculators were correct on one point. There was some truth to the notion that Hogan's investigation held out false hope to the Creeks and delayed removal. The fraud had gone on too long and was too extensive for the government ever to rectify it. By the spring of 1836, Opothle Yahola realized this and began to make other arrangements for paying his peoples' debts and getting them out of Alabama. With Hogan's help, along with that of subagent Leonard Tarrant, he and the other council chiefs sold the twenty sections of land set aside for Creek orphans by the Cusseta Treaty. Opothle Yahola and the three other leading headmen of Tuckabatchee—Little Doctor, Mad Blue, and Tuckabatchee Micco—had already sold their personal land reserves for a total of thirty-nine thousand dollars. The Lower Creeks, however, lacked such enlightened leadership, and numbers of these people were already planning to take back their land through force. Hogan failed to see this, largely because he allowed his personal conflicts with the speculators and removal contractors to cloud his judgment. He tended to discount the growing hostility of the Creeks and not only blamed their misdeeds on his own enemies but contended that all talk of an Indian uprising was merely another part of the speculators' plot to stop the land-fraud investigation. Thus, Hogan, the government's chief adviser in the Creek country, failed to give the Creeks credit for independent thinking and planning. Like many other whites, he infantilized the Natives and claimed speculators controlled them and guided their actions. Consequently, he did not see until it was too late that some of the Creeks meant to wage war.[33]

Certainly there were plenty of signs that war was possible, and indeed the Loachapoka Council meeting in late March probably provided the final spark that touched off the blaze. This council was bound to be a contentious one because the War Department made it clear that it would be the last such meeting of the Creek Nation in Alabama. At that point, only those Indians who still owned land and were willing to detach themselves from the Creek Nation and swear allegiance to the state of Alabama would be allowed to stay in the state; all others must leave. Then the government's agents added to all the tension and suspicion surrounding the council by meeting with the Upper and Lower chiefs in separate forums, as opposed to meeting altogether in the customary fashion. The agents did this because they believed that the Upper Creek leaders, with the exception of Tuskenea, would be amenable to their removal plans, while numbers of the Lower chiefs would not. Consequently, the agents did not want to address both groups of chiefs in a body, thus opening the door for unnecessary discord and needless debate that would only delay the proceedings. The Lower chiefs could not have been happy with this arrangement, but the government men carried on anyway. First, they distributed $43,740 to the Creek leaders, half to the Upper towns and half to the Lower ones. This money came from the sale of twenty-three half sections of land that were part of the twenty-nine sections allotted to the Creek people as a whole by the Cusseta Treaty. The agents then directed the chiefs to use this money to settle all their outstanding debts in preparation for their forthcoming removal to the West. The agents also told the Creek headmen that they would have to move their people into emigration camps scheduled to open in April. There would be five of these camps, they claimed, one each for the counties of Talladega, Coosa, Tallapoosa, Macon, and Russell.[34]

At that juncture, the agents saw their plans fall apart. The Upper Creek chiefs took their half of the money but found it sufficient to pay only three-fourths of the claims against them. The failed Texas land deal had placed them in arrears. Consequently, the Upper Creek headmen announced that they would have to await payment of their annuity before settling the debts completely and leaving the state. But the War Department had not intended to pay the annuity in Alabama and had not made the necessary arrangements to get the money. To do so would continue to delay removal. Then the agents heard even worse news from the Lower Creek chiefs. These leaders received their share of the land money and claimed to have paid their debts in full with funds left over, but Neah Micco and Efau Emathla declared flatly that they would not emigrate. At that point, Captain Page, Colonel Hogan, the removal contractors, and all other government operatives in attendance at Loachapoka began to exert pressure on the antiremoval chiefs. Page reminded them that 1836 was the last year they and their people could emigrate at government expense, and if they did not go, the whites who had bought almost all their land would certainly push them off. Then Page, at Hogan's insistence, demanded that the Lower chiefs reach a consensus on the removal question and deliver their answer to him at Fort Mitchell. According to Hogan, this demand "was like an electric shock to them; it changed the whole scene." And indeed it did. It is not hard to imagine that Neah Micco and the other antiremoval chiefs came away from the Loachapoka Council meeting fearing that the whites would use force against them if they continued to oppose removal. And this conclusion surely led some Creeks to believe that they should make a preemptive strike at their enemies. Furthermore, Loachapoka town, occupied as it was by Tallassee Creeks with a history of violent opposition to the settlers, was a poor site for this all-important council meeting. The atmosphere must have been volatile, and we should not be surprised that warriors living in this town went on to commit some of the first atrocities of the Second Creek War.[35]

More immediately, the Lower Creeks showed that they were not kidding about not leaving New Alabama. As Colonel Hogan toured their towns in the days following the council, he saw Indians building new homes. They were not going anywhere. Furthermore, the chief of the Ositchee Creeks went so far as to purchase a tract of land for his people to live on, and the Eufaulas demanded that the settlers in and around Irwinton give them some land to plant. When queried, most Lower Creeks informed Hogan that they would not go west until Neah Micco gave the word. However, other Indians to whom he spoke had become demoralized in the face of all the exploitation and faced the emigration deadline with a sort of fatalistic intransigence. Referring to the fact that a phrenologist had recently dug up a number of Creek skulls and carried them away for study, one elderly chief, possibly Neah Micco's brother, Efau Emathla, told Hogan that he would never leave Alabama. In fact, "He would stay and die here, and then the whites might have his skull for a water cup; they wanted everything, and when he was dead they might have his skull too." But the Creeks did not intend to die passively, nor did they mean to tolerate the obnoxious removal contractors any longer. In fact, the Hitchitees, Chehaws, and especially the Euchees, intimidated the agents of the Alabama Emigrating Company, a reorganized version of the Sanford Company, so much that these men would barely venture into those towns affiliated with the Seminole party. But still Hogan refused to see the signs of impending doom. He believed that once the Upper towns left the country, the Lower towns would soon follow, and he could get all the Indians out of Alabama by the fall of 1836. He seemed to think that the speculators and removal contractors were the only real obstacles he faced, but even so he could overcome their opposition, rectify the land frauds, and remove the Indians all in one summer.[36]

The settlers living around the Lower Creek towns knew better. They had observed their Indian neighbors for some time and had seen profound changes in their behavior as they reacted to colonization and economic exploitation. First, the Creeks wandered about in a state of shock. Then they entered a period of self-destruction marked by alcohol abuse, murders, and suicides. Next, they turned on the whites and engaged in acts of covert resistance such as thefts, destruction of property, and the occasional secretive murder. But in March and April 1836, the settlers saw another, even more disturbing, change in the mood and behavior of the Indians. Now the Creeks entered a state of heightened emotionalism and open, aggressive hostility to the settlers, who understood, intuitively, that this condition could only presage and culminate in some sort of violent outburst or catharsis. The settlers were correct, but what they did not know was that this Creek behavior was not unique. Oppressed Natives in other parts of the world responded to colonialism, driven by the spread of the world economic system, in much the same way as the Lower Creeks did. Those people also went through those same stages of shock, self-destruction, covert resistance, and heightened emotionalism. And then, they did something the Creeks were also about to do. They used the emotionalism to fuel an almost immediate armed revolt against their oppressors.[37]

The frightened settlers made their observations known to Governor Clay. They reported that their Creek neighbors had launched a concerted effort to intimidate them and to drive them out of the country. Whereas before the Indians had plundered only occasionally, secretly, and at night, the settlers now complained that Creeks appeared almost daily in armed parties, operating openly in broad daylight, breaking into houses and corncribs, collecting slaves, and driving off cattle "before the faces of their owners." The Indians also waged a campaign of wanton destruction, obliterating everything they could not carry away. They burned homes, tore down fences, and according to the settlers, shot even more cattle, hogs, mules, and dogs just for spite. Furthermore, the Indians confronted whites and threatened them with death if they did not leave the country. But worst of all, the behavior of some Natives grew more frenzied and erratic. They engaged in an increasing number of dances and stickball matches, and affected military displays. They assembled in the swamps in large numbers, painted themselves, fired off their guns to scare the settlers, and marched and countermarched over the country as if practicing for war. Seeing all this, some settlers did abandon the country and return to Georgia. Governor Clay responded to this news by again asking Secretary Cass to allow him to send "a body of well armed and equipped mounted men" to range through the Creek and Cherokee counties of Alabama.[38]

Certainly Creek resistors tried to scare settlers off the land, but their actions may have had a larger cultural significance that the whites did not understand or appreciate. In fact, their activities harkened back to the Red Stick revolt of 1813. That revolt took place, in part, because the recently opened Federal Road brought numerous travelers and their negative influences into the very heart of the Creek Nation. Viewing with alarm the actions of their accommodationist chiefs, their peoples' abject dependence on U.S. trade goods, and the rise in thievery and alcoholism among the young, the nativist Red Sticks attempted to stop the process of cultural disintegration by rehabilitating their social equilibrium and hardening the ethnic boundary between themselves and the whites, particularly the hated Georgians. They sought to do this first through religious revivalism, and then through armed conflict with the settlers and their traitorous allies within Creek society. In the process of purging themselves and seeking the spiritual power necessary to reconstitute their society, the Red Sticks shunned the accoutrements of white culture. They poured out whiskey, threw away their metal plows, and even killed off cattle herds, not for spite, but because livestock represented the Creeks' attachment to the market and all its negative consequences for their traditional way of life. The nativists also abandoned their log cabins and retreated to the woods and swamps to set up primitive camps in sacred places, such as at the forks of converging streams, places where the forces of the cosmos, the Upper and Under Worlds, convened and where sacred power ran especially strong. There their prophets exhorted, worked miracles, raised emotions to a fever pitch, and conducted rituals and ceremonies such as the Dance of the Lakes, which some Red Sticks believed would make them invincible against their enemies. Tecumseh and his entourage of Shawnee preachers and warriors had introduced this dance to the Creeks in 1811 as part of an effort to unite all the Native tribes and nations, north and south, in a religious and military movement aimed at restoring Indian moral strength and courage and pushing the whites out of the U.S. heartland.[39]

Tecumseh had warned the Creeks, indeed all the southern Natives, that the whites meant to enslave them in time just as they had done to the Africans. In the spring of 1836, it must have appeared to many

Creeks that the Shawnee's prediction was coming true. The cultural boundary the Red Sticks had fought to protect in 1813 and 1814 had completely crumbled with the establishment of New Alabama and the influx of settlers. Now Indians and whites lived virtually side by side, and many settlers believed that the Natives had no rights. Thus, they treated the Creeks cruelly, even to the point of whipping them as they did their black slaves. Some Indians could stand no more. The evidence suggests that once again Creeks were following their old trails to sacred places in the forests and meeting in large numbers to engage in religious revivals. Once again, they were questing for the power necessary to reestablish the space between themselves and the whites by driving the settlers and speculators out of New Alabama. But unlike the old-time Red Sticks, the Creek rebels of 1836 did not broadcast their intentions beforehand. The angrier Creeks did intimidate whites, but when worried settlers, land dealers, or government officials appeared at the increasing number of Indian councils to ascertain the Natives' intentions, they always encountered Creeks able to calm their fears. They returned to their fellows with the word that all was well. They saw only friendly, smiling Creeks. They saw no dancing Red Stick prophets, painted completely red, promising the destruction of the whites. Nor did they see or hear of any firebrands like Tecumseh, who never shied from proclaiming openly to all that Indians should fight for their land. Moreover, not all day-to-day encounters between settlers and Creeks seemed at all hostile. Indeed, during that planting season of 1836, some Indians showed more willingness than ever before to work in the settlers' cornfields, and they seemed not to care much about wages. But this was part of the subterfuge. Those Creeks capable of controlling their emotions meant to put the whites at ease, or at the very least keep them guessing, so they would lower their guards. At that point, these Creeks, along with their more hot-headed tribespeople, meant to rise up, drive settlers from the country, and, of course, appropriate their fine fields of corn.[40]

There are essentially two reasons why most whites failed to grasp the true cultural significance of the increased Creek ceremonialism they saw going on around them in the early months of 1836. First, these settlers were too concerned with their own economic advancement and too convinced of the superiority of their own culture. When, for example, John Howard Payne pressed frontier inhabitants for their interpretations of Indian customs, he discovered that "they really consider all study concerning them [the Creeks] as egregious folly, save only that of finding how much cotton their grounds yield, and in what way the greatest speculation can be accomplished with the smallest capital." However, the second, and perhaps most important, reason for the inability of even interested whites to comprehend the Indians involved Native deceptions. In fact, as with most colonized peoples living in close proximity to their oppressors, the Creeks became adept in the "arts of resistance," including subterfuge, dissimulation, and, of course, sabotage. They told the whites what they wanted to hear, then did as they pleased. Thus, both Colonel Hogan and the land speculators thought they had won the favor of the Creeks and could control and bend them to their wills. This was not the case. Moreover, when the Creeks conspired against the whites, they often did so in secret, meeting in the woods. But because few whites understood Native tongues, they could even lay plans right before the eyes of their enemies. And even the interpreters conversant in English and Muscogee found it difficult to fully understand Creek communications carried on in signs and symbolic language. The linksters admitted, for example, that the ceremonial language of the Creeks went well beyond their level of learning. As Payne explained of that linguistic variant, "It is a poetical, mystical idiom, varying essentially from that of trading and of friendly intercommunication, and utterly incomprehensible to the literal minds of mere trafficking explainers." Thus, the Creek resistors were able to create in various ways their own "hidden transcript" of life in New Alabama, a history far different in content and meaning than the "master transcript" passed down to us by the self-interested colonizers of New Alabama.[41]

But one does not have to understand another culture to sense real danger and take steps to avoid it, and such was the case with the Georgians. As part of the effort to guard the crossing points on the Chattahoochee to prevent Creeks from entering Georgia, Governor Schley sent Maj.

John H. Howard of the Georgia militia, along with 180 troops, to erect a state military post at Bryant's Ferry, the site of the battle the previous January. The Georgians called this post Fort Twiggs, but Howard had no sooner settled in when he saw that the Creek resistors had turned their attention to their white neighbors in Alabama. He then wrote to Governor Clay asking him to station two or three companies of mounted Alabama militiamen in the neighborhood of the Euchees, Hitchitees, and Chehaws in the northern part of Barbour and the southern part of Russell counties. Howard contended that these tribes were the most restless and opposed to emigration, but he and his troops, working in concert with a similar force of Alabamians, could hold them in check. However, a committee of citizens from Barbour and Russell demanded even more help. These people claimed that three notorious Creek troublemakers, who recently returned from Florida, were responsible for much of the restlessness among the Lower Creeks. These men—Jerry, Jim Henry, and Boson—were supposedly inciting their fellows to emulate the Seminoles in attacking their white neighbors. Consequently, the committee members requested that Clay send at least two thousand troops to overawe the Natives and remove them from the state. If only a small number of troops appeared, the citizens contended, the Indians would defeat them easily and then massacre all the settlers. The petitioners then reminded the governor that this was exactly the mistake the government had made in Florida in December when the Seminoles started to make trouble. They concluded that Clay should see to it that the resulting bloody scenes of the Seminole War did not repeat themselves in Alabama.[42]

Once again Clay asked the War Department for authority to raise troops, claiming that if "actual hostilities" did not exist, there was "evidently impending danger of them." He sent his correspondence from Creek country settlers along with his request. Federal army officers in New Alabama also bolstered his plea, forwarding their own descriptions of Indian depredations to Washington. One of these officers was Capt. John Page, who had, owing to Hogan's unpopularity with removal contractors and Georgia politicians, replaced that man as superintendent of Creek emigration. Given his new responsibility,

Page, who apparently spoke the Muscogee tongue, rode all over the Lower Creek country and reported to the War Department that the situation there was entirely out of hand. The state of Alabama, he declared, had never subjected the Natives to its laws, and, in fact, the settlers were afraid to punish the Indians. Furthermore, the Creeks would not emigrate on their own and must be removed by force. Otherwise, the settlers would have problems with them for years to come. Lieutenant McCrabb at Fort Mitchell concurred with Page and added that the Indians were determined to "engage in a desperate struggle to regain their land before they give up everything and move west." McCrabb declared that a military force must march to the scene of depredations to punish Indian leaders and to prevent more mischief by the Native resistors.[43]

But once again the secretary of war denied Clay's request. Astonishingly, he informed Clay that the president saw no "design to disturb the public tranquility, on the part of the Creeks, as to require the immediate organization of a force to keep them in subjection." In fact, it appears that Cass had by this point become somewhat leery about southern requests for military aid. He also refused a request by Gen. Edmund P. Gaines, commanding U.S. forces on the Texas-Louisiana border, for additional troops to resist a supposed Mexican-inspired invasion of Texas Indians. Cass believed that no such invasion would occur and that Texas land speculators had engineered the alarm to get the United States to aid them in their independence move from Mexico. This independence, in turn, would legalize their land claims in Texas. It is also likely that Cass refused Governor Clay's request in part because he believed Hogan's contention that land speculators were also creating alarm in Alabama to get a military force to push the Creeks off the land they coveted. However, Cass did send one company of federal troops from the arsenal at Augusta, Georgia, to Fort Mitchell. He also alerted troops stationed at Fort Monroe in Virginia to be ready to move south on short notice should the Creeks rise up in revolt. Finally, the secretary sent a message to Captain Page to circulate among the Lower Creek chiefs. The message warned them of the dire consequences they faced if they chose to resist removal and take up arms against the settlers.[44]

When Page went to deliver Cass's message, he found the chiefs assembled once again at Neah Micco's town. He sought the leaders out individually and gave them the warning in the harshest of terms, even telling them that the whites would exterminate their people if they did not leave Alabama. But the message came much too late. A number of the chiefs were beyond caring what the whites would do. They only knew what they meant to do. As Page would later claim, they had come together at Watoolahawka in late April to plan their war. They meant to rise up and drive all the settlers from their midst, as well as launch simultaneous attacks on the towns of Tallassee, a settler community named for the older Creek one, and, of course, the hated source of so much Indian misery, Columbus, Georgia. While most sources have accused Neah Micco, Efau Emathla, Neah Emathla, and other Lower Creek headmen as the prime movers in the plot, Hogan and Opothle Yahola also pointed the finger of blame at the fiery Tuskenea, Opothle Yahola's rival. However, a careful analysis of the historical evidence suggests that these prominent chiefs played ambivalent roles in the war. Certainly they wanted to resist removal and had encouraged their followers to do so in the past. They also knew that a plan was afoot to rise up in armed rebellion against the whites. They may have even helped formulate the plan. However, their subsequent actions raise doubts that they ever really meant to carry out it out. Rather these men appear to have been carried along by the tide of events, finally giving in to their angry, destitute followers, particularly those warriors of what the newspapers called New Alabama's "Seminole towns," the Hitchitee and Euchee speakers who wanted to emulate their relatives in Florida by going to war.[45]

Governor Clay knew nothing of the full extent of the rebel plan, but he believed the Creeks intended some sort of armed conflict. He did all he could to prepare for it. Knowing that Maj. Gen. Gilbert Shearer of Selma, the commander of Alabama's Sixth Militia Division, had recently raised a battalion of volunteers for the Seminole War, Clay notified the general to hold all other volunteer companies in his division in readiness to march into New Alabama. Should the Creeks start a war, the governor intended for Shearer's volunteers, drawn from counties just west of the Creek country, to hurry in and check the hostile advance. Then Clay would raise an overwhelming force of militia and personally lead them to a crushing victory over the hostile Natives. The governor also ordered Maj. Gen. William Irwin of the Fifth Division to raise a battalion of troops to hold in readiness on the southern border of New Alabama. Finally, Clay requisitioned two thousand muskets and accoutrements from the federal arsenal at Mount Vernon and had them brought up the Alabama River to Montgomery for distribution to his troops.[46]

Unfortunately, the governor encountered more resistance from the citizens of Old Alabama. In fact, even his friends and fellow Union Democrats doubted the need for troops in New Alabama. General Shearer informed Clay that he stood ready to obey his orders, but he believed that there was really nothing to fear from the Creeks "unless daily intrusion committed on them by whites should drive them to desperation." Similarly, Colonel Hogan, like Clay a strong Jackson supporter, contended that the large majority of Creeks had "no more disposition for hostilities than there is among the citizens of Washington." Hogan believed that such problems as existed were confined to the vicinity of Fort Mitchell, and even there the whole alarm was just another trick of the speculators, the same men who kicked up the fuss that resulted in the Bryant's Ferry fight in January. Hogan went on to claim that these men were using Jim Henry to instigate trouble among the Creeks, and as a result many New Alabama settlers had retreated back to Georgia. But in reality, Hogan claimed, the settlers faced no more danger than before. He admitted that the Indians were stealing some corn, and killing a beef or two, but he noted that they had been doing that for three years and still the settlers stayed in place. But now, Hogan concluded, a set of "designing white men" had imposed on and unduly frightened both the governor and the New Alabama settlers. Furthermore, the villains had done this simply because they wanted to stop the land-fraud investigation and induce the government to sweep the Creeks out of Alabama by force, leaving themselves in charge of the Creek domain.[47]

The most widespread critique of the war scare, however, came from

James Belser, another Jackson supporter and the editor of the *Montgomery Advertiser*. Belser always showed sympathy for the Creeks and, like Hogan, he tended to see land speculators and Jackson's political opponents, the states' rights nullifiers, as the real problem. In late April he published an editorial, reprinted in many southern newspapers, that declared, "The war with the Creeks is all a humbug. It is a base and diabolical scheme, devised by interested men, to keep an ignorant race of people from maintaining their just rights, and to deprive them of the small remaining pittance placed under their control, through the munificence of the government. We do trust, for the credit of those concerned, that these blood suckers may be ferreted out, and their shameful misrepresentations exposed."[48]

Such statements shocked the New Alabama settlers and made them cry out more loudly for help. In early May Dr. E. E. Park of Russell County appealed to General Shearer for military assistance and lamented that most people living in Old Alabama thought ill of New Alabamians and did not want to defend them against the Indians. Park complained of "slanderous publications" in Alabama newspapers and stated that it was "general opinion in the old part of the State, that the settlers are the individuals who are said to have swindled the Indians out of their lands." However, Park believed the settlers were innocent victims. They had given the speculators extravagant prices for their land, and now they were being abused by the Creeks and their fellow Alabama citizens. Furthermore, they would be the ones to die if the Creeks went to war, which, Park claimed, they would surely do. Park closed his communiqué to Shearer by telling the general that the friendly Indians had informed the settlers that the hostile party meant to wage a general war in the very near future. Word had gone out from High Log town, the Hitchitee and Euchee bastion on Hatchechubbee Creek, that all whites must leave the country in ten days or be shot.[49]

Both Governor Clay and the officers at Fort Mitchell believed what Park said. Maj. James S. McIntosh, the fort's new commander, promptly strengthened his post with a sturdy blockhouse and a strong stockade. Clay, however, could do nothing. Having applied a third and a fourth time to the War Department for permission to march troops into New

Alabama, he received yet another disappointing reply. On May 5 Lewis Cass told Clay he could not mobilize his forces because "recent information from Colonel Hogan leads to the belief that these Indians do not meditate hostilities." Nothing could have been further from the truth. Only two days after Cass penned these words, the Second Creek War erupted.[50]

Thus it was that the whites, socially, economically, and politically divided among themselves, failed to prevent the outbreak of war. Viewing the scene from Fort Twiggs, Maj. John Howard, the Georgia militia commander, summed up the situation well when he said, "I am persuaded that the various and diversified interests of the white population have produced representations which may induce the department [of war] to underrate the dangers reasonably to be apprehended." Howard might have added that it was those same various and diversified interests of the whites that created the conditions leading to war. In their competitive quest for land, wealth, and status, the European Americans had objectified, commodified, and depersonalized the Creeks, treating them and their possessions as "natural resources" to be exploited to the fullest. In the process, the whites unleashed an economic system in New Alabama that quickly cracked and splintered an already weakened society, as it sought to make Indians into individualistic, competitive economic creatures like the whites. Worse, the system reduced many Natives to abject poverty. It was predictable, then, that some members of Creek society would go to war, especially given the example of the Seminoles. And yet the whites were so competitive among themselves and had so infantilized the Creeks that they blamed even Indian misbehavior on one another and could not act in concert when the time came. They could produce only the various "representations" that misled President Jackson and Secretary Cass into underrating the danger of war in New Alabama.[51]

But that war occurred. While the whites argued among themselves, the antiremoval chiefs plotted, playing their enemies off against one another until they were ready to act. They made Hogan believe they were peaceful and might be induced to go west if he rectified the land frauds. But at the same time the chiefs had no confidence in the government or its investigation. They resolved among themselves not to leave Alabama and allowed their starving tribespeople to commit depredations on their white neighbors. The chiefs also accepted bribes and favors from the speculators and thwarted Hogan's investigation, yet at the same time they talked of killing the speculators and planters and destroying Columbus. Throughout the winter and spring of 1836 they conspired under the noses of the settlers, and by the second week in May their rebellion took on a life of its own. Their followers were ready to rise up and throw off the yoke of New Alabama's grinding economic system; they were ready to stop the removal process in its tracks and reclaim their lands and freedom from the whites. They were ready as well to teach the hated Georgians a lesson or two and perhaps use the war as a means of bringing unity and order to their fractured and fragmented society. Beyond that, the Creek resistors may have hoped to inspire a larger and more widespread conflagration, one in which the Lower Creeks would unite with Upper Creeks, Cherokees, and Seminoles in holding on to their homelands and stopping the settlers from achieving their main goal: making the Old Southwest the leading cotton producing region in the world.

5. Rebellion

The Creek rebels had a major advantage: the fragmented and disorganized enemy they faced. The Creek rebels also had a major disadvantage: the fragmented and disorganized nature of the Creeks. Indeed, both rebels and settlers sprang from the same pluralistic atmosphere where corruption, violence, and economic exploitation kept both Native and white communities unstable and created interethnic conflict and collusion as people looked for the best way to make do. Ironically, such an environment provided just the right conditions for producing a Native rebellion, but because the Creeks were not united and because so many had ties of one sort or another to the white community, it would be very difficult for a rebellion to succeed. The rebels would learn this in time, but not before they felt success within their grasp.

What little we know of the plot that led to war comes from Col. John Hogan and Opothle Yahola, and if their accounts are correct, the rebels' inability to act in concert became apparent from the outset. Hogan contended that Neah Micco, Neah Emathla, Tuskenea, and Octruchee Emathla, the Ositchee chief, planned to open the war with attacks on Fort Mitchell and Columbus. In anticipation, a large body of warriors congregated near the Russell-Barbour county line, about twenty-five miles south of Columbus. Then Neah Micco sent the "broken sticks" to Tuskenea designating the number of days before the attack was to begin. He also sent a message: "We are ready." But the Upper

Creek chief drew back. He sent word to Neah Micco that they should hold off "till roasting ear time" in the late summer. This reply may have meant that he wanted to delay the conflict until New Alabama's fields were full of corn to feed the rebel warriors and their families. He might also have had a religious motive in mind. The Creeks held their annual Busk ceremonies at the time of the new corn. It was a time of thanksgiving, cleansing, and renewal of the people's spiritual power. Tuskenea may have believed that the warriors would have their greatest physical and moral strength at the end of the Busk. Or, Tuskenea could have simply lost his stomach for war. Indeed, in the end his reasons are mysterious and may have been composed of a contradictory mix of traditional beliefs and more modern economic concerns. In this regard, he and other Creeks might not have been that different from their white neighbors. Surely settlers, and even speculators, professed a strong belief in Christianity, yet succumbed inevitably to the material demands of the growing market system. But no matter what Tuskenea thought, his hesitation hurt the rebel cause and helped the whites by saving both Columbus and Fort Mitchell from rebel sieges. Without the assistance of Tuskenea, the rebel Lower Creek chiefs were unwilling to attempt the assault. Moreover, Tuskenea never returned openly to the rebel party, and, in fact, he may not have intended to go to war in the first place. It is possible he pretended to go along with the idea only to appease all the impoverished Creeks he depended on for political support.[1]

It also appears Neah Micco found himself in the same situation. Probably he did not really want war but found himself unable to control all the angry, starving people in the Lower towns. And even if he did intend to take up the war club, Tuskenea's departure from the cause may have led him to lose his nerve and throw it down. Furthermore, Neah Micco had close ties to John Crowell, the former Creek agent, as well as other members of the white community. The elderly chief was a man accustomed to playing both ends against the middle, telling his people what they wanted to hear while at the same time doing business with the merchants and land speculators who so abused the Lower Creeks. Neah Micco had divided loyalties and ended up betraying the rebel cause. When he saw his people were determined to fight, he advised Crowell to leave his house and take up residence at Fort Mitchell or flee the Creek country altogether. He also told Crowell to "inform the citizens of Columbus that they could expect attack." On May 8 Crowell passed this word along to his neighbors in the Euchee Creek neighborhood of Russell County, and these people, obviously terrified, made one last appeal for help, but not to the state of Alabama. Instead, they beseeched General McDougald of the Georgia militia, one of the very speculators who caused the Indian problem. "We were many of us once Georgians," they cried, and "Our Governor [Clay] had done and will do nothing." Then they promised McDougald that if he came to them, "we shall hail you as our deliverers and our Women and children will rise and call you Blessed." But the Euchee Creek settlers did not sit on their hands while they waited for their deliverance. They collected at the home of Nimrod Long and worked day and night to construct a fort of split logs, which the local Indians derisively called the "wild cow pen." But the stockade protected them long enough. Neah Micco had saved their lives and placed the rebel warriors he promised to lead at a serious disadvantage.[2]

Nevertheless, many young Creek men wanted to wage war. Penned up and beaten down in New Alabama, they undoubtedly longed to assume their traditional roles as warriors, to win back their identities and self-respect. Moreover, the young men wanted to preserve their homeland and avoid the imminent removal to the West that Captain Page threatened. The military successes of their Seminole cousins in Florida encouraged them in this regard. But again, traditional cultural motives coalesced with raw economic necessity, for as one rebel leader later stated, he and his men fought primarily because their people were starving. In other words, these warriors felt they could survive only by rising up and taking back the country from the settlers. In this respect, the war marked the culmination of years of resource competition between Creeks and colonizers in New Alabama. During that time, endemic protests grew into an epidemic of outright rebellion, as it became clear that "the bonds of kinship or tribal solidarity" were "no longer a man's primary defense against the vagaries of his social environment." Only an armed uprising would do, and Creeks fought to keep from being totally absorbed into New Alabama society as an underclass of paupers, possibly even slaves. In sum, the Creek rebels saw war as the only alternative to two unacceptable paths: leaving their homeland to face a tenuous existence in the West or staying in New Alabama and treated as less than human. This microscopic view, although only a partial explanation for the war, is important in terms of understanding what made the Second Creek War distinctive in the whole panorama of Native revolts worldwide. Seen in macrocosm, the rebellion is exactly the same as many other Native rebellions in that it was the ultimate act of resistance against economic subordination and dependency within the larger world system.[3]

But how did the war actually begin? Hogan blamed a group of young warriors from Loachapoka for the first attacks. He claimed that these men had been visiting Neah Micco's village when the elderly chief sent the sticks to Tuskenea. They left the village with the understanding that the war would begin in two days. Consequently, on the second day, before reaching home, "they began to murder indiscriminately," not knowing that Tuskenea had caused a delay in the start of general hostilities. But Hogan was only partially correct. In truth, Tallassee warriors from the villages of Loachapoka and Sougahatchee began to kill people north of New Road on or about May 11. They struck both in eastern Macon County and in southern Chambers County, and two of the attacks were particularly shocking. In the vicinity of Black's store, ten miles south of LaFayette, the county seat of Chambers, the warriors killed a settler named Davis, his wife, and their seven children. Then they cut the heads off the youths and threw one child out into the cabin's dooryard, where "the hogs eat it nearly up." In the other attack, the rebels slaughtered the Jones family and hung their corpses in the trees around their home. In the wake of these atrocities by the Tallassee Creeks, the Chambers County settlers fled en masse to LaFayette and set up barricades for mutual protection.[4]

However, Colonel Hogan, perhaps because of his antipathy for Tuskenea, was wrong in blaming the Tallassees for beginning the Second Creek War. In reality, Lower Creek warriors had commenced the fray days earlier in Russell County, south of New Road. When their planned attack on Fort Mitchell failed to materialize, Hitchitees, Euchees, Ositchees, Chehaws, Sawoklis, and a number of Cussetas and Eufaulas moved out on their own to kill settlers, plunder houses, destroy livestock, collect slaves, and burn plantations. Naturally, the first deaths occurred in the vicinity of the Russell-Barbour county line, near where the warriors had been congregating. On the morning of Tuesday, May 5, one of the Glenns of the Glennville community fell victim. Subsequently, the rebels opened fire on the whole settlement. Later in the day, Maj. William "Billy" Flournoy, a former resident of Putnam County, Georgia, saddled his horse and set out for Columbus to spread the alarm. Seven miles north of his plantation, and seven miles south of Fort Mitchell, he passed through the Euchee town. Long known as the most hostile of the Lower Creeks, the Euchees may have learned the purpose of Flournoy's journey from a Creek boy who lived in the man's household. Consequently, they waited in ambush. But the Euchees may have had another reason to waylay the major. Earlier in the year, he and John Watson—the man who precipitated the Bryant's Ferry battle in January—visited Maj. Gen. Winfield Scott, commander of the army fighting the Seminoles, and talked him into receiving a contingent of five hundred Creek warriors to serve in Florida. Flournoy and Watson intended to command this force. But the Creek chiefs refused to help the two men recruit warriors, so the scheme fell through. Nevertheless, Flournoy's effort may have outraged Seminole partisans in the Lower Creek towns and earned him their enmity. In any event, the Euchees shot him and his horse dead, took his scalp, and stole his gold pocket watch. That same afternoon, Daniel Tarrant, one of Flournoy's neighbors, passed through the same Euchee settlement on his way home from Columbus. He simply disappeared. Two days later, on the night of May 7, a war party stole up to a log house where Mr. Watts, a white overseer, and a guest lay sleeping. They stuck their gun barrels into the spaces between the logs and fired. Watts died. His guest, unnoticed by the Indians, pulled up some floor boards and dropped to the ground below. Shivering and shaking, he hid beneath the house as the Creeks broke the door bolt and entered it. They dragged all of Watts's trunks outside, tore them open, and stole the contents. The guest waited until the Indians marched off, then he fled into the woods and remained there the rest of the night. He did not enjoy a peaceful repose, however. He heard gunfire in the direction of the two nearest plantations to Watts's house. On the morning of the eighth, the guest sneaked out of the woods, put Watts's corpse in a wagon, and carried it to Columbus. Flournoy's mangled body had arrived in town the previous day.[5]

These and several other of the initial casualties occurred south of Federal Road, but rather quickly small parties of Indians attacked settlers and burned houses all along both the Federal and New roads between Columbus and Tuskegee. The activity was particularly heavy around the bridges over the Big and Little Euchee creeks. In one incident, the rebels waylaid a body of settlers and killed the men among them. Then they scalped the women and children alive, placed them in a wagon, and tied fodder to the tails of the mules and the wagon wheels. This done, they set the fodder afire to make the mules run, and the injured women and children were thrown out of the wagon as they went. The Indians then burned the bridges to prevent both the escape of any other settlers and the ingress into the country of avenging troops or militiamen. It is difficult to say how many settlers died, but it is obvious the killing could have been much more extensive. Despite all the warning signs, the Creek uprising caught the settlers off guard. They had prepared no defense plan. They may have fallen for Neah Micco's double game, on the one hand professing friendship for the whites while on the other hand planning for war. More probably, however, the settlers were victims of their own aggressiveness and individualism. Preoccupied with exploiting the lands taken from the Creeks, they failed to cooperate in taking precautionary measures for the common defense. In fact, Governor Clay must have been shocked to discover that the citizens of Russell County, always the scene of the most intense Native-white conflict, had never even organized a militia. Without an effective militia or general defense plan, the settlers in the Lower counties of New Alabama had little recourse but to flee from the Indian attacks, and only their speed saved many from death.[6]

But some whites escaped slaughter because the Creeks were not unified in seeing all settlers as enemies. Some Natives and settlers lived as close neighbors and had grown mutually dependent on one another. Consequently, when the rebels began planning their attacks, numbers of other Indians warned their white friends of the impending doom and gave them time to escape. Tustenuggee Chopco, for example, the chief of Tallassee town, prevented the rebel warriors of his tribe from attacking the settler town of Tallassee at the falls of the Tallapoosa. Otherwise, the town would have been taken by surprise and destroyed. In the northern end of Russell County, a Creek woman, Katey Marthley, informed the settlers living around Wetumpka town that Tuscoona Fixico, the local rebel leader, meant to kill them; legend has it that a disabled Indian woman struggled five miles through the same county to tell Major Flournoy's family of his death and to warn them of their own peril. Similarly, an elderly Euchee named Estothlee repaid past kindnesses by warning the people of Glennville that the rebels had scheduled their village for destruction. Elsewhere in Barbour County, a compassionate elderly warrior came among the settlers every day scraping a cow horn with a stick to get their attention and holding up a number of fingers to alert the whites as to how many days remained before the rebel assault. Such kindness happened all over New Alabama and, indeed, all over the world where colonial revolts occurred. Natives always met settlers who were good people willing to do right by them. These Natives also came to see some of their own kind as problems, as well as the colonial society. Consequently, there was always a chance that respectable settlers and Natives could coexist. But alas, the press of the market eventually destroyed any middle ground of accommodation between the two, more often than not turning potential friends into adversaries.[7]

The Lower Creeks' campaign of terror sprang from this adversarial relationship, and it accomplished exactly what the warriors wanted it to. It shattered what remained of the settlers' sense of peace and security and caused them to vacate Indian land. Many Macon County settlers headed west into Old Alabama, making their way to Montgomery, or crossed the Tallapoosa River to seek refuge in white Wetumpka. The settlers living in the northern end of Russell County and the southern end of Chambers County rushed east to Georgia to join the settlers from farther south, who had left their homes along the Cowikee and Hatchechubbee creeks right after the initial attacks. Frightened settlers packed the bridge leading to Columbus and flocked to Hardaway's ferry station farther up the Chattahoochee. Most of these refugees had come from Georgia originally, and many simply moved into the interior of the state and returned to their old communities. However, some of the fleeing settlers lost their lives on the way out of New Alabama, and only their dogs returned to their old hometowns in Georgia. The appearance of these lonely animals gave notice to the town residents that their former neighbors had fallen to the Creeks.[8]

A large number of the refugees traveled only as far as the Georgia border towns to seek shelter. Scared settlers crowded into West Point, for example, but Columbus drew most of them, perhaps two thousand refugees. The *Columbus Enquirer* reported on May 13 that "this city presented a scene of confusion and distress, such as we have never witnessed. Our streets were crowded with wagons, carts, horses and footmen, flying for safety from the rifle and tomahawk of the Indians." The *Columbus Sentinel* described the pitiable condition of these people: "Wives separated from their husbands, parents from their children, all dismayed, all terror stricken." Having fled so precipitately, many New Alabama refugees left home with only the clothes on their backs. Now they stared complete economic failure in the face. According to the *Columbus Sentinel*, "Poverty, wretchedness and ruin must result to those unfortunate people who, having exhausted their last dollar in laying in their provisions for the year, are driven from their homes, destitute of every earthly comfort."[9]

In fact, it appears that the hungry Indians waited until the settlers stocked their pantries before they began running the whites from their homes. This left the refugees with no choice but to throw themselves on the mercy of the Georgians. Yet this situation worked a great hardship on refugees and border town residents alike. The people of LaGrange found themselves suddenly outnumbered by strangers needing assistance. Columbus residents took as many women and children into their homes as they could, but most of the refugees had to live in tent villages and shanty camps around the outskirts of the town. Food then became a problem. One local woman remembered having to cook for two hundred refugees camped near her home. Furthermore, the state government had no funds for such an emergency. Consequently, George W. B. Towns, one of Georgia's representatives, requested that the War Department provide rations to all the New Alabama refugees. Dixon Lewis, representing the New Alabama counties in Washington, introduced a resolution in Congress setting aside twenty thousand dollars for that purpose.[10]

Besides their hunger, the New Alabama refugees brought real fear to Columbus and the other border communities. Columbus residents now felt themselves in imminent danger of attack. General Lowe, the local militia commander, put every eligible male on his muster roll. Then the town fathers sent out messengers and letters requesting military aid from the federal government, as well as from the governors of Alabama and Georgia. Some of these men owned large plantations in New Alabama and faced severe financial losses if the rebellion continued. One planter, Anderson Abercrombie, punctuated his plea to Governor Clay with the words, "For God's sake, send us some help." Eli Shorter, the land speculator who now headed Columbus's defense committee, gave further evidence of the extent of the townspeople's fear, as well as his own ability to profit from tragedy, in a letter to the secretary of war. He declared, quite erroneously, that "four-fifths of the Creek nation are at heart, and in principle, hostile." Furthermore, he proclaimed that a large portion of the Cherokees were hostile and that both the Cherokees and Creeks had "an intimate understanding and concert of purpose" with the Seminoles. Thus, Shorter raised the specter of an extensive Indian conspiracy against southern whites. He claimed that "we must, we are fated to have a severe and sanguinary war with these people," and he asked that a force be sent "fully adequate to the purpose." But Shorter also took the opportunity to advance his own financial interests. He asked the secretary to remove the friendly Creeks from the country as soon as possible because even they could not be trusted, and the government should not bear the great cost of feeding them during the coming conflict. Moreover, Shorter knew that a massive intervention of troops, and a forced removal of Indians, would obliterate the evidence needed for a complete investigation of the Creek land frauds.[11]

Meanwhile, the Creek rebels, emboldened by their early success, extended their depredations and consolidated their hold on the Lower counties of New Alabama. The disaffected warriors spread destruction from Irwinton in the south to LaFayette in the north, from the banks of the Chattahoochee in the east to the outskirts of Tuskegee and Tallassee in the west. Those settlers who remained in the country "forted in" at these places and huddled together in fear, expecting attack at any moment. At LaFayette all noncombatants took up residence in the courthouse while the able-bodied men prepared to defend the town from attack. However, not all the men were brave enough for the task. When the town's military commander created a false alarm one night to test the competence of his troops, he found some hiding in the courthouse behind the women. Besides their momentary embarrassment, these poor cowards "were scorned to the end of their lives." At Irwinton, other men had to endure the same stigma. They were so afraid of the Creeks that they ran and hid in barrels when a company of their own militiamen made a noisy approach to town one evening.[12]

Seeing all this, the settlers in the Cherokee country of northern Alabama and Georgia also began to panic. Many Creeks, perhaps a few thousand, had moved to Cherokee territory to escape the turmoil in their own land, and the local whites believed that these Creek refugees, along with some disaffected Cherokees, would rise up to join in the rebellion. In Cherokee country, Alabama, a committee of white citizens met with the Creek community at Pole Cat Ground and learned from the residents that some of the rebels from the south had come among them on a recruiting trip. The terrified settlers wrote to Governor Clay asking for the authority to organize a company of men to disarm their Creek neighbors and place them under guard so no one could sell them liquor or guns. Similarly, the *Milledgeville Federal Union* reported that armed Creeks had moved into the Coosawattee Valley in Murray County, Georgia. According to local reports, these Indians avoided contact with whites and were "suspected of exasperating the Cherokees." From Walker County word came in that the Creek rebels had sent their women and children to that place "to be out of harm's way." The editor of the *Federal Union* recommended that the state take these people hostage. In Carroll and Paulding counties rumors began to circulate that the Cherokees were already following the Creek example and would devastate the white settlements in those counties if the state ordered their militiamen south to fight the Creek war. In actuality, the Georgians had little to fear from a Cherokee uprising, but their politicians and presses insisted on threatening the Cherokees with massive retaliation if they pursued a hostile course. Indeed, one suspects that some Georgians simply used the Creek rebellion as an excuse to finally bludgeon the Cherokees out of the state.[13]

While no armed hostilities occurred in the Cherokee country, the Native rebels did increase their numbers in the Lower Creek territory. More Apalachicolas, Sawoklis, and Eufaulas joined the Euchees, Hitchitees, Ositchees, Chehaws, Cussetas, and Tallassees in making war on the whites, increasing the hostile party to about three thousand warriors and their families. And with the accession of numbers came more destruction of property. The rebels began to demolish the plantations in the fertile Chattahoochee River bends near Fort Mitchell and Columbus. At Coweta Bend, they burned out the wealthy Abercrombies and John Crowell, the former Creek agent. They also destroyed the plantation of Paddy Carr, the Creek who associated almost exclusively with whites and gave such valuable assistance to the land speculators. At night the inhabitants of Columbus could look across the river and see the fires burning. The rebels also took the slaves from the plantations they demolished. Paddy Carr alone lost seventy blacks. Furthermore, the hostile warriors captured a good supply of arms, ammunition, food, and other necessities from all the deserted stores and homes they found. They secreted these supplies, along with their women and children, in the swamps along Big Euchee Creek. Then, to guard against any retaliation from the whites, the rebels set up a line of spies from the headwaters of the Big Euchee down to Irwinton, a distance of sixty miles. The rebels also sent their spies over the Chattahoochee to the outskirts of Columbus, and these spies occasionally shot whites who ventured beyond the town's limits.[14]

The rebels also moved to gain complete control of the Federal and New roads to prevent communication between the Georgians and Alabamians and to isolate Fort Mitchell. On the evening of May 13, the rebels pursued and overturned a stagecoach on the road and killed the passengers. During the next two days, they plundered and burned all the remaining houses and stagecoach stands on the highways between Tuskegee and Columbus. Then, on May 15, rebel warriors directed by Tuscoona Fixico of Wetumpka town set up an ambush near Frazier's stand and Brush Creek, twenty miles west of Columbus. Before the day's end, they had wrecked and burned two or more stagecoaches, and the next day, using the wreckage as a roadblock, they stopped and captured two more stages carrying sixteen passengers. They killed as many of these passengers as they could catch, again wrecked the stages, and also claimed a rich reward from the Great Western Stage Line. In consequence of the Indian difficulties, the managers of that company had decided to withdraw all their livestock from Alabama on that fateful weekend. Extra horses, some of the best in the country, trailed each coach, and the Indians captured most of them. In addition, the coaches' heavy mail sacks yielded cash, bank notes, and other securities. The Indians also took a considerable amount of cash and valuable paper from the dead passengers. One of the victims, Mr. Lackey, had come to Alabama as an agent for a group of orphans. He was returning home to Georgia with $1,500 of their money.[15]

The stage attacks alerted the outside world to the seriousness of the Creek rebellion. In closing down Federal Road, the Creeks stopped the east-west flow of travelers and mail across the Deep South. Thomas Abbott, one of the government's certifying agents, announced that he could no longer approve Creek land sales because his communication with Washington had been cut off "by the suddenness and unexpected extent" of the Creek uprising. More importantly, the people of Old Alabama and points west now felt inconvenienced, forced to recognize the Indian problem. As late as May 13, many residents of the older part of the state thought that the New Alabama settlers were merely crying wolf one more time. In fact, the postal manager in Montgomery had stated that "The alarm appears to have been unnecessarily great; and we hope that the symptoms of disorder and hostility will be promptly and effectually quelled without further bloodshed, and with such prudence as will not exasperate the Indians who have not been guilty of violence and disorderly conduct." Following the stage attacks, people outside the Old Creek Nation no longer spoke in such moderate tones. Now all Alabamians knew a real war was at hand.[16]

The stage attacks also revealed that in a white society divided by class and economic interests, the respectable citizens of Alabama and Georgia had more than the rebel Creeks to fear. A party sent to retrieve the mail sacks from the stage wreckage claimed that because the sacks and letters had been opened so carefully, and with so much discernment, a white man must have done the work. This observation turned out to be accurate. One Philander Broad assisted the rebel Creeks in the stage attacks. The residents of Girard, just across the river from Columbus, also jailed another white man for being an accessory to Indian depredations, but he made his escape from confinement, possibly with the aid of the Natives. Similarly, the inhabitants of white Wetumpka arrested yet another character thought to be in league with the rebel Creeks. In fact, suspicion fell on many more whites, particularly those who had made their living selling liquor to the Indians. The *Columbus Sentinel* declaimed against these "unprincipled white men" with the following words: "Having swindled and plundered the Indians in every shape and manner within their power, until nothing more was to be obtained from them, their next step has been to set the Indians to murdering and plundering the white man, and they appropriating the richest spoils to themselves." This statement was true, but only in one respect. Some whites had, indeed, found a way to turn even a war into one more branch of the lucrative Indian business. But these people did not "set the Indians to murdering and plundering." The Creeks did this themselves as part of their rebellion. Furthermore, some whites undoubtedly helped the Creeks because they too belonged to the underclass and had some sympathy for the Native cause. But newspaper editors or respectable whites generally could not admit this. They had to infantilize the Indians and blame the uprising on a few white roughs and/or land speculators, because to do otherwise would be to admit their own culpability as participants in an economic system that thrived on the aggressive exploitation of all available resources.[17]

But roughs were only part of the problem for respectable whites. The stage attacks also revealed that in a pluralistic society, knowledgeable Natives of mixed parentage could also be a threat. The fact that the rebels had attacked the stages on the exact day the Great Western line put extra coaches and horses on the road led the citizens of Columbus to suspect a conspiracy: someone had informed the Indians of the company's plans. The finger of suspicion fell on an enigmatic young man named Jim Henry, a bicultural individual, perfectly at home in a Creek cabin or a speculator's mansion. He was well-known on the streets of Columbus, walking about looking for all the world like any other tall, well-dressed, aspiring young U.S. businessman. Indeed, he had worked for one of the town's mercantile firms. He had also worked as an interpreter for the land speculators, and during that time he would have been privy to specific information about the stages. But it would appear that Henry left Columbus to join the Creek resistance well before the stage attacks. The settlers in Russell County had even accused him of going to Florida to consort with the Seminoles and then coming back to agitate the Creeks to war. This being the case, Henry would have found it difficult to venture into Columbus to get information once the war began.[18]

But Henry had been a popular figure in the town and had many friends there, some wealthy and highborn, others denizens of the underclass. As a result, the young rebel succeeded in forming a little network of spies among the blacks and poor whites in and around Columbus, and he could have heard about the stages from them. Henry, however, later denied this charge, although he would admit to other offenses. Furthermore, David Hardridge, Henry's Hitchitee friend and former classmate, also took up the rebel cause, much to the chagrin of his former friends in Columbus. The presence of such men in the hostile ranks also made the speculators and settlers very insecure, but such was the tenor of the times. Racial miscegenation and the competitive economy generated a tangled web of interethnic collusion and conflict, and no one knew whom to trust: a friend one day could be an enemy the next. But this was surely true in all areas of the world undergoing conquest, colonization, and incorporation in the world system. Occupiers could never really tell friend from foe, and oftentimes those well-acculturated and mixed-blood Natives who seemed so friendly and well adapted to the new day became, in the end, the most dangerous rebel leaders just because they knew the occupiers and their economy so well.[19]

It should not be surprising that the residents of Columbus became paranoid. In fact, their fear of Indians increased to near hysteria. Lurid accounts in the local newspapers fed the alarm. The *Columbus Republican*, for example, proclaimed that in "the Creek nation, at this moment, the scenes of Florida are being acted over. The wild savage, frenzied by the smell of blood in his nostrils, is prowling the wilderness." Then, in the midst of such reports, friendly Creeks came into town with the news that not only had the rebels allied themselves with the Seminoles in a war of extermination against the whites but that the Florida Indians had recently defeated the large army sent against them by the federal government. One can only imagine the looks on the faces of the Columbus folk as they gathered around to hear these tales. The Creek criers must have enjoyed the sight, and one can further imagine them waiting till they had the jittery whites completely enthralled before they delivered the pièce de résistance. Now, they warned, none other than Osceola himself would soon arrive from Florida to direct the war in Alabama and Georgia. The audience must have quaked at the mention of the name. Osceola had become nationally famous as a warrior. Every newspaper in the nation broadcast his exploits, real or imagined. The Columbus people also knew that Osceola had been born in Alabama, and they believed he still had relatives living in Chambers County, just across the line from West Point, Georgia. Therefore, it did not seem at all unlikely to the Georgians that the feared war chief would follow up his stunning victory in Florida by returning to his old homeland to cement the military alliance between Creeks and Seminoles. But then again, insecure and frightened people will believe almost anything.[20]

The Creek rebels also terrified the friendly Lower Creeks. Seeking to impose discipline and order on their fragmented society, the rebels tried to intimidate reluctant Indians into joining them in hostilities against the whites. Like the Red Sticks of old, the rebels of 1836 even vowed to destroy all Indians who opposed them and detained numbers of their more peaceable tribespeople at Neah Micco's town, twenty-five miles west of Columbus. They shot those who tried to escape. However, many Lower Creeks did manage to elude the rebels and seek asylum with the whites. The peaceful Tallassees moved close to the fort at white Tallassee town, while some Lower Creeks moved into Benjamin Marshall's camp just across the river from Columbus. Other Natives fled from the rebels and took up residence with the settlers at Tuskegee or moved into the friendly Upper Creek towns in Macon County. Still more Lower Creek refugees went to Fort Mitchell, where Captain Page promised food and protection to all Indians who renounced the rebel cause. On May 12 he wrote, "I see we are surrounded by these people; we have men, women, and children, more than we can get inside the pickets." Seeing all this, congressional representative George W. B. Towns called on the secretary of war to do more. Having already asked the federal government to feed the settlers fleeing New Alabama, he now wanted Cass to establish a retreat for friendly Indians in Georgia. Otherwise he feared those Natives could not maintain a neutral stance in the war. The rebels, or their own hunger, would eventually force them to take up arms against the whites.[21]

Furthermore, Towns may have realized that for Captain Page to promise the friendly Creeks protection at a post as vulnerable to attack as Fort Mitchell was laughable. The rebels controlled the country all around the fort. They had confined the Georgians to Columbus. They had cut off all communication between Fort Mitchell and the governor of Alabama. Less than one hundred troops ran the fort, which had no well within its gates. Even worse, the rebels knew everything about Fort Mitchell and the activities of its garrison. Some of the Euchees who had gone there seeking shelter were actually spies. Put out at night as sentries, they went into the surrounding woods to give information to their fellow rebels. The hostile chiefs knew they could take the fort anytime they chose, and they sent word to the Natives living there that they would share the same fate as the soldiers if they did not leave the outpost. Then, to give proof of their strength, rebel warriors often ventured as near as thirty yards to the stockade to carry off whatever they pleased from the fort's outbuildings. The soldiers did not venture out to stop them, for as the *Columbus Republican Herald* reported, "It was not deemed prudent." Despite his pledge to protect the friendly Indians, and his belief that the rebels could not take Fort Mitchell, Page lamented his inability to take positive action against the hostile party. Dejectedly, he concluded, "Our situation is a very unpleasant one, to have these people challenge and threaten us, and we unable to do anything."[22]

Humiliated by his impotence in the face of the rebel insurgency, Page could only complain to his superiors and assign blame for the disaster in New Alabama. He pointed to something that was both a local and national problem. He believed that the U.S. Army was simply too small to meet the demands of a growing nation. No tribe of Indians feared it, he declared, and gave as evidence his own situation. He had repeatedly asked for more regular troops to overawe the increasingly hostile Creeks, but the War Department could not spare them. With only three hundred men, Page declared, he could have prevented the Second Creek War and saved three million dollars in losses and many human lives. Furthermore, he opined that the want of regular troops had caused the failure of the recent Seminole campaign. And then, like so many military officers before and after him, Page focused the blame on the politicians in Washington. They were the ones who would rather depend on an antiquated and inefficient militia system and argue over the deposition of the nation's large surplus fund rather than spend a portion of that fund to augment the regular army.[23]

But at least Page did not pay with his own life for the politicians' mistakes. In the end, the Lower Creek rebels, having penned Page and his fellow soldiers up in Fort Mitchell, turned their attention to a more important task. They moved to open a line of communication with the Seminoles in Florida and to clear a path through southwestern Georgia to the Seminole country, should they need to retreat there. The first obstacle in their way was the village of Roanoke, Georgia, which stood across the Chattahoochee from the mouth of Cowikee Creek and commanded one of the Indians' favorite river crossing points. The settlers from surrounding farms and plantations had gathered in Roanoke for safety, erecting a small fort with a blockhouse and pickets. The Creek rebels determined to eliminate this nest of their enemies so they could move freely across the river, through Georgia's sparsely settled southern counties and into Florida Territory.

On Friday night, May 13, a scouting party of thirty warriors crossed the Chattahoochee to test Roanoke's defenses. They fought a brief skirmish with the settlers and withdrew. The apparent victory must have lulled the townspeople into a false sense of security. Many of them went off on a visit to Lumpkin, and when a force of three hundred Creek warriors returned to Roanoke early on the morning of May 15, they caught the village completely off guard. Twenty county militiamen slept by the cotton warehouse, and the remaining forty or fifty people in town slept peacefully in their homes, not in the stockade. The warriors carefully surrounded the village and stationed themselves at the door of every house. Then they began their attack. Nine whites and three blacks died in the initial gun blasts; eight or nine more Georgians suffered wounds. The other townspeople burst out of their houses and made for the woods, Indians shooting at them all the way. Miraculously, most of the surprised villagers survived and made their way to Lumpkin or up the river to Fort Twiggs, still commanded by Major Howard. The Indians looted Roanoke's homes, three stores, and warehouse; then they consigned all the buildings to the flames. The rebels also rounded up a considerable number of horses and slaves and very nearly claimed a steamboat, the *Georgian*, which lay at dock below the village at the time of the attack. The terrified crew barely managed to pull away into the river in time. The steamer then proceeded downriver to the tiny village of Fort Gaines, a place now "crowded with women and children flying from Savages to find protection."[24]

Like the stage attacks, the capture of Roanoke was an important event. It signaled the extension of the Second Creek War into Georgia and stood as a direct challenge to all the citizens of that state. In partial recognition of this fact, one Joel Crawford proclaimed from the town of Sparta that the Creeks were waging a war against whites, and none "have more of the Indian hate than Georgians." John Fontaine, the mayor of Columbus, sent friendly Indians to spy on the rebels and received the disturbing report that the insurgents intended not only to attack Columbus but to enter Georgia "in small bodies, secret themselves in swamps and thickets" and "make sudden eruptions into the settlements lying between the Flint and Chattahoochee to burn and massacre." Furthermore, the destruction of Roanoke served notice that the rebel Creeks meant to establish their control of the Lower Chattahoochee and its crossing points. In fact, the Indians commenced regular attacks on steamboat traffic the same day they took Roanoke. Twenty warriors, stationed on the Alabama side of the river eight miles south of Columbus, fired on the *Hyperion* as it descended the Chattahoochee. The boat's first pilot, Mr. Brockway, fell dead with a musket ball in his throat. Five others suffered wounds. The steamer then ran aground on the Georgia side of the river and "the passengers fled from her in terror and dismay." The Creeks followed this victory with attacks on other steamers, and the citizens of Columbus soon discovered that they could not carry on their river trade without military protection.[25]

The attack on Roanoke also revealed again how much the Georgians feared the Natives and how ill-prepared they were for cooperative effort. Like the New Alabama settlers, many Georgians living near the east bank of the Chattahoochee fled back from the river in terror, abandoning even more territory to the rebel Creeks. One traveler making his way from Columbus to Macon "found people on the road flying in all directions from the lower counties." And as these people ran, the rumor spread that the Indians had fortified Roanoke and had beaten off two relief parties of militiamen. Though untrue, this piece of information came as yet another stunning blow to the citizens of Columbus. Fearing that the town would be isolated and cut off from Georgia's interior by rampaging Creeks, the editor of the *Columbus Sentinel* urged the farmers south of the town to stay and fight. He proclaimed that he did not understand how Georgians could run from Indians, who were, according to the editor, a "constitutionally cowardly" people. But the rebels were certainly not cowards, and in all fairness, neither were some of the settlers of southwestern Georgia. Not all of them ran away to hide in the interior of the state. When Col. John Dill called up the militias of Randolph and Early counties, numbers of men responded. Col. Abenego McGinty mustered eighty men at Fort Gaines and built a better stockade there to protect the nearly three hundred women and children seeking refuge in the village. Then a party of mounted men began to scout the river bank between Fort Gaines and Irwinton on the Alabama side. However, all these Georgians knew they stood in harm's way. They realized that if the rebel Creeks decided to flee New Alabama, or were driven out, they would come right toward Fort Gaines on their way to Florida.[26]

But on the whole, settlers and townspeople in the Chattahoochee Valley did not distinguish themselves in the face of the Creek rebellion. The editor of the *Columbus Sentinel* even chided his own townspeople for their lack of courage and effort in defending the city. He declared that Columbus would be the military depot for the coming conflict, and it could not be allowed to fall into enemy hands. He called on Gov. William Schley to send troops and cannons. He urged his townspeople to organize a better defense for the city, lamenting the fact that the citizens had become lax since the initial Indian attacks in Alabama. He wanted the men to erect blockhouses for the protection of the women and children. He decried the fact that the number of men guarding the town at night had fallen from two hundred to a mere nineteen or twenty. Even more, he criticized the three companies of militia in Columbus for their poor organization and sense of readiness. The men had scattered themselves all over town and could not be assembled in half a day should the Indians attack. Despite the danger, the inhabitants of Columbus simply could not work together for the common good.[27]

But what was the common good in a competitive society divided along the lines of race and class? The editor's notion of a common good presupposed that all whites were, at the very least, on the same side in the war. This was not the case. When a company of local militiamen ventured back to Roanoke to spy on the enemy, they discovered that a white man led the small party of rebels who still occupied the destroyed village. Apparently, this party had remained on the scene to guard the loot not yet transported across the river to the Creek towns. The angry militiamen managed to shoot the white man to death and scatter the Natives. But who was this man? The Georgians wrote him off as just another outlaw, but he may have been more. He could have been a man who sympathized with the Indians, or he could have been an Indian himself, one of those adopted Indian countrymen who actually identified himself as a Creek. We will never know because the historical record, produced by writers like the *Sentinel*'s editor, hides so much from us. They believed in, and sought to impose, the social structure and racial ideology of the world system, so they could not let themselves believe in the legitimacy of the Creek rebellion or the fact that white persons, other than social deviants, could possibly share the Native point of view.[28]

But Governor Schley came to the editor's rescue. On May 19, he called twelve volunteer companies of troops into state service and drafted militiamen from twenty-eight Georgia counties to face the Creek rebels. He then directed these troops to rendezvous at three points on the Chattahoochee River: Columbus; Fort Twiggs, just south of Columbus; and West Point, twenty-five miles north of the town. Schley also made it clear to his officers that their purpose was to defend the soil of Georgia from invasion. Consequently, he prohibited them from taking offensive measures and moving into Alabama until the whole Georgia force was collected, supplied, and organized for war. That much done, the governor placed Brig. Gen. Henry H. Lowe in temporary command of the troops at or south of Columbus and took another week to decide who should command the whole host of Georgia troops. He finally determined that the man should be the former Creek land-sales agent, resigned congressional representative and removal contractor, Major General Sanford.[29]

But Schley was unhappy with the whole situation. Like many of his fellow Georgians, he felt his state had been wronged, but not only by the Indians. He believed the federal government should have removed the Creeks and Cherokees already, then Georgia would not have to pay for a call-up of state troops. In fact, Schley used the Creek rebellion as yet another opportunity to push for forced removal of the southern Indians and to criticize those northern representatives and humanitarians who showed sympathy for the Indians' plight and believed that forced removal violated the Natives' treaty rights. Schley believed that Georgia's critics should be more concerned about the murdered New Alabama settlers, and he contended that it was "idle to talk of treaties and national faith with such savages" as the Creeks. Furthermore, Schley now suggested his own solution to the troublesome problem of what to do with the federal government's great surplus fund. It should be used to finance the Indian removal so Georgia and the other southern states would have no more violent outbreaks of disaffected Natives. In short, Schley's response to the Creek rebellion showed considerable anger toward the federal government, northerners, and the Indians, perhaps reflecting Georgia's heavy involvement in New Alabama's settlement and economic development, as well as the state's long history of conflict with the Creeks and disapproval of federal policy toward those Natives.[30]

The Georgians' response to Schley's call for troops reflected another aspect of their mentality: anger toward the state of Alabama. In an address to the troops of Morgan and Clark counties, just prior to their march to the Chattahoochee, the speaker of the day told the volunteers that after appealing unsuccessfully to Governor Clay, the people of New Alabama now "turn with outstretched arms and beseeching looks, imploring succor from the brave, patriotic, chivalrous sons of Georgia." The editor of the *Columbus Enquirer* added, "We are proud that we are Georgians—and we sincerely regret that any of those who once were our fellow citizens, and yet share our sympathies and affections, should have been thrown into a state, unwilling to defend their rights—should have placed themselves under the protection of those who laugh at their misfortunes, and abandon them, their lives, their property, their children and wives, a prey to the merciless savage." Moreover, the *Enquirer* implicitly criticized President Jackson in its attacks on Clay, claiming that instead of acting like a man, Clay had "sent to Washington City, 700 miles, to know of his master whether he ought to protect his bleeding fellow citizens." Needless to say, such sentiments did not endear Georgians to the people of Old Alabama.[31]

But not all Georgians were ready to rush to the aid of the New Alabama settlers, or of the citizens of Columbus for that matter. In fact, some state citizens remained wholly unenthusiastic about the war. Their dissent most often found voice in the states' pro-Jackson Union Party organs. The *Milledgeville Federal Union*, for example, reported that "Some patriotic and high spirited men feel lukewarm in supporting the Creek War, because they believe that it has been caused by the dishonest speculations of our own citizens." Furthermore, the newspaper noted that this indignation over the "egregious frauds" committed by the "land sharks" was a "just and honorable sentiment." However, the paper warned that the residents of Georgia's interior should not indulge a "sickly sentimentality" for Indians whose hands reeked with the blood of men, women and children and who sought to "lay waste to the fertile and flourishing counties bordering on the Chattahoochee." Instead, Georgia's men should fly to the rescue of the state's border inhabitants.[32]

For the most part, Georgia's men took this advice. Eager volunteers began to arrive in Columbus even before Schley published his call for troops. Along with them came a cannon, ammunition, and 360 stands of arms. These first citizen soldiers came from nearby Upson, Talbot, and Harris counties, and they were anxious to get at the Indians. Along with the Columbus militiamen and companies of New Alabama settlers, they began almost immediately to venture across the river to retrieve property and prevent the Indians from doing more damage to nearby plantations. They also sought to track down and engage rebel parties, but they had no real success. Rebel spies kept their fellows well apprised of movements in and around Columbus. But not all the men venturing from Columbus wanted to fight. Some settlers wanted merely to return to New Alabama or their farms in southwestern Georgia to salvage their cotton and corn crops. Unfortunately, though, these people found that "General Green" had "taken full and entire possession" of their fields.[33]

The early volunteers soon realized that they could do little to win the war. Without sufficient men and arms to penetrate the rebel strongholds, they could not hope to engage any sizable body of Creek warriors.

Furthermore, some Columbus citizens feared for the safety of their homes if the volunteers ventured too far away. The *Columbus Enquirer* voiced the opinion that the refugees from New Alabama should be the ones to take the lead in combating the Indians; the Georgia volunteers should guard the town. A few of the braver New Alabamians agreed. They returned to their property determined to fight for it, and they urged their fellows to do the same. But their pleas often had little effect. Many of the refugees turned their backs on New Alabama and the war and returned to their old homes in Georgia for good.[34]

Then more Georgia troops arrived on the scene and their divisional commanders organized larger military expeditions against the rebels. But if these commanders expected to win the war, they were sadly mistaken. In fact, the larger expeditions had no more success than the earlier forays into Creek country. On May 21 Maj. Gen. S. A. Bailey of Georgia's Tenth Militia Division led a futile effort to drive the Chewackla Swamp for rebels. His force consisted of nearly eight hundred men, half of them friendly Creeks. Two days later, the Georgians organized a similar expedition to the Eight Mile Swamp. That detachment never reached its destination. At the same time, Lee County's militia commander assembled a force of four hundred men to take back Roanoke from the rebels and to cross the river to help Gen. William Irwin of the Alabama militia construct a fort near the mouth of Hatchechubbee Creek. The purpose of this fort was to protect public stores and to open a line of communication between Columbus and Irwinton. A company of Columbus residents participated in this last expedition and made a great show of leaving town by horseback and steamboat. At the head of the entourage rode the town's elite gang of planter-speculators, including General Abercrombie, Seaborn Jones, and "Major" Eli Shorter. On discovering the Indians had abandoned Roanoke, General Jones's expedition "fell apart" under a spirit of mutiny, and General Irwin, left stranded on the Hatchechubbee near a large body of rebels, had to return to Irwinton without erecting a fort. At that point, Schley's initial order prohibiting troop movements into Alabama reached Columbus and stopped the formation of any more expeditions, which was just as well. The Georgia militia had proved incompetent in the field, and General

Bailey, casting about for a scapegoat, blamed the junior officers for the problem. He reported to Governor Schley that "the inferior commands in the Militia, have not of late years been bestowed on those best qualified for them. Indeed their acceptance has almost brought disgrace, instead of conferring honor."[35]

From that point on, the Georgia troops merely stood guard, maintaining a defensive position against the Indians. General Jones convinced some of his soldiers to stay by the Chattahoochee for ten days to watch the river-crossing points until the governor's main force arrived. These troops took up residence at Fort Jones, just north of Roanoke; at Fort McCreary, a few miles north of that; and at Fort Twiggs, twenty miles south of Columbus. The men at Fort McCreary fought a brief skirmish with rebels who attacked the Brewer and Quarles plantations nearby, but most of the other troops sat idle. At Columbus the civilian soldiers settled into a boring routine uninterrupted by any attempt to fortify the town, much to the chagrin of all the local newspaper editors. However, a few citizen soldiers did venture over into Alabama to chase the once popular and now notorious Jim Henry, who set fire to the Federal Road bridges over the Euchee creeks, attacked the Victory plantation near Fort Twiggs, and according to most reports, had led the raid on Roanoke. These troops always returned to Columbus disappointed, however, and Henry remained at large.[36]

Not surprisingly, dissension arose among the troops and local citizens as they waited in Columbus for the rest of Georgia's army to arrive. In general, this unrest revealed the economic competitiveness and class consciousness of the society. The *Columbus Sentinel*, a Jacksonian paper expressing the views of the commoner, accused the rich people of the town of not doing their part to defend Columbus. The officers and troops of Harris County, Georgia, whose crops needed cultivation, also began to complain that they had been called in to protect the town so the rich merchants there could return to their stores to make money. Similarly, Randolph County troops complained of being ordered to Fort Twiggs to defend Columbus even though their own sparsely populated county stood in danger of Indian attack. Furthermore, these men claimed to know the reason for such an unjust assignment: "It is because men of influence ... live about Columbus and in that direction." Outside the town, the rumor spread that Columbus's wealthy families had completely deserted the place to seek safety and leisure at watering holes and "other fashionable places," allowing others to fight the war for them. Indeed, in both Alabama and Georgia, many people felt Columbus should not be defended by outsiders at all. As home of the worst land speculators, these people reasoned, Columbus was only getting what it deserved from the Indians. Seeing all this dissent, the states' rights *Columbus Enquirer* defended the town and its wealthy inhabitants, pointing to the fact that Shorter and other prosperous townspeople had gone south to face the Creeks on the river. Then the editor sought conciliation. He acknowledged that Georgians were a "divided people," but he contended that the war could help solve the problem. The common effort against the Creeks would lessen all distinctions and bind Georgians as "brethren." This was a telling statement. Again and again, the leaders of western societies would offer war as the cure for social divisions caused by their economic system. But the cure never worked for long. War offered only temporary relief. It distracted people from the problem rather than provide a real solution. Such would be the case with the Georgians.[37]

The *Enquirer* was also wrong on another point. The state of Alabama had not been inactive in prosecuting the war during this time. Indeed, by the time Schley issued his order for a troop call up, Alabama's forces were already advancing toward the scene of hostilities. Expecting some sort of Indian uprising, Governor Clay had been holding a battalion from Alabama's Fifth Militia Division in readiness since April 25. On May 11, soon after the outbreak of hostilities, he ordered Major General Irwin, commander of that division, to send the battalion to Irwinton in the southern end of New Alabama. He also called a regiment from the Sixth Division into service and directed its commander, Col. Edward Shackleford, to proceed with his men to Tuskegee. However, these troops, most of whom came from the Montgomery area, were only the vanguard of the Alabama army. Clay ordered them into the Creek Nation to give temporary relief to the settlers and to build forts and supply depots in preparation for the introduction of a larger force.[38]

Shortly after sending his advance guard on its way, the governor called up the remainder of his army: one battalion from the First Division, another battalion from the Second, three more companies from the Sixth, and a regiment from the Fourth. In all, Clay intended to hurl twenty-seven hundred men at the rebel Creeks, and his plan of operations called for the larger part of the Alabama force to move south from Tuskegee to attack the rebel strongholds, while the troops at Irwinton moved north to cut off the Natives' retreat to Florida. The governor gave overall command of the Alabama army to a Huntsville resident, Maj. Gen. John H. Patterson of the First Division. Clay also made Col. John Hogan his acting adjutant and inspector general, knowing full well that Hogan's opposition to the Creek land frauds had made the colonel numerous determined and violent enemies in and around Tuskegee. Nevertheless, Clay dispatched Hogan to that town and placed some weighty responsibilities on his shoulders. He ordered the colonel to muster Shackleford's regiment into the service; recruit five hundred or more friendly Indians as auxiliary troops and scouts; open a line of communication between Tuskegee, Columbus, and Fort Mitchell; organize local militia units; and establish quartermaster, forage master, and wagon master departments for the Alabama expeditionary force. In addition, Hogan had to recruit a party of vedettes to serve as express riders between Tuskegee and Montgomery, where Governor Clay intended to set up his war headquarters as soon as he could leave the state capital in Tuscaloosa.[39]

Though Clay acted decisively in getting Alabama troops into the field, the nation's inefficient military system caused delays in getting his army ready to fight. Though Clay had the power to order up state troops, he had to turn to the federal government to arm, equip, feed, and pay those troops. He notified Captain Harding at the federal arsenal at Mount Vernon that he needed subsistence stores for his men, forage for twelve hundred horses, and an additional supply of arms—two thousand muskets, four or five pieces of artillery, and enough pistols, swords, and other accoutrements to outfit a battalion of cavalry. But Harding informed the governor that he had no food or forage on hand. Furthermore, he lacked the money to purchase these items, because Congress had not yet made its yearly appropriation for the army. Harding also informed Clay that the Seminole War had depleted his military stores and he could not furnish the governor with all the arms and accoutrements he needed right away. However, the captain did send an agent to secure a loan from the state bank in Mobile so he could purchase supplies for the Alabama army. In the interim, he suggested that Clay use private contractors to furnish his troops with rations and forage. The governor wanted to take Harding's advice, but he had no contingency fund to make purchases for the state. Consequently, he had to borrow twenty thousand dollars from the state bank to finance his operations until the federal government could reimburse him. However, all the wrangling and negotiations and letting of contracts took time and this prevented the state from getting the necessary equipment and food to its troops so they could get on with the business of subduing the Creeks.[40]

Clay had another problem, one that would plague governors and conscientious military officers throughout the Creek and Seminole wars. In short, the culture of southern civilian soldiers often made it difficult for them to do the tasks enlisted men must do in a successful army. First of all, they were aggressively independent. Second, they wanted only to fight and would not turn their hands to menial labor in the service of their country. Consequently, Colonel Shackleford had to impress slave gangs to build the fort, prison stockade, and other structures necessary to turn Tuskegee into a military base. Shackleford also had to contend with the mutinous behavior of some of his troops. A portion of his command consisted of drafted militiamen who were especially hard to control. They questioned the right of the governor to order them into service. Furthermore, many of Shackleford's men had left home in great haste, agreeing to serve for only four weeks until reinforcements arrived in New Alabama. However, when it appeared the main portion of the army would be slow in reaching Tuskegee, some of the men began to fear they would be kept away from their farms and businesses all summer, which would ruin them economically. Other soldiers complained that Shackleford should get on with the fighting; otherwise, the reinforcements would get all the credit for whipping the

Indians. Amid all the dissatisfaction and complaining, the McDonald Troop of Montgomery County deserted, and it appeared other militiamen would follow. On hearing the news, Governor Clay suggested that Shackleford and his officers advertise a reward of ten dollars per head for the apprehension and delivery of defectors to Tuskegee.[41]

The situation was no better at Irwinton, where Gen. William Irwin had taken command even before receiving Clay's order. Irwin just happened to be traveling up the Chattahoochee on the day Roanoke fell, and he arrived in Irwinton to find the town residents "in a state of consternation." Irwinton sat on a bluff overlooking the Chattahoochee only eleven miles south of Roanoke. Consequently, the wounded refugees from the Georgia village made their way, or were carried, to Irwinton following the Indian attack. The sight of them terrified the inhabitants of the little Alabama community. They realized that their town held a rich supply of arms and provisions, yet lacked effective fighting men or any sort of military organization. Worse, the town residents had never gotten on well with the Indians, and several despised land speculators lived there. No one doubted the Indians would attack Irwinton next, and many women and children had already deserted the town. Those settlers who remained "feared slaughter at the hands of the savages."[42]

If anything, General Irwin was even more afraid. He had just returned from Florida the day before and he knew the state of the Seminole War. He believed the Seminoles had taken possession of East Florida and were moving north toward Tallahassee. He also believed the rebel Creeks now intended to move south, devastate all before them, and "force a junction with the victorious Seminoles." He saw their attack on Roanoke in that light, and he believed that only Irwinton stood in the way of the dreaded Creek-Seminole union. Beyond that, the general saw another threat. Barbour County held some of the best cotton lands in the state, and a large number of slaves lived both in Irwinton and out on the plantations that had been abandoned by whites. Irwin, perhaps the largest land and slave owner in the state, feared these Barbour County blacks "who have had uninterrupted intercourse with the Indians for a great length of time." He believed that they may have developed a plan of cooperation with the Indians in the taking of Irwinton. And if Irwinton fell, along with all its provisions and munitions of war, the whole country between New Alabama and Florida would become "one scene of devastation and ruin."[43]

Consequently, Irwin overreacted. He sent out a frantic call for the civilian soldiers in his division to come to Irwinton as fast as possible. By May 20 he had accumulated more troops than the single battalion authorized by Clay. Moreover, these men arrived without provisions for themselves or forage for their horses, and their presence soon taxed Irwinton's resources. The men cleaned out the stores and charged such items as cigars, liquor, and fine jellies to the government. Irwin, in turn, commandeered the town's supply of powder, shot, and tools, and when citizens seemed reluctant to furnish food for the men and horses, he took that as well. Then the general criticized the citizens for their lack of patriotism. Finally, Irwin applied to the governor for "pecuniary aid" so that he could maintain his troops in Irwinton. This request only irritated Clay, however, and he ordered Irwin to dismiss all the excess troops he had called into service. He also informed the general that a regiment of reinforcements from the Fourth Militia Division under Gen. John W. Moore would soon arrive in Irwinton, at which time Moore would take command of the war in that quarter. Much aggrieved, General Irwin promptly dismissed nearly all the troops in Irwinton, leaving that settlement without enough protection. Fortunately for him, no rebel Creeks attacked.[44]

The Alabamians were also fortunate, given their inability to respond quickly to the rebellion, that the most prominent Upper Creek leaders came out forcefully against the uprising. In Tallapoosa County one Upper Creek chief stationed armed warriors on the trails to prevent the ingress of rebels and to protect the whites. Similarly, Menawa, the former leader of the Red Sticks at the Battle of Horseshoe Bend, met with his white neighbors in that county to proclaim his friendship and to offer to give up his people's guns if necessary to allay the settlers' fears. Then Tustenuggee Chopco, the headman of Creek Tallassee, assisted in the incarceration of Tallassee Fixico, alias Oakfuskee Yahola, the leader of the rebel Tallassees of Sougahatchee village. Most importantly, Opothle Yahola took a decisive stand against the rebellion. He mustered three hundred warriors from Tuckabatchee and two other nearby Creek towns and moved them into the settlers' new town of Tallassee, both to protect the settlement and to show the peaceful intent of the Tuckabatchee party of Upper Creeks. He also sent off a dispatch to the War Department making it clear that he regretted the killing of settlers in the eastern part of the Creek country. In fact, he declared, "We disdain the idea of shedding a white man's blood; we look on them as our brothers and will treat them as such." With this language he demonstrated a sort of human universalism that the Red Sticks, and perhaps some of the more recent Creek rebels, would not have shared. The Red Sticks believed that whites and Indians were separate and distinct people, products of separate creations, in fact, and whites possessed an evil intent that should be resisted violently. Now, however, Opothle Yahola admitted that some of the Creeks were "bad people." He declared that Neah Micco, chief of the Lower Creeks, had opposed emigration and could not govern his followers, who frequently committed depredations on the whites "such as stealing and murders." He then promised that the friendly Indians would join the whites in "chastizing [sic]" those people.[45]

Despite Opothle Yahola's condemnation of the Lower Creek rebels, and his pledge of kinship to the whites, he and the other leaders of the Tuckabatchee party had some sound political and economic motives for moving quickly to aid the settlers against the rebels. First, some of the Upper Creeks were starving and their chiefs wanted food from the whites. Second, the headmen had to do something to ensure that U.S. retribution, when it finally arrived, would not fall on their own heads. They certainly remembered how Gen. Andrew Jackson had taken land from all the Creeks as compensation for the Red Stick uprising, and they must have feared what President Jackson would do now. Third, the Tuckabatchee chiefs wanted to reestablish order among the Lower Creeks and depose Neah Micco in the process. Fourth, these headmen may have wanted to complete a political break between the Upper and Lower Creeks that had been building for some time. In fact, it seems clear that when Opothle Yahola attempted to move his people to Texas, he had no intention of taking the Lower towns with him, and Captain Page declared, after meeting with Opothle Yahola when the rebellion began, that the chief had implied that "the Lower Creeks were almost a separate and distinct people from the Upper Creeks." But most importantly, the Tuckabatchee headmen volunteered themselves for the war as a way to win back some of the power they had lost as a result of the extension of state law over them and the federal government's failure to enforce the terms of the Cusseta Treaty. Indeed, Opothle Yahola, in his correspondence to the secretary of war, as much as blamed the federal government for the rebel outbreak, reminding the War Department that the Creek Council once had the power to stop such an occurrence, but the government had allowed Alabama to take away the council's laws and police powers. Furthermore, the government had dismissed the Creek agent in Alabama, said Opothle Yahola, and in the process eliminated something his people needed: a strong leader to guide them and make their complaints known in Washington. Obviously, Opothle Yahola wanted the government to correct all these mistakes for the good of the Creeks. But the Tuckabatchees also wanted more money from the War Department, and Opothle Yahola hoped to use the rebellion of the Lower Creeks to get it. He continued to complain, as he had done for some time, that the Lower Creeks, being fewer in number and, he implied, more troublesome than the Upper Creeks, should not continue to get half the annuity payment from the government. The Upper towns should get a larger share. Finally, the leader of the Tuckabatchee party announced that his people were ready to both fight the rebel Indians and emigrate to the West, but they must receive payment for their stolen lands as compensation. These were extensive demands; Opothle Yahola was a shrewd trader; the man who would become known as "Old Gouge" was earning his nickname.[46]

Now Creek factionalism became a real problem for the rebels. Realistically, they could never have expected support from the Tuckabatchees, but they may have been surprised that Opothle Yahola would offer to fight for the settlers. That was a stunning blow. Then, in the Lower towns, John Stedham of Sawokli; John Oponee of Chehaw; and Paddy Carr, James Islands, and Benjamin Marshall of Coweta came out against the rebellion, and while this certainly damaged the rebel cause, the insurgents would have expected little else from these acculturated, accommodationist leaders. But then Tuckabatchee Harjo, leader of the Cussetas living in Chambers County, condemned the uprising and offered to join Opothle Yahola in not only fighting but exterminating the hostiles. This had to have been the rebels' greatest disappointment. For the most part, these rebels came from the Seminole party towns and were members of the Hitchitee and Euchee elements of Lower Creeks. However, most Lower Creeks were Muscogees and hailed from the towns of Cusseta, Coweta, and Eufaula. Consequently, rebel success depended on enlisting a goodly number of Muscogees in their ranks. The rebels could never count on much support from the Cowetas, who were led by men with ties to the McIntosh family, but the insurgents did get considerable help from the Eufaulas. However, the Cussetas were the key. They were largest and most influential of the Lower Creek groups and they were Neah Micco's people. As the Cussetas went, so went the Lower Creeks. At first Neah Micco supported the rebellion, and the insurgents had every reason to believe that the Cussetas, many of them impoverished, would rise up en masse against the settlers. In fact, they must have depended on this happening. But when Tuckabatchee Harjo declared himself and his followers their enemy, he split the Cussetas in two. Now the insurgents could hope only to gain the assistance of those Cussetas who lived near Neah Micco or in the other villages in Russell County. But then Neah Micco did not seem to know if he was a rebel or not, meaning that, in the end, not all that many Cussetas joined in the uprising. This left the Hitchitean and Euchean insurgents in a difficult position.[47]

The Upper Creeks and the friendly Lower Creeks then made good on Opothle Yahola's promise of assistance to the settlers. In truth, they helped the whites carry out their only successful military actions against the rebels during the entire month of May. Col. Charles McLemore of Chambers County, a noted land speculator, led one of these forays. Seeing that the settlers were leaving their homes in droves, ruining all prospect for a successful crop in the fall, the colonel decided to stop the exodus by striking at the rebel Tallassees, who had precipitated the white flight from Chambers by killing numbers of settlers along the county's southern border. McLemore called up two companies of local militiamen for the task. Then Brig. Gen. Elias Beall joined the effort. Beall, a Georgia resident, commanded that state's Tenth Militia Division, but he also speculated in Creek lands and owned an Indian trading store or, rather, grog shop in Chambers County. Consequently, he moved to protect his business interests by leading a company of volunteers from Chambers and two more from Troup County, Georgia, to attack the rebels. And finally, Capt. Nimrod Doyle, an elderly Indian countryman also involved in land deals, offered his assistance, riding at the head of nearly one hundred Coweta and Cusseta warriors. On May 15, the day the rebels moved to close down traffic on the Federal and New roads, McLemore's Chambers County force destroyed Loachapoka in Macon County, the largest of the hostile Tallassee branch villages. In the process, the colonel's troops and warriors fought a couple of brief skirmishes, buried dead settlers, collected some beef cattle and other valuable property, and captured several prisoners, including Loachapoka's chief and town prophet. The whites concluded their successful effort by confining these prisoners in the LaFayette jail. However, the Creek auxiliaries proved indispensable to the victory. According to General Beall, they "executed every order with promptness and uniformly charged the swamps at every order." Unfortunately for the whites, however, most of the Loachapoka residents had deserted the town before the troops arrived, taking the greater part of their cattle and other possessions down to Big Swamp on Euphaubee Creek. This swamp, actually a rebel stronghold, sat in the southern end of Macon County, eight miles below Tuskegee, and, General Beall concluded, the rebels were moving south to prepare "for as long and as troublesome warfare as possible." But this was not Beall's only disappointment. As it turned out, the respectable settlers of Chambers County did not take part in the speculators' "conquest" and would, in fact, call for a federal investigation of the role Beall and his kind played in causing the Indian uprising.[48]

But the speculators turned soldiers were not done. While McLemore moved on the rebel Tallassees from the east, Capt. John Brodnax moved on them from the west. Brodnax, of course, was yet another land-dealing Indian countryman and the founder of white Tallassee. He led two companies of settlers from that town and two hundred friendly Tallassee and Tuckabatchee Creeks under Opothle Yahola. On the same day that the Chambers force entered Loachapoka, Brodnax arrived at the Tallassee village of Sougahatchee, which sprawled along the banks of Sougahatchee Creek several miles north of Loachapoka. And like McLemore's men, Brodnax's troops found that their enemies had taken flight. However, Opothle Yahola and his warriors followed the fleeing Tallassees and succeeded in killing one hostile chief and putting thirteen more rebels in irons. This came as another blow to the rebel Lower Creeks. They had hoped to attract Upper Creeks to their cause, but Opothle Yahola's actions undoubtedly had a chilling effect on any Upper Creeks inclined to join the rebel party.[49]

The operations conducted by McLemore, Brodnax, and their Indian allies essentially cleared Chambers County and the adjacent Upper Creek country of rebels, causing them to retreat south of New Road into Russell County. Colonel McLemore then moved to secure the southern border of the cleared territory by constructing three forts, evenly spaced along the thirty-seven-mile Russell-Chambers county line. He situated one, Fort Henderson, at the west end of the line at the abandoned Sougahatchee village site. Twelve miles east of that, McLemore erected Fort White Plains. Then twelve miles east of White Plains, he ordered the construction of Fort Gunn. This post sat on Halawakee Creek twelve miles inland from the Chattahoochee River. McLemore meant for these posts to serve as a line of defense, separating friendly country from that of the hostiles. The forts also served as bases for offensive strikes against the rebels to the south. In fact, Governor Clay's strategic plan called for the troops from these forts to march against the Creek rebels in concert with his Tuskegee force once assembled. In the meantime, the volunteer troops stationed at the forts began to venture out on search-and-destroy missions, and within a short time, they burned nearly every Indian dwelling between LaFayette and Tuskegee. Unfortunately, many of these dwellings belonged to friendly Creeks, some of whom had gone to Tuskegee to join Governor Clay's

Alabama army. Moreover, an angry Captain Brodnax reported to Clay that whites had burned the Creek town of Notasulga, knowing that it was not a rebel settlement. Obviously, some settlers had decided to use the Creek rebellion as an opportunity to drive as many Creeks as possible off their land.[50]

The peaceable Creeks must have been shocked by this treatment, and Governor Clay soon added insult to injury. Despite the fact that Opothle Yahola and other chiefs had assisted the settlers in striking at the rebels, Clay feared the insurgency would spread to the Upper Creek towns. Consequently, when he finally arrived in Montgomery to set up his war headquarters, he summoned Opothle Yahola and a delegation of ranking chiefs to his side. He wanted to deliver a proclamation that he had designed to impress on them the gravity of the situation. He emphasized that the Second Creek War was unique in the history of Indian-white conflict, and the chiefs should make sure their people chose the right side. The hostile Creeks, he said, were not engaged in an old-fashioned frontier war with the whites, because they were no longer an independent people living far from white settlements. On the contrary, they were now citizens of the state of Alabama. They had been incorporated into the state four years earlier. Their councils, conventions, and assemblies had been abolished. Their usages and customs contrary to those of white citizens were declared null and void. Now all Creeks were subject to state, not tribal, law and that law did not allow them to wage war on other state citizens. Consequently, the whites would not treat the hostile Creeks as "fair and open enemies" as they had in past times; now they would deal with them as mere traitors. If caught and convicted, they would be hanged. In other words, Clay declared that the Creek uprising was, in fact, a civil rebellion, and the rebels would suffer accordingly.[51]

But that threat was not enough; Clay's proclamation went further. It obligated the friendly Indians to assist the whites in enforcing state law and putting down the rebellion. In particular, it imposed on town chiefs the duty of handing over their hostile tribespeople to the state, along with all property stolen from the whites. In addition, these chiefs had to apprise state officers of the movements of hostile parties. And, finally, the proclamation stated that all friendly warriors, to allay the fears of their white neighbors and keep themselves from harm, should not venture forth from their towns with guns in their hands except to join the whites in battle against the rebels.[52]

Unfortunately, Clay's rather high-handed proclamation was unnecessary. Even worse, it threatened to undo all the good work local whites had done to secure the help of friendly Creeks. Clay's words insulted them and cooled their relations with the state. Furthermore, some whites began to tell the friendly Creeks that Clay's statement meant that they were required to take up arms against the rebels or be declared hostile themselves. The Indians found this piece of news particularly galling. Many of them did not wish to fight their rebel tribespeople, in part because they knew the hatred and bitterness of the conflict would linger on after all the Creeks left Alabama and would blossom into renewed intertribal violence in the West. Furthermore, the proclamation offended those warriors who had already gone to Tuskegee to join the Alabama army. Viewing the rather lethargic pace of the state's military movements, these warriors now became convinced that the whites meant to put them forward to do the real fighting of the war, and Clay's proclamation was basically a statement to that affect. Consequently, the friendly chiefs held a council at Echo Harjo's camp, a popular gathering place twelve miles from Tuskegee. There they determined that they would not fight the rebels. Their warriors began to pick up their belongings to go home.[53]

Observers at Tuskegee were aghast, and pummeled Clay with protests. Colonel Shackleford believed that more Creek warriors would take up the rebel cause in the wake of Clay's proclamation, and he urged the governor to send even more troops to Tuskegee as quickly as possible. One George Goldthwaite, equally distressed, proposed a typically New Alabama solution to the problem. He believed Clay should appeal to the economic self-interest of Opothle Yahola and the other Indian leaders, paying each of them "three or four thousand dollars contingent on them bringing in the hostile leaders for justice." The governor did not take this advice, but he did work through Colonel Hogan to patch up difficulties with Opothle Yahola and the other chiefs. He also sought to have the state pay compensation to all the friendly Creeks who lost homes and property to marauding troops. However, as the month of May drew to a close, the Alabamians, showing once again their tendency to work at cross purposes, failed to secure a firm commitment of military assistance from the Upper Creeks. And yet they knew such assistance would be invaluable in the upcoming invasion of the Lower Creek country. In fact, N. T. Collins, a prominent New Alabama settler, proclaimed that with the help of friendly Indians the war could end in a few days, but without them the whites would have to endure months of hard fighting.[54]

Fortunately for Governor Clay, some discerning settlers knew that to gain support from peaceable Creeks, as well as to allay the anger of rebels, whites would need to deal with what appeared to be the root cause of the war: hunger. One George T. Salli, writing to Secretary Cass from Mobile, reported that the destitute Indians "are driven to the remedy of either eating their dead, or taking by force from those who have to spare." He then contended that "the money laid out in a military expedition to hurry the work of death among them, if laid out in provisions would soon restore peace and brotherly love among them and would make them friends instead of enemies." In Coosa County, settlers reported much the same and blamed the removal contractors for the hunger problem. These settlers claimed that the contractors had promised the Indians that they would emigrate early in the spring. As a consequence the Creeks sold their corn, livestock, and farming equipment to prepare for the journey. But then the emigration agents failed to take them off, so they sat in place with starvation staring them in the face. Seeing all this, militia officers stepped forward to offer the Indians material rewards for their service against the rebels. Both Beall and Brodnax, for example, allowed their Creek allies to keep everything they took from Loachapoka and Sougahatchee. General Beall noted that this method of paying the friendly Indians also had the effect of further dividing them from the rebels, who would surely be displeased by the theft. Some white residents of the Upper Creek country also gave the Indians food to win their loyalty; when their resources ran low, Governor Clay stepped in with an offer to feed the friendly Creeks at government expense until the end of the war.[55]

Now Clay was on the right track. The offer of food helped the war effort, as evidenced by the fact that Upper Creeks, following the direction of their chiefs, began to assist the settlers in capturing rebel infiltrators from the Lower towns. Soon the jail at new Tallassee filled with prisoners, including a woman who allegedly carried the news of rebel successes to the Upper towns and urged her audiences to take up arms against the whites. In addition, some of the female relatives of the male prisoners gave the settlers valuable information that helped them recover a good deal of stolen money and property. Upper Creeks also helped the whites capture twenty-one more rebels and incarcerate them in the Montgomery jail. This group of inmates included five warriors and one white man charged in the stage attacks.[56]

However, the self-interested settlers did not make very good jailers. The citizens of Tallassee complained that they could not guard their town and all the prisoners at the same time. Yet they did not want to ask the friendly Creeks to assist them in watching the captives, because they claimed they did not have enough food for themselves and their Indian allies. But when offered the option of sending their captives to Shackleford's compound in Tuskegee, the citizens of Tallassee declined. They wanted to keep the rebel prisoners with them so they could extract more information on stolen property from them. Consequently, they asked Governor Clay to send them some help. It does not appear that he did so. He had a military expedition to worry about and left the Tallassee settlers to their own devices. They may have continued to whine, but they did manage to hold on to their prisoners. Such was not the case in Montgomery, where rebel prisoners pulled off an impressive escape. One night as their guard slept in a state of "brutish intoxication," they picked the locks holding the chains around their bodies, bent the bars on their cell windows with the chains, squeezed through to the prison yard, dug a hole under the fence, and disappeared into the darkness. Neither the other jailer nor the town sentinels knew the difference, and their negligence cost the whites dearly. One of the escapees, possibly the Tallassee prophet, made his way to southern Florida and became a feared leader of the Seminole resistance movement in that quarter.[57]

Even so, the rebellion did not spread to the Upper Creek towns, and this damaged the insurgency beyond measure. Had the rebels been able to draw a sizable number of Upper Creeks into their fold, they surely could have cleared New Alabama and a good portion of western Georgia of the fearful and disorganized whites. But the early defection of Tuskenea; the weakness of Neah Micco; and the forthright antirebel stance of Opothle Yahola, Tuckabatchee Harjo, and numerous other influential chiefs undoubtedly kept numbers of Upper and Lower Creeks from joining the rebellion. Consequently, the insurgents found themselves contained in the southern counties of New Alabama and threatened by a growing army of whites on both sides of the Chattahoochee. The incohesive, fragmented, and particularistic nature of Creek society had done what the Alabamians and Georgians could not do. It blunted the impact of the uprising and severely limited its future prospects.

But for the time being, the rebels ruled the day. They had driven the settlers off their lands. They were well fed for the first time in years. They had accumulated a good supply of arms and ammunition. They had cowed the hated land speculators and penned many of them up in Columbus. They had disrupted traffic on the Chattahoochee and cut off communication between Columbus and Montgomery, making it difficult for Georgians and Alabamians to coordinate their war efforts. Furthermore, the rebels saw no white force in the field ready to offer them serious opposition. Neah Micco, now feeling more courageous, proclaimed that the whites would not fight, and that he would take back all the old Creek land in Georgia, all the way east to the Ocmulgee River. Neah Emathla, leader of the Seminole party, also seemed confident. He knew his warriors must face an avenging army in time, but he had to wonder, given the experience of his Seminole cousins in Florida, how powerful and competent that army would be. He fortified his camp on Hatchechubbee Creek and sent a message to Captain Page announcing that his people were ready to meet the white troops in back of Cook's stand on Federal Road.[58]

Indeed, the rebels had to take satisfaction in the fact that they had struck fear into the hearts of their enemies and exposed an inherent weakness in the white society that had oppressed them. For from being the united, confident monolith marching ever westward to fulfill the nation's manifest destiny, the society the rebel Creeks faced was aggressive but individualistic and competitive, divided politically and economically, and above all, insecure. In the months leading to the Creek rebellion, the respectable citizens of Georgia and Alabama faced a world of enemies. State sons fought in Texas, attempting to take that province from Mexico and place it under the rule of the world system. But rumor had it that the Mexicans were inciting the western Indians against the European Americans and would send those Natives to harass the borders of Arkansas and Louisiana. Closer to home, Georgians and Alabamians feared the roughs and outlaws in their midst, as well as the northern abolitionists who had begun to send their literature south, thereby threatening to stir up slave revolts. And then, of course, there were the French. Newspapers warned that the United States and France might soon go to war, and French ships often appeared menacingly off the southern coasts. Then the Creeks and Seminoles attacked, killing more Georgians and Alabamians to go along with those slain by the Mexicans at Goliad and the Alamo. Worse still, it did not appear the whites could defeat these Indians. Thousands of southern troops went forth to fight the Seminoles in Florida, but their efforts proved ineffective, owing to poor organization, discipline, and the fact that the general government had no workable plan for defeating a Native guerilla force in a trackless, swamp-covered wilderness. And what would happen if the Ross faction of antiremoval Cherokees rose up in arms to defy the New Echota Treaty, uniting with the Creeks and Seminoles to turn back the tide of white settlement? Contemplating this possibility, many Georgians actually feared for the future of their civilization, believing that the Creeks, in particular, meant to return their state to a state of nature. Truly, these Georgians did not see themselves as the confident expansionists one might imagine. On the contrary, they saw themselves as victims of powerful enemies, both foreign and domestic.[59]

Confronted by their own weakness and shown the tragic results of their greed, all the whites could do was argue about who was to blame for the Second Creek War. Interestingly, they did not blame the Indians as much as they blamed one another. In late May seven hundred citizens living in New Alabama and the Georgia counties nearby signed and forwarded to the U.S. Congress a memorial calling for an investigation into the causes of the conflict. The memorialists claimed that they were surrounded by "the devastating horror of an Indian war brought into existence by an abandoned and heartless association of white men," who had not only enriched themselves by cheating the Creeks out of their lands but had influenced "some of the public presses of the country by their ill-gotten wealth, making them servile organs of misstatement and falsehood." Furthermore, the outraged petitioners accused the various "Land Companies" of deliberately planning the Creek uprising to block a federal investigation into their extensive business in fraudulent land contracts. According to the memorialists, enough evidence existed to warrant the immediate arrest of several individuals living near the disaffected Indian districts, and the government should do so. In so many words, the memorialists were saying that the Second Creek War was unique. It was not so much a traditional conflict between Native Americans and whites as it was a civil war between dishonest land speculators on one side and the government and respectable settlers on the other, with the speculators fomenting and using Indian hostilities as a cover for their nefarious practices. Once again, the Natives appear only as a commodity, an unthinking, unfeeling, natural resource to be used by whites in their unending economic competition with one another. Such was the ideology of the system.[60]

Governor Clay, Colonel Hogan, James Belser, and other prominent members of Alabama's pro-Jackson Union Party commiserated with the memorialists. In fact, Clay had come away from his conference with Opothle Yahola agreeing with the Upper Creek leader that the war had been produced by white men, the retailers of spirituous liquors, and the land speculators whom Opothle Yahola called "sandshakers." Therefore, on May 24, when Clay asked the commanding officer at Fort Mitchell to supply him with the names of all hostile Creek chiefs, he also requested that the officer capture and hold all white persons suspected of instigating the hostility until the state could review the evidence against them. Clay especially wanted evidence against the land speculators, Judge Shorter in particular. He had heard that one of Shorter's associates, Dr. John Scott, was reporting that in the days preceding the outbreak of the war, the judge had told some men in his Columbus office that "dust would be kicked up in the nation" to conceal the activities of the speculators and to cause President Jackson to come in and drive out the Indians. Furthermore, Shorter had reacted to Scott's comment that the government would not let the Indians be defrauded with a certain smug satisfaction. According to Scott, Shorter assured him that the government "would let things pass and use the war to excuse everything." An angry Clay ordered Colonel Hogan to interview Scott and the other members of Shorter's audience and to collect their sworn statements as evidence against the Columbus speculator.[61]

Meanwhile, Hogan had already begun work on an odd and interesting piece of the conspiracy theory. When Hogan and Opothle Yahola met shortly after the war commenced, the chief told the agent that just before the outbreak he had heard of a paper or letter circulating among the Creeks, sent from "a people beyond the seas." He also believed that Econchattee Micco, Neah Emathla, Neah Micco, and Tuskenea had received this letter and that it had inspired them to begin the war when they did. Closer investigation revealed that the letter was the same one sent to the Creeks during the War of 1812 by Sir George Cockburn, who commanded the British fleet operating in the Gulf of Mexico. At that time, Cockburn had urged the Creeks to rise up against the United States and promised them British support and protection. Hogan also discovered the man responsible for recirculating the letter in the Creek towns in the spring of 1836. His name was William Earle, a traveling silversmith, who translated the letter for the Indians without telling them that it did not represent current British policy. Subsequently, state authorities arrested Earle on suspicion of fomenting the Creek revolt and committed him to the Montgomery County jail. Hogan then interrogated the man and acquired more intriguing information. Earle, as it turned out, claimed to be the son of Josiah Francis, also known as Hillis Harjo, the leading prophet of the old Red Stick party and himself a silversmith. Francis had escaped to Spanish Florida with the Tallassee chief, Peter McQueen, at the close of the First Creek War in 1814 and continued to preach resistance to U.S. expansionism among the Florida Indians. He also sailed to England at one point, hoping to secure British protection for the southern Natives and their remaining lands. On his return, he participated in the First Seminole War and that led to his demise. As commander of the Seventh Military District of the U.S. Army, Gen. Andrew Jackson took it upon himself to invade Spanish Florida and hunt down his old Red Stick foes and their Seminole allies. He captured and hung Francis at St. Marks in 1818. But the prophet's dream of a British-Indian alliance did not die, for Earle, supposedly conceived by Francis in London, had returned to his father's people to introduce the notion once again. However, Earle claimed he merely translated Cockburn's letter for the Creeks he visited, implying that they received the missive from another source. Hearing this, Hogan naturally concluded that the land speculators were that source, and as part of their plan to drive the Indians to war, paid Earle to distribute and translate copies of the letter as he traveled about the Creek country selling his silver spurs, bracelets, and earrings. Unfortunately, Earle died before his trial and never confirmed Hogan's suspicions.[62]

Of course the speculators did not agree with Hogan's interpretation of events, nor did the states' rights supporters in Alabama and Georgia agree with Clay. In fact, they seized on the Creek conflict "as a weapon of party warfare." The editor of the *Columbus Enquirer* contended that the idea that the war was a trick of the speculators was ridiculous, and "no one with a thimble full of brains would believe such a thing." Furthermore, the paper's editor, as an obvious friend to the Shorter crowd, sought to place all blame for the Creek war on President Jackson's partisans. Once again, he excoriated Hogan for manufacturing the whole Creek land-fraud myth to serve his own financial interests. He also accused Hogan of inciting the Indians to violence against the whites by advising one warrior to cut the throat of a judicial officer who had seized his property. Then the editor moved on to Secretary Cass, condemning him for not sending federal troops to prevent the Indian uprising. He contrasted this failure with Cass's willingness to use troops to remove white settlers from the Creek country a few years earlier. In those days, said the editor, "The hills about Fort Mitchell were covered with soldiers and tents, as though war was about to be waged with some great nation." Therefore, the editor concluded, Cass actually favored the Creeks, who had "been treated with all the tenderness, respect and forbearance due to our people, and our people have been treated like outlaws and savages." The editor did not profess to know why Cass should act as he did, but he did note that the secretary of war had grown quite wealthy while in office. The implication here was that even Lewis Cass was somehow involved in New Alabama's infamous Indian business.[63]

Finally, the *Enquirer* fired a broadside at Jackson himself, thus relieving the citizens of Columbus of blame for the war while at the same time advancing the interests of the states' rights party in the upcoming state and presidential elections. First the paper pointed to the administration's failure in Florida, where Jackson had sent three major generals and an army of five thousand men against twelve hundred Seminoles. The result: "The Indians triumphant and the whole of Florida at their mercy." Then the paper described the fruits of the Creek War: "peaceable citizens murdered, commerce on the Chattahoochee interrupted, and the flourishing City of Columbus threatened with pillage." At last the editor concluded, "Oh! the Glory of the Administration."[64]

That President Jackson and his party stood to lose popularity in the South over the issue of Indian affairs was ironic. Old Hickory owed his initial rise to political power to his victories over the Creeks and Seminoles in 1814 and 1818. But since that time the nation and the South had changed. Settlers no longer lived apart from Indians, separated by a wide frontier of wilderness. By 1836 much of the Natives' land domain had been incorporated into the U.S. economic system. Natives and whites lived as near neighbors, their economic affairs entangled. The Second Creek War grew out of this situation and consequently it was not simply an Indian versus white conflict. Farmers, merchants, speculators, outlaws, and others saw the war differently according to the own political and economic interests. There was not so much uniformity of purpose as there was when Jackson led troops against the Red Sticks. Now, in a more highly politicized and economically competitive environment, the president's states' rights opponents, the hated nullifiers, were able to picture the Old Hero, the great Indian fighter, the father of the Indian Removal Act, as a liberal in Indian affairs, a man whose leniency toward the Creeks and unwillingness to dispatch troops to the Creek country had led to the deaths of U.S. citizens. With a presidential election in the offing and a controversial Martin Van Buren as the Democratic candidate, Jackson, as well as his followers in Alabama and Georgia, must have found the Indian outbreak very embarrassing. And perhaps this helps explain why the War Department's response to the Creek rebellion, when it finally came, was so overdone.[65]

6. The Federal Response

Secretary Cass set the federal operation in motion by marshaling a supply of money and troops. On hearing of the Creek rebellion, he sent a requisition to Congress calling for an appropriation of five hundred thousand dollars to finance the Seminole War and to suppress the uprising. Congress approved the appropriation almost immediately. Cass also urged the representatives to pass a bill, pending before them, that would authorize the president to raise ten thousand volunteer troops for twelve months to fight against the Creeks and Seminoles, and possibly against the Mexicans and Indians on the western frontier. Again, Congress granted the secretary's request. But Cass was not content to fight the Creek war with volunteers alone. He sent fourteen companies of regular troops, including four hundred marines, to Fort Mitchell from their stations in the North. Then the secretary brought the navy into play. He ordered five armed steamboats to the Chattahoochee to transport military supplies, protect commercial traffic, and intercept hostile bands attempting to cross the river.[1]

Next, Cass sought out someone to direct the federal operation. Before the worst of the Creek depredations, he had instructed Maj. Gen. Winfield Scott, commander of U.S. troops in Florida, to move north and direct the campaign against the Creeks should they commence open hostilities. Now, however, Cass thought the Creek conflict merited its own commanding general. Consequently, he assigned the task to

Thomas S. Jesup, the army's quartermaster general. Cass brevetted Jesup a major general and directed him "to take command of the troops of the United States and of the militia who may be called into service from Georgia and Alabama for suppression of hostilities in the Creek country." However, the secretary reminded Jesup that General Scott was his senior, and if Scott moved to take direct charge of the Creek war, Jesup would be his second-in-command. Though this part of Cass's instructions would prove a great mistake, Jesup accepted the secretary's decision without complaint and left Washington for the Creek country on May 20, approximately the same day that Governor Clay arrived in Montgomery to take charge of his part of the campaign. In fact, Cass wrote to Clay and Governor Schley to inform them of Jesup's arrival in their quarter and to ask that they cooperate with the general and furnish him with everything he needed to wage the war.[2]

But Cass gave Jesup a larger responsibility than simply winning the war. In fact, the secretary saw the war as an opportunity to end the whole Creek problem, a problem the Jackson administration had helped to create by failing to enforce the terms of the Cusseta Treaty of 1832. Cass's solution was the complete removal of all Creeks, both hostile and friendly, from New Alabama. Claiming that all Indians were unstable and violent and that it would be impossible to keep a majority of the Creeks at peace if any portion of them made war, Cass ordered Jesup to ignore previous treaty promises and to send all the Creeks west as a national security measure. He also instructed the general to remove the Lower Creeks first, taking care to place a significant part of his military force on the southern border of the Creek country to prevent any of them from fleeing to the Seminole country once the removal began. Finally, Cass directed Jesup to feed the Indians and to treat them kindly as he ushered them into the removal camps. However, the secretary stated firmly that the Creeks "must be removed by a military force if necessary." Cass then ordered Captain Page to collect the Indians' firearms and to send them ahead of the emigrants to Fort Gibson in the Western Territory.[3]

Cass also urged haste on Jesup. He wanted to end the Creek rebellion and clear New Alabama of Indians as quickly as possible so he could devote full attention to the Seminole conflict, which now threatened to be a costly, time-consuming, and humiliating affair. With this object in mind, he told Jesup that removal was to be his top priority and "other considerations must yield." Chief among these other considerations was the land-fraud investigation. Believing that Hogan and his associates could not conduct their inquires while the war raged, and now accepting the speculators' view that the investigation had only delayed removal and thereby encouraged rebellion, Cass informed Jesup that he was stopping the search for fraud. Subsequently, he dismissed Hogan and the other investigators.[4]

Of course, Cass wanted to continue all practices that facilitated removal, including the sale of Creek lands. However, he fired all of the civilian land-sales agents and made the supervision of contracts part of the military operation. Friendly Indians could still sell their reserves, Cass decreed, but now General Jesup would oversee the process. But the secretary was quick to point out that he would no longer allow the buying and selling of land to delay Creek emigration. He declared that when Jesup was ready to remove the Indians, they must go, whether they had sold all their lands or not. The government would then sell the remaining land for the Natives at a fair price and send the money to them. Cass also said that he would look into the matter of fraudulent contracts once the war ended; if any lands had been stolen from the Indians, the government would claim them and resell them for the original allottees. He would send that money west as well. However, none of these considerations applied to the hostile Creeks. The secretary declared that they had forfeited their claims to the land.[5]

Thus, Cass outlined an ambitious plan of action for General Jesup, but the task became even more difficult and complex when Jesup arrived in Augusta, Georgia, on May 27 to find Maj. Gen. Winfield Scott already there. His Seminole campaign having failed miserably, Scott decided to leave Florida to take charge of the Creek war as a means of redeeming his soiled military reputation. As a general of the old school, trained in the War of 1812, Scott believed that military success lay in strict organization. In his fight with the Seminoles he had attempted to assemble a superior force of well-equipped troops with which to surround and crush the enemy. However, he believed this plan had failed because of factors outside his control—supply problems, disease, inefficient volunteer troops, the guerrilla tactics of the Seminoles, and the insubordination of a competing general, Edmund Gaines. Consequently, Scott had not lost faith in his methods. He felt sure he would have better success with the Creeks because he assumed they were "accessible." Scott thought, for example, that the Creeks, unlike the Seminoles, lived in large towns that could be easily located and destroyed. Furthermore, while Florida remained difficult and unknown terrain for most whites, New Alabama was familiar territory to numerous settlers and military men, and while it held its fair share of swamps, the Creek country was much easier to traverse than Seminole Florida. Given these "facts," Scott took command of the Creek war, determined to prove that a well-organized, well-supplied army, with all its parts working together, could encircle and destroy a Native enemy relatively quickly and with minimal losses to the United States.[6]

Scott also hoped to do a better job of public relations in Georgia than he had done in Florida, for he had learned a good deal about the insecure and prickly nature of southern society. Witnessing the wholesale flight of settlers from the Seminoles in northeast Florida, Scott made the mistake of publicly accusing the refugees of cowardice. Furthermore, he pointed out to them that the Indians might not be their worst enemies. The general believed that white cattle thieves had caused much of the panic, spreading rumors of Indian advances so respectable settlers would desert their plantations and leave their livestock unattended. The Floridians responded to these accusations by burning the general in effigy on the streets of Tallahassee, as well as accusing him of calling off the Seminole campaign too early and disbanding his army. They complained that he had left them to the mercy of the victorious Indians. But this was not the general's biggest mistake. In one of his official letters, widely published, he expressed a preference for "good troops" over volunteers, a sentiment that gained him the ire of many citizen soldiers already dissatisfied with their service in Florida. Consequently, on arriving in Georgia, the general sought to explain away his comments in the state's newspapers to set aside any prejudice the Georgia volunteers and militiamen might have about serving under him in the Creek conflict. And even though many Georgians and Alabamians had fled from the Creeks, Scott did not criticize them for it.[7]

His public relations work done, the general now began to organize his new military campaign as if he expected to engage the British in the War of 1812 all over again. He intended to set up headquarters at Columbus, and as he expected several thousand regular troops, volunteers, and drafts to assemble at or near that town, he first took up the important task of arming and feeding such a host. Even before leaving Florida he appropriated rifles, tents, ammunition, accoutrements, and the like leftover from the Seminole debacle, then sent these articles by steamboat up the Altamaha and Ocmulgee rivers to Hawkinsville, Georgia—only seventy-five miles overland from Columbus. On arriving at Augusta, the general cleaned out the federal arsenal there and ordered some 150,000 rations from Savannah and Charleston. In addition, General Scott sent a requisition to the army's quartermaster and commissary departments in New Orleans for 250,000 more rations, forty or fifty sacks of salt, and four hundred felling axes. He also ordered arms, ammunition, and even cannons from the federal arsenal at Mount Vernon, Alabama. Then Scott contracted with local businesspeople to supply his army. He purchased ten wagon loads of subsistence in Augusta and made arrangements with parties in west Georgia for the daily delivery of two hundred bushels of corn to the Chattahoochee River posts already run by Georgians. Finally, the general stationed a commissary agent at Hawkinsville and instructed him to purchase sixty thousand pounds of bacon, 350 head of cattle, and up to 1,500 bushels of corn meal for all his soldiers.[8]

Strategy was the next important issue. Scott wanted to outline a plan of military operations that everyone would understand and follow. This had not been done in the Florida campaign, and Scott was determined that the mistake not be repeated. He and General Jesup left Augusta together, traveled down Federal Road to Milledgeville, Georgia's capital, and on the evening of May 28 met with Governor Schley to decide on a course of action. Scott was surprised, and pleased, that independent of each other the three men had already developed the same strategy for fighting the war. Very quickly, then, they agreed to a war plan designed to bring about the rapid destruction of the Creek rebels while at the same time prevent any retreating hostiles from reaching, and combining with, the Seminoles in Florida.[9]

The grand plan called for a division of the U.S. Army of the South into two parts. General Scott, as commander of the first corps would take charge of all the Georgia troops assembling about Columbus, as well as half the regulars marching in from points north. Then, assisted by Governor Schley, Scott would station a portion of the Georgia force at all the important river crossings between Columbus and Roanoke, forty miles to the south. These troops would keep the river open for navigation and protect the Georgia settlements from incursions by the rebel Creeks until Scott was ready to lead the main body of Georgia troops and regulars down the river to Irwinton, Alabama, or some other point south of the rebel Creek towns. In the meantime, General Jesup would take charge of the army's second corps, made up of all the Alabama troops and the other half of the regular force. After setting up his headquarters at Tuskegee and mustering all the Alabamians into the federal service, Jesup would take the majority of his troops to Irwinton to join Scott, and together the men would march north against the rebels. If the Natives decided to fight in a body, the army would destroy them. If the rebels decided to break and flee, they would have to run north into the heart of the Old Creek Nation, not south to Florida. However, should any of the hostiles attempt to escape across the Chattahoochee on the right flank of the advancing army, to reach Florida through southwestern Georgia, they would run head-on into all the troops previously stationed at the various river posts on the Georgia side. Thus contained, the rebels would have no choice but to die or give up their resistance.[10]

Scott, Jesup, and Schley set out for Columbus together the day after their discussion and arrived at their destination on the evening of May 30, much to the relief of the town's residents, whose anger and pessimism now turned to joy and a general sense of benevolence. The governor and the federal officers took up adjoining rooms in the upper floor of the McIntosh Hotel, and the town's newspapers began to sing their praises. The editor of the *Columbus Herald* proclaimed that seeing Scott and Jesup together awakened feelings of the "more chivalrous days," when the two men served together in the War of 1812. The states' rights *Enquirer*, however, went out of its way to compliment Schley, a Union supporter, stating, "what may have been our former prejudices against him, these are now forgiven. We see him as the governor of our State, prompt and decisive on an important occasion, and think him entitled to the thanks of the State." For his part, Schley appointed a number of states' rights supporters to his staff, and while his ranking officer, Major General Sanford, was a Union man, he was not unpopular with Columbus's ruling elite. Indeed, Sanford had probably endeared himself to Judge Eli Shorter and the other speculating nullifiers in Columbus by his lax, if not criminal, performance as a government certifying agent and Indian land-fraud investigator. In fact, the states' righters seemed to have sworn off state party politics for the duration of the Indian rebellion so they could come together with their fellow Georgians to wage a "War of no ordinary character." Instead, the editor of the *Enquirer* now turned his venom on northerners, particularly those northern editors who insinuated that the Creek war had been contrived "to squander a portion of the public money among the southern people." The Georgians, now briefly united in a common cause, did not want to hear such criticism from people who supported the hated tariff, a "specious system of legalized robbery" that absorbed the "South's treasure."[11]

Despite the warm reception by the townspeople, Scott, Schley, and Jesup immediately received word of the first of what would become a series of setbacks for their plan of operations. They discovered that Governor Clay, now ensconced in his headquarters at Montgomery, had drawn up war plans of his own and intended to attack the rebel Creeks on June 5, less than a week away. Scott believed he had to get control of Clay or see his own plan, and the war, spoiled. He did not want the Alabamians approaching on the hostiles from the north, scattering them to the winds. Yet the general knew he could not have all the Georgia troops and U.S. regulars mustered, equipped, and ready to march with the Alabamians by June 5. Therefore, he sent a letter to Clay, informing the governor that he was "opposed to any premature operations against the enemy" and asking him to delay the advance of his troops until June 15. Scott also received Schley's help in this regard. The Georgia governor wrote to Clay, telling him that the war would be over in a few weeks if he would only wait for Scott's plan to unfold. He also warned Clay that an early move on his part might cost lives and do little good.[12]

Scott then sent Jesup to take command of the Alabama army. Traveling with an escort of 120 Georgia cavalrymen and regular officers, the general galloped west along the dangerous New Road, passing within three miles of Neah Micco's town, to arrive at Tuskegee on the evening of June 5. Fortunately, he found the Alabama troops still sitting in place. On the morning of the seventh the general set out again, bound for Clay's headquarters in Montgomery. He did not have to travel that far. On reaching Line Creek, the border between Old and New Alabama, the general came face-to-face with Clay, who was making his way to Tuskegee to take command of his army and lead it against the Creek rebels. The two men dismounted and held a discussion on the spot, then rode to Tuskegee together the next day.[13]

Clay and Jesup established a rapport and seemed to agree on all important points. Both men supported the Jackson administration, and Clay was delighted to hear that Jesup meant to remove all the Creeks from Alabama. He was also glad to hear that the general would take over distributing food to the friendly Indians. Both men thought rations were necessary both to procure a Creek auxiliary force and to keep the rebellion from spreading to the hungry Upper Creek towns. Jesup and Clay also agreed on the causes of the war, blaming the speculators more than the Indians and declaring that the guilty parties should be brought to justice. Furthermore, the two men agreed on the competence of the unfortunate Colonel Hogan, whom Jesup authorized, along with Hogan's speculating enemies William Walker and Thomas Woodward, to recruit a force of friendly Creek warriors to participate in the drive against the rebels. More importantly, however, Jesup learned that the governor, who had already delayed the Alabama advance because of supply problems and the inability of Gen. John Moore and his Fourth Division troops to get to Irwinton on time, was now willing to turn the state's troops over to Jesup to command as he saw fit. Consequently, the two men came away from their meeting with a feeling of mutual respect and the ability to work well with one another.[14]

Unfortunately, on his return to Tuskegee, Jesup began to discover that local conditions, particularly the nature of southern civilian soldiers, would cause him serious problems. First, he found that Alabama's troops were proud, independent, and very particularistic. They mistrusted the "General Government" and refused to join the federal service. The Alabamians wanted to fight "on their own hook" under their own officers. Beyond that, they believed that if they entered into the U.S. service, Jesup would extend their three-month enlistments and march them off to fight the Seminoles once they were done with the Creeks. Fortunately, impassioned pleas by Governor Clay and Gen. John H. Patterson, commander of Alabama forces, overcame the men's intransigence and they finally agreed to muster into the federal service and accept Jesup as their leader. But then Jesup learned that he had to be careful what he ordered the Alabamians to do, for, as he complained to Cass, "Southern militia and volunteers cannot be induced to labor." To remedy this difficulty, the general recommended to the secretary that the army quartermaster department form "a corps of artificers and laborers" for use in the southern states. But this was not Jesup's most vexing personnel problem. He soon discovered that the independent Alabamians had little desire to cooperate with the Georgians in warring on the Creeks. Some even resented the Georgians for coming onto Alabama soil to attack the Indians. Furthermore, the Alabamians were impatient and wanted to get on with the fight according to Clay's original schedule. They pressed a sense of urgency on their new commander and made it difficult for him to wait for Scott and the Georgians to ready themselves for the main campaign.[15]

Jesup also had to contend with the concerns of an extremely fearful settler population. In fact, he entered New Alabama just as another wave of panic washed over these people. New reports of rebels entering the Creek camps in northeastern Alabama came in to Tuskegee and

Montgomery. The citizens of that area, residents of Benton, DeKalb, and Cherokee counties, believed that the Creeks, and some Cherokees, would surely attack them, and they wanted to raise troops to patrol the Indian settlements and stop the sale of alcohol to the Natives. Similarly, the citizens of Talladega and Tallassee were convinced the rebels meant to assail them, and Clay was forced to divert troops from Tuskegee to protect those towns. At the same time, Col. Charles McLemore reported that the situation had deteriorated in Chambers County. The rations the settlers had been giving the friendly Indians were growing scarce, more local Creeks had turned hostile, and McLemore feared that if he marched the county's troops to join Jesup's army, these Indians would start to massacre white families. Consequently, McLemore said he would not obey the governor's order to come to Tuskegee. Furthermore, the colonel objected to Jesup's plan to remove all the Creeks from Alabama as soon as possible, showing once again that New Alabama's whites were not united in their approach to Indian policy. McLemore, supposedly representing the respectable citizens of Chambers County, pointed out that many of his county's Indians had lost their lands to theft, and if the removal agents tried to make them go west before they recovered those lands or received a fair price for them, the injustice would cause even more Natives to turn hostile and the settlers of Chambers would suffer. Moreover, McLemore claimed that a quick military removal would protect the interests of the land thieves, who had always advocated such a removal "to secure their stolen lands against reversal." This argument made perfect sense, but McLemore had more than a concern for peace and justice in mind. Like some of the other land speculators who led the Alabama militia units, he wanted suspect land contracts reversed so he could repurchase the property from the Creeks before they left Alabama. A quick military removal would deny him this opportunity.[16]

Then disturbing news came in from the south. A group of Eufaula Creeks, formerly friendly, attacked settlers in the eastern end of Pike County in Old Alabama. On June 3 these Indians fired on an elderly farmer named Pugh and his two sons as they worked in a field. Pugh and one son fell critically wounded; the other son escaped. Later the same day the Eufaulas ambushed members of the Watson family as they herded their cattle away from the Indian border along Three Knotch Road, which connected Columbus with Pensacola in the Florida Territory. Thomas and Peter Watson were killed, along with Peter Watson's son-in-law. Another man, shot through the mouth, escaped with some unwounded family members. Pike County's citizens responded to these attacks by taking flight, much to the chagrin of General Moore, who happened to be marching through Pike County on his way to Irwinton when the murders took place. Moore arrived at Monticello, the county seat, on June 7 and was astonished to find that even though the village stood a good twenty-five miles from the Old Creek Nation boundary, all of its inhabitants had fled. Hearing that the Eufaulas were collecting in a large body somewhere near the Watson place and the headwaters of Pea River and intended to ravage Pike County, Moore notified Clay that he should send arms and ammunition to Monticello so the terrified whites could return and defend themselves. Then the general resumed his march to Irwinton, leaving two companies of troops behind at the Watson home to guard the border between Old and New Alabama.[17]

But bad news continued to follow Moore. He received a report that the rebel Creeks were amassing before Irwinton, preparing to finally wipe the place away. He responded to this news by making a forced march to the village, only to discover the report was false—another product of fear. Even worse, Moore found no provisions for his six hundred tired troops or forage for his horses. Expecting hot food, comfortable tents, and other conveniences at the end of their long journey, the general's men grew surly. Then, when they learned that they must swear into the federal service and take orders from General Scott, they became mutinous. Moore managed to calm them down for the time being, but he wrote to Clay that unless he received food and forage, he could not hold his men in line at Irwinton. Clay was mystified. In anticipation of Moore's arrival and the commencement of the Alabama campaign against the Creek rebels, he had sent ten or twelve wagonloads of flour and bacon to Irwinton, along with $1,500 for the purchase of corn for the horses. Now it was all missing, gone the way of the Creek lands.[18]

Hearing all this, and running low on food and forage himself, General Jesup decided he must leave Tuskegee and take some action against the rebels. As he would later explain, "a general panic pervaded the whole country; the Indians were plundering, murdering, and burning in all directions, and there seemed to me to be a great danger of several of the frontier counties breaking up entirely unless some decisive movements were made." Consequently, Jesup decided to march his men thirty miles up Federal Road to set up camp at Long's station, where he believed he would find corn and a small stockade. And because the Long place was only a few miles from Neah Micco's town, the general claimed that his camp there would intimidate the chief and his warriors and help end the recent rash of depredations on settlers and their property. However, Jesup meant to do more. On June 11 he wrote to the secretary of war that the line of communication with Columbus was in the hands of the enemy and that circumstance, along with the recent hostilities, inclined him to "strike a blow at once." The general never named the target of this blow, but it must have been Neah Emathla's war camp, which sat on the northern reaches of Hatchechubbee Creek between Tuskegee and Irwinton. Before advancing, however, Jesup sent out an Indian runner to Neah Micco's town to present the elderly chief one last chance to give up the rebel cause, declare himself friendly, and bring his people into an internment camp in Macon County. This camp sat alongside New Road near Echo Harjo's camp. Jesup also issued an order that all friendly Indians must move north of Federal Road; any Natives found south of the thoroughfare would be treated as hostiles by his advancing army.[19]

Of course, any attack on the Indians at this point would be a violation of Scott's orders, but General Jesup, given the dire circumstances he found in Alabama, believed he had the right to change the commanding general's plan. He also may have been moved to haste by Cass's instructions that he defeat the Creeks as soon as possible so the government could concentrate its efforts on the even more troublesome Seminoles. Unfortunately, Jesup failed to reveal all his motivations and plans to General Scott. Later Jesup would say that he wrote two letters to Scott explaining his decision and subsequent movements, but one letter was never mailed and the other, entrusted to an Indian runner, never reached Scott. In fact, the only report Scott received from his second-in-command during the first two weeks in June was one dated June 8. In this short, cryptic, unsatisfactory report, Jesup did say that the hostiles were committing outrages south of Tuskegee and he would need to make some sort of troop movement in that direction, but he never mentioned striking a blow at the heart of the Creek rebellion.[20]

General Scott was not a little distressed. Since arriving in Columbus, he had experienced his own set of problems. He found nothing organized and no magazines or stores in place in the town. Then he fell ill, confined to bed. And worst of all, he lost contact with Jesup and his second corps. Now reports reached his sick room that some of the Creek rebels, including the members of Jim Henry's band, were attempting to escape across the Chattahoochee. These people had decided not to face the invading troops and had assembled near the mouth of Hatchechubbee Creek to build rafts and canoes for transporting their families, captured slaves, and assorted plunder over to the Georgia shore. Simultaneously, they sent war parties against the Georgia river posts and plantations, attempting to clear a path for themselves and to steal horses for the overland trip to the Seminole country. Even before Jesup arrived in Tuskegee, rebel warriors crossed the river within one mile of Fort McCreary to loot and burn the Quarles and Brewster plantations before moving on to Florida. Then, on June 3, Georgia troops fired on a large party of Creeks coming over the river at Boykin's Ferry, twenty-five miles south of Columbus. Shortly thereafter, fifty rebels attacked the Watson plantation farther upstream and carried away three slaves. And finally, on June 9 Capt. Hamilton Garmany's troops from Gwinnett County fought a desperate battle with a reported 250 Indians at Shepherd's plantation, four miles north of Roanoke. These troops sustained serious losses, and only the timely arrival of reinforcements from forts McCreary and Jones saved them from annihilation.[21]

Scott heard all these reports with a good deal of frustration; he did not have enough efficient troops to counter the rebel move. By June 9 only one company of regular soldiers had arrived at Columbus, and while numbers of Georgia militiamen and volunteers poured in, they were not yet prepared to fight the enemy. In fact, Governor Schley had called up too many men. Approximately four thousand citizen soldiers descended on Columbus and West Point, many more than Scott could effectively supply. And even though the *Columbus Herald* praised the "chivalry and prowess" of these troops, most of the men turned up without muskets or rifles. Nor were many of them particularly good soldier material, if Jacob Rhett Motte, a regular army surgeon, is to be believed. To Motte, the Georgia civilian soldiers "presented a glorious array of dirks, pistols, and bowie-knives, with no scarcity of dirt." Furthermore, it seemed to the surgeon that "every ragamuffin of Georgia, deeming himself an invincible warrior, had enlisted under the standard of Mars, which many from their conduct must have mistaken for the standard of Bacchus, as they observed the articles of the latter god with much greater reverence." Apparently, General Sanford agreed. Initially, he set up his headquarters at Fort Ingersoll, just across the river from Columbus, but later he marched his host of Georgia troops three miles farther into Alabama, because a "town life did not well suit soldiers." Worse, the Georgians, like the Alabamians, objected to federal service and agreed to it only if they could enlist for three months. General Scott also had to promise them that he would not march them away to fight the Seminoles in Florida, especially not in the heat of summer.[22]

Nevertheless, Scott did the best he could under the circumstances. He armed the first six to eight hundred men to appear in Columbus, purchased ammunition from town merchants, and sent these troops downriver to forts Twiggs, McCreary, and Jones, as well as to all the other smaller guard posts between Columbus and Roanoke. Then, when Capt. William C. Dawson arrived in town with a volunteer company carrying their own arms, Scott ordered these men and a part of the Columbus artillery company to board a local steamboat, the *Metamora*, for duty. Scott instructed Dawson and his troops to cruise up and down the Chattahoochee, prevent any rebels from crossing the stream, and destroy all Indian "canoes, bateaux, flats, rafts, etc." He also told

Dawson to call at all the stations on the river, render assistance to the posts as needed, and spread the word of any enemy movements to all troops along the Chattahoochee.[23]

Unfortunately for Scott, most of the untrained and undisciplined Georgia troops did not distinguish themselves against the rebel Creeks. On seeing Indians they tended to shoot first and then retreat precipitately, later magnifying rebel numbers to justify their flight. Governor Schley was so used to this happening that when messengers reported that there were more than two hundred Indians at the Battle of Shepherd's Plantation, the governor noted sarcastically "that would do very well for 30 or 40." Similarly, a company of Monroe County troops, after fleeing from the Creeks at Turner's Field on June 16, claimed to have faced from two to three hundred warriors. However, Thomas J. Stell reported that he saw only twenty-five or thirty Indians and the Monroe troops refused orders to stand and fight, preferring to run for the safety of Fort Jones. When Stell sent word of the so-called battle to Columbus, he summed up his view of the war on the Chattahoochee with the words, "Worse and worse—just had a fight with the Indians—got whipped."[24]

But in all fairness, the civilian soldiers did have their successes. Dawson's steamboat patrols located and destroyed enough Native watercraft to keep many of the would-be rebel escapees confined to New Alabama. Furthermore, the use of steamboats allowed the whites to win at least one significant battle over the Creeks. This fight occurred on June 4, when 125 Georgia and Alabama troops concealed themselves on board the *Metamora* at Irwinton and set off upriver to lure the Creeks into a confrontation. The ploy worked. Two or three miles north of Roanoke, 150 Indians fired on the apparently unprotected steamer. The troops then raised up and returned fire, dropping rebel Creeks and a few of their black allies off the river bluff.[25]

General Scott took little pleasure in such victories. He wanted to put his grand plan in motion, but he could not arm and supply his army quickly enough given its large size, the relatively primitive state of transportation, and the insecurity and acquisitiveness of the local population. Heavy rains virtually closed the road from Augusta and

Milledgeville, two steamboats bringing supplies up the Ocmulgee River to Hawkinsville exploded, and the various federal arsenals and supply depots in the South found it difficult to meet the demand for arms and rations created by troop buildups on the Texas frontier and in Alabama, Georgia, and Florida. Captain Harding, for example, informed Scott he could not fill the general's order for ordnance from the Mount Vernon arsenal, because Governor Clay and his Alabama troops had already taken all his stores, including 6,800 muskets. Furthermore, Georgia businesspeople showed that they were just as willing to cheat the federal government as they had the Indians. Wagoners charged the army exorbitant rates for hauling provisions, and speculators moved into Columbus even before the army to buy up corn and bacon for resale to Scott and his supply officers at an excessive profit. Furthermore, the exaggerated fear of the frontier populace interfered with Scott's ability to feed and equip his troops. Inexplicably, Gen. William Irwin of the Alabama militia, already unduly afraid of a slave revolt in Irwinton, created yet another panic when he sent a letter to the Georgians informing them that two thousand hostile Creeks had crossed the Chattahoochee and were laying waste to the southern counties of Georgia, murdering men, women, and children indiscriminately. This wild tale caused more of the inhabitants of southwest Georgia to fly from their farms and villages, and the conductor of the wagon train carrying arms from Hawkinsville to Columbus, in an effort to avoid the imaginary Indians, took a circuitous route that delayed his arrival at Scott's headquarters for three or four days. Given all these difficulties, Scott would not have his first corps armed and ready to march downriver to Irwinton until June 21.[26]

Neither Jesup nor General Moore believed they could wait for Scott. In fact, Jesup was "anxious to secure the country and General Scott himself from the evil consequences of a plan there were neither means nor time to execute." Rather than trust the Georgia sentinels on the Chattahoochee to keep the rebels from flying to Florida, Jesup and Moore determined to seek the Indians in their camps and capture them before they had time to flee. Jesup led his troops out of Tuskegee on June 12 with the intention of setting up camp at Long's Station. He had previously sent word to Moore to bring his men north from Irwinton. Jesup meant to move south from Long's, link forces with Moore, march against the Creek strongholds, and defeat the enemy in ten to fifteen days. However, if the rebel force proved larger and stronger than supposed, then Jesup would combine his army with Scott's and bring the Indians into submission in a month. But unknown to Jesup, General Moore was already taking his own independent action against the Creeks. Responding to yet another rumor that a rebel force of two thousand warriors was assembling to attack Irwinton, Moore left the village on June 13 to attack High Log, the main Euchee settlement on Hatchechubbee Creek. He marched at the head of his mounted regiment of Fourth Division troops and four companies of infantry previously stationed at Fort Bell, a tiny guard post on the south fork of Cowikee Creek. General Scott knew nothing of this operation or of Jesup's new scheme for winning the Creek war. Before leaving Tuskegee, Jesup sent a letter purporting to explain his actions, but, mysteriously, this missive never reached Scott at Columbus.[27]

General Jesup had good reason to expect a victory, because the rebel party had started to come apart. A good portion of the rebels had decided not to stand and fight, and they left their strongholds to attempt escape across the Chattahoochee. Tuskenea sat safely ensconced at Tuskegee with the settlers, disclaiming any involvement in the war. Then, on June 10 Neah Micco made his final decision. Since the outbreak of war, he had played both ends against the middle. Early on he sent messages to Fort Mitchell denying his culpability in the rebellion and even dispatched peace emissaries to Columbus to discover what might be the penalties for surrender. But, at the same time, he harbored some of the more active rebel warriors in his town and even ordered his men to watch New Road in hopes of ambushing General Jesup's escort on their return to Columbus from Tuskegee. But now, sensing impending doom from an invading host and understanding from Jesup that he could come in and surrender without punishment, Neah Micco left Watoolahawka with some of his townspeople, declared himself at peace, and sought the protection of Echo Harjo's internment camp a few miles southeast of Tuskegee. Simultaneously, a few of the other leading chiefs of the Lower Creeks came in with their immediate followers. Cusseta Harjo, Alloe Harjo, and Esphany Emathla brought in more inhabitants of the various Cusseta villages. Tuckabatchee Fixico, one of the headmen of Ositchee, also turned up, along with Alock Micco, from Chewocollee, a branch village of Lower Eufaula. Then Yarginhar Micco, from Wetumpka, the main settlement of Broken Arrow town of Lower Creeks, made an appearance, followed by Ositchee Emathla, from Euchee, and Neharthlockko Harjo, from Tolowar Thlocko, an offshoot village of Apalachicola town. Finally, one of the headmen from Sawokli and another from Hatchechubbee, an Hitchitee settlement, came in to seek refuge with their people. These desertions, amounting to some 1,300 or 1,400 Indians, left the hardcore group of rebels concentrated along the Euchee, Hatchechubbee, and Cowikee creeks in Russell and Barbour counties.[28]

The loss of Neah Micco was followed by an even more stunning jolt to the rebel cause: the decision of Upper Creeks to join Jesup's army. As Jesup and General Patterson neared Long's Station with their 800 troops, 450 warriors rode up to join them. This body included Autosees, Upper Eufaulas, Tuskegees, and some Lower Creek Cussetas, all recruited by the land speculators and Indian countrymen Thomas Woodward, William Walker, and L. B. Strange. Echo Harjo and the Cusseta chief, Tuckabatchee Harjo, led these warriors along with "the celebrated Jim Boy," an Autosee chief who had once been a Red Stick warrior and had participated in the attack on Fort Mims during the First Creek War. But these 450 men were only the vanguard of the friendly contingent. An additional 1,200 more warriors were supposed to meet Jesup at Long's on June 16. Colonel Hogan had recruited this larger group of warriors at the white settlement of Tallassee, where many of the Upper townspeople congregated for safety and to receive food.[29]

Led by Opothle Yahola and Menawa—the elderly Oakfuskee chief who commanded the Red Sticks at their last stand at Horseshoe Bend in 1814—this last body of men left Tallassee on June 15 and proceeded to Warrior Stand on Federal Road, near the head of Big Swamp in the western part of Macon County. Big Swamp sat in the middle ground between the main Upper and Lower Creek towns, and several clusters of

Indian settlements rested along the edges of the swamp. These settlements now contained a considerable population of disaffected Indians. Besides the group that followed Neah Micco into Macon County, the rebels of Loachapoka and Sougahatchee, including the murderers of the Davis family and other settlers, also lived about Big Swamp. Before he led his warriors into Russell County to join Jesup, Opothle Yahola wanted to call on these people and warn them against any further hostile acts. Otherwise, he would be leaving a great number of his people, as well as many settlers, undefended at Tallassee, should the swamp dwellers decide to renew their attacks. Jesup concurred in this strategy and also wanted Opothle Yahola to stand between him and the subdued Indians in Macon County so they would not interfere when he drove on the rebel strongholds in Russell and Barbour counties. Then, to assure that no one would mistake his warriors for a massive rebel force, Jesup directed Opothle Yahola and his men to wear white scarves on their left arms and white bands around their heads as they marched to the fray.[30]

As far as convincing would-be rebels to keep the peace was concerned, Menawa certainly proved himself a great asset to Opothle Yahola. Having been nearly shot to pieces by General Jackson's troops twenty-two years before, Menawa was a large, scarred, and frightening man, and surely an intimidating presence as he rode into Big Swamp as a servant of President Jackson. His whole being gave testimony to the dangers of warring against the European Americans. And Menawa's transformation from enemy to ally, along with that of all the other former Red Sticks in the Alabama force, is not difficult to explain. Unlike many of the Lower Creeks, they knew firsthand the futility of fighting the whites. Moreover, the frontier line, or geographical buffer zone, that separated Creeks and whites in 1813 and afforded Indian towns some protection had now disappeared. Rebellion in the present time could lead to the complete destruction of all the Creeks. But most importantly, the Cusseta Treaty and the influx of speculators, liquor dealers, and settlers it inspired had finally broken down the Creeks' independence. They had become a dependent people. Many of them were starving and in debt, trapped in a downward economic spiral not of their own making. And whereas numbers of the Lower Creeks, along with a few of the Tallassees, sought to recapture independence through armed rebellion, the Upper Creeks by and large sought an alliance with the whites for much the same purpose. They knew they needed money to pay off their obligations, to buy food and clothes for their families, and to prepare themselves for their long and arduous journey to the West, where they could, at least for a time, live apart from whites and become self-sufficient once again. In this regard, General Jesup promised to pay friendly warriors for their service in the army and to deliver to them their annuity payment before they emigrated, including the share that would have gone to the Lower Creek rebels. Of more immediate importance, Jesup and Governor Clay promised to feed the warriors' families during their period of service. These were all strong inducements, and the Upper Creek fighters soon proved themselves well worth the investment.[31]

In fact, the Upper Creeks demonstrated their value as allies almost immediately. When Jesup's column arrived at Long's on June 14, the general discovered what he should have known all along: the rebels had stolen or destroyed all forage and provisions for miles around the station. Furthermore, the general found no stockade there. Apparently, the local settlers had fled, and the rebels had dismantled "the wild cow pen" they left behind. Jesup intended to leave all his baggage wagons under guard in this stockade before setting out to chase the enemy unencumbered. Now he had to change his plans. He decided to move directly on to Irwinton for food and supplies. However, since Neah Emathla's camp, situated in the swamp on the northern reaches of the Hatchechubbee, also lay near the road to Irwinton, the general meant to attack it along his way south. Marching ahead of the main body of troops, Jim Boy's warriors, early in the afternoon, arrived at the wide, well-worn trail that connected Neah Micco's town on Big Euchee Creek with Neah Emathla's camp eight miles to the south. These men turned onto this trail and followed it to Big Spring, a popular Indian campground located midway between the two Indian villages. They had just dismounted to rest and eat when, much to their surprise, they saw Neah Emathla himself, accompanied by his son and daughter, coming down the trail. Pretending to be friends, the Upper Creek warriors decoyed the chief into their midst and captured him. Now surrounded by his adversaries, many of whom cried out for his blood, the elderly veteran showed no sign of shock or despair, nor did he attempt to escape his captors. However, two of his rebel warriors, coming along behind the chief, witnessed his capture and rushed around the spring and on to the Hatchechubbee to warn of the enemy's approach. Nevertheless, Jesup now had the second of the rebels' two principal chiefs in custody—thanks to his Creek allies.[32]

The main body of troops came to Big Spring a short time after Neah Emathla's capture. Knowing that the rebels at Neah Emathla's town were warned and ready for his attack, Jesup decided to make camp until his reinforcements arrived. He knew Opothle Yahola's warriors were drawing near, as well as a fresh battalion of militiamen from northern Alabama. Jesup also wanted to open a line of communication with Scott. He wrote a letter to the general informing him of the Alabama army's position and finally told his superior officer of his intention to attack Neah Emathla's stronghold. He also told Scott that he would not be pushing on to Irwinton after all. Since he had only two days' provisions for his army, he would fall back on Fort Mitchell for supplies after attacking the Hitchitee camp. He asked General Scott to have corn and rations ready for him when he arrived.[33]

The troops may have been glad for the day of rest at Big Spring, but the friendly Creeks were not. Without telling Jesup about his plans, Jim Boy led one hundred of his warriors and three or four of their white friends away from camp. This party then traveled up the Indian trail to Neah Micco's town and entered it. Owing to Neah Micco's defection, most of his rebel followers had moved down to join Neah Emathla's people; only a few remained in their home village along with those of their tribespeople who had never taken up the rebel cause. Jim Boy's men encountered no opposition as they rode into a town loaded with plunder. The sight of it astonished one of the white men, William Baskin Stogner. Besides captured slaves and fine furniture, he saw such "niceties" as writing paper, china, and cut glass in abundance. The nature of this stolen property spoke volumes about the competitive and predatory nature of New Alabama society. First, it showed the wealth and refinement of some of the Indians' neighbors; second, it showed that the Indians believed they could sell such items to a different class of whites. Why else would the rebel Creeks, in a state of war, bother to carry off and store such items? Of more immediate importance, however, Jim Boy's warriors and their white friends found food: purloined beef, bacon, and pork in large quantities, both cooked and uncooked. They sat down for a much needed feast, and afterward Jim Boy took a few of his men across Euchee Creek into another part of the sprawling town. There the men killed a Euchee warrior and took twelve prisoners before returning to Big Spring.[34]

By the morning of June 17 the reinforcements had not arrived, so Jesup moved ahead without them. However, the difficulty of driving all the wagons over the rough road slowed the army's movement to a crawl. The men traveled only a few miles the whole day and had to make camp at the spot where the road crossed Hatchechubbee Creek, still nine miles from Neah Emathla's stronghold. But as they settled in for the night, Opothle Yahola and his warriors, along with a number of white men from Tallassee and other parts of Tallapoosa County, finally arrived. Now Jesup had a force of more than two thousand men, well armed and eager for battle. Unfortunately, a message also arrived in camp, bringing opposition from an unexpected quarter. The message came from General Scott, who had not received Jesup's message of the previous day but had heard about Jesup's expedition from a civilian traveler recently arrived in Columbus from Tuskegee. Scott also heard that General Moore was marching up the country from Irwinton. He was shocked. In fact, he could scarcely believe the news, for he had expressly forbidden any offensive measures until the entire force of Alabamians, Georgians, and regulars could move in unison. One can only imagine his anger as he hurried off a direct order to the commander of his second corps: "I desire you instantly to stop all offensive movements (if you are in command) on the part of the Alabamians until the Georgians are ready to act, say on the 21st instant, when the greater number of them will be armed and ready for the field."[35]

Jesup received the order but thought he had come too far to turn back. He feared the consequences if he tried to restrain his headstrong Alabama troops. Even more, Jesup believed his Native warriors would lose all confidence in him and leave his army if he stopped his advance against the enemy. Consequently, the general made a momentous decision. He would later write the secretary of war that, because General Scott was "unacquainted with the circumstances under which I was placed, I felt it my duty to disregard the order." Therefore, early the next morning, Jesup closed on Neah Emathla's village, which "was strongly fortified by nature, and one of the best selected spots for an Indian battle, in the whole Creek Nation." In fact, the village sat on a peninsula of land surrounded on three sides by creeks and swamps. The only open approach was from the north, through a sparse pine forest. This layout resembled the one Andrew Jackson faced at Horseshoe Bend in 1814, and Jesup chose to fight his battle the same way Old Hickory did back then. He sent his Indian auxiliaries across the creeks to the back of the camp, while he brought his troops and artillery down through the forest. He intended for the two divisions of his army to close on the town at once, catch the rebels in a vice, and defeat them, while at the same time denying them any avenue of escape.[36]

The strategy did not work this time. Having lost their leader, the rebels decided not to make a stand in the village. They moved out to a nearby swamp and waited, then took advantage of a flaw in Jesup's plan. Owing to the slow movement of the army's wagons and field pieces, the Upper Creek warriors entered Neah Emathla's village from the south before the white troops arrived. This left an avenue of escape for the rebels and they moved away from the troops unopposed. The women and children set out for the impenetrable swamps and canebrakes of the Cowikee creeks in Barbour County. The rebel warriors lingered to the rear to protect against pursuit and to look for a chance to strike a blow against the whites, should they camp too near the town's swamps. They never got the opportunity. Jesup drew his men back from the swamps to camp on high ground, while the friendly Creeks spent the night safely ensconced in the village. A few angry rebels prowled the outskirts of the place all night, and early the next morning they fired a few ineffective rounds at Jesup's allies before moving south to join their families.[37]

Jesup was disappointed by his failure to trap the rebels in Neah Emathla's village, but at the same time he must have considered himself fortunate. On inspecting the place, he gained a great deal of respect for Neah Emathla's military prowess. The elderly chief put the settlement in a spot where it would be easy to defend against superior numbers. In addition, he had constructed it as a fort, with stout houses arranged in a way that would give the inhabitants the best firing angles all around. In fact, Jesup stated that the Hitchitee camp was one of the strongest military posts he had ever seen. Neah Emathla meant to defend his ground if pressed, and had his followers remained in the town, they could have inflicted serious casualties on Jesup's army. Obviously the sudden loss of their chief broke their resolve, but Jesup and General Patterson also believed the rebels chose to flee because they did not want to fight other Creeks. In fact, the general gave most of the credit for his success to his Native allies, admitting that his troops would have encountered hard fighting and a much longer campaign without them. Furthermore, the rebel retreat in the face of Opothle Yahola and his sixteen hundred warriors tends to support the belief that a major part of the rebel plan for taking back and holding their country was to enlist the Upper Creeks in their cause. Failing to do this, they knew they could not hold their territory for long and a stout defense of their war camp was unnecessary. Indeed, the realization that the Upper Creeks would not take part in the rebellion may have led to Neah Micco's sudden capitulation as well, even before Jesup's expedition began.[38]

Certainly the general believed that the rebels were ready to quit. Shortly after he took Neah Emathla's town on June 18, the reinforcements from northern Alabama arrived, bringing his total force to more than three thousand men. With an army of this size, Jesup believed he could force the hostiles into a major battle within twenty-four hours and end the war entirely in a mere five days. All he had to do was continue his march toward Irwinton, which would carry him right to the Cowikee creeks, where the disillusioned rebels had fled. Furthermore, Jesup's troops found one hundred head of cattle and a considerable quantity of corn at Neah Emathla's town, freeing them to resume their march south without having to go back up-country to Fort Mitchell for provisions.[39]

But then General Scott did what the rebel Creeks could not. At this crucial point in the war he stopped Jesup's advance, giving the rebels a much needed respite. While on a visit to Fort Mitchell, Scott received Jesup's letter from Big Spring informing him that he was bringing his Alabamians to that post for provisions. Shocked for a second time, Scott dashed off a note to his wayward second corps commander. It said that Scott was astonished to learn that instead of proceeding straight to Irwinton as ordered, his trusted friend had marched down through the heart of the Indian country "seeking private adventures." Scott then accused Jesup of deliberately inverting his plan of operations by conducting a sweep through the hostile territory rather than north from Irwinton. Furthermore, Scott informed Jesup that he should not have assumed he could get supplies at Fort Mitchell. In fact, Scott likened Jesup's unauthorized advance into the Indian country and desperate appeal for provisions to General Gaines's foolhardy march on Fort King in Florida during the recent Seminole campaign, a march that Scott obviously believed had doomed his army's efforts to bring a quick end to that Indian uprising. Scott then told Jesup he could give him provisions at Fort Mitchell only by taking them from the Georgia soldiers who were already living hand to mouth. Those supplies would then have to be replenished before the Georgians could move downriver, and any further delay would cause untold trouble, as the Georgians were already near mutiny for being held in check. Worse still, Scott feared what his unruly troops would do when they discovered that the Alabamians were already operating and would soon appear at Fort Mitchell, forty-five miles out of position according to the general plan of attack. Therefore, to prevent such trouble, as well as stop any further "erratic movements" before his grand plan could take effect, Scott ordered Jesup to not only delay his march but encamp his force somewhere in the neighborhood of Fort Mitchell until further orders. As Jesup would later explain, he did not feel himself at liberty to disobey this second order from Scott. Consequently, he turned command of his troops over to General Patterson and rushed off to Fort Mitchell to reason with Scott and obtain his permission to continue his advance against the enemy.[40]

Jesup arrived at Fort Mitchell only to find that Scott had returned to Columbus. However, he did discover a steamboat loaded with eighty thousand rations tied up at the fort's landing on the Chattahoochee. Now Jesup, already angry, began to lose control of himself. He fired off a letter to Scott justifying his march on the grounds of necessity, to save the lives of Alabama citizens. He also accused Scott, his old comrade at arms, of treating him "with a degree of harshness which is cruel in the extreme." Then Jesup began to play politics. He wrote a letter to Francis P. Blair, editor of the *Washington Globe*, a Democratic Party organ. He complained that Scott had abused him and mishandled the Creek war, stating that the "scenes of Florida were enacted all over again." He blamed the Seminole failure on needless delay and said the same tactics threatened to ruin the Creek campaign. He contended that Scott could have put an end to the war only one week after his arrival had he used all the men available to him properly. Instead, Scott "thought it necessary to adopt a splendid plan of campaign upon paper, and make everything bend to it." Jesup then went on to say that he would ask to be relieved of command and would request an investigation of the war effort. Finally, he told Blair to "let the President see this letter; he, I am sure will approve the promptness with which I have acted, when he shall be sensible that I have, by the movement I have made, tranquilized the whole Alabama frontier."[41]

No one sentence could have caused more trouble in that day and time. President Jackson was already incensed over the conduct of the Florida war. In fact, he had accused the Florida settlers of being "Cowards And Breeders Of Cowards" for running from the Seminoles. Then he had seen the citizens of Georgia and New Alabama fly from the rebel Creeks, and General Scott, whom Jackson had once challenged to a duel, seemed unable to defeat the Indians. This was especially difficult for the president to understand as he had made short work of both the Creeks and Seminoles in 1814 and 1818, when both groups were more powerful. Jesup's letter gave Jackson proof that something had been mismanaged and convinced him to order a War Department investigation of both the Seminole and Creek conflicts. Moreover, Blair decided to publish Jesup's letter for the nation to see. In so doing, he turned a strategy disagreement between two generals into a national political issue, with Jackson's Democrats supporting Jesup and his Whig opponents backing Scott.[42]

However, that controversy lay a couple of months in the future. For the moment, Jesup and Scott reached an accommodation. They finally met on June 21, and Jesup presented a full report of his operations. Scott, not knowing of Jesup's letter to Blair, decided to accept Jesup's explanation of extenuating circumstances. Though Scott did not completely agree that the danger to Alabama citizens was as grave as Jesup said, he did conclude that the general acted as he thought he must and had not purposefully set out to disobey orders for his own aggrandizement. (Later, Scott would change his mind again and decide that this was exactly what Jesup did.) The two men parted on good terms, with Jesup agreeing to submit himself to Scott's command in all future endeavors.[43]

For the next few days Jesup presided over what he thought was the conclusion of the war. Following the capture of Neah Emathla's town, his Creek allies scoured the country south of Hatchechubbee Creek and brought in numbers of blacks, along with fifty or sixty Indian captives, including another rebel chief, Kia Motla. Jesup sent some of these captives back to the swamps to tell their families and friends that if they surrendered they would be treated fairly. As a result, on June 22, approximately three hundred warriors and more than five hundred women and children surrendered to General Patterson at his camp. These Indians also brought in a large number of horses and mules and more slaves to turn over to Patterson. The friendly Creeks then went to their camp and appropriated their other property and plunder, while Patterson marched the prisoners themselves to Fort Mitchell for safekeeping. A newspaper reporter "witnessed the grand entrée" of this "drove of savages" into the fort and reported that "they were all ages, from a month old to a hundred years—of all sizes, from the little papoosie [sic] to the giant warrior." Moreover, the elderly Blind King

(Micco Chooley) of the Euchees' High Log town "rode in the center of the throng, and although it had been many years since he beheld the light of day, yet his feelings of hostility continued to rankle at his heart." The soldiers penned the warriors inside the fort but allowed the women and children to camp outside its walls. Two days later, Jesup led six companies of mounted troops and sixty Indians under Jim Boy on a reconnaissance of the country between Fort Mitchell and the Hatchechubbee. He left Opothle Yahola stationed in the center of Russell County to protect the white settlements farther west from any rebels that might fly in that direction to escape this latest sweep of their country. In the course of this movement, Jesup and Jim Boy managed to capture 113 more rebels, led by the Chehaw chief, Yahola Harjo. These Indians apparently surrendered at Sawokli, located near the mouth of the Hatchechubbee. This town was a seat of the rebel party and had been the center of operations for all the Hitchitee horse thieves operating in Georgia before the war.[44]

Simultaneously, General Moore's troops had some success. After burning sixty or seventy homes at the abandoned High Log town on June 16, they went to work searching the branches of Cowikee Creek for rebels. Another detachment of Moore's men, stationed at Watson's farm, captured three hundred of the Eufaulas who threatened Pike County. In accordance with instructions received from General Jesup, Moore surrendered all his prisoners to William Walker and Jim Boy of the Upper Creek force. These prisoners included two hundred warriors—two of whom allegedly killed the Watsons—and five headmen, most notably Tustenuggee Harjo, the principal chief of Eufaula, and Yelker Harjo, who had been a loud critic of the land frauds. Another group of Eufaulas gave themselves up at Echo Harjo's camp in Macon County.[45]

By this time, June 25, Jesup had ended his operations and settled in at Fort Mitchell with about 1,200 prisoners. In fact, he believed that nearly all the hostiles had surrendered or been captured, with the exception of Jim Henry's small band of Euchees and Chehaws, and a few other distracted rebels who were "wandering without concert or object" waiting for "a favorable opportunity to come in." Neah

Micco and several hundred more prisoners still loitered about Echo Harjo's camp. But the friendly chiefs no longer recognized him as a Creek headman. As a follow-up to their activities against the rebels, these chiefs met in council at Big Spring and broke Neah Micco as a headman, lowering him to the status of a "common Indian." General Patterson thought this act finished the war, and he gave most of the credit to the Indian allies for the "bloodless" victory. He even wrote to Governor Clay, recommending that the state of Alabama give Jim Boy and Opothle Yahola a "public testimonial of appreciation." Thomas Abbott, Hogan's assistant, agreed and praised the force of friendly Creek warriors to the commissioner of Indian Affairs, saying that "their formidable presence and conduct is in no small degree to be attributed the speedy and happy termination of these difficulties." Meanwhile back in Tallassee, John Brodnax would be even more effusive in his praise of Opothle Yahola, the "prime minister" of the Upper Creeks. He informed Jesup that the Tuckabatchee chief had told the headmen of all the towns that "should the white people leave their homes through fear or otherwise and leave property it must be protected, that nothing was to be spoiled, all saved for the owners. That even the chicken and the egg must be saved." Furthermore, Brodnax credited Opothle Yahola with saving Tallassee from destruction at the hands of the rebels, giving talks to the Creeks that kept "thousands from being hostile" and lending military assistance that brought the war to a "speedy close."[46]

But General Scott was not so optimistic. He believed the rebels might be more numerous, and still troublesome. While Jesup thought he had defeated the Indians, Scott saw that no real battle had occurred. He believed that many of the rebels had scattered and gone into hiding. Furthermore, Scott received word from an "intelligent negro" recently escaped from the hostile camps that four or five hundred Indians were congregating on the southern reaches of the Hatchechubbee and Cowikee creeks to prepare for an escape across the Chattahoochee. More importantly, perhaps, the general now commanded more than four thousand Georgia troops and a considerable force of U.S. regulars, including approximately four companies of infantry and six companies of artillery. Yet few men in this mass of troops had seen any action. Scott must have known he could not simply send them home. Consequently, the general decided to follow through with his original plan. He intended to move down the Chattahoochee from Columbus, cross the river below the mouth of Cowikee Creek, and then lead his Georgians, regular troops, and Moore's Alabamians in a sweep up the country. He apprised Jesup and Patterson of this fact and ordered them to move their troops down from the Hatchechubbee at the same time. With this maneuver, Scott hoped to catch the remaining rebels in a vice and crush them.[47]

Scott would have liked to have employed Opothle Yahola's warriors in the operation but he could not. Once again, his own subordinates foiled his design. Just before marching down the Chattahoochee, he received word that Opothle Yahola's men had left their camp at Big Spring and gone home, because Jesup had not met his commitment to feed their families. Moreover, a few of the ragtag Alabama troops, in lieu of finding any hostiles to kill, had waylaid a scouting party of friendly Euchees sent out from the Big Spring encampment by Colonel Hogan. These troops knew the Indians and that they served in the army, but that did not matter. They led the Euchees to a spring near the road and gunned down three or four of them "for pure malice." These murders further discouraged the Upper Creeks from military service, and the chiefs warned Hogan that they would have a difficult time controlling their young men if the whites ignored the killings. General Patterson and many other Alabamians deeply regretted this episode, for, as one correspondent stated, all the good that had been done in the war to that point had been through the "instrumentality" of the friendly warriors. But the damage was done. Scott now lacked enough Creek scouts to find the rebels he sought. This fact hindered his grand expedition. Furthermore, it gave more evidence that the aggressively competitive and violent nature of local society not only caused conflict with the Natives but posed the greatest obstacle to defeating the rebels and moving the whole body of Creeks west.[48]

But Creek society was fractured as well, and Scott did succeed in recruiting some Creek allies. Not surprisingly, he gained the assistance of a company of acculturated Cowetas to serve as scouts and spies for the Georgians. Following the example of the late William McIntosh, these men took up arms in favor of the settlers, doing their part to defend the economic system and bring "civilization" to the Creek country. John Riley, John Chopco, Benjamin Marshall, and John Marshall offered their services to Scott, along with the redoubtable Maj. Paddy Carr, who brought one hundred of his followers to the general's aid.[49]

Joining Scott's troops for the march down the Chattahoochee, Carr, the Native planter and land speculator, presented an impressive picture of a cultural intermediary, a man living at the meeting point of two worlds becoming one. On the one hand, he looked and acted like an "Indian." He was handsome, well-built, and dark-skinned, with a face tattooed in ancient Creek fashion. He and his men wore buckskin leggings, calico hunting shirts, and scarlet turbans with strips of white cloth tied around the center to mark them as Scott's allies. Furthermore, everyone knew Carr was brave and generous. He accumulated wealth but practiced the traditional custom of redistribution by caring for his less fortunate tribespeople. It was said he was kind to strangers and the poor. But on the other hand, Carr also acted like the white plantation owners and slave holders around him. He was generous because generosity gave him power and won him followers. In fact, Carr associated mainly with whites, made himself the centerpiece of their balls and parties, sought after profit, and, of course, worked closely with the Columbus gang to take advantage of Creek land allotees. Carr could also be haughty and proud and quick to defend his honor. He possessed a violent streak and was indicted at least once for the murder of another Indian, but apparently never convicted. Letters sent to the War Department, supposedly written by Carr, say that he favored removal as the salvation of the Creeks, and he undoubtedly believed, like the other McIntosh party members and the acculturated Cowetas in general, that the Creeks must educate themselves and utilize the market system to survive.

But all that was easy for Carr and his fellows to say. Like the southern planters they mimicked, they had certain advantages their tribespeople lacked. Carr, for example, was a mixed-blood. His father was an

Irishman, who may have abandoned him. Consequently, the long-time Creek agent, John Crowell, took Paddy in tow and taught him how to be a success. Carr received good instruction in the ways of making money, most notably how to gain wealth by farming Creek tribal lands, free of charge, with slave labor. He also learned how to gain access to Creek annuity payments, as every year he saw John Crowell and his brother, Tom Crowell, who operated a store near the agency, put the Creeks in debt and then take off a healthy cut of the government money as their compensation. Carr became a trader himself and learned to marry well, tying himself to the wealthy bicultural families of Coweta town. He had three wives in the end, one being the daughter of the respected Lovett family and another the daughter of William McIntosh himself. By 1836 Carr had amassed a considerable fortune, including seventy to eighty slaves, and a large stock of cattle and horses. But he had lost much of this property to the rebellion, and now he marched with Scott to quell an uprising that sprang, in part, from his own participation in the Indian business, his own exploitation of tribal resources. In the end, Carr, and others like him, represented, in sociological terms, "points of weakness" in Native society, for by mortgaging themselves and their land to the colonizers and the economic system, they became the keys, not to a meaningful acculturation of Natives, but to a loss of tribal integrity and independence. Perhaps more than any other single individual, Paddy Carr's actions, indeed his very being, revealed the tangled and destructive nature of interethnic conflict and collusion in New Alabama.[50]

Scott sent his regular troops and Indian allies down the river on June 20. Paddy Carr's warriors led the way, followed by a small battalion of U.S. artillery. More artillerymen brought up the rear. Three days later a detachment of 450 marines arrived in Columbus, and Scott promptly dispatched them down to Bryant's Landing to construct a new picket post and supply depot called Fort Henderson on the Alabama side of the river. As all these troops set out, Georgia's newspapers made it appear as if the U.S. counterattack had just begun, completely ignoring all the work done by Governor Clay, General Jesup, and the friendly Creeks. One published public address urged the Georgians to "go, teach the people of Alabama, that if they can tamely submit to see the flag of their country insulted and degraded, you cannot." This same address, one of many with the same theme, then sought to bolster the pride of the troops by reminding them "that there never was, and never will be, a quality possessed by man that will so highly recommend him to the female sex as personal bravery." And finally, the papers suggested that the troops would be in for the fight of their lives, as "Osceola will probably appear to lead the Creeks." However, the soldiers were told not to worry if they got killed or scalped for "your fellows will avenge you."[51]

The troop movement was an impressive sight. Poised on a hilltop to the rear of the first column, Jacob Rhett Motte, the army surgeon, described the marching soldiers and Indian warriors as a huge snake winding its way along through the open pine woods near the river. The troops, marching double file and wearing sky blue fatigue uniforms, black leather caps, and white cross-belts, made up the glittering body of the serpent, while the mounted Indians in vivid attire resembled the head. Far ahead of the snake rode "Major Paddy" on a cream-colored horse covered with a scarlet blanket. A colorful beaded bullet pouch hung at his side, he swept the summer insects away from his face with a beautiful eagle feather fan, and his turban was "distinguished from the rest by the graceful floating of an eagle's feather."[52]

On June 22 the column reached Fort McCreary. Passing beyond, the troops immediately entered "the scene of Indian devastation," the place where the advance of Georgia's cotton culture collided with New Alabama's Native resistance movement. For eight miles before they reached Roanoke, the river road they traveled "presented nothing but a continued series of black heaps of ashes, all that remained to mark the once happy homes of many now homeless families." They arrived at the once beautiful village of Roanoke at sunset to find the most dramatic evidence of the Creek rebellion. According to Motte, "Nothing marked the place where once it [Roanoke] stood but [more] heaps of ashes and a few charred logs. Of many proud mansions which lately reared their fronts to the admiration of the beholder, not one was left." The site did not remain desolate, however. The five hundred federal troops set up Camp Gibson on the spot.[53]

Then came the Georgia civilian soldiers. After finally receiving a shipment of one thousand rifles from Hawkinsville, General Sanford and 2,000 of his militiamen and volunteers, 160 of them still unarmed, left Columbus on the same day the advance column of regulars reached Fort McCreary. Then, once Sanford was well away, General Scott marched out of town, leaving behind 600 men to guard the river passes north of Columbus and 400 more troops to protect Columbus itself. Another mounted battalion of Georgia troops remained in town to receive additional supplies and transport them down the river. This group of soldiers soon sent along more arms, accoutrements, and two huge flats for Scott's men to use in crossing the Chattahoochee.[54]

On the evening of June 24, General Sanford's troops arrived at Roanoke, marching up to Camp Gibson with their drums and fifes playing martial music and their "banners of gaudy hues waving before their eyes." Surgeon Motte was astonished. The large bustling camp of soldiers stood in striking contrast "to the dark and smoldering ruins around" and Motte, a southern aristocrat recently arrived from his comfortable home in Charleston, had trouble "identifying himself" with this frontier spectacle.[55]

Scott arrived at Camp Gibson the next day and prepared to cross the river. Unfortunately, he had to delay the move because of another wandering subordinate. General Moore had taken off on his own to attack the rebels congregating between the Hatchechubbee and Cowikee creeks. This move, like Jesup's before it, threatened to completely disrupt Scott's plans by giving the rebels an opportunity to escape downriver and make a crossing south of Scott's army. Consequently, Scott sent a messenger to find Moore and to tell him to move his force back below the south fork of the Cowikee to cover Scott's western flank as he made his push northward.[56]

On June 26 Scott led the federal troops and half of the Georgians across the river. The other Georgians remained behind to reinforce the various river posts. They would prevent any rebels seeking to escape Scott from crossing over to Georgia. Once in Alabama, Scott immediately set up Camp Sanford as a base of operations and promptly set off up the country to scour the Cowikee swamps, a "terra incognito" to all but Carr's friendly Creeks. The Georgians marched in two columns, one led by Scott and the other by Sanford. Gen. John R. Fenwick led the brigade of federal troops, which consisted of three small battalions of artillery. Owing to heavy rains, Scott could not take his wagons along on the trip. He left them at Camp Sanford, along with his sick men, under the protection of a lone militia company and a six-pound cannon. He then transported his army's supplies, including four days' rations, on packhorses.[57]

Dr. Motte also remained in camp, taking care of between sixty and seventy men, most of whom "suffered cases of dysentery and diarrhea from drinking the rotten lime-stone water of the country and the hardships of camp life." In addition, Motte found plenty of opportunities to observe the laziness and lack of discipline that made it so difficult for state militiamen to defeat the Creeks. In fact, Motte and the few other regulars in camp were so unwilling to trust their safety to militia sentinels that they stayed awake to do their own sentry duty, making "the grand rounds several times a night." Unfortunately, in doing this they ran a greater risk of being shot by the militiamen than the hostile Indians. Furthermore, on observing some of the night guards, Motte discovered that, despite all the danger, "the eyelids of these votaries of Morpheus had so great a desire of associating together, as to exclude all remembrance of their being on post."[58]

As it turned out, Scott's grand march was short and ineffective. General Moore never got to his correct position; General Jesup, having turned over command of the Alabama troops to General Patterson, remained at Fort Mitchell, preparing hostile captives for removal; General Patterson carried on business as usual from his camp north of the Hatchechubbee. If there were any rebel Creeks about, they defied Scott's plan by refusing to confront him, by not allowing themselves to be "accessible." For his part, the general had no desire to pursue the rebels into their hidden recesses. Consequently, he declared that no substantial body of hostiles remained in the wild in the Lower Creek country. He spent only two or three days in the swamps and arrived back at Fort Mitchell on July 2 with only one Indian and one black man captured. The only real achievement that might be attributed to the march was the capture of Jim Henry by Jim Boy on or around July 1. But again, friendly Creeks, not Scott's troops, performed this feat. For the most part, Jesup's earlier bold maneuver had turned Scott's march into a mere formality, an anticlimax. In fact, Jesup believed that Scott had only scared Indians into hiding, and when the Georgia army retired, they would come out and surrender to the friendly Creeks. But Scott's expedition did serve some purpose. It allowed the general to contend that he completed the plan of operations he drew up at Milledgeville. Now he was ready to announce what he could not let Jesup declare ten days before: "the war was virtually over" and the federal operation against the rebel Creeks was a success.[59]

But was it a success? Many New Alabama settlers and Indian countrymen knew that a significant number of rebel fighters remained unsubdued. In fact, one observer wrote from Fort Mitchell that the general impression that the war was nearly finished arose solely from the fact that "the hostiles have *now* no leader of a fierce, bold, and military genius, to plan, to execute, and to control them." Thus, the rebels could not concentrate for a fight, but small, scattered parties could still do damage to the whites. Given this evidence, one has to ask why Scott was so quick to declare victory. Why did he change his earlier assessment that the uncoordinated, piecemeal movement of fairly ineffective troops had only scattered the Creek rebels? Why did he fail to acknowledge that Jesup's "victory" resulted more from the fractured nature of Creek society than from the military prowess of his army? And why did he alter his belief that the war would not end until the rebels suffered a decisive defeat in battle? Perhaps the general pronounced his campaign a success to keep peace with Jesup, his old comrade. Perhaps his brief march through rebel territory actually convinced him that few hostile warriors remained on the loose. Or possibly General Scott simply needed a quick victory to salvage the prestige he lost in Florida. As to his motives, we can only speculate. But one fact stands out. The federal operation of June and early July 1836 did not result in the decisive victory both Jesup and Scott declared. It certainly did not end the Second Creek War.[60]

7. Flight through Southern Georgia

Local observers were correct: the Creek war was not finished. Because the Alabama and Georgia troops did not execute Scott's strategy, a significant number of rebels remained in the wild. Many of these people now set out for Florida, winding their way through the south Georgia swamps to the Seminoles, attacking settlers and fighting militiamen and volunteer troops all the way. In fact, the real combat of the Second Creek War began only after the supposedly decisive federal operation in June. Yet this part of the story has remained to this day largely untold. The engagements of July and August 1836 occurred in isolated swamps, hammocks, and fields scattered throughout the sparsely settled southern counties of Georgia. But no federal troops participated in these contests, hence few "official reports" reached Washington or the national periodicals. The war continued largely out of sight for most of the nation's citizens. In fact, it took place in the unobserved interspace between Jesup's removal efforts in Alabama and the dramatic Seminole War in Florida. For this reason, historians, writing from federal records, have focused on those two events, ignoring the full extent or significance of the second stage of the "minor" Creek conflict.

Actually, rebel Creeks broke out of Scott's trap even before he had time to set it. And they did so under his very nose. However, this realization was slow to dawn on the general. Stopping off at Fort Mitchell

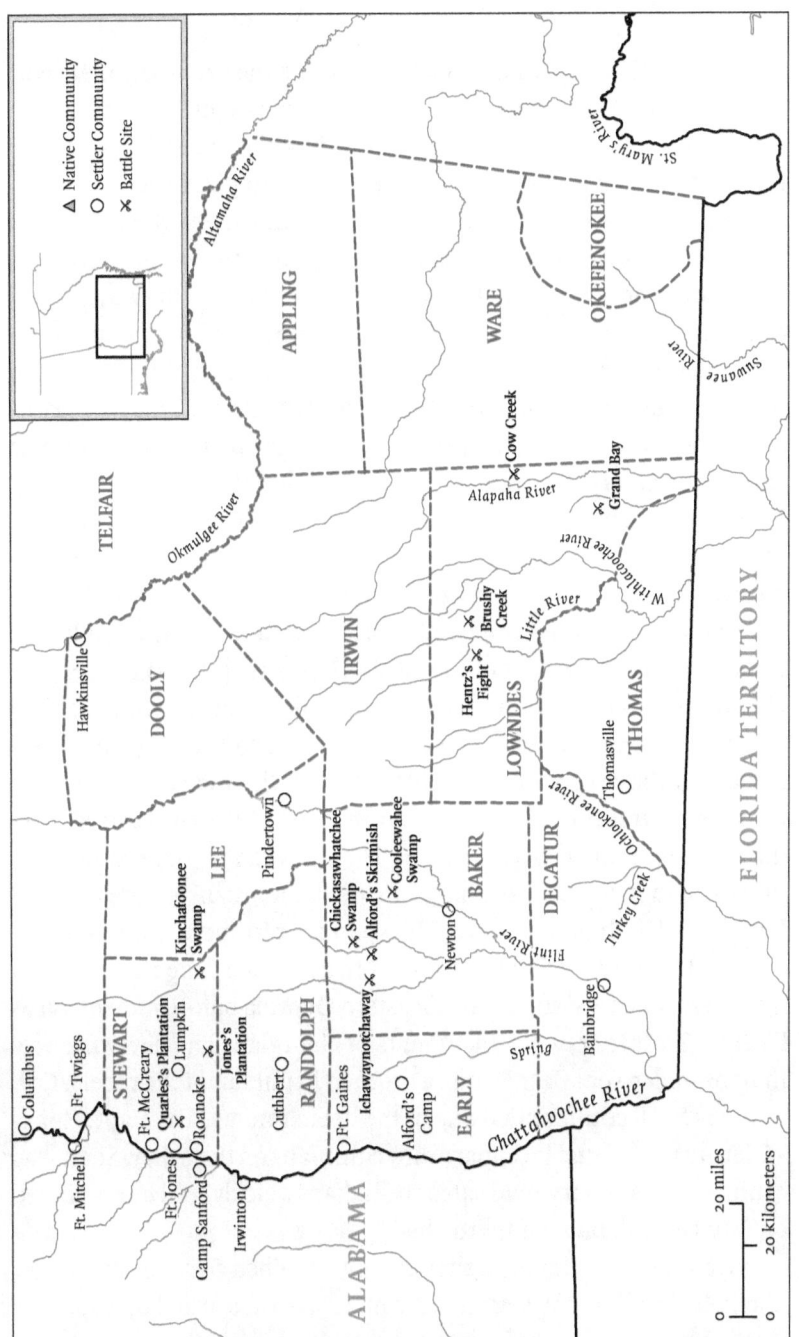

4. War in southern Georgia

to confer with Jesup on his march down the river to Roanoke, Scott learned that no less than eighty of the warriors who surrendered to Patterson and Jesup had fled from custody while the Alabama troops escorted them to Fort Mitchell. In fact, they had given themselves up without their weapons simply to get information about their enemies, and once achieving that object, they returned to the woods, retrieved their arms, and set out for Florida. Even worse as far as the whites were concerned, the rebels who remained in custody admitted that before surrendering they sold or gave their guns and ammunition to all those tribespeople who wanted to continue the resistance. This news concerned Scott, but he was not overly alarmed. Owing to all the outposts and armed Georgians on the river, he believed that few, if any, rebel Creeks had, or would, escape across the Chattahoochee.[1]

On arriving at Roanoke, Scott began to discover his mistake. He received reports that two Indian trails had been discovered south of Roanoke, one three and a half miles away and the other only one and a half miles away from the village. The first trail was only a day old and the second two days old. Both trails led away from the river in a southeasterly direction toward Florida. Scott was appalled. He attributed the escape of these Indians into the interior of Georgia to "some extraordinary neglect" on the part of the river guards. Yet the general retained his optimism. He believed that only about sixty Indians had made the crossing, mostly the more inveterate of Neah Emathla's Hitchitee warriors. His sources informed him that these men had "abandoned their families" to attempt a desperate flight to the Okefenokee Swamp in southeastern Georgia before moving on to Florida. Scott sent two detachments of Georgians and a few friendly Indians under Tom Carr, Paddy's brother, in pursuit of the rebels. Col. Thomas Beall commanded one of the detachments, and Capt. Henry W. Jernigan, a noted local partisan, commanded the other. Scott was confident these men would catch the Indians quickly, and he continued on into New Alabama unperturbed.[2]

But the bad news for the troops continued. When arriving back at Fort Mitchell after the completion of his march, Scott learned that another small party of warriors had just that day escaped across the river just a few miles south of the fort. The very next day militiamen in Stewart County, Georgia, found still another group of Indians, twenty-five to thirty, traveling in a southeasterly direction toward Florida. They engaged these Creeks in a three-day running battle through the Kinchafoonee Swamp before calling off the chase. Even worse, the men Scott sent to pursue the fleeing rebels south of Roanoke discovered that those Indians numbered not sixty individuals but as many as three hundred. Furthermore, they were mounted, well-armed, and supplied, and word traveled upriver to General Scott that many black Creeks, as well as slaves taken from New Alabama plantations, traveled with the Native rebels. The whole crowd was moving along the old Indian trail that led across the southwest corner of Georgia into Florida, passing through sparsely settled Baker and Thomas counties along the way.[3]

Most distressing of all, this last body of rebels did not try to pass by to the Seminole country unnoticed. They meant to exact vengeance on the Georgians as they went. They began by shooting a man near Cuthbert. Then, as they passed down the west bank of Chickasawhatchee Creek on Sunday morning, June 25, they began to slay Georgians in earnest. They killed a Mr. William Jones, his wife, and several children. They also murdered Joseph Hollowell and his children, along with the Nix family. Then they destroyed John Padgett, his child, and a widow named Hayes. By Sunday evening thirteen to fifteen whites lay dead; others nursed serious wounds. The Creeks scalped none of the victims, but the mangled appearance of the white children gave evidence that the rebels had beaten them to death "with sticks and lightwood knots." As word of the assaults spread, other families living in Baker County either fled to the center of Georgia or congregated in local stockades.[4]

The viciousness of the rebel attack on the Chickasawhatchee community suggests that the Lower Creeks bore the inhabitants of that locale some special animus. Some Chehaws, Ositchees, Hitchitees, and Euchees lived in the area prior to the Washington Treaty of 1826, and they had returned there often since their removal to New Alabama. Probably these Natives never got along well with the settlers who supplanted them on the Chickasawhatchee, and so they decided to settle old scores as they traveled to Florida. Certainly one white family died for this reason. When the Creeks attacked the Jones clan as they sat at their breakfast table on that Sunday morning, they did so because the family lived in a house formerly occupied by a man known to abuse Indians.[5]

Following the killings, the Creeks entered the Chickasawhatchee Swamp, forty miles east of the Chattahoochee and approximately one hundred miles south of Columbus. Said to be from fifteen to twenty-five miles long, and in places anywhere from one to eight miles wide, the swamp was a forbidding place. Colonel Beall and Captain Jernigan arrived in the vicinity of the swamp on June 28, riding at the head of a troop of mounted volunteers from Bibb, Monroe, Talbot, and Upson counties. This group was augmented along the trail by local militiamen from Baker County, as well as others from Early, Stewart, Thomas, and Pulaski counties, making a total force of about five hundred men. They began to search and probe the swamp for signs of the enemy.[6]

At first the scouting parties of local settlers and friendly Indians found little, but on July 1 they spotted a line of Indian pickets and realized the fugitives' camp lay somewhere in the swamp beyond. Beall stationed half of his men around the swamp and led the other half toward the Indian position. On the morning of July 2, these troops pulled off their coats, tied up their heads with handkerchiefs, and went into the morass with a rush. Then they slowed and trudged three or four miles "through briers, mud and water, sometimes up to the neck" before coming in view of the rebel stronghold. It sat on a hammock hard by Chickasawhatchee Creek. The men charged, and after twenty minutes of heavy fighting, succeeded in driving off the Indians and taking the camp. In the process they killed twelve Indians and wounded perhaps twenty or thirty more. The Indians broke up into small groups and fled in every direction into parts of the swamp so thick that the whites could not follow. Colonel Beall's men suffered seven casualties, two of them fatal.[7]

Along with the camp, Beall's men captured a large store of booty, much of it taken from Roanoke. According to one observer, "the Indians had 35 tents, and an incredible quantity of beef, bacon, horses, saddles, bridles, homespun, cooking utensils, etc." The soldiers also gathered up guns and a substantial supply of ammunition. Not having the means to transport most of this plunder out of the swamp, Colonel Beall ordered it burned. The horses were another matter. The Indians entered the swamp with fifty to seventy of them, and after the battle, a number of men appeared before Beall to make legitimate claims on animals stolen from them. But the horses disappeared before their rightful owners could identify them. According to Beall, the beasts "were carried off without [my] knowledge, by individuals who were not in the battle, nor under my command." This situation showed, once again, that the rebel Creeks were not the only people living by predation. It was part and parcel of the local ecnonomy.[8]

Despite the colonel's frustration with some of his fellow citizens, Chickasawhatchee was a significant victory for the Georgians. In fact, the Chickasawhatchee was the place where these men "met, fought and for the first time, whipped the Indians." But Beall wanted to finish the job he started. He believed the Creek survivors of his attack were still hiding in the swamp and intended to remain there for some time. He wanted to hunt them out, but he knew he could not find them without the assistance of more Indian scouts. On July 3 he asked General Scott to send Paddy Carr and one hundred of his warriors to the Chickasawhatchee. He also asked for three thousand cartridges, because the incessant rains, coupled with all the wading in the swamp, had ruined his supply of ammunition.[9]

Scott responded on July 6. He sent off two steamboats, the *Metamora* and *Reindeer*, from Columbus loaded with 40 Indians and 160 foot soldiers. The soldiers were all Columbus men, members of the town's various volunteer companies: the Columbus Guards, the Cadet Riflemen, the Muscogee Blues, and an artillery company. These troops stayed at home to guard Columbus during the New Alabama campaign, but they chafed at the inactivity, as well as at the constant criticism that Columbus men were more interested in making money than fighting. Consequently, when word of the Chickasawhatchee fight and Beall's request for more men reached Scott, Major Hoxie pleaded with the general to let the Columbus men go south to prove their mettle. The general consented and placed Hoxie in command of the relief force.

The troops then boarded the steamboats with the Creek scouts and traveled down the Chattahoochee to the mouth of the Flint River, then up the Flint to the vicinity of the Chickasawhatchee. There they made contact with Colonel Beall.[10]

Unfortunately for Scott, his order to Major Hoxie was his last significant act as commander of the Army of the South and chief prosecutor of the Second Creek War. In a sense, he became another casualty of the conflict. Dissatisfied with the conduct of both the Seminole and Creek campaigns, President Jackson ordered Scott's recall to Washington and gave General Jesup "command of the troops serving against the hostile Creeks." Scott left Columbus on July 8, but he did not feel defeated. Indeed, he still believed he had brought the Creek conflict to a close. In his parting report, he expressed confidence that the civilian troops would soon surround the fugitive Creeks in Georgia and force them to surrender. He also stated that the number of rebels still on the loose in New Alabama was "quite inconsiderable." Once again, and for the last time, General Scott underestimated his Native opponents.[11]

The battalion of Columbus troops, and the companies of local militiamen who joined them at the Chickasawhatchee Swamp, accomplished very little. After searching the morass for a week, they decided that no substantial body of Indians remained there. Then, when fresh signs were reported in the Cooleewahee Swamp some fifteen miles away, the battalion and a party of friendly Indians "marched to the place, entered that swamp of swamps, and searched it most elegantly." However, they succeeded in "only jumping up a few bears, rattlesnakes, and several alligators, who, no doubt, were not a little astonished at the visit paid them." Consequently, General White, who now commanded the Columbus battalion, decided that the Indians had left that part of the country and to continue to search for them in the swamps would only destroy the health of his "up-country troops." Therefore, the general ordered his men back to Columbus, where they made a spectacular entrance—"half military and half farsical [sic]"—on July 18 and 19. The Columbus troops led the way down Broad Street so sunburned, dirty, and thoroughly smoked, their neighbors hardly recognized them. Behind them rode their Creek allies in their "fantastic native costumes." The last man of the Indians carried the only real trophy of the expedition, "a little bob-tailed piney woods shoat... which squealed manfully at every step the Indian brought."[12]

Though the Columbus troops found no rebels to fight, the town's newspapers trumpeted the positive benefits of their expedition. According to the *Sentinel*, "The unexplored swamps of Baker county have at least one advantage—they furnish a desirable chance to change the quiet, easy living, and peaceful citizen of our cities into the hardy, laboring, and fear-naught soldier." The *Enquirer* went further, saying that the expedition had saved the reputations of the Columbus men, who at the outset of the war had been "promiscuously charged with cowardice." The expedition also improved the standing of the friendly Creeks in the eyes of the *Enquirer*, and the editor encouraged the town residents to treat them favorably and encourage them, "for without them, but little can be done against a foe that slips from his hiding place, does mischief and slips back again, so secret as to be almost unperceived."[13]

Whatever may have been the personal benefits of their field trip, the Columbus troops and Creek scouts left south Georgia too soon. Had they stayed a day or two longer, they could have joined in a fight with the same rebels Beall had engaged earlier in the Chickasawhatchee. The day after that battle, while Beall was writing to Scott for reinforcements to search the swamp, sixty of the surviving Creek warriors and their families came out of the morass and headed east. They crossed the Flint River, reposed for a week in another swamp, and then set off once more toward the expansive and mysterious Okefenokee. But now they moved more cautiously, committing no murders, and trying to stay out of sight of the settlers. Nevertheless, some Georgians spotted them forty miles north of Thomasville and sent out the alarm. Having just set out for Columbus, that town's brave troops missed the opportunity to respond.[14]

Instead, 136 militiamen from Thomas and Lowndes counties rushed to the scene. They caught up to the Indians just east of Little River, and on July 15 fought a two-hour engagement called the Battle of Brushy Creek. The rebels initially repulsed the whites, then broke before a vigorous charge. At that point the fight became a running struggle through cypress swamps, bay ponds, and hurricane falls. Throughout the contest the Indians "distinguished themselves by a boldness savages rarely exhibit," but in the end the whites claimed another victory. They lost three men killed and eight wounded; they killed twenty-two Indian warriors and two black ones. The civilian soldiers also captured nine women and nine children and placed these captives in the county jail in Thomasville. Those rebels not killed or wounded beyond recovery escaped into the Alapaha River Swamp and probably reached a safe haven in the Okefenokee.[15]

But then more Indians appeared in Baker County. Settlers sighted thirty mounted warriors ten miles north of the Chickasawhatchee battleground. Now the local inhabitants realized the full extent of their Indian problem. Fearing more attacks from Creeks passing through the county, they cried out for help. Taking up their cause, the *Columbus Sentinel* called for General Sanford, who had taken command of the Georgia corps of the Army of the South on Scott's departure, to recall troops into the service and station a body of them both in Baker County and at Fort Gaines on the Chattahoochee to protect the exposed citizens in the southern end of the state. Sanford responded by detailing troops under General White to Baker County. He seemed to think that would solve the problem. He wrote to Jesup asking that all remaining units of Georgia troops be discharged as "the war is over." He did, however, want to keep a squadron of mounted men in service to patrol the eastern bank of the Chattahoochee, and he declared that this small unit would be sufficient to restrain and subdue "the few wandering Indians that may still be lurking" near the river border with Alabama. He in no way believed these Creeks could assemble a force large enough to overpower that squadron.[16]

But Governor Schley was not so confident. Besides that, he had more than south Georgia to worry about when it came to Indian affairs. The Cherokees, who still occupied a sizeable portion of north Georgia and presented a fairly united front against removal under a group of talented leaders, concerned Schley and most of his constituents more than the Creeks making their way to Florida. These Georgians knew that the U.S.

Senate had recently ratified the New Echota Treaty, which obligated all the Cherokees to move west by the year 1838. Schley and his fellow citizens also knew most Cherokees were angry and did not feel bound by any treaty signed by an unauthorized minority of their leadership. This fact alone would have led Schley to fear a Cherokee uprising. But he became even more concerned when alarmed settlers in northern Georgia reported that a new wave of Creek refugees were leaving New Alabama and entering the Cherokee country. The *Milledgeville Federal Union* noted that armed Creeks had moved into the Coosawattee Valley in Murray County, Georgia, and according to local settlers, these Indians avoided contact with whites and were "suspected of exasperating the Cherokees." From Walker County word came in that the Creek rebels had sent their women and children to that place "to be out of harm's way" while they fought the whites in Alabama. The editor of the *Federal Union* recommended that the state take these people hostage. In Carroll and Paulding counties rumors began to circulate that the Cherokees were already following the Creek example and rising up; they would devastate the white settlements if local militiamen were sent to southern Georgia to fight recalcitrant Creeks there. Though most of these reports exaggerated the situation, and Georgians really had little to fear from a Cherokee uprising, the Creek rebellion kept the flames of panic burning and actually retarded new settlement in northern Georgia, because farmers and planters no longer wanted to go there. Realizing this, the state's presses insisted on threatening the Cherokees with massive retaliation if they pursued a hostile course in concert with the Creeks.[17]

But the respectable class of north Georgians had yet another concern with the Creek incursion. As people of property, they suspected that Creek refugees colluded with white roughs in running a troublesome theft ring throughout the Cherokee counties. Thus, they called for their governor not only to stop the ingress of Indians but to remove all Creeks from Georgia, for two important reasons. First, they wanted to prevent another outbreak of Indian warfare. Second, they wanted to be able to concentrate on disciplining and controlling the criminal element of their own society. Hearing all this, Schley believed he had

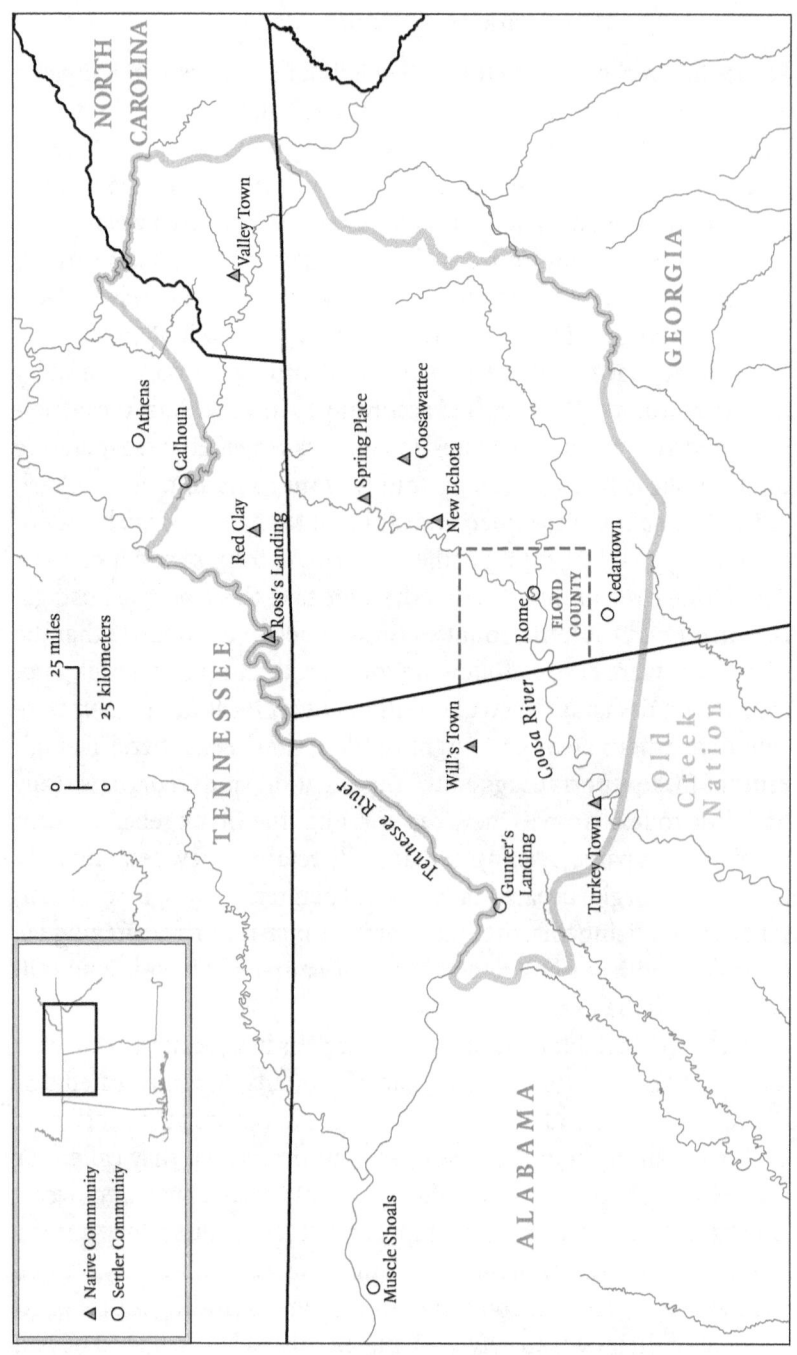

5. Cherokee Nation, 1835–38

to keep a strong military force in and near the Cherokee counties. Consequently, he stationed several companies of state troops at West Point, while another four companies under Maj. Charles H. Nelson set themselves up at Camp Lesley in Floyd County. Schley also dispatched troops to patrol the Alabama-Georgia line in the Cherokee district to prevent any more Creeks from entering his state.[18]

Unfortunately, the Georgians were too aggressive. The patrolling troops discovered that small parties of Upper Creeks had been passing into the state by way of an old Indian trail leading from Hillabee town in Tallapoosa County up between the Coosa and Tallapoosa rivers to Cedartown, Georgia. These Indians, coming mainly from Hillabee and Arbocochee towns, continued the migration that had begun the year before, of Creeks into Georgia and the Cherokee counties of Alabama. Moreover, they openly stated that they did not intend to move beyond the Mississippi and that the Cherokees had offered them asylum and protection. The already frightened north Georgians took this declaration to mean that the Cherokees and Creek refugees would fight to stay in the country they now occupied. Consequently, they treated both Creeks and Cherokees roughly in an effort to drive them out of the country. At one point, Georgia troops entered Alabama and captured thirty refugees near the head of Terrapin Creek, then took these Indians into Georgia for internment. Other Georgians began to disarm Cherokee men and otherwise abuse them. John Ridge, a proremoval Cherokee and one of the signers of the New Echota Treaty, reported to Washington that "the lowest classes of the white people were flogging the Cherokees with cowhides, hickories, and clubs." He also complained that "this barbarous treatment is not confined to men, but the women are stripped, also, and whipped without law or mercy." Consequently, Ridge put in his own call for troops, but he wanted U.S. regulars to protect the Cherokees from the Georgians.[19]

Meanwhile, over in Alabama, Governor Clay faced some of the same concerns about Creek-Cherokee collusion and armed resistance. He believed that five hundred to six hundred Creeks lived on Cherokee lands in his state, and he knew they terrified the settlers living near them. In Cherokee County, a committee of settlers met with the Creek community at Pole Cat Ground and learned from the Indians that, indeed, some of the rebels from the south had come among them on a recruiting trip. These alarmed settlers then asked Clay for permission to organize a company of men to disarm the local Creeks and watch over them until they could be removed from the state. They wanted to see to it that no one sold the Indians more liquor and guns. Clay agreed and went further. He held a couple of regiments from Alabama's First and Seventh Militia Divisions in service to patrol the Cherokee district and observe the interaction between Creeks and Cherokees. These regiments consisted of men who lived in north Alabama near the Cherokee border.[20]

Officials in the War Department also worried about the Cherokee-Creek connection. When the Second Creek War broke out, the secretary of war issued a call on the southern states for 10,000 troops to fight the Creeks and Seminoles, and possibly the Mexicans, western Indians, and Cherokees should the need arise. Secretary Cass required that the state of Tennessee furnish 2,500 of the total number of men, and Gov. Newton Cannon issued a proclamation to that effect on June 6, 1836. Troops from the middle and western part of the state assembled at Fayetteville, Tennessee, and formed a brigade of 1,550 under Gen. Robert Armstrong. This brigade then marched south to the scene of the Creek war. Troops from the eastern part of the state collected at Athens, Tennessee, on July 7 for service in the Cherokee Nation. These volunteers, led by Brig. Gen. Richard G. Dunlap, joined a small contingent of federal troops under Brig. Gen. John E. Wool, who assumed command of all forces in the Cherokee country. Wool divided his troops into two regiments and sent one to the mouth of Valley River in Macon County, North Carolina; the other regiment he sent to Ross's Landing on the Tennessee River. Wool believed that a large number of potentially hostile Cherokees lived near those locations and he wanted to establish a military presence in each area as soon as possible. He instructed his regimental commanders to visit as many of the Indians as possible with the message that any armed revolt against the New Echota Treaty would bring devastation on the Cherokee Nation. In particular, Wool told his officers to point to what was happening in the Creek country as an example of what the Cherokees should avoid. And finally, the general instructed his men to detain any Creeks they found who had escaped to the Cherokee domain to avoid punishment for their conduct in the recent hostilities in Alabama and Georgia.[21]

But Wool may not have called the Cherokees' attention to the Creek country had he realized that his fellow generals had not really defeated the rebellion there as they claimed. On July 7, shortly after Scott swept through Barbour and Russell counties, a detachment of Gen. John Moore's Alabama militiamen discovered a party of Indians at Cowikee Swamp, a known staging area for rebels seeking to cross the Chattahoochee. Since their arrival at Irwinton in early June, General Moore's regiment had conducted numerous searches of the three branches of Cowikee Creek without finding any Indians to fight. Now their sudden discovery of enemy warriors unnerved them and caused them to overreact. In truth, they initiated the sort of engagement that had become all too common in the Second Creek War. They fired on the rebels too quickly, and when the Natives ran to the swamp, the excited civilian soldiers foolishly chased after them. Almost too late they discovered the trap. Many more warriors lay in wait in the swamp, intent on ambushing the inexperienced troops. Finally realizing the danger, Moore's men drew back, but they did not retreat in an orderly military fashion. Instead, they did as so many of the Georgia troops had done when confronted with a superior Indian force. They fled in panic to spread the alarm and call for reinforcements. Yet when those reinforcements arrived, led by General Moore himself, they found that the rebel band had broken up into small parties and scattered into the thickest parts of the swamps, places where the whites could not follow. That was disappointing enough, but then some settlers told Moore of their suspicions that John McCrory, a white man living near the Barbour-Pike county line, had been aiding and abetting the group of hostile Creeks who ran the troops from the field.[22]

This missed opportunity, coming on the heels of so many fruitless searches, obviously frustrated General Moore and he lashed out, criticizing others for their handling of the Creek war. He wrote to Governor Clay to complain about General Jesup's conduct. Obviously, Moore believed, like Scott, that Jesup had attempted to win the war on his own without ever trying to coordinate his efforts with those of the Alabama troops at Irwinton. Furthermore, Moore claimed that Jesup had never acknowledged all the hard work Moore's troops had done. Moore also noted that the press had never publicized his men's efforts. But the general's chief complaint was that no one had furnished his regiment with Native trackers and scouts. Writing of his recent battle, Moore stated, "On this occasion, as on many others, had but a few friendly Indians been with this division of Troops, these Indians [rebels] might have been successfully pursued—their cunning in disguising their trails is so great, as to render it impossible for any white man who is not perfectly conversant with their habits, to discover the course they may have taken in the retreat." In so many words, Moore was admitting to what others had already discovered: despite all the claims of victory, the whites could never capture all the Creek rebels and end the Creek war by themselves.[23]

Jesup seemed to pay little attention to the renewed fighting. Having already declared the war "virtually over," he moved to consolidate his victory by reopening the southern counties of New Alabama to settlers. First, he recommenced the sale of Creek lands, assigning two army officers, Maj. Thomas Abbott and Lt. J. A. Chambers, along with the Creek subagent, Leonard Tarrant, to certify contracts between Indians and purchasers. Jesup also established two new military posts on New Road, one twelve miles west of Columbus and the other fourteen miles east of Tuskegee. The troops stationed there then went to work repairing bridges and making the highway secure for the mail and renewed travel. Reestablishing a white presence in the Lower Creek country was not an easy task, however, because of the extent of the destruction. As the federal troops moved out from Fort Mitchell to take up their new posts, they encountered nothing but burned homes, ruined stages and wagons, rows of newly made graves, and at one point, a number of empty coffins, "scattered in all directions by the Indians." One company of soldiers stopped at a deserted farmhouse to drink from a well standing out front. After they had taken their fill, the men received the "pleasing news" from a bystander that the Creeks had only recently killed the owner of the property and had thrown his corpse down the well. Such incidents did little to improve the morale of the regulars, many of whom came from the northern states and lacked enthusiasm for the Second Creek War. As one officer explained, "The army has been sent here to protect the rights of the citizens, which rights have been established wrongs."[24]

Having sent his regulars on their way, Jesup went to work on his most important task: Creek removal. In fact, the general believed that removal was "but the sequel" to the war and the only real way to bring "permanent peace and tranquility" to the country. Consequently, he disdained the futile task of chasing fugitive Creeks and concentrated his efforts on getting his rebel captives out of Alabama as quickly as possible. He began with the sixteen hundred war prisoners at Fort Mitchell. Since June 23, the day General Patterson and his Indian allies brought in most of these captives from the Hatchechubbee, Captain Page had been busy enrolling and preparing them for emigration. Similarly, the fort's blacksmiths had been hard at work making handcuffs and chains for the warriors, and county sheriffs had searched through the prisoners to find and arrest those rebels known to have committed crimes. At the same time, crowds of whites flocked to the fort to reclaim stolen horses and slaves brought in with the rebels or simply to gawk at the vanquished foe. These interested spectators, especially the newspaper correspondents, found chief Neah Emathla particularly fascinating. He had opposed the whites for a long time and possessed a high military reputation. He was eighty-six years old, and "something peculiarly striking in his countenance" impressed everyone who saw him. One reporter claimed that he was the only Indian he ever saw that could "look a white man full in the eye" when addressed. In fact, Neah Emathla showed remarkable courage in the face of defeat—which he blamed on Neah Micco—and even requested that the soldiers shoot him rather than bind him up in chains. He did, however, ask that they spare his son, a youth of seventeen or eighteen years. But General Jesup had no interest in executing any of the rebels; he only wanted them out of the country. Consequently, he sent them away from Fort Mitchell on July 2 with an escort of three companies of troops to begin their long journey to the West.[25]

The marching rebels presented a poignant spectacle. The men led the procession, walking in double file, handcuffed two together with a long chain passing down the center of the files, connecting all the pairs. The elderly Neah Emathla marched with the rest and, like the other warriors, showed no sign of the physical and mental anguish he must have been suffering. In fact, the only sound that came from the ranks of these men was "an emphatic 'ta' whenever two of them pulling in opposite directions would jerk one another by the wrists." Moreover, the courage and fortitude these Creek warriors displayed impressed observers and led some reporters to speculate about the bloody conflict that might occur when Neah Emathla and his Seminole party met the more acculturated McIntosh group in the western land. The Creek women, however, did not take the forced march to Montgomery in quite so stoic a fashion as the warriors. They followed their men "drowned in tears, and giving utterance to most distressing cries." Many youngsters walked with the women and cried in sympathy for their mothers. The smallest children, along with the oldest and most feeble of the party, brought up the rear, riding in wagons.[26]

The moving line of rebels also gave evidence of the high degree of racial and cultural miscegenation among the Lower Creeks, as well as of their complex relationship with the "whites" around them. According to a correspondent for the Army and Navy Chronicle, the rebel Creeks were "all complexions, shading through white, red, and black." Furthermore, some of the spectators who watched the rebels depart felt pity for them. Far from hating the Creeks, they understood their plight and the reasons for their rebellion. A reporter for the Milledgeville Federal Union expressed a common sentiment. "Surrounded by a white population, broken up in their nationality—wretched, and every way undone, this miserable remnant of a once powerful people, have at last yielded to the force of circumstances, and with a bitter curse upon the heads of their enemy, they have left us, for what we hope, a better country, and a happier condition." The mixed appearance of the rebels and the sympathetic reaction to their passing by numerous observers surely revealed that the Second Creek War was not a simple matter of secluded and primitive Natives facing aggressive, uncaring colonizers across a hard and fast racial and cultural boundary. No, the Creek uprising was, at least in part, a civil rebellion, and as is true of all civil rebellions, the opponents were not complete strangers. They shared elements of culture and even blood kinship.[27]

The people who watched the passing of the Creek rebels pictured them as defeated and subdued, their acts of resistance completely at an end. This was not exactly the case. Some of the more embittered prisoners would stage one final demonstration of their opposition to oppression. These Creeks did not believe it possible to find a better country or happier condition in the West. Unlike the mobile settlers, who saw land as a marketable commodity, many Creeks felt an organic attachment to their homeland and some could not bear to leave it. Furthermore, many of the older people, and those of all ages who still clung to the old Creek view of the cosmos, believed that the West was a woeful place where no one could be happy. The spirits of the dead dwelled in the West, and only sorrow, sickness, and death awaited those who ventured there. Now faced with forced exile to a dreaded place, some of the warriors took their rebellion to its ultimate extreme. They chose the most dramatic form of escape and protest. They committed suicide. One elderly man hanged himself the night before the departure from Fort Mitchell, and others soon followed his example. These incidents of self destruction among the rebels "served forcibly to exhibit how strong the 'amor patriae' burned in their breasts."[28]

Other members of the rebel party killed themselves to avoid imprisonment or execution for their crimes. When the procession of rebels reached Montgomery, where they were scheduled to board steamboats for passage down the Alabama River to Mobile, a detachment of Governor Schley's troops arrived to arrest some of the warriors suspected of committing depredations in Georgia. At that point one perturbed warrior drew a concealed knife and cut his own throat; another, using a duller knife, succeeded, after several attempts, in plunging it into his chest; and a third man killed one of his guards with a hammer, knowing full well he would be shot to death on the spot.[29]

But death was not the only way for Creek captives to resist forced removal or imprisonment. Escape was another alternative, as Jesup discovered when he attempted to remove Neah Micco's band of approximately fourteen hundred souls, including four hundred warriors, from New Alabama. Following the conclusion of his sweep of the Lower Creek country during the last week in June, Jesup remained at Fort Mitchell with all his prisoners for eight days to prepare their march to Montgomery and to give local authorities time to identify particular warriors accused of specific crimes. Then, as his prisoners set out for Montgomery, Jesup prepared to move his headquarters to Tuskegee and sent General Patterson and a battalion of his Alabama volunteers ahead to Echo Harjo's camp to disarm Neah Micco's people in preparation for their departure from the state. But this second body of rebels had by that time lost their fear of Jesup and his soldiers. They gave up only a portion of their weapons, concealed the remainder, and then disingenuously agreed to report to General Jesup at Tuskegee on July 7, at which time the general intended to send them off to Montgomery. But when the general arrived at Tuskegee on that date, he found only Neah Micco and a few of his followers. The rest of the chief's people had determined not to emigrate and fled to Tuckabatchee Harjo's town in Chambers County. Jim Henry, whom Jesup had chosen not to imprison for the moment, was also absent, having returned to the woods to retrieve his family members. Moreover, all the Sawoklis had "gone down the country." Similarly, when Maj. John C. Webb of the Chambers County militia arrived at Tallassee to escort the rebel prisoners there to Tuskegee for removal, he found that they too had fled, forcing Webb to send out a detachment under Capt. John Brodnax to round them up. Meanwhile, a furious Jesup ordered General Patterson to go after Neah Micco's people and secure them for removal, declaring, "The negotiation with Neo [sic] Micco has proved that the best argument with Indians is formed not of words, but of powder and lead." Then Jesup ordered out another company of troops to chase down the Sawoklis. A few days later, Patterson returned from Tuckabatchee Harjo's camp with most of the fugitives, and Jesup hurried them on to Montgomery. There, on July 14 they, along with Neah Emathla's band and a few additional parties of rebels brought in by the friendly chiefs and troops, boarded two small steamboats, and two barges pulled by the boats, and started off down the river to Mobile to await ships to take them along the Gulf Coast and up the Mississippi River to Arkansas. With the departure of these 2,498 rebel Creeks, consisting of Euchees, Cussetas, Eufaulas, Chehaws, and Hitchitees, General Jesup declared the war "entirely at an end," discharged most of General Moore's brigade along with the better part of three other regiments of Alabama troops, and began preparations to remove the friendly Creeks, most of whom had already entered several emigration camps throughout New Alabama.[30]

But Jesup was wrong again. Some rebels reposed in the friendly camps to hide from justice and await an opportunity to escape back to the swamps. Opothle Yahola even complained to Jesup that some Indians from Cubahatchee town in Macon County lived in his camp, and he did not want them for they were "bad characters" who had committed depredations on the whites. More alarmingly, about 200 of Neah Micco's people avoided the march to Montgomery and secreted themselves among the friendly Indians, who seemed reluctant to give them up. In fact, it appears that Tuckabatchee Harjo, Echo Harjo, and possibly Jim Boy used the turmoil surrounding the rebellion and forced removal to increase their number of followers, undoubtedly at the expense of Neah Micco, Tuskenea, and other rebel chiefs. Furthermore, several groups of unsubdued insurgents lay in hiding in the stretch of country between the Ositchee Bend of the Chattahoochee and the mouth of Cowikee Creek. Jesup had never discovered these people, because Patterson's mounted troops could not penetrate their swamps and hammocks, and the general's Creek scouts had refused to look. Upset by Jesup's inability to feed their families properly and the fact that some of the Alabama troops murdered a few friendly Indians, those scouts left Patterson's service without completing the necessary searches. Consequently, when Jesup dismissed the Alabama troops in late July, and they left their posts in Russell and Barbour counties, the undetected rebel parties came out of hiding, congregated in larger groups, set up well-stocked tents in the open pinewoods, and prepared to join the exodus to the Florida Territory. Moreover, some formerly friendly Creeks, who also wanted to avoid Jesup's forced removal, joined with rebel infiltrators in the friendly camps and moved out to the wilds, bound for Florida. Once again, the Georgia volunteers who occupied the river posts across from the mouths of the Hatchechubbee and Cowikee creeks began to hear the ring of axes and hammers as the resurgent rebels built new canoes and rafts for crossing the Chattahoochee.[31]

Then the war resumed in Georgia. On the night of July 22, a party of 250 rebels, consisting of refugees from Neah Micco's band, some Eufaula Creeks, and a few blacks, slipped across the river a few miles south of Fort McCreary. Nulkarpuche Tustenuggee, one of the Hitchitee headmen, led the group as they entered the Georgia woods and headed for Florida by a rather devious route, marching north and west at first before turning south. But the Georgians soon discovered their course. A slave boy happened upon their trail and reported the find to the garrison of mounted troops stationed at Fort McCreary. Then 98 of these men set off in pursuit, trailed the rebels for fifteen miles, and caught up to them at the Quarles plantation, eleven miles west of Lumpkin and twenty-two miles south of Columbus. On July 24 the company's advance guard attacked the Indians' rear guard and forced the Indians to retreat. The Georgians rushed in pursuit only to find that the rebel rear guard, once again, had decoyed them into the main rebel force. The two sides locked in a hard struggle, with the Creeks attempting to outflank the Georgians, first on one side and then the other. The Georgians fought off the flanking movements for an hour until some person in their rear called out the order, "To your horses!" At that point the Georgia line broke and the men ran, despite their commanding officer's best efforts to rally them. They left 5 dead troops behind. Their captain then reported that, although the Indians outnumbered his men two to one, the Georgians had killed 22 rebels. However, the Georgians were outnumbered only if one counts the Creek women and children as combatants. In reality, the Georgians probably met a force of warriors inferior to themselves and still managed to lose the Battle of Quarles Plantation.[32]

When word of this engagement reached Columbus and Milledgeville, both Governor Schley and General Sanford knew they had a serious problem. Because of the declarations of victory by Jesup and Scott, they had dismissed most of Georgia's army after the march through New Alabama, holding in service only one battalion of mounted men, under Maj. Julius C. Alford, for service in south Georgia. These troops operated out of Fort McCreary and patrolled the riverfront of Stewart County, the site of most Indian crossing attempts. But all along, Schley feared that the Creek rebels would reassemble in force once they saw the great majority of Georgia and Alabama troops go home. Consequently, he took the precaution of ordering troops from Telfair County, just north of the Okmulgee River, to assemble and station enough men in Baker County to intercept those Creeks who might pass by Alford's men on their way to Florida. But once again the insubordinate nature of Georgia's civilian soldiers interfered with Schley's ability to capture the fugitive Creeks. The Telfair troops refused to go to Baker County. As a result, there was no backup force in place when the rebels began their flight to Florida. A disappointed Schley wrote to Jesup and admonished him: "I think, therefore, you have mistaken the true state of the war, when you consider it at an end."[33]

Worse, the newspapers questioned the competency of Sanford's river guards. Besides the news of the large rebel party that engaged the troops at Quarles's plantation, the *Columbus Sentinel* began to receive almost daily reports of smaller parties of Indians crossing the Chattahoochee and "strolling off to the eastward!" Therefore, the paper's editor demanded to know: "Where are our horsemen? Are they at their posts? If so, why not stop this *Indian emigration*, which is taking altogether a wrong course?" This alone was a telling criticism, but the editor coupled it with an even darker specter. If the rebel Creeks reached Florida, he said, they would stay there only until the United States launched its upcoming campaign against the Seminoles. Then they would return to south Georgia and New Alabama to continue their harassing warfare for "God only knows how long!" Thus, the editor proclaimed, something must be done to stop the rebel flight and finally end the Creek war. "Let those in command see to this matter," he demanded.[34]

Now Sanford knew he had to take decisive action. He could not let more Creeks escape. He ordered all the militia and volunteer companies in south Georgia to prepare themselves for action. Then he ordered Stewart County's local hero, the former captain turned major, Henry Jernigan, to pursue the hostiles and hold them in check until reinforcements arrived. He also directed the militiamen stationed at Fort Gaines to move to take the Chickasawhatchee. Finally, General Sanford took to the field himself, leading four mounted companies and a battalion of Columbus infantrymen south to Fort McCreary. As he left town, he announced that he would not return empty-handed. He was determined "to pursue the enemy to the *South keys* of Florida" if necessary.[35]

But Sanford's task would not be easy because of the indifferent quality of Georgia's troops. Even as Sanford marched, Major Jernigan was having problems in this regard. The morning after the clash at Quarles's plantation, Jernigan received word that the Creeks had turned to the southeast and had crossed Cuthbert Road just seven miles south of his company headquarters at Lumpkin. This meant that once again the rebels were headed for the Chickasawhatchee Swamp, and Jernigan knew he had to cut them off before they reached that tangled expanse of territory. He started after the Creeks immediately and put out a call for his Stewart County Rangers to gather themselves together and join him along the way. He also sent word to the officers at Fort McCreary, asking that they fly to his aid with their garrison. They did not come. But Jernigan kept to the trail and soon overtook the Creeks at Jones's plantation. By that time some of his rangers had joined him, along with a number of civilians from Stewart and Randolph counties. Still undetected by the Indians, Jernigan ordered his men to dismount and steal through a cornfield to the rebel camp. But his advance guard engaged the enemy too early and spoiled the surprise. A tough battle ensued, and Jernigan might have gained the day but for the inconsistency of his men. At a crucial moment in the contest, they refused his order to charge the Indians. This gave the rebels time to seek superior cover and Jernigan had to order his exposed troops to retreat, leaving three dead on the field. Fortunately for the whites, the Creeks did not pursue them. They continued on their way to Florida, claiming the Battle of Jones Plantation as another victory for their rebellion.[36]

The Georgia troops were not the only problem, however. From the Georgian point of view, General Jesup's strategy of focusing on Creek removal in Alabama and virtually ignoring the war across the Chattahoochee made the situation much more difficult. In fact, by late July Jesup had a good number of federal troops, Alabama militia, and Tennessee volunteers at his disposal, but he chose to use them to keep the peace in New Alabama and watch over the Indians as they accumulated in the emigration camps. Obviously, the general took a calculated risk. He certainly knew the importance of kin and town relationships to the Creeks, and he believed, along with Governor Clay and others, that if the mass of tribespeople left Alabama quickly, the scattered groups of rebels would soon quit the fight, give themselves up, and follow their own to the West. Jesup also believed that if he sent his forces off to prosecute the war in Georgia, the peaceful Creeks he had worked so hard to concentrate for removal would scatter and perhaps start to commit depredations themselves. Therefore, he decided that the removal project was the most effective way to employ his troops to bring peace and security to the region. Consequently, Jesup announced by way of a formal order on July 14 that General Sanford would have to rely solely on Georgia troops to defend his state.[37]

By the end of the month, Jesup had systematically redeployed his troops to facilitate Creek removal. He instructed Gen. Andrew Moore of the Alabama militia to stay in service in the Cherokee country. He also directed Moore to set up a removal camp near Gunter's Landing on the Tennessee River. Moore's troops were to keep peace between Indians and settlers in that neighborhood, as well as collect refugee Creeks and confine them to a removal camp. Jesup also called on Maj. Charles Nelson, stationed with four companies in north Georgia, to scour the Cherokee settlements of both Georgia and Alabama for Creek refugees and drive them into Moore's camp. Furthermore, Jesup instructed his troops in the Cherokee country to inform the Indians that all Creeks who had not reported to removal camps by August 20 would be treated as hostiles. Then Jesup turned his attention back to his immediate locale. He sent two battalions of General Patterson's Alabama troops to Coosa County's largest emigration camp. Two more battalions of Patterson's men he stationed at Line Creek in Macon County as a reserve force, ready to move in any direction needed. Next, Jesup ordered all his companies of marines, and one volunteer company from far-off Washington DC to Opothle Yahola's burgeoning removal camp at Tallassee. This done, the general divided his regular army force between Fort Mitchell, Tuskegee, and Tuckabatchee Hargo's town in Chambers County. He also sent his newly arrived contingent of Tennessee volunteers to the two posts on New Road between Tuskegee and Columbus. Then, with all these troops in place, Jesup ordered all Lower Creeks encamped about Fort Mitchell, or living anywhere south of New Road, to present themselves immediately to the Tallassee camp. He also announced that all Indians caught south of that road after August 1 would be treated as hostile, with the exception of warriors employed by the government. Then, to back up this threat, regular troops from Fort Mitchell, along with two companies of Tennessee volunteers, conducted yet another sweep of the Hatchechubbee and Cowikee creeks in early August to drive out or destroy all hostiles they found hiding there.[38]

Jesup's forced removal policy only made the rebels more determined than ever to resist capture, and their determination caused more problems for those Georgians trying to prevent Creeks from escaping to Florida. Major Jernigan was the first to note this fact. On the morning of July 26, he rallied his men and started after the Indians who had defeated him at Jones's plantation. He chased them to the outskirts of the Ichawaynotchaway Swamp, which sat at the southwest end of the Chickasawhatchee Swamp. More and more of his rangers joined him as he rode, and by the time he made camp that evening, his force numbered three hundred men. He roused his troops before sunrise on the twenty-seventh and put them on the march without breakfast for two reasons: "First, no time to cook; and second, nothing to cook." A mere three-mile march brought them near the enemy as they crossed Turkey Creek at its main confluence with Ichawaynotchaway Creek. Seeing the whites, the rebels turned about and made a stand on a hammock within the swamp. The Georgians eventually overran the Creek position, killing eighteen rebels and capturing a large store of goods, but the battle was long and hard. In fact, the troops came away from the contest awestruck. Before the battle, the fatalistic Primitive Baptist members of Jernigan's group announced that they would not hide behind trees when facing the Creeks, for if they were meant to die "they would be killed anyhow, tree or no tree." On seeing the fierceness of the Indians, however, the Primitives "ran for the biggest trees on the battle field," and there they stayed for the remainder of the fight. For his part, Jernigan claimed that the Creeks at Ichawaynotchaway "fought with more desperation and gave up the ground with more reluctance than any battle I have had with them."[39]

However, the fugitive Creeks did not want to demonstrate their bravery and courage unless they had to do so. They knew that their greatest strength lay in their ability to conceal themselves in the Georgia swamps, as General Sanford would soon discover. He arrived at the Ichawaynotchaway on the evening of the battle, and the next day he put his mounted men to work searching the Chickasawhatchee for the remaining members of Nulkarpuche Tustenuggee's party or any other Natives who might be passing through the swamp on their way to Florida. Five more companies of mounted troops soon joined his command, and the general directed these men to scour the Ichawaynotchaway and Kinchafoonee swamps, as well as the Chickasawhatchee. At the same time, Sanford ordered Major Hoxie, who had brought his battalion of Columbus foot soldiers up Flint River by steamboat, to position his command between Chickasawhatchee and the Flint to cut off any rebels. Meanwhile, Florida volunteers stationed themselves on the Suwanee River to meet any fugitives who might escape Hoxie. The search lasted two weeks, and though Sanford's men found many fresh tracks, the Creeks for the most part eluded them. In fact, all the activity resulted in only one skirmish. On August 5, Maj. Julius Alford's battalion of river guards fought a brief battle with a party of more than one hundred Indians east of the Chickasawhatchee. After the battle, Alford's men found bloody litters beside the trail of the escaping rebels, but they could not locate any corpses. Actually, Sanford's whole campaign resulted in only one confirmed kill. An elderly Creek man, making his way out of the Chickasawhatchee, passed too near a settler cabin and some young boys shot him dead. Alford, for want of anything else to praise, described this act as being "very much to the honor of these little warriors."⁴⁰

Unable to find any Indians or significant trails to follow, Sanford returned to Columbus on August 11, along with Major Hoxie and the town's troops. However, the general did leave men at strategic points in southwestern Georgia to stop the Indian flight and to protect the white citizenry. He instructed Major Alford and his battalion, consisting of several mounted companies, to set up a post near Chickasawhatchee and form various flying camps to chase down and exterminate any rebels sighted between the Chattahoochee and the Chickasawhatchee. Sanford also ordered two more mounted companies to station themselves near a strategic point in Lee County and to keep alert for any signs of the Indians along the Kinchafoonee. Then the general sent more men to reinforce Major Jernigan's troops near Lumpkin. And finally, Sanford stationed an additional company at Fort McCreary and charged another detachment of troops under Capt. Michael Hentz with the task of tracking down the rebel party Alford had engaged in the Chickasawhatchee. This done, Sanford confidently, and erroneously, reported to Jesup that only about 250 Indians had crossed into Georgia in the last few weeks and most of these had probably returned to Alabama after their confrontation with Georgia's troops. Those who had not done so, he claimed, had scattered themselves in small groups over many hundreds of square miles, and if they dared embody, the Georgia men would overtake and expel them, owing to the "character of gallant soldiery" and the "chivalric spirit of the officers."⁴¹

But the civilian soldiers still could not stop the rebels. Captain Hentz soon discovered the trail of a large Indian party coming out of the Chickasawhatchee and followed it east across the Flint near Newton, Georgia. Realizing that the Natives outnumbered his company of troops, he sent word to Alford's camp near the head of Spring Creek that he would need reinforcements. Hentz then trailed the rebel party another thirty miles to the vicinity of Little River, where on August 13 he found that the Creeks had stopped, turned about, and now stood ready to fight their pursuers. Furthermore, they occupied an advantageous position. The eighty warriors of the party had formed an extended line of defense across the mouth of a bushy swamp that sat securely in the fork of a creek. The only approach to the swamp lay across an open pine flat. Nevertheless, Hentz ordered an attack on the Indians' position. After the first fire, many of the captain's men broke and ran. Worse, they not only left the battlefield but kept riding until they reached their distant homes. A dejected Hentz and a few others made camp, and as they waited for Major Alford's reinforcements, they dressed their wounds and undoubtedly lamented this latest example of Georgian cowardice and Indian determination.[42]

Now Alford tried his hand. He arrived at Hentz's camp that evening, and led another advance on the Indians. True to form, however, the rebels broke up into smaller parties and fled across Little River toward Grand Bay on the eastern branch of the Withlacoochee. Lacking the ability to track small, crafty parties of fugitives, Alford did just as he had done at the Chickasawhatchee: he simply gave up the chase and headed back to his base camp. Along the way, he stopped by the county jail at Thomasville to pick up thirty-one Indian prisoners for transport back to Fort Mitchell. The Georgians had captured eighteen of these people at the Brushy Creek fight and three on the Alapaha River. The remaining ten, however, were new captives, part of yet another large party of Creeks making their way to the Okefenokee on a parallel course with those Hentz fought at Little River. Alford chose to ignore this band of Natives and marched for Fort Mitchell as if he had finished his task.[43]

Then, as Jesup and Scott had done before him, Alford simply declared himself victorious. On August 25 he wrote to Sanford and pompously proclaimed that his battalion of troops had "effected at the point of the bayonet, what heretofore no array of force, or parade of men could otherwise accomplish: the total expulsion of the Indians from Chickasawhatchee swamp." Furthermore, Alford claimed that all the swamps of Baker County "are now more clear of Indians, than they have been for five years." The major also contended that all those Creeks who had escaped through south Georgia had taken refuge in the Okefenokee, and according to the captive women taken from Thomasville, they would remain there two months before descending into Florida.

Therefore, Alford informed his superior, "not one Indian has [yet] gone to Florida." Then, with his battalion's term of enlistment about to expire, Alford marched his troops to Lumpkin to await their discharges from the service.[44]

Like all the other victory proclamations, Alford's statement was premature, if not deliberately deceptive. He had no sooner issued it than some Baker County fishermen happened upon a camp of Creeks on Flint River at the back of Guy's plantation, six miles south of Pindertown, formerly an Indian settlement now occupied by Georgians. The fishermen called for assistance and a troop of thirty or forty civilian soldiers subsequently chased down and charged these fugitives in some open pine woods in Irwin County. In the process, they claimed to have killed from eighteen to twenty-three of the Indians without a single white man sustaining a wound. This report seems all the more incredible considering the soldiers' statement that the Creeks "fought desperately, clubbing their rifles, and fighting man to man." Nevertheless, some sort of skirmish occurred, and the militiamen did take three wounded women and two children prisoners. Moreover, seven women lay dead on the field because they "so resembled the men in their dress" that the Georgians could not "discriminate between them in the engagement." But those women did not want the whites to discriminate; they, like other Creek women during this time, fought alongside their men and asked for no special consideration or quarter. They meant to achieve freedom for themselves and their children or die in the effort. Furthermore, one of the females taken captive in the Irwin County fight contradicted Alford's claims. This defiant woman spoke English and was well-known to the settlers in Pindertown. She told her captors that many small parties of Indians remained unsubdued. These people were still stealing their way through the swamps to Florida, and numbers of Creeks had already arrived there.[45]

The truth of her statement soon became obvious. For the remainder of the month of August and into September, Georgians living in Lowndes and Ware counties saw groups of Indians traveling toward Florida. Similarly, the settlers in Middle Florida were "kept in a state of great alarm by the continual passing of parties of Creek Indians on their way to the country occupied by the Seminoles." According to the *Tallahassee Floridian*, hundreds of Creeks had penetrated Florida despite the effort of the territorial militia to stop them. But these parties tried to be as secretive as possible. They avoided confrontations with the whites, and in most cases, did not seek to murder them. They did loot deserted plantations to survive, carrying off "cattle, horses, clothing, and provisions." In some cases, they plundered the outbuildings of farms without disturbing the families living there. Nevertheless, the settlers feared for their lives and stayed constantly on guard. According to local tradition, some of the farm families slept in their cow pens to avoid being surprised by parties of Indians in the night. The cattle could detect the coming of the Indians well in advance, and once let out of their pens, they would always retreat in the opposite direction, leading their owners through the darkness and out of harm's way.[46]

Unfortunately, Georgia troops were not content to let the Indians pass by unmolested. The mounted volunteers kept up their searches and numerous skirmishes occurred. The largest of the late summer fights took place on August 27, when a company of sixty-five Georgians fought thirty-three rebel warriors and their families at Cow Creek near the line between Ware and Lowndes counties. The whites dispersed the Indians, killed a few, and captured four, but as always, most of the fugitives escaped and continued on to the Okefenokee or directly to the Florida Territory.[47]

In fact, the constant pursuit only made the Creeks more determined to escape, even to the point of killing their offspring. The desperate fugitives sometimes suffocated hungry, crying infants to prevent soldiers from hearing them. The troops found these babies with their mouths and noses packed full of moss and dry grass. The Creeks also killed larger children to avoid encumbrance. One group of captive women, en route to Fort Mitchell for removal, poisoned all their children in the night so they could make good their escape. However, this was not selfish behavior. The rebel Creeks obviously believed death was a better fate for their young than falling into the hands of the whites, whose acquisitive, commodifying behavior applied to Indian youngsters as well. After the Ichawaynotchaway battle, for example, the civilian soldiers not only distributed ten or twelve packhorse loads of captured goods among themselves, they also divided the Indian infants they found abandoned or orphaned in the woods. According to Major Jernigan's final report, the men who took these babies "seemed pleased to have them." And, indeed, one wonders just how many Creek youngsters ended up in the slave quarters of Alabama, Georgia, and Florida before the war ended. Truth be told, the Creeks' long-standing fear of enslavement helped inspire their rebellion in the first place. After witnessing the workings of the whites' economic system over the centuries, they surely had good reason to believe that even if they emigrated west that system would ultimately reduce them to slavery, something worse than death.[48]

The determination of the rebels and their success in escaping capture increased the level of fear among the whites, but this fear turned to panic when they realized that the rebel flight was only a part of a larger war strategy. Captured Indian women informed the settlers that their retreat to Florida, and the fact that they had forsworn attacking white people along the way, did not mean that the Creek war was over for the Georgians. In fact, the rebel warriors intended only to deposit their women and children in the Seminole country before returning to Georgia with some of the Seminole warriors to renew the conflict. Furthermore, the Georgians believed that the Creeks had no intention of simply using the Okefenokee Swamp as a temporary camping ground before moving into Florida. It now appeared the Creeks meant to establish permanent base camps and staging areas there for their upcoming raids in the south Georgia counties. In fact, Ware County militiamen, after having fought engagements with Indians along the Florida border in early September, followed their trail into "the dismal and almost impassable bogs of the Okefenokee" and discovered a large Indian campground on an island in the swamp. The Georgians believed raids from such strongholds would begin in the fall when the Creeks and Seminoles moved north from Florida in numbers to escape the next campaign of U.S. troops there.[49]

The citizens of south Georgia cried out to Governor Schley for help in averting the fall disaster. A committee of respectable citizens in

Decatur County expressed a common sentiment: "We the undersigned citizens of Decatur County considering ourselves, families, and property in a state of immediate danger from the inroads of the Indians, and knowing that in our present state of defense nothing but an over-ruling Providence prevents the savage from murdering our wives and children, burning our houses and laying waste our farms; do feel it our duty to address your Excellency on the subject of an immediate and so far as consistent and adequate defense." More specifically, the south Georgians wanted troops sent to their aid and a military post built on the edge of the Okefenokee to watch for Indian movements in and out of the swamp. Schley wanted to comply but he found himself in a difficult position. He had already raised large contingents of volunteers to serve in Florida, and the enlistments of most of the Georgia volunteers serving against the Creeks would expire in September. Raising a sufficient force to protect south Georgia from the Creeks would require drafting militiamen, which Schley had already discovered was a very unpopular, costly, and ineffective way to fight Indians. Volunteer companies were more successful, but the state lacked funds to support them. In Thomas County, for example, each volunteer company patrolled the Georgia-Florida border for about ten days before turning the task over to another unit of volunteers. These men had to use their own horses, provisions, and guns, and this cost them dearly. They complained that many of them were poor and could not sustain themselves as soldiers. Furthermore, their crops suffered from want of attention, and some men lost their crops entirely. They begged Schley for arms, ammunition, and money, but he was unable to comply. Consequently, he decided to call on the federal government for assistance. He asked General Jesup to station federal troops in Ware and Lowndes counties, as they were "the least populous and most defenseless portion of the country through which the Indians were passing." Fortunately for the Georgians, Jesup agreed. He sent two hundred regular troops to the Georgia-Florida border. These men marched out of Irwinton on September 29, followed the general route of the flying Creeks through southwestern Georgia, and set up camp in Lowndes County near the western fringe of the Okefenokee Swamp.[50]

By that time the fighting in southern Georgia had ceased, but Jesup's response to Schley's request was a tacit admission that neither his march against the rebels in New Alabama nor his forced removal effort had ended the Second Creek War. In fact, his efforts made the rebels only more desperate and determined to resist two unacceptable alternatives: incorporation into the white socioeconomic system as slaves or removal to the West. The flight to Florida and the continuation of the war in southern Georgia was an expression of this rebel tenacity. Now, as the fall approached, it appeared that the Creek resistance movement, united with that of the Seminoles, would become larger and more destructive than ever before. In fact, the federal garrison at Newnansville, Florida, reported seeing numerous small parties of Creeks passing by them, going south to the Seminoles. And some of these Creek refugees began to attack settlers in northern Florida, thereby drawing pursuit from the troops at Newnansville, as well as from those regular troops Jesup posted at the Okefenokee. The editor of the *Columbus Enquirer* lamented all this and summed up the events of July and August in words that were more perceptive than he realized: "It is a remarkable fact, in the history of the recent difficulties with the savages, that the whites generally believe the war at an end, about the time it fairly commences. Whether this arises from a want of knowledge, among the commanding officers, *of the real character of the Indians*, we do not pretend to say."[51]

8. Recriminations

Despite the fears of an even larger war with Creeks and Seminoles in southern Georgia and Alabama, the late summer and fall of 1836 brought a temporary cessation of armed hostilities—a lull in the eye of the storm. Yet conflict did not end. In the aftermath of fighting between Indians and whites, the whites continued to engage in an intraethnic conflict, arguing constantly among themselves. Revealing once again the economic and political competitiveness that had helped bring on the Indian war, the whites now clashed with each other on issues rising out of the Creek rebellion. The conduct of the Creek removal, the punishment of rebel leaders and warriors, the disposition of the remaining Creek lands, and the assignment of blame for a war all thought disgraceful continued to be topics of hot dispute even after the shooting died down.

The debate showed that many Georgians and Alabamians viewed the Creek war and removal as negative experiences, not as triumphs. They knew that something had gone awry. Some felt guilty for the injustices done to the Natives. Many even pitied the Creeks as they marched from their ancient homeland. Most were ashamed of the conduct of the war, knowing they had not performed well. Yet few citizens assumed personal responsibility for the situation. They blamed others for the debacle, or they passed the whole sorry state of affairs off as one of the mysteries of history. They saw the sad dispossession and removal of the Creeks as an unfortunate yet somehow unavoidable episode in the ongoing struggle between "savagery" and "civilization." They even wrote it all off as the unfathomable will of their God. They could not acknowledge that their economic system repeatedly produced such results. They also could not admit that they were both products and creators of such a system, which had been in operation so long and had become so powerful that it seemed to be an uncontrollable force of nature rather than a mere creation of humankind. Indeed, the system that had been imposing itself on the Creeks since the sixteenth century seemed omnipotent and had become a source of worship for many European Americans, whether they would admit it or not.

Still, the fact that so many southerners lamented the course of events and did not seek to glorify the Creek war and removal is surprising. While many historians have detailed the negative impact of the removal era on Native Americans, few if any have studied the impact on whites at the grassroots level where the removals took place. The view implicit in most historical accounts is that a united body of aggressive, remorseless white southerners pushed for removal, were relieved and happy when it happened, and benefited economically as a result. After all, the Indian removals facilitated the expansion of cotton cultivation into the Deep South, and as a consequence, cotton production became not only the South's leading industry but the cornerstone of the nation's "market revolution." Given this situation, one would expect that southerners would have extolled the removals after the fact and even mythologized events like the Second Creek War. But this did not happen. The Creek case reveals that whites were not so united in purpose, not so remorseless, and definitely not all happy to see the Natives go the way they did. And far from dressing up the Creek war, most local observers saw it for what it was: a failure. They did not, however, take the next logical stop and admit that this failure was an indictment of the acquisitive and competitive nature of their entire society and its economic system.

Once the smoke of battle cleared in the late summer and early fall of 1836, the citizens of Alabama and Georgia had time to stop and think more about the causes of the stunning Creek rebellion and war. Naturally, they were angry and wanted to punish those responsible for the costly and humiliating affair. Yet they could not agree who the responsible parties actually were. Two schools of thought arose. Governor Schley and many Georgians simply blamed the rebel warriors and chiefs and wanted to chastise them with executions and prison terms. Governor Clay and the Alabamians, however, seemed more interested in bringing the land speculators and liquor dealers before the bar of justice. When the fighting temporarily ended and the Creek removal began, these two groups clashed, and President Jackson sent a special commission to Alabama to settle the issue of war causation and culpability.

General Jesup's removal policy brought the controversy to a head. Because Secretary Cass had charged him with the larger tasks of winning the Creek war, removing the Creeks from Alabama, and supporting the fight against the Seminoles, Jesup had little interest in punishing rebel captives. Furthermore, he believed that the peace and security of the country demanded that the speedy removal of the Creeks must take priority over all other considerations. Consequently, the general rushed his rebel prisoners out of the country before county officers in Georgia and Alabama could arrest all the Indians they suspected of crimes. These officers managed to claim and incarcerate some of the rebels, but prosecuting them proved difficult because Jesup's hasty removal of other Native witnesses interfered with the collection of incriminating evidence. In fact, Jesup allowed both Neah Micco and Neah Emathla, the men who led the Creek rebellion, to leave Alabama without being arrested or seriously questioned by local sheriffs and prosecutors. In excusing this action, the general claimed that no real evidence existed against most of the hostile leaders, so he saw no reason to keep them in Alabama. Thus, he detained only Jim Henry, the man both Alabamians and Georgians blamed for the more outrageous crimes committed during the rebellion.[1]

Ironically, just as the outbreak of the war had covered over the misdeeds of the land speculators, now Jesup's removal policy tended to cover over the misdeeds of the Indians. This incensed the Georgians, who had a long history of conflict with both the Creeks and the federal government and who believed that they had borne the brunt of rebel hostilities without any chance of seeking proper retribution. Furthermore, the Georgians had feared all along that once pressed by a mass of troops, the rebel leaders and warriors would simply declare their innocence and the federal government, as it had often done in the past, would be lenient and let them escape just punishment. Jesup's speedy removal policy realized their fears. The Georgia newspapers, particularly the states' rights party organs, roundly criticized the federal government's negligence. The *Columbus Enquirer* even blamed the renewal of the war in southern Georgia in July on the fact that Jesup had failed to cower the common Indians by inflicting immediate and severe punishment on their captured leaders. In fact, the paper accused the government of "coaxing, begging, and persuading Indians to keep the peace" and warned that if the rebel chiefs were allowed to go freely to the West, they would simply continue their war against the whites on that frontier.[2]

Governor Schley was especially angry with Jesup. On June 28, shortly after General Patterson marched Neah Emathla's band into Fort Mitchell, Schley called for all offended parties to step forward with evidence against the captives. He then asked General Jesup to delay the removal of the rebel warriors until such time as he could accumulate all the evidence he needed to convict the ringleaders. But Jesup did not want to wait. He sent Neah Emathla's people off to Tuskegee on July 2 and made a political enemy of Schley in the process. The angry governor was able to claim only nine members of Neah Emathla's group, although one of these men was the chief's son-in-law, the notorious David Hardridge, whom the Georgians blamed for planning the attack on Roanoke. With Hardridge and the others secure in the Columbus jail, Governor Schley tried on July 8 to get nineteen more rebels out of the Russell County, Alabama, jail so he could try and punish them in Georgia. Apparently, he was unsuccessful in this effort, but he did not stop trying to secure Native prisoners. With a little more evidence in hand, he dispatched sixty mounted men to Tuskegee on July 9 to claim more of Neah Emathla's warriors for trial. On arriving in Tuskegee, however, these men found that the rebel removal party had already set out on the road west. Undeterred, these diligent troops rode on to Montgomery. There they caught up to the Indians, gathered twelve suspects, and carried them back to Columbus. Several more of the suspects committed suicide rather than return to Georgia.[3]

Still, Schley and his Georgians were not satisfied. They wanted the only major rebel leader remaining in the country, Jim Henry. The *Columbus Enquirer* characterized Henry as "a villain, more conspicuous than any other in the nation throughout the war." Schley held the same view and demanded that General Jesup turn Henry over to him, claiming that he led the war party that burned Roanoke and had "committed many murders, robberies and arsons in Georgia." According to Schley, Henry was "amenable to the laws of Georgia, against which he has notoriously offended." However, Governor Clay had made a previous request for the rebel leader, and as Henry was a resident of Alabama, Jesup handed him over to the sheriff of Russell County on the charge of stage robbery and murder. The sheriff placed Henry with the county's other rebel prisoners, including the ringleaders in the stage robberies, in the county jail at Girard, which sat just across the Chattahoochee from Columbus. But this provoked the Georgians, who now believed that Jesup, by denying Schley's order, was trying to screen Henry from punishment. Indeed, so great was the feeling of indignation that the Georgians were willing, should Schley give the word, to cross the river and seize Henry by force. To prevent this, General Sanford, the first corps commander, placed a strong military guard around the Russell County jail. For his part, Governor Schley asked Governor Clay to rearrest Henry should he be acquitted by the Alabama court and to deliver him to Schley's agents to stand trial again in Georgia. Clay agreed, but the Alabamians promptly moved Henry to a more secure jail in Chambers County, where he received medical attention for shoulder wounds received in the fighting. Clay obviously wanted to give Henry special protection for a couple of reasons. One, in keeping with his view that the hostile Creeks were Alabama citizens, who had committed an armed rebellion against the state, the governor wanted to try, convict, and punish one of the major leaders of the rebellion in Alabama. But Clay also believed, along with Hogan and probably Jesup, that land speculators, the Columbus men in particular, conspired in fomenting the rebellion to cover over their thefts. Therefore, Clay wanted to keep Henry out of their hands and alive so he could fully explain the plot and give evidence against culpable white men.[4]

That Jim Henry should become such a center of attention showed not only how tangled the local communities of Indians and whites had become but also how much the competitive whites mistrusted the commercial motivations of their own society. Unlike the rebels Neah Micco and Neah Emathla, Henry was an acculturated mixed-blood. The best evidence suggests that he was the son of a Chehaw mother and a Scottish trader named McHenry and he lived at or near Pindertown in southwestern Georgia before the Georgia Creeks moved into Alabama in the late 1820s. Furthermore, Henry was only about twenty years old at the time of the war and had a fair amount of education for the day and time. Like David Hardridge, also a trader's son, Henry attended the Asbury Methodist mission school near Fort Mitchell, an institution generally opposed by old-line Creek conservatives. In later life he would call himself James McHenry and become a Methodist preacher; a Mason; a member of the progressive McIntosh, or Southern, party; and even a major in the Confederate army. Then, after the Civil War, when the Creeks established a constitutional government on the U.S. plan, McHenry served as president of the Creek Senate, called the House of Kings. Reverend McHenry also became a successful farmer and trader in the Indian Territory, but he began his business life in Columbus, first as a clerk and interpreter for Indian customers in Stewart and Fontaine's store, then as a small store owner himself. He also worked, along with Hardridge, as an interpreter for the land speculators before deciding to take a rebel stand. In fact, Fontaine and Stewart were major land buyers, holding title to forty-nine thousand acres of the Creek domain. In addition, Fontaine served as mayor of Columbus during the speculation episode and war. Ironically, then, it was probably Henry's close association with important white men that led them to see him as a major Indian leader. After all, Henry was tall, handsome, and popular, often dressing "more like a courtier than a warrior" in "clothes of finest broadcloth and casimere [sic]." With their own racial prejudices and acquisitive instincts in mind, the Georgians must have felt that only an acculturated Indian like Henry could be the brains of the Native rebellion, and he must have done so to increase his own personal fortune. Years after the war, the story persisted that he had staged the revolt as a means of cornering the valuable Indian trade. But in accusing Jim Henry, the whites were actually indicting the economic practices of many of their own people. They projected their own motives onto the young Chehaw, then sought to punish him for their own sins.[5]

But Henry was not an important Creek leader, and, in fact, the rebel chiefs may have used him as a foil and scapegoat as well. It also appears that this realization dawned on General Jesup sometime after he began his march on the insurgents' strongholds. At first, he and the Alabamians believed the tales of Henry's role in the war and condemned the young warrior as roundly as the Georgians. Jesup even ordered his Creek allies to capture Henry as soon as possible and simply execute him on the spot as a means of squashing rebel resistance. But by the end of the expedition Jesup's mood changed, and he allowed Henry to surrender without summary execution or even imprisonment. Thus, the young man ventured back to Euchee Creek, retrieved his family, and remained free until Neah Micco's party marched off to Montgomery. Only then did the Alabama authorities take full custody of Henry, and his tearful farewell to his young wife as she departed with the other emigrants for the West touched the hearts of all observers. Moreover, when General Patterson sat down to interview Henry, he concluded that the so-called rebel genius did not deserve his reputation. In fact, Patterson discovered that "public report has greatly exaggerated the consequences and capability of Jim Henry: the position he seems to have occupied among the Indians, by no means warrants the anxiety with which the pursuit after him has been viewed. He is young, and possesses none of those qualities calculated to give him sway over the tribe." Yet the other rebel chieftains were more than willing to let Henry appear to be an important headman, because, as Thomas Woodward explained, "The Indians soon learn whom the whites look upon as being their leaders, and not being as ambitious of distinction as the whites generally are, when any talking or compromising is to be done, those persons are put forward. Such was the case with Jim Henry and others, in 1836." Thus, Henry and Hardridge, men who had always had close contact with the whites, stayed behind to face the bar of justice, while Neah Micco, Neah Emathla, and others emigrated and escaped punishment.[6]

But in the end, it appears the authorities realized their mistake and did not convict Henry or Hardridge of any crimes. Placed before an examining justice in Russell County on July 12, Henry denied most of the atrocities attributed to him. He admitted robbing some homes and carrying off the county sheriff's slaves, but he denied robbing the stages or committing any murders whatsoever. Furthermore, Henry said he had not participated in the sacking and burning of Roanoke—one of the main accusations against him—but he did claim to have led the rebel warriors in battle against the Georgians at Shepherd's plantation, Turner's Field, and the attack on Fort Jones. This hardly seems likely, however, owing to Henry's youth, and he may have been bragging because his fellow warriors did well in these contests. But even as he admitted his part in the rebellion, he pleaded extenuating circumstances. He claimed that his people were starving; they had to rise up or die. In the end, the justice decided that all he could do was charge Henry with "negro stealing" (a capital offense) and bind him over for a grand jury hearing. Sure enough, the jury did indict the young man and the judge scheduled him for trial at the next meeting of the circuit court. By that time, however, Henry had decided to stop boasting and incriminating himself, and he gained the able services of two attorneys at law, Messrs. Underwood and Harris. These men succeeded in changing the venue of his trial from the scene of the hostilities in Russell County to Montgomery in Old Alabama, where Henry remained for several months before being remanded back to Russell County for trial because of some "defect in the proceedings." Then, surprisingly, the court acquitted the young man sometime in the later months of 1837 and turned him over to the Georgians. Then he and Hardridge stood trial in Columbus in January 1838, but once again juries acquitted both men, undoubtedly for lack of real evidence. Captain Page, the removal superintendent, attended the trial and quickly secluded the two men in his hotel room until he could turn them over to Benjamin Marshall for removal to the West. According to Page, he afforded Henry and Hardridge shelter because there was "so much excitement about their being acquitted that if they had been turned loose in the country they would have been murdered."[7]

Admittedly, Henry's escape from all punishment must have looked highly suspicious to all those angry citizens who saw a dark conspiracy lying behind the Creek war. Certainly they knew of Henry's close association with the land speculators, and they must have taken his acquittals as proof that the land thieves had put him up to instigating the Indian uprising and then used their money and political power to keep him silent and free from retribution. After all, Henry had worked for Stewart and Fontaine. Then, Charles McLemore, the head of a speculating group holding 131, 686 acres of Creek land, helped get Henry transferred to the Chambers County jail and supposedly wrote a letter to President Jackson on the young man's behalf. Next, Henry received expert, and no doubt expensive, counsel from Underwood and Harris, as well as a fortuitous cooling-off respite in Montgomery. Then came the shocking acquittals, first in Russell County, then in Columbus itself, the very nest of the speculators. And at that point, Captain Page, whom Colonel Hogan had long since charged with being in league with the land buyers, conveniently sheltered Henry from vigilante justice. To complete the escape, Benjamin Marshall, interpreter for speculators and a member of the notorious emigration company, also made up of speculators, took charge of the young man and whisked him away to the West. Surely this scenario made a compelling argument for the conspiracy theory at the time, and hindsight makes the theory look even better. After all, Henry went on to join the accommodationist McIntosh Party, which continued to ally its fortunes with those of the wealthiest white citizens in the South, even to the point of joining and fighting for the Southern Confederacy.[8]

But, in the end, the conspiracy theory hardly seems credible. The Creeks, not whites, planned the rebellion, and the speculators suffered from the uprising along with settlers of lesser means. Consequently, Henry's acquittals occurred because the courts realized he was not really a great criminal, although this conclusion does not rule out the possibility that the speculators aided his defense to keep him quiet about their nefarious business practices prior to the war. Furthermore, the treatment of all the other rebel prisoners tends to support this view of Henry's case. In fact, almost all of the rebel prisoners in Georgia and Alabama, some fifty-seven in number, eventually went free for want of evidence, and apparently only six received the death penalty for their part in the uprising. And oftentimes important men wanted these Indians convicted but lacked the power to get it done. Gen. J. S. Watson, for example, went to Fort Mitchell in early July 1836 and secured fifteen warriors he knew had attacked his plantation south of Columbus and shot several of his slaves. But in November, he stood by helplessly as the superior court in Columbus acquitted all fifteen men at once. Thus, Henry was not alone in receiving what appeared to be leniency from the courts. Indeed, one might make the case that the Russell County court executed the six rebels it did only as a token gesture to appease the mass of angry citizens in the Chattahoochee Valley. These six unfortunate men, all residents of Wetumpka town, were convicted of participating in the stage robberies and murders on New Road the previous May. Tuscoona Fixico, one of the town chiefs, led them in the enterprise. The whites hanged these men at Girard, Alabama, on November 25, 1836, but even their deaths failed to satisfy a crowd of hundreds who had "left their homes, eager to witness the breaking of an Indian's neck." In fact, the condemned rebels turned their executions into a dramatic rite of passage and last act of passive resistance, which according to the *Columbus Enquirer*, was "well calculated to draw forth the sympathies of the white man in behalf of these deluded and unhappy people." On their way to the scaffold, the warriors stopped by a burned pine stump to smear their faces and bodies with black smut—the color of death in the Creek cosmos. Then, on mounting the scaffold, Tuscoona Fixico fully and bravely declared his guilt before the assemblage but proclaimed the other Indians completely innocent. Tuscoona also stated that he committed his crimes only in accordance with instructions given him by Neah Emathla and Neah Micco, men whom the *Enquirer* described as now "quietly reposing in the forests of Arkansas." Finally, the chief and his five compatriots faced their deaths stoically and heroically, singing several songs and giving a final "whoop" before taking the fatal leap. All of this had a sobering effect on the observers and left a reporter for the *Columbus Herald* to lament that, while "the most prominent actors in the bloody drama" had escaped, "doubtless some unlucky son of the forest suffered in the very midst of his innocence." And yet the reporter concluded, "it cannot be helped—blood for blood, life for life, is the golden maxim; the wail of widow, and the cry of the orphan, sued for revenge in tones of thunder."[9]

Yet despite this cry for revenge, the fact that settlers in the Chattahoochee Valley convicted so few rebels proves that they did not hate the Creeks to the point of letting their desire for retribution overcome the rule of law. Furthermore, the lack of legal convictions, as well as the absence of vigilante justice, indicates that many citizens, even in Georgia, understood the real reason for the Native rebellion. Certainly this was the case in Alabama, as evidenced by General Patterson. Shortly after taking Neah Micco, Neah Emathla, and Jim Henry into custody, he informed Governor Clay, "It is becoming the general impression that the hostile Creeks have been driven to the perpetration of these outrages by a mass of wrong & injury suffered by them from a portion of our citizens disgraceful to the age in which we live & a lasting stigma upon our country." Then he added, "I do not ask that the arms of the law should be weakened but I speak, I am sure the sentiment of my command when I suggest that these considerations ought not to be disregarded in the question of their punishment." Clay obviously agreed. Despite having declared the Indian uprising an act of treacherous rebellion against the state of Alabama, the governor did not seek sweeping retribution on the captive warriors and chiefs. He asked General Jesup to surrender only "hostile criminals" to the county authorities, not all rebel leaders and fighting men. And while Clay was willing to let the courts try these Indian criminals for various offenses, he ordered the judge and solicitor of the circuit court embracing the New Alabama counties where the uprising took place to rigorously prosecute only known murderers. The governor seemed willing to let other offenses pass by unnoticed.[10]

But some Alabamians did not think leniency toward the Creeks was enough; they wanted to punish the white men who either caused the war or participated in it on the side of the hostile Indians. Indeed, even James Van Ness, the prosecuting attorney in the stage-attack trials, proclaimed that the Creeks were being removed and trying a relative few of them for the rebellion was not worth the time and money. But, he said, all the whites involved in the stage attacks and rebellion should be prosecuted, otherwise they would remain in Alabama to "pose a lingering danger to a civilized community." James E. Belser of the *Montgomery Advertiser* then led a verbal attack on those he saw as culpable. He wrote to President Jackson to give him "especial notice" of the "system of villainy" the speculators had practiced on the Indians, accusing Eli Shorter and Benjamin Tarver, both residents of Columbus, of heading the combination of "land pirates" who drove the Creeks to war. Then Belser set his sights on the Columbus press, claiming that the town's newspapers were "principally in the hands of speculators," who covered "their own vile deeds" by attacking Alabama's chief executive. Finally, Belser attacked the town of Columbus itself, with which Montgomery competed for control of the produce of New Alabama. Revealing some of the tension surrounding this economic rivalry, Belser contended that there was "not within our knowledge such a brothel of corruption as is contained within the limits of our celebrated sister-town. If the righteous could be extracted from it, there is good reason why it should be blotted out from the book of remembrance."[11]

John Hogan also stepped forward to call for retribution against the speculators, by publishing correspondence he had received from John S. Scott, a defector from the speculators' camp. One of these letters, written by Shorter during the height of the speculations, proclaimed that "stealing was the order of the day" and outlined the methods Shorter and his partners used to swindle the Indians out of their lands in Chambers County. Another letter, written by Benjamin B. Tarver, gave even more dramatic proof of fraud by impersonation and pretended payment. "There is nothing going on at this time, but stealing of land with about fifty Indians. Pay them ten dollars or five when certified, and get all the balance back, and get four hundred or five hundred contracts certified with fifty Indians, is all the game." Then Tarver concluded, "Hurrah boys—here goes it—let's steal all we can. I shall go for it, or get no lands—now or never."[12]

Hogan also attempted to produce evidence that speculators had planned the war to stop the government's investigation of their schemes and to provoke a forced removal of the Creeks. After holding talks with Opothle Yahola and the rebel chief Hotulgar Harjo, Hogan published the outlines of the plot he discovered. He proclaimed that two of the leading rebels, Neah Micco and Tuskenea, had never operated as free agents in directing Creek affairs. The company of land speculators headed by Thomas Woodward and William Walker had always controlled Tuskenea, while Luther Blake and Paddy Carr and their group dictated policy to Neah Micco. These speculators had used these chiefs to secure control of Creek land, and after concocting the Creek war "in high council" in Columbus, they instructed their puppet chiefs as to how the uprising should proceed. Then Woodward, who attended the council under the pretext of going to the Columbus horse races, returned home to Tuskegee to spread the word among friends and neighbors that a war was about to occur and they should protect themselves. And once the war broke, according to Hogan, Woodward and Walker continued to hold secret councils with Tuskenea, even as they marched out with Jesup's expeditionary force to put down the rebellion they themselves created.[13]

Hogan's explanation of events hardly seems reliable. The speculators did try to influence Creek leaders, but Hogan gave these chiefs no credit for independent thinking, preferring to blame the whole rebellion on a plot concocted by white men. More to the point, Hogan ignored the fact that Columbus became a prime target of the rebellion. The speculators, as corrupt as they may have been, surely would not turn Indians loose on the town and its surrounding plantations where they and their friends lived. It seems much more likely that the Creek rebels targeted Columbus and its environs for attack because they considered the speculators their enemies, not their friends and coconspirators. Nevertheless, Hogan's conspiracy theory flourished in Alabama and even in the war-ravished section of Georgia. Both Governor Clay and General Jesup suspected Judge Shorter and Paddy Carr of instigating the Creek war, and even those citizens who doubted Hogan's full account still blamed the speculators for causing the war and sought to censure them. At public dinners held to honor war veterans, men raised their glasses and expressed such sentiments. In Stewart County, Georgia—the site of several battles and extensive Creek depredations—Thomas Stuckey proposed the toast: "Maj. Eli S. Shorter, together with all those who have been participants in the late Indian frauds, be forever damned in the estimation of every honest and intelligent citizen." In Pike County a celebrant added, "May the time soon roll round when the hostile Indians that have killed the innocent be brought to justice, and those that have stolen their lands be hung by the neck until they are dead, and then be buried together as murderers and dishonest men." Then in Fayette County, Larkin Burnitt issued an even more creative salute to the "land stealers of the Creek nation."

> May angry corns beset their toes,
> 'Till blood at every step may flow,
> And narrow shoes their feet to wear,
> 'Till savage yells are heard no more.[14]

All the complaints soon reached Washington, including a document titled "A Memorial of the People of East Alabama and the Western Frontier of Georgia." This memorial, containing seventeen pages of signatures, not only blamed the land companies for plotting the Creek war but called on Congress to investigate the matter. This request found attentive ears in the House of Representatives, especially among President Jackson's opponents from the North and South. John Quincy Adams and other northern abolitionists believed that southern slaveholders had precipitated the conflict so the federal government would drive the Creeks out of a rich cotton country. They also believed that Jackson's forced removal policy violated the treaty rights of the friendly Creeks. Consequently, Adams attempted to block an appropriation of funds for the Creek removal until Congress conducted a full investigation of the war and its causes. Jackson's southern opponents also wanted an investigation of the war because they believed the president's policies were to blame. Dixon Lewis of Alabama even accused Jackson of being too favorable to the Indians, of placing their rights ahead of New Alabama's settlers. Lewis believed this leniency and permissiveness toward the Natives had emboldened them and encouraged them to go to war against their white neighbors. Ironically then, both the abolitionist Adams and the proslavery Lewis joined forces to push for a congressional investigation of the Creek conflict. Furthermore, they proposed that either the Committee on Indian Affairs or a special committee selected by the House should conduct the inquiry. However, the majority of representatives, including Jackson's partisans, voted against this proposal and decided to let the president handle the matter. On July 1 the House forwarded a resolution to Jackson calling on him to look into the causes of the Creek war, specifically the alleged misdeeds of the land companies, and to pursue the prosecution of those who may have broken the law.[15]

On July 7 the War Department, pursuant to the resolution, commissioned two men, T. Hartley Crawford and Alfred Balch, as government investigators. The president, through Secretary Cass, then gave the commissioners a twofold task: first, to investigate the causes of the war; second, to inquire into the Creek land frauds and determine if the president should approve or disapprove the land contracts made in McHenry's and Sanford's districts of the Old Creek Nation. The rebellion had cut short Hogan's investigation into Sanford's contracts, and although he had submitted his final report on the McHenry contracts—most of which were fraudulent—Jackson thought the document too sketchy and generally unsatisfactory. The president did not wish to overturn land contracts on what he thought was flimsy evidence of wrongdoing. Consequently, Crawford and Balch had to do the work in McHenry's district all over again. The commissioners arrived in New Alabama in September, set up shop near Tuskegee, and began their investigations by placing notices in the regional newspapers, informing all parties holding unconfirmed, disputed, or reversed contracts on Creek land to provide evidence within forty days of the validity of their claims. They also wrote to governors Schley and Clay, and all other informed parties, asking for evidence of land frauds and information that might enlighten the commissioners on the causes of the Creek war. In particular, they wanted to find out if some conspiracy had brought the conflict about, for the president had specifically directed them "to ascertain what steps have been taken by any white persons to excite the Indians to war."[16]

Unfortunately, Crawford and Balch, like Hogan before them, encountered numerous obstacles in their path. Again, the speculators launched a letter-writing and newspaper campaign against the government investigation. An angry Balch complained of the "high toned nature of Shorter's correspondence" and lamented that certain wealthy parties had the power to influence, obfuscate, and cajole public officials and opinion. General Sanford, in fact, did a complete turnaround in his testimony on the frauds. In 1834, when he worked as a land-sales agent, Sanford was the first person to notify the government of frauds, but by the time of the investigation in 1836, he was saying that "there was little or no fraud in his district." But Crawford and Balch had an even bigger problem than the speculator campaign. They lacked the power to coerce. They could not compel anyone to give testimony or tell the truth. When, for example, they visited the Montgomery jail to interrogate William Earle about the incendiary British proclamation he circulated among the Creeks just prior to the uprising, the man would not tell them why he did it or who, if anyone, put him up to it. Furthermore, the commissioners encountered a general lack of enthusiasm for the investigation on the part of important Georgians. While Governor Clay showed a willingness to help in the inquiry, providing what evidence he could and blaming the war on the land frauds and the intemperance introduced to the Indians by a "class of white men," Governor Schley refused to provide any useful information. In his brief reply to the commissioners' questions, he simply passed over the wrongdoing of the land pirates and liquor dealers—many of them Georgians—and blamed the Indians for the war, calling the Natives "idle, dissolute vagrants, many of whom had for a long time, been subsisting on provisions stolen from the people of Georgia living on and near the Chattahoochie." But perhaps the greatest problem the commissioners faced was the Creek removal. With the Indians departing and the settlers coming in, New Alabama was like a "moving camp," and evidence against the speculators was difficult to obtain. Thus, the removal tended to shield both Indians and whites from punishment for their parts in the Creek war.[17]

Faced with all these difficulties, the commissioners could not do a satisfactory job. After spending the fall in Alabama, they published a report assigning partial blame for the war on the speculators, stating, "It is shocking to reflect on the disclosures elicited. They embrace men of every degree. Persons, heretofore deemed respectable, are implicated in the most disgraceful attempts to defraud those who were incapacitated from protecting their own interests." The commissioners also recommended that the president reject a large number of questionable land contracts. However, the commissioners could prove no conspiracy on the part of the speculators to start the war, nor were they able to compile enough proof to bring any one individual or group before the bar of justice for any particular crime. Even so, President Van Buren, Jackson's successor, did not follow their recommendations. In the end, he approved most of the fraudulent land contracts. The commissioners had to content themselves with the somewhat absurd observation that as of October, 1836, the government policy of allotting the Creek domain in severalty and allowing individual holders to sell their land had resulted in a fair number of legitimate contracts, giving the Indians $890,400 free and clear to begin their new lives in the West. However, they failed to note that land included in these legitimate sales amounted to only 774,400 acres; the federal government had allotted the Creeks an estimated 2,187,200 acres. Had the Creeks been able to sell all this land for a fair price, they would have been far better off. Furthermore, much of the money the Natives received from the fair contracts went almost directly into the hands of lawyers, merchants, liquor dealers, and all the others operating the notorious Indian business. Again, Balch and Crawford failed to make this clear. Their reports did, however, tend to clear the government of any wrongdoing, which may have been the sole purpose of the investigation all along.[18]

For his part, Crawford placed the heaviest blame for the war on the Creeks. In his highly condescending report, he referred to them as "imbecile and dependent beings," who rose up in armed rebellion to resist removal. However, their aversion to removal, he claimed, did not stem so much from an attachment to their native soil as from "that indolence so natural to them." Or, in other words, the Creeks would rather fight than go to the trouble of moving to a better place for themselves. Crawford also stated that most Creeks had sold their lands, some of them years ago, and planted no more crops. The Indians simply stopped feeding themselves, he implied. Furthermore, they squandered the money they received for their reserves, because, Crawford said, they were "ignorant of the true value of money." Thus, these Indians, "untaught in the ways of morality, unbound by the ties of social life, and not feeling or recognizing ties of any kind, unless they yield personal gratification, endeavored to supply the wants their own vices had created, by depredation and theft." The Creeks, Crawford declared, were "children of impulse" who on seeing the Seminoles rise up, decided to follow suit without fully considering the consequences. And while Crawford did admit that "numerous and glaring frauds" had been perpetrated against the Indians, he also noted that the inhabitants of some of the Creek towns where the worst frauds occurred remained "most peaceful." Then, shockingly, Crawford implied that the Creeks bore responsibility even for land frauds, because they were so incompetent in the handling of land or money. Indeed, he asserted that the president had not wanted to allot individual reserves to the Creeks as he knew certain individuals would move in to amass fortunes. But the chiefs had insisted on the reserves, and despite all the safeguards the government imposed, it could not in the end protect the Indians and their property from themselves and those who sought to prey on them. Then the commissioner concluded his remarks with a statement that both highlighted his view of the Indians' inability to cope and justified the government's removal policy: "It is late in the Indian's day, and his sun, it is to be feared, will soon set. The only atmosphere through which it can longer light its way, is west of the great river."[19]

In actuality, Crawford summarized perfectly the racial ideology used to justify the expropriation, of both land and resources, that lay at the heart of world-system colonialism. In the end, this ideology allowed the speculators to prevail in taking the lion's share of Creek property. Eli Shorter's statement, made the year before, came true: "The government would let things pass and use the war to excuse everything." And that was really the only way it could be, because after everything was said and done, both the speculators and the government, along with most of the New Alabama settlers, wanted the same goals: Indian land and Indian removal. By the end of the year 1836, the whites had these in hand, and many seemed satisfied with that, disdaining the desire for retribution and wanting only to enjoy the newfound bounty of a rich land finally free of its Native population. As Crawford stated, "The ordinary pursuits of life once more occupy the white inhabitants, who speak of the late robberies, conflagrations, and murders as matters of history." Those citizens who still wished to see the land speculators punished for the Creek war, along with those who had cried out for the blood of all the rebel leaders, had to sit by and stew in their disappointment. In the end there would be no satisfactory punishment for the men most responsible for all the death and destruction on both sides of the Chattahoochee River.[20]

However, some angry settlers did gain a measure of revenge. They ostracized the land speculators and punished some of the roughs who assisted the Creeks in their rebellion. Shortly after the six Indians met their deaths at Girard, the U.S. District Court in Mobile convicted Philander Broad for his part in the stage attacks and sentenced him to death by hanging. Apparently, militiamen captured Broad at his house in June and found letters taken from the stage bags in his possession. They then incarcerated the man in the Chambers County jail before transferring him to Mobile. There the testimony of one Adams, a stage driver, proved crucial to the conviction. Adams actually knew Broad and declared that he saw him directing a party of fifty of sixty Creek warriors, who burst out of a house beside New Road to attack the stage. Rumors persisted that Broad worked for the land speculators, and mysterious figures visited him in jail and attended his trial, but, again, no one could prove the conspiracy. Broad faced his punishment alone, as did Thomas Chambers of Cherokee County, Alabama. Settlers brought him in for interrogation, and after he confessed to helping the local Creeks plan an attack on them, the settlers "turned him loose in the woods," a euphemism meaning killed but denied a burial. The aggrieved New Alabamians also developed a popular myth as compensation for their inability to bring the speculators before courts of law. They simply proclaimed that God would not allow the land pirates to reap the rewards of their crimes. Johnson Jones Hooper, Chambers County resident and local colorist, gave voice to this myth in his book *Some Adventures of Captain Simon Suggs*. Hooper declared that in the ten years following the Creek removal most all of the speculators "lost money, lands, character, everything!" while those who yet retained some of their "lordly possessions" strove in vain "to avert their irresistible fate—an old age of shame and beggary." Finally, Hooper concluded, "They are cursed, all of them—blighted, root and trunk and limb! The Creek is avenged!" The facts did not justify such a sweeping judgment, but it certainly was true that some of the more infamous speculators did not enjoy their spoils for long. Judge Shorter died before the end of 1836, as did William Walker, who perished in Apalachicola, Florida, on his way south to join in the Seminole War. Thomas Woodward, after being sold out twice by the county sheriff, left Alabama in 1841 to pursue a less than happy life in Louisiana and Arkansas. Gen. Daniel McDougald and other speculators lost money when the Columbus banks they controlled failed during the economic depression that began to spread over the nation in 1837.[21]

However, the punishment of those responsible for causing the war was only one of the issues that sparked controversy among Georgians and Alabamians in the late summer and fall of 1836. These citizens were ashamed as well of the conduct of the Creek war, and they wanted to assign blame to everyone but themselves. Not surprisingly, Maj. Gen. Winfield Scott became a prime target. When he left Columbus in July, the general thought he had concluded the war successfully, but on arriving in Washington, he discovered the real reason Jackson relieved him of command: Jesup's critical letter to Francis Blair, editor of the *Washington Globe*. Scott called the letter a "treacherous instrument which . . . stabbed me in the dark," and he launched a crusade to clear his name. He wrathfully demanded a court of inquiry into his conduct in both the Creek and Seminole conflicts, and the nation's Whig newspapers, looking for anything they could use against the administration during a presidential election year, took his side in the controversy. When the court convened in Frederick, Maryland, in November, Scott accused Jesup of trying to build his military reputation by deliberately defying the orders of his superior officer. Furthermore, Scott contended that there had been no real danger to the frontier justifying Jesup's premature advance and that his unwise maneuver had caused the hostile Creeks to flee across Georgia, carrying more death and destruction with them. Then Scott cataloged in great detail all the supply problems that delayed his offensive against the rebels. He also called on Governor Schley, General Sanford, and other noted Georgians to support his testimony. The court finally cleared the general of any wrongdoing or incompetence in handling the Creek and Seminole conflicts, but many people in Georgia, Alabama, and the Florida Territory continued to blame him for all the failures. On the whole, they seemed to prefer Jesup's aggressiveness to Scott's deliberate attention to detail. Said one observer, "General Scott is too slow and systematic for Indian warfare, and is abused from Columbus to Mobile—not without cause." Despite the verdict of the court of inquiry, the popular sentiment prevailed that Scott's "Northern laurels" won against the British in the War of 1812 had now turned to "Southern willows" against the Creeks and Seminoles. However, General Jesup was not without his severe critics as well, especially in Georgia. These people, including Governor Schley, blamed Jesup for not allowing the Georgians full participation in the war, being lenient on rebel captives, and, of course, causing the war in southwest Georgia by allowing so many Creek rebels to escape from New Alabama.[22]

Schley also came under attack for his role in the conflict. Many state citizens submitted claims to the state for property destroyed by the Indians or appropriated by all the troops who took to the field against the Creeks. The governor had sole responsibility for adjusting these claims; he discovered many fraudulent and unjust ones, and these he refused to pay. In so doing, he saved the state money, but he also lost some votes in the 1837 gubernatorial election. Furthermore, some members of his own Union Party turned against him because, as a political expedient, he had appointed members of the opposition states' rights group to important military posts during the war.[23]

The vituperation continued as the citizens of Georgia and Alabama turned on themselves. They knew they had not fought the war well, and they found all the displays of cowardice and timidity particularly distressing. In Alabama, Governor Clay's political opponents used his supposed ineffectiveness as a protector of the state's people against him in the fall elections. Meanwhile, Gen. John Moore continued to claim that his regiment had performed better than any other troops, but without reward or recognition from the state or federal government. In Georgia, some critics castigated the New Alabama settlers for their incontinent flight in the face of the rebel uprising, saying they should have stayed at home to defend themselves rather than relying on others to do it for them. These Georgians, represented by O. P. Cheatham of Stewart County, wanted the rich soil of New Alabama "settled by a braver and more honorable set of men" now that the war was done. Other Georgians complained that they had come to the defense of the Creek Nation settlers, and had done most of the fighting against the rebels, without proper appreciation or cooperation from the Alabamians or the federal government. But the Georgians also pointed fingers at one another in the aftermath of so many humiliating engagements with the Creeks. Officers who had participated in those battles where the Creeks ran the whites from the field argued with one another as to who was a coward and who was not. The competition and level of condemnations grew to the point that the *Columbus Enquirer* was forced to call a halt, saying of the recriminations, "We shall therefore feel bound hereafter to publish nothing of the kind evidently personal, leaving the contending parties to convey their abuse, threats, challenges, &c., through some other channel." Members of the Georgia legislature also got caught up in the controversy, and so they decided in the fall of 1836 to completely revamp and reform the state's militia system to make it more effective in the future. However, M. T. Chapin, a Yankee lawyer living in Irwinton, attributed the disappointments of the war to a larger problem: the inferior quality of southern society. Writing home to Rhode Island, he proclaimed, "The War has been most miserably managed. The secret is the men are cowards. They don't consider how serious a matter is till they get into the woods and hear the yell of the savage. . . . So away they run and fill the country with reports as wild and false as their conduct is base and cowardly." Hearing all the insults passing back and forth, Mansfield Torrance, who had served with Jesup's Indian brigade, summed up the popular disgust with the conduct of the conflict: "The Creek War, may its history never be written but if written may it be *ex-punged*."[24]

But the conduct of the Creek war was not the greatest source of embarrassment to Alabamians during the late months of 1836. Surprisingly, the Creek removal, which the war inspired and facilitated, became an even more controversial issue. After all the death and destruction of the summer, one would expect that the state's citizens would have been overjoyed to see the Natives finally leave Alabama and would have cooperated freely with federal officials in sending them on their way. This was not always the case, as General Jesup would soon discover.

Having shipped his rebel captives from Alabama by mid-July, the general turned his attention to the systematic removal of the mass of friendly Creeks. He moved his headquarters from Tuskegee to Tallassee and stationed his force of regular troops along with Alabama and Tennessee volunteers at various posts throughout New Alabama. He intended that these troops maintain law and order between the settlers and Indians until the Natives were ready to leave the state; at that time the troops would escort them on the first leg of their journey west. Then Jesup ordered all the Creeks into removal camps north of Federal Road and warned them that if they ventured south of the highway into what had been rebel territory, they would be considered hostile by the troops and treated accordingly. Finally, Jesup ordered Opothle Yahola to assemble the people of Tuckabatchee and all its affiliated towns at Tallassee and have them ready to march west by August 10. Obviously, the general believed that if he could get the speaker of the Upper Creeks out of the country, the other leaders and towns would follow in short order. In fact, Jesup hoped to have the remainder of the Creeks, 18,000 to 20,000 people, removed from Alabama by the end of the summer, including the 1,500 to 2,000 Indians who had taken up residence near the Cherokees in Benton and Cherokee counties. He warned this group of refugee Natives, who now seemed the most troublesome and ill-tempered of the Upper Creeks, that they too would be treated as rebels if they did not move west when he gave the order.[25]

But Jesup soon learned that the Indians were not the major obstacle to his plans. Opothle Yahola and his Tuckabatchees, numbering about 2,700 souls, tried to leave Alabama as early as August 1. Another group of 1,170 Creeks, including 400 captured among the Cherokees in Tennessee, attempted to leave the vicinity of Talladega on August 6. On that same day a third detachment of 3,022 Creeks, headed by William McGillivrey, marched out of Wetumpka. However, these Indians found the path west blocked by sheriffs, lawyers, creditors, and an assortment of greedy whites. According to Jesup, "Suits were multiplied against the Indians—their negroes, horses, and other property taken—themselves driven almost to desperation by the difficulties which surrounded them." And, indeed, the Indians faced even more problems. Whiskey peddlers infested the Indian camps, spreading lies and "false stories," to keep the Indians, their good customers, from leaving Alabama. Other whites accused the Creeks in Jim Boy's Thlobthlocco town of being rebels to get at their land reserves when, in fact, those Indians had served in Jesup's expeditionary force. Numbers of Creeks could not return to their homes from the removal camps to retrieve valuable possessions and buried money for fear of being mistaken for wandering rebels and gunned down by anxious militiamen. One elderly woman, named Tocooche, had amassed considerable funds from her own industry, selling horses and cattle, but being under guard, she had to enlist Opothle Yahola's aid in securing her buried treasure before she marched off to the West. Even more bad news came in from Cherokee County, Alabama, where one Jesse Duran stood in the way of removal. The county's respectable settlers complained to Jesup that Duran had induced the Creeks to come into the Cherokee country in the first place, so that he might profit "by bringing them to want and starvation." He sold goods and liquor to the Indians and now proclaimed that he would not allow them to enroll for the removal unless he got the appointment as enrolling agent. Exasperated by the actions of Duran and others like him, Jesup concluded, "I find more difficulty than I apprehended in removing the Indians, & all the difficulties, or nearly all, arise from the interference of white men." Worse, the general believed that because of that opposition, the long-suffering Upper Creeks, heretofore friendly, "may yet be persuaded to hostilities."[26]

Gen. John Wool faced the same situation. Jesup had charged him with the task of removing all refugee Creeks living on Cherokee land in Alabama, Georgia, North Carolina, and Tennessee. He, along with the volunteer troops under his command, tried to follow orders, diligently rooting out Creeks and sending them to Gunter's Landing for transfer west. But Wool also learned that the stubborn Creek refugees were not his greatest concern. Similar to Jesup's experience, Wool found that Indian removal was a complex affair and that while some whites wanted the South swept clean of all its Native inhabitants, others wanted them to stay for a variety of economic reasons. In fact, Wool stated, "the worst Indians" he had to contend with were the whites living among the Indians. Besides the grog shop and grocery operators, who wanted to retain good Cherokee and Creek customers, many whites purposefully traded with the Indians in the Cherokee country and lent them money so they could run them into debt, just as had been done in New Alabama. These opportunistic creditors then presented their bills to the Cherokee agent for payment out of the Creek annuity funds, or they simply hauled the indebted Indians into court and stripped them of everything they possessed, including their farms, houses, and cattle herds. In some cases local sheriffs imprisoned Indian men until their frightened families agreed to vacate their homes and move away. Seeing this, Wool concluded that the Cherokees were "the prey of the most profligate and the most vicious of the white men," and "the whole scene, since I have been in this country, has been nothing but a heart-rending one, and such a one as I would be glad to get rid of as soon as circumstances will permit." In truth, the situation caused a complete reversal in Wool's attitude about the Indian service in the South. He came to the Cherokee country initially to protect settlers from Indian hostilities and to urge the Cherokees to uphold their treaty obligation and move west. By the end of the summer of 1836, however, he realized the New Echota Treaty was a fraud and saw protecting Indians from whites as his major task. And while he would continue to press removal on the Cherokees and the Creeks among them, he did so for a different reason. He now believed the Indians could save themselves from utter ruin only by disentangling themselves from their white neighbors and fleeing as quickly as possible to a safe haven beyond the Mississippi. Furthermore, Wool agreed with Jesup about the possibility of a renewed Creek war. He also believed the Cherokees might join the Creeks in the new uprising because of the abuse they suffered at the hands of local whites.[27]

Hearing all this, Governor Clay could barely contain his anger. Like other Alabama politicians, he had been urging the federal government to remove the Creeks for many years. Yet he had seen his own citizens delay the process. First they had prevented Colonel Hogan from taking the Creeks away. Then, in his opinion, they purposefully fomented a costly war. Now they resisted the efforts of both Jesup and Wool to clear Alabama's soil of its Indian population. Worse, the governor knew he could do nothing about the problem. Alabama law did not give him the power to punish whites who interfered with the federal removal project. Therefore Clay took a radical step. He urged Jesup to use his war powers to arrest and discipline those who stopped the Indians from emigrating. That a southern governor, during a time of growing sectionalism and states' rights sentiment, would advocate the use of federal power against his own citizens shows just how frustrating the Creek situation had become for Alabama's respectable citizens.[28]

Jesup did not take Clay's advice. Perhaps he feared that using his troops against the citizens of Alabama would set off a federal-state conflict even greater than the one in 1833, when President Jackson tried to remove all the unauthorized settlers from the Creek Nation. Instead, Jesup chose to hasten Creek removal by a method more appropriate to local economic conditions. Like Hogan before him, he decided to get the Indians out of Alabama by "enabling them to pay the just demands against them and defending them against those which were doubtful or unjust." In other words, Jesup wanted to get more money into the hands of the Tuckabatchee chiefs and the other leading men of the Upper Creeks so they could buy their way out of their own country. Furthermore, he saw a way to do this that would also help win the Seminole War. He had received orders from Washington directing him to take charge of the war in Florida as soon as he completed the Creek removal, and he intended to take a force of Creek warriors with him to fight the Seminoles. He knew he owed his success against the Creek rebels to friendly Indians, and he wanted to duplicate this success against the Florida Indians. Jesup also knew that using Creek warriors against the Seminoles would be much less expensive than a like number of white troops. Furthermore, the general thought the Creeks more expendable. The heat and disease of Florida took a terrible toll on white troops, and the general knew the use of Native warriors would save many white lives. Consequently, he asked the Creek chiefs to raise a regiment of six hundred to one thousand mounted warriors for twelve months service in Florida. In return, Jesup promised to advance them their annuity payment of $31,900, plus a $10,000 bonus for good and faithful performance in the Seminole country. The general also promised that the warriors would receive the pay, emoluments, and equipment of U.S. soldiers as well as any "plunder" they might take from the Seminoles, including black Seminoles. Then, Jesup believed, the Creeks would have enough resources to emigrate.[29]

However, Jesup could not claim sole credit for the idea of paying Creeks to serve in Florida so they could purchase their leave from Alabama. Opothle Yahola actually maneuvered Jesup into the thought. Using the general's need for Creek warriors as leverage, he meant to pry substantial concessions out of the government. The chief began the negotiations by objecting to sending his men to Florida, claiming that the Upper Creeks did not know the terrain there as well as the Lower Creeks. Opothle Yahola also insisted that his men wanted to stay with their families during removal and help them plant their fields in the "strange country" to the west. Then the Creek headman put Jesup on the defensive. He complained to the general that the Creeks had never intended to leave Alabama when they signed the Cusseta Treaty. They wanted to remain in Alabama as state citizens, but their reserves were sold out from under them and they had no money to pay their debts and the expenses of removal. Moreover, the land-fraud investigations would not result in any substantial payments of money to them until they arrived in the West, which was too late. Thus, the Upper Creek headman insisted that Jesup pay the Indians their annuity before they left Alabama. But Opothle Yahola did not stop there. He informed Jesup that he had been in council with a company of land speculators who wanted to purchase all the unsold and disputed reserves of the Tuckabatchees and surrounding towns for a lump sum, payable immediately. Not only would such a sale put money in Creek pockets right away, it would also free them of all legal entanglements involving the land and put those problems on the backs of the speculators. And with that much said, Opothle Yahola proposed his deal. If Jesup agreed to give his people the money he requested, then "the arrangements for the Florida War can be made, and the Creeks can go quickly to the West."[30]

Jesup acquiesced. He authorized the land sale previously negotiated between Opothle Yahola and the speculation group headed by James C. Watson, president of the Insurance Bank of Columbus. On August 28 Watson and his partners paid the Creek chiefs of Tuckabatchee and surrounding towns seventy-five thousand dollars for more than two hundred thousand acres of land taken from the Indians by fraud but returned to them as a result of Hogan's investigation. Not surprisingly, some of the members of the Watson Company were the same men who stole the land in the first place, and the new land contract allowed them to get back not only what Hogan had taken from them, but at a mere 37.5 cents per acre. Furthermore, the contract gave Watson and his associates an option to purchase all the rest of the Indians' unsold lands at appraised prices. General Jesup actually entertained strong doubts that the chiefs had the right to make such an agreement, selling land that belonged to individual Indians and their families. However, the deal gave the chiefs a substantial sum of money to pay their tribal debts, so Jesup kept his reservations to himself. The general also gave into the Creek demand that the families of the warriors and chiefs who served in Florida would not be removed from Alabama until their men returned to assist and lead them. Though this condition meant that approximately three thousand Natives would remain in the state for another year, Jesup had to concede the point. Thus, the Creeks signed a contract with the government to furnish warriors for the Florida war on the same day they inked the land deal with Watson. Now Opothle Yahola and his fellow headmen finally had enough money to buy the majority of their people out of the grasp of the whites. Seeing this, the editor of the *Montgomery Advertiser* concluded, "When we see how carelessly the country views the atrocious crimes that have been practiced upon the Indians, we are not astonished at the conclusion they have adopted [to take any money they could and get out of Alabama]."[31]

One should not suppose, however, that Jesup and Opothle Yahola alone put together the Creek brigade transaction. As with most everything else associated with the war, a desire for economic gain on the part of numerous interested parties stood behind the formation of the Creek force. President Jackson actually called Jesup to his home outside Nashville and advised him to recruit Creek warriors for service in Florida. Indeed, Jackson had used a large contingent of Creek warriors when he invaded the Seminole country in 1818, and he must have thought that Jesup could duplicate his success. But one should recall that, in the earlier Seminole conflict, Jackson's Creek warriors, led by the ever-acquisitive William McIntosh, went to Florida to take slaves from the Seminoles, as well as to punish the Red Sticks who had taken refuge there. Subsequently, McIntosh rounded up numbers of blacks, took them back to Fort Mitchell, and sold them off to the Georgians. However, some of these slaves ran away from their new owners and returned to Florida. The Georgians wanted them back. Furthermore, the Creeks signed a treaty with the government in 1821, which obligated the government to pay the citizens of Georgia $250,000 for depredations committed by the Creeks over time, including the theft of slaves. But the Creeks claimed that many of these slaves had run off to Florida as well, and since they had to pay the Georgians for them, they wanted them back. Thus it was that by 1837 both the

Georgians and the Creek leadership wanted to get into the Seminole country to reclaim slaves, including those blacks who fled to Florida with the rebel fugitives in 1836 and 1837. A new Creek auxiliary force provided the means.[32]

Not surprisingly, then, market-oriented headmen such as Paddy Carr and Jim Boy helped form the brigade, and speculators such as the Indian countrymen William Walker and Thomas Woodward signed up to go along as officers, hoping to include the reclamation of escaped slaves into the whole pantheon of enterprises making up their Indian business. And Jesup must have known all this, for he objected to Woodward and Walker serving in the brigade. But President Jackson made him relent, which is quite surprising in that Jackson did not like the speculators who subverted the object of his Cusseta Treaty. He also found Woodward, who had served under McIntosh in the first Florida invasion, personally distasteful, once calling him "a damned long, Indian-looking son-of-a-bitch." But perhaps Jackson thought Walker and Woodward, given their close relationship with some of the Creeks, would do useful service in Florida, or as a slave-owner and astute businessperson himself, the president, soon to leave office, may have had some personal financial interest in the expedition, stemming all the way back to his earlier invasion of Florida. He has, after all, been accused of mixing his own speculations with his official duties on other occasions.[33]

President Jackson also made sure that Jesup included "three talented and influential Creek chiefs" in the brigade, men who Jackson knew had family connections among the Seminoles and Creek refugees in Florida. The first of these individuals, Yahola Micco, was the head chief of the Upper Creek town of Eufaula. He had long been an advocate of accommodation with the whites, and while he undoubtedly had relatives and acquaintances among the Lower Creek Eufaulas who fled to Florida in the summer of 1836, he was also the nephew of the famed Jumper, a former Red Stick who escaped to Florida in 1814 and had become an important Seminole headman. Jesup's second emissary of note was Echo Harjo, the man who convinced so many of the Creek rebels in Alabama to give up the fight. Obviously, he would hold some sway with the Lower Creeks who fled to Florida, but more importantly, as far as the general was concerned, this chief claimed kin to two of the Seminole war party's main firebrands: Osceola, war chief of the Tallassees in Florida, and Holatti Micco, the head chief of that band of old-time Red Stick nativists. Finally, the general called on John Oponee, a leader of the Lower Creek Chehaws, most of whom, including Jim Henry, had taken up the standard of the rebel party. Potentially, Oponee and his associate, Yahola Harjo, the headman of Chehaw town, could be the most useful to Jesup. These men surely knew all the Lower Creek refugees in Florida, as well as many of the Seminoles. Indeed, Oponee had once lived in the territory; his daughter and other close relatives still lived there. Consequently, Oponee, along with Yahola Harjo, could appeal to the Creek fugitives to give themselves up and might even have some influence with the feared Mikasukis, a Seminole tribe descended from the Chehaws. The revolt of the Mikasukis surely encouraged the Chehaws to rise up against the settlers in Alabama, and perhaps Jesup hoped to reverse the process by sending the acculturated and peace-loving Chehaw, John Oponee, to calm his Florida cousins.[34]

In any event, Jesup got his Creek brigade, solved part of the Creek land-fraud problem, and aided removal by getting more money into Creek pockets, all in one package deal. However, as with everything involving the Creeks and their lands, Jesup's schemes did not go uncontested. Competing companies of speculators wanted the Upper Creek reserves, and they began to complain loudly about the Watson contract. Irvin Lawson, James S. Calhoun, and the other members of a Columbus-based company would allege that the deal had been struck "in a private room, and after the hour of midnight," without any notice to competing interests. Yet another group of speculators, Ware, Dougherty, and Company, asserted the principle that Jesup had kept to himself, that the Creek chiefs had no right to sell land for their people and therefore the Watson contract could not be valid. Even the federal commissioners, Balch and Crawford, recommended that the president disapprove the Watson deal. However, Watson eventually reached a compromise with his chief opponents by admitting them to membership in his land company, and the government ratified the Creek land purchase despite all objections.[35]

Then Jesup's plan for enlisting Creek allies against the Seminoles came up for debate. Generally speaking, the supporters of Jackson's administration favored it and the opponents did not. The Jacksonian *Columbus Sentinel* stated, "This scheme seems to be a measure of sound policy, particularly when we reflect how serviceable the celebrated chief Jim Boy and his command were to General Jesup in fighting the Lower Creeks." The *Columbus Herald* was even more optimistic: "When the eagle eyes of Osceola, Carr and Jim Boy shall flash on each other, there will be a war-whoop that will stir with new life the blood of the red man, and produce a fight which we believe will put a final stop to all Indian disturbances on this side of the Mississippi." However, the states' rights *Columbus Enquirer* was not so sanguine, taking, as always, a more anti-Jackson, anti-Indian, and strongly pro-Georgian point of view. According to the *Enquirer*'s editor, Jesup's policy of using Creeks against Seminoles "looks a little like stooping to conquer." Then he asked, "Shall it be said that the United States with a population of Sixteen Millions of people are unable to conquer and put down a handful of Seminoles without a band of Creeks?" Yet this was only part of the problem. What bothered the states' rights Georgians most was that Jesup's plan delayed the complete removal of the Creeks. The *Enquirer*'s editor feared that leaving the few thousand relatives of the Creek regiment in New Alabama might be "the occasion of future disturbances." If so, said the editor, "we wonder if Gen. Jesup and Col. Hogan will be able to shuffle the blame again on the people of Georgia? They are apt to try."[36]

Events would prove that Jesup's opponents had a good point: marching the Creeks against the Seminoles was a mistake. The general was determined, however, and proceeded with his plan to use the Creeks to win the Florida war. He was so confident, in fact, that he informed the War Department that his Indian force would probably put an end to the Seminole War by October. Thus, the Creek regiment, 750 warriors strong, left Fort Mitchell by steamboat in early September. They traveled down the Chattahoochee, out into the Gulf of Mexico, and on to federal army headquarters at Tampa Bay. A number a prominent Creeks served as officers for the volunteer force, including David Moniac, a resident of Tuskegee town who also happened to be a graduate of West Point. A group of white officers also rode with the regiment, and Col. John Foote Lane of the regular army commanded the force as a whole. The warriors' families remained behind in three camps: one in Russell County near Fort Mitchell, another at Echo Harjo's camp on New Road in Macon County, and the other at Pole Cat Springs on Federal Road near the Old Alabama boundary.[37]

While Lane's regiment moved south, most of the remainder of the Creeks began the march to their new homes beyond the Mississippi. Opothle Yahola and the Tuckabatchees started the journey west on September 2, with the town's holy men marching a mile ahead of the main body, carrying the sacred medals that had been buried beneath the Tuckabatchee square for generations. The day after the Tuckabatchees left their camp at Tallassee, William McGillivrey, headman of Hickory Ground town, led a party of more than three thousand souls from the Wetumpka camp in Coosa County. On September 5, a couple of thousand more Indians set out from Tallassee. Then nearly two thousand Lower Creek Coweta and Cusseta tribespeople left Tuckabatchee Harjo's camp hard by the white settlement of Cusseta in Chambers County. More than one hundred truculent rebel Creeks emerged from hiding and joined this party of emigrants after it got underway. Simultaneously, approximately two thousand Indians moved out from Talladega and marched north to Gunter's Landing on the Tennessee River, where the two thousand Creeks who had been living near the Cherokees in DeKalb, Benton, and Cherokee counties joined with them in crossing the river and marching on to Memphis. Presumably, this host of Creek refugees from the Cherokee country also included some Creeks recently removed from among the Cherokees in north Georgia, Tennessee, and North Carolina under the direction of General Wool. A month after this grand procession of Indians crossed the Tennessee River, another removal party from Talladega, consisting of 2,330 individuals, followed along the same path to Gunter's Landing and on to the Mississippi. This was the last group of the 14,609 Creeks who left

Alabama before the end of 1836. An army officer conducted each of the removal parties west and the Alabama Emigrating Company supplied food, wagons, and when necessary, steamboat transportation for the Indian travelers. This company, which included Thomas Woodward, William Walker, and some of the more infamous land speculators and members of the Watson land company, charged the government $28.50 for each Creek emigrant. Even after the Natives left Alabama, these men continued to profit at their expense.[38]

The exodus from the lands of the Old Creek Nation was a terrible experience for the Indians. The "squalid, forlorn and miserable" Tuckabatchees left their homes reluctantly "under the influence of deep melancholy and deep dejection." Another party of Indians so loved their country that on moving they "carried with them every article they could lay their hands on that they ever owned, whether of any value or not, as keepsakes, such as old irons, broken jugs, jars &c." Other Creeks tore down their cabins so the whites could not use them and cut down the fruit trees growing over the graves of their children so the settlers could not enjoy the produce of their labors and their sorrows. Menawa gave Colonel Hogan a picture of himself painted by the celebrated Charles Bird King when the chief visited the nation's capital. He told Hogan to hang it in his house and tell his children when they looked at it what he, Menawa, had been. Then, despite their friendship, the Oakfuskee chief informed Hogan that when he crossed the great river, his desire was to "never again see the face of a white man." And when Hogan reminded him that he may have trouble with the McIntosh party in the West, because Menawa had led the men who executed William McIntosh, the chief replied, "I know there will be blood shed, but I am not afraid. I have been a man of blood all of my life." But Menawa also said that in his old age he wanted peace, and he and some of the other Creeks sought to find just a bit of it before they left their homeland. A few Indians lingered behind the moving parties to meditate alone among the deserted towns, to touch the rocks and trees one last time, and to bid a final farewell to the fields and streams of Alabama. The day before his departure, Menawa received permission to leave his emigration camp to spend his last night at the site of his silent and empty Nuyaka town. The next day, after setting out on the journey with his people, he acted distracted and uneasy. Asked if he had forgotten something and needed to return, he replied in the negative: "No! . . . No other evening will come, bringing to Menawa's eyes the rays of the setting sun upon the home he has left forever!" But some of the elder Creeks were even more dejected, and determined not to leave at all. They took up posts on the high hills where they sat gazing out on their ancient homeland until they starved to death. Menawa died somewhere on the way west, along with many other Creeks.[39]

Unfortunately, some whites, usually the rougher element of society, made the ordeal much worse for the Creeks; they saw the removal as a joyous spectacle and one last grand opportunity to torment and exploit the Natives. Lt. John T. Sprague of the U.S. Marines, the man Jesup charged with the task of removing the Coweta and Cusseta Creeks, reported that "a large number of white men were prowling about" his emigrating party, robbing the Indians of "their horses and cattle and carrying among them liquors which kept up an alarming rate of intoxication." Another observer watched a party of Creeks making their way over the Coosa River and recounted that "some low-down white men stood on the bank and shot the dogs of the Indians as they were swimming across." This observer also "saw many an Indian shed tears as his dog was killed."[40]

And then there was Wiley Williams of Marion County, Georgia. He had gotten in trouble before the war for keeping a considerable number of Euchees on his plantation as near-slaves in contravention of the law barring Creeks from living in Georgia. Then when the Creek removal began, he angered his neighbors once again by shielding his Euchees from the process. He meant to keep them on his plantation so he could continue to exploit their labor. Finally, Governor Schley ordered Williams to deliver his Indians to Fort Mitchell for removal, and the county authorities placed the planter on trial for his numerous counts of violating Georgia law. However, it appears Williams got around his difficulties by simply crossing the Chattahoochee and taking up residence in New Alabama. He took the Indians with him and put them to work on another plantation. They did not emigrate in 1836, and one wonders how many other planters and farmers either helped Indians avoid removal or used some form of coercion to keep them from leaving. After all, the system did demand labor, and lots of it.[41]

However, other whites deplored the mistreatment of the Indians and showed pity and compassion for their Native neighbors. Whitney Anthony, a local historian, never forgave Charles H. Nelson, the Georgia officer who marched the Creeks out of Cherokee County, Alabama, for shooting an Indian who disobeyed one of his orders. In Macon County, some whites held a dance for the Creeks the day before they were to depart for the West. In Talladega County, Melton Lewis, a prominent white citizen, married an Indian woman, packed up his possessions, and left Alabama with her people. Other white men with Creek wives followed his lead. Meanwhile, all over the old Creek country respectable Alabamians watched sadly as the Natives passed and, like the citizens of Tuscaloosa, "expressed many a heartfelt regret . . . at the necessity which compelled us to remove them to the far West." Undoubtedly, some of this sympathy for the Creeks stemmed from the fact that they had contact with European Americans for a long period of time and consequently resembled the whites in many respects. Besides the obvious light skin color of many emigrating Creeks, a correspondent for the *New York Observer* reported that the travelers consisted of "all ages, sexes, and sizes, and of all the varieties of human intellect and condition, from the civilized and tenderly nourished matron and misses, to the wild savage, and the poorest of the poor." Certainly northerners would have applied this description equally well to all the Alabamians the Creeks left behind.[42]

Unfortunately, though, most sympathetic whites refused to take personal responsibility for what had happened. They knew the removal was a tragedy but they believed it was necessary to preserve the "doomed Red man," who, the apologists claimed, tended to adopt the vices of white civilization but not its virtues. The respectables could not admit that removal was simply a product of their own expansionistic and acquisitive culture, particularly their desire to achieve wealth through the increased production of cotton. In fact, they seemed strangely detached from the whole process, as evidenced by one writer in the

Mobile Commercial Register. His description of the Creek removal was echoed by many presses across the South: "This spectacle of a moving people, could not be more affecting.... We gaze as upon a great drama, in which we are less actors than spectators, wherein the fortunes of millions have been guided, upon principles not yet developed to our understanding,—full of obscure judgments, and incomprehensible dispensations of Providence, moving kingdoms and states as by the power of an unseen but irresistible and acknowledged Destiny."

What a maddening statement! There was no incomprehensible dispensation of Providence here. He was describing the world system at work, and Alabamians were actors in the drama, not powerless spectators devoid of responsibility for how the play turned out. And insofar as respectable whites did feel guilty about what had happened, they were able to project this guilt onto the speculators and roughs who were more directly involved in exploiting the Creeks and taking their land. Perhaps this fact explains the high level of vituperation against the speculators and liquor dealers in the months following the Creek uprising. In fact, this same writer in the *Commercial Register* called for punishment of the speculators and a reversal of their schemes, to "redeem the character of our people" and "carry some comfort to the Creek in the farthest wilds of Arkansas." Respectable whites also called for financial compensation for the Creeks, believing like any commercial people that they could reduce Native lives and suffering to a dollar amount and then make satisfactory restitution without ever coming to grips with the real root of the problem.[43]

But to their credit, most whites never glorified or mythologized the Creek war and removal, as victors often do in such circumstances. The early county historians, men such as Whitney Anthony and F. L. Cherry, told the story as it actually happened. While they did see a certain inevitability in the triumph of their own Christian civilization, they tended to regard sinful whites, not the Indians, as the greatest opponents of that civilization. In the process of describing the growth of their respective communities, they pictured speculators, faro dealers, horse thieves, and drunks as the real enemies, not the Indians. Furthermore, they blamed the Native corruption they observed on members of their own race. As one aristocratic young writer in Irwinton commented, "The problem with the Indians was that they tended to associate with lower class whites." Obviously, then, the continuing conflicts among the whites themselves in the aftermath of the Creek rebellion and removal reveals that these events are not explainable in the simple, traditional context of whites versus Indians.[44]

But no matter what the contentious citizens of Alabama and Georgia thought of one another, they were all relieved to be free of Indian warfare. General Jesup was also relieved. Having set the mass exodus of Creeks in motion, he once again declared the Creek war officially ended and turned to the task of defeating the Seminoles. In early October he marched his regular troops out of the Alabama interior and encamped them around Fort Mitchell. Then, when the steamboats that had taken the Creek regiment to Tampa Bay returned, these men sailed off to Florida. General Jesup traveled not far behind and assumed command of the Seminole War from John Call, the governor of the Florida Territory. Now it appeared peace had come to New Alabama at last. There were no more war whoops or gunshots, and by December much of the argument between the white citizens had died away. Finally, settlers looked forward to developing the fine country they had acquired from the Creeks.[45]

Unfortunately, the late summer and fall of 1836 was but the lull in the eye of the storm as far as the Second Creek War was concerned. The conflict was far from finished. In fact, the "spectators" of the "great drama" of the Creek war and removal would see a few more acts before the final curtain fell.

9. The War Revives in New Alabama

The months of peace following the federal operation against the Lower Creeks, coupled with the removal of so many Indians during the fall of 1836, stimulated a new rush of people into New Alabama. Many of these people were returning settlers, those who could afford to rebuild destroyed homes, replace stolen property, and start afresh. However, many more of the settlers were new arrivals who purchased property from the land companies or from earlier residents. In some cases, the original settlers sold because they could not afford to return to Alabama, but others sold because the new immigration drove up land prices. These last individuals made a profit by selling their farms and plantations and used the money to finance new starts for themselves in Mississippi, Louisiana, Texas, or Arkansas. They moved west along with the Indians and became part of the mass of migrants who, in the years prior to the Civil War, occupied and developed the South as a distinctive agricultural region within the world system.[1]

Newspapers promoted the new immigration into New Alabama by praising the potential productivity of the country and advertising the towns of Montgomery, Wetumpka, Columbus, and Irwinton as ideal places for the marketing and shipment of cotton and other agricultural products. In turn, these towns began to grow as never before, owing to a new influx of merchants and others coming to profit in a developing country. The growth of Irwinton was the most dramatic.

During the late months of 1836 and early 1837, a number of wealthy cotton planters from Virginia, the Carolinas, and Old Alabama moved in to set up operations on the fertile lands bordering Hatchechubbee, Cowikee, and Barbour creeks. Some of these planters, however, chose to live in Irwinton and built fine homes there. At the same time, brick stores began to appear along the streets near the waterfront. In addition, the Alabama Assembly granted charters for the establishment of male and female academies in the town, and the state of Georgia issued a permit to the Irwinton Bridge Company to build a structure across the Chattahoochee. Another company constructed an expensive racetrack for the town, and W. G. M. Davis started the community's first newspaper, a weekly, the *Irwinton Herald*. Thus, what had been a little frontier outpost on the Chattahoochee began to take on the trappings of an aristocratic cotton port, a place that would produce in time more than its share of Alabama governors and other wealthy and influential people.[2]

Surely the citizens of the New Alabama counties were optimistic about their future, but they still had an Indian problem. They believed far too many Creeks remained in the country. Some of them had fled to the Chickasaws in Mississippi; who knew how many had succeeded in making their way into Florida to join the Seminoles; a few still lived in the swamps of southwestern Georgia; several families of Indians remained at various places in Coosa, Tallapoosa, Benton, and Cherokee counties. The Creeks in these last two counties were part of a group seeking refuge in the Cherokee Nation, and while local settlers seldom saw them, they found constant signs of these fugitives in their corn and potato fields. The state of Alabama kept a couple of volunteer companies in service to protect settlers from these Creeks and to compel their emigration. Meanwhile, Gen. John Wool and the federal removal agents continued their efforts to extract from the country the even larger body of Creeks living deeper within the confines of the Cherokee domain. While Wool and his men had by the end of 1836 succeeded in removing about 1,500 individuals of this group, perhaps as many as 3,000 remained. Possibly a third of these people lived in "the wild and mountainous track of country extending from near New

Echota and Coosawatie to the neighborhood of the Valley town in North Carolina," and had become so well integrated into Cherokee society that Wool feared they could not be extracted by force without causing violence to the Cherokees. In fact, he protested to the War Department that some Creeks had lived in the Cherokee country for twenty years and were so connected to their hosts by blood and marriage that they should "not be hunted and dragged to the emigration camps like so many wolves."[3]

The situation of one Oke-wo-nat, the Cherokee widow of one of the Creeks, serves as an example here. The troops captured this woman and a half dozen of her children for removal, but according to the matrilineal kinship systems of both Creeks and Cherokees, this woman and her offspring were seen as Cherokees and entitled to stay in their homeland at least until the removal date mandated by the New Echota Treaty. But white society was patrilineal in structure, and thus the men who held Oke-wo-nat believed her Creek husband was the head of her family, and she and her children must be considered Creeks as a consequence. This sort of cultural confusion, and the possibility of bloody confrontations springing therefrom, deeply troubled General Wool. He yet feared a wide-ranging war pitting Cherokees and Creek refugees against the citizens of Tennessee, North Carolina, Georgia, and Alabama. Nevertheless, the general persisted in his efforts, and during the late spring and early summer of 1837, succeeded in shipping about two thousand more Creeks out of the Cherokee territory.[4]

Ironically, Wool's persistence led to his downfall. Believing that white businesspeople were holding the Creeks in place, the general attempted to close grog shops catering to Indians in northern Alabama. The white residents immediately accused him of the unauthorized use of federal power, and the War Department recalled him from the field to answer those charges. Ironically, Governor Clay, himself a resident of northern Alabama, led the protests against Wool's actions, even though he had earlier called on Jesup to use troops to arrest all those whites who interfered with the removal of Creeks from New Alabama. Here one can only speculate as to the governor's motives, but he was campaigning for the U.S. Senate, and perhaps he needed to curry favor with states' rights voters. Or, perhaps, some of Clay's loyal supporters had ties to the Indian business in the Cherokee country. In any event, General Wool found himself replaced by Col. William H. Lindsay, who believed that the key to getting the remaining Creeks out of their mountain retreats lay in the Cherokee Council. Consequently, Lindsay approached John Ross, the Cherokee chief, and asked him to help get the Creeks to come into removal camps. Ross, in turn, took the matter up with the Cherokee Council members when they gathered at Red Clay, Tennessee, for their annual meeting in September 1837.[5]

However, the Creek headmen also sought aid from John Ross and the Cherokee Council:

> We speak to you as the Chief of the Cherokee Nation. It has been the custom of our fathers and our forefathers to go freely into each others' country. With this knowledge we came in the Cherokee country. We came here to escape the evil of War. In time of trouble we came to the Cherokees as the home of a brother. When we came, we were treated kindly. Our red brethren made no objection. They did not tell us to leave the country. But we have been pursued by the White Men and treated harshly, without knowing that we were guilty of any crime. While living here we planted corn in the season but the white man destroyed it and took away our other property. In this bad treatment two of our men were killed, one man shot through the thigh and arm and three children lost in the flight of their mothers and have not been found. We do not want to be put in the hands of these Men. We ask the favor of you to permit us to reside with you. We ask your pity and protection. We put ourselves into your hands. We ask you to speak for us to the President, our father, that he may order his men not to hunt us through the country. We hope you will pity us. We want to live with you. We are willing to obey your laws.

And Ross took the plea to heart. He informed Lindsay that he had advised the Creeks to emigrate but he could not violate custom by giving them over to the troops. The colonel did not press the matter. In fact, he decided that the immediate removal of the remaining Creeks would not be necessary. Realizing the rapid approach of the May 1838 deadline for Cherokee emigration, he saw no harm in granting the Creeks' request to stay in place and leave the country with their Cherokee friends and relatives. And fortunately for the refugees, the secretary of war agreed.[6]

But by that time, the Cherokee Creeks mattered little to the settlers of the southern section of New Alabama. Their attention had long since been drawn to the four thousand Creeks living in the three remaining removal camps in Russell and Macon counties. The Fort Mitchell camp contained the families of the Coweta, Cusseta, and other Lower Creek warriors who followed Paddy Carr and General Jesup to Florida to fight the Seminoles. The Macon County camps—one at Pole Cat Springs and the other bordering Big Swamp—contained the families and townspeople of the warriors serving against the Seminoles under the direction of Jim Boy and Echo Harjo. According to their original agreement with General Jesup, all the Creek warriors, 776 in number, were obligated to stay in Florida for twelve months. However, Jesup's initial operations against the Seminoles went well, and the general then promised the Creeks he would release them from service on February 1, 1837, at which time they could return to Alabama, settle their business affairs, and immediately emigrate west with their families and friends. But as that deadline approached, Jesup changed his mind and decided to keep his Creek allies in Florida to help with Seminole removal. He believed they were better suited for that task than white troops. Moreover, he did not want to take on the trouble and expense of raising a sufficient number of volunteers to replace the warriors. But again, Jesup assured his men that their families would not be sent west without them. They would remain in Alabama, waiting. In addition, Jesup promised his warriors that the government would feed their families throughout their first year in the West to make up for the fact that they would be leaving Alabama too late to prepare and plant fields in their new country. The Creeks agreed to the deal, but New Alabama settlers did not. They did not want to delay the closing of the emigration camps in their midst. They believed that they would never know peace and develop their full economic potential until all the Creeks left the state. Furthermore, they could not understand why Jesup had not completed the task in the late summer and fall of 1836 when he sent the great majority of Creeks on their way to the Western Territory.[7]

But this was not the general's greatest mistake. He committed a much graver error when he declared victory in the Second Creek War too soon. As it turned out, he had not subdued and removed all the rebel Creeks hiding in New Alabama's swamps, and this failure would have tragic consequences. Settlers noticed that the federal removal camps grew in size in the late months of 1836, and they believed that as many as four hundred hostile Creek warriors had come out of hiding with the departure of the troops and moved into the camps to feed at government expense. Even more alarming, Indians continued to slaughter the settlers' cattle. The frightened whites became convinced that the removal camps must be closed and the last of the Creeks taken from the state. Otherwise, the Indians might launch another attack on New Alabama's farmers and planters and cause them to lose yet another year's crop. But again, there was no general consensus of opinion among the citizens of Alabama. Some Old Alabamians, as well as the federal officers who directed the removal camps, believed that the settlers only wanted to persecute the friendly Indians who lived in those camps. They saw the militia, made up of these settlers, as the real aggressors and troublemakers, men who were merely looking for any excuse to strip the friendly Creeks of their last possessions before driving them from the state. But no matter how one viewed this situation, the potential for violence was obvious. Jesup should have taken this fact into consideration before he decided to extend the enlistments of his Creek warriors. By leaving so many of their friends and family members in New Alabama in unguarded removal camps, the general was asking for a tragedy. More specifically, he set the stage for a revival of the Second Creek War.[8]

The trouble began in early December 1836 when Marine Lt. John G. Reynolds, director of the Creek camp at Pole Cat Springs, issued a pass to one of his charges. This pass allowed the man to return to land he

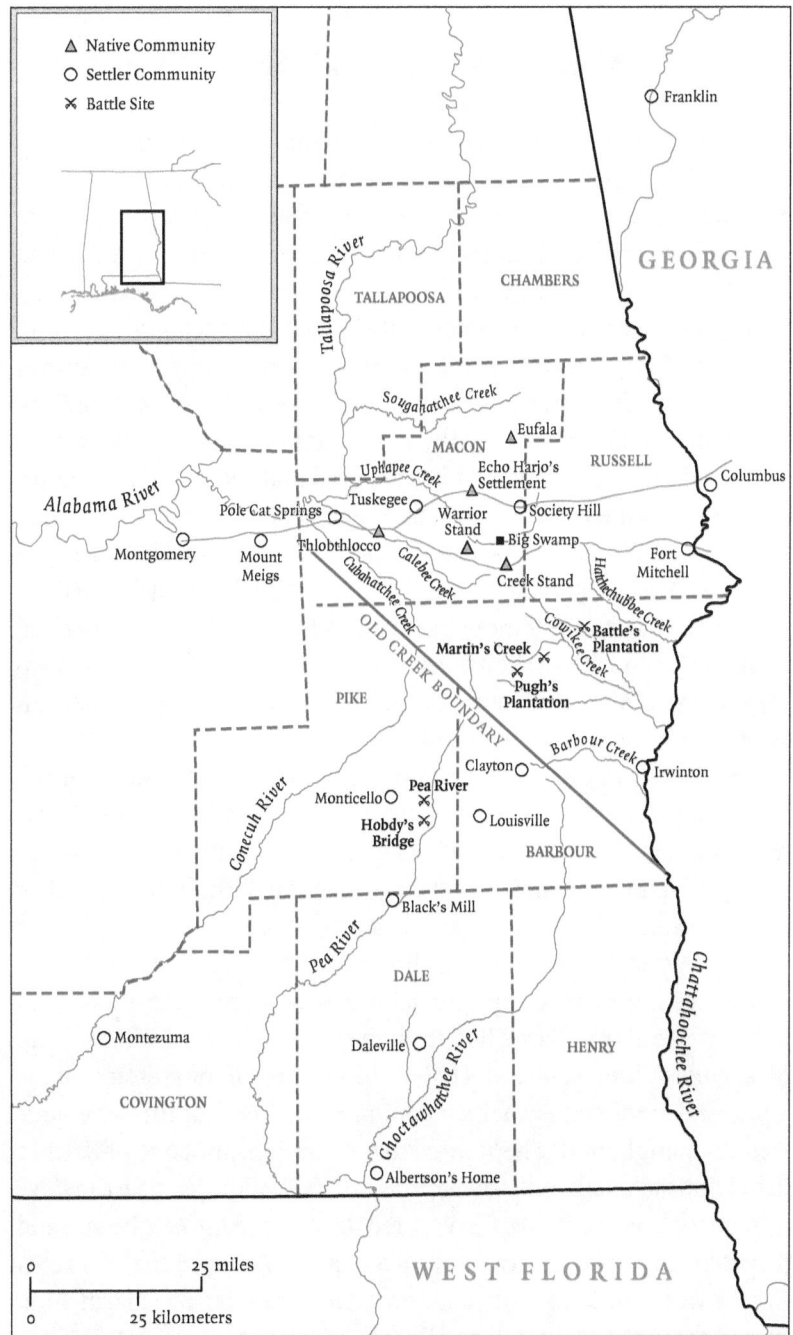

6. New Alabama, 1837

once owned on Sougahatchee Creek to collect his cattle and move them closer to the removal camp. He was engaged in this chore when a gang of whites murdered him. Certainly there was no justification for this crime, but it might be explained by the fact that the Sougahatchee had been the home of the rebel party among the Tallassee Creeks and perhaps a seat of Red Stick nativism since 1812. In fact, one fearful settler had reported to Clay previously that "those Indians who have been raised on Lockupokee creek [Sougahatchee Creek] are the most hostile of any in the nation," implying that those Natives resented European Americans even before settlers entered New Alabama. However, by late 1836 that section of Macon County between the Sougahatchee and Euphaubee creeks contained few settlers, and whites believed that some of the Tallassee rebels still haunted this area. The murderers may have thought the man from Reynolds's camp was one of these hostile Creeks. On hearing of the crime, Reynolds's commanding officer at Fort Mitchell directed the lieutenant to secure testimony and have the perpetrators apprehended by the civil authorities. The officer even vowed to send federal troops to help Alabama officials capture the murderers if necessary. However, it does not appear the killers ever came before the bar of justice.[9]

The Creeks in Reynolds's camp did not retaliate for the murder, but the settlers soon suffered for the killing in another quarter of New Alabama. On the afternoon of December 29, a half-dozen warriors used a horse-lot fence to shield their advance on the home of Dr. Cullen Battle, a Barbour County planter who lived on the north fork of Cowikee Creek between Fort Mitchell and Irwinton. The Creeks approached to within twenty-five yards of the dwelling when a servant girl saw them and gave the alarm. Battle fled from the house with the Indians firing their guns at him as he ran. He left the warriors in possession of his home and smokehouse, which contained the meat of fifty-one hogs recently slaughtered. They looted the plantation, shot one of Battle's field hands to death, and then burned all the buildings, save the slave cabins, to the ground. Battle reported the news to his neighbors, and they fled south toward Irwinton in a panic, convinced that the rebel Creeks were about to launch a new series of raids. The alarm soon spread throughout Russell and Barbour counties.[10]

Two days after the attack, a company of men from Battle's neighborhood, along with another company from Irwinton, set out from the plantation in pursuit of the Indians. The men found that herds of mules, cattle, and hogs had obliterated the warriors' trail but they "believed" that the Indians had proceeded toward the removal camps in Macon County. Consequently, they struck out in that direction and, after a ride of approximately twenty-five miles, arrived at the Big Swamp camp (Echo Harjo's settlement). This camp, commanded by Lt. T. P. Sloan, sat along the side of New Road and contained houses "as good as any Indian ever builds." Its residents numbered eleven or twelve hundred souls, more than two hundred of them warriors. The settlers called on Lieutenant Sloan to inquire into his management of the place and were shocked to find that he exercised hardly any control over his charges. He issued some food to the families every four days, but for the most part, the Indians came and went as they pleased with no troops to restrain them. Furthermore, they had guns, ammunition, and plenty of money, and often strayed to grog shops, where they "drank as much as they pleased." The settlers informed Sloan of their intention to search his camp for hostile Indians, but when the lieutenant warned them that they might scare the Creeks away from the place and scatter them in the woods, the white men desisted and returned to their homes in an angry mood.[11]

The leader of the expedition, Dr. Levi T. Wellborn—relative of the land buyer, William Wellborn—wrote an account of his adventure for the *Columbus Enquirer* and complained again about the treatment of the New Alabama settlers at the hands of the state and federal governments. He contended that the authorities had ignored the settlers' pleas for help in the days preceding the war, and, as a result, the Indians had plundered them to the point of poverty. And now, as farmers and planters worked to rebuild their homes and struggled to survive, the Indians, well fed and unregulated by the government, were again plotting their ruin. Wellborn concluded that only the complete removal of the Creeks would restore peace to New Alabama, and he threatened that if the government did not act, the settlers would take matters into their own hands and give the Indians "a quietas." The editor of the

Enquirer, ever ready to support the interests of settlers and land buyers, as well as condemn the policies of Union Party members, weighed in on Wellborn's side. Once again attacking Alabama's governor, he asked, "What is that poor lump of Clay about, that he does not order out the militia of the State and arrest or prevent the flow of blood?" Then he went after the new administration in Washington: "The election of Van Buren is now over, and it is sincerely hoped that the powers that be will turn their attention, at least for a time, from the villainous scenes of an electioneering campaign, to the protection of our suffering countrymen. *Remove* these Indians forthwith, is and ought to be the watchword."[12]

Throughout the month of January, individual settlers and citizens' committees also howled in protest. First they sent petitions to Washington through their favorite congressional representative and states' rights advocate, Dixon Lewis. In all these petitions, they outlined complaints against the Creeks, followed by lists of suggested remedies. They claimed that numerous rebel warriors had emerged from hiding and gone into the removal camps since Jesup and his troops departed for Florida and that these Indians only pretended to be friendly so they could enjoy the security of the removal camps and eat at government expense. But at the same time these Creeks prowled about the country carrying guns, doing mischief, and keeping the settlers "in a painful state of excitement." In particular, the settlers complained of losing livestock to the Indians, and they feared the emboldened residents of the camps would now rise up again to destroy people along with property. The petitioners proclaimed that they could not afford to lose another season's crop to such an uprising, yet they could not protect their frightened women and children and still farm at the same time. Consequently, the settlers declared that the federal government and Governor Clay must take action to save them. First, they wanted all the Creeks disarmed, moved to a single camp near the western border of New Alabama, and placed under guard. Next the settlers demanded that the government disarm and recall all the Creek warriors from Florida and place them in the camp as well. Then, at that point, said the petitioners, the whole lot of Creeks should be removed permanently from the state. Furthermore, the settlers believed they had the right to make these demands because Clay had been tardy in assisting them before and Jesup had promised them that his operations of the summer had ended the Creek rebellion. Finally, just as Levi Wellborn had done, the settlers and citizens' committees closed their letters with the threat that if Clay and the federal authorities did not act, they would take matters into their own hands. Some petitioners even went so far as to state that they and their fellow citizens, "exasperated by repeated outrages," might resort to the indiscriminate slaughter of all the New Alabama Creeks.[13]

However, not everyone was so quick to point the finger of blame at the camps. The removal superintendent, Capt. John Page, conducted his own investigation of the Battle affair and discovered the identities of two of the warriors involved. These men had entered one of the slave cabins to get fire to burn down the plantation house. A sick black woman lay on a bed in the room. For a moment, the warriors looked her right in the face and laughed. She identified them to Page as Yuchi Charley and Lame John, men she had seen almost every day for two years prior to the war. Page knew these men as well, and after consultation with his Creek informants, he concluded that they had never been in any of the removal camps. He believed that they had returned only recently from the hard fighting and starving times in Florida. In fact, Georgians had reported seeing Indians traveling toward Alabama from Flint River with packs and guns. Page relayed all these findings to Carey A. Harris, the commissioner of Indian Affairs, "to do away the suspicion that rests upon the friendly Indians, and that the guilty may be punished." Nevertheless, Page took steps to protect the settlers from future depredations. He commanded only a small company of regular troops at Fort Mitchell, so he mustered two companies of Alabama volunteers into the federal service. One of these companies, led by Capt. Benjamin Young of Macon County, he stationed at Echo Harjo's camp. The other company of Barbour County men, under Capt. William Wellborn, Page stationed at the Hatchechubbee Swamp south of Fort Mitchell.[14]

Lieutenant Sloan, the federal officer in charge at Echo Harjo's camp, also took steps both to ease settler fears and to protect his Indians against unwarranted retaliation from whites. Consequently, he moved all the Indians close to his quarters, making sure that they camped within a half-mile square plot of ground. Then Sloan called on the warriors to surrender their arms. Sixty men did so but forty-two others, formerly members of the hostile party, refused. They quit the encampment and did not return.[15]

This put Sloan in a difficult position. He had attempted to disarm his warriors to show the settlers how peaceful and manageable they were, but he had done just the opposite. It now appeared he had, indeed, been sheltering a group of unreformed rebels, who had now taken to the woods. Their flight also reflected badly on the friendly Creeks in Echo Harjo's camp, as the whites could accuse them of aiding and abetting the rebels. However, the lieutenant and the warriors loyal to him soon found a way to attempt to redeem themselves, as well as draw a sharp line of demarcation between the peaceful camp residents and the rebel interlopers. In early February, Sloan and thirty warriors sneaked up on and attacked a rebel camp on Loachapoka Creek some twenty miles north of Sloan's headquarters. They killed two men, captured all the women and children present, and returned to Echo Harjo's camp with their prisoners. But this did them little good. The settlers were not impressed and continued to declaim against all Creeks, hostile or not. Moreover, Sloan had let most of the rebel warriors escape, and now they turned on him and the friendly Indians in earnest. They began to skulk around the outskirts of Echo Harjo's camp at night, lying in wait near Sloan's headquarters and the houses of the camp's headmen, hoping to take their revenge on the lieutenant and his toadies. Needless to say, Sloan unlocked his storehouse and returned the guns to his warriors.[16]

Lieutenant Reynolds at the Pole Cat Springs camp also tried to allay the fears of the settlers, while at the same time separate the friendly Creeks resident at his camp from the hostile party. On hearing the news from Battle's plantation, he too asked his warriors to surrender their firearms. The warriors of the Thlobthlocco and Eufaula towns did so willingly, as their chiefs, Jim Boy and Yelker Harjo, were leaders of the Creek expeditionary force serving in Florida. Not surprisingly, however,

Reynolds encountered problems with Tuskenea's men. When the time arrived for them to hand over their guns, Tuskenea, who did not wish to help the whites in Florida nor emigrate to the West before he had to, would not let his people cooperate with the marine lieutenant. As usual, Reynolds thought self-interested whites influenced Tuskenea in his intransigence, and in part this may have been true. Tuskenea owned a considerable amount of property, including slaves, and this fact, along with his business dealings with whites, undoubtedly influenced his desire to stay in place as long as possible and resist the dictates of the government. However, Tuskenea had always resisted federal authority as a show of his people's independence and because government officials tended to favor his political opponent, Opothle Yahola. But first and foremost, Tuskenea must have realized that, given the dangerous state of affairs in New Alabama, his warriors needed weapons to defend themselves and their families. Yet these same conditions meant that Reynolds, walking a fine line between Creeks and settlers, could not afford to have his orders disobeyed. Therefore, he rode to Tuskenea's residence at Warrior Stand, arrested him, and jailed him in Tuskegee for three days. After that, Tuskenea relented and Reynolds succeeded in collecting the guns of the warriors under his command.[17]

However, Governor Clay could not act as swiftly and decisively. The state legislature had adjourned for the winter without making an appropriation of funds the governor could use to raise and pay troops. However, Clay was not entirely convinced a call-up of state troops was necessary. Given the limited extent of current Indian depredations, he believed the citizens of the affected counties had the power to defend themselves. In response to a petition from the people of Irwinton, he suggested that in the event of further outrages the citizens should promptly assemble, pursue, and punish the Indians. That, according to the governor, would "condure [sic] more to their safety than the troops which have been ordered into service." Clay then informed Russell County residents that their county sheriff and his deputies had the necessary power to deal with Indians. He also expressed surprise and dismay at the fact that Russell County, the scene of most of the Indian disturbances in New Alabama, still had no organized militia, only groups of armed men acting on their own. Nevertheless, Clay did believe, like his petitioners, that all the remaining Creeks should leave Alabama for the good of the state and themselves. He asked George Whitman and the other members of the emigration company to remove the Creeks as soon as possible, despite Jesup's promise that they could stay. He also directed Whitman, commander of a volunteer company called the Montgomery Guards, to offer the services of his troops to Captain Page at Fort Mitchell.[18]

President Van Buren did much more. Obviously stung by the protests of New Alabama's citizens, and not wishing to repeat Jackson's mistake of failing to send troops to the area in time to prevent a war with the Creeks, the new president ordered Clay to call up a whole battalion of volunteers for service in the Old Creek Nation. Clay issued the call on January 20, and by the second week of February, Captain Page had fulfilled the quota, mustering into service four companies of mounted volunteers and one company of infantry. These volunteers then elected William Wellborn of Irwinton as their commanding officer with the rank of colonel. They also elected Benjamin Young second-in-command, according him the rank of major. Page also accepted two companies of Georgians into the service, and these companies stationed themselves on the east bank of the Chattahoochee to protect the settlers on the Georgia frontier should any of the Creeks attempt once again to cross the river and march toward the Seminole country.[19]

At this point it appeared that the authorities might be overreacting to the Battle incident. In fact, George Whitman, the removal contractor and member of Wellborn's battalion, was quite skeptical of the furor surrounding the Battle attack and other alleged depredations by the Creeks. Reflecting the animosity some Old Alabama residents felt for all the Georgians colonizing New Alabama, Whitman informed Governor Clay that he had heard from a recent traveler through the Creek country that all the excitement was "a humbug—and another Georgia Trick." He went on to say that the Georgians "could not live without a disturbance with the Indians and when they have [to] I do not know what they will do for a substitute." However, the rebel Creeks soon justified all the precautions the authorities had taken.[20]

THE WAR REVIVES IN NEW ALABAMA

On January 26 a party of perhaps sixty warriors invaded Lewis Pugh's plantation on the western end of Barbour County. They shot the overseer, Jacob Herron, from the top of a house, then killed Pugh and four or five of his slaves. The next day twenty settlers went to the scene to survey the damage. They saw a few Indians milling about the plantation house and immediately opened fire on them. At that point the larger body of Creeks emerged and drove the whites off, killing two of them in the process. The Indians then left Pugh's place and moved toward the headwaters of the middle prong of Cowikee Creek. In the process they burned the homes of two settlers named Martin and Murphy and also destroyed a store. By that time, Colonel Wellborn and twenty-one of his Barbour Rangers had taken up the chase. On January 28 they overtook the warriors in a swamp at the intersection of Martin's Creek and the Cowikee. The ensuing fight raged for thirty minutes before Wellborn ordered a retreat, giving way to the Creeks' superior numbers. In fact, one soldier declared that he was "run to the eye-brows" to get away from the pursuing Indians. The Rangers lost one man killed, and four or five others suffered wounds, including Colonel Wellborn, who lost the tip of his forefinger to a musket ball. One of Wellborn's lieutenants, also a resident of Irwinton, lost an arm in the fray.[21]

News of the Pugh attack and the Battle of Martin's Creek caused many settlers in the southern counties of New Alabama to flee their homes and take up residence in stockades scattered about the countryside. It also raised a new round of protests from the states' rights camp. The *Columbus Enquirer* proclaimed that the New Alabama settlers could no longer look to "Granny Clay" and the "General Government" for support and predicted that the Georgians would have to fly to the rescue and salvage the situation as they had done the previous summer. One of Barbour County's Union Democrats, Charles Lewis, wrote Clay that his opponents in the area were actually withholding information from the governor so they could continue to curse him for his inactivity. Lewis begged Clay to travel to the community of Clayton, Barbour's county seat, to take charge of the situation, saying that "you can do more at this moment to serve the State and your self by coming to this place than at any other time." The governor, however, chose to stay in Tuscaloosa.[22]

News of the latest disturbance also led the settlers to believe that they must force a tighter discipline on the Creek removal camps, whether or not Clay or the federal government approved. Captain Page contended that the warriors Wellborn fought were more hostiles recently returned from Florida, along with a few others from Echo Harjo's camp "that have been loitering in the edge of the swamps and would never come forward to be enrolled" for removal. Nevertheless, the settlers mistrusted all the Creeks in the camps; at the very least, they did not know which ones were friendly and which ones were not. Certainly they remembered that earlier in the year Neah Micco and other rebel Creeks had professed friendship for the whites at the same time they attacked them. Furthermore, Colonel Wellborn and others mistrusted the federal officers in charge of the camps. They believed that these men, either knowingly or unknowingly, were feeding large numbers of rebel Creeks living near the camps. Consequently, the settlers decided to tolerate the situation no longer. They resolved to place all the Creeks in camp under guard until the government removed them from Alabama. Now Page realized he had lost control of the situation and of all the volunteer companies he had mustered into the federal service. These companies and various citizen committees thronged his house "from morning till night," pressing him to join with them in forcing all the Creeks out of Alabama. Moreover, he feared the settlers would soon commence a wholesale slaughter of Indian women and children. Consequently, he assembled all the Creeks under his care in and close around Fort Mitchell so he could protect them. He also directed Lieutenant Reynolds at Pole Cat Springs to place a chain of sentinels around his people.[23]

Interestingly, the Georgians made the first move on the camps. On receiving word of the Battle of Martin's Creek, Maj. Henry Jernigan, hero of the Chickasawhatchee fight, quickly assembled a company of men and crossed the Chattahoochee south of Irwinton to assist Wellborn in tracking down the Indians. He joined the colonel and another company of Georgians from the town of Franklin at Martin's plantation, and together the three companies began to search for the trail of the enemy. Captain Page would later report that the tracks of the warriors who left Martin's Creek led northeast toward Fort Mitchell, but Wellborn and Jernigan chose to follow yet another trail. They discovered fresher tracks, assumed they were made by hostile Creeks, and followed them to the northwest, in the direction of the removal camp at Echo Harjo's settlement. They did not follow the trail directly to the camp, however, but "decided" that the Indians had either gone into the camp or were using the camp to "screen themselves from punishment." They stopped their pursuit at Creek Stand on Federal Road, seven miles east of the camp, and sent a message to Lieutenant Sloan asking that he come out to meet them. When Sloan arrived, Wellborn informed him that the troops wanted to move his camp "away from the dense swamps that surrounded it to a more elevated location where all communication with hostile and supposed friendly Indians could be cut off." Sloan, however, objected strenuously, saying that he knew the Creeks in his camp were friendly and harmless. Furthermore, all the camp Indians lived near his headquarters and he had already disarmed the sixty warriors presently in residence. Faced with this protest from a regular army officer, Wellborn dropped the idea of moving the camp and returned with his company to Barbour County. The Georgians, however, refused to let the matter rest. They elected Jernigan as their new commander and determined to carry out the original plan with the assistance of a rough and irregular company of men recently arrived from Russell County. Dr. E. E. Parks led this last company.[24]

According to Jernigan's account of the operation, his men surrounded the camp on February 5, and despite Sloan's outcries, drove the Indians up to the lieutenant's headquarters in the center of the camp. The troops caught ninety-two effective warriors in their web, not the sixty Sloan had claimed. They also discovered forty guns and a good supply of ammunition, though Sloan had said his charges were unarmed. The troops held the Creeks at the headquarters overnight; the next day they marched the warriors north to Tuskegee and placed them in a strong stockade at Maj. Benjamin Young's cantonment on New Road. They left the women, children, and old men with Sloan. That finished the task. Jernigan left Tuskegee and returned with his company to Georgia, stopping by Fort Mitchell long enough to explain to Captain Page what he had done. The removal superintendent had little choice but to approve the act, as did the *Columbus Enquirer*, which accused the regular army officers stationed at the camps of "indirectly conniving at the atrocities of the savages."[25]

Lieutenant Sloan told a different story in his report to General Jesup. He claimed that the troops pillaged the homes of the Indians and carried away money and property, including the best Indian guns taken from Sloan's storehouse. The volunteers also held the Creeks overnight with no provisions and only a few blankets to shield them from the inclement weather. Then, by placing so many of the warriors in prison in Tuskegee, which they had no right to do, Jernigan's men left the removal camp largely unprotected from mobs of whites who began to take away the Indians' livestock—herds of horses, mules, and ponies. But the depredations on Native property did not end here. Some of the Georgia and Russell County volunteers did not go home after taking the warriors from Sloan's station. Joined by other volunteer companies, they continued to move through the countryside looking for Indians to torment. A group of Barbour County men, for example, rode down Federal Road to Pole Cat Springs to intimidate the residents there, and along the way, they attacked the plantation of Anne Cornell, a well-known Creek woman. They took two free blacks and an Indian boy from her, presumably to enslave them, and then burned her buildings and fodder stacks. Indeed, Sloan's account of all this seems to reveal another reason, besides the security of the country, for the whites' move against the removal camps. Some settlers obviously wanted the camps broken up and the Indians pushed out of Macon County so they could claim Indian property, perhaps even the land that some of the friendly Creeks still owned. After all, the five-year trust period of the Cusseta Treaty was about to expire, and despite the War Department's removal decree, it was conceivable that those Creeks who still held their land allotments might try to secure deeds from the government, as the treaty allowed, and then register those deeds in their county courts. Should that happen, those Indians would become freeholders and citizens of the state of Alabama. As such, they could claim important legal protections from the state and possibly even the right to vote.

Some settlers certainly found this possibility unacceptable and moved to divest the camp residents of everything they had and push them out of the state as soon as they could. Or, in other words, the desire to milk the Creeks of all their resources, the continued operation of the old Indian business, certainly explains some of the aggression toward the predominately friendly Indians of Macon County.[26]

Yet the drive against the camps, coupled with the economic exploitation that accompanied it, proved counterproductive. Rather than pacifying the Creeks, white aggression increased Creek hostility and ignited the second phase of the Second Creek War. Following Jernigan's operation, fights between small groups of whites and Creeks broke out in Macon County. Colonel Wellborn blamed this fighting on what he called Jernigan's premature move on Sloan's camp. According to Wellborn, the Georgian did not have enough men to surround Echo Harjo's settlement and capture all its inhabitants. Wellborn believed that Jernigan had flushed a considerable number of hostile warriors from the camp, perhaps as many as two hundred, and now those warriors were attacking local settlers. On one point Wellborn was correct: Jernigan did not have enough men for the job. Echo Harjo's settlement actually straggled along the outskirts of Big Swamp for a distance of nine miles. It would have taken two or three regiments to run the Indians scattered through that space. However, the colonel was wrong in thinking that many rebel warriors escaped Jernigan's grasp. Most of the warriors Jernigan left behind were friendly; if they fought the settlers, which some undoubtedly did, they probably did so to protect the property of their townspeople or to keep the whites from capturing them and taking them to the Tuskegee stockade. Thus, the move on Sloan's camp probably turned some friendly Creek warriors hostile, and rather than crippling the rebel party, Jernigan's action actually increased the numbers and strength of that group.[27]

Then Governor Clay duplicated Jernigan's mistake. On February 4, the day before Jernigan entered Sloan's camp, Clay, not knowing anything of the operation, took steps to "restore peace and safety" in New Alabama. He gave his adjutant and inspector general, John A. Campbell, a set of orders to transmit to the company commanders of the volunteer battalion recently called into the Creek service. Clay directed that the troops disarm all the Indians awaiting removal and place them in one camp under guard. The governor also instructed the troops not to permit the Creeks to roam from the camp they created, and any Natives found outside the camp should be treated as hostiles. Shortly after the issuance of Clay's order, Captain Page disarmed the friendly Indians living around Fort Mitchell and enclosed them in pickets. He then directed Lieutenant Reynolds at the Pole Cat Springs camp to disarm all of his Indians, box their guns, and send the weapons to Montgomery for shipment to the West. That done, Page ordered Major Young, stationed at Tuskegee, to take troops to Reynolds's camp and to erect a stockade to hold the camp's warriors until they could be removed from the state. Despite Clay's order, Page determined that it would not be practical to concentrate all the Indians at Tuskegee as the governor directed.[28]

Now the tragedy began to unfold. Following orders, Major Young left Tuskegee with his company, bound for the Pole Cat Springs camp. Along the way, more citizen soldiers joined the march: two companies of Barbour County men under Colonel Wellborn and Dr. Parks's Russell County volunteers. Ominously, Parks's men were probably the ones who committed the thefts at Sloan's camp, and unlike the other troops, they declined being mustered in to the federal service. They obviously resented federal authority and wanted to operate against the Indians unencumbered by any legal or moral restraints. They also had something to prove. The settlers of Russell County, always among the worst abusers of the Creeks, had been accused of cowardice during the summer war, of fleeing the country and allowing others to do their fighting for them. Now Parks and company wanted to salvage their tarnished reputations at the expense of the camp Indians. Captain Page undoubtedly realized this fact and tried to dissuade Parks from going to Pole Cat Springs. He also cautioned the Russell County men to watch their behavior if they did go, "lest they should do acts, that would bring disgrace upon themselves." Unfortunately for the friendly Creeks at Pole Cat Springs, as well as for the respectable settlers of New Alabama, Parks's irregular company paid no attention to the captain.[29]

The troops reached Federal Road and called a halt shy of the Pole Cat Springs camp. Then, just as he had done at Echo Harjo's camp, Wellborn sent a messenger ahead to Pole Cat Springs to inform Lieutenant Reynolds that he meant to scour his camp thoroughly and make prisoners of all the warriors he found there. However, he requested that Reynolds come out to meet him at Durant's stage stand on the edge of the Calebee Swamp so they could coordinate a plan for the operation. Fearing what Wellborn and his men intended to do to his warriors, Reynolds quickly repaired to the site and discovered that the colonel already had six or eight of the Creek men in custody. Incensed, the lieutenant demanded of Wellborn his authority for invading the removal camp, whereupon the colonel simply replied, "the people."[30]

Now Reynolds realized he had to cooperate with the Alabama volunteers, but he chose to do so in a way that would prevent great alarm among his charges and keep them from rushing headlong into the swamps and the welcoming arms of the rebel party. He informed Wellborn that he mustered the camp's warriors every other day for roll call, and he would do so again at the appointed time. Then, when he had all the men assembled, he would secretly send for Wellborn so he and his volunteers could ride in quickly and take custody of all the warriors at once. That way the colonel could achieve his objective without scaring any warriors off and Reynolds could preserve his standing with the Indians by pretending surprise and loudly protesting the sudden and unwarranted appearance of Alabama troops.[31]

The plan worked perfectly. When Wellborn's men surrounded Reynold's headquarters on February 19, the 253 congregated warriors, knowing they had done nothing wrong, "jumped upon logs and appeared quite amused, at the unnecessary measures adopted to make prisoners of them." Reynolds then called his roll, showing that all his male residents, save a few old men, were in attendance. Colonel Wellborn then took custody of the inmates and secured them under guard for the evening. At that point, all appeared well. But then Parks's men went to work. During the night they attacked the defenseless Indian homes. They stripped them of provisions, raped the women, shot and wounded a young Eufaula girl who resisted their advances, and murdered an inoffensive elderly man by shooting him in the chest and mashing his head to a paste with musket butts. This man and many of the other molested Creeks belonged to Jim Boy's Thlobthlocco town. Thus, Jim Boy's people suffered while he fought for the United States against the Seminoles in the wilds of Florida—a place the Russell County roughs would not dare go.[32]

The next morning Reynolds found himself in a terrible fix. His sullen warriors blamed him for the atrocities. They grew even angrier on learning that the Alabama troops meant to separate them from their families and confine them in Tuskegee. In desperation, the lieutenant sought to save face and appease the warriors in some way. He demanded that Wellborn disarm Parks's company and arrest all those who committed crimes against the Indians. Most of the men in the other Alabama companies disapproved the actions of the Russell County gang and supported Reynolds in his call for their arrest. Seeing this, Dr. Parks and his officers apologized to the Creeks for what some of their men had done, but neither Parks nor any of his crew would consent to disarmament or the possibility of arrest and confinement. Consequently, they soon quit the camp and headed for home. Before leaving, however, they rounded up eight or ten Indian ponies to take with them. They also beat up a white man in the public employ so they could steal the Indians' subsistence rations in his care.[33]

Surely Reynolds breathed a sigh of relief with the departure of Parks and his company, but he still had to prevent the separation of the Creek warriors from their families. He informed Wellborn that such a separation would only endanger the Indians and their property, and insofar as the Creeks were the colonel's prisoners now, he had the obligation to protect them. Fortunately, Reynolds found a subdued Wellborn willing to listen to reason. They sat down together and agreed to a compromise that would assure the safety of both Creeks and settlers. The warriors and their families would not be divided. Instead, Reynolds and Wellborn would move the whole camp of Indians out of New Alabama altogether, away from the scene of recent clashes between settlers and Creeks. That much decided, Reynolds rode west on Federal Road, crossed Line Creek, the border between Old and New Alabama, and located a suitable campsite near Mount Meigs. However, he then had to ask permission of the local residents to bring the Indians there. Interestingly, he had little trouble gaining their assent, showing once again that Old and New Alabamians did not see the Creeks in quite the same light.[34]

Now Reynolds had to get his Native charges to agree to the deal, and he knew that regaining the trust of the women would be crucial. Traditionally these women headed their households and made the important decisions regarding their families, but their authority would have been even greater in the removal camps because so many of their men were in Florida. And now these women were hurting, sorely abused by the Alabama volunteers. During the attacks on their homes at Pole Cat Springs, the women had to endure rape, along with the lesser offense of having their blankets and other property stolen. Then, adding insult to injury, their assailants snatched the women's prized earrings from their lobes. Not surprisingly, these terrified women gathered up their children and fled to the swamps to hide, making Reynold's task all the more difficult. He had to use every stratagem at his disposal to draw the women out for a council, including parading through the camp carrying a pole draped in white muslin—white being a color symbolizing peace and friendship in the Creek system of thought. Finally, the lieutenant believed he had won the women's approval, and so he turned to the warriors. He gave these men a choice of confinement under guard at Tuskegee or moving with the women and children to Mount Meigs. The warriors chose the latter, and all the Creeks immediately began selling off all but their most essential possessions in preparation for the move. Undoubtedly, settlers took advantage of this situation and picked up livestock, farm implements, and other goods at very reasonable rates. In a mere thirty-six hours after making the decision to relocate, Lieutenant Reynolds and the 1,900 residents of the Pole Cat Springs camp were on their way to Mount Meigs.[35]

Yet the relocation of Lieutenant Reynolds's camp, the largest in Macon County, did little to bring peace to New Alabama. Settlers on the Black Belt prairie in the vicinity of the former campsite still complained of Indians in the area and continued to clash with them along

Cubahatchee Creek. However, some of the so-called hostile Creeks were friendly Creeks who had fled from Pole Cat Springs in the wake of the mistreatment they received from the volunteers. Indeed, some of the camp's women surely must have decided that they would never trust the whites again and determined to resist removal at all costs. Beyond that, Governor Clay feared the reaction of Jesup's warriors in Florida, arguably the best fighting men in the Creek Nation. He asked Captain Page to send word to these men that the state of Alabama disapproved of the outrages committed on their friends and relatives at the removal camps. He also ordered the state solicitor, George D. Shortridge, to collect evidence for the prosecution of all those members of the Parks company who committed outrages on the Creeks. Shortridge, however, cautioned against such a move, given "the established and bitter prejudices of the people of the new counties" against the "unfortunate" Creeks. The solicitor also stated that anyone attempting to prosecute the offenders "would be put down by the weight of public odium." Consequently, Clay backed down, concluding that under the circumstances prosecutions might not serve "the cause of public justice."[36]

But apparently Clay did believe that closing the Creek camps altogether would serve the cause of public justice, for he contended that breaking up the so-called friendly camps would deny the rebel Creeks "a source of subsistence, and of refuge, and hasten a termination of hostilities." As early as February 1 he wrote the War Department requesting the authority to remove the encamped Indians from Alabama, despite Jesup's promise that they could stay where they were until their warriors returned from Florida. In three weeks Clay had his reply. Joel Poinsett, the new secretary of war, ordered him to move all the Indians down the Alabama River to Mobile Point on the Gulf Coast. There they would await the return of their warriors from Florida before taking passage on steamboats to the mouth of the Mississippi and up that river to Arkansas. On receiving this good news, the governor ordered his volunteers to move the Creeks from Mount Meigs, Tuskegee, Fort Mitchell, and Echo Harjo's settlement into yet another removal camp a mile east of Montgomery. By March 8 all the Creeks had been transferred, and nine days later, 650 of them embarked for Mobile Point on the steamboat *John Nelson*. The next day 800 more Creeks left Montgomery on the *Chippeway*, and another 480 departed on the *Bonnets O' Blue*. Then 1,000 more Natives set off on March 20, and during the next week, all the remaining Indians headed down the Alabama River. Captain Page, the removal superintendent, also left Fort Mitchell, as the War Department had ordered him to accompany the Creeks on their journey. In his absence, Colonel Wellborn assumed command of all the troops in the field in the southern counties of New Alabama.[37]

This hasty removal afforded greedy whites their last opportunity to exploit the Creeks, one final chance to pursue the Indian business that had done so much to cause the war. The volunteer troops gave the Creeks little notice before marching them out of the camps, and during the move, thieves moved in to strip them of their possessions. At Echo Harjo's settlement, for example, the women, children, and old ones had only thirty minutes to vacate the premises. Having no wagons to transport their property, they left it locked in Lieutenant Sloan's headquarters until the officer could send it along to them. That did not happen. Whites broke into the buildings and took almost everything of value. These thieves also stole the Indians' remaining livestock. In fact, the removal cost Sloan's charges "145 ponies, 60 head of cattle, 200 hogs, 100 bushels of corn, 100 beehives, cooking and farming utensils and crockery ware, 63 guns," and a goodly sum of money.[38]

Governor Clay may have thought that he was serving "public justice" by breaking up the removal camps, but James Belser of the *Montgomery Advertiser*, representing the more thoughtful residents of Old Alabama, saw the truth. On observing the Creeks just prior to their departure from his town, he stated that "The spectacle exhibited by them is truly heart rending.... While our citizens are rolling in ease and luxury, those who are natives of the country are in the most abject poverty, dependent for subsistence on the charity of the government." But Belser went no further. He did not lament the condition of enslaved blacks or that Montgomery owed its prosperity to the cotton these slaves produced. Nor did he decry the fact that many whites were as poor as the Indians. Belser was certainly more liberal than the average Alabamian but even he could not see the larger picture. He could not see, or would not admit, that Alabama was part of the periphery of the world system, and as such its people lived by extracting resources from the land to feed the system. But this extraction, whether in the U.S. South, Africa, or Latin America, always resulted in a dispossession of the Native population, exploitation of the labor supply, social injustice based on a maldistribution of wealth, and, of course, an abundance of violence and bloodshed.[39]

Viewed from the larger perspective, it is apparent that clearing the Creek removal camps did not serve "public justice." Moreover, Alabama's move against the camps made General Jesup's job much more difficult. Governor Clay had not consulted him about transporting the Creeks to Mobile Point, and he had learned of the event, along with the brutal treatment of the Indians, only after the fact. The news put him in an unenviable position. He had promised the Creek warriors serving with him in Florida that their families could stay in Alabama under federal protection until the men returned to take them west. Now the general had to inform the warriors that the United States had broken yet another promise. He tried to explain to them that moving the camps was the only way to prevent even greater harm to their friends and families in Alabama, but the explanation did not fully satisfy the men. Worse, Jesup wondered what effect the news would have on all the Seminoles who had surrendered to him under promise of fair treatment and now awaited removal in the Florida camps. Undoubtedly fearing wholesale desertions by the Creeks and Seminoles, the general exerted himself to see to it that his allies received remuneration for all the property lost in Alabama. He also sought to speed up the process of shipping his Seminoles off to the West, followed closely by the Creek warriors who would join their families at Mobile Point.[40]

The clearing of the Alabama camps had another evil consequence. It did not remove all the Creeks from New Alabama, and consequently it did not terminate the hostilities as Clay had hoped. A substantial number of Indians never enrolled themselves at the removal camps or made the march to Montgomery. Others dropped off along the way to the town. Still more fled their encampment at Montgomery just before their fellows boarded the steamboats for Mobile Point. This whole group of fugitives amounted to several hundred and perhaps one thousand people, and the citizens of Macon County complained loudly to Governor Clay that they still encountered dangerous Indians in the swamps bordering their Black Belt prairie lands. Furthermore, they knew the full economic potential of this rich prairie could not be realized if Indians retarded white settlement. Thus, they called on Clay to raise even more troops to ferret out the intractable Creeks. But these Indians had no intention of remaining in New Alabama. The renewal of hostilities, as well all the troop movements associated with it, stimulated a flight out of the area by both rebel Creeks and formerly friendly camp inmates. In fact, this flight had begun as early as January, with a few small parties of travelers leading the way. Then, with the closing of the camps in February, the flight picked up momentum, with larger parties of Indians attempting to escape New Alabama. However, the Creek refugees of 1837 did not run to the Chattahoochee and across southwest Georgia to the Seminole country in East Florida. Unlike the rebel migrants of the previous year, these Creeks knew they would find no shelter among the besieged Seminoles. Instead, they traveled due south toward West Florida, a region yet untouched by the war and largely uninhabited by whites. There the refugees hoped to find peace and security, not to mention avoiding removal beyond the Mississippi. But first they had to get through southern Alabama, and this was no easy trip. The settlers there were not content to let Indians pass by unmolested. They now saw all refugee Creeks as a threat to their existence and resolved to kill or capture for removal every Native they could find. Consequently, the southern migration of Indian refugees in the winter and spring of 1837 resulted in some of the bloodiest fighting of the Second Creek War.[41]

Small parties of Creek refugees moved south by three distinct routes: one trail led from Macon County down the Conecuh River through Pike and Covington counties to the Florida line; a second trail, farther to the east, led from the headwaters of the Cowikee creeks in Russell and Barbour counties down the Pea River through Pike and Dale counties;

and a third trail followed the high ground or ridge line between the other two routes. The counties through which these trails passed were part of Old Alabama, but they contained relatively few settlers. In fact, Indians traveling these routes would pass near only three significant white communities: Monticello in Pike County, Montezuma in Covington, and Daleville in Dale. The Creeks moved quietly along the outskirts of these settlements, trying to slip out of Alabama undetected. They did not molest local farmers or their property, though they did try to preserve the secrecy of their movements by killing the occasional unlucky white hunter who happened upon them in the woods.[42]

In February the situation changed. The Indian traffic through the southern border counties increased owing to the activity of the militiamen farther north. Now settlers in Dale, Covington, and Pike counties discovered an alarming number of tracks, and they determined to stop the Creeks from moving through their section of the state. Capt. Jack Cooper of Louisville in Barbour County took the first step. On receiving word of a large party of Indians coming down the Pea River trail, he gathered a company of one hundred men and on February 10 attacked the Indians at Hobdy's Bridge, eight miles east of Monticello. In the fight that followed, the Creeks fired nails from their muskets, and as their nails filled the swamp with screeching and howling noises as they flew through the air, the whites were disconcerted for a time. But in the end, Cooper's men drove the Indians from their position, killing four or five. The remainder of the Creeks scattered and ran, leaving a considerable amount of plunder behind in their camp, including bolts of calico taken from a store near Martin's Creek. This cloth identified the Creeks that Cooper fought as the same ones engaged by Wellborn two weeks before. The militiamen continued their pursuit of the Indians for two days and skirmished with them again at Black's Mill farther down the Pea. This time one of the whites died. The Indians then left the river and its swamps, ascended to higher ground, and escaped.[43]

On February 28 the flying Creeks retaliated for Cooper's attacks. They killed a Mrs. Albertson and her sister at the Albertson home on the east bank of the Choctawhatchee River, approximately fifty miles south of Hobdy's Bridge. Subsequently, local settlers chased the Creeks into Florida and captured a woman and two boys. They placed their captives in the Daleville jail, a rustic structure made of round logs, to await removal from the state. However, one moonlit night, a man, presumably Mr. Eli Albertson, husband of the deceased, sneaked up to the jail, stuck his gun barrel through one of the open spaces between the logs, and killed the woman. Now it was apparent that the migration of fugitive Creeks to West Florida would be a quiet affair no longer; the Second Creek War had begun in Alabama's southernmost counties.[44]

Following the Albertson killings, the residents of Dale County fought another skirmish with a party of two or three hundred passing Creeks and found even more Indian signs on the trails. Greatly alarmed, community leaders decided it was time to notify Governor Clay and ask for his help. They wanted permission to form volunteer companies paid for by the state and to station these troops at key points to intercept parties of Creek travelers. They explained that these troops were necessary because trying to assemble men and track down the Indians after some sighting or depredation occurred did not work. The Creeks always managed to elude pursuit, no matter how large the white force. Anticipation and ambush were necessary to defeat the foe. Furthermore, the men justified their request on the grounds that now the frightened residents of their county were fleeing their farms, and if they did not plant in the spring, severe want would ensue. Also, Clay's petitioners believed that if the Creeks reached Florida, they would stay there only until the Alabamians relaxed their guard. Then, they would return to their "old haunts" in New Alabama and once again do harm to the whites. Finally, the citizens warned that the Seminole War was winding down, that Jesup would soon press the Florida Indians into submission, and when that happened, some Seminoles would escape to West Florida, unite with the refugee Creeks there, and together they would harass Alabama's border counties. Dale's citizens charged Clay with the responsibility of preventing this potential disaster by stopping the Creek flight.[45]

Clay was surprised. Obviously, he had underestimated the number of Indians still at large. Rather quickly after hearing of their movements, he devised a plan to bring them to bay. He charged Colonel Wellborn with the overall defense of the state's southern counties and asked the colonel to supply him with a full report of the numbers and movements of both Alabama troops and fugitive Creeks. In addition, he ordered Wellborn to intercept southbound Creeks by stationing members of his battalion at appropriate points along the paths to West Florida. Then Clay ordered captains Whitman and Young to scour the swamps bordering Macon County and drive any remaining Indian residents of those swamps down toward Wellborn's troops. The governor also authorized the raising of a new company to operate in Dale County and told Captain Whitman to repair to that county with his troops following their searches in Macon County. Whitman would then take charge of the defense of Dale and construct a fort there for storing arms and provisions. Finally, Clay insisted that his men push ahead with their assignments and kill or capture all the "straggling Creeks." He believed it was necessary to deal with the Indians before the leaves filled out in the spring. Otherwise, it would be impossible to find them in the dense swamp cover, and the Creek war would drag on for several more months.[46]

Clay also begged assistance from General Jesup, who had been conducting an aggressive campaign against the Seminoles. Throughout the winter of 1837, the general kept detachments of troops constantly in motion destroying Native villages, cattle herds, and large stores of coontie—the root from which the Seminoles made their flour. Jesup's men also captured pony herds, killed Indians when they could, and took many more prisoners. In fact, the troops exerted so much pressure on the Natives that Micanopy, the principal chief of the Seminoles, sued for peace. He gave himself up to Jesup along with other important headmen, including Jumper, Alligator, Davey, and Negro Abraham. These leaders met with Jesup at Camp Dade on March 6, 1837, and signed a treaty whereby they agreed to cease hostilities and bring their followers to Tampa Bay by April 10 to board transports for the West. As part of this treaty, Jesup promised that the Natives would not have to surrender black Seminoles to the whites, and this provision, while unpopular with the Floridians, convinced many more

Indians and blacks to move into the general's removal camps. Seeing this success, Governor Clay, and most other observers, thought that the Seminole War was finished. Consequently, Clay informed Jesup that the Second Creek War had recommenced, that he was not pleased with the performance of the Alabama militiamen, and that he wanted Jesup to release the battalion of Alabama volunteers serving in Florida so they could help subdue the fugitive Creeks in southern Alabama. The governor asked Jesup to ship the troops home by way of the Choctawhatchee River, which led from Choctawhatchee Bay on the Gulf Coast north into Alabama. Clay intended to order these seasoned soldiers to disembark from steamboats near the Alabama line, then march up the country toward Montgomery scouring the swamps for hidden Creeks as they went. However, the governor did not want Jesup's regiment of friendly Creek warriors to return to New Alabama. He believed their presence would upset the citizens of the Lower counties and lead to more violence. Despite Jesup's promise that the warriors could return to their old home ground to settle their business affairs, Clay asked the general to send them directly to Mobile Point to join their families.[47]

Yet not everyone in the state agreed that military action was the way to rid the state of its aboriginal inhabitants. Captain Whitman conveniently used his duties as an emigration agent to avoid further military service in southern Alabama, for he did not believe such service was necessary. In fact, he thought that the continued pursuit of the Creeks was only prolonging the removal process and continuing the war. Whitman and the other members of his Montgomery Guards contended that many of the fugitive Creeks in Macon County and elsewhere wanted to come into the removal camps, but the marches and countermarches of the Alabama troops were scaring them away. Whitman also implied that the Indians were now fighting for their own survival when placed under attack; no longer were they actively pursuing a war with the white citizens of Alabama. Furthermore, Whitman's own experiences had taught him that searching for Indians in the swamps was useless. He likened the task to "chasing phantoms." The whites almost never found the Indians, and when they did, the Natives most often repelled their attacks. Whitman obviously believed it was in the state's best interest to leave the remaining Creeks alone. Furthermore, his Montgomery Guards were mostly businessmen, and given the poor economic conditions the nation was beginning to experience in 1837, these men wanted to get back to their banks and stores. Whitman's first lieutenant even announced that he would not return to the Creek service if ordered. Fortunately for him and the rest of the Montgomery Guards, Whitman's removal duties kept him occupied until their enlistments expired. They did not have to chase phantoms any longer.[48]

The argument over the best method to capture the Creek fugitives and remove them from the country continued for the duration of the Second Creek War. Federal army officers and Indian agents contended that peaceful coercion was the best policy. They wanted to send friendly Indians out to find the frightened fugitives and persuade them to surrender themselves for removal with promises of food, clothing, and federal protection. Settlers, however, continued to urge constant pursuit by armed troops as the only solution to the Indian problem. They wanted to either kill all the Creek fugitives or force them to give themselves up for removal. During the last years of the war, whites used both methods. However, in Alabama during the early months of 1837, the more militant course prevailed and resulted in one of the most bloody and decisive fights of the war.

The series of events leading to the Battle of Pea River began in mid-March when Colonel Wellborn learned that a number of Creeks had deserted the Indian camp at Montgomery just before their scheduled departure for Mobile Point. He believed that these Indians had joined others hiding in the Cubahatchee and Big swamps of Macon County. Consequently, he sent out a call for all of the companies of his battalion to join him at Stone's plantation near Creek Stand for a search-and-destroy mission. He examined the Cubahatchee first but found no Creeks. On March 20 he set out to attack a reported Indian camp in Big Swamp, though only seventy-two members of his battalion joined him for the assault. En route, he happened upon the Indians attacking the plantation of one Mr. Ellison and discovered that they had already burned the buildings and killed the overseer and one slave. Wellborn charged the Indians and ran them away. He then followed their "bloody trail" but failed to overtake them. In two days he gave up the search and returned to Stone's to await the arrival of the remainder of his troops.[49]

At that point, Wellborn received an express telling him that a company of his Barbour Rangers working in concert with some Georgia volunteers had flushed a party of approximately three hundred Indians from their hiding place on the middle fork of Cowikee Creek. Now these troops were pursuing those Creeks to the west toward Pea River. Wellborn decided to join the chase. He left two companies in place to protect the settlers of Macon County, then headed south to Pea River, leading one company of troops. On reaching the headwaters of the river, Wellborn was able to track the Indians by the houses they left burning in their wake. On March 23 he arrived at the fork of Pea River and Pea Creek, where the Indians had set up camp in a swamp four miles north of Hobdy's Bridge—the site of Captain Cooper's earlier battle with the Creeks. The Barbour Rangers and Georgia volunteers were already on the scene, along with a company of men from Pike County and two irregular companies of citizens who "turned out on the occasion." Many of these citizens had come over to the river from Irwinton. Wellborn now commanded a little more than two hundred men, and he determined to attack the Creek fugitives.[50]

On the morning of March 24, Wellborn divided his command in two parts for the assault. From south of the Indian camp, the colonel sent approximately half of his men across the Pea with orders to march upriver to a point opposite the Indian position. There they were supposed to move into the swamp on the river's edge and open fire on the Creeks. By this means Wellborn hoped to draw the fugitive warriors out of their camp and toward the river, while he and the rest of his command crossed Pea Creek and marched up to invest the camp from the south. Apparently Wellborn hoped that once the warriors saw that he had captured their women, children, old people, and supplies, they would lay down their arms and surrender.[51]

The plan did not work as expected. The warriors saw the troops coming up the west bank of the river and crossed the stream to drive them away. The troops stood their ground for awhile, then broke and ran.

Some of the whites scurried into the thickets to hide, others mounted their horses and fled all the way to Monticello, eight miles away. Even there they did not feel safe. The Creek warriors, having chased the whites some two miles, started back for their camp in what must have been a joyous mood. Meanwhile, Wellborn was slow to reach the enemy camp, his men having to swim Pea Creek and then wade through waist-high swamp water and mud just to reach a place where they could see the high ground on which the camp reposed. But when they finally came in sight of the camp, the Creek women put up "a most deafening shout" and alerted their men, who were able to rush back to the camp before Wellborn arrived. The two sides then commenced firing on one another across a lagoon that protected the camp to the east and south. The Indians had chosen their position well.[52]

The fight lasted nearly four hours, and Wellborn believed "but few battles in modern times have been more severe." The warriors fought fiercely, charging several times in an attempt to drive the whites back from the banks of the lagoon. Some fired bullets made from pewter plates melted down by their women. One of their rounds struck James H. Wellborn, the colonel's son, in the head, and he fell beside a small poplar tree. He writhed and moaned in agony for some time before he expired, and a fellow soldier crouching next to him said the sight made him feel that he "would just about as soon be at home." Undeterred by young James's death, and seeing that his troops were running out of ammunition, Colonel Wellborn ordered his men to move around the lagoon for a charge on the enemy's western flank near the river. This charge succeeded and the whites entered the Creek camp, where the fighting became hand to hand, with some of the Indian women joining the fray. Several of them surrounded one of the whites and he had to extricate himself from the trap with a Bowie knife. Finally the Indians broke and fled, at which point "the slaughter became unparalleled." The troops cut down men, women, and children alike and chased the Indians over to the west side of the river. The foot-log the Creeks used to cross the Pea was covered in blood. In the end, the volunteers killed forty-two Indians and one black man "dressed as an Indian" in and around the campsite. They and the enemy wounded "hung in grotesque forms over logs." Others fell into the river and died, floating in the sluggish stream. Wellborn was unable to report exactly how many fugitives died that day, but he did state that his troops did their duty and "I trust did execution." Certainly more than fifty Indians perished in the attack, and many more may have died later. In the aftermath of the clash, one trooper explained that his shoulder was so sore from the repeated kicking of his flintlock musket that he could scarcely use his arm. Furthermore, he lost all his eyebrows and eyelashes from the powder flashing in the gun's pan. Even more telling, his pants were as bloody as if he had been killing hogs. Another trooper claimed that the most strenuous fighting he did in the battle was with another soldier, whom he tried to stop from killing an Indian woman. The frustrated executioner struck him in the head with a gun butt.[53]

The Battle of Pea River was a decisive and profitable victory for the settlers. In addition to killing so many Indians, the troops also claimed all of their packs and provisions, as well as twenty horses. In addition, the whites took at least six captives, mostly children. Individual soldiers carried these captives to their homes and, according to an eye witness, enslaved them. Two of these youngsters were the children of Cheske Micco, the Indians' leader. This man, called "bold and fearless" by Wellborn, was a chief of Loachapoka town, one of the original hostile Tallassee settlements in the Creek rebellion of 1836. Both he and his wife died in the battle. The whites lost five killed and nine wounded. William Wellborn, though losing his son, gained the respect of the entire state, on top of the wealth he had amassed selling the land in and around the town of Irwinton, land he acquired from the Eufaula Creeks at a mere five or ten dollars per half section. Toward the end of 1837, he added to his prizes a seat in the state senate. Once again, the Creeks had proved to be a valuable natural resource for aggressive and ambitious whites.[54]

More importantly, the Pea River fight ended the Second Creek War in New Alabama, the place it began. Some overly optimistic settlers may have hoped the battle ended the war altogether. After all, only scattered groups of Creeks remained in the swamps of Macon, Russell, Pike, and Barbour counties. These groups stayed firmly hidden, and those who moved into West Florida now did so very quietly and carefully. New Alabama's whites lived in fear for some time after the battle, but gradually they realized the fugitive Creeks were no longer a threat to them. Similarly, the settlers on the Old Alabama side of Pea River, having fled from the southward-moving Creeks, now returned to their farms in time to save the year's crop. Governor Clay maintained troops at Society Hill on New Road and on the middle prong of Cowikee Creek to give confidence to the settlers and to encourage the continued migration of people into Alabama. Clay also gave Colonel Wellborn discretionary authority in dealing with the fugitive Natives and urged him to stay in the field "till every Creek Indian is killed, or captured and removed." However, the troops in New Alabama had little to do but chase the occasional party of six or seven frightened Indians seen running across the road.[55]

But the Pea River fight did not end the Second Creek War. Jesup's failure to quell rebel resistance and remove all the Creeks from Alabama in the summer and fall of 1836 continued to have adverse effects. In fact, the Pea River affair only shifted the locus of the conflict to West Florida and the Alabama border counties of Covington and Dale. Consequently, Colonel Wellborn could not release all his troops from service. He continued to keep six companies of troops in the field to guard the Alabama-Florida line.[56]

10. Seeking Refuge in West Florida

The movement of Creeks south into Florida in 1837 was the culmination of a migration that had been going on by fits and starts for well over one hundred years. In part, this migration was a natural aspect of Creek expansionism: the disease, colonial warfare, and slave trade caused by the entry of Europeans and their economic system into the Southeast had nearly extinguished Florida's original Native population. The robust Creeks simply moved into the void, the vacant environmental niche, to take up abandoned cornfields and hunting grounds. However, Creeks tended to move to Florida in times of stress. Some individuals went there to avoid punishment for crimes; others went as part of whole communities when they could no longer countenance the policies of the Creek Council, or when they found it difficult to live in peace with other Creek towns. But perhaps most Creeks moved to Florida simply to avoid European American expansionism, to get out of the way of the Georgians and others who sought constantly to encroach on the Creek Nation and bend its people to their will. To the Creeks, Florida was a place of refuge. And this was certainly the case in 1837, when the last beleaguered parties of Creeks made their way out of Alabama and into the "Land of Flowers." Florida was also the land of the Seminoles, themselves former Creek émigrés, who along with a few members of the original Native population of Florida, had undergone a process of ethnogenesis to form a separate tribal nation.[1]

One of the first government officials to notice that a new wave of refugee Creeks were entering West Florida was Archibald Smith, U.S. agent to the Apalachicola Indians, a branch band of the Seminoles living on the Apalachicola River, which divided West from East Florida. In January 1837, even before the break-up of the removal camps in Alabama, he alerted the War Department that eighty Creek warriors and their dependents had encamped near the mouth of Black Water Bay on Santa Rosa Sound. To anyone who dared inquire, these people claimed to be a peace-loving neutral party. They had come to the Florida coast, they said, because they did not wish to emigrate west or take part in the war against the whites. As further proof of their friendliness, these Creeks pointed to the fact that three white men had come from Alabama with them and would act as their intermediaries and protectors. And with the help of these men, they hoped they could stay on indefinitely in Florida, hunting and fishing along the stretch of coast from the town of Pensacola to the mouth of the Choctawhatchee River, an "entire wilderness without any [white] inhabitants," according to Smith. But the agent did not believe what he heard. He received numerous complaints from white Floridians that the eighty warriors and their families on Black Water Bay were rebels and fugitives from justice, people who had left their homes in Alabama the previous August when the war there went against them. Furthermore, these Indians stood accused of killing three men in Pike County on their way south and defeating a squad of ten or twelve more settlers who tried to trail them down the Choctawhatchee River into Florida. Moreover, the fact that white men lived with these Indians must have aroused further suspicion for, similar to the Alabama situation, interethnic collusion for nefarious purposes had become a distinguishing characteristic of life on the Florida frontier.[2]

In fact, Smith was not above such collusion himself, nor did he ever miss an opportunity to extol his virtues as an Indian agent to the War Department. He informed his superiors in Washington that all the settlers were afraid to approach the Black Water Creeks, but that he was not. He even bragged that he had been raised on the frontier since age nine and his "knowledge of the Indian character" was "perfect."

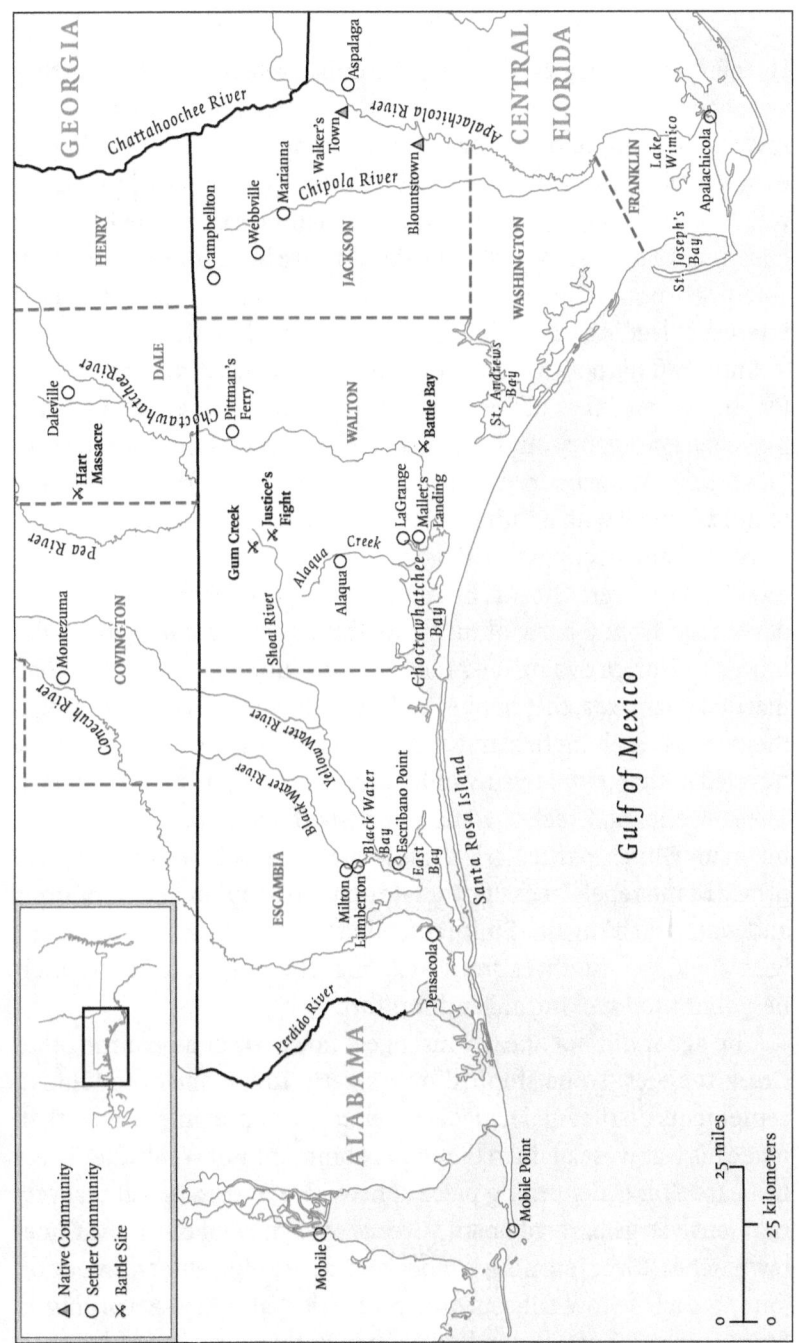

7. War in West Florida

He then promised not only to visit the Indian refugees to see what they were about but also to lure them back to his agency on the Apalachicola River so they might be removed from the country. Again praising his own knowledge of Native character, he pompously stated that there was "a certain manner in which the Indian race can be led without coercion." The War Department should have been forewarned. That sort of self-promotion usually meant someone had a personal business interest in leading the Indians, or appearing to lead them.[3]

Smith left his home in the little community of Chattahoochee, Florida, on the morning of February 27, 1837, and headed west toward his Aspalaga Agency on the Apalachicola River with two purposes in mind: first, he meant to visit the Black Water Creeks; then, he wanted to hold council with another group of Indians living in their vicinity. This last band occupied a village on Escribano Point on Black Water Bay. They too were Creeks, but older residents of West Florida. They descended from a party of migrants from Tuckabatchee town, who moved to Florida during the American Revolution. Some of them had married Spaniards, they spoke English fairly well, and they supported themselves catching fish and oysters for the Pensacola market. They traveled to that town, twenty miles across the bay, in small sailboats. These Escribano Creeks had never given offense to the local settlers, but many whites, particularly those in Alabama, believed that they had provided the rebel Creeks farther north with supplies and munitions and would do so again. Smith intended to warn them not to consort with any Creek fugitives from Alabama who might come into their neighborhood seeking aid and comfort.[4]

The agent did not speak Muscogee, however, or any of the other Creek tongues, so he stopped by Walker's Town, one of the Indian settlements on the Apalachicola River, to pick up an interpreter, then made his way west again to the settler community of Webbville. There he heard a most disturbing piece of news. He learned that at that very moment a large party of hostile Creeks were moving down the Choctawhatchee River, stealing canoes and attacking settlers, intent on joining their fellow tribespeople on Black Water Bay. According to Smith's informants, the Indian women in this party had killed their small children to ease their flight and were fighting as fiercely as their men. Obviously, these exaggerated reports referred to the same group of fugitives who fought Captain Cooper's Alabama volunteers at Hobdy's Bridge on the Pea River on February 10. And while Smith did not identify these Indians by tribe or town, the Alabamians thought them Eufaulas. Furthermore, the Webbville residents warned Smith that if he continued on his present course toward the bay he might very well run head-on into these Indians and lose his life. But this information only made Smith more determined to reach his destination ahead of the fugitives, and so he rushed to Pittman's Ferry on the Choctawhatchee. He crossed the river safely, but on that very night of February 28, the Creeks murdered the family of Arthur Albertson just two miles north of the ferry stand. Undeterred, the agent pushed on and "brought the sad news to every settlement" in his path until he finally reached Black Water Bay on the night of March 3.[5]

Early the next morning, Smith dashed off a hasty letter to a friend in Pensacola, telling him all the latest news and requesting that the town authorities suspend "the sale of powder and lead to all Indians and also to all white men who might be suspected of selling to Indians." Then Smith procured a yawl and three deckhands and sailed out to the Escribano village. He immediately informed the residents that hostile Creeks had broken away from the removal camp at Fort Mitchell and could not be far behind him on their way to the bay. He could have saved his breath. His hosts already knew about the fugitives. One of their women had encountered two strange Indian boys in the woods, and these boys informed her that they belonged to a large party of Coweta Creeks who occupied four different camps only a few miles back. The boys also informed the woman that more Indians would be coming south to join them and they were all "resolved to die rather that emigrate to Arkansas." That Coweta Creeks were part of the fugitive population must have startled Smith, for the Cowetas were Paddy Carr's people and had never been a part of the rebel party of 1836. Furthermore, most of the Cowetas had emigrated in the fall of that year. Some, however, had stayed behind at the Fort Mitchell removal camp. But now some of those people had broken away and come to Florida, determined to die before going west. On listening further, Smith determined that the Coweta camps held some three hundred people, and he had to wonder just how many Creeks had or would come to West Florida and what level of violence would result. He gave evidence of his concern in a statement to Carey A. Harris, the commissioner of Indian Affairs in Washington: "From what I have seen I am fearful that distress will pervade the most part of West Florida for some time."[6]

Smith did take some consolation from the fact that the Escribano Indians promised that they would conduct themselves well and stay away from the fugitives, even to the point of abandoning their village and retreating to Pensacola if necessary. However, Smith now faced the more immediate problem of safely getting back to his home in the hamlet of Chattahoochee, Florida. He had no desire to return the way he had come and run into a gauntlet of angry Indians. Consequently, he decided to travel due north, cross the Alabama line, and then turn east to travel across the southern counties of that state, avoiding the Florida counties altogether. However, he could not have felt much safer as he rode along, for he found all the southern Alabama settlers frightened and "forted in," owing to the passing Indians. Nevertheless, Agent Smith arrived home in one piece and reported all the latest events to the War Department.[7]

Meanwhile, the settlers of northwestern Florida took steps to defend themselves from harm. The entire militia force of Walton and Washington counties assembled and prepared for action. The citizens of Pensacola also raised a volunteer company, which proceeded to the Black Water River to protect the farmers in that vicinity. Joseph Bonifay, a prominent and knowledgeable inhabitant of the area, rode east from the Black Water on a reconnaissance mission, gathering all the information he could on recent Indian movements and activities.[8]

Simultaneously, federal military personnel joined in the defense effort, trying to find as many of the elusive Creek fugitives as they could. Soldiers and sailors from Pensacola established a supply depot named Camp Dallas at the head of East Bay, and a thirty-six-man mounted company used the camp as a base of operations. This company searched the country between the Yellow and Shoal rivers for Indians but found only one abandoned camp. Another small force operated from the U.S. steamboat *Constellation*, searching the bays, bayous, and rivers for Creeks, but with little to show for its efforts. The government's spies and agents riding into the interior alone or in parties of two or three were more successful, however. They located a band of thirty-five fugitive Creeks and convinced them to come in peacefully. Army Maj. Henry Wilson, the commanding officer at Mobile Point, came over to Pensacola to meet this group of Indians and to escort them back to his removal camp. Later, Major Wilson and Lt. John Reynolds, the Marine officer who had been in charge of the emigration camp at Pole Cat Springs, Alabama, would return to Escribano Point to oversee the government's efforts to establish contact with all the fugitive bands through friendly Indian emissaries. Wilson and Reynolds intended to promise the fugitives protection, food, and clothing if they would give themselves up and go to Mobile Point. These officers believed that peaceful coercion was the best method of bringing in the runaway Creeks and preventing harm to the settlers.[9]

But then the general fear of a hostile Indian invasion dissipated in West Florida. As the month of March progressed, no large bodies of Creeks showed themselves. Neither did the refugees commit any depredations of note. Farther north, the migrating parties referred to by the two Coweta boys found it difficult to escape from Alabama under the vigilant watch of Wellborn and the companies of Dale County men who roamed the Florida border. These men used the newly constructed Fort Dale as a supply depot and base of operations. News of the activity of Wellborn's troops and his decisive defeat of the fugitives at the Battle of Pea River on March 25 must have encouraged white Floridians to believe that they might escape harm. Certainly the *Pensacola Gazette* took such a view and attempted to ease the fears of its readers by downplaying the danger of Indian attacks.[10]

But, again, the whites proved to be their own worst enemies when it came to Indian affairs. The settlers and frontier roughs simply would not leave the refugee Creeks alone. They began to push the frightened, hungry Creeks to defend themselves. When several bands of Indians did turn up at Mallet's Landing on LaFayette Bayou, an offshoot of

Choctawhatchee Bay, one settler tried to hire them as farm laborers so he could capture them for removal. Another settler succeeded in taking four Indians as prisoners. Surprisingly, the Mallet's Landing inhabitants expressed no fear of being killed by the Creeks. They knew that the Natives wanted only to hide from the authorities. Yet the settlers were concerned that starving Indians would kill their cattle, and they wanted troops to come in and relieve them of their unwanted neighbors.[11]

Similar situations occurred throughout West Florida. Indian-white relations deteriorated rapidly, and on April 15, 1837, a climactic event took place. A group of eight to ten Creek fugitives went into the village of Lumberton, Florida, near the mouth of the Black Water River, to buy supplies. When they finished their business, some roughs tried to detain them. The Indians ran and the whites shot one in the leg. Rather than submit to imprisonment, the wounded Creek cut his own throat with a knife and threw the knife to his young son, indicating that the boy should kill himself in the same manner. The lad, approximately ten years old, tried to obey, but the roughs took the knife from him. Some of the men then grabbed the wounded father, secured a rope around his neck, threw him in the river, and dragged him under a raft of floating logs until he finally expired. The roughs also managed to seize an Indian woman and another boy during the melee.[12]

Some respectables deplored this incident and feared that the fugitive Creeks would retaliate. Cdre. Alexander J. Dallas, commander of the Pensacola Navy Yard, dispatched federal troops to protect the Black Water settlers. Lt. Neil M. Howison, leader of the troops, then sent a captured Creek woman, along with two Native interpreters, to open a dialogue with the fugitives camped in the Black Water neighborhood. The emissaries soon returned to Howison with the disappointing news that the fugitives were "very much exasperated" by the Lumberton incident. So much so, in fact, that they had threatened to shoot the interpreters and had kept the Indian woman, not allowing her to return to the whites. The fugitives' feelings were not improved when a company of Walton County militiamen captured a party of Indians on Black Creek, sixteen miles from LaGrange.[13]

Then Commodore Dallas's fears became reality. On April 23 the Creek fugitives began to strike back, opening the Second Creek War in West Florida and also renewing that conflict in the southernmost counties of Alabama. Just before dawn warriors attacked the camp of seven cow hunters on Gum Creek, a tributary of Shoal River, near the Alabama line in Walton County. They killed five of the cowmen, but the other two escaped to tell the tale. One week later, Creeks on horseback returned to Dale County, Alabama, established a camp on Pea River, and assailed the homes of settlers on the main road from Daleville to Montezuma, forty miles north of the Gum Creek incident. In one particularly ghastly attack, the Indians massacred seven members of the Josiah Hart family and left their mangled bodies in a heap in a cow pen. Hart's neighbors dug a common grave for the family, lined it with cow skins, deposited the corpses, covered the dead with more cow skins, and filled in the dirt. They then notified Governor Clay, who also received reports of Indian attacks in Covington County to the west of Dale. Clay was shocked, for he admitted that he thought the war was finished in his state.[14]

A company of Dale County troops led by Capt. Arch Justice quickly took up the Indian trail and followed it back into Florida and down to Shoal River. Justice had distinguished himself at the Battle of Pea River and, following that fight, traveled down the Pea in a canoe at night looking for Indian campsites in the swamps. These heroic acts, plus his ability to track down straggling parties of Natives, endeared him to the citizens of Dale County. In Florida, he enhanced his reputation even more. He and his men succeeded in running down the flying murderers of the Hart family, besieged their camp, and killed fourteen of the fugitives. Justice intended to move farther down the river to attack another Indian camp, but he never got the opportunity. Colonel Wellborn arrived on the scene two hours after the battle with reinforcements from his battalion. He sent Justice and his exhausted company back to their post, Fort Dale, and continued the pursuit of the Creeks himself. The Indians, however, managed to escape Wellborn.[15]

The outbreak of war in West Florida revealed the deep cultural divide between Indians and settlers in the region, but it also highlighted social and cultural differences in the white community itself. While the isolated settlers of Walton County saw themselves as the victims of Creek aggression, Benjamin Drake Wright, the editor of the *Pensacola Gazette*, took another view. In doing so, he represented the perspective of a respectable class of citizens removed from the Indian frontier. Wright tended to blame the coming of the war on other whites, saying "These misguided savages were seeking concealment. They were not disposed to shed blood of a white man, but the outrage committed at Black Water, has exasperated them to the last degree, and we may now look for a savage war with all its attendant horrors." Wright went on to say, quite prophetically, that many valuable lives would be lost before the troops drove the Natives from their hiding places. He concluded with the question: "On whose head rests the blood of these victims?"[16]

Soon Wright had the opportunity to chastise his fellow Floridians again, this time illustrating more vividly the contempt that many respectables held for frontier roughs. In early May a gaggle of white men murdered an Indian at Mallet's Landing in Walton County. But this Indian, named Jim, was a long-time and well-known resident of the area. Moreover, he had served the settlers as a guide and interpreter. Wright responded to the murder with a rather shocking denunciation: "These heroes are supposed to have been drunk when they perpetrated this outrage—they are the very last persons to go out with their neighbors against the hostile Indians, and expend their heroism upon those who are inoffensive and friendly! It is high time that these unprincipled wretches should be made to pay with their lives, the penalty of thus violating the laws of the land, and shedding human blood. The Indian, when friendly and peaceable, is as much entitled to the protection of our laws, as the best man in the community."[17]

With editorials of this sort, Wright established himself as a relatively moderate voice in West Florida, as an upholder, if somewhat condescendingly, of Indian rights in the heat of a war. In this respect, he resembled James Belser of the *Montgomery Advertiser* and, of course, John Hogan, the former removal agent and land-fraud investigator. These men were able to see that the pilfering of Indian lands and the injustices of the removal process had a degenerative effect on whites as well as Natives. And while they continued to support Indian removal, they most certainly did not believe that removal was a cure-all for the ills of the country. Reflecting, perhaps, the classism engendered by their economic system, these respectables believed that other whites, not Indians, posed the greatest obstacles to bringing true civilization and economic development to the South.

But Wright and his fellow respectables had little impact on the situation. The Indians meant to stay in West Florida, and the settlers were just as determined to drive them out. More bloodshed resulted. The main body of Creek refugees took up residence on the Choctawhatchee River and the bayous of Choctawhatchee Bay in Walton County, and according to local settlers, the Natives did so with a definite military strategy in mind. They meant to control Choctawhatchee Bay, thereby cutting off the settlers' main line of communication and supply from Pensacola. At the same time, the Creeks established their own supply line to the town through Spanish traders and Indians the whites considered friendly. Thus, firmly ensconced in Walton County, the Creeks, according to settler reports, began to raid at will. During the month of May, they committed numerous depredations in Walton County and killed twelve whites. The settlers lived in a state of panic and sent out cries for help in every direction. In fact, aged county residents remembered that the period of Indian warfare in Walton was more terrible than the years of the Civil War, when the Choctawhatchee became a base of operations for outlaws and Union guerrillas.[18]

General Jesup, among others, heard the appeals of the West Florida settlers. He also heard about the closing of the New Alabama emigration camps and the relocation of Creeks to the Gulf Coast, and he must have realized at that point, if not before, that he had rushed off to Florida without really finishing the war in the Creek country. In fact, Governor Clay said as much when he reminded the general that his huge army of regulars and volunteers had actually killed very few rebel warriors during the summer of 1836. Surely this reminder of a job left unfinished stung Jesup, for his campaign against the Seminoles had not gone as well as expected either. In fact, the wholesale Seminole surrender he thought he had achieved fell through, owing in part to the interference of self-interested white and black Floridians who conspired to keep the war going as an economic enterprise, a part of their own Indian business. Now fully exasperated and embarrassed, Jesup moved to make amends to Clay. He complied with the governor's earlier request and dismissed a regiment of Alabama volunteers from his service. These veteran troops, led by Lt. Col. David Cawlfield, traveled back to their state by way of the Florida panhandle so they could assist local militiamen in tracking down the Creek fugitives there.[19]

Florida's territorial governor, Robert Keith Call, also answered the cries for help coming out of West Florida. Since the Choctawhatchee seemed to be the center of Indian activity, Call ordered Col. Leavin Brown, a prominent resident of Jackson County, to raise a body of state troops and to take charge of the war effort on that river. Call also accepted into service two companies of knowledgeable citizen soldiers living near the river. These Walton County men, commanded by Col. John L. McKinnon, were Scottish pioneers for the most part, and they began their service by constructing a fort in the central part of their county. Then, using the redoubt as a base of operations, they began to scour the southern part of the river and the bayous of Choctawhatchee Bay in an attempt to dislodge Creek fugitives. Finally, Call authorized the Escambia County settlers to form a company of men to patrol the panhandle west of the Choctawhatchee to the Yellow Water River. Undoubtedly, the governor's call for troops pleased the West Florida settlers, but the friendly Creeks who had lived in the area for years must have felt a bit uneasy about what Colonel Brown would do with his newfound power. Before the outbreak of war, the Apalachicolas accused Brown of attempting to steal their blacks in concert with slave dealers out of Columbus, Georgia.[20]

Indeed, Columbus businesspeople did not confine their land speculations and exploitations of Indians and their resources to New Alabama alone. Their operations extended into Florida, Mississippi, Louisiana, and even Texas. In fact, James Walker Fannin Jr. of Columbus, one of the heroes of the Texas Revolution, was one of Eli Shorter's partners in land speculation and quite possibly in the illegal African slave trade. Furthermore, when volunteers from Columbus marched through Montgomery on their way to fight the Mexicans in 1835, the Alabamians chided them for carrying a flag sporting the words "Texas and Liberty" and suggested that the Georgians change the motto to "Texas and Land" to conform to their true motive for going to war. Not even realizing the insult, the leader of the volunteers, William Ward, a slaveholder and ardent states' rights nullifier, actually thought the change in wording might be a good idea.[21]

Colonel Wellborn of Alabama, who also had ties to the Columbus network of speculators, now decided that he too would enter the fray in West Florida, hoping once again to take the removal process out of the hands of the federal government, just as he had done in his home state. Agitated by the recent murders in Dale and Covington counties, the colonel wrote to Governor Clay on May 12 asking for permission to raise two hundred additional troops for a march into Florida to end the Indian hostilities. Wellborn claimed that he could not use the troops presently under his command for such an invasion because Indians still remained in the Alabama swamps and settlers needed protection from them. The colonel also assured the governor that he could end the hostilities in Florida fairly quickly if allowed to hunt down the fugitives. Furthermore, Wellborn implied that haste was necessary because the federal officers in Florida were trying to achieve peace by "begging" the hostile warriors to come in and surrender. If this policy persisted, the colonel said, the warriors would sue for peace, gain a respite for themselves, hide their women and children more deeply in the swamps, and then return to Alabama to desolate Dale County. Or, as one of Wellborn's supporters claimed, the warriors would move their families into government removal camps for a time to feed and arm themselves at federal expense before taking off on the war path again. The only real way to achieve peace, Wellborn concluded, was to chase and hound the fugitives constantly until they gave up their resistance unconditionally. But what the colonel did not say to the governor was that the key to his invasion plan was to break up the peaceful Creek village at Escribano Point on Black Water Bay. Wellborn and his supporters in Alabama believed the Escribano Indians were supplying the Creek fugitives, and if the troops cut off that source of supply, the fugitives could not hold out for long against their persistent pursuers. Once again, Wellborn sought to blame a band of friendly Creeks for the success of the hostiles. But more than this, Wellborn may have had hidden economic motives for taking Alabama troops to Florida. Just the previous year, the chief of the northernmost Apalachicola town, Econchattee Micco, had accused Wellborn's partner in the New Alabama land speculations, Alexander Robinson, of stealing twenty of the Apalachicola's slaves, together valued at about fifteen thousand dollars. Wellborn may have had his eye on Creek possessions in Florida as well.[22]

Fortunately for all concerned, Wellborn's ill-conceived assault on the Escribano Indians did not take place. Had he been allowed to proceed, he would have repeated the mistake he made at Pole Cat Springs. He would have had another confrontation with Lieutenant Reynolds, the federal removal agent, and undoubtedly would have frightened a number of the friendly Escribano people into joining the fugitive party. Furthermore, the fugitives would have kept on hiding and fighting with or without arms and food from the Native community at Escribano Point. And as far as hounding those fugitives into submission, that would have been a very difficult task in West Florida, a region that contained more hiding places and fewer settlers than most of Alabama. Governor Clay may have realized this fact, prompting him to deny Wellborn's request. More likely, the colonel could not get money for his expedition. The stingy Alabama Assembly would not have funded a hunt for Indians in Florida, seeing that as a federal responsibility, yet no federal officer in Florida would have approved or recommended funding for Wellborn's meddling in their affairs.

Meanwhile, Col. Leavin Brown opened his campaign on the Choctawhatchee. On May 6 he mustered seventy-three drafted militiamen into service at Marianna in Jackson County. He then marched north to Campbellton near the Alabama line to obtain supplies, moved over to Pittman's Ferry on the river, and began his explorations of the stream and its hiding places. Finding no Indians, the colonel moved south again to the Walton County courthouse, arriving on May 19. On that very day Colonel McKinnon and the Walton troops, operating on the lower Choctawhatchee, fought a serious engagement with the Creeks at Battle Bay near the Cow Ford on the river. These troops captured sixteen of the fugitives and sent them on to Pensacola for shipment to Mobile Point. Brown heard of McKinnon's fight only a short time before he received an express from one J. J. Harrison, telling him that a group of Creeks had taken up residence around his home on Alaqua Creek, another tributary of Choctawhatchee Bay. On May 22 Brown's troops took to their horses and rode the fifteen miles to Harrison's place in great haste.[23]

At that point, one more controversial episode in the Second Creek War in West Florida began to take shape. The men approached the Harrison home at night to avoid detection by the Indians. They found Harrison in the house along with seventeen fugitive Creeks who had decided to spend the night with him. Brown made these people prisoners, left them at the house under guard, and set out after the other fugitives in the neighborhood. He learned from Billy, a friendly Indian, that the Alabama Creeks occupied two camps on the Alaqua, one a half mile from Harrison's home and the other some two miles up the stream. Brown found the first camp easily and captured its occupants, one warrior and nine women and children. With this group of prisoners in tow, Brown headed for the second camp but found an impenetrable swamp standing in the way. The captive warrior informed the whites that he could show them another way to the camp and they let him take the lead. Brown's men followed the Indian all night with no sign of the camp. In the morning they realized the warrior had duped them, and because they could not find the remaining Alaqua fugitives on their own, Brown ordered them to return to Harrison's house. Then tragedy struck. Tired, angry, and disappointed, one of Brown's companies turned their guns on the captive warrior and executed him. Then, according to the colonel's report to Governor Call, the Creek women and children took fright and fled. To prevent this escape, the troops shot them all down. Moving on, the men collected their prisoners from Harrison's place, with the exception of one warrior who had poisoned himself, and marched to the village of LaGrange for supplies. That night, while their fatigued guards slept, the only three warriors in the party of sixteen Creek captives managed to escape.[24]

Some whites found the news that militiamen had killed Indian woman and children disturbing. Benjamin Wright and other newspaper editors reported that Brown's men slew twelve Indians, not the ten the colonel reported. Furthermore, these editors questioned the necessity of such an act. However, Lieutenant Reynolds soon turned their questions into outright condemnations when he reported his investigation of the incident. Reynolds happened to be traveling along the north shore of Choctawhatchee Bay shortly after the killings occurred, and he turned from his path to inspect the death site. He was shocked by what he discovered. The troops had killed the Indians in a spot "not more than fifteen feet in diameter." Moreover, they had scalped several of the dead and slit the ears of some to get at their silver earrings, always a prized commodity. Reynolds and the friendly Indians who accompanied him believed that Brown's men penned the captives up and slaughtered them like cattle. The inhabitants of a cabin not far away heard the shrieks of the children when the massacre occurred. Contrary to Brown's report, Reynolds concluded that the militiamen had committed "one of the most outrageous acts civilized men could be guilty of."[25]

The Alaqua Creek massacre and Reynolds's exposé of it further revealed the different ways federal officers and state troops saw the Creek issue. Even worse, the whole affair contributed to the general feeling of animosity between the two groups, delayed the removal process, and lengthened the war. Lieutenant Reynolds claimed that the fugitive Creeks were so frightened by "the worse than savage cruelty and treachery" of the settlers that they would either "fight or fly" whenever numbers of whites came near them. The frontiersmen, however, tended to blame the federal government's penury and weakness for all the difficulties, claiming that the authorities in Washington should have sent large numbers of federal troops to the Southeast before beginning the removal process. That would have kept the Creek and Seminole wars from starting in the first place. Some West Floridians focused their anger on Lieutenant Reynolds for exposing the Alaqua massacre.

The rumor spread that a man named Lawrence, having lost a wife and possibly other relatives to the Indians, instigated the Alaqua killings and also intended to assassinate Reynolds when the opportunity presented itself. The officer took this threat seriously and must have been disappointed to see so many settlers come out in support of Colonel Brown's actions in the affair. At a Fourth of July celebration in Marianna, the orator of the day claimed that the shooting of the Indians was necessary and that the normal rules of war did not apply to Indians who surrounded cabins and butchered everyone inside.[26]

But Reynolds was not the only critic of the West Florida militia. During this time, Jesup's reinforcements, led by Lt. Colonel Cawlfield, arrived at LaGrange, hoping to find supplies and Colonel Brown there. They found neither. In fact, the Alabamians could locate no West Florida troops to "link up with" and had to go out and look for Indians to fight on their own. They had no better luck, and after marching up and down the panhandle, Cawlfield concluded, like Reynolds, that the Creeks were trying only to hide out, did not feel safe surrendering to the settlers, and would only fight their pursuers if they could not otherwise escape. In fact, given the economic recession of 1837, Cawlfield believed the West Florida settlers were much more worried about lack of money and provisions than they were of Indians. Furthermore, he believed that because of the lean times the men entered military service more out of economic necessity than a desire to serve the country. He informed Jesup that the members of local militia companies subdivided themselves into squads by neighborhood. Then the squads took a short "scout" one day a week and went on with their regular business the rest of the time, all the while drawing government pay and rations. Yet they were not at all grateful to the government and complained of the administration's financial policies that obligated them to pay taxes and buy land from the government with specie when all they had by way of currency were bank notes. The Florida settlers also took "pleasure in abusing Jesup" for his conduct of the war and Indian removal. Obviously angry, Cawlfield informed Jesup that "the whole matter of Indian hostilities in this country is pretty much a story of moonshine, the object of which I leave others to conjecture for the present." Then, with his men "worn down and dispirited by performing laborious duty in an unhealthy climate with no advantage to the country," the colonel, without Jesup's permission, returned with his command to his home in north Alabama.[27]

But the criticism did not deter Colonel Brown. He planned an even larger military operation for the summer of 1837. He asked Governor Call to transfer all the Escambia County volunteers to Walton for use against the Creeks living along the Choctawhatchee, but the executive had to deny the request because settlers continued to see small parties of fugitive Creeks in the far western end of the territory between the Yellow and Black Water rivers. Therefore, Call had to keep troops in the vicinity of Pensacola as a defense against attacks. Not only that, the large Creek emigration camp at Mobile Point had, quite ironically, become a problem. The New Alabama settlers had demanded the break-up of the Creek removal camps in their vicinity as a necessary security measure. But the government responded in March 1837 by consolidating all these camps on the coast at Mobile Point, located only twenty miles from the western border of Florida and just sixty miles from the Black Water River. In other words, the federal officers and civilian removal contractors sat their charges down right in the same general area where the Creek fugitives had retreated to avoid removal. Thus, the government simply replicated the problematic New Alabama situation and increased the security concerns of settlers in the coastal region. Now citizens living between Mobile and Pensacola notified the War Department that small parties of from five to twenty Indians were leaving their new camp at Mobile Point and heading east through the extensive and sparsely settled pine barrens, trying to reach their tribespeople in West Florida. Moreover, they had begun to kill cattle to feed themselves and had even attacked and driven off two stockmen who stood in their way. Consequently, a whole new group of terrified settlers fled their properties and fired off petitions to Washington that resembled those sent earlier by New Alabama residents. They demanded that the War Department recall all of Jesup's Creek warriors immediately, then send those men and their families straight away to Arkansas. These distressed citizens also asked Governor Clay for assistance in keeping the Creeks confined to Mobile Point until the federal government woke up and closed the camp. Clay responded by sending out a company of volunteers from Alabama's Fourth Militia Division to serve at the emigration camp.[28]

Yet the petitioners did not blame the wandering Indians alone for their problems. They admitted that many of their own people were "reckless characters," who might very well commit "rash acts" against the Indians, which would have fatal consequences for all concerned. Furthermore, the writers recognized the role of interethnic collusion in the Indians' efforts to resist removal. They noted that all the Indians they encountered had both guns and money, and oystermen operating out of Bon Secour, Alabama, kept the Natives well supplied with ammunition, whiskey, and everything they required to stay in the country. But again, the petitioners concluded that this harmful intercourse between Indians and white roughs could be broken only by shutting down the Mobile Point camp.[29]

It appears the petitioners made a reasonable request, for the officers in charge at Mobile Point agreed with them. Capt. Mark W. Batman, who took over duties as superintendent of Creek emigration from Captain Page in June 1837, reported that the camp Indians had become discontented with their location and should be moved immediately. Batman reported that the camp sat in an unhealthy location that was difficult to supply. Moreover, the hard economic times resulted in high prices for fresh beef and other foodstuffs, in some cases too high for the emigration company to supply without losing money. And this the company would not do. As a result of all this, malnutrition and disease killed from eight to fourteen Indians each day. Even the military officers and government agents operating the camp sickened and found it difficult to perform their duties there. The Creeks grew more and more discontented, and they escaped from the site to avoid the curse of evil spirits. Moreover, the ever-observant John Hogan, having returned to his hometown of Mobile after his sojourn in New Alabama, visited the removal camp, which lay across the bay from the town, and informed the War Department of another reason for Indians leaving the camp. The renowned Jim Boy, having come to the camp on furlough from his service with General Jesup, informed his tribespeople there that the Seminole War was not going well for the whites. This news, according to Hogan, encouraged some of the Creeks at Mobile Point to prolong their emigration by fleeing into the interior of the country. And the officers in charge—Captain Batman, Captain Wilson, Captain Page, Lieutenant Sloan, and Lieutenant Reynolds—could not stop them. They had no body of troops to keep the Indians from returning to New Alabama, joining other Creek fugitives in West Florida, or flying all the way to the East Florida peninsula to join the Seminoles.[30]

Captain Batman decided to find a new campsite for his charges, one that would provide the Indians with a healthier environment and place more distance between them and the fugitive Creeks and Seminoles in Florida. He sent Captain Page and a boatload of fifty Indians, presumably some of the more influential members of the Mobile Point community, in search of such a place. This party explored Dauphin Island and other offshore locations but eventually decided on Pass Christian, Mississippi, as the best place for the new emigration camp. That done, Batman and his fellow officers went to work transferring the three thousand residents of Mobile Point over to Mississippi to await the arrival of their warriors from East Florida, at which time the whole group would board ships to take them over to New Orleans and then up the Mississippi River to the Arkansas River and out that stream to their new homes in the Indian Territory. Major Wilson, however, wanted to use the waiting period to bring in more fugitives. Consequently, he left for Pensacola with a few of the Creeks to collect all the Natives he could locate in West Florida. At the same time, Captain Page set out to gather in some seventy Indians awaiting removal at Fort Claiborne, Alabama, a small town located approximately eighty miles north of Mobile on the Alabama River. Some of these people were fugitives General Wellborn and others had captured in the southern counties of Alabama; others may have been members of a colony of acculturated Creeks living in the general vicinity of Fort Claiborne since the early 1800s, some of the same people whose relatives the Red Sticks killed at Fort Mims in 1813.[31]

The move to Pass Christian did not go smoothly because the removal contractors attempted it with only one steamboat. Loading so many sick Indians on one boat proved difficult. Some died as soon as they embarked, others perished on the way to Mississippi, and all the burials delayed the return of the vessel to Mobile Point to pick up the healthy Creeks. Then, as these people waited at the wharf, a two-day rainstorm set in, exacerbating their misery. Yet they had completed all the rituals necessary for embarking on the journey, so when Captain Page told them to return to their camp for shelter, they refused, claiming that going back would "spoil their physic." More sickness developed as the Indians deliberately faced exposure to the elements, and Page was dumbfounded. Though he had served among the Creeks and Seminoles for years and spoke the Muscogee tongue, he had little understanding of the Native view of the cosmos and how it operated. He wrote their complex ceremonialism off to superstition and thus found it quite difficult to get along with his charges. Nevertheless, he and his fellow officers did succeed in getting the Indians relocated to Pass Christian, and while some Creeks continued to die, the general health of the emigrants gradually improved at their new camp.[32]

Meanwhile, Colonel Brown, with Governor Call's help, launched his summer campaign in West Florida. Call dispatched volunteers from the coastal towns of St. Joseph and Apalachicola to Pensacola and placed them under Brown's command. A battalion of Georgia volunteers also came to help, led by Charles Nelson, the same officer who had spent the last few months rounding up Creek fugitives in the Cherokee country. This increase in his force allowed Brown to put an ambitious military maneuver into effect. He ordered the St. Joseph's and Apalachicola townspeople to sweep east into Walton County from the Black Water River while he and the rest of his men marched west from the Choctawhatchee. He hoped to catch the runaway Creeks in a vice. Unfortunately for the colonel, this strategy did not work as well as he had hoped. However, his relentless search for Indians did lead to the discovery of one of the original rebel bands of 1836. On July 4, the same day the citizens of Marianna turned out to show him their support, Brown detected fresh tracks by Shoal River and soon came up with a party of 125 fugitives on the edge of a hammock. The colonel ordered a charge and killed ten Creeks before they escaped into a nearby swamp. These Indians left all their packs behind, and in one of them Brown found "an elegant gold watch and safety chain." This watch bore an inscription: "William Flournoy, August 22, 1834." Brown's men knew that Flournoy's murder in Russell County, Alabama, in early May 1836 had opened the Creek war. They also knew that the Euchees who killed Flournoy had done much of the mischief during the rebellion, including the destruction of Roanoke, Georgia. The watch and other evidence told Brown that not all of the troublesome Euchees had gone west in chains or joined the Seminoles in East Florida. Some had taken up residence right there in Walton County.[33]

Brown continued the chase. He tracked the Euchees from the Shoal River battlefield north to the Alabama line where the Indians scattered. They also set fire to the woods for several miles near the border to shield their retreat. Brown broke off the pursuit and turned south again to the Shoal. There he located the tracks of another large Indian party going south. He followed these Natives from camp to camp down toward Choctawhatchee Bay and even discovered a village site where some fugitives had lived undetected for several months. Here the Creeks had cleared a large field to use as a stickball ground. Brown did not tarry, however, but kept after the Indians until they came to rest in the Alaqua Swamp. After spotting the smoke from their fires on the morning of July 19, the colonel divided his command and attacked the Creeks from two directions, killing three and wounding many more. The whites lost one man killed and a few wounded. Brown claimed to have engaged at least seventy warriors in the Alaqua Swamp fight, but again, most of the fugitives escaped death or capture.[34]

Nevertheless, by summer's end, Brown's military operations coupled with Major Wilson's peaceful overtures to the fugitives through Creek emissaries seemed to be having an effect. Wilson collected about fifty men, women, and children on the Perdido River and Escambia Bay and sent them off to Pass Christian. He then learned from a fugitive brought in from Walton County that several parties of Indians there, including some who fought Brown at the Alaqua Swamp, wanted to surrender to the whites. In fact, they had tried to do so on several occasions but "instead of extending the hand of friendship," the settlers "invariably gave them the discharge of the rifle." Consequently, these apprehensive Natives wished to meet with some Creeks the whites considered friends so they could give themselves up, as the skirmishes with troops had depleted their numbers and they were "destitute, dispirited, and nearly broken down with fatigue." Hearing this, Wilson immediately set out for Walton County. He went first to LaGrange to consult with Brown and then proceeded to the Cow Ford on the Choctawhatchee, where he sent out his Creek emissaries to search the river banks for any sign of the fugitives. Within two or three days, the scouts located a party in a swamp between Pine Log Creek and the river and delivered Wilson's message: he would receive all who surrendered with friendship, protect them, and send them on to their people at Pass Christian, with whom they would emigrate west. Sixteen or eighteen members of the band accepted the terms and walked into LaGrange in late August to capitulate, led by their chief, Cosa Fixico, and his wife. The villagers were impressed. One observer called the chief a "fine, noble-looking man," and his wife became a center of attention in LaGrange. The same observer said that she had "a distinguished air" and noted that she was the daughter of Peter McQueen, the late Tallassee war chief and one of the famed Red Stick leaders in the First Creek War. This information surely made Cosa Fixico's wife all the more interesting to Brown and Wilson, who conversed with their dignified prisoners at some length. During the course of the discussion, the chief informed the men of another group of fugitives located on Yellow Water River who, he believed, he could convince to surrender if allowed to visit them along with Wilson's Creek scouts. Wilson agreed and told the chief to meet him in ten days at the mouth of Yellow Water River on East Bay with as many of the fugitives he could gather. The major would then transport those people by boat to a camp at Escribano Point and then eventually to Pass Christian.[35]

At that point, it appeared that the fugitive Creeks, not finding in West Florida the place of refuge they sought, were giving up. Simultaneously, the government's removal project gained new life. By September 11, 1837, Jesup had sent all the warriors of his Creek brigade on to Pass

Christian after attempting to settle a number of financial matters with them. He ordered lieutenants Reynolds and Sloan, for example, to submit inventories to the War Department of all Creek property lost in the New Alabama camps; then he asked the secretary of war to submit a claim to Congress so that body could indemnify his aggrieved warriors and their people for their losses. Jesup also allowed the Creeks to sell all the Seminole livestock and property they captured as per their enlistment agreement, and apparently paid a reward of twenty dollars per head for the thirty-five slaves of the whites the warriors captured among the Seminoles. The general also attempted to buy the eighty black Seminoles they brought in for a sum of eight thousand dollars. However, the Creeks disappointed Jesup in this transaction by selling these captives to none other than James C. Watson, the leading New Alabama land speculator and member of the Alabama Emigration Company—the same man who bought all the disputed and unsold land reserves from Opothle Yahola and his coterie of chiefs. But it would appear Jesup's warriors had no right to sell the whole group of black Seminoles. J. W. O. Casey, one of the government's emigrating agents at Tampa Bay, claimed that the Creeks captured only eighteen of the eighty blacks in question. The remainder had surrendered voluntarily to claim Jesup's offer of freedom, but Jim Boy, a brigade officer, sold them off anyway, causing Casey to proclaim that he was "grieved to see one African Seminole go west, for I have always urged their removal to Africa, but still less do I wish the success of such scoundrels as Jim Boy who combine all the vices of white, Indian and negro without the virtues of any." Yet Casey must have taken some comfort in the fact that Watson's group of speculators also came up short in the deal, for the army mistakenly shipped the blacks off to the West before those men could take custody of them. For years thereafter Watson would try to claim the blacks through the courts, often appealing to Opothle Yahola, Jim Boy, and other Creek leaders for their assistance. In the end, this imbroglio would call forth a congressional investigation.[36]

But for the time being, the members of the Creek brigade had money, and once they reached Pass Christian, the second round of Creek emigration began. The Indians left Mississippi by steamboat in increments, the first departing in September and the last arriving at Fort Gibson in the Indian Territory in late December. During this time, a portion of the Apalachicola Indians, under the direction of their removal agent, Daniel Boyd, also boarded steamboats for the West, and some five hundred Creeks who had fled to the Chickasaw country in northern Mississippi began their trip to the Indian Territory with their emigration agent, R. E. Clements. This man claimed that his charges were outlaws who had left their towns in Alabama to escape punishment for murder and other crimes—committed, no doubt, amid the turmoil, squalor, and frustration brought on by the operation of the Indian business in that state. Clements also noted that the Chickasaw Creeks continued to exercise "eye for eye vengeance" and commit "savage and inhuman acts," sometimes murdering one another in the most brutal fashion. Withal, the agent thought them the "most hostile and savage Indians" he had ever known. Some of this language may have been hyperbole, of course, written by a man who found it difficult to get his charges to obey his commands. Nevertheless, he did finally get these Indians on their way to the Indian Territory.[37]

At about the same time, a federal commission created to investigate citizens' claims for damages against the Creek and Seminole Indians in Georgia, Florida, and Alabama finished its "long hot summer task" and filed a final report with the War Department. While in the field, the commissioners—L. T. Pease, Thomas Gibson, and J. M. Smith—held court at Columbus as well as in the Alabama communities of Shady Grove, Tuskegee, Irwinton, and Florence. There they heard claims from nine in the morning until the midday meal and from then until six in the evening, trying to determine what claims the government should pay. Finally, after determining that a majority of the Creeks had committed some hostilities and/or depredations on property, they still settled on the very conservative figure of $356,167.79 as the amount of damages. The government, however, would be reluctant to pay out even this comparatively small amount of money.[38]

Even more disappointing to southern settlers, the Creek removal remained incomplete. Some five hundred Creeks remained in the Cherokee highlands by the end of 1837, sheltered from the searching eyes of federal troops and state volunteers by Cherokee friends and relatives, self-interested or compassionate whites, and the wooded mountains themselves. More surprisingly, perhaps, Creeks remained in southern Alabama as well. Some lived as fugitives skulking about the swamps, others had become slaves, and still more carried on their lives as they had always done, working as hired hands for planters or farming independently and sometimes prosperously. On the lower Alabama River, a community of acculturated Creeks continued to live on lands they held legally under federal and state law long before the Cusseta Treaty of 1832. Moreover, Paddy Carr returned to Russell County following his service with Jesup in Florida, and along with a few other wealthy Indians, resumed work as planters and merchants. Undoubtedly, these New Alabama Creeks, while still obligated to leave Alabama, gained a respite or dispensation from the government so they could settle their financial affairs without absorbing devastating losses. Then, of course, there were all the Creek refugees in Florida, who now dashed the hopes of the government's removal agents not only by refusing to surrender for emigration but also for renewing their violent clashes with the whites.[39]

In fact, the Creek war, having seemingly died in the summer of 1837, sprang back to life just as the removals from Pass Christian got underway. Numbers of West Florida fugitives came out of hiding and conducted their own emigration movement, but they went east instead of west. They began moving out of Walton County toward the Apalachicola River and the Seminole country beyond. On September 10 word came in from St. Andrews Bay that 125 members of the Euchee band with whom Cosa Fixico had been associated were making their way down the coast. Apparently 5 Euchees already living with the Seminoles had come to West Florida to find their kinspeople and had convinced them to follow them back to the wilds of the peninsula where they would be free of the press of white settlers. Unfortunately, these same settlers did not want to let the Euchees go. On September 16 a company of 50 volunteer soldiers left Marianna to cut the fugitives off at the Apalachicola. They failed, but two weeks later, friendly Creeks captured 17 members of another flying party of fugitives on the

Apalachicola twenty-five miles south of the Alabama line. A company of 160 from the town of Quincy set off to pursue the remainder of this party. Meanwhile, Governor Call sent one of the Apalachicola Creek chiefs, John Walker, to scout the country west of the Apalachicola to the Ochlockonee River and south to the seashore. Call had received information from some of the Indian captives that this area of the territory, "unfrequented and entirely unknown to whites," was a refuge for a number of Creek warriors and their families. This information was entirely correct, and Walker surely knew where the fugitives were, but he told Call he could not find them. Then, in early October Indian scouts sighted a camp of runaway Creeks in the Chipola Swamp, just west of the Apalachicola, and the governor sent another body of troops to capture them, but to no avail.[40]

But not all the West Florida fugitives attempted to run east toward the Seminole country. One group of Creeks, undoubtedly starving, returned to Dale County, Alabama, to take food and other supplies from the whites. It appears they also felt compelled to avenge loved ones killed by pursuing militiamen. First they killed a man named Wilkinson near Pierman's Ferry on Pea River, and during the next few months, they murdered several families in the county. The surviving settlers responded as they always did; they retreated to stockades and abandoned their crops to the Indians just at harvest time. According to Maj. Gen. Jonathan P. Booth, the commanding officer of Alabama's Fifth Militia Division, the whole county was devastated. Furthermore, Dale's citizens felt abandoned. Wellborn had taken his seat in the state senate; Governor Clay had gone to Washington to serve in the U.S. Congress; the federal government seemed concerned only with the Seminole problem; and when General Booth raised a company to protect Dale's citizens, he found the state assembly reluctant to pay the bill. In November A. Warren, the county's representative in the state legislature, appealed to Gov. Arthur P. Bagby, Clay's successor, for help. Bagby authorized William Pouncey, a veteran Indian fighter, to recruit a company of mounted rangers to patrol the county and to provide the security necessary for the citizens to return to their farms. Later, Jeremiah Pate commanded this ranger company, which was active well into the year 1838. By that time the Indians had retreated back into Florida, and the county experienced no more armed conflict. Nearly two years after it began, the Second Creek War closed in the state of Alabama.[41]

Interestingly, though, the hostilities in Alabama may have ended at this time because Florida's territorial governor decided to change his tactics. He finally realized that ordering militiamen and volunteers out to chase Indians and force them into submission did not work; it led only to desperation and bloodshed. Therefore, he decided to try diplomacy, believing he might convince the Indians to surrender by promising them food, shelter, medical care, and protection from the very troops and settlers he first sent after them. Consequently, Call ordered Colonel Brown to suspend his military operations in West Florida and placed Stephen Richards in charge of contacting and negotiating with the fugitives. Richards had served as an interpreter during the Treaty of Payne's Landing negotiations in 1832, had the confidence of the Apalachicola Indians, and knew the lay of the land well. He recruited a company of forty Apalachicolas and seventeen white men and set out to find the fugitives. He located a camp of thirty-three Creeks, nearly all warriors, at the head of Lake Wimico, near the mouth of the Apalachicola. While fleeing an earlier pursuit by troops, members of this party had "evinced their indomitable spirit by destroying their infants in order to effect their escape," but Richards found them all starving and sick and they gave themselves up to him. Their leader, Coa Harjo, also agreed to help find other gangs of fugitives so he could deliver Call's message to them. This was not an easy task, however, because of the number of Indians still at large and the location of their hideouts. Over the next several months, Richards reported finding Indians in camps containing anywhere from one to forty individuals, "scattered in the most miserable wilderness and swamps that this country affords." He also said that the situation surpassed "anything I ever saw in my life all tho I am an old Traviler."[42]

Moreover, the *Tallahassee Floridian* announced that an entirely new group of Indians had been discovered along the coast. This band, made up of people from nearly every tribe in the Creek Nation, had come from Alabama in the summer of 1836 to settle on the narrow peninsula of land between Choctawhatchee Bay and the gulf. They had lived there unmolested ever since, only making their presence known in late November 1837 when three of them rowed their canoe out in the bay to board a keelboat and purchase corn and other supplies. They paid cash for what they bought and asked the boat's captain to bring them gunpowder, saying that they would pay one dollar per pound for it in hard money. They also informed the captain that they intended to remain peaceful, but they would resist to the last if the whites fired on them. Richards and Coa Harjo had quite a job on their hands.[43]

Nevertheless, Richard's diplomatic mission in West Florida began to show signs of real success in ending the war there and clearing the region of Indians. During the first two months of 1838, Richards and Coa Harjo convinced 130 Creek fugitives to come into the Apalachicola agency. They also collected a very important personage, namely Checote Emathla, who was, according to Richards, a very intelligent individual and the principal chief of all the fugitives in the western district of the territory. Checote Emathla also provided Richards with an interesting bit of information, namely that affronts to Creek sovereignty caused a continuation of the war even more than the Indians' desire to escape removal. Checote Emathla, in fact, said that he had never opposed emigration but had come to Florida because his people had been robbed of all their possessions in Alabama, and the whites even demanded that he and his warriors give up their arms as evidence of their complete submission. This, he said, was too much to take, so he had come south to Florida with a band of 200 warriors "resolved to die with their arms sooner than part with them." However, the chief informed Richards that he was now prepared to help the captain bring in the remainder of the Creeks in West Florida as long as none of the Indians would be shipped west until they had all reunited and congregated in one camp. He also said the task might take some time to accomplish, as about 150 Creeks remained at large, dispersed over a district more than two hundred miles. Richards took Checote Emathla up on his offer and formed an encampment for the fugitives about six miles from the town of Chattahoochee on the west side of the Apalachicola River close by Walker's Town, one of the Apalachicola Indian settlements. Presumably, this camp also served as Richards's headquarters, which he called Camp Relief.[44]

Governor Call himself came to the camp to interview Checote Emathla and was so impressed by what the chief had to say that he rode with the man and some of his warriors to LaGrange, where he intended to wait until the Creek chief and his men collected their fellow fugitives in that quarter. Call then wrote to Daniel Boyd, the Apalachicola emigration agent, that he was confident that all the Indians could be assembled and removed. But neither Boyd nor Archibald Smith agreed. They visited the fugitive camp near Walker's Town and questioned the Indians there. One sixty-year-old grandmother informed them that she had come to Florida because her chief told his people that Arkansas was too cold for them, and they would all die their first winter there. Consequently, she and her family had set out for the coast just east of Pensacola, where whites were few and game, fish, and oysters plentiful. But she had ended up living in swamps, sick and destitute, and she only wished her tribespeople could see how well she lived now. If so, they would quit the swamps and come in to receive Agent Smith's hospitality. However, this woman was still not ready to go west and expected to remain right where she was with the Apalachicola Indians. Furthermore, the other Creeks in camp had "no idea of going to Arkansas" and claimed they surrendered only in the belief that they could stay in Florida on the Apalachicola lands. Even more alarming to the whites, these Indians had retained their firearms as a condition of their surrender—undoubtedly at Checote Emathla's insistence—and they were yet "determined to die rather than go west of the Mississippi." Consequently, Agent Boyd would not even tell the Creeks who he was or that the government had sent him to remove them along with the Apalachicolas. He also complained that the government had not given him enough money to feed and remove all the Indians in West Florida, and he requested that both Governor Call and General Jesup provide him with troops to contain the fugitives in camp and assist in their removal when the time came. But this request disturbed Call, and he reiterated to the agent that coercion would not work. The

Indians would only disperse and commit more depredations. This had to be avoided, for, as the governor said, "A renewal of hostilities with an enemy concealed in the very bosom of our country would be fatal to hundreds of our people and would cost the government an immense sum of money to expel them." Call also did not want Boyd to remove any of the fugitives until all were assembled in conformity with the promise made to Checote Emathla by Richards. Otherwise, the governor feared those Indians presently in camp would not go. He reminded Boyd that the fugitive encampment sat next to woods and hammocks into which they could retreat at the slightest appearance of aggressive movements on the part of whites. Call also hoped that once the Creek fugitives emigrated, the Apalachicolas would soon follow. But Boyd and Smith clung to their doubts.[45]

Governor Call also let others know of his concerns about continued Indian warfare in West Florida. The amount of damage the conflict had caused troubled him deeply, as did an apparent lack of federal concern for the problem. Writing to Washington, Call informed the president and the secretary of war that many of the region's farmers were destitute. The sparse white population of Walton and Washington counties had been unable to tend their farms for several months because of the Indian danger. In addition, the Creeks had destroyed many of their cattle. Furthermore, most of the men had been called into the military service at one time or the other, but the federal government had been slow in paying them. In fact, numbers of men had to sell their pay claims to speculators at a discount. In some cases, the governor himself had to assume financial responsibility for calling up troops. Otherwise, the men would not serve and contractors would not supply forage and provisions, which were scarce and expensive throughout Florida. As a matter of fact, said Call, many of West Florida's people now depended on a federal rations program for their sustenance. The government had started this program early on during the Seminole War to feed Florida's indigent population—all those hunters, trappers, fishermen, cattle herders, and subsistence farmers whose precarious livelihoods the Seminoles threatened. Yet, as Call pointed out, the War Department had issued orders to its officers to end the subsistence program on February 15, 1838. Call demanded that Poinsett extend this deadline, allowing the eligible citizens of Florida to draw government subsistence until they could plant and harvest a crop. Indeed, the governor stated that the government actually owed the West Floridians such help because the U.S. Army had driven the Creeks out of Alabama and into Florida, then did little to get them out, leaving that task to state troops. Call concluded his argument with the exaggerated claim that if the government did not aid Florida's farmers, they would have no choice but to abandon the whole territory to the Indians.[46]

Poinsett granted Call's request and extended the rations program, but with some restrictions. The secretary denied the benefits of the program to those Floridians who sold whiskey, kept gambling houses, or engaged in "notoriously immoral conduct." Poinsett also decreed that if an able-bodied man refused to enter military service when called upon, or do work assigned to him by the authorities, the government would withhold rations from him and his entire family. But for the most part, Call got his way on the rations issue. Still, he was not happy, for he knew that the rations program was not really the point; ending the war was, and he could never hope to bring it to a close as long as his own citizens, pursuing selfish interests, kept it going. Throughout the early months of 1838, for example, whites harassed both the friendly Apalachicola Creeks and the former Creek fugitives camped near Aspalaga, the Apalachicola agency. These settlers and speculators coveted the valuable reservation lands on the Apalachicola and wanted to drive the Indians away from them. This gave Call pause. He knew that as a condition of their surrender, the fugitives retained their firearms and other weapons, and Call feared that they would react to all the pressure they felt by renewing their attacks on whites. He also feared they would draw the friendly Apalachicolas into the conflict on their side, so he tried to intervene to solve the problem. He advised the Apalachicolas to sell their land reserves back to the government and move west. However, both he and Agent Smith wanted to get the fugitives out of the way first and begged the War Department to remove them as soon as possible. Smith recommended shipping the Creeks to Tampa Bay, St. Augustine, or even Charleston, where they could be fed and guarded by a sufficient number of troops until they emigrated with the Seminoles. Smith did not get his wish, but by the spring of 1838, Call believed he had solved the problem. The former fugitives living at Walker's Town on the Apalachicola agreed to board the government's steamboats and leave for New Orleans in early May, and General Jesup ordered a detachment of regular troops to help see them off. Much relieved, Agent Boyd set out for Washington to report the good news to the War Department and to procure funds for the emigration.[47]

Then came the shock. On the night of April 30, just a few days before they were supposed to depart for the West, while Boyd was still on his way back from Washington, one hundred of the Creeks at Walker's Town became fugitives once again. They quickly deserted their camp, leaving many of their possessions, boarded a raft, floated down the Apalachicola for a few miles, and landed on the eastern bank. From there they fled into the woods of Middle Florida toward the Ochlockonee River country, intent on linking up with the Seminoles. Governor Call soon learned from the Creeks who remained behind that Archibald Smith and other whites had a hand in the escape. In fact, Smith and his fellows told the fugitives that instead of sending them west as promised, the government intended to kill all the warriors and confine the women in chains. Smith even showed the Indians a pile of chains intended for that purpose. John Walker, the Apalachicola chief, warned the Creeks that Smith gave them "bad talks" but he advised them to flee from their present situation nonetheless, and they took the advice. Even Checote Emathla took part in the escape. He told his people to appear merry until they were ready to go, and Walker's followers, who, in fact, were in the habit of stealing cattle from the whites, gave the fugitives beef for the trip. Then John Reilly, an Apalachicola subchief, let them use his boat to float silently away from their camp. Yet another Apalachicola headman, well acquainted with the country east of the river, went with the fugitives as a guide. As fast as he could, Call sent troops after the runaways but feared they would elude the pursuit through information "derived from abandoned white men, whose interests are opposed to removal."[48]

By blaming the incident on abandoned white men, the governor showed himself to be a little naive in a couple of respects. First of all, the Apalachicolas colluded with the fugitive Creeks for their own reasons, not just because Smith used them as tools to help in the escape. Many Apalachicolas did not want to emigrate and they probably believed that as long the Creeks remained at large and the war continued, they would face less pressure from the government to go. Furthermore, since the outbreak of the conflict, Apalachicola warriors had made money as scouts for the whites, searching the woods for Creeks and Seminoles. These warriors may have wanted to draw out this sort of employment as long as possible by keeping fugitive Creeks free in the wild. Then, too, the Apalachicola men were warriors, men who could increase their social status, both among Indians and whites, by winning fame in warfare. Thus, they did what they could to see to it that the armed conflict continued. But these are not the only explanations for the actions of the Apalachicolas. It is possible that they simply wanted to get rid of the troublesome fugitives, who caused angry whites to harass even friendly Indians all the more. But no matter what motivated the Apalachicolas, Call failed to recognize the central role these Indians played in the fugitive flight. More importantly, he failed to acknowledge the part played by the Creeks themselves. Like many whites on the southern frontier, he may have seen the Indians as childlike and malleable, while whites were competitive and crafty. Therefore, when he talked to Checote Emathla, he actually believed the man intended to emigrate, and if the chief and his people suddenly departed, it had to be because self-interested whites tampered with the Natives. In truth, many of the fugitives entered the agency camp because of Coa Harjo's persuasiveness, as well as to escape pursuit and to obtain food and recuperate at government expense. They never intended to go west and believed they could simply stay on in Florida living with the Apalachicolas. Then, when they learned they must emigrate, they simply told Call what he wanted to hear, that they would go. But all the while they prepared to return to the woods, and it may not be a coincidence that Coa Harjo, the fugitive leader who cooperated most closely with the whites, met his death shortly before the Creeks took flight. One report claimed some

Apalachicolas killed him in a drunken brawl, and the Apalachicola chiefs gave the perpetrators over to the fugitives for punishment in the traditional manner. However, Agent Boyd claimed that one of the Creeks "assassinated" Coa Harjo, leaving open the possibility that his own people wanted to make sure he would not try to hold any of them in place or alert the whites of the planned escape.[49]

But the governor was not entirely wrong in blaming the flight on the interests of white men. He would discover that Archibald Smith operated a "tipling shop" near the Apalachicola villages, and the Indians who frequented this shop often became "so intoxicated and riotous" that they alarmed the whole neighborhood, Indians and settlers alike. Furthermore, Smith sold gun flints and possibly ammunition to the fugitives encamped at his agency. Worse, the Apalachicolas complained that Smith paid them their last government annuity in depreciated bank notes, not specie, implying that he kept that for himself. George Walker, Call's representative to the Apalachicolas, informed the governor that Smith opposed Indian emigration and was using his influence to prevent it so he could continue to make a good living off of his charges.[50]

However, the governor displayed his naivety once again when he singled men like Smith out for blame and called them "abandoned." Smith was only doing what many residents of Florida were doing: profiting from the war and the removal process. Truth be told, Call served many constituents who did not want the armed conflict to end too soon or have all the Indians removed too quickly. Indeed, Andrew Jackson himself saw that the Floridians did not want to fight the Seminoles too aggressively and stated angrily that Florida's men "had better run off or let the Indians shoot them, that the women might get husbands of courage, and breed up men who would defend the country." But cowardice was not the problem; the need for money in a growing market economy was. After all, Florida was a territory with no cities, a relatively small population, little or no manufacturing, and as yet no large-scale agricultural production. War was Florida's biggest industry, its very own version of New Alabama's Indian business. The federal government had established military posts and supply depots throughout the territory, as well as roads, bridges, and causeways. The government employed many civilians as clerks, mechanics, carpenters, blacksmiths, guides, interpreters, and the like. Furthermore, the government brought thousands of soldiers to Florida: regular troops, state militiamen, and volunteers. These men had to be paid and they spent money with Florida merchants. In addition, the government sheltered settlers at its military posts and fed many civilians through its rations program. In some cases, the government put whole communities of men and their horses on the public payroll, then let those men simply stay at home as part of a "sedentary" defense force. In other cases, wealthy men drew government rations and, at the same time, sold the services of their slaves to the army at exorbitant rates. These slaves worked on government construction projects, largely because southern troops thought hard labor beneath their dignity. Worse still, in May 1836, regular army officers accused these southern troops of committing two-thirds of the murders in Florida "in order to keep up the excitement." But these troublesome troops fed at the public trough, and the government purchased large amounts of food and supplies from Florida contractors and farmers to fill the trough. More federal money went into the upkeep of regular troops, Indian allies, and all those Seminoles awaiting removal in camps. In all, the government poured millions of dollars into the territory in one form or the other, and many Floridians, especially politicians like Call, depended on this financial boon in the late 1830s and early 1840s, when the entire nation suffered from an economic depression. Furthermore, Florida's Natives needed arms and provisions to continue their resistance, and some disgruntled Spaniards, Cuban fishermen, blacks, and white roughs profited by trading with them. Undoubtedly, Smith and the others who frightened the fugitive Creeks away from the Apalachicola agency belonged, then, not to a small class of "abandoned" Floridians but to a very large group of acquisitive ones. But, again, this situation was not unique. Supplanting Native populations through warfare, disarticulating local economies, and commodifying and exploiting all available resources with government help have all been part and parcel of the process of drawing frontier regions into the world market.[51]

But no matter who was responsible for the Creek fugitives leaving the Apalachicola agency, Jesup felt the need to do something about it. As one of his last official acts before resigning his command and leaving the burden of the Seminole War to others, he dispatched three companies of regular troops under Capt. George C. Hutter to the port of St. Marks to help search for the Creek escapees. Hutter and his men traveled by steamboat from St. Marks west to Dog Island at the mouth of the Crooked River, then proceeded to examine the Crooked, Ocklockonee, and New river basins for a distance of thirty miles into the interior of Middle Florida. Finding no sign of the Indians, Hutter went back to Dog Island, where he made contact with Daniel Boyd on the last day of May, 1838. Together they proceeded up the Apalachicola with their interpreter, Stephen Richards, to the Indian towns to collect the few Creek fugitives still living there. These people they transported back to Dog Island and set them up in a new emigration camp, which Boyd intended to use as a collecting point for all the other fugitives once captured. The agent knew that the island, sitting a few miles offshore, would contain the otherwise elusive Indians until he could send the whole body off to the West.[52]

That much done, Boyd turned back to his main task: removing the Apalachicola Indians. These people had led a rather precarious existence for years. The Upper Creeks had occasionally ventured into their territory to take cattle and slaves. The whites had consistently abused them as well. Their only allies had been some of the Lower Creek towns and the proemigration Seminole towns under Charley Emathla and Holatta Emathla, but most of these people had departed for the West, leaving the Apalachicolas alone to face their aggressive white neighbors and the occasional Seminole raiding party. This gave Boyd the leverage he needed. He pointed out to John Walker and Econchattee Micco, the two leading chiefs of these people, that if they chose to stay in Florida they would do so without annuities from the government and without government protection from their enemies, both white and Seminole. Facing this eventuality, the chiefs finally agreed to sell the land reserves of their respective towns to the government and move west, with the understanding that individual Indians would receive compensation for their improvements to the land—fences, houses, fruit trees, and so on. However, Boyd knew a substantial portion of the Apalachicolas still had no desire to emigrate, for having assisted the whites so often in their contests against both Upper Creeks and Seminoles, they feared settling among those peoples in the West. Therefore, Hutter kept a close check on the Apalachicolas throughout the summer, both to break their continuing communication with the Creek fugitives and to see to it that none of them ran away from their towns. In fact, Boyd issued an edict that any Apalachicolas caught off their land reserves would be treated as hostile and promptly removed from Florida. But the agent continued to have problems keeping these people in line. Despite the federal law prohibiting liquor sales to Indians in the territory, grog shops ran full tilt and Apalachicolas drank heavily and wandered from their towns all summer. Consequently, Boyd had difficulty compiling a complete roll of their names for emigration purposes. He did learn, however, that more than half of the two hundred inhabitants of Walker's Town were actually Creeks who came to Florida during the hard year of 1835 in New Alabama. Therefore, the agent asked permission of the War Department to treat these people as fugitives, not Apalachicolas, so he could remove them immediately. His superiors in Washington demurred, however, probably because these Creeks had not gone to war in 1836 and because their sudden incarceration might upset the whole body of Apalachicolas to the point of causing them to take up arms against Boyd and rush out to join all the hostile Indians in the territory. This news must have disappointed the agent, all the more so because he never stopped the interaction between the Apalachicolas and the Creek fugitives. Indeed, some of these people had actually intermarried and certainly had no intention of breaking off contact with one another. Then Boyd received more disappointing news. Colonel Wellborn, now General Wellborn, had taken seven Creek children captive during the fighting in Alabama, and Boyd asked that he send them down to the Apalachicola for removal. Wellborn would not give them up. Nevertheless, by the end of August, Boyd had set up his headquarters in Chattahoochee, Florida, and had 274 Apalachicolas registered and ready to emigrate. In addition, he and Captain Hutter, after a couple of arduous searches, managed to capture and deposit for emigration on Dog Island some fifty Creek fugitives.[53]

The main body of refugees escaped detection, however, and augmented their numbers with a few members of Jesup's old Creek brigade. These men were undoubtedly related to the Apalachicolas and had deserted the U.S. service on hearing of the poor treatment of their friends and relatives in the New Alabama removal camps. But even more disturbing, as far as the settlers were concerned, the fugitive band became much more aggressive and violent as the summer wore on. On July 26, for example, they rowed up to the home of a Mr. Laschley on the Ocklockonee River in four large canoes, killed the elderly gentleman and his daughter, slaughtered seven of his beeves, gathered thirty or forty bushels of corn from the field and took another twenty bushels from the corncrib. They then shelled all the corn, loaded the plunder in the canoes, and slipped silently away down the stream. When militiamen arrived from the town of Quincy, they found "the whole premises had been reduced to ashes—the domestic animals, such as horses, dogs, &c. which had all been killed, were lying around the smoking ruins, and everything gave evidence of the most wanton cruelty and mischief." Then the fugitives extended their forays back to the plantations by the Apalachicola, causing more death and destruction.[54]

The attack on the Laschley homestead was a highly significant event. By crossing the Apalachicola River to attack settlers in East Florida, the Creek fugitives essentially merged the Second Creek War with the Second Seminole War. Moreover, other Creek bands, made up of people who had come through Georgia into the Florida Territory in the summer of 1836, now came out of hiding to assist the Seminoles in a conflict that stretched from the outskirts of Tallahassee, north to the Okefenokee Swamp and south to the Everglades. Significantly, Creeks took a whip hand in the fighting and by the year 1841 they carried the war almost by themselves. In fact, Gen. William J. Worth, the officer in charge of the war at that time, wrote to the adjutant general in Washington that the Creeks alone remained "as objects of apprehension or harm to the settlements."[55]

Creek fugitives also perpetrated one of the last, if not the last, attack on Florida settlers during the course of the war. And, again, this attack occurred in West Florida. About fifty Creeks of a group that had laid low between the St. Andrews and Choctawhatchee bays for a long time ventured forth on the morning of August 31, 1842, to attack the home of Stephen Perkins near Orange Hill in Washington County. These Indians murdered the entire Perkins family, save for one boy who managed to escape. White Floridians found this attack particularly shocking because they thought General Worth had ended the war a little earlier in the year. Governor Call now proclaimed that the army's peace treaty with the Seminoles did not apply to the Creeks, and sounded the familiar call for more troops, as did David Levy, Florida's congressional delegate. The War Department responded by ordering Col. Josiah H. Vose, standing in for General Worth, to send two infantry companies from his headquarters on Cedar Key to Washington County to protect the settlers and track down the Indians, who seemed to have disappeared from the face of the earth after attacking the Perkins family. John C. Spencer, the secretary of war, also authorized Vose to employ fifty local men as guides and offer them a two hundred dollar reward for every warrior they took and fifty dollars for every other Indian. But Colonel Vose procrastinated. He believed the treaty did apply to the Creeks, and if the Indians committed murders in West Florida, they did so out of ignorance of the accord. Consequently, he sent a messenger to find the Indians and apprise them of the facts before ordering out yet another search-and-destroy mission. Vose also believed that a pursuit of the Creeks at that point might upset the newly established peace with the remainder of Florida's Natives.[56]

By that time, however, the Washington County settlers had heard of the War Department's order from Delegate Levy, so they organized a company of mounted volunteers and set out after the Creeks themselves. But then Secretary Spencer suspended his troop order, owing to the official end of hostilities, and refused to recognize the formation of the Washington County company as legal. And that was the end of the matter as far as the War Department was concerned. However, local legend asserts that Spencer's new order angered the company of settlers and they continued to pursue the Indians, finally surprising them at a camp near Wright's Creek. This shocked the white men, for the Creeks had never before allowed themselves to be caught unawares. Nevertheless, the settlers took full advantage of their good fortune by killing twenty-two of the Indians. If this story is true, it is reasonable to suppose that the Creeks had finally heard of the peace accord, hence their lack of caution. It is also reasonable to suppose that no official report or newspaper account of the attack exists because the settlers feared they were operating illegally and had violated the peace treaty by essentially murdering the Indians. Consequently, they told no outsiders what they had done.[57]

In truth, the Washington County incident may be but one of many "unreported" assaults on the Indians at this time. Indeed, Vose may have wanted to delay operations against the West Florida Creeks not only because those Indians lacked knowledge of the treaty but because he suspected they had been provoked into attacking the Perkins family. He certainly did not think the Indians anywhere in Florida were the greatest threats to peace. He assigned that odium to the territory's poor whites, the people known as "vagabonds" and "crackers." They were the subsistence farmers, hunters, fishermen, and herders whom General Jesup once referred to as "indigents," the people who took government rations because the Indian war kept them from taking to the woods and fields to make their livings. Vose believed these poor whites, who lived much like the Seminoles, hated the Indians and the Indians hated them, and he and other army officers saw that this implacable animosity was both a cause and a major reason for the continuation of the war.[58]

Indeed, Gen. Alexander Macomb had concluded as early as 1838 that the Seminoles had given up attacking regular troops, or even unguarded army wagon trains, but continued to assail the Florida poor whites at every opportunity. Yet, quite interestingly, Florida newspapers did not report Indian attacks on poor whites or their assaults on the Natives. Only the deaths of respectable farm families made the newspapers. Thus, the number of killings resulting from the backwoods war between Indians and poor whites remains wholly unknown. And, more interesting still, respectable officers such as Vose and Macomb further revealed the deep cultural and class divisions that existed in white society by actually favoring the Indians over the poor whites. One of Worth's lieutenants, for example, described these whites as always "dirty, ragged and dusty, seated upon long-tailed and short-eared horses, with the deadly rifle resting in front and a short jacket, long beard and hair, and a broad-brim white hat." Capt. Jacob Rhett Motte, a veteran of both the Creek and Seminole wars, wrote in his memoirs that the poor whites in Florida and Georgia were the dumbest people in the world and excelled in no "duties except those involved in begetting ugly little white-haired responsibilities." But the vagabonds proved particularly upsetting to Colonel Vose because they plundered Indian camps and fields. In truth, Vose feared the poor whites might overturn his whole peace settlement. He wrote to Washington complaining that these people had not dared defend themselves during the war, but now that most of the Natives were peaceful and retiring, "a most unaccountable desire for the toils and glory of the field" had appeared among the poor white class. Surprisingly, the adjutant general noted on Vose's letter that the colonel should repel any attack on the peaceful Indians by force. The Natives, and the peace process, must be protected. This reply raised the specter of federal troops fighting poor white frontierspeople and showed again how difficult it was for a divided white population to end a war against Indians.[59]

Interestingly, those Creek fugitives who ran from the Apalachicola agency in 1838 to spread the Creek conflict into East Florida were the last actively hostile Natives to capitulate and give up the fight as far as the Seminole War was concerned. A man named Pascofar led the band, and Col. Ethan Allan Hitchcock determined to gain his surrender through peaceful means. Hitchcock, like many other regular army officers, had become an opponent of the war and meant to establish amicable relations with Pascofar and remove his people from Florida "without the shedding of blood." At first he tried to exploit the interethnic collusion that existed alongside conflict on the Florida frontier. He offered to pay five hundred to one thousand dollars to two white men for their help in setting up a meeting between Hitchcock and the chief. These men had been in communication with Pascofar and his people for years, all the while the army had been unable to locate them. In the end, though, Hitchcock simply set out on his own with a small detachment of men to locate Pascofar.[60]

In December 1842 the colonel and his men boarded a steamboat headed down the Apalachicola River. For some months past the Indians had been pillaging along the stream, and Hitchcock thought it would be the best place to find them. Using two friendly Indians as scouts and emissaries, Hitchcock made contact with one of Pascofar's young warriors. Through that young man, the officer gained an audience with the chief. Then, with kind words and gifts of food, liquor, and blankets, Hitchcock won Pascofar's confidence. The chief admitted that his people were poor and could not continue to live in isolation. Furthermore, they were in constant danger from the whites. Finally, Pascofar agreed to surrender his people for removal. However, he said that the members of his band were afraid to come out of hiding and show themselves on the Apalachicola because of all the depredations they had committed there. He promised Hitchcock that they would give themselves up on Ochlockonee Bay. Hitchcock agreed and later met the Indians there. He took the fifty-one members of the band on board his boat for transport to the Horse Key, another island internment camp. Then, on January 26, 1843, General Worth shipped the Creeks to New Orleans.[61]

Hitchcock was well pleased. He wrote in his diary, "But now the Indian War is finished—ended—closed for the last time. The Indians have been talked out of Florida." Governor Call was even more elated. He appeared before the territorial legislature to proclaim, "All apprehension of danger is now removed—not an Indian remains. The last war whoop has been heard on our southwestern border and peace and security are permanently restored in that quarter."[62]

Hitchcock and Call were not entirely correct. The Second Creek War was not completely finished. Fugitive Creeks remained along the coast of West Florida, and not all of them were content to live in peace at all times. For much of the remainder of the antebellum era, these Natives occasionally robbed homes, killed livestock, looted postal stations, and took what they needed from the settlers' cornfields and vegetable gardens to survive. They also committed murders in the few years following the peace treaty, usually in the course of robberies or to keep their exact whereabouts from becoming known to the authorities. In late 1843, for example, Indians committed "outrages" near St. Andrews Bay, and the adjutant general in Washington grew livid when he learned no federal troops had gone to capture the Creeks and deport them. Then, approximately a year later, on December 31, 1844, three white men, along with a black woman and boy, found themselves shipwrecked on the coast some eighteen miles west of St. Andrews Bay, near Phillip's Inlet. The party lived on the beach for a few days and had to hunt and fish to feed themselves. In the course of their excursions away from camp, two of the men came upon two boats containing animal skins and pots, which appeared to belong to Indians. The other man, Henry A. Nunes, discovered a small path and followed it to some planted fields and living quarters situated in a very thick hammock. Shortly thereafter, the Creeks, obviously realizing they had been discovered, visited the shipwrecked party on the beach, presenting themselves as friendly neighbors. The charade went on for a couple of days until the white men completely lowered their guard; then the Indians struck. They killed the black woman and one of the white men and severely wounded another. They may have also killed another of the men and the black boy; the record is unclear. We do know, however, that Nunes escaped, rounded up ten men to help him, and returned to the beach, where they found all the property he had managed to salvage from the ship either missing or destroyed. The War Department, on hearing of the incident, sent two detachments of troops to the area. These troops searched the shores of Choctawhatchee, West, and St. Andrews bays, as well as the creek basins leading into the bays, but failed to find any Indians. They did find evidence of Natives in several places, however, and some of this evidence indicated a recent occupation.[63]

We know little of these fugitive Indians, a remnant of the once proud Creek Confederacy in the East. We do not know their thoughts, feelings, or motivations. What we do know of their activities comes down in a few scattered documents and by word of mouth in the white community, which gives us a biased and often unflattering picture of a brave people who held out against removal. Such is the account of the death of Old Joe, who apparently led the band of Indians that roamed the West Florida coast between St. Joseph's and East Pass in the years following the peace treaty. As the story goes, a man named Kage King left the town of Apalachicola one day in 1848, carrying a roll of calico on his shoulder. As he walked along the road leading from St. Joseph's Bay to St. Andrews, he passed Old Joe and his son, a boy of about sixteen. They spoke and all seemed well. But, according to King, Old Joe must have wanted the bolt of calico. The two men had walked only a short distance from each other when Joe turned and fired at King, his ball striking the roll of cloth. King fell, then recovered his footing and fired at Joe but missed. At that point, each man drew his knife and closed in on the other. A fierce hand-to-hand struggle followed, and at one point King thrust his blade toward Joe's head and connected. The blow had no immediate effect, however, and the men continued to fight. King threw Joe to the ground. Joe came back and managed to get King down. They rose again, and King pushed Joe away. At that point the boy rushed up to help his father, but Joe ordered him to run away. Realizing his strength was failing, Joe also retreated, loping after his son, leaving King alone. Obviously relieved, the white man hurried home but returned to the scene a few days later with some companions. And there, only a short distance from where the men fought, Old Joe lay dead. King's blade had entered his brain.[64]

Joe's death seems to have ended violent conflicts between Indians and whites in West Florida, and in that sense we might say his demise finally ended the Second Creek War. However, Creeks would remain in the area and prey on the settlers in times of hardship. In fact, marauding Creeks stole so much corn there in 1854 that the state legislature made a special appropriation to compensate the local farmers. And only after this event did the citizens of West Florida stop speaking of Indians as being any kind of threat to their existence. Therefore, one might say that the Second Creek War did not really die away until this time, nearly twenty years after it began and only a few years before the beginning of the larger conflagration known as the Civil War.[65]

Epilogue
The Legacy of the Second Creek War

The fight against the Creeks and their Seminole cousins was a costly affair in terms of both money and lives. Between the years 1835 and 1843, Congress appropriated between thirty and forty million dollars for the suppression of Indian hostilities in Alabama, Georgia, and Florida. It is hard to draw the line between Creek and Seminole war expenditures because the appropriation bills made no designations, but chasing and fighting Creeks in three different states must have demanded a healthy portion of the total sum. Furthermore, both the federal government and the state of Florida continued to expend funds in tracking down Creeks well after 1843. Worse, the Creek and Seminole wars caused untold numbers of whites and Indians to die in the war, most from hardship and disease rather than from direct combat. In fact, the Creek fugitives may have lost all of their children during the years of their flight from Alabama to Middle Florida. When, for example, Col. Ethan Allen Hitchcock finally rounded up Pascofar's band at Ochlockonee Bay, he noted that the group included no children between the ages of four and fifteen years of age.[1]

Still, the Indian conflict, waged at national expense, benefited southern planters and an economic system based on slavery. First of all, the war resulted in the forced removal of the large majority of Creeks, ending the existence of a Creek Nation in the Southeast. Their absence, in turn, contributed to the whites' sense of security and bolstered economic development in Georgia, Florida, and Alabama. As more settlers moved onto land vacated by the Indians, Alabama's non-Native population doubled in the decade of the 1830s. Moreover, the state's cotton production more than tripled, largely because the famed Black Belt opened to plantation agriculture. Consequently, economic and political power shifted toward the southern part of Alabama, and Montgomery became the state's capitol and most influential city in the decade of the 1840s. Simultaneously, Mobile grew in importance. After nearly burning to the ground in 1827, that town rose from the ashes in the 1830s to experience one of the greatest boom periods in its history. In fact, Mobile became one of the leading cotton ports in the South, owing not only to Creek removal but to that of the Cherokees, Chickasaws, and Choctaws as well. Sitting near the Gulf of Mexico at the mouth of the Alabama-Tombigbee river drainage system, Mobile handled the cotton coming from millions of acres of land once owned and occupied by these Native peoples. Already by 1837 the Mobile branch of the Second Bank of the United States had more money on deposit than any other branch in the whole country, and the city did so much business that its warehouses proved inadequate to house all the cotton and other produce it gathered in from the hinterlands by raft and steamboat. Conversely, though, some New Alabama towns—Tallassee, for example—declined with Creek removal because they had grown dependent on Indian trade and especially the "Indian business."[2]

Creek removal also facilitated the economic growth of the Chattahoochee-Apalachicola river system. This system, which includes the Flint and Chipola rivers and numerous other tributary streams, traverses thousands of acres of good farmland. With the end of the Creek war, plantations and new towns sprang up all along the system, particularly in southwestern Georgia, where roaming Creeks and Seminoles had caused white settlers problems for decades. The city of Columbus, located at the fall line of this river system, became an even more important commercial center, just as its residents had hoped when they set out to grab the Creek lands in New Alabama. Columbus merchants prospered from the buying and selling of cotton from all the new fields in Georgia and Alabama, and they used the money to make Columbus a manufacturing hub. In fact, Columbus would become, along with Richmond, Virginia, one of the two leading textile manufacturing centers in the South. Furthermore, the city acquired ironworks, steamboat factories, and other establishments that produced steam engines, cotton gins, firearms, and iron railing. The Columbus merchants, along with those of Irwinton, Albany, Bainbridge, Marianna, and other inland ports on the Chattahoochee-Apalachicola system, shipped all the cotton they collected downriver to the town of Apalachicola, located at the mouth of the waterway on the Gulf of Mexico. There other businesspeople sent all the cotton produced on lands once claimed by the Creeks to the North and to Europe. During the 1840s Apalachicola boomed and bustled with activity and became the third largest cotton port and international trading center on the Gulf Coast, behind only New Orleans and Mobile.[3]

But Indian removal was not the only beneficial economic result of the Creek war. During the years 1835 to 1843, federal expenditures helped local economies. Besides construction of new roads and other internal improvement projects in Florida, the war provided valuable publicity for the territory, and many settlers purchased land there once the conflict ended. Some of these settlers were war veterans who returned with their families to a country they found exotic and delightful. Similarly, the presence of so many soldiers and the availability of government contracts benefited the town of Columbus and its environs in 1836. Money gained from these sources, along with all the business brought to Columbus by a rush of new settlers on the Creek lands, helped see the town through the Panic of 1837. Not as many businesses "went by the board" in Columbus as in other U.S. cities and towns.[4]

But the war's legacy was not a beneficial one for all the white residents of the Chattahoochee Valley, at least not in the long run. Certainly the opening of the Old Creek Nation to settlement seemed a great boon at first. Even though speculators sold lands to incoming settlers at a considerable profit and wealthy planters purchased the very best tracts, small farmers wishing to acquire fertile acreage had an opportunity to do so. The abundance of property and the fact that speculators took it from the Indians so cheaply tended to hold land prices down to a rate that, while still high, was not wholly beyond the reach of many farmers. At the same time, rising cotton prices on the world market made land and slaves such good investments that those farmers had little trouble securing loans for their purchase. Numbers of these fortunate farmers then became prosperous planters, achieving the southern dream. However, the Panic of 1837, based in part on underfunded banks lending too much money to land speculators and farmers, ushered in a severe depression that closed off economic opportunity and upward social mobility to most residents of the Chattahoochee Valley. Cotton prices plummeted with the panic and continued to fall into the early 1840s. Many farmers could not meet their loan payments and lost their lands and slaves to repossession. Now once independent and proud agriculturalists fell into the poor, white class as sharecroppers, tenant farmers, or simply hired help.[5]

The cotton market finally recovered in the late 1840s, but by that time wealthy slave owners had consolidated their hold on nearly all the good cotton ground in the valley. Impoverished farmers were left to eke out a mere subsistence. And the gulf between rich and poor continued to widen through the 1850s. Planters bought up even more land, pushing real estate prices higher and higher, farther out of sight of the commoner—the same commoner Andrew Jackson sought to benefit by pushing Indian removal. Indeed, for a time it looked as if the small farmer class would disappear from the land altogether, just like the Indians those farmers had once displaced. In fact, the expanding poor, white class of the Chattahoochee Valley lived much like the Creeks. They grew their own vegetables and hunted, fished, or raised a few head of livestock for meat. Most could not read or write, lived in log structures with dirt floors, undoubtedly drank a little too much, engaged in a bit of criminal activity on the side, and occasionally hired themselves out to their more affluent planter neighbors who either pitied or despised them. Those poor whites who drifted into Columbus seeking work as common laborers, as so many destitute Creeks had before them, found themselves little better off. In fact, the fortunate members of the Columbus community so detested factory workers that they once devised a plan to move them out of the town and house

EPILOGUE

them on the other side of the Chattahoochee in Alabama, all reminiscent of the time when Creeks were allowed to visit Columbus by day but had to be across the bridge and back to their own hovels at night. Indeed, one wonders if the poor whites of the Chattahoochee Valley ever recognized the irony in their situation.[6]

It was just such a society many Creeks hoped to escape by moving west, but in the end, they too found it difficult to shake off the negative consequences of the Second Creek War or pull free from the South's economic system. The Lower Creek rebels who went west in chains did not fare well in their new country. In fact, the Lower towns continued the process of social disintegration begun in New Alabama, partly because so many Lower Creek leaders gravitated toward the accepted norms of southern white society and deserted traditional Creek customs. The members of the McIntosh party, for example, some of the earliest arrivals in the West, established plantations and ranches and used slaves as well as hired workers, some of them white, to produce corn, cattle, cotton, and even rice for distant markets. Benjamin Marshall, after assisting the land speculators in Alabama and joining the Alabama Emigration Company to profit from Creek removal, continued his pursuit of wealth in the West with the help of one hundred slaves. In 1847 Creeks like Marshall even exported thousands of bushels of corn to famine-plagued Ireland. But as the Lower Creek leaders embedded themselves in the market economy, joined Methodist and Baptist churches, sent their children off to boarding schools, and in other ways looked and acted like members of the South's white aristocracy, Lower Creek town life, with its complex ceremonialism and communalism that gave traditional Indian life structure and meaning, deteriorated even more. As a result, extreme poverty, drunkenness, and general demoralization persisted among many of the Lower Creeks and probably even more so among the former rebels, who surely arrived in the West poorer, less healthy, and even more defeated than the rest.[7]

The Upper Creeks immigrants fared better, at least at first. Ethan Allen Hitchcock, the army officer who gained the surrender of Pascofar, visited the Creek Nation in the West in 1841 and found that the Upper Creeks, who had emigrated peacefully in 1836, were clinging to their old customs, including communal farming and cooperative construction projects about their towns. In fact, the residents of the Upper towns held their axes and hoes as common community property, and the town chiefs looked out for the general welfare of the people. One of the Tuckabatchee chiefs, for example, told Hitchcock that "when we order out the people to make a public fence, if they don't turn out we send and take away their gun, or horse; or something else to punish them." The chief also explained that when widows or orphans needed help, the leaders mustered the people to build houses for them, plant fields for their use, or otherwise see to their needs. Working together in traditional fashion, while at the same time allowing individual economic enterprises, these Upper Creeks began to prosper in their new country. By the time of Hitchcock's visit, they were growing large quantities of cotton and corn and tending herds of horses, cattle, and hogs. At one spot by the Canadian River, these Indians worked one vast field of corn three miles wide and eight miles long. Thus, it appeared the Upper Creeks wisely escaped their old homeland to preserve their culture and social order, and, in turn, the strength of these traditions allowed them to reestablish themselves successfully in the West. Furthermore, the Upper Creek Council members acted forcefully to protect their people from the agents of disintegration that had plagued them for so long. They passed a law excluding whites, free blacks, and whiskey from their country.[8]

While the Creeks as a whole showed remarkable resilience in stabilizing and rebuilding their nation in the West, they could not escape U.S. expansionism. Indeed, the world system made this expansionism absolutely necessary to keep itself alive and increasingly productive. A constant supply of new territory fed resources and raw materials into the system, while at the same time provided an outlet for the excess population, manufactured goods, and investment capital the system constantly created. But the argument between northerners and southerners about the extension of slavery into the West helped bring on a civil war, and the Creeks found themselves caught up in the conflict. Once again, factionalism rose to the fore, most notably the old division between the McIntosh and Tuckabatchee parties. As a general rule, the McIntosh faction, along with acculturated Creeks in both Upper and Lower Creek towns, sided with the Southern Confederacy and attempted to consolidate their hold over the entire Creek Nation by attacking more conservative Creeks who wished to stay out of the whites' war on either side. Opothle Yahola led this group of peaceful Creeks, once again showing his abhorrence of both the McIntosh crowd and the whole idea of rebellion. Undoubtedly, Opothle Yahola was wise enough to see that armed uprisings against the U.S. government could only hurt his people. Accordingly, he sided against the Red Sticks in 1813, the Lower Creek insurgents in 1836, and the pro-South Creeks in 1861. However, assault by the progressive, pro-South party ultimately drove Opothle Yahola and the conservatives into the arms of the Union and caused another intertribal war that destroyed much of the progress numerous Creeks had made since emigrating to the Indian Territory.[9]

Similarly, the Creeks who remained in the Southeast at the end of the Second Creek War faced a problematic existence, principally because whites still wanted to exploit them as a cheap source of labor. Green Beauchamp, a pioneer citizen of Barbour County, stated that after the Battle of Pea River in March 1837, Wellborn's troops enslaved all the Creek women and children they captured. The same conduct occasionally happened during the course of fighting throughout southern Alabama, Georgia, and Florida, and the militiamen and volunteers fortunate enough to capture Indians were reluctant to let them go. Similarly, planters who, even before the war, housed and fed destitute Indians in return for their labor did not want to lose their services. The Williams family of Russell County, Alabama, stands as a notable example of these sorts of planters. They lived in Lee County, Georgia, before the war and conflicted with state officials there for keeping as many as seventy Euchee Indians on their plantations as workers, all in contravention of a Georgia law prohibiting Creeks from living in the state. At some point, the Williams family and their Euchees moved into Alabama, but when the Creek war broke, most all of the Indians ran off to join the rebel party. The Williams clan somehow managed to maintain the services of about twenty Euchees, however, probably because the Indians were frightened and felt they needed sanctuary in those troubled times. Furthermore, it appears that the Williams family kept them so isolated and secluded that they never knew they had the opportunity to emigrate when the time came. The Williamses also used threats and intimidation to hold the Indians in place, as well as promising to pay them for their work one day, money they would never see if they left the plantation. In any event, the Creeks lived with the blacks on the Williams place, and for all practical purposes served as dutiful slaves, until one day in 1839. Luther Blake, a resident of the Society Hill community who had a long association with the Creeks, was riding past the Williams plantation on that day when, to his surprise, the Euchees confronted him on the road. Prior to that time, he had no idea of their existence and he listened intently as they told him of their plight and asked him to inform the government that they wanted to join their tribespeople in the West. They did, however, caution Blake not to alert the Williamses of their intentions because they feared the family might then take the matter to court, exert some legal claim to their labor, and continue to hold them in place. Blake did as they asked.[10]

On hearing from Blake that Indians yet lingered in Alabama, the commissioner of Indian Affairs, T. Hartley Crawford—formerly one of the government investigators looking into the causes of the Creek war—decided in 1841 to revive the Creek removal program. He began by enlisting the aid of Alabama's governor, Arthur Bagby, and others in determining the exact number of Indians the War Department would need to relocate. But this was no easy task. Some informants claimed only fifty Creeks remained; others said seven hundred. No one seemed to know for sure. Furthermore, actually laying hands on the Indians and moving them out of state threatened to be an even more difficult job than counting them. When, for example, Governor Bagby sent a letter to Jonathan P. Booth of Irwinton asking him about Indians held captive in that vicinity, he received a rather prickly reply. Booth had been the commanding general of Alabama's Fifth Militia Division at the war's end, and he readily admitted that he and several other leading citizens of Barbour and Dale counties continued to hold

Indian captives. However, Booth claimed that he had rescued the young Indian girl living in his household, her family having died in battle on their flight to Florida. He also said he would be willing to give the girl up for emigration when she was old enough to decide for herself if she should go west or stay in Alabama with his family. In addition, Booth contended that William Wellborn, the war's hero, was raising a young Indian he too would be willing to give up. However, General Booth warned Bagby that the release of all the other Indian captives was "very questionable." He was correct. Alabama's economic system required lots of workers, and some whites would never surrender the Creeks they had taken such pains to capture, especially given the rising price of black slaves. Green Beauchamp, an early chronicler of Barbour County, observed that as late as 1870 Indian captives, grown to adulthood, still lived among the whites and blacks in Eufaula (formerly Irwinton) and its environs.[11]

However, it does not appear that most whites thought of their Indian servants in the same way they did their black slaves. Indeed, those Creeks who stayed in the Southeast seemed to occupy a shady, second-class position between whites and blacks. The life of an Indian woman named Ailsey—one of General Booth's captives—gives testimony to this fact. For whatever reason, Booth never surrendered Ailsey to the authorities for removal. Instead, he reared her with his own children, educated her after a fashion, never enslaved her in any formal sense, and did not let her keep company with slaves. However, neither the Booths nor the other white residents of Eufaula allowed Ailsey to associate with them on terms of equality. Consequently, Ailsey became a hired servant for the whites and "a noted laundress of fine linens and laces." She also lived in her own log house and married a black man.[12]

Ailsey's situation was not unique. We have a couple of other examples of this peculiar relationship between whites and their Creek captives. The first illustration comes from Dale County, Alabama. There the redoubtable Arch Justice, an Indian fighter famous for his exploits in the West Florida theater of the Creek war, kept a Native boy and girl he captured in the course of his numerous border forays. But Justice fell on hard times, probably as a result of the Panic of 1837, and the county sheriff, one Levi Skipper, took the male youngster away from Justice on a *writ of detinue*. Then, to pay off Justice's debt, Skipper placed the lad on the local slave block for sale to the highest bidder. This act, however, did not sit well with Justice and he acted forcefully to stop the process. "Drawing his gun he walked up to the block and said to the Indian, 'Come down off that block, you are a free man.'" The sheriff, taken aback, did not resist and the Indian walked away a free person, though obviously not the social equal of the county's whites. And the same might be said of "Indian Peggy" over on Pea River. Back in 1837 a family named Clark found a dark-skinned Creek infant abandoned in their cotton field by her fugitive tribespeople. The Clarks named the girl and brought her up as one of their own. However, she never left their home to make her own way in the world. She served the Clarks as a cook and housekeeper, associated little with other whites or blacks, and never married. She died at age thirty-seven.[13]

So how would the whites have classified these captives who appeared to be neither slaves nor entirely free? Perhaps a good explanation of the status of Ailsey and Peggy and other such individuals comes from John L. McKinnon, author of the *History of Walton County, Florida*. In describing two captive boys who tended cows on the McKinnon's West Florida homestead, the writer simply called them "interesting pets." However, an elderly Indian living near Jacksonville, Alabama, gives us a little better idea of his community's racial ranking system, and in the process implies that Natives could get along fairly well in piedmont Alabama, as long as they understood and conformed to that system. According to this elderly man, the order of classification was "white man, Indian, dog, and Negro."[14]

But regardless of the Indians' status, Commissioner Crawford wanted to complete the difficult task of finally removing all the Creeks from their ancient homeland. In 1845, after years of delay caused by lack of funds and the inability to collect necessary information, Crawford finally granted a removal contract to one Moses K. Wheat, agreeing to pay him $47.25 for each Indian sent west. Interestingly, Representative Dixon H. Lewis, the states' righter who had been so instrumental in extending Alabama's authority over the Creeks in the early 1830s, was

Wheat's "good friend" and manipulated the contract process to both men's advantage. This maneuvering showed that the Indian business was still alive and well in Alabama, as did the fact that Wheat and his partners encountered considerable opposition from their fellow citizens in getting Creeks out of the state. When, for example, the removal contractors collected some Indians in Coosa and Tallapoosa counties and attempted to march them off to a holding camp in Montgomery, the Creeks suddenly broke and ran away "because interfering whites told them they were going to be chained and sold as slaves." Nevertheless, by January 1846 the contractors assembled 102 Indians in Montgomery, intending to transport them by steamer down to Mobile and over to New Orleans. But now the contractors had trouble keeping the Creeks in camp. The Indians often wandered off, "enticed by whites who wanted their labor." The contractors also reported, as previously noted, that there were a number of children in possession of the whites "who hold them for the benefit of their present and future services."[15]

Yet the contractors did have some success. They took off twelve families of Creeks, about 70 people in all, and delivered them to the Creek Agency West in February. Then, in March, the contractors reported to the agency with a party of 103 Indians. But most of these Creeks appear to have been independent, acculturated, and reasonably prosperous people, not the impoverished and/or enslaved captives who really needed rescue. In fact, one of the Indians, Abraham Foster, took thirty slaves with him to his new homeland. And, as further proof of the acculturation and prosperity of these 1846 emigrants, James Logan, the Creek agent, reported in May that all the new arrivals were healthy, hard at work farming, and would set a good example for the other Creeks and be an asset to their nation.[16]

But Wheat's contract expired before he could complete the task of getting all the Creeks out of Alabama. When Luther Blake rode out on a scout through the southern part of the state, he discovered more Indians, mostly orphans held as slaves in Barbour, Henry, Dale, Covington, and Pike counties. He also found adult Creeks anxious to emigrate but needing to arrange their affairs so they could do so. These Indians, again mostly acculturated individuals of the "better class," ultimately decided to conduct their own emigration, billing the government for their expenses when they arrived in the West. In February 1847 the Carr and Rogers families finally left Russell County. The famed Paddy Carr himself led this group, which included eleven Indians and eight blacks. Then in June William Walker and his wife, "respectable Creek Indians residing in the vicinity of Montgomery," arrived at the Creek agency. And finally, in the fall, Ward Cochemy, a Creek who had gone west two years before, returned to his former home in Wetumpka, Alabama—the place he was reared and educated—to reclaim relatives left behind and take them back with him to the Indian Territory. He discovered, however, that their connections with the whites were such that they could not leave Alabama without losing their property, meaning, most probably, that far from being slaves or even social outcasts, these Indians had done a good job of integrating themselves into the state's economic system. Realizing this, Cochemy told them to settle their affairs and he would return for them later.[17]

Cochemy, who would in time become the principal chief of the Creek Nation, did return the following year in 1848, secured permission from the War Department to remove all the Indians he could collect, and borrowed enough money from his white friends in Wetumpka to finance the project. He then visited all the Creeks he could and succeeded in assembling, besides his relatives, about forty individuals from Autauga, Bibb, Coosa, and Talladega counties. This done, he left Montgomery on May 30 with sixty-five people, including Echo Fixico of Chehaw town, a gentleman over one hundred years old, whom Cochemy called "the oldest man I ever saw." But still Creeks remained in central Alabama, mostly slaves living in deplorable conditions, according to Cochemy. He even noted that a Christian minister, Rev. William Hays of Autauga County, held a number of Indians. Cochemy had tried his best to lay hands on these unfortunate Natives, but "was prevented from doing so by threats of their would be masters." Nevertheless, he declared that he would get them in time.[18]

But neither Ward Cochemy nor anyone else ever got all the Creeks out of Alabama, or Georgia or Florida for that matter. Some straggling Indians continued to move west for many years, but others would never leave the old haunts of their ancestors. And yet those scattered groups of Indians who managed to evade removal and captivity and stayed on in the Southeast as free people still suffered some unfortunate consequences resulting from the Second Creek War. First and foremost, the war, by making Creek removal mandatory as a national defense measure, meant that most of these Indians would be illegal aliens in their own native land. Second, whites would continue to fear them. In fact, Commissioner Crawford chose to revive Creek removal in part because he heard that forty or fifty Indians in Coosa County, Alabama, had long been "pilfering and intruding upon the settlers in such a way that it would be dangerous to offend them lest they would revenge themselves" upon the whites' families or property. As late as 1858 this view of Indians as dangerous aliens persisted, as evidenced by one Charles Mackay, a traveling chronicler. He noted that Alabama was still not totally free of Indians and their presence recalled to whites the horrible incidents of the former war. Consequently, those Creeks who wanted to stay on in the South faced a third and even more terrible consequence of the war. To escape removal and not be perceived as a threat by others, Indians in the South would have to pretend not to be Natives. They would have to give up much of their culture and their original identities to blend into the social landscape.[19]

A closer look at the eastern end of old Macon County, Alabama (an area presently included in Lee County), reveals this blending process. Rev. F. L. Cherry, a nineteenth-century county historian, stated that two years after the Creek removal there were still as many Indians as whites living in this area. They had avoided removal by being "very quiet." Writing about the same location in the twentieth century, Alexander Nunn, another county historian, stated, "When I was a boy ... many families of Indian ancestry could still be found amongst us; some were of mixed white and Indian blood, some of Indian and Negro ancestry. Probably there are even more with Indian blood in their veins today but the proportion of Indian blood has been so much diluted that distinctly Indian features have almost disappeared." This description suggests that amid the turmoil and violence of New Alabama's economic life, some Creeks may have sought out blacks and whites as allies and mates in the contest to survive and prosper—a contest that cut across racial lines. These Creeks may have used their affiliations with black and white families as a successful strategy for going underground and evading removal. They chose collusion over conflict. However, the cost over time was the nearly complete loss of themselves as Natives. They resisted removal only to be assimilated into the black and white communities. The same happened in West Florida, the last resort of the remaining Creek resistance fighters. In time even these people had to emerge from their bayous and swamps, give up their lives of predation, and gradually blend in with blacks or whites. By 1900 most of Florida's Creeks, both old settlers and rebel refugees, had forgotten, or sought to cover up, their Indian ancestry.[20]

And yet, why, in the final analysis, is the Second Creek War really a significant historical event? What is its most important legacy? Part of the answer lies in the fact that in recent years Creeks, some of them descendants of the old rebel party, have reemerged from their hiding places in the Southeast. The civil rights movement and the opportunity to receive reimbursement for lost tribal land through the federal government's Indian Claims Commission (established in 1946) prompted many Creek descendants in the southern states to come forward and reassert themselves as Native Americans. Some have also tried to reclaim various aspects of their lost culture. The Poarch band of Creeks centered in southern Alabama and the Florida tribe of Eastern Creeks are the two most noticeable groups, but others are also seeking recognition. Their efforts show that the children of the Creek resistance fighters, as well as of those who resisted removal by more peaceful means, can claim at least a partial victory in the Second Creek War. Moreover, these and other Native Americans have won the respect of southerners in general because they resisted, because they fought for their land and way of life. Today thousands of people in the South claim Indian ancestry, perhaps more per capita than in any other region of the country. In Alabama alone, at least a quarter of the population claims Native ancestry, and in 1985 one of the members of Alabama's Indian Affairs Commission, a Native American who grew up on a reservation in California, made the surprising statement that Alabamians were more tolerant of Indians than some westerners because so many Alabamians "have some Indian blood."[21]

But is this really true that many Alabamians have Native blood flowing in their veins? It is possible but it may not be true. After all, only a comparative few individuals can prove Indian ancestry to the degree required to receive Claims Commission money. So why would so many other southerners, Alabamians in particular, claim Indian descent? Could it be that they feel some element of guilt stemming from removal, some subconscious understanding that all the South has and is rests on taking the best land from its aboriginal population and sending that population off on the tragic Trail of Tears? If that is the case, then claiming kinship to the oppressed would allow southerners to escape guilt for reaping the long-term benefits of that oppression. But it may be that white and black southerners are simply more culturally akin to Indians than the people of other areas. The southern Indian nations were larger than other Native groups, and the Choctaws, Cherokees, Chickasaws, Seminoles, and Creeks lived in close proximity to whites and blacks for a long time before the removal era. There must have been significant cultural exchange taking place, and this exchange may have given a decidedly Native cast to southern culture as a whole. Indeed, various scholars have gone to great pains to explain southern distinctiveness and the southern personality. They have talked about African influences, the impact of climate, Celtic heritage, the persistence of frontier conditions in the South, the existence of slavery, paternalism, codes of honor, and so on, but few if any have seen that both conflict and collusion with Natives in the South's formative era may be a significant factor in making Southern culture and personality distinctive. Moreover, there may have been a concerted effort on the part of southern elites to cover up this cultural affinity with Natives, just as the record of the Second Creek War was conveniently expunged. Following removal, respectable whites did set about the task of ushering in the reign of King Cotton. In the process they created a picture of the Cotton South, the *Gone with the Wind* South, that captivated southern historians and the world, so much so that many enthralled voyeurs lost sight of the frontier period, when Indians were an important part of southern society. But it could be that latter-day southerners know better on some deep psychological level. Thus, they claim Native blood when in fact they mean to claim a cultural descent from Natives that they can neither fully understand nor articulate in any other way than to say something one hears continually in the South: "My great-grandmother was a full-blooded Indian."[22]

Notes

ADAH   Alabama Department of Archives and History
ASPIA   American State Papers, Class 2: Indian Affairs
ASPMA   American State Papers, Class 5: Military Affairs
CA   Creek Agency
CVCC   Chattahoochee Valley Community College
GDAH   Georgia Department of Archives and History
GJ   General Jesup
LGM   Local Government Microfilm
LR   Letters Received
MP   Microfilm Publication
NARA   National Archives and Records Administration
OAG   Office of the Adjutant General
OIA   Office of Indian Affairs
PB   Papers and Books
RG   Record Group
SS   Seminole Superintendency
WD   War Department

Introduction

1. The standard view of the Creek conflict comes from Rogin, *Fathers and Children*; Foreman, *Indian Removal*; Green, *Politics of Indian Removal*; Young, *Redskins, Ruffleshirts, and Rednecks*; and Debo, *Road to Disappearance*. J. L. Wright, in his book *Creeks and Seminoles*, gives a different view of the war. His ethnohistoric account places the conflict in the context of an ongoing civil war between two competing moieties in Creek society.

2. Eby's *That Disgraceful Affair* is a good example of literature on the Black Hawk conflict, and Mahon's *Second Seminole War* is still the most comprehensive of a number of works on the Seminole struggle.

3. A couple of earlier journal articles and a master's thesis did explain parts of the war, but none of these works comprehended the full scope of the war or its real meaning. See Valliere, "Creek War of 1836"; Rucker, "Creek Indian Crisis"; Pepper, "Creek Indian Question."

4. Ortega y Gassett, *Man and Crisis*, 122. The idea of the world economic system and its impact on traditional societies comes from Wallerstein: "The mark of the modern world is the imagination of its profiteers and the counter-assertiveness of the oppressed. Exploitation and the refusal to accept exploitation as either inevitable or just constitute the continuing antimony of the modern era, joined together in a dialectic which has far from reached its climax in the twentieth century" (*Modern World-System*, 233). For capitalism and commodification in the Old South, see Rogin, *Fathers and Children*, 252–53; Genovese, *Political Economy of Slavery*, 19–31; and Kulikoff, *Agrarian Origins*, 5–7.

5. According to Foner, "capitalism is profoundly antitraditional," and one cannot logically defend social conservatism and the unregulated market at the same time (*Story of American Freedom*, 310).

6. The traditional interpretation of aggressive white southerners pushing Indian removal on oppressed Natives probably began with Turner's *Rise of the New West*, 65, 67–68. Since that time, many books have utilized and strengthened the theme. Their point of departure has been Andrew Jackson's role in the removal drama. Some historians blame Jackson for not enforcing treaties that protected Indian rights (see Van Every, *Disinherited*). Other historians exonerate the president, claiming that he could not resist the land hunger of southern whites and had no choice but to remove the Indians for the good of the nation and themselves (see Prucha, *Great Father*, 1:191–98). A review of the literature on this subject appears in Schoenleber's "Rise of the New West," 1–8. Schoenleber himself falls in the anti-Jackson camp, contending that the president's leadership was crucial to removal and that southerners and their representatives in Congress could not have accomplished it without him. However, Schoenleber shows that southerners were not as united behind removal as many historians have supposed. In the case of the Creeks, all of the works mentioned in note 1 follow and help delineate the traditional theme.

7. Thompson and Lamar, "Comparative Frontier History," 7–10 (quote on 7).

8. Merrell outlines the "New World" theme in *Indians' New World*. He claims the American frontier was a "New World" for all ethnic groups, who had to adapt to one another and the changing landscape and times. One of the better examples of "Middle Ground" literature is R. White's *Middle Ground*. See also Ethridge, *Creek Country*.

9. Peterson, "Old South," 129. Those scholars who have taken Peterson's advice when looking at the Old South usually focus on the period before the 1830s. Consequently, they do not examine the era when the most Native, white, and black people lived in the closest proximity. Usner's *Indians, Settlers, and Slaves* is an example of one of these studies of the preremoval era.

1. Creek Politics and Confinement

1. Doster, *Creek Indians*, 1:244–65, 2:35–38; Owsley, *Struggle*, 9–13; Edmunds, *Quest for Indian Leadership*, 148–52.

2. Doster, *Creek Indians*, 1:244–65, 2:35–38; Owsley, *Struggle*, 9–13; Edmunds, *Quest for Indian Leadership*, 148–52.

3. Doster, *Creek Indians*, 1:244–65, 2:35–38; Owsley, *Struggle*, 9–13; Edmunds, *Quest for Indian Leadership*, 148–52.

4. J. W. Martin, "Southeastern Indians," 316–20. See also Braund, *Deerskins and Duffels*.

5. Henri, *Southern Indians*, 268; Owsley, *Struggle*, 12; Sugden, *Tecumseh*, 118–19.

6. Hahn, *Creek Nation*, 48–49, 75–76. See also Gallay, *Indian Slave Trade*.

7. Champagne, *Social Order*, 117–18; Ethridge, "Contest for the Land," 193, 336–38; Saunt, *New Order of Things*, 227–28, 233–35, 241–43, 250–51, 257; Doster, *Creek Indians*, 2:42; Pound, *Benjamin Hawkins*, 24–40.

8. For a more complete socioreligious explanation of the nativist movement and the subsequent war, see J. W. Martin, *Sacred Revolt*; Doster, *Creek Indians*, 2:66–96, 111–12; Owsley, *Struggle*, 34–41; and Dowd, *Spirited Resistance*, 186–90.

9. Champagne, *Social Order*, 87; Saunt, *New Order of Things*, 250, 255, 259, 264, 272; Braund, "Creek Indians," 633–35; Doster, *Creek Indians*, 2:206–17; Owsley, *Struggle*, 184–85.

10. Hahn, *Creek Nation*, 273; Owsley, *Struggle*, 11; Wallerstein, *Modern World-System*, 238; Rogin, *Fathers and Children*, 12–14, 251–54.

11. Green, *Politics of Indian Removal*, 50–51; Owsley, *Struggle*, 194; Pickett, *History of Alabama*, 635. For the rise of Andrew Jackson and removal sentiment, see Remini, *Course of Empire*, chs. 13–14. For the views of the Georgians, see Schoenleber, "Rise of the New West," chs. 4, 7.

12. Griffith, *McIntosh and Weatherford*, 195–211; McBride, *Opothleyahola*, 38. Numerous scholars have discussed the conservative/progressive schism so common among Native American tribes and nations. See Metcalf, "Rule at Home," and Lowie, "American Aborigines." Green gives a good account of the Indian Springs Treaty in *Politics of Indian Removal*, ch. 4. See also "Federal-State Conflict," ch. 6.

13. Green, *Politics of Indian Removal*, 54–55, 57, 70–72, 82, 88; Braund, "Creek Indians," 635; J. L. Wright, *Creeks and Seminoles*, 185–214; Doster, *Creek Indians*, 2:189; Cotterill, *Southern Indians*, 214. The U.S. Congress ended the international slave trade to this country in 1808 but allowed domestic slavery and an internal slave trade to continue.

14. Swanton, "Social Organization," 308–9; McBride, *Opothleyahola*, 35; Elkin, "Reaction and Interaction," 45–46.

15. A. K. Frank, *Creeks and Southerners*, 96–113.

16. Ethridge, "Contest for the Land," 329; Young, *Redskins, Ruffleshirts, and Rednecks*, 37; Green, *Politics of Indian Removal*, 96–99, 111, 113, 133; Doster, *Creek Indians*, 2:274–84; McBride, *Opothleyahola*, 61; Wallerstein, *Capitalist World-Economy*, 217–18.

17. Ethridge, "Contest for the Land," 329; Young, *Redskins, Ruffleshirts, and Rednecks*, 37; Green, *Politics of Indian Removal*, 96–99, 111, 113, 133; Doster, *Creek Indians*, 2:274–84; McBride, *Opothleyahola*, 61; Wallerstein, *Capitalist World-Economy*, 217–18.

18. Green, *Politics of Indian Removal*, 117, 121, 124, 133, 139, 155, 156; Champagne, *Social Order*, 125; Ethridge, "Contest for the Land," 300, 312–14; Young, *Redskins, Ruffleshirts, and Rednecks*, 20, 37; Doster, *Creek Indians*, 1:242; Rogin, *Fathers and Children*, 6; McBride, *Opothleyahola*, 61. The connection between the Creek cession controversy and the rise of states' rights sentiment in Georgia is a major theme in two important books on antebellum Georgia politics: Paul, *Whig Party in Georgia*, and U. Phillips, *Georgia and States Rights*. The accords the headmen signed are the Washington Treaty, January 24, 1826; the Supplementary Article to the Washington Treaty, March 31, 1826; and the Creek Agency Treaty, November 15, 1827.

19. Champagne, *Social Order*, 128; Ethridge, "Contest for the Land," 59, 94, 155–56; Green, *Politics of Indian Removal*, 38–39, 141–42, quote on 150–51; Foreman, *Indian Removal*, 151.

20. Doster, *Creek Indians*, 2:14, 17, 20, 28; Cherry, "History of Opelika," 317; Clements, *History of Irwin County*, 35–36; J. L. Wright, *Creeks and Seminoles*, 9–10; Crowell to Randolph, July 7, 1831, reel 221, MP 234, RG 75, CA, LR, OIA, WD, NARA, 520–22. Hobsbawn speaks of the "universal and virtually unchanging phenomenon" of "peasant protests against oppression and poverty." See his *Primitive Rebels*, 5.

21. Champagne, *Social Order*, 80, 48–49; McBride, *Opothleyahola*, 75; Rogin, *Fathers and Children*, 2–13; Green, *Politics of Indian Removal*, 115–56; Wallace, *Long, Bitter Trail*, 6–8; Page to Gibson, September 15, 1834, *ASPMA* 6:763–64.

22. Champagne, *Social Order*, 80, 48–49; McBride, *Opothleyahola*, 75; Rogin, *Fathers and Children*, 2–13; Green, *Politics of Indian Removal*, 115–56; Page to Gibson, September 15, 1834, *ASPMA* 6:763–64.

23. Champagne, *Social Order*, 80, 48–49; McBride, *Opothleyahola*, 75; Rogin, *Fathers and Children*, 2–13; Green, *Politics of Indian Removal*, 115–56; Page to Gibson, September 15, 1834, *ASPMA* 6:763–64.

24. Champagne, *Social Order*, 169–70; C. White, "Opothleyahola," 95, 139–40, 143–48; Meserve, "Chief Opothleyahola," 444, 451–53; Woodward, *Reminiscences*, 100; Lanny to Troup, March 10, 1825, *ASPIA* 2:764–66; McBride, *Opothleyahola*, 10, 11, 25; Martin, McKane Mauldin, and McGirt, *Totkv Mocvse—New Fire*, xix.

25. Green, *Politics of Indian Removal*, 150–51, 158–59.

26. Green, *Politics of Indian Removal*, 150–51, 158–59.

27. Green, *Politics of Indian Removal*, 129–30, 138, 159; U.S. Congress, *House Documents*, 20th Cong., 1st sess., March 28, 1828, no. 219, "Creek Indian Broke," 7–8 (hereafter cited as *House Doc.* 219).

28. Green, *Politics of Indian Removal*, 132, 164–65; Crowell to Barbour, August 12, 1827, reel 221, MP 234, RG 75, CA, LR, OIA, WD, NARA, 232–35; Resolution of Upper Creek Chiefs, February 17, 1827, reel 221, MP 234, RG 75, CA, LR, OIA, WD, NARA; *Alabama Journal*, February 12, 1830, 2; *House Doc.* 219, 3, 5–6.

29. Green, *Politics of Indian Removal*, 132, 164–65; Crowell to Barbour, August 12, 1827, reel 221, MP 234, RG 75, CA, LR, OIA, WD, NARA, 232–35; Resolution of Upper Creek Chiefs, February 17, 1827, reel 221, MP 234, RG 75, CA, LR, OIA, WD, NARA; *Alabama Journal*, February 12, 1830, 2; *House Doc.* 219, 3, 5–6.

30. Doster, *Creek Indians*, 2:1, 14, 220–21, 227; Yamaguchi, "Macon County," 4, 27–29, 32, 36, 41; Swanton, *Early History*, 215, 243–46, 266; Sugden, *Tecumseh*, 247–48; Woodward, *Reminiscences*, 103; Halbert and Ball, *Creek War*, 91–93.

31. Ethridge, "Contest for the Land," 307; Swanton, *Early History*, 245–46; Brannon, "Indian Tribes and Towns," 190, 214; Green, *Politics of Indian Removal*, 39, 41–42; Doster, *Creek Indians*, 1:199; Yamaguchi, "Macon County," 11.

32. Green, *Politics of Indian Removal*, 137, 162; Tuskenea to Secretary of War, October 1835, reel 224, MP 234, RG 75, CA, LR, OIA, WD, NARA, 310.

33. Saunt, *New Order of Things*, 218–21; Braund, *Deerskins and Duffels*, 140; Green, *Politics of Indian Removal*, 172; McBride, *Opothleyahola*, 63–64; *House Doc.* 219, 6; Page to Gibson, May 9, 1835, *ASPMA* 6:766; Hogan to Gibson, May 14, 1835, *ASPMA* 6:725–26.

34. Bartram, *North and South Carolina*, 388; Hodgson and Hawkins, *Creek Indian History*, 59; U.S. Congress, *Senate Documents*, 23rd Cong., 1st sess., 1835, no. 512, "Indian Removal," 4:359 (hereafter cited as *Senate Doc.* 512).

NOTES TO PAGES 32–45

35. Bartram, *North and South Carolina*, 388; Hodgson and Hawkins, *Creek Indian History*, 59; *Senate Doc.* 512, 4:359.

36. J. L. Wright, *Creeks and Seminoles*, 220–21, 234–37, 265–66; Stiggins, *Creek Indian History*, 32–33; Doster, *Creek Indians*, 2:186, 200, 262–64; Yamaguchi, "Macon County," 40, 44–45; J. L. Wright, *American Frontier*, 179–80.

37. Champagne, *Social Order*, 168; Griffith, *McIntosh and Weatherford*, 268; McIntosh to Troup, *ASPIA* 2:764; Kappler, *Indian Affairs*, 214–15; McKenney, *Indian Tribes*, 132–33.

38. A. Walker, *Russell County in Retrospect*, 41–63. For more on Indian countrymen, see Woodward, *Reminiscences*, and A. K. Frank, *Creeks and Southerners*.

39. Ethridge, "Contest for the Land," 286–91, 293; Prucha, *American Indian Policy*, 30–33; Ethridge, *Creek Country*, 196–97; Braund, "Creek Indians," 605.

40. A. K. Frank, *Creeks and Southerners*, 92, 129–32; Saunt, *Black, White, and Indian*, 36; Champagne, *Social Order*, 169; Green, *Politics of Indian Removal*, 131, 152; Wallerstein, *Modern World-System*, 231.

41. "Chiefs Resist Removal," *Alabama Journal*, April 9, 1830, 1; Editorial, *Alabama Journal*, January 29, 1830, 2; "James B. Reed vs. Opothleyaholo and Jim Boy," *Alabama Journal*, March 19, 1830, 2; Creek Chiefs to Secretary of War, August 2, 1827, reel 221, MP 234, RG 75, CA, LR, OIA, WD, NARA, 172–74; Green, *Politics of Indian Removal*, 131, 148, 153, 158; Chiefs to U.S. Commissioners, December 11, 1824, *ASPIA* 2:571; McBride, *Opothleyahola*, 32; Foreman, *Indian Removal*, 151n29.

42. Compere to McKenny, date illegible, reel 221, MP 234, RG 75, CA, LR, OIA, WD, NARA, 703–7; Saunt, *Black, White, and Indian*, 35–36; C. White, "Opothleyahola," 143, 145; J. L. Wright, *Creeks and Seminoles*, 224.

43. A. K. Frank, *Creeks and Southerners*, 124; Champagne, *Social Order*, 166; Ethridge, "Contest for the Land," 160, 165; Braund, "Creek Indians," 601, 608, 631; A. Walker, *Russell County in Retrospect*, 60; Green, *Politics of Indian Removal*, 63–65; Yamaguchi, "Macon County," 26–27; U.S. Congress, *House Reports*, 19th Cong., 2nd sess., March 3, 1827, no. 98, "Report of the Select Committee on the Georgia Question Relative to Creek Indian Lands," 24, 35, 50–51, 68–69, 72.

44. Saunt, *Black, White, and Indian*, 16–17, 23, 33, 38, 43, 48–49 (quote on 33).

45. Hamilton, *Men and Manners*, 2:333–39.

46. Dunaway, *First American Frontier*, 51; Aiken, *Digest of the Laws*, 223–24; An Act to Extend Criminal Jurisdiction over Alabama Courtier, reel 221, MP 234, RG 75, CA, LR, OIA, WD, NARA, 191; An Act to Prevent Crime and Disorder, reel 221, MP 234, RG 75, CA, LR, OIA, WD, NARA, 192–93.

47. Green, *Politics of Indian Removal*, 145–47; Wallerstein, *Capitalist World-Economy*, 219–20.

48. Green, *Politics of Indian Removal*, 145–47; Wallerstein, *Capitalist World-Economy*, 219–20.

49. Green, *Politics of Indian Removal*, 143–44, 146–47; Schoenleber, "Rise of the New West," chs. 4, 7.

50. Green, *Politics of Indian Removal*, 143–44, 146–47; Schoenleber, "Rise of the New West," chs. 4, 7; Aiken, *Digest of the Laws*, 224–25; Saunt, *Black, White, and Indian*, 39.

51. "Creek Indians," *Niles Weekly Register* 40 (July 16, 1831): 344; Foreman, *Indian Removal*, 108; "From the *Columbus Democrat*," *Alabama Journal*, July 16, 1831, 3.

52. Garrison, *Legal Ideology of Removal*, 3–4, 151–68; Foreman, *Indian Removal*, 233; Richardson, *Messages and Papers*, 982, 1020.

53. Garrison, *Legal Ideology of Removal*, 3–4, 151–68; Foreman, *Indian Removal*, 233; Richardson, *Messages and Papers*, 982, 1020.

54. Young, *Redskins, Ruffleshirts, and Rednecks*, 14.

2. The Cusseta Treaty of 1832

1. Ellisor, "Like So Many Wolves," 1–3; Kappler, *Indian Treaties*, 2:341–43; Herring to Cass, June 6, 1836, *ASPMA* 6:575; Foreman, *Indian Removal*, 107–12; Green, *Politics of Indian Removal*, 169–73.

2. Green, *Politics of Indian Removal*, 171–72.

3. Foreman, *Indian Removal*, 111–12; Rogin, *Fathers and Children*, 228.

4. Foster-Carter, "Modes of Production Controversy"; Quataert, *Social Disintegration*, 3; Banton, *Racial and Ethnic Competition*, 119–25. See also A. G. Frank, *Capitalism and Underdevelopment*.

5. Cass to Picket, May 14, 1832, reel 223, MP 234, RG 75, CA, LR, OIA, WD, NARA, 278–79.

6. Hudson, *Southeastern Indians*, 259, 313; Parsons to Secretary of War, October 16, 1832, reel 223, MP 234, RG 75, CA, LR, OIA, WD, NARA, 281–82.

7. *Senate Doc.* 512, 3:631

8. Cass to Abert and Parsons, May 2, 1833, reel 223, MP 234, RG 75, CA, LR, OIA, WD, NARA, 432–38.

9. *Senate Doc.* 512, 3:498, 637.

10. *Senate Doc.* 512, 3:434, 469, 516; J. L. Wright, *Creeks and Seminoles*, 217.

11. *Senate Doc.* 512, 3:574–76.

12. *Senate Doc.* 512, 3:525; Foreman, *Indian Removal*, 111–12; Abert to Cass, January 14, 1836, *ASPMA* 6:608–10.

13. Kappler, *Indian Treaties*, 2:341–43; *Senate Doc.* 512, 2:806–7.

14. *Senate Doc.* 512, 2:822.

15. *Senate Doc.* 512, 3:310.

16. Foreman, *Indian Removal*, 109, 115, 117; Hogan to Cass, May 14, 1835, *ASPMA* 6:725–26; *Senate Doc.* 512, 3:440, 543.

17. *Senate Doc.* 512, 3:440, 453, 454.

18. *Senate Doc.* 512, 3:440, 453, 454.

19. *Senate Doc.* 512, 3:413, 440, 454, 485.

20. *Senate Doc.* 512, 3:410, 453–54.

21. *Senate Doc.* 512, 3:464.

22. *Senate Doc.* 512, 3:522–23, 483–84.

23. Young, *Redskins, Ruffleshirts, and Rednecks*, 74–76; McHenry to Cass, March 12, 1834, *ASPMA* 6:639.

24. Citizens to Cass, October 2, 1832, reel 223, MP 234, RG 75, CA, LR, OIA, WD, NARA, 369–71; Certificate of Edward Croft, August 24, 1832, reel 223, MP 234, RG 75, CA, LR, OIA, WD, NARA, 373.

25. The terms "respectables" and "roughs" come from Collins, *White Society*, ch. 10; *Senate Doc.* 512, 3:528; Citizens to Cass, October 11, 1832, reel 223, MP 234, RG 75, CA, LR, OIA, WD, NARA, 225–26; Watkins to Cass, October 18, 1832, reel 223, MP 234, RG 75, CA, LR, OIA, WD, NARA, 335–38; Citizens to Cass, October 18, 1832, reel 223, MP 234, RG 75, CA, LR, OIA, WD, NARA, 369–71.

NOTES TO PAGES 66–77

26. Statement of John Elliott, November 5, 1832, reel 223, MP 234, RG 75, CA, LR, OIA, WD, NARA, 189–91; Crawford to Kurtz, December 6, 1832, reel 223, MP 234, RG 75, CA, LR, OIA, WD, NARA, 61–62; Senate Doc. 512, 2:957.

27. Senate Doc. 512, 3:550, 565; Crawford to Kurtz, December 6, 1832, reel 223, MP 234, RG 75, CA, LR, OIA, WD, NARA, 61–62.

28. Senate Doc. 512, 2:961–63; King, Mardis, and Clay to Cass, December 6, 1832, reel 223, MP 234, RG 75, CA, LR, OIA, WD, NARA, 215–16; Cass to Moore, December 8, 1832, reel 223, MP 234, RG 75, CA, LR, OIA, WD, NARA, 66–67; Crowell to Cass, December 5, 1832, reel 223, MP 234, RG 75, CA, LR, OIA, WD, NARA, 178–79.

29. Copy of Standard Bond, n.d., reel 223, MP 234, RG 75, CA, LR, OIA, WD, NARA, 939; Perry to Abbot and Parsons, June 14, 1833, reel 223, MP 234, RG 75, CA, LR, OIA, WD, NARA, 941; Senate Doc. 512, 3:612.

30. Senate Doc. 512, 3:396, 400, 422–24.

31. Cass to Abert and Parsons, May 2, 1833, reel 223, MP 234, RG 75, CA, LR, OIA, WD, NARA, 432–38; Senate Doc. 512, 3:686–88; Young, *Redskins, Ruffleshirts, and Rednecks*, 80–81; Foreman, *Indian Removal*, 119–21.

32. Abert to Cass, May 17, 1833, reel 223, MP 234, RG 75, CA, LR, OIA, WD, NARA, 385–86; Abert to Cass, May 20, 1833, reel 223, MP 234, RG 75, CA, LR, OIA, WD, NARA, 389–92; Abert to Cass, June 2, 1833, reel 223, MP 234, RG 75, CA, LR, OIA, WD, NARA, 399–405.

33. Creek Chiefs to Parsons and Abert, June 30, 1833, reel 223, MP 234, RG 75, CA, LR, OIA, WD, NARA, 427–29; Chiefs to President, July 1, 1833, reel 223, MP 234, RG 75, CA, LR, OIA, WD, NARA, 430–31; Senate Doc. 512, 3:453–54.

34. Senate Doc. 512, 4:236–37; Chiefs to Cass, May 5, 1833, reel 223, MP 234, RG 75, CA, LR, OIA, WD, NARA, 642–44.

35. Abert to Robb, June 29, 1833, reel 223, MP 234, RG 75, CA, LR, OIA, WD, NARA, 411; Watson to Jackson, July 14, 1833, reel 223, MP 234, RG 75, CA, LR, OIA, WD, NARA, 1104–6; Report of the Commissioners, n.d., reel 223, MP 234, RG 75, CA, LR, OIA, WD, NARA, 968–76; Senate Doc. 512, 3:448–53, 455, 543, 704.

36. Senate Doc. 512, 3:448–53 (quote on 450).

37. Senate Doc. 512, 3:448–53. Mississippian culture refers to a series of chiefdoms existing across the Southeast during the late prehistoric period, ca. 900 to 1600 CE. Mississippian towns were noted for their palisades, flat-topped temple mounds, ornate public buildings, extensive trade networks, and vast corn fields. The Mississippian people also developed elaborate religious rituals and a complex belief system, parts of which their descendants, members of the later southeastern Indian confederacies such as the Creeks, continued to practice. See Shaffer, *Native Americans before 1492*.

38. Senate Doc. 512, 3:267.

39. Senate Doc. 512, 2:853–54; Senate Doc. 512, 3:23–24; Secretary of War to Commissioners, August 2, 1832, reel 223, MP 234, RG 75, CA, LR, OIA, WD, NARA, 148–50; Brodnax to Secretary of War, July 25, 1832, reel 223, MP 234, RG 75, CA, LR, OIA, WD, NARA, 33–39; Creek Chiefs to Secretary of War, January 17, 1832, reel 223, MP 234, RG 75, CA, LR, OIA, WD, NARA, 73–75; Chiefs to Secretary of War, February 8, 1832, reel 223, MP 234, RG 75, CA, LR, OIA, WD, NARA, 82–83.

40. Senate Doc. 512, 2:853–54; Senate Doc. 512, 3:23–24; Secretary of War to Commissioners,

August 2, 1832, reel 223, MP 234, RG 75, CA, LR, OIA, WD, NARA, 148–50; Brodnax to Secretary of War, July 25, 1832, reel 223, MP 234, RG 75, CA, LR, OIA, WD, NARA, 33–39; Creek Chiefs to Secretary of War, January 17, 1832, reel 223, MP 234, RG 75, CA, LR, OIA, WD, NARA, 73–75; Chiefs to Secretary of War, February 8, 1832, reel 223, MP 234, RG 75, CA, LR, OIA, WD, NARA, 82–83.

41. Secretary of War to Commissioners, August 2, 1832, reel 223, MP 234, RG 75, CA, LR, OIA, WD, NARA, 148–50; Chiefs to Secretary of War, September 27, 1832, reel 223, MP 234, RG 75, CA, LR, OIA, WD, NARA, 95–98; Parsons to Cass, October 12, 1832, reel 223, MP 234, RG 75, CA, LR, OIA, WD, NARA, 299–301; *Senate Doc.* 512, 3:467–70, 483–84; *Senate Doc.* 512, 2:938.

42. Creek Delegation to Decide Claims, 1st Monday in Jan. 1833, reel 223, MP 234, RG 75, CA, LR, OIA, WD, NARA, 896; Parsons and Crowell to Cass, 1st Monday in Jan. 1833, reel 223, MP 234, RG 75, CA, LR, OIA, WD, NARA, 914–29; Creek Chiefs to Cass, February 18, 1833, reel 223, MP 234, RG 75, CA, LR, OIA, WD, NARA, 637–39; *Senate Doc.* 512, 5:102–4.

43. Crowell to Cass, April 4, 1833, reel 223, MP 234, RG 75, CA, LR, OIA, WD, NARA, 930–33; Schedule of Claims, n.d., reel 223, MP 234, RG 75, CA, LR, OIA, WD, NARA, 943; *Senate Doc.* 512, 3:150.

44. Parsons and Crowell to Cass, April 4, 1833, reel 223, MP 234, RG 75, CA, LR, OIA, WD, NARA, 914–29; *Senate Doc.* 512, 4:471; Woodward, *Reminiscences*, 168.

45. *Senate Doc.* 512, 4:472–73; *Senate Doc.* 512, 3:626–27, 729; Parsons to Herring, June 7, 1833, reel 223, MP 234, RG 75, CA, LR, OIA, WD, NARA, 1025–27.

46. Austill to Cass, July 26, 1833, reel 223, MP 234, RG 75, CA, LR, OIA, WD, NARA, 508–13; *Senate Doc.* 512, 3:455–56.

47. *Senate Doc.* 512, 3:461, 469.

48. Austill to Cass, July 31, 1833, reel 223, MP 234, RG 75, CA, LR, OIA, WD, NARA, 515–17; Gayle to Crawford, n.d., reel 223, MP 234, RG 75, CA, LR, OIA, WD, NARA, 579; Foreman, *Indian Removal*, 112–18, 121–23; Green, *Politics of Indian Removal*, 175–80; McCorvey, *Alabama Historical Sketches*, 40–46; C. Williams, *Early History of Montgomery*, 121–22.

49. Austill to Cass, August 5, 1833, reel 223, MP 234, RG 75, CA, LR, OIA, WD, NARA, 519–21; Austill to Cass, August 6, 1833, reel 223, MP 234, RG 75, CA, LR, OIA, WD, NARA, 523; Austill to Cass, August 10, 1833, reel 223, MP 234, RG 75, CA, LR, OIA, WD, NARA, 525; Austill to Cass, September 22, 1833, reel 223, MP 234, RG 75, CA, LR, OIA, WD, NARA, 528–29. In late 1832 a South Carolina state convention nullified the federal tariff laws of 1828 and 1832, claiming that those laws violated the state's rights and were therefore unconstitutional. This move provoked a huge controversy with President Jackson, who threatened to use armed force to bring South Carolina back in line with his view that federal law was supreme and could not be voided by individual states. The immediate controversy passed, but more southerners adopted the Doctrine of Nullification over time, and this fact set the stage for the eventual secession of southern states and the Civil War. See Freehling, *Prelude to Civil War*.

50. *Senate Doc.* 512, 3:448, 506–19.

51. Cass to Crawford, August 26, 1833, reel 223, MP 234, RG 75, CA, LR, OIA, WD, NARA, 590–94; Robb to Parsons, October 8, 1833, reel 223, MP 234, RG 75, CA, LR, OIA, WD, NARA, 1046–49; *Senate Doc.* 512, 3:757.

52. *Senate Doc.* 512, 3:547–48, 573, 610–11; Wyche to Secretary of War, September 28, 1833, reel 223, MP 234, RG 75, CA, LR, OIA, WD, NARA, 1114–16; Austill to Cass, October 26, 1833, reel 223, MP 234, RG 75, CA, LR, OIA, WD, NARA, 536.

53. *Senate Doc.* 512, 3:616–18; Scott to Cass, November 20, 1833, reel 223, MP 234, RG 75, CA, LR, OIA, WD, NARA, 1052–61.

54. Crawford to Cass, October 23, 1833, reel 223, MP 234, RG 75, CA, LR, OIA, WD, NARA, 620–22.

55. Cass to Crawford, November 2, 1833, reel 223, MP 234, RG 75, CA, LR, OIA, WD, NARA, 624; Key to Cass, November 11, 1833, reel 223, MP 234, RG 75, CA, LR, OIA, WD, NARA, 818–21; McCorvey, *Alabama Historical Sketches*, 48–49; Thornton, *Politics and Power*, 28–31; Jack, "Federal Government."

56. *Senate Doc.* 512, 3:655, 703–5; Key to Cass, November 11, 1833, reel 223, MP 234, RG 75, CA, LR, OIA, WD, NARA, 818–21; McCorvey, *Alabama Historical Sketches*, 48–49; Thornton, *Politics and Power*, 28–31.

57. Clay to Cass, October 8, 1833, reel 223, MP 234, RG 75, CA, LR, OIA, WD, NARA, 554–59.

58. A Friend to the Union to Jackson, October 3, 1833, reel 223, MP 234, RG 75, CA, LR, OIA, WD, NARA, 493–94; A Friend to the Union to Cass, December 10, 1833, reel 223, MP 234, RG 75, CA, LR, OIA, WD, NARA, 496–97; *Senate Doc.* 512, 3:632.

59. Cass to Crawford, November 2, 1833, reel 223, MP 234, RG 75, CA, LR, OIA, WD, NARA, 624; Key to Crawford, December 1832, reel 223, MP 234, RG 75, CA, LR, OIA, WD, NARA, 832–36; Key to Abert, December 18, 1833, reel 223, MP 234, RG 75, CA, LR, OIA, WD, NARA, 837–38; Key to Gayle, December 16, 1833, reel 223, MP 234, RG 75, CA, LR, OIA, WD, NARA, 839–44; Elliott to Cass, December 28, 1833, reel 223, MP 234, RG 75, CA, LR, OIA, WD, NARA, 684–85; McCorvey, *Alabama Historical Sketches*, 48–49; Thornton, *Politics and Power*, 28–31. For further information on Key's visit to Alabama, see McCorvey, "Key's Mission," and Owsley, "Key's Mission."

60. Young, *Redskins, Ruffleshirts, and Rednecks*, 99–100; Foreman, *Indian Removal*, 112.

3. Commodifying the Creek Domain

1. Foreman, *Indian Removal*, 129; Abert to Cass, January 14, 1836, ASPMA 6:609; Government Agents, January 14, 1836, ASPMA 6:590; Herring to Bright, March 18, 1834, ASPMA 6:586.

2. U.S. Congress, *House Documents*, 25th Cong., 2nd sess., 1838, no. 452, "Alleged Frauds on Creek Indians," 72–73 (hereafter referred to as *House Doc.* 452); Young, "Creek Frauds," 422–23.

3. *House Doc.* 452, 72–73; Young, "Creek Frauds," 422–23.

4. *House Doc.* 452, 72–73; Young, "Creek Frauds," 422–23.

5. Abert to Sanford, November 20, 1834, Sanford Papers, ADAH.

6. *House Doc.* 452, 62–63.

7. H. King, "Historical Sketches," 198, 201; *House Doc.* 452, 62–63; Upper Creek Chiefs to Secretary of War, September 4, 1836, ASPMA 6:641–42; Tarrant to Cass, March 27, 1835, ASPMA 6:781; Hogan to Gibson, April 8, 1835, ASPMA 6:723–24; Hogan to Gibson, May 9, 1835, ASPMA 6:724–25; Hogan to Gibson, June 18, 1835, ASPMA 6:729; Meserve, "Chief Opothleyahola," 442.

8. *House Doc.* 452, 62–63.

9. Foreman, *Indian Removal*, 129–32; *House Doc.* 452, 20; McHenry to Cass, March 12, 1834, ASPMA 6:639; Creek Chiefs to Secretary of War, March 16, 1835, ASPMA 6:645–46; McHenry to Herring, March 15, 1835, ASPMA 6:648; McHenry to Cass, April 17, 1835, ASPMA 6:651; Hogan to Gibson, July 5, 1835, ASPMA 6:430; Herring to Cass, June 6, 1836, ASPMA 6:576.

10. U.S. Congress, *House Documents*, 24th Cong., 2nd sess., 1837, no. 154, "Hostilities with Creek Indians," 27 (hereafter referred to as *House Doc.* 154); *House Doc.* 452, 19, 65, 97–99.

11. *House Doc.* 452, 57, 63–65; *House Doc.* 154, 58.

12. *House Doc.* 452, 47; *House Doc.* 452, 33–35, 55.

13. *House Doc.* 452, 22, 29–31; *House Doc.* 154, 39–43.

14. Tallapoosa County Bicentennial Committee, *Tallapoosa*, 37, 121; Lindsay, *Reason for the Tears*, 34–35.

15. *House Doc.* 452, 8, 18, 32–33, 36–38; Foreman, *Indian Removal*, 133; *House Doc.* 154, 29.

16. *House Doc.* 452, 39–43.

17. *House Doc.* 452, 39–43.

18. Young, *Redskins, Ruffleshirts, and Rednecks*, 86–87; Citizens to President, May 19, 1835, ASPMA 6:655–56; McHenry to Cass, May 23, 1835, ASPMA 6:656; Hogan to Cass, March 8, 1836, ASPMA 6:751.

19. *House Doc.* 452, 97–99; Sanford to Cass, May 15, 1835, ASPMA 6:654; Harris to McHenry, June 18, 1835, ASPMA 6:599; Sanford to Cass, June 22, 1835, ASPMA 6:660–61; McHenry to Cass, July 22, 1835, ASPMA 6:622; Sanford to Secretary of War, August 18, 1835, ASPMA 6:622; Creek Chiefs to President, August 25, 1835, ASPMA 6:662–63.

20. Foreman, *Indian Removal*, 134; Hogan to Cass, March 31, 1835, ASPMA 6:722; Hogan to Gibson, April 3, 1835, ASPMA 6:722–23; McHenry to Cass, April 17, 1835, ASPMA 6:651; Hogan to Gibson, May 9, 1835, ASPMA 6:724–25; Hogan to Gayle, June 2, 1835, ASPMA 6:727.

21. For the flight of Creeks to the Cherokee and Chickasaw nations, see Foreman, *Indian Removal*, 114, 126, 142, 188, 190. For the Tuskenea-Walker plan, see Hogan to Gibson, June 3, 1835, ASPMA 6:726; Hogan to Gibson, June 8, 1835, ASPMA 6:726–27; Hogan to Gibson, July 5, 1835, ASPMA 6:430; Hays, Creek Indian Letters, 1830–39, GDAH, pt. 4, 717.

22. Page to Gibson, May 9, 1835, ASPMA 6:766; Hogan to Gibson, May 14, 1835, ASPMA 6:725–26.

23. Bean to Cass, February 24, 1833, *Columbus Enquirer*, June 19, 1835, 2; Blue to Hogan, July 4, 1835, ASPMA 6:731; Hogan to Gibson, July 5, 1835, ASPMA 6:430–31; Hogan to Gibson, July 8, 1835, ASPMA 6:731; Sommerville to Hogan, July 10, 1835, ASPMA 6:733; Meserve, "Chief Opothleyahola," 442–43.

24. Hogan to Gibson, July 12, 1835, ASPMA 6:733–34; Hunter to Hogan, July 13, 1835, ASPMA 6:736; Hogan to Gibson, June 18, 1835, ASPMA 6:729.

25. *House Doc.* 452, 97–99; Hogan to Gibson, July 5, 1835, ASPMA 6:430–31; Creek Chiefs to President, August 25, 1835, ASPMA 6:661–62.

26. Cass to Lower Creek Chiefs, September 9, 1835, ASPMA 6:600; Cass to Hogan, September 9, 1835, ASPMA 6:600; Herring to Tarrant, September 18, 1835, ASPMA 6:602; Hogan to Herring, October 15, 1835, ASPMA 6:667; *House Doc.* 154, 29.

27. Hogan to Gibson, November 6, 1835, ASPMA 6:746; Hogan to Gibson, July 25, 1835, ASPMA 6:735; Sommerville to Hogan, July 25, 1835, ASPMA 6:738; Hogan to Gibson, July 26, 1835, ASPMA 6:736; War Department to Hogan, September 21, 1835, ASPMA 6:777–78; Sanford and Company to Gibson, April 3, 1836, ASPMA 6:761.

28. Blue to Hogan, July 13, 1835, ASPMA 6:732–33; Hunter to Hogan, August 12, 1835, ASPMA 6:739–40; Hogan to Gibson, August 24, 1835, ASPMA 6:738; "Col. William C. Dawson," *Columbus Enquirer*, October 27, 1836, 2.

29. Sanford to Gibson, September 30, 1835, *ASPMA* 6:753–54; Hogan to Gibson, October 12, 1835, *ASPMA* 6:741; Sanford and Company to Gibson, October 23, 1835, *ASPMA* 6:754–55; Hogan to Herring, January 6, 1836, *ASPMA* 6:645.

30. Sanford and Company to Gibson, September 30, 1835, *ASPMA* 6:754; Hogan to Gibson, October 24, 1835, *ASPMA* 6:743; Sanford and Company to Gibson, October 29, 1835, *ASPMA* 6:755; Dougherty to Herring, June 5, 1835, *ASPMA* 6:558–59.

31. Brewer, *History of Coosa County*, 262; *House Doc.* 154, 17.

32. Hogan to Secretary of War, October 28, 1835, *ASPMA* 6:670; Sanford and Company to Gibson, October 29, 1835, *ASPMA* 6:755; Hogan to Jackson, November 3, 1835, *ASPMA* 6:671; Hogan to Gibson, November 4, 1835, *ASPMA* 6:743; Collins to Cass, January 29, 1836, reel 243, MP 234, RG 75, CA, LR, OIA, WD, NARA; Foreman, *Indian Removal*, 129; Hogan to Jackson, September 1835, *ASPMA* 6:663–64; *House Doc.* 154, 17.

33. Sanford to Secretary of War, November 3, 1835, *ASPMA* 6:756; Blue to Hogan, November 5, 1835, *ASPMA* 6:745; Sanford to Hogan, November 3, 1835, *ASPMA* 6:745–46; Sanford and Company to Hogan, November 5, 1836, *ASPMA* 6:746; Sanford and Company to Gibson, December 3, 1835, *ASPMA* 6:757; Hogan to Gibson, November 6, 1835, *ASPMA* 6:746.

34. Hogan to Gibson, December 5, 1835, *ASPMA* 6:747; Herring to Hogan, January 18, 1836, *ASPMA* 6:612; "By Letter," *Mobile Commercial Register*, January 19, 1836, 2; "Twenty Sections of Creek Land, for Sale," *Columbus Enquirer*, February 19, 1836, 3; Hogan to Cass, March 18, 1836, *ASPMA* 6:617; Herring to McHenry, January 10, 1836, *ASPMA* 6:607; Cass to Hogan, January 15, 1836, *ASPMA* 6:611.

35. Hogan to Herring, January 6, 1836, *ASPMA* 6:645; Hogan to Herring, January 22, 1836, *ASPMA* 6:686–87; Hogan to Herring, February 14, 1836, *ASPMA* 6:690; *House Doc.* 154, 7, 45–51.

36. *House Doc.* 154, 13–14; J. A. Campbell, "Creek Indian War," 166.

37. Hogan to Gibson, July 5, 1835, *ASPMA* 6:430; Hogan to Herring, January 11, 1836, *ASPMA* 6:685; Hogan to Cass, February 1, 1836, *ASPMA* 6:613; Hogan to Herring, February 14, 1836, *ASPMA* 6:690; "For the Enquirer," *Columbus Enquirer*, April 22, 1836, 3.

38. *House Doc.* 154, 13, 34; Shorter to Secretary of War, November 10, 1835, *ASPMA* 6:673–75; Land Companies to President, November 18, 1835, *ASPMA* 6:676; Shorter to Secretary of War, January 9, 1836, *ASPMA* 6:684; Herring to Shorter, January 18, 1836, *ASPMA* 6:612; Herring to Hogan, January 18, 1836, *ASPMA* 6:612; Hogan to Gibson, January 23, 1836, *ASPMA* 6:748; Shorter to Secretary of War, February 18, 1836, *ASPMA* 6:690; Citizens to Cass, February 20, 1836, *ASPMA* 6:692–93; Citizens to Secretary of War, February 20, 1836, *ASPMA* 6:690–91; Page to Gibson, April 9, 1836, *ASPMA* 6:767; Howard to Cass, May 9, 1836, *ASPMA* 6:654. One outraged land buyer expressed another common question in his letter to Washington: "Is it indeed true that the Government is more partial to the *Indians* than to its own *citizens*?" (Bissell to Secretary of War, March 8, 1836, reel 243, MP 234, RG 75, CA, LR, OIA, WD, NARA).

39. Cass to Hogan, January 16, 1836, *ASPMA* 6:611–12; Gibson to Sanford and Company, January 30, 1836, *ASPMA* 6:697; War Department to Burney and Anderson, February 16, 1836, reel 243, MP 234, RG 75, CA, LR, OIA, WD, NARA; Hogan to Cass, March 8, 1836, *ASPMA* 6:751; Cass to Hogan, Burney, and Anderson, March 8, 1836, *ASPMA* 6:614–15; Cass to Sanford and Company, March 12, 1836, *ASPMA* 6:780; Hogan to Herring, March 30, 1836, *ASPMA* 6:618–19; Hogan to Cass, April 3, 1836, *ASPMA* 6:620; War Department to Lyon, May 9, 1836, *ASPMA* 6:621; Prucha and Carmody, "Memorandum of Lewis Cass."

40. Cass to Mardis, December 26, 1834, ASPMA 6:592; "We are pleased," *Columbus Enquirer*, March 18, 1836, 2; Page to Gibson, April 9, 1836, ASPMA 6:767; "For the Enquirer," *Columbus Enquirer*, April 22, 1836, 3; Hogan to Cass, April 22, 1836, ASPMA 6:707–8; *House Doc.* 154, 16.

41. For information on Creek estates, see reel 26, LGM 26, vol. A, Deed Records, 1833–37, Miscellaneous Probate Records, Talladega County, ADAH; reel 21, LGM 27, vol. A, Will Records, 1833–41, Talladega County, Miscellaneous Probate Records, Talladega County, ADAH; reel 2, LGM 28, vol. C-1, Orphans Court Minutes, 1843–47, Miscellaneous Probate Records, Talladega County, ADAH; reel 21, LGM 114, Indian Estate Records 1834–46, Miscellaneous Probate Records, Chambers County, ADAH; Lindsay, *Reason for the Tears*, 78; J. P. Wright, *Glimpses into the Past*, 128. For Creek inheritance problems, see Collins to Cass, January 29, 1836, reel 243, MP 234, RG 75, CA, LR, OIA, WD, NARA; Foreman, *Indian Removal*, 129; Hogan to Jackson, September 1835, ASPMA 6:663–64. For information on the Creeks and the county courts, see Yamaguchi, "Macon County," 66, and Orr, "History of Lafayette," 11–12.

42. Hogan to Gibson, May 9, 1835, ASPMA 6:724; McHenry to Cass, March 17, 1834, ASPMA 6:639; Yamaguchi, "Macon County," 52, 57.

43. Swanton, "Green Corn Dance," 179; Foreman, *Indian Removal*, 125–26, 142; Martineau, *Society in America*, 1:292; Power, *Impressions of America*, 2:137–38.

44. Swanton, "Green Corn Dance," 184; Indictment, October 16, 1834, Gayle Pardons, Paroles, and Clemency Files, 1831–35, Russell County, ADAH; Goldthwaite to Gayle, November 11, 1834, Gayle Pardons, Paroles, and Clemency Files, 1831–35, Russell County, ADAH; Grenshaw to Gayle, October 15, 1834, Gayle Pardons, Paroles, and Clemency Files, 1831–35, Russell County, ADAH.

45. Foreman, *Indian Removal*, 138; Hooper, *Captain Simon Suggs*, 69; Hogan to Gibson, June 18, 1835, ASPMA 6:729. Vandiver tells of the stickball games in "Pioneer Talladega," 44. See also Cherry, "History of Opelika," 191.

46. For the whites' use of Indian land, see Cherry, "History of Opelika," 317, 445, 464; Vandiver, "Pioneer Talladega," 16; Yamaguchi, "Macon County," 49. For the settlers' use of Indian labor, see "For the Enquirer," *Columbus Enquirer*, April 22, 1836, 3; Hogan to Clay, January 30, 1836, ASPMA 6:749; Smartt, *History of Eufaula*, 21.

47. Hogan to Gibson, May 9, 1836, ASPMA 6:725; Sommerville to Hogan, July 25, 1835, ASPMA 6:738. Hogan also reported that when the Creek subagent, Leonard Tarrant, announced at the Creeks' summer council meeting in 1835 that the government would make only one more annuity payment to the Indians in Alabama, the news "flew like wildfire among the whites, for nearly every second man on the ground had his pockets filled with accounts against the Indians, and these scamps are the very men that retard the emigration, although they make great professions in favor of their removal" (Hogan to Gibson, June 18, 1835, ASPMA 6:728–29). See also Foreman, *Indian Removal*, 141, for a list of forces working against the Creek removal.

48. A. Walker, *Backtracking in Barbour County*, 19, 77; Cherry, "History of Opelika," 186; Crawford to Cass, January 26, 1834, ASPMA 6:635–36; Crawford to Cass, March 2, 1834, ASPMA 6:638; Creek Chiefs to Secretary of War, March 16, 1835, ASPMA 6:645; Hogan to Cass, March 8, 1836, ASPMA 6:751; Foreman, *Indian Removal*, 130; Featherstonhaugh, *Slave States*, 152–53.

49. See Scott, *Arts of Resistance*, 140–42. For the Creeks' self-destruction, see Foreman, *Indian Removal*, 120; Page to Harris, December 24, 1836, reel 237, MP 234, RG 75, CA, LR, OIA, WD, NARA. For examples of destitution, see Foreman, *Indian Removal*, 108–10, 115; Burney and Anderson to Cass, June 10, 1836, reel 243, MP 234, RG 75, CA, LR, OIA, WD, NARA.

4. Resistance

1. Sociologists and social anthropologists have produced a substantial literature on this sort of resistance, as well as on rural rebellions in Europe, Africa, and Asia. However, scholars seldom if ever explore Native American uprisings in this context. Welch, *Anatomy of Rebellion*, is an interesting example of scholarship in this area. For particular acts of Creek resistance, see "From the Flag of the Union," May 10, 1836, repr., *Mobile Commercial Register*, May 16, 1836, 2; Howard to Cass, May 9, 1836, ASPMA 6:578; Howard to Mitchell, May 9, 1836, ASPMA 6:653; Coulter, *People Courageous*, 3.

2. Lumpkin to Cass, February 5, 1834, ASPMA 6:636–37; Citizens to Lumpkin, May 27, 1834, ASPMA 6:641; Lumpkin to Cass, June 7, 1834, ASPMA 6:641; Lumpkin to Cass, June 28, 1834, ASPMA 6:642; Tarrant to Cass, August 20, 1834, ASPMA 6:642.

3. "Difficulties of a Serious Character," *Columbus Enquirer*, February 6, 1835, 3. For information on the extreme winter of 1835, see *Columbus Enquirer*, January 10, 1835, 3; February 13, 1835, 3; March 6, 1835, 2; March 13, 1835, 3. For depredations, see Hays, Creek Indian Letters, 1830–39, GDAH, pt. 4, 1191–95, 1201–4, 1222, 1225, 1229, 1233, 1238.

4. Both Rogin, *Fathers and Children*, and Sellers, *Market Revolution*, discuss the growth of the United States' market economy and the fracturing impact it had on society. However, Rogin looks primarily at psychological effects, while Sellers deals with the nation's institutions. For New Alabama's people, see Featherstonhaugh, *Slave States*, 151–53; Hamilton, *Men and Manners*, 2:332; Buckingham, *Slave States of America*, 258.

5. The terms "respectables" and "roughs" come from Collins, *White Society*, ch. 10. For class conflict on the U.S. frontier, consult R. Brown, "American Vigilante Tradition," 131–32. For vigilance in Alabama, see Orr, "History of Lafayette," 16; R. Brown, "American Vigilante Tradition," 99–100; Bragg, "Captain Slick," 124–34.

6. For the association of Creeks and roughs, see Cherry, "History of Opelika," 208–13; Hays, Creek Indian Letters, 1830–39, GDAH, pt. 4, 1222, 1236; Anthony, "Cherokee County," 34; M. Thompson, *Barbour County*, 49; "Case of Negro Stealing," *Milledgeville Federal Union*, August 8, 1835, 2; Lindsay, *Reason for the Tears*, 77. For information on the Fannin murder and the subsequent jail break, see Elliott to Gayle, September 9, 1835, Gayle Pardons, Paroles, and Clemency Files, 1831–35, Russell County, ADAH; "Mr. William Fannin," *Columbus Enquirer*, April 17, 1835, 3. "Strikers" was the name the land speculators gave to the blacks they sent into the Indian country to do their bidding. Military officers also called their paid servants strikers, which suggests the speculators saw their campaign to take the Creek domain as a near military operation.

7. Gayle to Cass, May 27, 1835, Gayle Executive Letter Book, ADAH; Foreman, *Indian Removal*, 138; E. Thompson, *English Working Class*, 615–16.

8. Mitchell to Howard, May 7, 1836, ASPMA 6:576, 654; Irwin to Clay, May 20, 1836, Clay Administrative Files, Creek War, ADAH; Irwin to Clay, May 25, 1836, Clay Administrative Files, Creek War, ADAH; Cherry, "History of Opelika," 326–28; Petition for Neah Micco, n.d., Gayle Pardons, Paroles, and Clemency Files, 1831–35, Russell County, ADAH.

9. Hamilton, *Men and Manners*, 2:259–60, 333–39; Martineau, *Society in America*, 1:292; Power, *Impressions of America*, 2:137–38.

10. Ingram, *History of Tallapoosa County*, 4; Lindsay, *Reason for the Tears*, 77; Page to Clay, April 5, 1836, ASPMA 6:705; Page to Clay, April 5, 1836, Clay Administrative Files, Creek War, ADAH; Hogan to Gayle, June 2, 1835, ASPMA 6:728; Woodward to Clay, February 18, 1836, ASPMA 6:698;

A. Walker, *Backtracking in Barbour County*, 77. The citizens of Jacksonville, Alabama, were afraid of the local Creeks and Cherokees and claimed that out of a population of one thousand people in their town "there are not sixty guns." Martin to Clay, February 12, 1836, ASPMA 6:697. For the hanging incident, see Vandiver, "Pioneer Talladega," 29–30; Featherstonhaugh, *Slave States*, 151–53; "Report from *Columbus Enquirer*," repr., *Tallahassee Floridian*, May 2, 1835, 3.

11. John Gayle to Lewis Cass, May 27, 1835, *Columbus Enquirer*, June 19, 1835, 2; H. King, "Historical Sketches," 203–4, 208–9; Hudson, *Southeastern Indians*, 229–31.

12. Hays, Creek Indian Letters, 1830–39, GDAH, pt. 4, 307–9, 310, 1246; Hogan to Gibson, May 9, 1835, ASPMA 6:725. For the Seminole outbreak, see "Letter from a Savannah Volunteer," *Milledgeville Federal Union*, January 9, 1836, 2; "The Contest Now Promises," *Tallahassee Floridian*, January 9, 1836, 3; "Volunteers for Florida," *Mobile Commercial Register*, January 13, 1836, 2; "Florida," *Mobile Commercial Register*, January 18, 1836, 2; "A Correspondent of the Courier," *Mobile Commercial Register*, January 28, 1836, 2; "Arson in Columbus: At Midnight on Wednesday," *Columbus Enquirer*, February 5, 1836, 3; "A Plot to Burn and Plunder Columbus," *Tallahassee Floridian*, February 6, 1836, 3.

13. "From Columbus Paper," *Mobile Commercial Register*, January 18, 1836, 2; "Public Meeting," *Columbus Enquirer*, January 22, 1836, 3; Resolution of Russell County Citizens, January 23, 1836, ASPMA 6:698; "Meeting for Purpose of Forming a Night Guard," *Columbus Enquirer*, January 29, 1836, 3; Hogan to Gibson, January 17, 1836, ASPMA 6:748.

14. Hays, Creek Indian Letters, 1830–39, GDAH, pt. 4, 1262.

15. "An Act," *Milledgeville Federal Union*, January 8, 1836, 1; Hogan to Gibson, January 30, 1836, ASPMA 6:748–49; Hogan to Cass, February 1, 1836, ASPMA 6:613; Hays, Creek Indian Letters, 1830–39, GDAH, pt. 4, 1235–37.

16. "During the Excitement," *Columbus Enquirer*, January 29, 1836, 2.

17. McCrabb to Jones, January 27, 1836, ASPMA 6:580; "The Major General," *Columbus Enquirer*, January 29, 1836, 2; Hogan to Gibson, January 30, 1836, ASPMA 6:748–49; Hogan to Clay, January 30, 1836, ASPMA 6:749.

18. Hogan to Gibson, February 1, 1836, ASPMA 6:749; Hogan to Gibson, February 1, 1836, ASPMA 6:750; Sanford and Company to the Commissary General, February 2, 1836, ASPMA 6:758; "On Monday Last," *Columbus Enquirer*, February 5, 1836, 3; Pledge of the chiefs, ASPMA 6:750; Hays, Creek Indian Letters, 1830–39, GDAH, pt. 4, 1251.

19. H. King, "Historical Sketches," 204–5, 214–15; Brewer, *History of Coosa County*, 18, 263; Swanton, "Green Corn Dance," 194–95.

20. H. King, "Historical Sketches," 215.

21. Citizens to Clay, February 4, 1836, ASPMA 6:698; Hogan to Cass, February 5, 1836, ASPMA 6:749; Stogner to Clay, February 16, 1836, ASPMA 6:698; "The War in Florida," *Milledgeville Federal Union*, February 19, 1836, 3.

22. Woodward to Clay, February 18, 1836, ASPMA 6:697–98.

23. Truman to Clay, March 5, 1836, Clay Administrative Files, Creek War, ADAH.

24. Garrett to Clay, January 25, 1836, Clay Administrative Files, Creek War, ADAH; Citizens' Resolution, Cherokee County, February 6, 1836, ASPMA 6:695; Hook to Clay, February 8, 1836, ASPMA 6:693–94; Martin to Clay, February 12, 1836, ASPMA 6:697; Garrett to Clay, March 3, 1836, ASPMA 6:700–701; Martin to Clay, March 3, 1836, ASPMA 6:700; Garrett to Father, March 10, 1836, Clay Administrative Files, Creek War, ADAH; Officers to Clay, March 15, 1836, ASPMA

6:697–98; "From the *Flag of the Union*," *Tallahassee Floridian*, April 2, 1836, 2; "The Creeks," *Milledgeville Federal Union*, March 25, 1836, 2; Foreman, *Indian Removal*, 269.

25. Garrett to Clay, January 25, 1836, Clay Administrative Files, Creek War, ADAH; Citizens to Clay, n.d., *ASPMA* 6:694–95.

26. "An Act to Authorize the Formation of One or More Companies of Cavalry..." *Milledgeville Federal Union*, January 1, 1836, 3; "Arrest of John Howard Payne," *Milledgeville Federal Union*, January 1, 1836, 3; "An Act to Amend the Militia Laws," *Milledgeville Federal Union*, January 1, 1836, 3; *Milledgeville Federal Union*, February 19, 1836, 3; "An Act to Amend Laws Dealing with Slaves and Free Persons of Color," *Milledgeville Federal Union*, February 19, 1836, 3; "Georgia, Harris County," *Milledgeville Federal Union*, February 19, 1836, 3.

27. "Depredations by Creek Indians," *Milledgeville Federal Union*, January 22, 1836, 3.

28. Clay to Miller et al., March 19, 1836, Clay Administrative Files, Creek War, ADAH.

29. Scott to Jones, January 31, 1836, *ASPMA* 7:224; Clay to Cass, February 25, 1836, *ASPMA* 6:695; "From the *Tuscaloosa Intelligencer*," February 20, 1836, repr., *Columbus Enquirer*, March 11, 1836, 2; Clay to Harding, March 2, 1836, Clay Administrative Files, Creek War, ADAH; "From the *Montgomery Advertiser*," March 8, 1836, repr., *Milledgeville Federal Union*, March 25, 1836, 3.

30. King to Clay, March 14, 1836, Clay Administrative Files, Creek War, ADAH; Clay to Officers, March 19, 1836, Clay Administrative Files, Creek War, ADAH; Cass to Clay, March 19, 1836, *ASPMA* 6:226–27.

31. Hogan to Cass, March 8, 1836, *ASPMA* 6:751–52; Cass to Clay, March 12, 1836, *ASPMA* 6:627.

32. The *Columbus Enquirer* served as the voice of the speculators and published the most criticisms of Hogan. See "Indian Affairs," *Columbus Enquirer*, March 11, 1836, 2.

33. "Twenty Sections of Creek Land, for Sale," *Columbus Enquirer*, February 19, 1836, 3; Hogan to Cass, March 18, 1836, *ASPMA* 6:617; Creek Chiefs to President, reel 243, MP 234, RG 75, CA, LR, OIA, WD, NARA.

34. Nunn, "On Moving the Creek Indians West," June 13, 1976, Articles, Alexander Nunn Collection, CVCC.

35. Nunn, "On Moving the Creek Indians West," June 13, 1976, Articles, Alexander Nunn Collection, CVCC.

36. Hogan to Cass, March 8, 1836, *ASPMA* 6:752–53. Furthermore, the War Department had assigned two men to help him in the investigations, J. W. Burney and George W. Anderson ("The Creeks," *Southern Advocate*, May 3, 1836, 3).

37. Fanon sees resistance and self-destruction (autodestruction) among colonized people as part of the same process, leading ultimately to armed revolt against the colonizers. The same stage of shock, self-destruction, heightened emotionalism, and outright revolt that Fanon witnessed among the Algerians under French rule were evident among the Lower Creeks during the years 1832 to 1836 (*Wretched of the Earth*, 54–58).

38. Clay to Cass, March 22, 1836, *ASPMA* 6:697; Glenn to Howard, March 29, 1836, *ASPMA* 6:705; McCrabb to Jones, April 4, 1836, *ASPMA* 6:579; Page to Clay, April 5, 1836, *ASPMA* 6:705; Abercrombie and Carey to Clay, April 9, 1836, *ASPMA* 6:702–3; "Committee to Clay," April 12, 1836, *ASPMA* 6:709–10; "From the *Flag of the Union*," n.d., repr., *Mobile Commercial Register*, May 16, 1836, 2.

39. J. W. Martin, *Sacred Revolt*, 143–44; Wickman, *Tree That Bends*, 47.

40. H. King, "Historical Sketches," 216; *House Doc.* 154, 27.

41. Swanton, "Green Corn Dance," 181, 183. The concept of the hidden transcript comes from Scott, *Arts of Resistance*.

42. "Military," *Columbus Enquirer*, March 11, 1836, 2; Howard to Clay, April 2, 1836, Clay Administrative Files, Creek War, ADAH; Abercrombie and Carey to Clay, April 9, 1836, *ASPMA* 6:702–3.

43. McCrabb to Jones, April 4, 1836, *ASPMA* 6:579; Page to Gibson, April 9, 1836, *ASPMA* 6:767–68; Clay to Cass, April 15, 1836, *ASPMA* 6:704.

44. Cass to Clay, April 15, 1836, *ASPMA* 6:626; "Letter from General McComb to Secretary of War," April 25, 1836, repr., Milledgeville Federal Union, June 2, 1836, 1.

45. Page to Gibson, May 20, 1836, *ASPMA* 6:771–72.

46. Clay to Harding, April 17, 1836, Clay Administrative Files, Creek War, ADAH; Clay to Shearer, April 18, 1836, *Mobile Commercial Register*, May 13, 1836, 2; Clay to Irwin, April 25, 1836, Clay Administrative Files, Creek War, ADAH.

47. Shearer to Clay, May 2, 1836, Clay Administrative Files, Creek War, ADAH; Hogan to Cass, April 24, 1836, *ASPMA* 6:709.

48. "Creek Difficulties," Milledgeville Federal Union, May 5, 1836, 2.

49. "The Lower Creeks," Milledgeville Federal Union, May 12, 1836, 3.

50. Clay to Cass, April 18, 1836, *ASPMA* 6:706–7; Clay to Cass, April 25, 1836, *ASPMA* 6:710; McIntosh to Jones, May 2, 1836, *ASPMA* 6:579; Cass to Clay, May 5, 1836, *ASPMA* 6:628.

51. Howard to Mitchell, May 9, 1836, *ASPMA* 6:653.

5. Rebellion

1. "John B. Hogan to the Editor," *Montgomery Advertiser*, June 1, 1836, repr., Milledgeville Federal Union, July 12, 1836, 2; *House Doc.* 154, 41.

2. H. King, "Historical Sketches," 216–17; Hays, Creek Indian Letters, 1830–39, GDAH, pt. 4, 1280.

3. *House Doc.* 154, 15; Salli to Cass, May 13, 1836, reel 225, MP 234, RG 75, CA, LR, OIA, WD, NARA, 150–52; Hobsbawn, *Primitive Rebels*, 3–5.

4. "Hogan to Editor," *Montgomery Advertiser*, June 1, 1836, repr., Milledgeville Federal Union, July 12, 1836, 2; Hays, Creek Indian Letters, 1830–39, GDAH, pt. 4, 1289–90; "From the Columbus Sentinel," May 27, 1836, repr., Milledgeville Federal Union, June 2, 1836, 3; Cherry, "History of Opelika," 518; Page to Gibson, May 16, 1836, *ASPMA* 6:771; Columbus Enquirer Extra, n.d., repr., Milledgeville Federal Union, May 19, 1836, 2; Citizens Committee to Clay, Wetumpka, May 13, 1836, Clay Administrative Files, Creek War, ADAH; Nunn, *Yesterdays in Loachapoka*, 8, 60.

5. "Creek War and Massacre," *Columbus Enquirer*, May 13, 1836, 3; McIntosh to Adjutant General, May 7, 1836, *ASPMA* 6:580; Page to Gibson, May 8, 1836, *ASPMA* 6:768; Mitchell to Howard, May 7, 1836, *ASPMA* 6:576, 654; M. Thompson, *Barbour County*, 62; A. Walker, *Russell County in Retrospect*, 126–28; Nunn, "On Moving the Creek Indians West," June 13, 1976, Articles, Alexander Nunn Collection, CVCC; McCann, "Aunt Susan Thomas."

6. "From the *Columbus Sentinel*," May 27, 1836, repr., Milledgeville Federal Union, June 2, 1836, 3; Cherry, "History of Opelika," 518; Page to Gibson, May 16, 1836, *ASPMA* 6:771; Columbus Enquirer Extra, May 10, 1836, repr., Milledgeville Federal Union, May 19, 1836, 2; Citizens Committee to Clay, May 13, 1836, Clay Administrative Files, Creek War, ADAH; Nunn, *Yesterdays in Loachapoka*, 8, 60; Clark to Clay, January 4, 1837, Clay Administrative Files, Creek War, ADAH.

7. Abbott to Herring, May 31, 1836, reel 243, MP 234, RG 75, CA, LR, OIA, WD, NARA; Cherry, "History of Opelika," 249, 296, 291, 325–26, 531–33; A. Walker, *Russell County in Retrospect*, 128; Nunn, "Indian Uprising, 1836," April 4, 1976, Articles, Alexander Nunn Collection, CVCC; Fanon, *Wretched of the Earth*, 144–46.

8. Mitchell to Howard, May 7, 1836, ASPMA 6:576; Cherry, "History of Opelika," 337; S. King, *Georgia Voices*, 96.

9. "Creek War and Massacre," *Columbus Enquirer*, May 13, 1836, 3; "Indian Wars and Murders," *Columbus Sentinel*, May 6, 1836, repr., *Milledgeville Federal Union*, May 19, 1836, 2; "To the Editor," *Columbus Sentinel*, May 6, 1836, repr., *Milledgeville Federal Union*, May 19, 1836, 2.

10. "Creek War and Massacre," *Columbus Enquirer*, May 13, 1836, 3; "Indian Wars and Murders," *Columbus Sentinel*, May 6, 1836, repr., *Milledgeville Federal Union*, May 19, 1836, 2; "To the Editor," *Columbus Sentinel*, May 6, 1836, repr., *Milledgeville Federal Union*, May 19, 1836, 2; Cherry, "History of Opelika," 434, 506; Bailey to Schley, May 13, 1836, *Milledgeville Federal Union*, May 19, 1836, 2; "Creek War and Massacre," *Columbus Enquirer*, May 13, 1836, 3; "The Creeks," *Columbus Enquirer*, June 9, 1836, 3; Towns to Cass, May 24, 1836, ASPMA 6:556–57; Cass to Towns, May 25, 1836, ASPMA 6:225.

11. "An Appeal," *Columbus Enquirer*, May 13, 1836, 3; Foreman, *Indian Removal*, 145; "Indian Wars and Murders," *Columbus Sentinel*, May 6, 1836, 2; Fretwell, *This So Remote Frontier*, 240; Shorter to Cass, May 13, 1836, ASPMA 6:712.

12. Orr, "History of Lafayette," 14; Richards, "Chambers County," 438–39; Beeson, *History of Eufaula*, 12–13.

13. Citizens to Clay, May 30, 1836, Clay Administrative Files, Creek War, ADAH; "The Cherokees," *Milledgeville Federal Union*, June 9, 1836, 3; "Our Indian Neighbors," *Milledgeville Federal Union*, June 2, 1836, 2; "The Cherokees Are Up!!!" *Milledgeville Federal Union*, June 16, 1836, 3.

14. "From the Columbus Herald," May 21, 1836, repr., *Milledgeville Federal Union*, June 2, 1836, 2; "Postscript," *Columbus Enquirer*, May 20, 1836, 3; "Report of Captain William Davis," *Columbus Enquirer*, May 28, 1836, 2.

15. *Mobile Commercial Register*, May 19, 1836, 2; "From the Macon Messenger," June 6, 1836, repr., *Milledgeville Federal Union*, June 16, 1836, 2; Shackleford to Clay, May 19, 1836, Clay Administrative Files, Creek War, ADAH; "From the Macon Telegraph," May 19, 1836, repr., *Milledgeville Federal Union*, May 26, 1836, 2; "From the Columbus Enquirer," May 20, 1836, repr., *Milledgeville Federal Union*, May 26, 1836, 2; "From the Columbus Sentinel," May 20, 1836, repr., *Milledgeville Federal Union*, May 26, 1836, 2; Cherry, "History of Opelika," 384, 293–95, 518.

16. "Statement of Rev. J. E. Dawson," *Columbus Enquirer*, May 14, 1836, 2; Abbott to Herring, May 31, 1836, reel 243, MP 234, RG 75, CA, LR, OIA, WD, NARA; *Mobile Commercial Register*, May 19, 1836, 2; "Letter from N. Blue," *Mobile Commercial Register*, May 16, 1836, 2. One Russell County settler complained of neglect by the people of Old Alabama with the words, "My God! are we, the honest settlers of this new country, to be branded with disturbing the peace of the citizens of Alabama by crying for help, when we are daily witnessing scenes of barbarity at which the basest savage should shudder!" ("B. H. Baker to Editors," *Columbus Enquirer*, May 20, 1836, 3).

17. "By a Letter," *Columbus Enquirer*, June 3, 1836, 2; "Extract of a letter," *Milledgeville Federal Union*, June 23, 1836, 2; "From the Columbus Enquirer," June 1, 1836, repr., *Milledgeville Federal Union*, June 2, 1836, 2; Stone to Clay, May 20, 1836, Clay Administrative Files, Creek War, ADAH; Citizens to Clay, May 28, 1836, Clay Administrative Files, Creek War, ADAH; "From the Columbus Sentinel," June 2, 1836, repr., *Milledgeville Federal Union*, June 9, 1836, 2; *House Doc.* 154, 56.

18. Cherry, "History of Opelika," 294; "From the Columbus Enquirer," May 20, 1836, repr., *Milledgeville Federal Union*, May 26, 1836, 2; Harold Coulter, "The Creek War of '36," *Columbus Enquirer*, August 11, 1974, 5; Foreman, *Indian Removal*, 145.

19. Cherry, "History of Opelika," 294; "From the Columbus Enquirer," May 20, 1836, repr., *Milledgeville Federal Union*, May 26, 1836, 2; Harold Coulter, "The Creek War of '36," *Columbus Enquirer*, August 11, 1974, 5; Foreman, *Indian Removal*, 145.

20. *Columbus Enquirer Extra*, May 10, 1836, repr., *Milledgeville Federal Union*, May 19, 1836, 2; "Indian Wars and Murders," *Columbus Sentinel*, May 6, 1836, repr., *Milledgeville Federal Union*, May 19, 1836, 2; "Creek War Incidents," *Columbus Republican Herald Extra*, May 16, 1836, repr., *Milledgeville Federal Union*, May 19, 1836, 2; Hays, Creek Indian Letters, 1830–39, GDAH, pt. 4, 1289–90; Lindsay, *Reason for the Tears*, 74.

21. "Postscript," *Columbus Enquirer*, May 20, 1836, 3; Page to Gibson, May 12, 1836, ASPMA 6:771; Towns to Cass, May 24, 1836, ASPMA 6:656–57.

22. "Postscript," *Columbus Enquirer*, May 20, 1836, 3; Page to Gibson, May 20, 1836, ASPMA 6:772; "From the Columbus Republican Herald," May 31, 1836, repr., *Milledgeville Federal Union*, June 9, 1836, 2.

23. Page to Gibson, May 20, 1836, ASPMA 6:771–72.

24. Scott to Jones, June 26, 1836, ASPMA 7:350; "From the Columbus Republican Herald," May 31, 1836, repr., *Milledgeville Federal Union*, June 9, 1836, 2; "Corrected Account of Roanoke Attack," *Columbus Enquirer*, May 20, 1836, repr., *Milledgeville Federal Union*, May 26, 1836, 2; "Massacre at Roanoke," *Columbus Enquirer*, May 20, 1836, repr., *Milledgeville Federal Union*, June 2, 1836, 2; Hays, Creek Indian Letters, 1830–39, GDAH, pt. 4, 1297.

25. "From the Columbus Enquirer," May 20, 1836, repr., *Milledgeville Federal Union*, May 26, 1836, 2; "The Creek Indians," May 20, 1836, repr., *Milledgeville Federal Union*, May 19, 1836, 2; Hays, Creek Indian Letters, 1830–39, GDAH, pt. 4, 1283, 1307.

26. "Creeks," *Columbus Enquirer*, May 28, 1836, 2; "From the Columbus Sentinel," May 20, 1836, repr., *Milledgeville Federal Union*, May 26, 1836, 2–3; Hays, Creek Indian Letters, 1830–39, GDAH, pt. 4, 1297, 1300–1301, 1310.

27. "Creeks," *Columbus Enquirer*, May 28, 1836, 2; "From the Columbus Sentinel," May 20, 1836, repr., *Milledgeville Federal Union*, May 26, 1836, 2–3; "From the Columbus Enquirer," May 20, 1836, repr., *Milledgeville Federal Union*, May 26, 1836, 2; *Columbus Enquirer*, May 27, 1836, 3.

28. "Further News from Roanoke," *Columbus Enquirer*, May 20, 1836, 2.

29. Schley to Bailey, May 19, 1836, *Columbus Enquirer*, June 16, 1836, 3; "General Orders," *Columbus Enquirer*, May 29, 1836, 3.

30. "General Orders," *Milledgeville Federal Union*, May 19, 1836, 3; Schley to Cass, May 12, 1836, ASPMA 6:712; Schley to Cass, May 17, 1836, ASPMA 6:46.

31. "Tribute to the Brave," *Milledgeville Federal Union*, June 23, 1836, 2–3; "Troops," *Columbus Enquirer*, May 20, 1836, 3.

32. "On to the Rescue," *Milledgeville Federal Union*, May 26, 1836, 3.

33. "Troops," *Columbus Enquirer*, May 20, 1836, 3; Cherry, "History of Opelika," 400; "Wednesday, May 18," *Columbus Enquirer*, May 20, 1836, 2; "From the Columbus Sentinel," May 20, 1836, repr., *Milledgeville Federal Union*, May 26, 1836, 2; "From the Columbus Enquirer," May 20, 1836, repr., *Milledgeville Federal Union*, June 2, 1836, 2; "From the Macon Telegraph," June 2, 1836, repr., *Milledgeville Federal Union*, June 2, 1836, 2; Hays, Creek Indian Letters, 1830–39, GDAH, pt. 4, 1320.

34. "We Are Literally Doing Nothing," *Columbus Enquirer*, May 28, 1836, 2; "The Excitement," *Columbus Enquirer*, May 13, 1836, 3; "Published by Request," *Columbus Enquirer*, June 3, 1836, 3; "Many Families," *Milledgeville Federal Union*, June 16, 1836, 2.

35. "From the *Columbus Enquirer*," n.d., repr., *Milledgeville Federal Union*, June 16, 1836, 2; "From the *Columbus Republican Herald*," n.d., *Milledgeville Federal Union*, May 22, 1836; "Head Quarters," *Columbus Enquirer*, June 3, 1836, 3; "From the *Columbus Herald*," May 21, 1836, repr., *Milledgeville Federal Union*, June 2, 1836, 2; "From the *Columbus Sentinel*," May 27, 1836, repr., *Milledgeville Federal Union*, June 2, 1836, 3; "From the *Macon Telegraph*," June 2, 1836, repr., *Milledgeville Federal Union*, June 9, 1836, 2; Irwin to Clay, May 25, 1836, Clay Administrative Files, Creek War, ADAH; Hays, Creek Indian Letters, 1830–39, GDAH, pt. 4, 1319.

36. "Head Quarters," *Columbus Enquirer*, May 30, 1836, 3; "From the *Columbus Sentinel*," May 27, 1836, repr., *Milledgeville Federal Union*, June 2, 1836, 3; "From the *Columbus Herald*," May 31, 1836, repr., *Milledgeville Federal Union*, June 9, 1836, 2; "From the *Columbus Sentinel*," June 2, 1836, repr., *Milledgeville Federal Union*, June 9, 1836, 2; "Troops," *Columbus Enquirer*, May 27, 1836, 3; "From the *Macon Telegraph*," June 2, 1836, repr., *Milledgeville Federal Union*, June 9, 1836, 2; "From the *Columbus Enquirer*," June 3, 1836, repr., *Milledgeville Federal Union*, June 9, 1836, 2.

37. "Troops," *Columbus Enquirer*, May 20, 1836, 3; "Troops," *Columbus Enquirer*, May 27, 1836, 2–3; "From the *Columbus Sentinel*," May 27, 1836, repr., *Milledgeville Federal Union*, June 2, 1836, 3; "We Sincerely Regret," *Columbus Enquirer*, June 9, 1836, 2–3; Hays, Creek Indian Letters, 1830–39, GDAH, pt. 4, 1323.

38. Clay to Abercrombie, May 19, 1836, Clay Administrative Files, Creek War, ADAH; Orders, Pickett, n.d., Clay Administrative Files, Creek War, ADAH. Shackleford's troops included the Montgomery Cavalry, the Montgomery Guards, and the Rifle Rangers. He also led about one hundred civilian soldiers from Autauga. "Letter from Montgomery," *Mobile Commercial Register*, May 18, 1836, 2.

39. Clay to Abercrombie, May 19, 1836, Clay Administrative Files, Creek War, ADAH; Orders, Pickett, n.d., Clay Administrative Files, Creek War, ADAH; Clay to Shackleford, May 24, 1836, Clay Administrative Files, Creek War, ADAH; Orders, Clay, May 21, 1836, Clay Administrative Files, Creek War, ADAH; Orders, No. 8, Pickett, May 24, 1836, Clay Administrative Files, Creek War, ADAH; Clay to Cass, June 3, 1836, Clay Administrative Files, Creek War, ADAH.

40. Clay to Abercrombie, May 19, 1836, Clay Administrative Files, Creek War, ADAH; Clay to Harding, May 20, 1836, Clay Administrative Files, Creek War, ADAH; Clay to Martin, May 16, 1836, Clay Administrative Files, Creek War, ADAH; Harding to Clay, May 24, 1836, Clay Administrative Files, Creek War, ADAH; Clay to President and Director of the Branch Bank at Montgomery, May 20, 1836, Clay Administrative Files, Creek War, ADAH; Clay to Moore, May 24, 1836, Clay Administrative Files, Creek War, ADAH; Campbell to Hubbard, May 26, 1836, Clay Administrative Files, Creek War, ADAH; Clay to Harding, June 4, 1836, Clay Administrative Files, Creek War, ADAH.

41. "Turnipseed Letter," *Mobile Commercial Register*, May 19, 1836, 2; Shackleford to Clay, May 22, 1836, Clay Administrative Files, Creek War, ADAH; Hall to Clay, May 25, 1836, Clay Administrative Files, Creek War, ADAH; Clay to Shackleford, May 26, 1836, Clay Administrative Files, Creek War, ADAH; Pickett to Officers, May 27, 1836, Clay Administrative Files, Creek War, ADAH.

42. Irwin to Clay, May 25, 1836, Clay Administrative Files, Creek War, ADAH; Irwin to Clay, May 20, 1836, Clay Administrative Files, Creek War, ADAH.

NOTES TO PAGES 211–219

43. Irwin to Clay, May 25, 1836, Clay Administrative Files, Creek War, ADAH; Irwin to Clay, May 20, 1836, Clay Administrative Files, Creek War, ADAH.

44. Irwin to Clay, May 25, 1836, Clay Administrative Files, Creek War, ADAH; Irwin to Clay, May 20, 1836, Clay Administrative Files, Creek War, ADAH; Clay to Irwin, May 21, 1836, Clay Administrative Files, Creek War, ADAH; Clay to Scott, May 23, 1836, Clay Administrative Files, Creek War, ADAH; Booth to Clay, May 25, 1836, Clay Administrative Files, Creek War, ADAH; Lewis to Clay, May 25, 1836, Clay Administrative Files, Creek War, ADAH.

45. Shackleford to Clay, May 21, 1836, Clay Administrative Files, Creek War, ADAH; Citizens to Clay, May 24, 1836, Clay Administrative Files, Creek War, ADAH; Creek Chiefs and Warriors to Clay, May 30, 1836, Clay Administrative Files, Creek War, ADAH; Page to Gibson, May 29, 1836, *ASPMA* 7:953; Opothle Yahola to Secretary of War, n.d., reel 225, MP 234, RG 75, CA, LR, OIA, WD, NARA, 46–48.

46. Page to Cass, May 9, 1836, *ASPMA* 6:766; Opothle Yahola to Secretary of War, n.d., reel 225, MP 234, RG 75, CA, LR, OIA, WD, NARA, 46–48; Nunn, "On Moving the Creek Indians West," June 13, 1976, Articles, Alexander Nunn Collection, CVCC; Hogan to Cass, March 28, 1836, *ASPMA* 6:617; Clay to Butler, January 14, 1837, reel 238, MP 234, RG 75, CA, LR, OIA, WD, NARA.

47. Webb to Jesup, June 9, 1836, Letters Received relating to Creek and Seminole Indian Affairs in Alabama and Florida, box 24, RG 94, GJ 159, PB, OAG, NARA.

48. Citizens of Chambers County to Clay, May 24, 1836, Clay Administrative Files, Creek War, ADAH; "Beall's Report," *Columbus Enquirer*, May 27, 1836, 3; "S. J. Morris to Enquirer," *Columbus Enquirer*, June 3, 1836, 3; "From the *Columbus Enquirer*," *Milledgeville Federal Union*, June 2, 1836, 2; Beall to Clay, May 18, 1836, Clay Administrative Files, Creek War, ADAH; Citizens of Chambers to Clay, May 22, 1836, Clay Administrative Files, Creek War, ADAH; McLemore to Clay, May 23, 1836, Clay Administrative Files, Creek War, ADAH; "The War," *Columbus Enquirer*, May 21, 1836, 2; Hays, Creek Indian Letters, 1830–39, GDAH, pt. 4, 1293; Lindsay, *Reason for the Tears*, 62.

49. Brodnax and Committee to Clay, May 22, 1836, Clay Administrative Files, Creek War, ADAH; Shackleford to Clay, May 21, 1836, Clay Administrative Files, Creek War, ADAH.

50. McLemore to Clay, May 23, 1836, Clay Administrative Files, Creek War, ADAH; "From the *Columbus Enquirer*," June 3, 1836, repr., *Milledgeville Federal Union*, June 9, 1836, 2; Brodnax to Clay, May 26, 1836, Clay Administrative Files, Creek War, ADAH; Webb to Jesup, June 19, 1836, Letters Received relating to Creek and Seminole Indian Affairs in Alabama and Florida, box 24, RG 94, GJ 159, PB, OAG, NARA; Richards, "Chambers County," 427; Hays, Creek Indian Letters, 1830–39, GDAH, pt. 4, 1330.

51. "Governor's Proclamation," May 20, 1836, *Columbus Enquirer*, May 27, 1836, 3.

52. "Governor's Proclamation," May 20, 1836, *Columbus Enquirer*, May 27, 1836, 3.

53. Collins to Walker and Woodward, May 20, 1836, Clay Administrative Files, Creek War, ADAH; Goldthwaite to Campbell, May 23, 1836, Clay Administrative Files, Creek War, ADAH; Shackleford to Clay, May 23, 1836, Clay Administrative Files, Creek War, ADAH; "From the *Columbus Herald*," May 23, 1836, repr., *Milledgeville Federal Union*, June 2, 1836, 2.

54. Collins to Walker and Woodward, May 20, 1836, Clay Administrative Files, Creek War, ADAH; Goldthwaite to Campbell, May 23, 1836, Clay Administrative Files, Creek War, ADAH; Shackleford to Clay, May 23, 1836, Clay Administrative Files, Creek War, ADAH; "From the *Columbus Herald*," May 23, 1836, repr., *Milledgeville Federal Union*, June 2, 1836, 2; Campbell to Brodnax, May 27, 1836, Clay Administrative Files, Creek War, ADAH.

55. Clay to Shortridge et al., June 1, 1836, Clay Administrative Files, Creek War, ADAH; Clay to Butler, January 14, 1837, Clay Administrative Files, Creek War, ADAH; Graham et al. to Cass, May 18, 1836, reel 225, MP 234, RG 75, CA, LR, OIA, WD, NARA, 56–60; Salli to Cass, May 13, 1836, reel 225, MP 234, RG 75, CA, LR, OIA, WD, NARA, 150–52.

56. Brodnax to Clay, May 26, 1836, Clay Administrative Files, Creek War, ADAH; "The Montgomery Journal," *Columbus Enquirer*, June 3, 1836, 2.

57. Brodnax to Clay, May 26, 1836, Clay Administrative Files, Creek War, ADAH; Goldthwaite to Clay, June 4, 1836, Clay Administrative Files, Creek War, ADAH; Sworn Statement of Daniel Partridge, n.d., Clay Administrative Files, Creek War, ADAH.

58. "The War," *Columbus Enquirer*, May 21, 1836, 2; "From the *Georgia Telegraph*," June 2, 1836, repr., *Milledgeville Federal Union*, June 9, 1836, 2; Page to Scott, May 31, 1836, Clay Administrative Files, Creek War, ADAH.

59. "To the People of Georgia," *Milledgeville Federal Union*, June 2, 1836, 2; "Major General Alexander Macomb to Cass," April 25, 1836, *Milledgeville Federal Union*, June 2, 1836, 1; "Cass to C. C. Camereleno," May 4, 1836, *Columbus Enquirer*, May 20, 1836, 3; "Florida," *Columbus Enquirer*, May 20, 1836, 3; "How Is This?" *Milledgeville Federal Union*, June 9, 1836, 2; "On to the Rescue," *Milledgeville Federal Union*, May 26, 1836, 3; "Relations with France," *Milledgeville Federal Union*, January 15, 1836, 3; Mitchell, *Georgia Land and People*, 220; Elizer, "Administration of William Schley," 18–20; "From Florida," *Milledgeville Federal Union*, January 29, 1836, 2; "The Florida Campaign," *Milledgeville Federal Union*, May 19, 1836, 3.

60. Foreman, *Indian Removal*, 149.

61. Clay to Cass, June 3, 1836, Clay Administrative Files, Creek War, ADAH; Clay to Commanding Officer, May 24, 1836, Clay Administrative Files, Creek War, ADAH; Pickett to Hogan, June 12, 1836, Clay Administrative Files, Creek War, ADAH.

62. *House Doc.* 154, 17, 41, 55; Earle's Statement, n.d., Clay Administrative Files, Creek War, ADAH.

63. *Mobile Commercial Register*, May 14, 1836, 2; "Troops," *Columbus Enquirer*, May 27, 1836, 2–3.

64. "The Great Glory of This Administration," *Columbus Enquirer*, June 3, 1836, 3.

65. Jackson's troops gave him the nickname Old Hickory because of his personal toughness and the hardness of the discipline he imposed on his men.

6. The Federal Response

1. "Dixon H. Lewis to the Editor," *Columbus Enquirer*, June 3, 1836, 3; "Dixon H. Lewis to the Editor," *Columbus Enquirer*, June 9, 1836, 3; Cass to Schley, May 13, 1836, ASPMA 6:629; Cass to Schley, May 25, 1836, ASPMA 6:625–26; "Cass to Lewis," May 17, 1836, *Columbus Enquirer*, May 27, 1836, 3; Cass to President, n.d., ASPMA 6:434–35; Cass to Shorter, May 21, 1836, ASPMA 6:631; Statement of the Number, June 1836, ASPMA 7:115; Recapitulation, Adjutant General's Office, July 18, 1836, ASPMA 7:354.

2. Cass to Jesup, May 19, 1836, ASPMA 6:622–23; Cass to Jesup, May 25, 1836, ASPMA 6:631; Cass to Schley, May 20, 1836, ASPMA 6:629.

3. Cass to Jesup, May 19, 1836, ASPMA 6:623; Cass to Jesup, May 25, 1836, ASPMA 6:631–32; Cass to Call, May 23, 1836, ASPMA 6:441; Cass to Armstrong, May 20, 1836, ASPMA 6:630.

4. Cass to Jesup, May 19, 1836, ASPMA 6:623; Cass to Hogan, Anderson, and Burney, May

19, 1836, ASPMA 6:623–24; Herring to Cass, May 20, 1836, ASPMA 6:630; Gibson to Hogan, May 20, 1836, ASPMA 6:776.

5. Extract from Instructions, War Department, May 19, 1836, ASPMA 6:446.

6. Scott's Address, January 19, 1837, ASPMA 7:202; Scott to Clinch, February 26, 1836, ASPMA 7:244; Scott to Jones, May 22, 1836, ASPMA 7:313; Document 263, n.d., ASPMA 7:358; Gadsden's Statement, n.d., ASPMA 7:135.

7. "General Order No. 48," Milledgeville Federal Union, June 2, 1836, 2–3; White to Jackson, May 28, 1836, ASPMA 7:296–97; Scott to Schley, May 26, 1836, ASPMA 7:314–15; "Scott to F. M. Robertson," May 26, 1836, Columbus Enquirer, June 3, 1836, 2; "Scott to Jones, Adjutant General," Milledgeville Federal Union, June 9, 1836, 2.

8. Scott to Schley, May 26, 1836, ASPMA 7:314–15; Scott to Clark and Grayson, May 28, 1836, ASPMA 7:316; Scott to Clark and Grayson, May 26, 1836, ASPMA 7:315; Scott to Beard, May 27, 1836, ASPMA 7:315.

9. Schley's Deposition, n.d., ASPMA 7:174; Kenan's Deposition, November 27, 1836, ASPMA 7:170; Kirby's Testimony, December 19, 1836, ASPMA 7:168; Orders No. 1, Jesup, June 9, 1836, Clay Administrative Files, Creek War, ADAH; Jesup to Clay, May 31, 1836, Clay Administrative Files, Creek War, ADAH.

10. Schley's Deposition, n.d., ASPMA 7:174; Kenan's Deposition, November 27, 1836, ASPMA 7:170; Kirby's Testimony, December 19, 1836, ASPMA 7:168; Orders No. 1, Jesup, June 9, 1836, Clay Administrative Files, Creek War, ADAH; Jesup to Clay, May 31, 1836, Clay Administrative Files, Creek War, ADAH.

11. "From the Columbus Herald," May 31, 1836, repr., Milledgeville Federal Union, June 9, 1836, 2; Schley's Deposition, n.d., ASPMA 7:175; "The War," Columbus Enquirer, June 3, 1836, 3; "Since Our Last," Columbus Enquirer, June 9, 1836, 2.

12. "From the Columbus Herald," May 31, 1836, repr., Milledgeville Federal Union, June 9, 1836, 2; Schley's Deposition, n.d., ASPMA 7:175; "The War," Columbus Enquirer, June 3, 1836, 3; "Since Our Last," Columbus Enquirer, June 9, 1836, 2; Scott to Clay, May 31, 1836, ASPMA 7:318–19; Scott to Jesup, June 1, 1836, ASPMA 7:319; Schley to Clay, May 31, 1836, Clay Administrative Files, Creek War, ADAH.

13. Jesup to Cass, June 25, 1836, ASPMA 7:347; Clay to Hopothle Yoholo, June 7, 1836, Clay Administrative Files, Creek War, ADAH.

14. Clay to Moore, June 6, 1836, Clay Administrative Files, Creek War, ADAH; Clay to Hopothle Yoholo, June 7, 1836, Clay Administrative Files, Creek War, ADAH. Jesup charged Hogan with the task of feeding the families of the friendly warriors who agreed to serve as auxiliaries. Hogan apparently continued the system begun by Clay of allowing private individuals to feed the Indians, subsequently submitting their bills to the government for payment. F. G. McConnell fed the Creeks camped about Talladega during the war; Harrison Young fed the Kowaligi Creeks, procuring bacon from the merchants at Wetumpka; and Mr. Russell supplied the Indians at Tallassee. These and other individuals submitted their claims to Captain Page after the war ended and they had handed over their Native charges to the removal contractors. Jesup to Clay, June 16, 1836, Clay Administrative Files, Creek War, ADAH; Page to Gibson, November 3, 1836, reel 227, MP 234, RG 75, CA, LR, OIA, WD, NARA, 614; Page to Harris, November 15, 1836, reel 227, MP 234, RG 75, CA, LR, OIA, WD, NARA, 615; Page to Harris, November 23, 1836, reel 227, MP 234, RG 75, CA, LR, OIA, WD, NARA, 617; Chambers to Page, November 1, 1836, reel 227, MP 234, RG 75, CA, LR, OIA, WD, NARA, 618.

15. Jesup to Cass, June 11, 1836, *ASPMA* 7:325; Clay to Patterson, June 6, 1836, Clay Administrative Files, Creek War, ADAH; Valliere, "Creek War of 1836," 477; "To the Public," June 25, 1836, *Columbus Enquirer*, June 30, 1836, 3.

16. Hindmon to Clay, June 7, 1836, Clay Administrative Files, Creek War, ADAH; Clay to Garrett, June 19, 1836, Clay Administrative Files, Creek War, ADAH; Garrett to Clay, June 21, 1836, Clay Administrative Files, Creek War, ADAH; Brodnax to Clay, May 26, 1836, Clay Administrative Files, Creek War, ADAH; Clay to Nicks, June 1, 1836, Clay Administrative Files, Creek War, ADAH; Clay to Patterson, June 3, 1836, Clay Administrative Files, Creek War, ADAH; Clay to Patterson, June 6, 1836, Clay Administrative Files, Creek War, ADAH; Scott to Jones, June 2, 1836, *ASPMA* 7:317; McLemore to Clay, June 5, 1836, Clay Administrative Files, Creek War, ADAH; "S. J. Morris to Editors," June 12, 1836, *Columbus Enquirer*, June 16, 1836, 2.

17. Citizens to Clay, June 4, 1836, Clay Administrative Files, Creek War, ADAH; Clay to Commanding Officer, June 5, 1836, Clay Administrative Files, Creek War, ADAH; Clay to Stanley et al., June 5, 1836, Clay Administrative Files, Creek War, ADAH; Moore to Clay, June 7, 1836, Clay Administrative Files, Creek War, ADAH; Jesup to Scott, n.d., *ASPMA* 7:338.

18. Moore to Clay, June 11, 1836, Clay Administrative Files, Creek War, ADAH; Huger to Clay, June 12, 1836, Clay Administrative Files, Creek War, ADAH; Clay to Jesup, June 13, 1836, Clay Administrative Files, Creek War, ADAH.

19. Jesup to Cass, June 11, 1836, *ASPMA* 7:325; Jesup to Cass, June 25, 1836, *ASPMA* 7:347; "To the Public," June 25, 1836, *Columbus Enquirer*, June 30, 1836, 3; Yamaguchi, "Macon County," 223.

20. Jesup to Scott, June 20, 1836, *ASPMA* 7:337–38; Jesup to Scott, June 8, 1836, *ASPMA* 7:325.

21. Scott's Statement, January 19, 1837, *ASPMA* 7:204–5; Scott to Jones, July 2, 1836, *ASPMA* 7:350; *Columbus Enquirer*, June 3, 1836, 2; "Creek War," *Milledgeville Federal Union*, June 23, 1836, 2; "Several Skirmishes," *Columbus Enquirer*, June 9, 1836, 2; "From the *Columbus Sentinel*," June 9, 1836, repr., *Milledgeville Federal Union*, June 16, 1836, 2–3; "One of the Most Serious," *Columbus Enquirer*, June 16, 1836, 2; "Maj. Howard's Report to Gen'l Sanford, Steam Boat *Metamora*," June 13, 1836, *Columbus Enquirer*, June 23, 1836, 2.

22. Scott's Statement, January 19, 1837, *ASPMA* 7:204–5; Kirby's Testimony, December 19, 1836, *ASPMA* 7:169; Sanford's Deposition, December 17, 1836, *ASPMA* 7:172; Schley's Deposition, n.d., *ASPMA* 7:176; "Creek War Incidents," *Columbus Herald*, June 7, 1836, repr., *Milledgeville Federal Union*, June 16, 1836, 2; Motte, *Journey into the Wilderness*, 3; "Creek War," *Milledgeville Federal Union*, June 16, 1836, 2; Scott to Call, July 1, 1836, *ASPMA* 7:351; Scott to Jones, June 12, 1836, *ASPMA* 7:327.

23. Scott's Statement, January 19, 1837, *ASPMA* 7:202–5; Dawson's Deposition, January 16, 1836, *ASPMA* 7:173.

24. "Schley to Maj. H. W. Jernigan," June 15, 1836, *Columbus Enquirer*, June 23, 1836, 3; "A. B. Pope to Mr. Miller," June 16, 1836, *Columbus Enquirer*, June 23, 1836, 3; "From the *Republican Herald*," July 2, 1836, repr., *Milledgeville Federal Union*, August 9, 1836, 3; "Thomas J. Stell to Editors," August 6, 1836, *Columbus Enquirer*, August 18, 1836, 3; "Ezekiel Ward to Editors," *Columbus Enquirer*, July 14, 1836, 3.

25. Scott to Jones, July 2, 1836, *ASPMA* 7:350; Booth to Clay, June 18, 1836, Clay Administrative Files, Creek War, ADAH.

26. Scott's Statement, January 19, 1837, *ASPMA* 7:204; Betts's Deposition, n.d., *ASPMA* 7:177; Harding to Scott, June 14, 1836, *ASPMA* 7:321; Huson's Deposition, December 17, 1836, *ASPMA* 7:173.

27. Order No. 263, n.d., *ASPMA* 7:359; Moore to Clay, July 11, 1836, Clay Administrative Files, Creek War, ADAH; Jesup to Scott, June 12, 1836, *ASPMA* 7:338.

28. "From the *Columbus Sentinel*," June 3, 1836, repr., *Milledgeville Federal Union*, June 9, 1836, 2; "From the *Columbus Herald*," June 8, 1836, repr., *Milledgeville Federal Union*, June 23, 1836, 2; "From the *Columbus Sentinel*," June 17, 1836, repr., *Milledgeville Federal Union*, June 23, 1836, 2; Collins to Capt. W. Walker, May 20, 1836, Clay Administrative Files, Creek War, ADAH; Captain John Page to Jesup, June 11, 1836, Letters Received relating to Creek and Seminole Indian Affairs in Alabama and Florida, box 24, RG 94, GJ 159, PB, OAG, NARA; Collins to Jesup, July 31, 1836, Letters Received relating to Creek and Seminole Indian Affairs in Alabama and Florida, box 24, RG 94, GJ 159, PB, OAG, NARA; "Letter of Colonel Felix G. Gibson," *Southern Advocate*, July 5, 1836, 3.

29. Jesup to Cass, June 11, 1836, *ASPMA* 7:325; Jesup to Cass, June 25, 1836, *ASPMA* 7:347; "To the Public," June 25, 1836, *Columbus Enquirer*, June 30, 1836, 3; Clay to Hopothle Yahola et al., June 10, 1836, Clay Administrative Files, Creek War, ADAH; Clay to Jesup, June 12, 1836, Clay Administrative Files, Creek War, ADAH; "From an Act Making Further Appropriations," *Tallahassee Floridian*, July 30, 1836, 2. The larger group of Upper Creek warriors came from Tuckabatchee, Tallassee, Chot-lock-sof-ka, Upper Creek Eufaula, Nuyaka (New York), Fish Pond, Hatchet Creek, Kowaligi, Hillabee, and Oakfuskee. Clay to Jesup, June 14, 1836, Clay Administrative Files, Creek War, ADAH; Foreman, *Indian Removal*, 148; Opothle Yahola to Jesup, June 16, 1836, Letters Received relating to Creek and Seminole Indian Affairs in Alabama and Florida, box 24, RG 94, GJ 159, PB, OAG, NARA; Order No. 3, June 11, 1836, in Orders, June 1836 to February 13, 1837, box 45, RG 94, GJ 159, PB, OAG, NARA.

30. Jesup to Cass, June 11, 1836, *ASPMA* 7:325; Jesup to Cass, June 25, 1836, *ASPMA* 7:347; "To the Public," June 25, 1836, *Columbus Enquirer*, June 30, 1836, 3; Clay to Hopothle Yahola et al., June 10, 1836, Clay Administrative Files, Creek War, ADAH; Clay to Jesup, June 12, 1836, Clay Administrative Files, Creek War, ADAH; "From an Act Making Further Appropriations," *Tallahassee Floridian*, July 30, 1836, 2; Clay to Jesup, June 14, 1836, Clay Administrative Files, Creek War, ADAH; Foreman, *Indian Removal*, 148; Opothle Yahola to Jesup, June 16, 1836, Letters Received relating to Creek and Seminole Indian Affairs in Alabama and Florida, box 24, RG 94, GJ 159, PB, OAG, NARA; Webb to Jesup, June 19, 1836, Letters Received relating to Creek and Seminole Indian Affairs in Alabama and Florida, box 24, RG 94, GJ 159, PB, OAG, NARA; Orders No. 3, June 11, 1836, in Orders, June 1836 to February 13, 1837, box 45, RG 94, GJ 159, PB, OAG, NARA.

31. Jesup to Cass, June 11, 1836, *ASPMA* 7:325; Jesup to Cass, June 25, 1836, *ASPMA* 7:347; "To the Public," June 25, 1836, *Columbus Enquirer*, June 30, 1836, 3; Clay to Hopothle Yahola et al., June 10, 1836, Clay Administrative Files, Creek War, ADAH; Clay to Jesup, June 12, 1836, Clay Administrative Files, Creek War, ADAH; "From an Act Making Further Appropriations," *Tallahassee Floridian*, July 30, 1836, 2; Clay to Jesup, June 14, 1836, Clay Administrative Files, Creek War, ADAH; Foreman, *Indian Removal*, 148; Opothle Yahola to Jesup, June 16, 1836, Letters Received relating to Creek and Seminole Indian Affairs in Alabama and Florida, box 24, RG 94, GJ 159, PB, OAG, NARA; Webb to Jesup, June 19, 1836, Letters Received relating to Creek and Seminole Indian Affairs in Alabama and Florida, box 15, RG 94, GJ 159, PB, OAG, NARA; Orders No. 3,

June 11, 1836, in Orders, June 1836 to February 13, 1837, box 45, RG 94, GJ 159, PB, OAG, NARA; Clay to Butler, January 14, 1837, reel 238, MP 234, RG 75, CA, LR, OIA, WD, NARA.

32. Jesup to Cass, June 25, 1836, ASPMA 7:347; "To the Public," June 25, 1836, *Columbus Enquirer*, June 30, 1836, 3.

33. Jesup to Cass, June 25, 1836, ASPMA 7:347; "To the Public," June 25, 1836, *Columbus Enquirer*, June 20, 1836, 3; Clay to Garth, May 29, 1836, Clay Administrative Files, Creek War, ADAH; Jesup to Scott, June 15, 1836, ASPMA 7:332.

34. "To the Public," June 25, 1836, *Columbus Enquirer*, June 30, 1836, 3.

35. Jesup to Cass, June 25, 1836, ASPMA 7:347; Scott to Jesup, June 16, 1836, ASPMA 7:330–31.

36. Jesup to Cass, June 25, 1836, ASPMA 7:347; "Indian War," *Milledgeville Federal Union*, June 23, 1836, 3; "To the Public," June 25, 1836, *Columbus Enquirer*, June 30, 1836, 3.

37. Jesup to Cass, June 25, 1836, ASPMA 7:347; "Indian War," *Milledgeville Federal Union*, June 23, 1836, 3; "To the Public," June 25, 1836, *Columbus Enquirer*, June 30, 1836, 3.

38. "Creek War Incidents from the *Columbus Herald*," June 28, 1836, repr., *Milledgeville Federal Union*, July 7, 1836, 2; "Patterson to Clay," July 25, 1836, *Milledgeville Federal Union*, August 16, 1836, 2; Thomas Abbott, Hogan's assistant, agreed with Jesup as to the value of the Upper Creeks as allies. He wrote to the commissioner of Indian Affairs that "their formidable presence and conduct is in no small degree to be attributed the speedy and happy termination of these difficulties" (Abbott to Herring, July 9, 1836, reel 243, MP 234, RG 75, CA, LR, OIA, WD, NARA). General Patterson believed Jim Boy and Opothle Yahola deserved a "public testimonial of appreciation" (Patterson to Clay, June 22, 1836, Clay Administrative Files, Creek War, ADAH).

39. Jesup to Blair, June 20, 1836, ASPMA 7:336; Jesup to Scott, June 19, 1836, ASPMA 7:334.

40. Scott to Jesup, June 17, 1836, ASPMA 7:332–33; Scott to Jesup, June 19, 1836, ASPMA 7:335; Jesup to Cass, June 25, 1836, ASPMA 7:347.

41. Jesup to Scott, June 19, 1836, ASPMA 7:334; Scott to Jesup, June 19, 1836, ASPMA 7:335; Jesup to Blair, June 20, 1836, ASPMA 7:336.

42. "Florida to Become a State," *Tallahassee Floridian*, May 13, 1837, 3; Kieffer, *Maligned General*, 141–42; Bassett, *Correspondence of Andrew Jackson*, 419.

43. Jesup to Scott, June 20, 1836, ASPMA 7:337–38; Jesup to Cass, June 25, 1836, ASPMA 7:347; Scott to Jesup, June 21, 1836, ASPMA 7:339; Scott to Jesup, June 23, 1836, ASPMA 7:340; Scott to Jones, June 23, 1836, ASPMA 7:340.

44. Jesup to Cass, June 25, 1836, ASPMA 7:347–48; "To the Public," June 25, 1836, *Columbus Enquirer*, June 30, 1836, 3; "Movements of General Jesup," *Milledgeville Federal Union*, July 7, 1836, 2; "The War," *Milledgeville Federal Union*, June 30, 1836, 2; Patterson to Clay, June 22, 1836, Clay Administrative Files, Creek War, ADAH; Jesup to Scott, June 23, 1836, ASPMA 7:346; "Patterson to Clay," July 25, 1836, *Milledgeville Federal Union*, August 16, 1836, 2; A. Walker, *Russell County in Retrospect*, 132, 152; Jesup to Opothle Yahola, June 21, 1836, Letters Received during the Creek War, 1836–38, from Fort Mitchell Letters, box 15, RG 94, GJ 159, PB, OAG, NARA.

45. Moore to Clay, July 11, 1836, Clay Administrative Files, Creek War, ADAH; Moore to Scott, June 23, 1836, ASPMA 7:343; Moore to Jesup, July 12, 1836, Letters Received relating to Creek and Seminole Indian Affairs in Alabama and Florida, box 24, RG 94, GJ 159, PB, OAG, NARA.

46. Patterson to Clay, June 22, 1836, Clay Administrative Files, Creek War, ADAH; Abbott to

Herring, July 9, 1836, reel 243, MP 234, RG 75, CA, LR, OIA, WD, NARA; Jesup to Jones, July 12, 1836, Letters Received during the Creek War, 1836–38, box 17, RG 94, GJ 159, PB, OAG, NARA; Brodnax to Jesup, August 19, 1836, Letters Received from Governors of Alabama and Georgia, 1836–38, box 17, RG 94, GJ 159, PB, OAG, NARA; "The Creek War," *Columbus Sentinel*, June 17, 1836, repr., *Milledgeville Federal Union*, June 23, 1836, 2.

47. Scott to Jesup, June 19, 1836, ASPMA 7:335; Scott, Orders No. 15, June 21, 1836, ASPMA 7:344. Scott to Jones, June 21, 1836, ASPMA 7:333; Scott to Jones, June 23, 1836, ASPMA 7:337; Scott to Jones, June 24, 1836, ASPMA 7:345–46.

48. "Letter from Fort Mitchell," June 29, 1836, *Milledgeville Federal Union*, July 7, 1836, 3; Clay to Jesup, June 14, 1836, Clay Administrative Files, Creek War, ADAH; Hogan to Jesup, June 25, 1836, Camps and Forts, box 15, RG 94, GJ 159, PB, OAG, NARA; *House Doc.* 154, 26.

49. Muster Roll of Benjamin Young's Spy Company, n.d., General Scott's Operations in Florida and the Creek Country, box 37, RG 94, GJ 159, PB, OAG, NARA.

50. Scott to Jesup, June 21, 1836, ASPMA 7:336; Motte, *Journey into the Wilderness*, 8; Brannon, "Alabama Indian Chiefs," 67; Elkin, "Reaction and Interaction," 46; Schoolcraft, *History, Condition and Prospects*, 2:23–24.

51. Scott to Jones," June 21, 1836, ASPMA 7:333; "United States' Marines," *Columbus Sentinel*, July 1, 1836, repr., *Milledgeville Federal Union*, July 7, 1836, 2; Scott to Jesup, June 21, 1836, ASPMA 7:336, 339; "Tribute to the Brave," *Milledgeville Federal Union*, June 23, 1836, 2.

52. Motte, *Journey into the Wilderness*, 11.

53. Motte, *Journey into the Wilderness*, 11–12.

54. Scott to Jones, June 21, 1836, ASPMA 7:333; Scott to Jones, June 23, 1836, ASPMA 7:337; Orders No. 17, Lee, June 22, 1836, ASPMA 7:344.

55. "Camp Gibson, near Roanoke," *Columbus Republican Herald*, July 5, 1836, repr., *Milledgeville Federal Union*, July 12, 1836, 2; Motte, *Journey into the Wilderness*, 12–13.

56. Scott to Jesup, July 26, 1836, ASPMA 7:348–49.

57. Scott to Jones, July 2, 1836, ASPMA 7:349–50; Motte, *Journey into the Wilderness*, 15.

58. Scott to Jones, July 2, 1836, ASPMA 7:349–50; Motte, *Journey into the Wilderness*, 15–16.

59. Scott to Jones, July 2, 1836, ASPMA 7:349–50; Scott to Call, July 1, 1836, ASPMA 7:350–51; "The Notable Jim Henry," *Columbus Republican Herald*, July 5, 1836, repr, *Milledgeville Federal Union*, July 12, 1836, 2; "Patterson to Clay," July 25, 1836, *Milledgeville Federal Union*, August 16, 1836, 2; Jesup to Scott, June 24, 1836, General Scott's Operations in Florida and the Creek Country, box 37, RG 94, GJ 159, PB, OAG, NARA.

60. "Letter from Ft. Mitchell," June 29, 1836, *Milledgeville Federal Union*, July 7, 1836, 3; Scott to Jones, June 24, 1836, ASPMA 7:345–46; "The War," *Columbus Enquirer*, June 30, 1836, 2.

7. Flight through Southern Georgia

1. "Letter from Ft. Mitchell," June 29, 1836, *Milledgeville Federal Union*, July 7, 1836, 3; Scott to Jones, June 24, 1836, ASPMA 7:345–46; "The War," *Columbus Enquirer*, June 30, 1836, 2; Scott to Jones, July 2, 1836, ASPMA 7:349–50.

2. "Letter from Ft. Mitchell," June 29, 1836, *Milledgeville Federal Union*, July 7, 1836, 3; Scott to Jones, June 24, 1836, ASPMA 7:345–46; "The War," *Columbus Enquirer*, June 30, 1836, 2; Scott to Jones, July 2, 1836, ASPMA 7:349–50; Scott to Call, July 1, 1836, ASPMA 7:350–51.

3. Scott and Kenan to Jones, July 4, 1836, ASPMA 7:352; "D. Stapleton to Editors," *Columbus*

Enquirer, July 14, 1836, 3; "Michael Hentz to Governor," n.d., extract, *Milledgeville Federal Union*, July 7, 1836, 2; "The Creeks Crossing the Chattahoochee," *Georgia Telegraph*, June 30, 1836, repr., *Milledgeville Federal Union*, July 7, 1836, 2; Scott to Jones, July 6, 1836, ASPMA 7:353.

4. "Michael Hentz to Governor," n.d., extract, *Milledgeville Federal Union*, July 7, 1836, 2; "Indian Depredations and Murders," *Macon Messenger*, June 30, 1836, repr., *Milledgeville Federal Union*, July 7, 1836, 2.

5. Thronateeska Chapter, *Dougherty County*, 3–4.

6. "From the *Columbus Herald*," July 12, 1836, repr., *Milledgeville Federal Union*, July 19, 1836, 2; "Thomas N. Beall to Scott," *Milledgeville Federal Union*, July 12, 1836, 2; "Colonel Beall's Report," *Columbus Enquirer*, July 28, 1836, 2–3; G. White, *Historical Collections of Georgia*, 262.

7. "Colonel Beall's Report," *Columbus Enquirer*, July 28, 1836, 2–3; J. H. Martin, *Columbus, Georgia*, 74.

8. "In Our Last," *Columbus Enquirer*, July 14, 1836, 2; "Colonel Beall's Report," *Columbus Enquirer*, July 28, 1836, 2–3.

9. Thronateeska Chapter, *Dougherty County*, 3; "By Col. Henry Mumford," *Columbus Enquirer*, July 21, 1836, 3; "Beall to Scott," *Milledgeville Federal Union*, July 12, 1836, 3.

10. Scott to Hoxie, July 6, 1836, ASPMA 7:355; "We Have at Length," *Milledgeville Federal Union*, July 12, 1836, 3.

11. Macomb to Scott, Washington, June 28, 1836, ASPMA 7:355; Macomb to Jesup, July 7, 1836, ASPMA 7:356; Scott to Macomb, July 8, 1836, ASPMA 7:356; Order No. 29, July 7, 1836, ASPMA 7:356; "Order No. 30," July 9, 1836, *Milledgeville Federal Union*, July 19, 1836, 3; Jesup to Blair, June 20, 1836, ASPMA 7:336–37; "Gen. Scott's Recall," *Milledgeville Federal Union*, August 9, 1836, 3.

12. "From the *Columbus Sentinel*," July 22, 1836, repr., *Milledgeville Federal Union*, July 26, 1836, 2.

13. "From the *Columbus Sentinel*," July 22, 1836, repr., *Milledgeville Federal Union*, July 26, 1836, 2; "The Army," *Columbus Enquirer*, July 21, 1836, 2.

14. "Gallant Affair," *Milledgeville Federal Union*, August 16, 1836, 2; Hays, Creek Indian Letters, 1830–39, GDAH, pt. 4, 1409–10.

15. "Gallant Affair," *Milledgeville Federal Union*, August 16, 1836, 2; Hays, Creek Indian Letters, 1830–39, GDAH, pt. 4, 1409–10; "Indians in Thomas County," *Columbus Enquirer*, July 24, 1836, 3.

16. "From the *Columbus Sentinel*," July 22, 1836, repr., *Milledgeville Federal Union*, July 26, 1836, 2; Sanford to Jesup, July 12, 1836, Headquarters, Army of the South, box 17, RG 94, GJ 159, PB, OAG, NARA.

17. "The Cherokees," *Milledgeville Federal Union*, June 9, 1836, 3; "Our Indian Neighbors," *Milledgeville Federal Union*, June 2, 1836, 2; "The Cherokees Are Up!!!" *Milledgeville Federal Union*, June 16, 1836, 3; "Letter from a Friend in Walker County," *Milledgeville Federal Union*, August 30, 1836, 2; Hays, Creek Indian Letters, 1830–39, GDAH, pt. 4, 1401–2, 1417; Sanford to Jesup, July 12, 1836, Headquarters, Army of the South, box 17, RG 94, GJ 159, PB, OAG, NARA.

18. "The Cherokees," *Milledgeville Federal Union*, June 9, 1836, 3; "Our Indian Neighbors," *Milledgeville Federal Union*, June 2, 1836, 2; "The Cherokees Are Up!!!" *Milledgeville Federal Union*, June 16, 1836, 3; "Letter from a Friend in Walker County," *Milledgeville Federal Union*, August 30, 1836, 2; Hays, Creek Indian Letters, 1830–39, GDAH, pt. 4, 1401–2, 1417; Sanford to Jesup, July 12, 1836, Headquarters, Army of the South, box 17, RG 94, GJ 159, PB, OAG, NARA.

19. Ellisor, "Like So Many Wolves," 6; Hays, Creek Indian Letters, 1830–39, GDAH, pt. 4, 1402, 1417; U.S. Congress, Senate Documents, 25 Cong., 2nd sess., 1838, no. 120, "Cherokee Treaty of 1835," 607–8 (hereafter cited as Senate Doc. 120).

20. Citizens to Clay, May 30, 1836, Clay Administrative Files, Creek War, ADAH; Clay to Jesup, June 28, 1836, Governors' Letters, box 17, RG 94, GJ 159, PB, OAG, NARA.

21. Ellisor, "Like So Many Wolves," 7–8; Statement of the Number . . ., n.d., ASPMA 7:115; R. H. White, Governors of Tennessee, 126–27; Senate Doc. 120, 141–43.

22. "From the Columbus Herald," July 12, 1836, repr., Milledgeville Federal Union, July 19, 1836, 2; "From the Columbus Herald," July 16, 1836, repr., Milledgeville Federal Union, July 19, 1836, 3; Moore to Clay, July 11, 1836, Clay Administrative Files, Creek War, ADAH; Moore to Patterson, July 9, 1836, Letters Received relating to Creek and Seminole Affairs in Alabama and Florida, box 24, RG 94, GJ 159, PB, OAG, NARA.

23. "From the Columbus Herald," July 12, 1836, repr., Milledgeville Federal Union, July 19, 1836, 2; "From the Columbus Herald," July 16, 1836, repr., Milledgeville Federal Union, July 19, 1836, 3; Moore to Clay, July 11, 1836, Clay Administrative Files, Creek War, ADAH.

24. "Thomas J. Lee to Post Master," July 2, 1836, Milledgeville Federal Union, July 12, 1836, 2; Jesup to Clay, July 5, 1836, Clay Administrative Files, Creek War, ADAH; Scott to Jesup, June 26, 1836, ASPMA 7:348–49; Motte, Journey into the Wilderness, 21; "Florida War," Army and Navy Chronicle 4 (July 28, 1836): 124, 127; Van Ness to Scott, July 2, 1836, Letters Received relating to Creek and Seminole Indian Affairs in Alabama and Florida, box 24, RG 94, GJ 159, PB, OAG, NARA; House Doc. 452, 12.

25. Jesup to Clay, July 5, 1836, Clay Administrative Files, Creek War, ADAH; "From the Columbus Sentinel," June 24, 1836, repr., Milledgeville Federal Union, June 30, 1836, 2; "Letter from Columbus," June 25, 1836, repr., Milledgeville Federal Union, June 30, 1836, 3; "Creek War," Columbus Herald, June 28, 1836, repr., Milledgeville Federal Union, July 7, 1836, 2; "Letter from Camp Gibson," Columbus Republican Herald, June 28, 1836, repr., Milledgeville Federal Union, July 12, 1836, 2; Motte, Journey into the Wilderness, 20–21.

26. Page to Commissary General, July 2, 1836, ASPMA 7:753; Foreman, Indian Removal, 152–53; Motte, Journey into the Wilderness, 20; "The Western Frontier," Milledgeville Federal Union, September 27, 1836, 3.

27. Foreman, Indian Removal, 151; "Florida War," Army and Navy Chronicle 4 (July 28, 1836): 126; "Westward Ho!" Milledgeville Federal Union, July 12, 1836, 2.

28. Motte, Journey into the Wilderness, 19–20; Foreman, Indian Removal, 153–54.

29. Motte, Journey into the Wilderness, 19–20; Foreman, Indian Removal, 153–54.

30. "Patterson to Clay," July 25, 1836, Milledgeville Federal Union, August 16, 1836, 2; Jesup to Scott, July 7, 1836, ASPMA 7:357; Jesup to Clay, July 5, 1836, Clay Administrative Files, Creek War, ADAH; Jesup to Secretary of War, July 17, 1836, ASPMA 7:951; "Patterson to Clay," July 25, 1836, Milledgeville Federal Union, August 16, 1836, 2; Jesup to Schley, August 28, 1836, ASPMA 7:365; Jesup to Scott, July 7, 1836, ASPMA 7:357; "Remarks on Richmond Courier and Enquirer by J. F. Lane," Creek Country, August 8, 1836, ASPMA 7:358–60; Foreman, Indian Removal, 154; Lewis to Clay, July 29, 1836, Clay Administrative Files, Creek War, ADAH; Lewis to Clay, August 4, 1836, Clay Administrative Files, Creek War, ADAH; "Letter to the Editor," June 29, 1836, Milledgeville Federal Union, July 7, 1836, 3; "From the Columbus Sentinel," July 29, 1836, repr., Milledgeville Federal Union, August 2, 1836, 2; Hays, Creek Indian Letters, 1830–39, GDAH, pt. 4, 1444; Fretwell, This

So Remote Frontier, 244–45; Webb to Jesup, July 8, 1836, Letters Received relating to Creek and Seminole Indian Affairs in Alabama and Florida, box 24, RG 94, GJ 159, PB, OAG, NARA; Jesup to Jones, July 12, 1836, Letters Received from the Creek War, Headquarters, Army of the South, box 17, RG 94, GJ 159, PB, OAG, NARA; [?] to Jesup, September 29, 1836, Letters Received from Fort Mitchell, box 15, RG 94, GJ 159, PB, OAG, NARA.

31. "Patterson to Clay," July 25, 1836, Milledgeville Federal Union, August 16, 1836, 2; Jesup to Scott, July 7, 1836, ASPMA 7:357; Jesup to Clay, July 5, 1836, Clay Administrative Files, Creek War, ADAH; Jesup to Secretary of War, July 17, 1836, ASPMA 7:951; "Patterson to Clay," July 25, 1836, Milledgeville Federal Union, August 16, 1836, 2; Jesup to Schley, August 28, 1836, ASPMA 7:365; Jesup to Scott, July 7, 1836, ASPMA 7:357; "Remarks on Richmond Courier and Enquirer by J. F. Lane," Creek Country, August 8, 1836, ASPMA 7:358–60; Foreman, Indian Removal, 154; Lewis to Clay, July 29, 1836, Clay Administrative Files, Creek War, ADAH; Lewis to Clay, August 4, 1836, Clay Administrative Files, Creek War, ADAH; "Letter to the Editor," June 29, 1836, Milledgeville Federal Union, July 7, 1836, 3; "From the Columbus Sentinel," July 29, 1836, repr., Milledgeville Federal Union, August 2, 1836, 2; Hays, Creek Indian Letters, 1830–39, GDAH, pt. 4, 1444; Fretwell, This So Remote Frontier, 244–45; Batman to Jesup, July 1, 1836, Letters Received relating to Creek and Seminole Indian Affairs in Alabama and Florida, box 24, RG 94, GJ 159, PB, OAG, NARA; Opothle Yahola to Jesup, July 16, 1836, Letters Received relating to Creek and Seminole Indian Affairs in Alabama and Florida, box 24, RG 94, GJ 159, PB, OAG, NARA; Webb to Jesup, July 15, 1836, Letters Received relating to Creek and Seminole Indian Affairs in Alabama and Florida, box 24, RG 94, GJ 159, PB, OAG, NARA; Jesup to Jones, July 12, 1836, Letters Received from the Creek War, box 17, RG 94, GJ 159, PB, OAG, NARA.

32. Page to Commissary General, July 26, 1836, ASPMA 7:954; Jesup to Clay, August 1, 1836, Clay Administrative Files, Creek War, ADAH; "Camp at McClendon's," Columbus Enquirer, August 28, 1836, 3; "The War Not Yet Ended," Columbus Sentinel, July 29, 1836, repr., Milledgeville Federal Union, August 2, 1836, 3.

33. "Alford to Sanford," July 23, 1836, Columbus Enquirer, July 28, 1836, 3; "From the Columbus Sentinel," July 1, 1836, repr., Milledgeville Federal Union, July 7, 1836, 2; "Schley to Jesup," Columbus Enquirer, July 7, 1836, 3.

34. "From the Columbus Sentinel," July 22, 1836, repr., Milledgeville Federal Union, July 26, 1836, 2; "Creek War Not Over," Columbus Enquirer, July 28, 1836, 2.

35. "Order No. 130," July 25, 1836, Milledgeville Federal Union, August 2, 1836, 3; "From the Columbus Sentinel," July 22, 1836, repr., Milledgeville Federal Union, July 26, 1836, 2; "Creek War Not Over," Columbus Enquirer, July 28, 1836, 2; Orders No. 131, July 25, 1836, Headquarters, Army of the South, box 17, RG 94, GJ 159, PB, OAG, NARA; Orders No. 134, July 25, 1836, Headquarters, Army of the South, box 17, RG 94, GJ 159, PB, OAG, NARA.

36. "Major Jernigan's Official Report," Milledgeville Federal Union, August 30, 1836, 3.

37. Orders No. 40, July 14, 1836, Orders, box 38, RG 94, GJ 159, PB, OAG, NARA.

38. Orders No. 39, Tuskegee, July 13, 1836, Orders, box 38, RG 94, GJ 159, PB, OAG, NARA; Orders No. 42, July 16, 1836, Orders, box 38, RG 94, GJ 159, PB, OAG, NARA; Orders No. 47, July 21, 1836, Orders, box 38, RG 94, GJ 159, PB, OAG, NARA; Orders No. 49, July 24, 1836, Orders, box 38, RG 94, GJ 159, PB, OAG, NARA; Orders No. 53, July 29, 1836, Orders, box 38, RG 94, GJ 159, PB, OAG, NARA; Deas to Harris, May 19, 1837, reel 238, MP 234, RG 75, CA, LR, OIA, WD, NARA; Senate Doc. 120, 26, 162, 670.

39. Orders No. 39, Tuskegee, July 13, 1836, Orders, box 38, RG 94, GJ 159, PB, OAG, NARA; Orders No. 42, July 16, 1836, Orders, box 38, RG 94, GJ 159, PB, OAG, NARA; Orders No. 47, July 21, 1836, Orders, box 38, RG 94, GJ 159, PB, OAG, NARA; Orders No. 49, July 24, 1836, Orders, box 38, RG 94, GJ 159, PB, OAG, NARA; Orders No. 53, July 29, 1836, Orders, box 38, RG 94, GJ 159, PB, OAG, NARA; Deas to Harris, May 19, 1837, reel 238, MP 234, RG 75, CA, LR, OIA, WD, NARA; *Senate Doc.* 120, 26, 162, 670; "Creek War Incidents," *Columbus Republican Herald*, August 2, 1836, repr., *Milledgeville Federal Union*, August 9, 1836, 3; Cherry, "History of Opelika," 401.

40. "Major Jernigan's Official Report," *Milledgeville Federal Union*, August 30, 1836, 3; "Creek War Incidents," *Columbus Republican Herald*, August 2, 1836, repr., *Milledgeville Federal Union*, August 9, 1836, 3; "From the Columbus Herald," August 16, 1836, repr., *Milledgeville Federal Union*, August 23, 1836, 3; "Tho's Hoxey to Editors," July 27, 1836, *Columbus Enquirer*, August 11, 1836, 2; "Julius C. Alford to Gentlemen," August 6, 1836, *Columbus Enquirer*, August 11, 1836, 2; "Alford to Sanford," August 25, 1836, *Milledgeville Federal Union*, September 13, 1836, 2.

41. "From the *Columbus Herald*," August 16, 1836, repr., *Milledgeville Federal Union*, August 23, 1836, 3; "The Troops," *Columbus Enquirer*, August 18, 1836, 3; Sanford to Jesup, August 12, 1836, Headquarters, Army of the South, box 17, RG 94, GJ 159, PB, OAG, NARA.

42. "Alford to Sanford," August 25, 1836, *Milledgeville Federal Union*, September 13, 1836, 1–2.

43. "Alford to Sanford," August 25, 1836, *Milledgeville Federal Union*, September 13, 1836, 1–2.

44. "Alford to Sanford," August 25, 1836, *Milledgeville Federal Union*, September 13, 1836, 1–2.

45. "Another Skirmish," *Milledgeville Federal Union*, August 30, 1836, 3; Hays, Creek Indian Letters, 1830–39, GDAH, pt. 4, 1418–19.

46. Motte, *Journey into the Wilderness*, 69; "The Creeks," *Tallahassee Floridian*, August 27, 1836, repr., *Milledgeville Federal Union*, September 6, 1836, 3; "Florida," *Tallahassee Floridian*, August 27, 1836, repr., *Milledgeville Federal Union*, September 13, 1836, 3; *Tallahassee Floridian*, August 6, 1836, 2; Pate, *History of Turner County*, 37; Hays, Creek Indian Letters, 1830–39, GDAH, pt. 4, 1412–13.

47. "Levi J. Knight to Schley," August 30, 1836, *Milledgeville Federal Union*, September 20, 1836, 3.

48. "Jernigan's Report," *Milledgeville Federal Union*, August 30, 1836, 3; Motte, *Journey into the Wilderness*, 69–70; "From the *Columbus Herald*," August 16, 1836, repr., *Milledgeville Federal Union*, August 23, 1836, 3.

49. "Indians in Lowndes," *Milledgeville Federal Union*, August 30, 1836, 3; "Alford to Sanford," August 25, 1836, *Milledgeville Federal Union*, September 13, 1836, 2; "Jernigan's Official Report," August 5, 1836, *Milledgeville Federal Union*, August 30, 1836, 3; Hays, Creek Indian Letters, 1830–39, GDAH, pt. 4, 1447–48.

50. "From the *Columbus Herald*," August 16, 1836, repr., *Milledgeville Federal Union*, August 23, 1836, 3; "Citizens to Schley," August 30, 1836, in Jones, *History of Decatur County*, 126–27; "United States' Troops in Lowndes," *Milledgeville Federal Union*, September 27, 1836, 3; Motte, *Journey into the Wilderness*, 31, 34, 38–39, 42–43; Hays, Creek Indian Letters, 1830–39, GDAH, pt. 4, 1424–25, 1453.

51. "Indian War," *Army and Navy Chronicle* 3 (September 24, 1836): 172; "The Creek War," *Columbus Enquirer*, August 4, 1836, 2; Hays, Creek Indian Letters, 1830–39, GDAH, pt. 4, 1469 (my emphasis).

8. Recriminations

1. Clay to Abercrombie, July 9, 1836, Clay Administrative Files, Creek War, ADAH; Pickett to Clay, July 15, 1836, Clay Administrative Files, Creek War, ADAH; Pickett to Clay, July 19, 1836, Clay Administrative Files, Creek War, ADAH.

2. "From the *Columbus Sentinel*, July 8, 1836, repr., *Milledgeville Federal Union*, July 12, 1836, 2; "Creek War," *Columbus Herald*, July 19, 1836, repr., *Milledgeville Federal Union*, July 26, 1836, 2; *Columbus Enquirer*, July 28, 1836, 2.

3. Jesup to Schley, August 2, 1836, *ASPMA* 7:364–65; Jesup to Schley, August 28, 1836, *ASPMA* 7:365; "From the *Columbus Sentinel*," July 1, 1836, repr., *Milledgeville Federal Union*, July 7, 1836, 2; "From the *Columbus Enquirer*," July 7, 1836, repr., *Milledgeville Federal Union*, July 12, 1836, 2; "From the *Columbus Sentinel*," July 8, 1836, repr., *Milledgeville Federal Union*, July 12, 1836, 2–3; "From the *Columbus Herald*," July 19, 1836, repr., *Milledgeville Federal Union*, July 26, 1836, 2; "From the *Columbus Herald*," July 16, 1836, repr., *Milledgeville Federal Union*, July 26, 1836, 2.

4. *Columbus Enquirer*, July 7, 1836, 2; Schley to Jesup, July 3, 1836, Clay Administrative Files, Creek War, ADAH; "Jesup to Schley," July 4, 1836, *Milledgeville Federal Union*, July 12, 1836, 2; "From the *Columbus Herald*," July 12, 1836, repr., *Milledgeville Federal Union*, July 19, 1836, 2; "Letter from Columbus," July 7, 1836, repr., *Milledgeville Federal Union*, July 12, 1836, 3; "From the *Columbus Herald*," July 16, 1836, repr., *Milledgeville Federal Union*, July 19, 1836, 2; Schley to Clay, September 13, 1836, Clay Administrative Files, Creek War, ADAH; Clay to Schley, September 26, 1836, Clay Administrative Files, Creek War, ADAH; "The Indians Confined," *Milledgeville Federal Union*, August 16, 1836, 2; Lindsay, *Reason for the Tears*, 64–65.

5. Foreman, *Indian Removal*, 152–53; West, *History of Methodism*, 376–78; Tuggle, *Shem, Ham, and Japheth*, 42, 44, 46, 130; Cherry, "History of Opelika," 294; House Doc. 452, 60; Cross, "On the Trail," 58, 60–61; "Henry Captured," *Army and Navy Chronicle* 3 (August 3, 1836): 88.

6. "Patterson to Clay," July 24, 1836, *Milledgeville Federal Union*, August 16, 1836, 2; Woodward, *Reminiscences*, 45 (my emphasis).

7. "From the *Columbus Herald*," July 16, 1836, repr., *Milledgeville Federal Union*, July 19, 1836, 2; "The Indian Prisoners," *Milledgeville Federal Union*, November 22, 1836, 1; Tuggle, *Shem, Ham, and Japheth*, 130; Foreman, *Indian Removal*, 55, 190.

8. For a good review of the conspiracy theory, see Cross, "On the Trail," 55–63.

9. "From the *Columbus Herald*," November 15, 1836, repr., *Milledgeville Federal Union*, November 22, 1836, 2; "Execution of Indians," *Columbus Herald*, November 29, 1836, repr., *Milledgeville Federal Union*, December 6, 1836, 2; "Six Creek Indians," *Columbus Enquirer*, December 1, 1836, 2; Cherry, "History of Opelika," 202.

10. Patterson to Clay, June 22, 1836, Clay Administrative Files, Creek War, ADAH; Clay to Moore, June 28, 1836, Clay Administrative Files, Creek War, ADAH; Clay to Pickett and Shortridge, July 9, 1836, Clay Administrative Files, Creek War, ADAH.

11. Foreman, *Indian Removal*, 149, 183–84; Belser to Jackson, June 12, 1836, reel 243, MP 234, RG 75, CA, LR, OIA, WD, NARA; "The Montgomery Advertiser," *Columbus Enquirer*, June 30, 1836, 2. Unfortunately for Belser, the loyal Jackson man, the commercial emporium of Montgomery, like Columbus, held a preponderance of states' rights supporters and nascent Whigs. Therefore, when the editor ran for the state legislature on August 1, he was badly beaten. The *Columbus Enquirer* crowed over the fall of the "censor general of the west," but proclaimed that Belser was now "on the high road to promotion; it having become the settled policy of the government

to cherish and feed every worthless wretch that the people condemn and reject." The Enquirer went on to predict that Vice President Van Buren would give Belser an office before six months expired ("A Great Man Has Fallen," *Columbus Enquirer*, August 11, 1836, 2); Van Ness to Jesup, July 2, 1836, Letters Received relating to Creek and Seminole Affairs in Alabama and Florida, box 24, RG 94, GJ 159, PB, OAG, NARA.

12. Hogan, letter to the editor, *Montgomery Advertiser*, June 11, 1836, repr., *Milledgeville Federal Union*, July 12, 1836, 2.

13. Hogan, letter to the editor, *Montgomery Advertiser*, June 11, 1836, repr., *Milledgeville Federal Union*, July 12, 1836, 2; Clay to Jesup, July 13, 1836, Clay Administrative Files, Creek War, ADAH; Jesup to Clay, July 18, 1836, Clay Administrative Files, Creek War, ADAH.

14. Young, *Redskins, Ruffleshirts, and Rednecks*, 113; "Stewart County Celebration," *Columbus Enquirer*, September 8, 1836, 3; "Public Dinner, Zebulon, Pike County," *Milledgeville Federal Union*, September 6, 1836, 3; "Fayette County Festival," *Milledgeville Federal Union*, September 27, 1836, 3.

15. "Memorial of the People of East Alabama and the Western Frontier of Georgia," reel 225, MP 234, RG 75, CA, LR, OIA, WD, NARA, 128; "Remarks of Dixon Lewis on the Indian Appropriation Bill," *Columbus Enquirer*, June 30, 1836, 2; "Resolved," *Milledgeville Federal Union*, August 2, 1836, 1.

16. War Department to Brown, July 15, 1836, reel 243, MP 234, RG 75, CA, LR, OIA, WD, NARA; "Letter from *Columbus Sentinel*," July 8, 1836, repr., *Milledgeville Federal Union*, July 9, 1836, 3; Young, *Redskins, Ruffleshirts, and Rednecks*, 90–91; Foreman, *Indian Removal*, 149–50; House Doc. 154, 2.

17. Balch to Cass, August 1, 1836, reel 243, MP 234, RG 75, CA, LR, OIA, WD, NARA; Crawford and Balch to Butler, August 1, 1836, reel 243, MP 234, RG 75, CA, LR, OIA, WD, NARA, 190–91; Schley to Balch and Crawford, September 26, 1836, Clay Administrative Files, Creek War, ADAH; Foreman, *Indian Removal*, 149–50; House Doc. 154, 18; Sanford to Harris, June 25, 1839, Sanford Papers, ADAH.

18. Young, *Redskins, Ruffleshirts, and Rednecks*, 74, 91–96; Balch and Crawford to Harris, October 14, 1836, reel 243, MP 234, RG 75, CA, LR, OIA, WD, NARA; Harris to Crawford and Balch, October 28, 1836, reel 243, MP 234, RG 75, CA, LR, OIA, WD, NARA; House Doc. 154, 14, 51; House Doc. 452, 14.

19. House Doc. 154, 51–54, 57, 60.

20. House Doc. 154, 50.

21. "Broad Convicted," *Columbus Enquirer*, December 29, 1836, 2; Anthony, "Cherokee County," 38–39; Hooper, *Captain Simon Suggs*, 69–70; "Tribute of Respect," *Columbus Enquirer*, December 13, 1836, 2; Young, *Redskins, Ruffleshirts, and Rednecks*, 108–9; Testimony against Philander Broad, n.d., reel 243, MP 234, RG 75, CA, LR, OIA, WD, NARA, 1335; "Indian War," *Army and Navy Chronicle* 2 (June 30, 1836): 382; "Philander Broad," *Army and Navy Chronicle* 3 (December 24, 1836): 318.

22. Scott's Statement, January 19, 1837, ASPMA 7:204, 207, 211; Elliott, *Winfield Scott*, 323–25; Sanford's Deposition, December 17, 1836, ASPMA 7:171–72; Dawson's Deposition, January 16, 1837, ASPMA 7:174; Schley's Deposition, n.d., ASPMA 7:176; Pronouncement of Macomb and Cooper, n.d., ASPMA 7:178–80. For local opinion on Scott, see "General Scott," *Columbus Enquirer*, July 14, 1836, 2; *Tallahassee Floridian*, July 16, 1836, 3; Gayle to Clay, July 18, 1836, Clay Administrative Files, Creek War, ADAH; "Letter from Columbus," *Milledgeville Federal Union*, July 12, 1836, 3.

23. Elizer, "Administration of William Schley," 28, 66.

24. "From the Tuscaloosa Flag of the Union," August 10, 1836, repr., Milledgeville Federal Union, August 16, 1836, 2; Moore to Clay, July 10, 1836, Clay Administrative Files, Creek War, ADAH; "To the Settlers in the Creek Nation from Wm. Baskin Stogner," July 13, 1836, Milledgeville Federal Union, July 14, 1836, 2; "Toasts," Columbus Enquirer, September 15, 1836, 3; "Dinner for Baldwin Hussars, Corporal William House," Milledgeville Federal Union, August 23, 1836, 3; "Stewart County Celebration, O. P. Cheatham," Columbus Enquirer, September 8, 1836, 3; "To the Public," Columbus Enquirer, August 25, 1836, 3; "Flewellen's Reply," Columbus Enquirer, August 8, 1836, 3; "For Some Weeks Past," Columbus Enquirer, September 8, 1836, 2; Chapin to Bicknell, July 30, 1836, Chapin Collection, ADAH; "4th of July Toasts, Mansfield Torrance," Milledgeville Federal Union, July 7, 1836, 2; Elizer, "Administration of William Schley," 29 (my emphasis).

25. "From the Columbus Sentinel," July 29, 1836, repr., Milledgeville Federal Union, August 2, 1836, 2; Jesup to Scott, July 7, 1836, ASPMA 7:357; Jesup to Secretary of War, July 24, 1836, ASPMA 7:951; Garrett to Clay, July 1, 1836, Clay Administrative Files, Creek War, ADAH; Jesup to Clay, July 18, 1836, Clay Administrative Files, Creek War, ADAH; Jesup to Clay, August 23, 1836, Clay Administrative Files, Creek War, ADAH. The settlers in the northern counties of Alabama had always been afraid of the Creek refugees there, and some believed that the hostile escapees from the Lower Creek country had fled to the mountains around the Creek camp on Town Creek. In August many settlers were about to flee their homes in that vicinity until more Alabama troops arrived to protect them. Moore to Clay, August 20, 1836, Clay Administrative Files, Creek War, ADAH.

26. Ellisor, "Like So Many Wolves," 9; Foreman, Indian Removal, 160–63; Garrett to Clay, June 27, 1836, Clay Administrative Files, Creek War, ADAH; Jesup to Clay, July 18, 1836, Clay Administrative Files, Creek War, ADAH; Opothle Yahola to Jesup, July 17, 1836, Letters Received relating to Creek and Seminole Affairs in Alabama and Florida, 1818–53, box 24, RG 94, GJ 159, PB, OAG, NARA; Sprague to Jesup, August 28, 1836, Letters Received relating to Creek and Seminole Affairs in Alabama and Florida, 1818–53, Camps and Forts, box 15, RG 94, GJ 159, PB, OAG, NARA.

27. Ellisor, "Like So Many Wolves," 12–13; Senate Doc. 120, 29, 626, 646.

28. Clay to Jesup, August 31, 1836, Letters Received relating to Creek and Seminole Affairs in Alabama and Florida, 1818–53, Camps and Forts, box 15, RG 94, GJ 159, PB, OAG, NARA; Clay to Jesup, July 25, 1836, Letters Received relating to Creek and Seminole Affairs in Alabama and Florida, 1818–53, Camps and Forts, box 15, RG 94, GJ 159, PB, OAG, NARA.

29. Foreman, Indian Removal, 160–62; Orders, August 28, 1836, reel 237, MP 234, RG 75, CA, LR, OIA, WD, NARA; Jesup to Harris, September 28, 1836, reel 237, MP 234, RG 75, CA, LR, OIA, WD, NARA; Macomb to Poinsett, September 19, 1837, ASPMA 7:518–19; Rogin, Fathers and Children, 241. Lewis Cass also wanted Jesup to raise Creek warriors for the Florida service and proposed this to the general as early as July 11. Cass to Jesup, July 11, 1836, ASPMA 7:519.

30. Creek Chiefs to Jesup, August 20, 1836, Camps and Forts, box 15, RG 94, GJ 159, PB, OAG, NARA; Opothle Yahola to Jesup, August 26, 1836, Camps and Forts, box 15, RG 94, GJ 159, PB, OAG, NARA.

31. "Creek Lands," Milledgeville Federal Union, August 23, 1836, 3; Young, Redskins, Ruffleshirts, and Rednecks, 90–91; Jesup to Harris, September 28, 1836, reel 237, MP 234, RG 75, CA, LR, OIA, WD, NARA; "Stolen Lands," Montgomery Advertiser, September 2, 1836, repr., Milledgeville Federal Union, September 13, 1836, 3; Orders, Tallassee, August 28, 1836, reel 237, MP 234, RG 75, CA,

LR, OIA, WD, NARA; Jesup to Harris, September 28, 1836, reel 237, MP 234, RG 75, CA, LR, OIA, WD, NARA; Macomb to Poinsett, September 19, 1837, *ASPMA* 7:518–19; Foreman, *Indian Removal*, 161–62; Rogin, *Fathers and Children*, 241.

32. Everett to Eaton, May 25, 1829, reel 222, MP 234, RG 75, CA, LR, OIA, WD, NARA, 147; Thompson to Duval, January 1834, *ASPMA* 6:453; Jesup to Butler, January 19, 1837, *ASPMA* 7:826; Jesup to Jones, June 17, 1837, *ASPMA* 7:839; Jesup to Jones, July 19, 1837, *ASPMA* 7:840; "Creek Brigade," *Army and Navy Chronicle* 4 (July 2, 1836): 10; Mahon, *Second Seminole War*, 209; Wallace, *Long, Bitter Trail*, 4–5; Remini, *Andrew Jackson*, 180.

33. Everett to Eaton, May 25, 1829, reel 222, MP 234, RG 75, CA, LR, OIA, WD, NARA, 147; Thompson to Duval, January 1834, *ASPMA* 6:453; Jesup to Butler, January 19, 1837, *ASPMA* 7:826; Jesup to Jones, June 17, 1837, *ASPMA* 7:839; Jesup to Jones, July 19, 1837, *ASPMA* 7:840; "Creek Brigade," *Army and Navy Chronicle* 4 (July 2, 1836): 10; Mahon, *Second Seminole War*, 209; Wallace, *Long, Bitter Trail*, 4–5; Remini, *Andrew Jackson*, 180.

34. Jesup to Poinsett, June 15, 1837, *ASPMA* 7:874–76; Jesup to Poinsett, October 17, 1837, *ASPMA* 7:885–86; Sprague, *Florida War*, 162; Swanton, *Early History*, 401; Jesup to Wilson, April 3, 1837, reel 238, MP 234, RG 75, CA, LR, OIA, WD, NARA.

35. Young, *Redskins, Ruffleshirts, and Rednecks*, 90–91; Shorter to Abert, November 17, 1836, reel 243, MP 234, RG 75, CA, LR, OIA, WD, NARA.

36. "From the *Columbus Sentinel*," August 5, 1836, repr., *Milledgeville Federal Union*, August 16, 1836, 2; "The Creeks against the Seminoles," *Columbus Herald*, September 5, 1836, repr., *Milledgeville Federal Union*, September 13, 1836, 3; "Rather Slim," *Columbus Enquirer*, September 1, 1836, 2; *Columbus Enquirer*, September 15, 1836, 3.

37. "The Creeks against the Seminoles," *Columbus Herald*, September 5, 1836, repr., *Milledgeville Federal Union*, September 13, 1836, 3.

38. Debo, *Road to Disappearance*, 106; Harris to Poinsett, February 5, 1838, *ASPMA* 7:952; Foreman, *Indian Removal*, 161–63, 167; "Creeks in Cherokee," *Milledgeville Federal Union*, August 9, 1836, 2–3; "On Sunday Last," *Milledgeville Federal Union*, August 23, 1836, 3; Jesup to Harris, August 21, 1836, reel 237, MP 234, RG 75, CA, LR, OIA, WD, NARA; "Removal of the Creeks," *Columbus Sentinel*, August 16, 1836, repr., *Milledgeville Federal Union*, August 23, 1836, 3; Young, *Redskins, Ruffleshirts, and Rednecks*, 90. The Creek removal camp in the Cherokee section of Alabama was situated in Town Creek in the vicinity of Gunter's Landing on the Tennessee River. Moore to Clay, August 15, 1836, Clay Administrative Files, Creek War, ADAH; Moore to Clay, August 22, 1836, Clay Administrative Files, Creek War, ADAH. For a more thorough account of the removal of Creeks from the Cherokee country, see Ellisor, "Like So Many Wolves."

39. Foreman, *Indian Removal*, 162; Cherry, "History of Opelika," 406; Motte, *Journey into the Wilderness*, 254; Lindsay, *Reason for the Tears*, 67.

40. Foreman, *Indian Removal*, 167; Anthony, "Cherokee County," 42.

41. "The Citizens of Marion County vs. Williams and His Uchee Indians," *Milledgeville Federal Union*, July 7, 1836, 3; Williams, letter to the editor, *Columbus Enquirer*, August 4, 1836, 2.

42. Nunn, *Yesterdays in Loachapoka*, 96; Anthony, "Cherokee County," 42; Foreman, *Indian Removal*, 162; Orr, "History of Lafayette," 16; "Letter to the Editors," August 4, 1836, *Columbus Enquirer*, August 8, 1836, 2; *Columbus Enquirer*, August 11, 1836, 2; "Letter from Little Rock," December 25, 1836, *New York Observer*, February 11, 1837, 4.

43. "From the *Commercial Register*," repr., *Tallahassee Floridian*, July 30, 1836, 3; Rogin, *Fathers and Children*, 243.

44. Anthony, "Cherokee County," 42; M. Thompson, *Barbour County*, 49. Typical of all the early Alabama historians, Vandiver calls Indian removal "one of the darkest tragedies that ever stained the pages of the history of the United States government, or sullied the reputation of the American people" ("Pioneer Talladega," 63).

45. Orr, "History of Lafayette," 15.

9. The War Revives in New Alabama

1. Cherry, "History of Opelika," 412, 526–27.

2. H. Owens, "History of Eufaula," 11, 19, 27, 34; Beeson, *History of Eufaula*, 13–14; "Irwinton, Barbour County, Alabama," *Columbus Enquirer*, February 9, 1836, 2.

3. Ellisor, "Like So Many Wolves," 15; Deas to Harris, March 30, 1837, reel 238, MP 234, RG 75, CA, LR, OIA, WD, NARA; *Senate Doc.* 120, 668–69; [?] to Jesup, September 29, 1836, Fort Mitchell Letters, box 15, RG 94, GJ 159, PB, OAG, NARA.

4. Ellisor, "Like So Many Wolves," 15; *Senate Doc.* 120, 668–69.

5. Ellisor, "Like So Many Wolves," 20; Deas to Harris, August 2, 1837, reel 238, MP 234, RG 75, CA, LR, OIA, WD, NARA.

6. Ellisor, "Like So Many Wolves," 20–21; Creeks to Ross, August 14, 1837, reel 238, MP 234, RG 75, CA, LR, OIA, WD, NARA; Deas to Harris, September 19, 1837, reel 238, MP 234, RG 75, CA, LR, OIA, WD, NARA; Deas to Harris, September 23, 1837, reel 238, MP 234, RG 75, CA, LR, OIA, WD, NARA; Lindsay to Deas, September 20, 1837, reel 238, MP 234, RG 75, CA, LR, OIA, WD, NARA.

7. Foreman, *Indian Removal*, 179–80. "Creek Indians," *Milledgeville Federal Union*, January 17, 1837, 3; Page to Harris, February 9, 1837, reel 238, MP 234, RG 75, CA, LR, OIA, WD, NARA; Jesup to Jones, March 6, 1837, *ASPMA* 7:834; Jesup to Butler, March 7, 1837, reel 238, MP 234, RG 75, CA, LR, OIA, WD, NARA.

8. Foreman, *Indian Removal*, 179–80; "Creek Indians," *Milledgeville Federal Union*, January 17, 1837, 3; Page to Harris, February 9, 1837, reel 238, MP 234, RG 75, CA, LR, OIA, WD, NARA; Jesup to Jones, March 6, 1837, *ASPMA* 7:834; Jesup to Butler, March 7, 1837, reel 238, MP 234, RG 75, CA, LR, OIA, WD, NARA.

9. Washington to Reynolds, December 18, 1836, Clay Administrative Files, Creek War, ADAH; Reynolds to Clay, January 3, 1837, Clay Administrative Files, Creek War, ADAH. The Tallassee offshoot villages of Sougahatchee and Loachapoka sat along the banks of Sougahatchee Creek. Volunteer troops from Chambers County and a mixed force of whites and friendly Creeks under Opothle Yahola attacked the inhabitants of these villages shortly after the outbreak of war in May 1836 (Harper to Clay, January 28, 1836, Clay Administrative Files, Creek War, ADAH).

10. Page to Harris, December 30, 1837, reel 237, MP 234, RG 75, CA, LR, OIA, WD, NARA; Currie, Forty-second Regiment, to Clay, December 31, 1836, Clay Administrative Files, Creek War, ADAH; Page to Clay, January 3, 1837, Clay Administrative Files, Creek War, ADAH; "Indian Difficulties," *Columbus Enquirer*, January 19, 1837, 2.

11. Page to Harris, December 30, 1837, reel 237, MP 234, RG 75, CA, LR, OIA, WD, NARA; Currie, Forty-second Regiment, to Clay, December 31, 1836, Clay Administrative Files, Creek War, ADAH; Page to Clay, January 3, 1837, Clay Administrative Files, Creek War, ADAH; "Indian Difficulties," *Columbus Enquirer*, January 19, 1837, 2.

12. "Indian Difficulties," *Columbus Enquirer*, January 19, 1837, 2; Page to Harris, December

30, 1837, reel 237, MP 234, RG 75, CA, LR, OIA, WD, NARA; Currie to Clay, December 31, 1836, Clay Administrative Files, Creek War, ADAH; Page to Clay, January 3, 1837, Clay Administrative Files, Creek War, ADAH.

13. Citizens to Clay, January 2, 1837, Clay Administrative Files, Creek War, ADAH; Irwinton Committee to Clay, January 4, 1837, Clay Administrative Files, Creek War, ADAH; Clark to Clay, January 4, 1837, Clay Administrative Files, Creek War, ADAH; Feagin to Clay, January 10, 1837, Clay Administrative Files, Creek War, ADAH; Keener to Clay, January 11, 1837, Clay Administrative Files, Creek War, ADAH; Clark to Clay, January 12, 1837, Clay Administrative Files, Creek War, ADAH; "Indian Disturbances," *Columbus Enquirer*, January 19, 1837, 2; Tate to Lewis, January 8, 1837, reel 238, MP 234, RG 75, CA, LR, OIA, WD, NARA; Resolutions of Russell County Citizens, January 7, 1837, reel 238, MP 234, RG 75, CA, LR, OIA, WD, NARA.

14. Page to Harris, January 15, 1837, *ASPMA* 7:954–55.

15. Sloan to Jesup, March 31, 1937, reel 238, MP 234, RG 75, CA, LR, OIA, WD, NARA.

16. Sloan to Page, February 7, 1837, reel 238, MP 234, RG 75, CA, LR, OIA, WD, NARA.

17. Reynolds to Wilson, March 31, 1837, reel 238, MP 234, RG 75, CA, LR, OIA, WD, NARA.

18. Clay to Commanding Officer, January 14, 1837, Clay Administrative Files, Creek War, ADAH; Clay to Clark, January 14, 1837, Clay Administrative Files, Creek War, ADAH; Clay to Whitman, January 14, 1837, Clay Administrative Files, Creek War, ADAH; Clay to Irwinton Committee, January 31, 1837, Clay Administrative Files, Creek War, ADAH; Clay to Butler, February 2, 1837, Clay Administrative Files, Creek War, ADAH.

19. Clay to Brigadier General Thomas B. Scott, Commanding the Fifth Division, Alabama Militia, January 20, 1837, Clay Administrative Files, Creek War, ADAH; Clay to Page, January 20, 1837, Clay Administrative Files, Creek War, ADAH; George to Clay, January 27, 1837, Clay Administrative Files, Creek War, ADAH; Clay to Irwinton Committee, January 31, 1837, Clay Administrative Files, Creek War, ADAH; Page to Clay, February 11, 1837, Clay Administrative Files, Creek War, ADAH; Page to Clay, February 12, 1837, Clay Administrative Files, Creek War, ADAH.

20. Whitman to Clay, January 22, 1837, Clay Administrative Files, Creek War, ADAH.

21. Hunter to Clay, January 28, 1837, Clay Administrative Files, Creek War, ADAH; Keener to Clay, January 28, 1837, Clay Administrative Files, Creek War, ADAH; Goldthwaite to Clay, January 31, 1837, Clay Administrative Files, Creek War, ADAH; Page to Clay, February 3, 1837, Clay Administrative Files, Creek War, ADAH; "Indian Affairs," *Columbus Enquirer*, February 9, 1837, 2.

22. Lewis to Clay, February 3, 1837, Clay Administrative Files, Creek War, ADAH; "Indian Affairs," *Columbus Enquirer*, February 9, 1837, 2.

23. Lewis to Clay, February 3, 1837, Clay Administrative Files, Creek War, ADAH; "Indian Affairs," *Columbus Enquirer*, February 9, 1837, 2; Page to Harris, February 9, 1837, reel 238, MP 234, RG 75, CA, LR, OIA, WD, NARA.

24. Lewis to Clay, February 3, 1837, Clay Administrative Files, Creek War, ADAH; "Indian Affairs," *Columbus Enquirer*, February 9, 1837, 2; Page to Harris, February 9, 1837, reel 238, MP 234, RG 75, CA, LR, OIA, WD, NARA.

25. Lewis to Clay, February 3, 1837, Clay Administrative Files, Creek War, ADAH; Page to Harris, February 9, 1837, reel 238, MP 234, RG 75, CA, LR, OIA, WD, NARA; "Indian Affairs," *Columbus Enquirer*, February 9, 1837, 2.

26. Sloan to Jesup, March 31, 1837, reel 238, MP 234, RG 75, CA, LR, OIA, WD, NARA; Reynolds

to Wilson, March 28, 1837, reel 238, MP 234, RG 75, CA, LR, OIA, WD, NARA; Foreman, *Indian Removal*, 180–82; Yamaguchi, "Macon County," 224.

27. Brunson to Clay, February 4, 1837, Clay Administrative Files, Creek War, ADAH; Whitman to Clay, February 7, 1837, Clay Administrative Files, Creek War, ADAH; Wellborn to Clay, March 2, 1837, Clay Administrative Files, Creek War, ADAH; Nunn, *Lee County*, 298. The *Columbus Herald* reported that as many as two hundred warriors broke free from Sloan's camp when the whites approached ("From the *Columbus Herald*," January 20, 1837, repr., *Milledgeville Federal Union*, January 24, 1837, 3).

28. Clay to Campbell, February 4, 1837, Clay Administrative Files, Creek War, ADAH; Clay to Page, February 4, 1837, Clay Administrative Files, Creek War, ADAH; Clay to Currie, February 21, 1837, Clay Administrative Files, Creek War, ADAH; Page to Clay, February 27, 1837, Clay Administrative Files, Creek War, ADAH.

29. Young to Clay, February 19, 1837, Clay Administrative Files, Creek War, ADAH; Page to Clay, February 27, 1837, Clay Administrative Files, Creek War, ADAH; Park to Bagby, April 18, 1838, Bagby Militia Files, 1837–41, ADAH; Page to Harris, February 21, 1837, reel 238, MP 234, RG 75, CA, LR, OIA, WD, NARA.

30. Reynolds to Page, February 19, 1837, reel 238, MP 234, RG 75, CA, LR, OIA, WD, NARA; Reynolds to Wilson, March 31, 1837, reel 238, MP 234, RG 75, CA, LR, OIA, WD, NARA.

31. Reynolds to Page, February 19, 1837, reel 238, MP 234, RG 75, CA, LR, OIA, WD, NARA; Reynolds to Wilson, March 31, 1837, reel 238, MP 234, RG 75, CA, LR, OIA, WD, NARA.

32. Reynolds to Page, February 19, 1837, reel 238, MP 234, RG 75, CA, LR, OIA, WD, NARA; Reynolds to Wilson, March 31, 1837, reel 238, MP 234, RG 75, CA, LR, OIA, WD, NARA; Young to Clay, February 19, 1837, Clay Administrative Files, Creek War, ADAH.

33. Reynolds to Page, February 19, 1837, reel 238, MP 234, RG 75, CA, LR, OIA, WD, NARA; Reynolds to Wilson, March 31, 1837, reel 238, MP 234, RG 75, CA, LR, OIA, WD, NARA; Young to Clay, February 19, 1837, Clay Administrative Files, Creek War, ADAH; Foreman, *Indian Removal*, 180–82.

34. Reynolds to Page, February 19, 1837, reel 238, MP 234, RG 75, CA, LR, OIA, WD, NARA; Reynolds to Wilson, March 31, 1837, reel 238, MP 234, RG 75, CA, LR, OIA, WD, NARA; Young to Clay, February 19, 1837, Clay Administrative Files, Creek War, ADAH; Foreman, *Indian Removal*, 180–82.

35. Reynolds to Page, February 19, 1837, reel 238, MP 234, RG 75, CA, LR, OIA, WD, NARA; Reynolds to Wilson, March 31, 1837, reel 238, MP 234, RG 75, CA, LR, OIA, WD, NARA.

36. Settlers to Clay, March 6, 1837, Clay Administrative Files, Creek War, ADAH; Clay to Page, March 7, 1837, Clay Administrative Files, Creek War, ADAH; Shortridge to Clay, March 20, 1837, Clay Administrative Files, Creek War, ADAH; Clay to Shortridge, March 23, 1837, Clay Administrative Files, Creek War, ADAH; Clay to Schley, March 23, 1837, Clay Administrative Files, Creek War, ADAH.

37. Foreman, *Indian Removal*, 184; Clay to Shortridge and Booth, February 24, 1837, Clay Administrative Files, Creek War, ADAH; Clay to Page, March 7, 1837, Clay Administrative Files, Creek War, ADAH; Clay to Macon Citizens, March 13, 1837, Clay Administrative Files, Creek War, ADAH; H. Wilson to J. Wilson, March 13, 1837, Clay Administrative Files, Creek War, ADAH; Whitman to Clay, March 18, 1837, Clay Administrative Files, Creek War, ADAH; Clay to Jesup, March 30, 1837, Clay Administrative Files, Creek War, ADAH; Page to Clay, March 4, 1837, Clay Administrative Files, Creek War, ADAH.

38. Foreman, *Indian Removal*, 182.
39. Foreman, *Indian Removal*, 182–84.
40. Jesup to Poinsett, April 11, 1837, reel 238, MP 234, RG 75, CA, LR, OIA, WD, NARA.
41. Citizens to Clay, February 24, 1837, Clay Administrative Files, Creek War, ADAH; Brodnax to Clay, March 2, 1837, Clay Administrative Files, Creek War, ADAH.
42. Citizens to Clay, February 24, 1837, Clay Administrative Files, Creek War, ADAH.
43. Citizens to Clay, February 24, 1837, Clay Administrative Files, Creek War, ADAH; A. Walker, *Backtracking in Barbour County*, 48–50; Beauchamp, "Early Chronicles," 52–54; Farmer, *History of Pike County*, 11; Brunson, *Pea River Reflections*, 5.
44. Warren to Clay, March 8, 1837, Clay Administrative Files, Creek War, ADAH; Foster to Clay, March 12, 1837, Clay Administrative Files, Creek War, ADAH; Clay to Wellborn, March 13, 1837, Clay Administrative Files, Creek War, ADAH; Brunson, *Pea River Reflections*, 5; McGhee, *Claybank Memories*, 18–19. Eli Albertson lived on the upper edge of the Broxton settlement, east of the Choctawhatchee and between the present-day towns of Geneva and Daleville. Watson, *Piney Woods Echoes*, 13–14.
45. Citizens to Clay, February 24, 1837, Clay Administrative Files, Creek War, ADAH; Warren to Clay, March 8, 1837, Clay Administrative Files, Creek War, ADAH; Foster to Clay, March 12, 1837, Clay Administrative Files, Creek War, ADAH.
46. Clay to Page, March 3, 1837, Clay Administrative Files, Creek War, ADAH; Clay to Wellborn, March 13, 1837, Clay Administrative Files, Creek War, ADAH; Clay to Warren, March 13, 1837, Clay Administrative Files, Creek War, ADAH; Clay to Young, March 13, 1837, Clay Administrative Files, Creek War, ADAH; Clay to Holcomb, March 15, 1837, Clay Administrative Files, Creek War, ADAH; Clay to Foster, March 20, 1837, Clay Administrative Files, Creek War, ADAH.
47. Mahon, *Second Seminole War*, 199–200; Sprague, *Florida War*, 166–67, 177–78; Clay to Jesup, March 30, 1837, Clay Administrative Files, Creek War, ADAH; Clay to Warren, March 31, 1837, Clay Administrative Files, Creek War, ADAH.
48. Whitman to Wellborn, March 15, 1837, Clay Administrative Files, Creek War, ADAH; Whitman to Clay, March 18, 1837, Clay Administrative Files, Creek War, ADAH; Clay to Whitman, March 30, 1837, Clay Administrative Files, Creek War, ADAH; Means to Clay, April 2, 1837, Clay Administrative Files, Creek War, ADAH; Whitman to Clay, April 17, 1837, Clay Administrative Files, Creek War, ADAH.
49. Warren to Clay, March 24, 1837, Clay Administrative Files, Creek War, ADAH; Wellborn to Clay, April 6, 1837, Clay Administrative Files, Creek War, ADAH.
50. Warren to Clay, March 24, 1837, Clay Administrative Files, Creek War, ADAH; Wellborn to Clay, April 6, 1837, Clay Administrative Files, Creek War, ADAH; Skinner and Booth to Clay, March 25, 1837, Clay Administrative Files, Creek War, ADAH; M. Thompson, *Barbour County*, 63–65.
51. Wellborn to Clay, April 6, 1837, Clay Administrative Files, Creek War, ADAH; M. Thompson, *Barbour County*, 63–65; A. Walker, *Backtracking in Barbour County*, 49–55; Beauchamp, "Early Chronicles," 55–58.
52. Wellborn to Clay, April 6, 1837, Clay Administrative Files, Creek War, ADAH; M. Thompson, *Barbour County*, 63–65; A. Walker, *Backtracking in Barbour County*, 49–55; Beauchamp, "Early Chronicles," 55–58.
53. Wellborn to Clay, April 6, 1837, Clay Administrative Files, Creek War, ADAH; M. Thompson, *Barbour County*, 63–65; A. Walker, *Backtracking in Barbour County*, 49–55; Beauchamp, "Early Chronicles," 55–58; Fretwell, *This So Remote Frontier*, 246–47.

54. Wellborn to Clay, April 6, 1837, Clay Administrative Files, Creek War, ADAH; M. Thompson, *Barbour County*, 63–65; A. Walker, *Backtracking in Barbour County*, 49–55; Beauchamp, "Early Chronicles," 55–58.

55. Hunter to Clay, March 30, 1837, Clay Administrative Files, Creek War, ADAH; Clay to Skinner and Booth, April 3, 1837, Clay Administrative Files, Creek War, ADAH; Clay to Brodnax, April 6, 1837, Clay Administrative Files, Creek War, ADAH; Currie to Clay, April 8, 1837, Clay Administrative Files, Creek War, ADAH; Clay to Booth, April 14, 1837, Clay Administrative Files, Creek War, ADAH; Clay to Poinsett, April 17, 1837, Clay Administrative Files, Creek War, ADAH; Warren to Clay, April 20, 1837, Clay Administrative Files, Creek War, ADAH.

56. Clay to Wellborn, April 15, 1837, Clay Administrative Files, Creek War, ADAH.

10. Seeking Refuge in West Florida

1. Sturtevant, "Creek into Seminole," 92.

2. Smith to Harris, January 15, 1837, reel 290, MP 234, RG 75, SS, LR, OIA, WD, NARA, 229–31.

3. Smith to Harris, January 15, 1837, reel 290, MP 234, RG 75, SS, LR, OIA, WD, NARA, 229–31.

4. Smith to Harris, March 12, 1837, reel 290, MP 234, RG 75, SS, LR, OIA, WD, NARA, 229–31.

5. Smith to Harris, March 12, 1837, reel 290, MP 234, RG 75, SS, LR, OIA, WD, NARA, 229–31; Buford to Clay, February 24, 1837, Clay Administrative Files, Creek War, ADAH.

6. Smith to Harris, March 12, 1837, reel 290, MP 234, RG 75, SS, LR, OIA, WD, NARA, 229–31.

7. Smith to Harris, March 12, 1837, reel 290, MP 234, RG 75, SS, LR, OIA, WD, NARA, 229–31.

8. Rucker, "Creek Indian Crisis," 323; "The Creeks," *Tallahassee Floridian*, March 18, 1837, 2.

9. Rucker, "Creek Indian Crisis," 323, 326; "The Military," *Tallahassee Floridian*, March 25, 1837, 2.

10. Rucker, "Creek Indian Crisis," 323–24; Clay to Whitman, March 30, 1837, Clay Administrative Files, Creek War, ADAH.

11. Rucker, "Creek Indian Crisis," 324.

12. Rucker, "Creek Indian Crisis," 324.

13. Rucker, "Creek Indian Crisis," 324–25; "From the *Tallahassee Floridian*," May 21, 1837, Clay Administrative Files, Creek War, ADAH.

14. Rucker, "Creek Indian Crisis," 325; McKinnon, *Walton County*, 110–15. For the Hart massacre and resumption of war in southern Alabama, see Citizens to Clay, May 5, 1837, Clay Administrative Files, Creek War, ADAH; Wellborn to Clay, May 12, 1837, Clay Administrative Files, Creek War, ADAH; Clay to Jones, May 12, 1837, Clay Administrative Files, Creek War, ADAH; Lewis to Clay, May 18, 1837, Clay Administrative Files, Creek War, ADAH; Brunson, *Pea River Reflections*, 23–27.

15. Wellborn to Clay, May 12, 1837, Clay Administrative Files, Creek War, ADAH; Brunson, *Pea River Reflections*, 26–27.

16. Rucker, "Creek Indian Crisis," 325–26; "White Man's Murder," *Pensacola Gazette*, April 29, 1837, 3.

17. Rucker, "Creek Indian Crisis," 327–28; "Another White Man's Murder," *Pensacola Gazette*, May 13, 1837, 3.

18. McKinnon, *Walton County*, 118–24; "News from the Army," *Tallahassee Floridian*, May 20, 1837, 3.

19. Clay to Jesup, March 20, 1837, Clay Administrative Files, Creek War, ADAH; Jesup to Jones, June 17, 1837, ASPMA 7:839; Jesup to Jones, June 24, 1837, ASPMA 7:839–40; Jesup to Jones, Ft. Heilman, July 25, 1837, ASPMA 7:843; Jesup to Poinsett, June 5, 1837, ASPMA 7:238–39; Jesup to Poinsett, June 15, 1837, ASPMA 7:874–75; Poinsett to Jesup, July 25, 1837, ASPMA 7:811–12; Motte, *Journey into the Wilderness*, 304–5, 305n7.

20. Rucker, "Creek Indian Crisis," 327; Walker, Chief Enachitohustern to Thompson, July 28, 1835, ASPMA 6:463.

21. Davis, "Georgia Battalion," 27, 32–33.

22. Wellborn to Clay, May 12, 1837, Clay Administrative Files, Creek War, ADAH; Lewis to Clay, May 18, 1837, Clay Administrative Files, Creek War, ADAH; Petition of Econchattee Micco to Congress, April 2, 1836, ASPMA 6:462–63.

23. Rucker, "Creek Indian Crisis," 327; "Report of Colonel Brown," May 24, 1837, *Tallahassee Floridian*, July 1, 1837, 2.

24. Rucker, "Creek Indian Crisis," 327; "Report of Colonel Brown," May 24, 1837, *Tallahassee Floridian*, July 1, 1837, 2.

25. Rucker, "Creek Indian Crisis," 328–29.

26. Rucker, "Creek Indian Crisis," 328–29; "Oration," *Tallahassee Floridian*, July 29, 1837, 2; "The Citizens of Florida," *Tallahassee Floridian*, July 29, 1837, 3; Reynolds to Harris, January 31, 1837, reel 239, MP 234, RG 75, CA, LR, OIA, WD, NARA; Carswell, *Homesteading*, 33.

27. Cawlfied to Jesup, July 7, 1837, Letters Received from Cawlfield, Alabama Volunteers, 1837, box 23, RG 94, GJ 159, PB, OAG, NARA; Cawlfied to Jesup, July 22, 1837, Letters Received from Cawlfield, Alabama Volunteers, 1837, box 23, RG 94, GJ 159, PB, OAG, NARA; Cawlfield to Jesup, July 15, 1837, ASPMA 7:843; Harris to Reynolds, June 29, 1837, reel 239, MP 234, RG 75, CA, LR, OIA, WD, NARA.

28. Petition of Baldwin County Citizens to Poinsett, June 17, 1837, reel 238, MP 234, RG 75, CA, LR, OIA, WD, NARA; Toulmin to Clay, June 11, 1837, Clay Administrative Files, Creek War, ADAH.

29. Petition of Baldwin County Citizens to Poinsett, June 17, 1837, reel 238, MP 234, RG 75, CA, LR, OIA, WD, NARA; Toulmin to Clay, June 11, 1837, Clay Administrative Files, Creek War, ADAH.

30. Reynolds to Harris, June 12, 1837, reel 238, MP 234, RG 75, CA, LR, OIA, WD, NARA; Batman to Harris, June 18, 1837, reel 238, MP 234, RG 75, CA, LR, OIA, WD, NARA; Hogan to Indian Office, June 18, 1837, reel 238, MP 234, RG 75, CA, LR, OIA, WD, NARA; Hogan to Harris, July 22, 1837, reel 238, MP 234, RG 75, CA, LR, OIA, WD, NARA; Page to Harris, July 17, 1837, reel 238, MP 234, RG 75, CA, LR, OIA, WD, NARA; Wilson to Campbell, May 11, 1837, reel 238, MP 234, RG 75, CA, LR, OIA, WD, NARA; Campbell to Wilson, May 11, 1837, reel 238, MP 234, RG 75, CA, LR, OIA, WD, NARA.

31. Iverson to Harris, June 18, 1837, reel 238, MP 234, RG 75, CA, LR, OIA, WD, NARA; Batman to Harris, July 20, 1837, reel 238, MP 234, RG 75, CA, LR, OIA, WD, NARA; Page to Harris, July 27, 1837, reel 238, MP 234, RG 75, CA, LR, OIA, WD, NARA; Reynolds to Harris, August 17, 1837, reel 238, MP 234, RG 75, CA, LR, OIA, WD, NARA.

32. Iverson to Harris, June 18, 1837, reel 238, MP 234, RG 75, CA, LR, OIA, WD, NARA; Batman to Harris, July 20, 1837, reel 238, MP 234, RG 75, CA, LR, OIA, WD, NARA; Page to Harris, July 27, 1837, reel 238, MP 234, RG 75, CA, LR, OIA, WD, NARA; Reynolds to Harris, August 17, 1837, reel 238, MP 234, RG 75, CA, LR, OIA, WD, NARA; Woodfin to Reynolds, August 26, 1837, reel 238, MP 234, RG 75, CA, LR, OIA, WD, NARA; Hogan to Harris, July 22, 1837, reel 238, MP 234, RG 75, CA, LR, OIA, WD, NARA.

33. Rucker, "Creek Indian Crisis," 329–31; Toulmin to Clay, June 11, 1837, Clay Administrative Files, Creek War, ADAH; Clay to Bates, June 29, 1837, Clay Administrative Files, Creek War, ADAH; "Leven Brown's Report," *Tallahassee Floridian*, July 15, 1837, 2; "The Creeks," *Tallahassee Floridian*, September 16, 1837, 3; "Florida War," *Army and Navy Chronicle* 5 (July 14, 1837): 329.

34. Rucker, "Creek Indian Crisis," 331; "Report of Colonel Brown," *Tallahassee Floridian*, August 5, 1837, 2.

35. Rucker, "Creek Indian Crisis," 331; "From the *Pensacola Gazette*," *Tallahassee Floridian*, September 9, 1837, 2; Wilson to Harris, September 4, 1837, reel 238, MP 234, RG 75, CA, LR, OIA, WD, NARA.

36. Jesup to Poinsett, October 17, 1837, ASPMA 7:885–86; Jesup to Poinsett, June 15, 1837, ASPMA 7:873–75; Jesup to Butler, January 19, 1837, ASPMA 7:826; Jesup to Jones, July 19, 1837, ASPMA 7:841; Miller to Jesup, July 16, 1837, ASPMA 7:842; Jesup to Harris, July 18, 1837, reel 238, MP 234, RG 75, CA, LR, OIA, WD, NARA; Jesup to Poinsett, September 22, 1837, ASPMA 7:882; Jesup to Searle, September 9, 1837, reel 290, MP 234, RG 75, SS, LR, OIA, WD, NARA; Creek Chiefs to Harris, May 8, 1838, reel 225, MP 234, RG 75, CA, LR, OIA, WD, NARA, 667; Sloan to Harris, May 6, 1838, reel 225, MP 234, RG 75, CA, LR, OIA, WD, NARA, 682; Harris to Cooper, May 9, 1838, reel 225, MP 234, RG 75, CA, LR, OIA, WD, NARA, 699–700; Harris to Poinsett, July 19, 1838, reel 225, MP 234, RG 75, CA, LR, OIA, WD, NARA, 702–3; Casy to Clark, July 14, 1836, reel 291, MP 234, RG 75, SS, LR, OIA, WD, NARA, 606–10; House Resolution, 25th Cong., 2nd sess., January 28, 1839, reel 291, MP 234, RG 75, SS, LR, OIA, WD, NARA, 186–87; Creek Delegation to Harris, April 23, 1838, reel 225, MP 234, RG 75, CA, LR, OIA, WD, NARA, 475–76; Arbuckle to Poinsett, September 28, 1838, reel 225, MP 234, RG 75, CA, LR, OIA, WD, NARA, 489–90; Arbuckle to Reynolds, June 13, 1838, reel 225, MP 234, RG 75, CA, LR, OIA, WD, NARA, 497–98.

37. Page to Harris, October 27, 1837, reel 238, MP 234, RG 75, CA, LR, OIA, WD, NARA; Page to Harris, December 28, 1837, reel 238, MP 234, RG 75, CA, LR, OIA, WD, NARA; Boyd to Crawford, January 26, 1838, reel 291, MP 234, RG 75, SS, LR, OIA, WD, NARA; Clements to Harris, November 1, 1837, reel 238, MP 234, RG 75, CA, LR, OIA, WD, NARA; Clements to Harris, November 18, 1837, reel 238, MP 234, RG 75, CA, LR, OIA, WD, NARA; Foreman, *Indian Removal*, 187, 190; Muster Roll of Emigrant Creeks, First Quarter, 1838, reel 239, MP 234, RG 75, CA, LR, OIA, WD, NARA.

38. Claims Commission Report, November 28, 1837, reel 225, MP 234, RG 75, CA, LR, OIA, WD, NARA, 291–98; Smith to Secretary of War, October 6, 1837, reel 225, MP 234, RG 75, CA, LR, OIA, WD, NARA, 375–76; Spierin to [?], October 9, 1837, reel 225, MP 234, RG 75, CA, LR, OIA, WD, NARA, 393–94; Notice, Commissioner's Office, June 21, 1837, reel 225, MP 234, RG 75, CA, LR, OIA, WD, NARA, 288.

39. Ellisor, "Like So Many Wolves," 19–22; Paredes, "Federal Recognition," 120–21.

40. Rucker, "Creek Indian Crisis," 332; "By a Letter," *Tallahassee Floridian*, September 9, 1837,

3; "Fugitive Creeks," *Tallahassee Floridian*, September 16, 1837, 3; "On Wednesday Last," *Tallahassee Floridian*, October 7, 1837, 2; "A Party of Friendly Indians," *Tallahassee Floridian*, October 14, 1837, 3; "The Party of Friendly Indians," *Tallahassee Floridian*, October 28, 1837, 2; "From the West," *Tallahassee Floridian*, November 18, 1837, 3; Wilson to Harris, September 4, 1837, reel 239, MP 234, RG 75, CA, LR, OIA, WD, NARA.

41. Citizen's Petition, Dale County, n.d., Clay Administrative Files, Creek War, ADAH; Booth to Bagby, November 1, 1837, Bagby Militia Files, 1837–41, ADAH; Lewis to Bagby, November 4, 1837, Bagby Militia Files, 1837–41, ADAH; Warren to Bagby, November 23, 1837, Bagby Militia Files, 1837–41, ADAH; Pouncey to Bagby, December 12, 1837, Bagby Militia Files, 1837–41, ADAH; Pate to Bagby, February 12, 1838, Bagby Militia Files, 1837–41, ADAH.

42. Richards to Boyd, Camp Relief, March 6, 1838, reel 239, MP 234, RG 75, CA, LR, OIA, WD, NARA.

43. "The Fugitive Creeks," *Tallahassee Floridian*, December 2, 1837, 2; "We Understand," *Tallahassee Floridian*, January 6, 1838, 2.

44. Richards to Boyd, Camp Relief, March 6, 1838, reel 239, MP 234, RG 75, CA, LR, OIA, WD, NARA; Call to Boyd, March 7, 1838, reel 239, MP 234, RG 75, CA, LR, OIA, WD, NARA.

45. Richards to Boyd, March 6, 1838, reel 239, MP 234, RG 75, CA, LR, OIA, WD, NARA; Call to Boyd, March 7, 1838, reel 239, MP 234, RG 75, CA, LR, OIA, WD, NARA; Smith to Harris, February 7, 1838, reel 239, MP 234, RG 75, CA, LR, OIA, WD, NARA; Boyd to Harris, February 20, 1838, reel 239, MP 234, RG 75, CA, LR, OIA, WD, NARA; Boyd to Harris, February 25, 1838, reel 239, MP 234, RG 75, CA, LR, OIA, WD, NARA; Smith to Harris, February 26, 1838, reel 239, MP 234, RG 75, CA, LR, OIA, WD, NARA; Boyd to Harris, March 1, 1838, reel 239, MP 234, RG 75, CA, LR, OIA, WD, NARA; Call to Boyd, March 7, 1838, reel 239, MP 234, RG 75, CA, LR, OIA, WD, NARA; Boyd to Harris, March 8, 1838, reel 239, MP 234, RG 75, CA, LR, OIA, WD, NARA.

46. "Legislative Council," *Tallahassee Floridian*, January 30, 1838, 1; "Call to Poinsett," October 14, 1837, *Tallahassee Floridian*, January 30, 1838, 1; "Call to Poinsett," January 17, 1838, *Tallahassee Floridian*, January 30, 1838, 1; "Call to Van Buren," January 18, 1838, *Tallahassee Floridian*, January 30, 1838, 1.

47. Walker to Harris, January 25, 1838, in Carter, *Territorial Papers*, 25:458–59; "The Creeks," *Tallahassee Floridian*, July 21, 1838, 2; *Tallahassee Floridian*, October 28, 1837, 2; Smith to Harris, January 4, 1838, reel 290, MP 234, RG 75, SS, LR, OIA, WD, NARA; Jesup to Poinsett, April 2, 1838, reel 290, MP 234, RG 75, SS, LR, OIA, WD, NARA, 239; Boyd to Harris, May 20, 1838, reel 290, MP 234, RG 75, SS, LR, OIA, WD, NARA, 239.

48. "We Learn," *Tallahassee Floridian*, May 5, 1838, 2; "The Creeks," *Tallahassee Floridian*, July 21, 1838, 2; Statement of Sally and Silversmith, On Board the Francis, n.d., reel 239, MP 234, RG 75, CA, LR, OIA, WD, NARA; Boyd to Harris, May 24, 1838, reel 239, MP 234, RG 75, CA, LR, OIA, WD, NARA.

49. Boyd to Harris, May 24, 1838, reel 239, MP 234, RG 75, CA, LR, OIA, WD, NARA; *Tallahassee Floridian*, April 21, 1838, 2; Smith to Harris, January 5, 1837, reel 290, MP 234, RG 75, SS, LR, OIA, WD, NARA, 221.

50. Walker to Harris, January 25, 1838, in Carter, *Territorial Papers*, 25:458–59.

51. Sprague, *Florida War*, 268–70; Mahon, *Second Seminole War*, 244, 247–49, 301; Franklin, *Militant South*, 28; "We Learn," *Tallahassee Floridian*, May 5, 1838, 2; "The Creeks," *Tallahassee Floridian*, July 21, 1838, 2; "Three Companies," *Tallahassee Floridian*, April 28, 1838, 2; "General

Orders No. 7," *Tallahassee Floridian*, April 28, 1838, 2; Levy to Secretary of War, January 5, 1841, in Carter, *Territorial Papers*, 26:416; White to Knowles, February 15, 1837, in Carter, *Territorial Papers*, 26:378–79.

52. Boyd to Hutter, May 31, 1838, reel 239, MP 234, RG 75, CA, LR, OIA, WD, NARA; Boyd to Harris, June 3, 1838, reel 239, MP 234, RG 75, CA, LR, OIA, WD, NARA; Boyd to Harris, June 6, 1838, reel 239, MP 234, RG 75, CA, LR, OIA, WD, NARA.

53. Smith to Harris, November 3, 1837, reel 290, MP 234, RG 75, SS, LR, OIA, WD, NARA, 241; Boyd to Hutter, May 31, 1838, reel 239, MP 234, RG 75, CA, LR, OIA, WD, NARA; Boyd to Harris, June 3, 1838, reel 239, MP 234, RG 75, CA, LR, OIA, WD, NARA; Boyd to Harris, June 6, 1838, reel 239, MP 234, RG 75, CA, LR, OIA, WD, NARA; Boyd to Harris, June 13, 1838, reel 239, MP 234, RG 75, CA, LR, OIA, WD, NARA; Treaty, Econchattee Micco's Town, June 20, 1838, reel 290, MP 234, RG 75, SS, LR, OIA, WD, NARA; Boyd to Harris, August 8, 1838, reel 290, MP 234, RG 75, SS, LR, OIA, WD, NARA; Boyd to Harris, August 24, 1838, reel 290, MP 234, RG 75, SS, LR, OIA, WD, NARA; Harris to Boyd, August 29, 1838, reel 290, MP 234, RG 75, SS, LR, OIA, WD, NARA; Boyd to Richards, September 3, 1838, reel 290, MP 234, RG 75, SS, LR, OIA, WD, NARA; Estimate of Funds, October 1, 1838, reel 291, MP 234, RG 75, SS, LR, OIA, WD, NARA; Boyd to Harris, October 2, 1838, reel 291, MP 234, RG 75, SS, LR, OIA, WD, NARA; Muster Roll, October 20, 1838, reel 291, MP 234, RG 75, SS, LR, OIA, WD, NARA; Boyd to Harris, October 28, 1838, reel 291, MP 234, RG 75, SS, LR, OIA, WD, NARA; Covington, "Federal Relations," 140; Smith to Harris, February 19, 1837, reel 290, MP 234, RG 75, SS, LR, OIA, WD, NARA, 227–28.

54. "Hutter to Call," *Tallahassee Floridian*, August 4, 1838, 2; "A Portion of the Indians," *Tallahassee Floridian*, June 9, 1838, 2; "From St. Augustine," *Tallahassee Floridian*, June 23, 1938, 2; "From the Frontiers," *Tallahassee Floridian*, July 21, 1838, 2; "More Indian Murders," *Tallahassee Floridian*, July 28, 1838, 2; "The War Nearly Ended," *Tallahassee Floridian*, July 28, 1838, 2; "More Victims to Savage Barbarity," *Tallahassee Floridian*, July 28, 1838, 3; "Indians in the Okefenokee," *Tallahassee Floridian*, July 28, 1838, 3; "The Creeks," *Tallahassee Floridian*, August 4, 1838, 2. For the Lashley attack, see "C. H. Dupont, Colonel Commanding 5th Regiment Florida Militia, to Call," *Tallahassee Floridian*, August 4, 1838, 2.

55. Worth to Adjutant General, December 15, 1841, in Carter, *Territorial Papers*, 26:410–11; Sprague, *Florida War*, 331, 347, 394–95, 440, 470; Mahon, *Second Seminole War*, 305.

56. Sprague, *Florida War*, 495–96; Mahon, *Second Seminole War*, 316; Adjutant General to Vose, September 12, 1842, in Carter, *Territorial Papers*, 26:538–39; Vose to Adjutant General, October 6, 1842, in Carter, *Territorial Papers*, 26:555–56; Secretary of War to Long, November 28, 1842, in Carter, *Territorial Papers*, 26:572.

57. Carswell, *Washington*, 45–49.

58. Jesup to Poinsett, October 15, 1837, *ASPMA* 7:885; Vose to Adjutant General, September 26, 1842, in Carter, *Territorial Papers*, 26:548–49; Vose to Adjutant General, September 29, 1842, in Carter, *Territorial Papers*, 26:551.

59. Jesup to Poinsett, October 15, 1837, *ASPMA* 7:885; Vose to Adjutant General, September 26, 1842, in Carter, *Territorial Papers*, 26:548–49; Vose to Adjutant General, September 29, 1842, in Carter, *Territorial Papers*, 26:551; Mahon, *Second Seminole War*, 256, 317; Sprague, *Florida War*, 494, 496; Motte, *Journey into the Wilderness*, vii, xiv.

60. Sprague, *Florida War*, 500; Peters, *Florida Wars*, 257, 259.

61. Peters, *Florida Wars*, 259–61.

62. Peters, *Florida Wars*, 262.

63. Carswell, *Washington*, 49–50; Adjutant General to Arbuckle, February 6, 1844, in Carter, *Territorial Papers*, 26:850.

64. McKinnon, *Walton County*, 124–28; Carswell, *Washington*, 50–51.

65. McKinnon, *Walton County*, 124–28; Rucker, "Creek Indian Crisis," 333.

Epilogue

1. Mahon, *Second Seminole War*, 326; Foreman, *Indian Removal*, 383.

2. Jordan, *Ante-Bellum Alabama*, 9–12; Flynt, *Montgomery*, 18; Tallapoosa County Bicentennial Committee, *Tallapoosa*, 121.

3. Jordan, *Ante-Bellum Alabama*, 10. Willoughby chronicles the economic development of the country between Columbus and the Gulf of Mexico in *Fair to Middlin'*.

4. Mahon, *Second Seminole War*, 326; J. H. Martin, *Columbus, Georgia*, 80–81.

5. D. Williams, *Rich Man's War*, 16–17.

6. D. Williams, *Rich Man's War*, 16–17; Jordan, *Ante-Bellum Alabama*, 16.

7. Debo, *Road to Disappearance*, 110–11; Warde, *George Washington Grayson*, 28.

8. Foreman, *Traveler in Indian Territory*, 111–23; Debo, *Road to Disappearance*, 110–11; Armstrong to Harris, July 13, 1838, reel 225, MP 234, RG 75, CA, LR, OIA, WD, NARA, 502.

9. Warde, *George Washington Grayson*, 53–85.

10. Blake to Lewis, June 27, 1839, reel 240, MP 234, RG 75, CA, LR, OIA, WD, NARA; Blake to Lewis, February 8, 1840, reel 240, MP 234, RG 75, CA, LR, OIA, WD, NARA; Blake to Abert, May 8, 1841, reel 240, MP 234, RG 75, CA, LR, OIA, WD, NARA; Crawford to Blake, May 31, 1841, reel 240, MP 234, RG 75, CA, LR, OIA, WD, NARA; Blake to Crawford, June 25, 1841, reel 240, MP 234, RG 75, CA, LR, OIA, WD, NARA.

11. Crawford to Poinsett, July 23, 1839, reel 239, MP 234, RG 75, CA, LR, OIA, WD, NARA; Crawford to Blake, September 5, 1839, reel 239, MP 234, RG 75, CA, LR, OIA, WD, NARA; Crawford to Blake, May 31, 1841, reel 240, MP 234, RG 75, CA, LR, OIA, WD, NARA; Booth to War Department, May 30, 1841, reel 240, MP 234, RG 75, CA, LR, OIA, WD, NARA; Blake to Crawford, June 25, 1841, reel 240, MP 234, RG 75, CA, LR, OIA, WD, NARA; Varner and Lewis to Crawford, January 14, 1845, reel 240, MP 234, RG 75, CA, LR, OIA, WD, NARA; Beauchamp, "Early Chronicles," 58; Booth to Bagby, May 26, 1841, Bagby Militia Files, 1837–41, ADAH.

12. Smartt, *History of Eufaula*, 19; M. Thompson, *Barbour County*, 54–55; Booth to Bagby, May 26, 1841, Bagby Militia Files, 1837–41, ADAH.

13. Watson, *Piney Woods Echoes*, 14–15; Brunson, *Pea River Reflections*, 27–29.

14. McKinnon, *Walton County*, 120; Nixon, *Lower Piedmont Country*, 8.

15. Wheat to Medill, May 8, 1846, reel 240, MP 234, RG 75, CA, LR, OIA, WD, NARA; Crawford to Lewis, April 9, 1844, reel 240, MP 234, RG 75, CA, LR, OIA, WD, NARA; Blake to Abert, September 9, 1843, reel 240, MP 234, RG 75, CA, LR, OIA, WD, NARA; Cherry to Crawford, August 28, 1845, reel 240, MP 234, RG 75, CA, LR, OIA, WD, NARA; Medill to Cherry, January 11, 1846, reel 240, MP 234, RG 75, CA, LR, OIA, WD, NARA; Medill to Commissioner of Indian Affairs, January 20, 1846, reel 240, MP 234, RG 75, CA, LR, OIA, WD, NARA.

16. Muster Roll, Creek Agency, February 15, 1846, reel 240, MP 234, RG 75, CA, LR, OIA, WD, NARA; Logan to Medill, Creek Agency, March 5, 1846, reel 240, MP 234, RG 75, CA, LR, OIA, WD, NARA; Abstract of Provisions, March 31, 1846, reel 240, MP 234, RG 75, CA, LR, OIA, WD, NARA; Logan to Medill, May 19, 1846, reel 240, MP 234, RG 75, CA, LR, OIA, WD, NARA.

17. Medill to Commissioner of Indian Affairs, January 26, 1846, reel 240, MP 234, RG 75, CA, LR, OIA, WD, NARA; Lovett and Carr to Lewis, December 15, 1846, reel 240, MP 234, RG 75, CA, LR, OIA, WD, NARA; Muster Roll of Major Carr's Party, September 30, 1847, reel 240, MP 234, RG 75, CA, LR, OIA, WD, NARA; Logan to Medill, November 9, 1847, reel 240, MP 234, RG 75, CA, LR, OIA, WD, NARA; Cochemy to Medill, April 7, 1848, reel 240, MP 234, RG 75, CA, LR, OIA, WD, NARA.

18. Cochemy to Medill, April 7, 1848, reel 240, MP 234, RG 75, CA, LR, OIA, WD, NARA.

19. Lewis to Lewis, December 12, 1843, reel 240, MP 234, RG 75, CA, LR, OIA, WD, NARA; Mackay, *Life and Liberty*, 289–90.

20. Cherry, "History of Opelika," 224; Nunn, *Yesterdays in Loachapoka*, 8; Ellsworth and Dysart, "West Florida's Forgotten People," 433; Wells, *Searching for Red Eagle*, 8.

21. Ellsworth and Dysart, "West Florida's Forgotten People," 433; Paredes, "Federal Recognition," 136–39; J. L. Wright, *Creeks and Seminoles*, 318.

22. "Commission Seeks to Aid State Indians," *Montgomery Advertiser*, February 9, 1985, 1–2; J. L. Wright, *Only Land They Knew*, 246, 252, 289; Clark and Guice, *Frontiers in Conflict*, xi, 188, 252; DeLoria, *Custer Died*, 2–5.

Bibliography

Unpublished Sources
Alabama Department of Archives and History (ADAH), Montgomery AL
Bagby, Arthur P. Militia Files, 1837–41.
Chambers County. Miscellaneous Probate Records. Indian Estate Records, 1834–46. Local Government Microfilm 114, reel 21.
Chapin, M. T. Chapin Collection.
Clay, Clement C. Administrative Files, Creek War.
Gayle, John. Executive Letter Book.
Gayle, John. Pardons, Paroles, and Clemency Files, 1831–35. Russell County.
Sanford, John W. A. Papers.
Talledega County. Miscellaneous Probate Records. Deed Records, 1833–37. Vol. A. LGM 26, reel 26.
———. Probate Records. Orphans Court Minutes, 1843–47. Vol. C-1. LGM 28, reel 2.
———. Probate Records. Will Records, 1833–41. Vol. A. LGM 27, reel 21.

Chattahoochee Valley Community College (CVCC), Phenix City AL
Nunn, Alexander. Articles. Alexander Nunn Collection.

Georgia Department of Archives and History (GDAH), Atlanta GA
Hays, Louise Frederick, ed. Creek Indian Letters, part 4, 1830–39.

National Archives and Records Administration (NARA), Washington DC
Office of the Adjutant General. Papers and Books. General Jesup. Record group 94.
War Department. Office of Indian Affairs. Letters Received. Creek Agency. Record group 75, microfilm publication 234, reels 221, 223, 224, 225, 237, 238, 239, 240, 243.
———. Office of Indian Affairs. Letters Received. Seminole Superintendency. Record group 75, microfilm publication 234, reels 290, 291.

Newspapers and News Periodicals
Alabama Journal, 1830–31.
Army and Navy Chronicle, 1837.
Brunswick Advocate, 1838.

Columbus Enquirer, 1835–37.
Milledgeville Federal Union, 1835–37.
Mobile Commercial Register, 1836–37.
Montgomery Advertiser, 1985.
New York Observer, 1837.
Niles Weekly Register, 1828, 1831.
Pensacola Gazette, 1837.
Tallahassee Floridian, 1835–38.

Published Sources

Aiken, John G. *A Digest of the Laws of the State of Alabama*. Tuscaloosa AL: Woodruff and Smith, 1836.

Anthony, J. D. "Reminiscences of Cherokee County, 1835–1875." In *Early History of Northeast Alabama and Incidentally of Northwest Georgia*, edited by W. Stanley Hoole and Addie S. Hoole, 29–58. Tuscaloosa AL: Confederate, 1979.

Applebome, Peter. *Dixie Rising: How the South Is Shaping American Values, Politics, and Culture*. San Diego: Harcourt Brace, 1997.

ASPIA (American State Papers, Class 2: Indian Affairs), 2 vols. Washington DC: Gales and Seaton, 1832–34.

ASPMA (American State Papers, Class 5: Military Affairs), 7 vols. Washington DC: Gales and Seaton, 1832–61.

Banton, Michael P. *Racial and Ethnic Competition*. Cambridge: Cambridge University Press, 1983.

Bartley, Nunan V. *The Creation of Modern Georgia*. Athens: University of Georgia Press, 1983.

Bartram, William. *Travels through North and South Carolina, Georgia, East and West Florida*. Philadelphia: Jones and Johnson, 1791.

Bassett, John Spencer. *The Correspondence of Andrew Jackson*. Vol. 5. Washington DC: Carnegie Institution, 1931.

Beauchamp, Green. "Early Chronicles of Barbour County." *Alabama Historical Quarterly* 33, no. 1 (Spring 1971): 37–74.

Beaud, Michael. *A History of Capitalism 1500–1980*. New York: Monthly Review, 1983.

Beeson, J. A. B. *History of Eufaula, Alabama: The Bluff City of the Chattahoochee*. 1875. Reprint. Spartanburg SC: Reprint Company, 1976.

Boles, John B. *The South through Time: A History of an American Region*. Englewood Cliffs NJ: Prentice-Hall, 1995.

Bragg, James W. "Captain Slick, Arbiter of Early Alabama Morals." *Alabama Review* 11, no. 2 (April 1958): 124–34.

Brannon, Peter A. "Alabama Indian Chiefs." *Alabama Historical Quarterly* 13, no. 1 (January 1951): 5–91.

Braund, Kathryn E. Holland. "The Creek Indians, Blacks, and Slavery." *Journal of Southern History* 57, no. 4 (1991): 601–36.

———. *Deerskins and Duffels: The Creek Indian Trade with Anglo-America, 1685–1815*. Lincoln: University of Nebraska Press, 1993.

———. "Guardians of Tradition and Handmaidens to Change: Women's Roles in Creek Economic and Social Life during the Eighteenth Century." *American Indian Quarterly* 14 (Summer 1990): 239–58.

Brewer, George Evans. *History of Coosa County*. Montgomery AL: State Department of Archives and History, 1955.

Brown, Philip M. "Early Indian Trade in the Development of South Carolina: Politics, Economics,

and Social Mobility during the Proprietary Period, 1670–1719." *South Carolina Historical Magazine* 76 (October 1975): 118–28.
Brown, Richard Maxwell. *The American Vigilante Tradition*. Edited by Hugh Davis Graham and Ted Robert Gurr. Vol. 1 of *Violence in America: Historical and Comparative Perspectives of Violence in America*. Washington DC: Government Printing Office, 1969.
———. *Strain of Violence: Historical Studies of American Violence and Vigilantism*. New York: Oxford University Press, 1975.
Brunson, Marian Bailey. *Pea River Reflections: Intimate Glimpses of Area Life during Two Centuries*. Tuscaloosa AL: Portals, 1975.
Buckingham, James Silk. *The Slave States of America*. Vol. 1. London: Fisher, Son, and Company, 1842.
Campbell, John. "The Seminoles, the 'Bloodhound War,' and Abolitionism, 1796–1865." *Journal of Southern History* 72, no. 2 (May 2006): 259–302.
Campbell, John Archibald. "The Creek Indian War of 1836." *Alabama Historical Society Publications* 3 (1898–99): 162–66.
Carswell, E. W. *Homesteading: The History of Holmes County, Florida*. Tallahassee FL: Rose, 1986.
———. *Washington: Florida's Twelfth County*. Tallahassee FL: Rose, 1991.
Carter, Edwin, ed. *The Territorial Papers of the United States*. Vol. 25, *The Territory of Florida 1834–1839*. Washington DC: National Archives, 1960.
———. *The Territorial Papers of the United States*. Vol. 26, *The Territory of Florida, 1839–1845*. Washington DC: National Archives, 1960.
Caughey, John Walton. *McGillivray of the Creeks*. Norman: University of Oklahoma Press, 1938.
Champagne, Duane. *Social Order and Political Change: Constitutional Governments among the Cherokee, the Choctaws, the Chickasaws, and the Creeks*. Stanford CA: Stanford University Press, 1992.
Cherry, F. L. "The History of Opelika and Her Agricultural Tributary Territory, Embracing More Particularly Lee and Russell Counties, from the Earliest Settlement to the Present Date." *Alabama Historical Quarterly* 15, nos. 2–4 (1953): 176–537.
Clark, Thomas D., and John D. W. Guice. *Frontiers in Conflict: The Old Southwest, 1795–1830*. Albuquerque: University of New Mexico Press, 1989.
Clements, J. B. *History of Irwin County, Georgia*. Spartanburg SC: Reprint Company, 1978.
Cohen, M. M. *Notices of Florida and The Campaigns*. 1836. Reprint. Gainesville: University of Florida Press, 1964.
Coleman, Kenneth, ed. *A History of Georgia*. Athens: University of Georgia Press, 1977.
Coles, Arthur Charles. *The Whig Party in the South*. 1914. Reprint. Gloucester MA: Smith, 1962.
Collins, Bruce. *White Society in the Antebellum South*. London: Longman, 1985.
Corkran, David H. *The Creek Frontier 1540–1783*. Norman: University of Oklahoma Press, 1967.
Cotterill, Robert Spencer. *Southern Indians: The Story of the Civilized Tribes before Removal*. Norman: University of Oklahoma Press, 1971.
Coulter, Harold S. *A People Courageous: A History of Phenix City, Alabama*. Columbus GA: Howard, 1976.
Covington, James W. "Federal Relations with the Apalachicola Indians: 1823–1838." *Florida Historical Quarterly* 42, no. 2 (October 1963): 125–41.
Crane, Verner W. *The Southern Frontier, 1670–1732*. Ann Arbor: University of Michigan Press, 1929.
Croffut, W. A., ed. *Fifty Years in Camp and Field: Diary of Major-General Ethan Allen Hitchcock*. New York: Putnam and Sons, 1909.
Cross, Richard H. "On the Trail of Jim Henry." *Muscogiana* 3, nos. 3–4 (Fall 1992): 55–63.
Davenport, E. Garvin. *The Myth of Southern History: Historical Consciousness in Twentieth-Century Southern Literature*. Nashville TN: Vanderbilt University Press, 1970.

BIBLIOGRAPHY

Davis, Robert S., Jr. "Goliad and the Georgia Battalion: Georgia Participation in the Texas Revolution, 1835–1836." *Journal of Southwest Georgia History* 4 (Fall 1986): 25–55.

Debo, Angie. *Road to Disappearance*. Norman: University of Oklahoma Press, 1941.

DeLoria, Vine. *Custer Died for Your Sins: An Indian Manifesto*. New York: Macmillan, 1969.

DeRosier, Arthur H., Jr. *The Removal of the Choctaw Indians*. Knoxville: University of Tennessee Press, 1970.

Dobyns, Henry F., and William R. Swaggerty, eds. *Their Number Become Thinned: Native American Population Dynamics in Eastern North America*. Knoxville: University of Tennessee Press, 1983.

Doherty, Herbert J. "Richard K. Call vs. the Federal Government of the Seminole War." *Florida Historical Quarterly* 31, no. 3 (January 1953): 163–80.

Doster, James F. *The Creek Indians and Their Florida Lands, 1740–1823*. 2 vols. New York: Garland, 1974.

Dowd, Gregory Evans. *A Spirited Resistance: The North American Indian Struggle for Unity, 1745–1815*. Baltimore: John Hopkins University Press, 1992.

Dunaway, Wilma A. *The First American Frontier: Transition to Capitalism in Southern Appalachia, 1700–1860*. Chapel Hill: University of North Carolina Press, 1996.

Eby, Cecil. *"That Disgraceful Affair": The Black Hawk War*. New York: Norton, 1973.

Edmunds, R. David. *Tecumseh and the Quest for Indian Leadership*. Boston: Little, Brown, and Company, 1984.

Elizer, Marshall Ridley. "Georgia under the Administration of William Schley, 1835–37." Master's thesis, University of Georgia, 1940.

Elkin, A. P. "Reaction and Interaction: A Food Gathering People and European John T. Settlement in Australia." In *Beyond the Frontier: Social Process and Cultural Change*, edited by Fred Plog and Paul Bohannon, 43–70. New York: Natural History, 1967.

Elliott, Charles W. *Winfield Scott: The Soldier and the Man*. New York: MacMillan, 1937.

Ellis, Joseph J. *Founding Brothers: The Revolutionary Generation*. New York: Knopf, 2001.

Ellisor, John T. "'Like So Many Wolves': Creek Removal in the Cherokee Country, 1835–1838." *Journal of East Tennessee History* 71 (1999): 1–24.

———. "The Second Creek War: The Unexplored Conflict." PhD diss., University of Tennessee, 1996.

Ellsworth, Lucius F., and Jane E. Dysart. "West Florida's Forgotten People: The Creek Indians from 1830 until 1970." *Florida Historical Quarterly* 59 (April 1981): 422–39.

Ethridge, Robbie Franklyn. "A Contest for the Land: The Creek Indians on the Southern Frontier, 1786–1816." PhD diss., University of Georgia, 1996.

———. *Creek Country: The Creek Indians and Their World*. Chapel Hill: University of North Carolina Press, 2003.

Fanon, Frantz. *The Wretched of the Earth*. 1961. Reprint. New York: Grove, 1978.

Farmer, Margaret Pace. *History of Pike County, Alabama*. Ann Arbor: Edwards Brothers, 1953.

Featherstonhaugh, George William. *Excursion through the Slave States from Washington on the Potomac to the Frontier of Mexico: With Sketches of Popular Manners and Geological Notices*. 1844. Reprint. Negro Universities Press, 1968.

Flynt, J. Wayne. *Montgomery: An Illustrated History*. Woodland Hills CA: Windsor, 1980.

Foner, Eric. *The Story of American Freedom*. New York: Norton, 1998.

Foreman, Grant. *Indian Removal*. Norman: University of Oklahoma Press, 1932.

———, ed. *A Traveler in Indian Territory: The Journal of Ethan Allen Hitchcock, Late Major-General in the United States Army*. Cedar Rapids IA: Torch, 1930.

Foster-Carter, Aiden. "The Modes of Production Controversy." *New Left Review* 107 (January–February 1978): 47–77.

Frank, Andre G. *Capitalism and Underdevelopment in Latin America*. New York: Monthly Review, 1967.
Frank, Andrew K. *Creeks and Southerners: Biculturalism on the Early American Frontier*. Lincoln: University of Nebraska Press, 2005.
Franklin, John Hope. *The Militant South, 1800–1861*. Boston: Beacon, 1964.
Freehling, William W. *Prelude to Civil War: The Nullification Controversy in South Carolina*. New York: Harper and Row, 1966.
Fretwell, James. *This So Remote Frontier*. Tuscaloosa: University of Alabama Press, 1980.
Gallay, Alan. *The Indian Slave Trade, 1670–1717*. New Haven: Yale University Press, 2003.
Galloway, Patricia. "Confederacy as a Solution to Chiefdom Dissolution: Historical Evidence in the Choctaw Case." In *The Forgotten Centuries*, edited by Charles Hudson and Carmen Chaves Tesser, 393–420. Athens: University of Georgia Press, 1994.
Garrison, Tim Alan. *The Legal Ideology of Removal: The Southern Judiciary and the Sovereignty of Native American Indians*. Athens: University of Georgia Press, 2002.
Genovese, Eugene D. *The Political Economy of Slavery: Studies in the Economy and Society of the Slave South*. New York: Pantheon Books, 1965.
Giddings, Joshua R. *The Exiles of Florida; or, The Crimes Committed by Our Government against the Maroons, Who Fled from South Carolina and Other Slave States, Seeking Protection under Spanish Law*. 1858. Reprint. Gainesville: University of Florida Press, 1964.
Green, Michael D. "Alexander McGillivray." In *American Indian Leaders: Studies in Diversity*, edited by R. David Edmunds, 41–63. Lincoln: University of Nebraska Press, 1980.
———. "Federal-State Conflict in the Administration of Indian Policy: Georgia, Alabama, and the Creeks, 1824–1834." PhD diss., University of Iowa, 1973.
———. *The Politics of Indian Removal: Creek Government and Society in Crisis*. Lincoln: University of Nebraska Press, 1982.
Griffith, Benjamin W., Jr. *McIntosh and Weatherford, Creek Indian Leaders*. Tuscaloosa: University of Alabama Press, 1988.
Hackney, Sheldon. "Southern Violence." *American Historical Review* 74, no. 3 (February 1969): 906–25.
Hahn, Steven C. *The Invention of the Creek Nation, 1670–1763*. Lincoln: University of Nebraska Press, 2004.
Halbert, Henry S., and Timothy H. Ball. *The Creek War of 1813 and 1814*. 1895. Reprint, edited by Frank L. Owsley Jr. Tuscaloosa: University of Alabama Press, 1995.
Hall, Joseph M., Jr. "Making an Indian People: Creek Formation in the Colonial Southeast, 1590–1735." PhD diss., University of Wisconsin, 2001.
Hamilton, Thomas. *Men and Manners in America*. 2 vols. 1833. Reprint (2 vols. in 1). New York: Kelly, 1968.
Hassig, Ross. "Internal Conflict in the Creek War." *Ethnohistory* 21, no. 3 (Summer 1974): 251–71.
Hawkins, Benjamin. *Letters of Benjamin Hawkins 1796–1816*. Savannah: Georgia Historical Society, 1916.
Henri, Florette. *The Southern Indians and Benjamin Hawkins, 1796–1816*. Norman: University of Oklahoma Press, 1986.
Hobsbawn, Eric J. *Primitive Rebels: Studies in Archaic Forms of Social Movements in the 19th and 20th Centuries*. New York: Praeger, 1963.
Hodgson, William B., and Benjamin Hawkins. *Creek Indian History*. Americus GA: Americus Book Company, 1938.
Hoole, Stanley, and Addie S. Hoole, eds. *Early History of Northeast Alabama and Incidentally of Northwest Georgia*. Tuscaloosa AL: Confederate, 1979.

Hooper, Johnson Jones. *Some Adventures of Captain Simon Suggs*. 1858. Reprint. Upper Saddle River NJ: Gregg, 1970.

Horseman, Reginald. *The Origins of Indian Removal, 1815–1824*. East Lansing: Michigan State University Press, 1967.

Hudson, Charles M. "The Genesis of Georgia's Indians." *Journal of Southwest Georgia History* 3 (Fall 1985): 1–16.

———. *Knights of Spain, Warriors of the Sun: Hernando de Soto and the South's Ancient Chiefdoms*. Athens: University of Georgia Press, 1997.

———. *Southeastern Indians*. Knoxville: University of Tennessee Press, 1976.

Ingram, William Pressley. *A History of Tallapoosa County*. Bessemer AL: American Calendar and Novelty Company, 1951.

Jack, Theodore H. "Alabama and the Federal Government: The Creek Indian Controversy." *Mississippi Valley Historical Review* 3 (December 1916): 301–17. Reprint. New York: Kraus Reprint, 1964.

Jane, Cecil, ed. *The Four Voyages of Columbus*. 2 vols. New York: Dover, n.d.

Jones, Frank S. *History of Decatur County, Georgia*. 1971. Reprint. Spartanburg SC: Reprint Company, 1980.

Jordan, Weymouth T. *Ante-Bellum Alabama: Town and Country*. Tallahassee: Florida State University, 1957.

Kappler, Charles J., ed. *Indian Affairs: Laws and Treaties*. Washington DC: Government Printing Office, 1975–1979.

———, ed. and comp. *Indian Treaties 1778–1883*. 4 vols. 1904. Reprint (4 vols. in 1). New York: Interland, 1972.

Kieffer, Chester L. *Maligned General: The Biography of Thomas Sidney Jesup*. San Rafael CA: Presidio, 1979.

King, H. M. "Historical Sketches of Macon County." *Alabama Historical Quarterly* 18, no. 2 (1956): 187–217.

King, Spencer B., Jr. *Georgia Voices: A Documentary History to 1872*. Athens: University of Georgia Press, 1966.

Knight, Vernon James, Jr. "The Formation of the Creeks." In *The Forgotten Centuries*, edited by Charles Hudson and Carmen Chaves Tesser, 373–92. Athens: University of Georgia Press, 1994.

———. *Tuckabatchee: Archaeological Investigations at an Historical Creek Town, Elmore County, Alabama*. Tuscaloosa: Office of Archaeological Research, Alabama State Museum of Natural History, University of Alabama, 1984.

Kulikoff, Allan. *The Agrarian Origins of American Capitalism*. Charlottesville: University of Virginia Press, 1992.

Lancaster, Jane F. *Removal Aftershock: The Seminole's Struggles to Survive in the West, 1836–1866*. Knoxville: University of Tennessee Press, 1994.

Lindsay, Bobby L. *"Reason for the Tears": A History of Chambers County, Alabama*. West Point GA: Hector Printing Company, 1971.

Littlefield, Daniel F. *Africans and Creeks: From the Colonial Period to the Civil War*. Westport CT: Greenwood, 1979.

Lowie, Robert H. "Some Aspects of Political Organization among the American Aborigines." *Journal of the Royal Anthropological Institute* 78 (January 1948): 11–25.

Mackay, Charles. *Life and Liberty in America*. Vol. 1. London: Smith, Elder, and Company, 1859.

Mahon, John K. *History of the Second Seminole War, 1835–1842*. Gainesville: University of Florida Press, 1967.

Martin, Bessie. *A Rich Man's War, A Poor Man's Fight: Desertion of Alabama Troops from the Confederate Army*. Tuscaloosa: University of Alabama Press, 2003.

Martin, Jack B., Margaret McKane Mauldin, and Juanita McGirt, eds. *Totkv Mocvse—New Fire: Creek Folktales by Earnest Gouge*. Norman: University of Oklahoma Press, 2004.

Martin, J. H., comp. *Columbus, Georgia: From Its Selection as a Trading Town in 1827 to Its Partial Destruction by Wilson's Raid in 1865*. Columbus GA: Gilbert, 1874.

Martin, Joel W. *Sacred Revolt: The Muskogees' Struggle for a New World*. Boston: Beacon, 1991.

———. "Southeastern Indians and the English Trade in Skins and Slaves." In *The Forgotten Centuries*, edited by Charles Hudson and Carmen Chaves Tesser, 304–24. Athens: University of Georgia Press, 1994.

Martineau, Harriet. *Society in America*. 3 vols. 1837. Reprint. New York: AMS, 1966.

Marx, Karl. *Capital: A Critical Analysis of Capitalist Production*. Vol. 1. Moscow: Progress, 1965.

Mathis, Ray. *John Horry Dent: South Carolina Aristocrat on the Alabama Frontier*. Tuscaloosa: University of Alabama Press, 1979.

Matter, Robert Allen. "Missions in the Defense of Spanish Florida, 1566–1710." *Florida Historical Quarterly* 54 (October 1975): 18–38.

McBride, Lela J. *Opothleyahola and the Loyal Muscogees: Their Flight from Kansas in the Civil War*. Jefferson NC: McFarland, 2000.

McCaffrey, James M. *The Army in Transformation, 1790–1860*. Westport CT: Greenwood, 2000.

McCann, R. B. "An Interview with Aunt Susan Thomas, An Old Slave, On the Early History of Russell County." *Arrow Points* 11, no. 1 (July 1925): 3–6.

McCorvey, Thomas C. *Alabama Historical Sketches*. Charlottesville: University of Virginia Press, 1960.

———. "Key's Mission." *Transactions of the Alabama Historical Society* 4 (1899–1903): 141–65.

McGhee, Val. *Claybank Memories: A History of Dale County, Alabama*. Ozark AL: Dale County Historical Society, 1989.

McKenney, Thomas L. *History of the Indian Tribes of North America*. Philadelphia: Rice and Clark, 1842.

McKinnon, John L. *History of Walton County, Florida*. Gainesville: Palmetto Books, 1968.

McReynolds, Edwin C. *The Seminoles*. Norman: University of Oklahoma Press, 1957.

Merrell, James H. *The Indians' New World: Catawbas and Their Neighbors from European Contact to the Era of Removal*. New York: Norton, 1989.

Meserve, John Bartlett. "Chief Opothleyahola." *Chronicles of Oklahoma* 9 (December 1931): 439–53.

Metcalf, P. Richard. "Who Should Rule at Home? Native American Politics and Indian-White Relations." *Journal of American History* 61 (December 1974): 651–65.

Milanich, Jerald T. "Franciscan Missions and Native Peoples in Spanish Florida." In *The Forgotten Centuries*, edited by Charles Hudson and Carmen Chaves Tesser, 276–303. Athens: University of Georgia Press, 1994.

Miller, Susan A. *Coacoochee's Bones: A Seminole Saga*. Lawrence: University of Kansas Press, 2003.

Mitchell, Francis Letcher. *Georgia Land and People*. Atlanta: Franklin, 1893.

Morgan, Edmund Sears. *American Slavery, American Freedom: The Ordeal of Colonial Virginia*. New York: Norton, 2003.

Motte, Jacob Rhett. *Journey into the Wilderness: An Army Surgeon's Account of Life in Camp and Field during the Creek and Seminole War, 1836–1838*. Edited by James F. Sunderman. Gainesville: University of Florida Press, 1953.

Nash, Gary B. *Red, White, and Black: The Peoples of Early America*. Englewood Cliffs NJ: Prentice-Hall, 1974.

Nixon, H. C. *Lower Piedmont Country*. New York: Duell, Sloan and Pearce, 1946.

Nunn, Alexander, ed. *Lee County and Her Forebearers*. Montgomery AL: Jones, 1983.

———. *Yesterdays in Loachapoka and Communities Nearby*. Alexander City AL: Outlook, 1968.
Oakes, James. *The Ruling Race: A History of American Slaveholders*. New York: Knopf, 1982.
O'Donnell, James H. *Southern Indians in the American Revolution*. Knoxville: University of Tennessee Press, 1973.
Orr, Nell Hart. "A History of Lafayette, Alabama, 1833–1933." Master's thesis, Auburn University, 1950.
Ortega y Gassett, José. *Man and Crisis*. New York: Norton, 1962.
Owens, Harry Philpot. "A History of Eufaula, Alabama 1832–1882." Master's thesis, Auburn University, 1963.
Owens, Thomas M. "Indian Tribes and Towns in Alabama." *Alabama Historical Quarterly* 12, no. 3 (1950): 118–241.
Owsley, Frank L. "Key's Mission." *Alabama Review* 23 (July 1970): 181–92.
Owsley, Frank Lawrence, Jr. *Struggle for the Gulf Borderlands: The Creek War and the Battle of New Orleans 1812–1815*. Gainesville: University Presses of Florida, 1981.
Paredes, J. Anthony. "Federal Recognition and the Poarch Creek Indians." In *Indians of the Southeastern United States in the Late 20th Century*, edited by J. Anthony Paredes, 120–39. Tuscaloosa: University of Alabama Press, 1992.
Pate, John Ben. *History of Turner County, Georgia*. 1933. Reprint. Spartanburg SC: Reprint Company, 1979.
Paul, Murray. *The Whig Party in Georgia, 1825–1853*. Chapel Hill: University of North Carolina Press, 1948.
Penick, James Lal, Jr. *The Great Western Land Pirate: John A. Murrell in Legend and History*. Columbus: University of Missouri Press, 1981.
Pepper, Pearl. "The Creek Indian Question in Alabama, 1832–1837." Master's thesis, Auburn University, 1942.
Perdue, Theda. *Slavery and the Evolution of Cherokee Society 1540–1866*. Knoxville: University of Tennessee Press, 1979.
Peters, Virginia Bergman. *The Florida Wars*. Hamden CT: Archon Books, 1979.
Peterson, John H., Jr. "The Indians in the Old South." In *Red, White, and Black: Symposium on Indians in the Old South*, edited by Charles M. Hudson, 116–33. Athens: University of Georgia Press, 1971.
Phillips, Paul C. *The Fur Trade*. 2 vols. Norman: University of Oklahoma Press, 1961.
Phillips, U. B. *Georgia and States Rights*. 1902. Reprint. Yellow Springs OH: Antioch, 1968.
Pickett, Albert James. *History of Alabama and Incidentally of Georgia and Mississippi from the Earliest Period*. 1851. Reprint. Sheffield AL: Randolp, 1903.
Porter, Kenneth. "Billy Bowlegs in the Seminole War." *Florida Historical Quarterly* 45, no. 3 (January 1967): 219–42.
———. *The Black Seminoles: History of a Freedom-Seeking People*. Gainesville: University of Florida Press, 1996.
———. "Florida Slaves and Free Negroes in the Second Seminole War, 1835–1842." *Journal of Negro History* 28, no. 4 (October 1943): 390–421.
Pound, Merritt B. *Benjamin Hawkins: Indian Agent*. Athens: University of Georgia Press, 1951.
Power, Tyrone. *Impressions of America*. 2 vols. London: Bentley, 1836.
Prucha, Francis Paul. *American Indian Policy in the Formative Years: The Indian Trade and Intercourse Acts, 1780–1834*. Cambridge: Harvard University Press, 1962.
———. *The Great Father: The United States Government and the American Indians*. 2 vols. Lincoln: University of Nebraska Press, 1984.
Prucha, Francis Paul, and Daniel Carmody. "A Memorandum of Lewis Cass concerning the

Regulation of Indian Affairs." *Wisconsin Magazine of History* 52, no. 1 (Autumn 1968): 36–40.

Quataert, Donald. *Social Disintegration and Popular Resistance in the Ottoman Empire, 1881–1908: Reactions to European Economic Penetrations.* New York: New York University Press, 1983.

Rau, Charles. *Ancient Aboriginal Trade in North America.* Washington DC: Smithsonian Institution, 1873.

Rawick, George P. *From Sunup to Sundown: The Making of the Black Community.* Westport CT: Greenwood, 1972.

Remini, Robert V. *Andrew Jackson and His Indian Wars.* New York: Viking, 2001.

———. *Andrew Jackson and the Course of Empire, 1767–1821.* New York: Harper and Row, 1977.

Richards, E. H. "Reminiscences of the Early Days in Chambers County." *Alabama Historical Quarterly* 4, no. 3 (Fall 1942): 417–45.

Richardson, James D. *A Compilation of the Messages and Papers of the Presidents.* Vol. 2. New York: Bureau of National Literature and Art, 1910.

———, ed. and comp. *Indian Affairs: Laws and Treaties.* Washington DC: Government Printing Office, 1974–79.

Rogin, Michael Paul. *Fathers and Children: Andrew Jackson and the Subjugation of the American Indian.* New York: Knopf, 1975.

Rucker, Brian R. "West Florida's Creek Indian Crisis of 1837." *Florida Historical Quarterly* 69, no. 3 (July 1991): 315–34.

Sahlins, Marshall David. *Tribesmen.* Englewood Cliffs NJ: Prentice-Hall, 1968.

Satz, Ronald N. *American Indian Policy in the Jacksonian Era.* Lincoln: University of Nebraska Press, 1975.

Saunt, Claudio. *Black, White, and Indian: Race and the Unmaking of an American Family.* Oxford: Oxford University Press, 2004.

———. *A New Order of Things: Property, Power, and the Transformation of the Creek Indians, 1733–1816.* Cambridge: Cambridge University Press, 1999.

Schafer, Daniel L. "U.S. Territory and State." In *The New History of Florida*, edited by Michael Gannon, 207–30. Gainesville: University Press of Florida, 1996.

Schoenleber, Charles Herbert. "The Rise of the New West: Frontier Political Pressure, State-Federal Conflict, and the Removal of the Choctaws, Chickasaws, Creeks and Cherokees, 1815–1837." PhD diss., University of Wisconsin, 1986.

Schoolcraft, Henry R., ed. *Information respecting the History, Condition and Prospects of the Indian Tribes of the United States: Collected and Prepared under the Direction of the Bureau of Indian Affairs, per Act of Congress of March 3rd, 1847.* 5 vols. Philadelphia: Lippincott, Grambo, 1853.

Scott, James C. *Domination and the Arts of Resistance: Hidden Transcripts.* New Haven: Yale University Press, 1990.

Sellers, Charles Grier. *The Market Revolution: Jacksonian America, 1815–1846.* London: Oxford University Press, 1991.

Shaffer, Lynda N. *Native Americans before 1492: The Moundbuilding Centers of the Eastern Woodlands.* Armonk NY: Sharpe, 1992.

Sheehan, Bernard. *Seeds of Extinction: Jeffersonian Philanthropy and the American Indian.* Chapel Hill: University of North Carolina Press, 1973.

Shofner, Jerrel H. *Jackson County, Florida: A History.* Marianna FL: Jackson County Heritage Association, 1985.

Smartt, Eugenia Persons. *History of Eufaula.* Birmingham AL: Roberts and Son, 1933.

Smith, Marvin T. "Aboriginal Depopulation in the Postcontact Southeast." In *Forgotten Centuries*, edited by Charles Hudson and Carmen Chaves Tesser, 257–75. Athens: University of Georgia Press, 1994.

Sprague, John T. *The Origin, Progress, and Conclusion of the Florida War*. 1848. Reprint. Gainesville: University of Florida Press, 1964.

Stiggins, George. *Creek Indian History: A Historical Narrative of the Genealogy, Traditions and Downfall of the Ispocogi or Creek Indian Tribe of Indians*. Edited by Virginia Pound. Birmingham AL: Public Library Press, 1989.

Sturtevant, William C. "Creek into Seminole." In *North American Indians in Historical Perspective*, edited by Oestreich Lurie, 92–128. New York: Random House, 1971.

Sugden, John. *Tecumseh: A Life*. New York: Henry Holt, 1998.

Swanton, John R. *Early History of the Creek Indians and Their Neighbors*. Washington DC: Government Printing Office, 1922.

———. "Green Corn Dance." *Chronicles of Oklahoma* 10 (June 1932): 170–95.

———. *The Indians of the Southeastern United States*. Washington DC: Bureau of American Ethnology, 1946.

———. *Social Organization and Social Usages of the Indians of the Creek Confederacy*. In *Forty Second Annual Report of the Bureau of American Ethnology to the Secretary of the Smithsonian Institution*, 279–325. Washington DC: Government Printing Office, 1928.

Tallapoosa County Bicentennial Committee. *Tallapoosa: A History*. Alexander City: Service Printing Company, 1976.

Thompson, Edward P. *Making of the English Working Class*. New York: Pantheon Books, 1964.

Thompson, Leonard, and Howard Lamar. "Comparative Frontier History." In *The Frontier in History: North America and Southern Africa Compared*, edited by Leonard Thompson and Howard Lamar, 1–13. New Haven: Yale University Press, 1981.

Thompson, Mattie Thomas. *History of Barbour County, Alabama*. Eufaula AL: privately printed, 1939.

Thornton, J. Mills. *Politics and Power in a Slave Society*. Baton Rouge: Louisiana State University Press, 1978.

Thronateeska Chapter, Daughters of the American Revolution. *Reminiscences of Dougherty County, Georgia*. Spartanburg SC: Reprint Company, 1978.

Tuggle, W. O. *Shem, Ham, and Japheth: The Papers of W. O. Tuggle Comprising His Indian Diary, Sketches and Observations, Myths, and Washington Journal, in the Territory and at the Capital, 1879–1882*. Edited by Eugene Current-Garcia, with Dorothy B. Hatfield. Athens: University of Georgia Press, 1973.

Turner, Frederick Jackson. *Rise of the New West, 1819–1829*. 1906. Reprint. New York: Collier Books, 1962.

U.S. Congress. House Documents. No. 154, "Hostilities with Creek Indians." 24th Cong., 2nd sess., 1837.

———. *House Documents*. No. 219, "Creek Indian Broke." 20th Cong., 2nd sess., 1833.

———. *House Documents*. No. 452, "Alleged Frauds on Creek Indians." 25th Cong., 2nd sess., 1838.

———. *House Reports*. No. 98, "Report of the Select Committee on the Georgia Question Relative to Creek Indian Lands." 19th Cong., 2nd sess., 1832.

———. *Senate Documents*. No. 120, "Cherokee Treaty of 1835." 25th Cong., 2nd sess., 1838.

———. *Senate Documents*. No. 512, "Indian Removal." 5 vols. 23rd Cong., 1st sess., 1835.

———. *Statutes at Large of the United States of America, 1789–1873*. "An Act to Regulate Trade and Intercourse with the Indian Tribes, and to Preserve Peace on the Frontiers." 23rd Cong., 1st sess., June 30, 1834.

Usner, Daniel. *Indians, Settlers, and Slaves in a Frontier Exchange Economy: The Lower Mississippi Valley before 1783*. Chapel Hill: University of North Carolina Press, 1992.

Valliere, Kenneth L. "The Creek War of 1836: A Military History." *Chronicles of Oklahoma* 57 (Winter 1979–80): 463–85.
Vandiver, Wellington. "Pioneer Talladega: Its Minutes, and Memories." *Alabama Historical Quarterly* 16, no. 1 (Spring 1954): 9–155.
Van Every, Dale. *Disinherited: The Lost Birthright of the American Indian.* New York: Morrow, 1966.
Walker, Anne Kendrick. *Backtracking in Barbour County: A Narrative of the Last Alabama Frontier.* Richmond VA: Dietz, 1941.
———. *Russell County in Retrospect: An Epic of the Far Southwest.* Richmond VA: Dietz, 1950.
Walker, Laura Singleton. *History of Ware County, Georgia.* Macon GA: Burke, 1934.
Wallace, Anthony F. C. *The Long, Bitter Trail: Andrew Jackson and the Indians.* New York: Hill and Wang, 1993.
Wallerstein, Immanuel. *The Capitalist World-Economy.* Cambridge: Cambridge University Press, 1979.
———. *The Modern World-System: Capitalist Agriculture and the Origins of the European World-Economy in the Sixteenth Century,* Text Edition. New York: Academic Press, 1976.
———. "What Can One Mean by Southern Culture?" In *The Evolution of Southern Culture,* edited by Numan Bartley, 1–13. Athens: University of Georgia Press, 1988.
Ward, May McNees. "The Disappearance of the Head of Osceola." *Florida Historical Quarterly* 33, nos. 3 and 4 (January–April 1955): 193–201.
Warde, Mary Jane. *George Washington Grayson and the Creek Nation, 1843–1920.* Norman: University of Oklahoma Press, 1999.
Waselkov, Gregory A. "Changing Strategies of Indian Field Location in the Early Historic Southeast." In *People, Plants, and Landscapes: Studies in Paleoethnobotany,* edited by Kristen J. Gremillion, 179–94. Tuscaloosa: University of Alabama Press, 1997.
———. "Historic Creek Indian Responses to European Trade and the Rise of Political Factions." In *Ethnohistory and Archaeology: Approaches to Postcontact Change in the Americas,* edited by J. Daniel Rogers and Samuel M. Wilson, 123–32. New York: Plenium, 1993.
Watson, Fred S. *Piney Woods Echoes: A History of Dale and Coffee Counties, Alabama.* Elba AL: Elba Clipper, 1949.
Weisman, Brent Richards. *Like Beads on a String: A Culture History of the Seminole Indians in Northern Peninsular Florida.* Tuscaloosa: University of Alabama Press, 1989.
Welch, Claude E. *Anatomy of Rebellion.* Albany: State University of New York Press, 1980.
Wells, Mary Ann. *Searching for Red Eagle.* Jackson: University Press of Mississippi, 1998.
West, Anson. *A History of Methodism in Alabama.* Nashville: Methodist Episcopal Publishing, 1893.
White, Christine Schultz. "Opothleyahola, Factionalism, and Creek Politics." PhD diss., Texas Christian University, 1986.
White, George. *Historical Collections of Georgia.* 1855. Reprint. Genealogical Publishing, 1969.
White, Richard. *The Middle Ground: Indians, Empires, and Republics in the Great Lakes Region, 1650–1815.* New York: Cambridge University Press, 1991.
———. *The Roots of Dependency: Subsistence, Environment, and Social Change among the Choctaws, Pawnees, and Navajos.* Lincoln: University of Nebraska Press, 1983.
White, Robert H., ed. *Messages of the Governors of Tennessee, 1835–1845.* Vol. 3. Nashville: Tennessee Historical Commission, 1945.
Wickman, Patricia. *The Tree That Bends: Discourse, Power, and the Survival of the Maskoki People.* Tuscaloosa: University of Alabama Press, 1999.
Williams, Clanton Ware. *The Early History of Montgomery and Incidentally of the State of Alabama.* Tuscaloosa AL: Confederate, 1979.

Williams, David. *Rich Man's War: Class, Caste, and Confederate Defeat in the Lower Chattahoochee Valley.* Athens: University of Georgia Press, 1998.

Willoughby, Lynn. *Fair to Middlin': The Antebellum Cotton Trade of the Apalachicola/Chattahoochee Valley.* Tuscaloosa: University of Alabama Press, 1993.

Woodward, Thomas S. *Woodward's Reminiscences of the Creek, or Muscogee Indians.* Montgomery AL: Barrett and Wimbish, 1859.

Worth, John E. *The Timucuan Chiefdoms of Spanish Florida.* Vol. 1, *Assimilation.* Gainesville: University of Florida Press, 1998.

Wright, Albert Hazen. *Our Georgia-Florida Frontier: The Okefenokee Swamp, Its History and Cartography.* Ithaca NY: Wright, 1945.

Wright, J. Leitch, Jr. *Britain and the American Frontier, 1783–1815.* Athens: University of Georgia Press, 1975.

———. *Creeks and Seminoles: The Destruction and Regeneration of the Muscogulge People.* Lincoln: University of Nebraska Press, 1986.

———. *The Only Land They Knew: The Tragic Story of the American Indians in the Old South.* New York: Free Press, 1981.

———. *William Augustus Bowles: Director General of the Creek Nation.* Athens: University of Georgia Press, 1967.

Wright, John Peavy. *Glimpses into the Past from My Grandfather's Trunk.* Alexander City AL: Outlook, 1969.

Wright, Ronald. *Time among the Maya: Travels in Belize, Guatemala, and Mexico.* New York: Werderfield and Nicolson, 1983.

Yamaguchi, Elizabeth H. "Macon County, Alabama: Its Land and Its People from Pre-History to 1870." Master's thesis, Auburn University, 1981.

Young, Mary E. "The Creek Frauds: A Study in Conscience and Corruption." *Mississippi Valley Historical Review* 42 (June 1955–March 1956): 411–37.

———. *Redskins, Ruffleshirts, and Rednecks: Indian Allotments in Alabama and Mississippi, 1830–1860.* Norman: University of Oklahoma Press, 1961.

Zamora, Margarita. *Reading Columbus.* Berkeley: University of California Press, 1993.

Index

Abbott, Thomas J., 50, 56, 60, 193, 256
Abert, John J., 69, 70, 73, 86–87, 95, 98, 100–101
Adams, John Quincy, 17–18, 45, 310–11
Alabama Emigrating Company, 170, 330
Alabama Fifth Militia Division, 207
Alabama Fourth Militia Division, 211, 389
Alabama Seventh Militia Division, 164–65, 276
Alabama Sixth Militia Division, 177–78, 207
Alaqua Creek massacre, 385–87
Alaqua Swamp, 392
alcohol. See grog shops; liquor
Alford, Julius C., 285, 289–92
annuity payments: and Creek removal, 76–77, 114–15, 122, 123–24, 169, 323; and depredations, 163; exploitation of, 132, 444n47; and tribal politics, 15, 18, 30–31
Apalachicola Indians, 372, 385, 398, 402–5, 407–9
Austill, Jeremiah, 66, 82–86, 88, 89, 96

Bailey, S. A., 155, 205–6
Balch, Alfred, 311–13
Batman, Mark W., 389–90
Battle, Cullen, 342
Battle of Brushy Creek, 271–72
Battle of Bryant's Ferry, 154
Battle of Jones Plantation, 286
Battle of Martin's Creek, 349, 350

Battle of Pea River, 366–70, 379
Battle of Quarles Plantation, 284
Battle of Shepherd's Plantation, 240, 242
Beall, Elias, 215, 219, 268–70
Belser, James, 179, 308, 359–60, 463n11
Big Fellow. See Tuskenea
Big Spring campground, 247–49, 256, 257
Big Swamp stronghold, 215, 245–46, 339, 343; as removal camp, 329, 343, 345–46, 351–53, 359
Big Warrior, 12, 14, 26, 27
Bird, Henry C., 109–10
Black Water Creeks, 372
Blair, Francis P., 253–54
Blake, Luther, 34, 424, 427
Blind King, 254–55
Booth, Jonathan P., 397, 424–25
Boyd, Daniel, 400–401, 407–9
Brashears, Samuel, 53–54
Bright, James, 97
Bright, William, 95
Broad, Philander, 194, 315
Brodnax, John H., 34, 47, 80, 94–95, 108–9, 215–17, 256
Brown, Leavin, 382, 384–86, 388, 391–93
Busk ceremony, 156–57, 183

Caldwell v. Alabama, 45
Call, Robert Keith, 382, 388, 397, 398, 400–405, 410, 413

491

INDEX

Camp Dallas, 376
Camp Gibson. *See* Roanoke
Camp Sanford, 261–62
capitalism. *See* world system
Carr, Paddy, 33, 79, 81, 124, 126, 192, 258–59, 260, 396, 428
Casey, J. W. O., 394
Cass, Lewis: and Creek debt fund, 76, 78; and Creek removal, 113, 117–19, 128–29, 136; and Creek reserves, 50; and Creek resistance, 165, 176, 180; criticism of, 225–26; and intruder removal, 57–58, 65–71, 82–83, 87–88; and land sales, 97–98, 99–100; sending of troops by, 228–30, 276
Cawlfield, David, 387–88
census commissioners, 51, 52, 53–57, 67, 68–69, 70, 73–75, 96
Chapin, M. T., 318–19
Charley, Yuchi, 345
Chehaw Indians, 154, 175, 255, 327
Cherokee Indians: and Creek politics, 14, 17, 25–26, 103; and Creek refugees, 55–56, 160–63, 191–92, 287, 320–22, 336–39; and Georgia, 272–77
Cherokee Nation v. Georgia, 44–45
Chickasawhatchee, 267–71, 286, 289–91
Chickasaw Indians, 395
children: capture and enslavement of, 408, 423, 425–26, 427; education of, 37; exploitation of, 132; killing of, 267, 293–94, 386, 417; matrilineal descent of, 51, 337
Choctawhatchee Bay, 381, 382, 384–85, 392, 399, 410, 414
Chooley, Micco. *See* Blind King
Chopco, Tustenuggee, 28, 188, 211
Christianity, 37–39
Clay, Clement C.: and Andrew Jackson, 66–67, 93–94; and Cherokee Creeks, 275–76, 337–38, 347–48; and Creek resistance, 158, 159–65, 171, 175, 177–78, 179–80; and Florida war, 381, 388–89; and land speculators, 223–24, 301–2, 307, 312, 322; and removal camps, 353–54, 358–59, 363–65, 370; and war strategy, 203, 207–10, 211, 216–18, 219–20, 234–38
Cochemy, Ward, 428
Cockburn, George, 224–25

Columbus: in Creek rebellion, 152, 189–90, 196, 200, 201, 204–7, 233–34; and land speculators, 63, 112, 133; and war in southern Georgia, 269–71, 309; war's impact on, 419, 420–21
Columbus Enquirer, 150, 203, 207, 225–26, 234, 296, 300, 318, 328
Columbus Herald, 307, 328
Columbus Land Company, 65, 73, 92, 103–4, 125, 127–28
Columbus Republican, 196
Columbus Sentinel, 194, 200, 201, 285, 328
Compact of 1802, 14
Cooper, Jack, 362
cotton, 13, 48, 58, 298, 418–19, 420
courts. *See* justice system, Alabama; justice system, Creek
Cow Creek skirmish, 293
Coweta Indians, 214, 258, 375–76
Coweta town, 29, 33
Cowikee Swamp, 261–62, 277, 283
Crawford, Robert L., 57–61, 66, 87–88, 89–90
Crawford, T. Hartley, 311–15, 424, 426, 429
Creek Council: and Creek disintegration, 69; and Cusseta Treaty, 46, 61, 70; and debt fund, 77–78, 79; Lower, 72, 79; and missionaries, 66; protection of tribal lands by, 17, 33, 36–37, 43–45, 46, 71–72; and race, 39; and removal, 101–3, 120, 168–69; and speculators, 103; and Tuskenea, 26–27; Upper, 26–27, 72, 79, 422; Western, 81–82
Crowell, John, 26, 29, 34, 38, 47, 64, 79, 94–95, 183–84, 259
Crowell, Thomas, 34, 259
Cusseta Indians, 29–31, 126, 214
Cusseta party, 29, 30, 116–17
Cusseta town, 46, 104–5
Cusseta Treaty of 1832, 165, 324, 352; as blunder, 90, 96; and Creek census, 51–57, 67; and Creek debt fund, 71, 75–78; and Creek reserves, 96; and intruder removal, 51–67, 82–83; and John Brodnax, 94; negative effects of, 68–69; provisions of, 47–50

Dance of the Lakes, 172
Dawson, William C., 241–42

INDEX

debt fund commission, 76, 78–79
Doyle, Nimrod, 34, 99, 215
Duran, Jesse, 320–21

Earle, William, 224–25, 312
Elliott, John, 65
Emathla, Checote, 399–400, 403
Emathla, Efau, 29, 169, 170
Emathla, Fushatchee, 60
Emathla, Neah, 32–33, 37, 177, 221, 247–51, 279–80, 299
emigration. *See* removal, Creek; removal, settler
Escribano Indians, 374, 375–76, 383–84
Euchee Indians, 126, 177, 184, 186, 197, 257, 331, 392, 396; as labor source, 153, 423–24; and Seminole party, 31–32
Eufaula Indians, 59–60, 65–66, 83, 126–27, 154, 237–38, 255, 284
Eufaula town, 58, 126–27

Federal Road, 143, 172, 193, 293, 319
First Creek War, 12–13, 15, 28, 29, 31, 32, 55, 212, 225; and Creek politics, 23–24; and First Seminole War, 12–13, 28; similarities of, with Second Creek War, 172–73
Fixico, Cosa, 393
Fixico, Tallassee. *See* Yahola, Oakfuskee
Fixico, Tuscoona, 193, 306–7
Flournoy, William "Billy," 186–87, 392
Fontaine, John, 200, 302
Fort Gaines, 199, 201
Fort Gunn, 216
Fort Henderson, 216
Fort Jackson Treaty of 1814, 12, 32, 71
Fort Mitchell, 59, 60, 66, 82, 89, 113, 124, 153, 179, 223–24, 228, 252–53, 279, 281, 288, 300; and Creek resistance, 155–56; as removal camp, 329, 339, 350, 354, 375
Fort Twiggs, 206
Fort White Plains, 216
France, 222
Francis, Josiah, 224–25

Gayle, John, 85, 88, 90, 92–93, 95, 146–47, 150–51
General Chinubbee, 55–56
Georgia Guards, 162
Goldthwaite, George, 218

Grace, John, 82–83
Great Western Stage Line, 193, 195
grog shops, 64–65, 69, 86, 88, 133–34, 146–47, 153, 337, 408. *See also* liquor

Harding, E., 164–65, 208–9, 243
Hardridge, David, 195, 300, 304–5
Harjo, Coa, 398–99, 404–5
Harjo, Echo, 245, 283, 326–27; camp of, 218, 244–45, 329, 345–46, 351–52, 359
Harjo, Hillis. *See* Francis, Josiah
Harjo, Tuckabatchee, 214, 245, 283
Harjo, Yahola, 255, 327
Harjo, Yelker, 60, 255
Hawkins, Benjamin, 9–10, 31, 80–82
Hawkins, Samuel, 33, 80–81
Henry, Jim, 195, 206, 240, 255, 263, 282, 299, 301–6
Hentz, Michael, 290–91
Herring, Elbert, 68
High Log, 179, 244, 255
Hitchcock, Ethan Allan, 412–13, 421–22
Hitchitee Indians, 31, 142–43, 145
Hogan, John B., 151, 152–53, 155, 165–70, 178, 230, 235, 444n47, 454n14; and Creek resistance, 168–70, 178; as fraud investigator, 118–21; and land speculators, 224–25, 308–9; at Mobile Point, 389–90, 444n47, 454n14; as removal superintendent, 113–16, 122–30; in war, 182, 185, 208
Hooper, Johnson Jones, 316
horse stealing, 22
Howard, John H., 175, 180
Howison, Neil M., 378
Hoxie (major), 269, 289–90
Hutter, George C., 407–8
Hyperion, 200

Ichawaynotchaway Swamp, 288–89
Indian Springs Treaty, 14–15, 17, 33, 40
Indian Trade and Intercourse Act of 1834, 163
Irwin, William, 61, 205, 210–11, 243
Irwinton, 58–60, 65–66, 83, 126–27, 149–50, 191, 210–11, 335–36
Islands, James, 33, 99

Jackson, Andrew, 12–13, 22, 36, 71, 76, 87,

493

INDEX

Jackson, Andrew (cont.)
    113, 136, 165, 225, 311, 405, 434n6; and
    Cusseta Treaty, 48–49; drop in popularity
    of, 226–27; and John Gayle, 90–91; and
    land fraud, 117–19; and Seminole War,
    253–54, 325–26
Jernigan, Henry W., 268, 286, 288–89,
    350–52, 353
Jesup, Thomas S.: Creek campaign of, 229–
    30, 233–37, 239–40, 243–46, 247–55,
    263, 270; and Creek regiment, 323–29,
    334, 339–40; in Creek removal, 278–79,
    282–85, 299–300, 303, 319–21; and Geor-
    gia war, 287–88, 295–96; as Seminole
    War commander, 360, 364–65, 381–82,
    393–94, 407; and Winfield Scott, 317
Jim Boy, 245, 247–49, 255, 263, 283, 328,
    389–90, 394
Jones, Seaborn, 92, 205–6
Justice, Arch, 379, 425–26
justice system, Alabama, 149, 301, 321, 352–
    53, 394, 395; and Creek trials, 83, 89, 129;
    and federal courts, 65–66, 131–32; and
    Jim Henry, 304–7; jurisdiction of, over
    Creeks, 40, 43–44, 45
justice system, Creek, 69, 150–51, 154

Key, Francis Scott, 91–93, 95–96
Kinchafoonee, 267, 289–90
King, Kage, 415
King, William Rufus, 66–67

LaFayette, 191
Lame John, 345
land speculators. *See* speculation
Lewis, Dixon H., 41–42, 61, 311
Lindsay, William H., 338–39
liquor, 146, 162, 194, 320, 408; and Alabama
    law, 149; Creek addiction to, 62, 65, 69,
    88, 121, 133–35; Native dealers in, 138;
    and theft, 153. *See also* grog shops
Loachapoka, 29, 168–69, 185, 215, 346
Lower Creek territory, 21
Lumberton incident, 378
Lumpkin, Wilson, 142, 143

Mardis, Samuel W., 66
Marshall, Benjamin, 33, 79, 81, 118, 213–14,
    305, 421

Marshall, Joseph, 33
McCrabb, John W., 155, 176
McDougald, Daniel, 125, 155, 166–67, 316
McGillivray, Alexander, 30
McGillivray, William, 116, 329
McHenry, Robert, 97, 98–99, 104–5, 107,
    109–10, 112
McIntosh, Chilly, 33, 80–82
McIntosh, James S., 89, 179
McIntosh, William, 14–17, 28, 80–81
McIntosh party, 33, 35, 37, 39, 54, 80–81,
    305, 421, 422–23
McKenney, Thomas L., 22, 26
McKinnon, John L., 382, 385, 426
McLemore, Charles, 34, 106, 214–16, 237
McQueen, Peter, 28, 393
Meigs, Return J., 99–100
Menawa, 81, 211, 245–47, 330–31
Metamora, 241–42
Mexican-American Treaty of 1831, 115
Mexico, 115, 176, 222
Micanopy, 364
Micco, Autosee, 72
Micco, Cheske, 369
Micco, Econchattee, 384, 407–8
Micco, Hoboithle. *See* Tame King
Micco, Neah, 43, 132; arrest of, 148; and
    Creek debt, 77, 78–80, 115; and Creek
    politics, 29–30, 31, 35; and Cusseta
    Treaty, 61; and land speculators, 117, 125;
    and removal, 282–99; war role of, 182–84,
    214, 221, 239, 244–45, 251, 255–56
Micco, Neah (Fat King), 30
Micco, Toma, 72
Micco, Yahola, 326
Mikasuki Indians, 327
Milton, John, 81–82
miscegenation, 39, 53, 195–96, 280–81,
    302, 429
missionaries. *See* Christianity
Mississippian Indians, 75, 439n37
Mitchell, David B., 14, 15
Monticello, 238
Moore, Andrew, 287
Moore, John W., 211, 238, 243–44, 249, 255,
    261, 277–78
Motte, Jacob Rhett, 241, 260–62
Moultrie Creek Treaty, 32
Mount Vernon, 164–65, 208, 243

494

INDEX

Muscogee Indians, 11, 29, 31, 116–17, 214

Nelson, Charles H., 287, 332
New Echota Treaty, 161, 273, 276, 322, 337
Notasulga, 217

Okefenokee Swamp, 266, 291, 294
Oke-wo-nat, 337
Old Gouge. *See* Yahola, Opothle
Old Joe, 415
Oponee, John, 72, 213–14, 327
Osceola, 28, 196, 328
Owens, Hardiman, 84–85, 89, 92, 96

Page, John: as removal agent, 128, 129, 169, 175–77, 304–5, 345, 359, 390–91; war role of, 197–98, 345, 348, 350–51, 354
Parks, E. E., 179, 351, 354, 355–56, 358
Parsons, Benjamin S., 50–51, 53, 56, 73, 79, 80
Parsons, Enoch, 61–63, 73, 79–80, 87
Pascofar, 412–13
Patterson, John H., 208, 245, 251, 254, 256, 262, 282, 303, 307
Payne, John Howard, 157, 162, 174
personation, 103–5, 107, 308–9. *See also* speculation
Peterson, John H., Jr., 6
Poinsett, Joel, 358, 402
Pole Cat Springs removal camp, 329, 339, 340–42, 346–47, 354–58
Pugh, Lewis, 349

race, 35, 39–40, 53–54. *See also* miscegenation
Red Stick War. *See* First Creek War
removal, Creek, 203, 229–30, 237, 279–83, 287, 313, 350, 366; Andrew Jackson's view of, 22; as cause of war, 158, 165–66, 168–70; and Cherokee Creeks, 336–40; and Creek morality, 86–87; Creek opposition to, 37, 71–72; and Cusseta Treaty, 48–49; difficulties with, 121–24; in 1841, 424; and John B. Hogan, 113–20; and land fraud, 129–30; new approach to, 4–5; from removal camps, 388–91, 426–30; as source of profit, 136; and Thomas Jesup, 299–300, 319–25, 329–33; and western Creeks, 81–82

removal, settler, 57–67, 82–84, 87, 88, 93–94
Reynolds, John G., 340–42, 346–47, 354–57, 377, 386–87
Richards, Stephen, 398–400
Ridge, John, 14, 275
Roanoke, 199–200, 205, 210, 260–61, 266
Robinson, Alexander J., 127, 384
Ross, John, 161, 162, 338–39
Russell County volunteers, 352, 354, 355–56

Salli, George T., 219
Sanford, John W. A.: and land fraud, 97, 100, 104, 110, 112–13, 117, 312; in removal company, 117–20, 122–23; war role of, 202, 234, 241, 261, 272, 284–86, 289–90
Sawokli Indians, 145, 282
Sawokli town, 255
Schley, William, 175, 202–3, 233–35, 241–42, 272–75, 284–85, 295, 300–301, 312, 317–18
Scott, John, 34, 73, 82, 224, 308
Scott, Winfield: Alabama blockade of, 89; and court of inquiry, 316–17; as Creek War commander, 228–29, 230–35, 240–44, 249, 252–54, 256–59, 261–63, 264–67, 269–70; as Seminole War commander, 164
Seale, Arnold, 106–7
Second Seminole War, 2, 409
Selochta. *See* General Chinubbee
Seminole Indians: Creek flight to, 294, 296; and Creek regiment, 323, 328, 339; and Creek resistance, 152, 155, 157, 158–59, 164, 175, 196, 210; as party in Creek Nation, 31–33, 72, 142, 186, 214; resistance of, in Florida, 222, 230–31, 253; Thomas Jesup's campaign against, 364–65, 381–82, 389–90
Shackleford, Edward, 207, 209–10, 218
Shawnee Indians, 10, 172–73
Shearer, Gilbert, 177–78
Shorter, Eli S., 92, 103–6, 127–28, 143, 190–91, 224, 308, 310, 316
Shortridge, George D., 358
slavery: and army slave gangs, 209; and Creek regiment, 325–26, 394; and Creeks as slavers, 11, 15, 56–57, 147–49; Creeks threatened by, 37–40, 119, 137, 172–73,

slavery (cont.)
294; and enslavement of Creeks in Alabama, 428; and states' rights, 41–42; and taking of slaves, 130–32, 267
Sloan, T. P., 343, 345–46, 351–52, 359
Smith, Archibald, 372–76, 400, 402–3, 405
Sougahatchee, 29, 185, 216, 246, 342
Spanish Florida, 13, 14
speculation, 215; and Alabama development, 419; in Cherokee country, 163; in county seats, 131–32; in Creek lands, 49, 65, 67, 73, 81, 90, 92, 96, 99–100, 103–13; and fraud investigation, 124–29, 165–68, 178–79; by Indian countrymen, 34–35; and Jim Henry, 305; and removal, 118–21; role of, in starting war, 155, 204, 223–24, 225, 308–13, 315–16; in South, 382–83; and states' rights, 234; and Tuckabatchee land deal, 324, 327; and war profits, 243
Spencer, John C., 410
states' rights, 146, 234; and Georgia, 41–43; and Indian lands, 34–35, 128, 166–67, 225–26; and intruder controversy, 84–86, 89, 91, 93, 95; and removal camps, 328; and state law, 149; and war criticism, 300, 349
Stedham, John, 72, 213
Stell, Thomas J., 242
stickball, 134–35

Tallassee Indians, 27, 29, 169, 185, 188, 197, 211–12, 214–16, 467n9
Tallassee settlement, white, 177, 188, 212, 220, 256, 418
Tallassee town, Creek, 27–29, 120, 288
Tame King, 27–28, 30
Tarrant, Leonard, 97, 110, 124, 278
Tarver, Benjamin B., 308–9
Tecumseh, 9–12, 172–73
Tenskwatawa, 9–10
Texas, 102–3, 115, 176, 382–83
Totalugulnar. *See* Watoolahawka
Towns, George W. B., 190, 197
Troup, George M., 16–18, 42
Truman, O. K., 160
Tuckabatchee Indians, 23–28, 33, 102, 124, 319–20, 329–30, 422
Tuckabatchee party, 23, 26–27, 29–31, 72, 79–80, 81, 120, 212–13

Tuckabatchee town, 9–12, 14, 23, 72, 85, 122, 132, 329
Tuskenea: and Creek debt, 77, 78–80; as Creek headman, 26–30, 61; in removal camp, 347; removal opposition of, 114, 119, 120; and speculators, 110–11; war role of, 182–83, 244
Tustenuggee, Etomme, 33
Tustenuggee, Nulkarpuche, 284, 289

U.S. party, 33–35

Van Buren, Martin, 313, 348
Van Ness, James, 308
Vose, Josiah H., 410, 411–12

Walker, John, 397, 403, 407
Walker, William, 34, 110–11, 114, 123, 316, 326, 428
Walker's Town, 400, 403, 408
War Department: and Creek removal, 123, 168–69; and Creek War investigation, 311; and Cusseta Treaty, 48; and intruder removal, 66, 90, 101, 117; and land sales, 68, 82, 99; and search for Florida Creeks, 410, 414; and sending of troops to Cherokee country, 276
Ware, Robert J., 111
War of 1812, 12, 13–14, 224
Washington Treaty of 1826, 21, 75, 267
Watkins, Lewis, 65
Watoolahawka, 124–25, 165–66, 177
Watson, John H., 154, 186
Watson, J. S., 306
Wellborn, Levi T., 343–44
Wellborn, William, 127, 349–51, 353, 355–56, 364, 366–70, 379, 383–84, 408
West Point, 83, 108, 131
Wheat, Moses K., 426–27
White (general), 270
white roughs, 64, 144–47, 153, 194–95, 222, 273, 315, 333, 377–78, 380
Whitman, George, 348, 364, 365–66
Williams, John J., 106
Williams, Wiley, 153, 331–32
Williams family (Russell County), 423–24
Wilson, Henry, 377, 390, 392–93
women: as captives in Alabama, 425; as Florida refugees, 393, 400; and fraud

investigation, 125–26; and matrilineal descent, 26, 51–53, 337; protection of settlers by, 188; as rebel combatants, 220, 292, 293, 368; in removal camps, 320, 352, 357; sexual exploitation of, 134; and slavery, 15

Woodward, Thomas S., 34, 94–95, 110–11, 123, 159–60, 309, 316, 326, 330

Wool, John E., 276–77, 321–22, 336–38

world system: and Civil War, 422; and colonialism and commodification, 49–50, 137–38, 171, 223, 360; and Creek annuities, 30–31; and Creek land, 45–46; Creek resistance to, 180, 185, 196; as historical context, 3–4, 13; impact of, on Lower Creeks, 21–22; lower class resistance to, 144, 147, 434n4; racism of, 35–36, 38–40, 315; as religion, 298, 333; role of, in co-opting Native practices, 16–17; and slavery, 10–11, 294; and warfare, 207

Wright, Benjamin Drake, 380–81, 386

Yahola, Assi. *See* Osceola

Yahola, Oakfuskee, 125, 211

Yahola, Opothle: in Civil War, 423; and Creek debt, 79, 81–82; and Creek regiment, 319–20, 323–25, 329; as defender of Creek land, 35–37; and fraud investigation, 107–11; and Neah Micco, 30, 31; and removal, 72, 167; as slaveholder, 38; and speculators, 224; and Texas, 102–4, 115–16; as Tuckabatchee party chief, 14, 23–24; and Tuskenea, 25–26, 27, 30; and U.S. party, 35; war role of, 212–13, 216–17, 245–46, 249, 255–56, 283

Yargee, 38, 156

Young, Benjamin, 348, 354

IN THE INDIANS OF THE SOUTHEAST SERIES

The Payne-Butrick Papers, Volumes 1, 2, 3
The Payne-Butrick Papers, Volumes 4, 5, 6
Edited and annotated by
William L. Anderson, Jane L. Brown,
and Anne F. Rogers

*Deerskins and Duffels: The Creek Indian
Trade with Anglo-America, 1685–1815*
By Kathryn E. Holland Braund

*Searching for the Bright Path: The Mississippi
Choctaws from Prehistory to Removal*
By James Taylor Carson

*Demanding the Cherokee Nation: Indian
Autonomy and American Culture, 1830–1900*
By Andrew Denson

*A Kingdom of Water: Adaptation
and Survival in the Houma Nation*
By J. Daniel d'Oney

*The Second Creek War: Interethnic Conflict
and Collusion on a Collapsing Frontier*
By John T. Ellisor

*Cherokee Americans: The Eastern Band
of Cherokees in the Twentieth Century*
By John R. Finger

*Creeks and Southerners:
Biculturalism on the Early American Frontier*
By Andrew K. Frank

Choctaw Genesis, 1500–1700
By Patricia Galloway

*The Southeastern Ceremonial Complex:
Artifacts and Analysis
The Cottonlandia Conference*
Edited by Patricia Galloway
Exhibition Catalog by David H. Dye
and Camille Wharey

The Invention of the Creek Nation, 1670–1763
By Steven C. Hahn

*Rivers of Sand: Creek Indian Emigration,
Relocation, and Ethnic Cleansing in
the American South*
By Christopher D. Haveman

*Bad Fruits of the Civilized Tree: Alcohol and
the Sovereignty of the Cherokee Nation*
By Izumi Ishii

*Epidemics and Enslavement:
Biological Catastrophe in the
Native Southeast, 1492–1715*
By Paul Kelton

*An Assumption of Sovereignty:
Social and Political Transformation among
the Florida Seminoles, 1953–1979*
By Harry A. Kersey Jr.

*Up from These Hills:
Memories of a Cherokee Boyhood*
By Leonard Carson Lambert Jr.
As told to Michael Lambert

*The Caddo Chiefdoms:
Caddo Economics and Politics, 700–1835*
By David La Vere

The Moravian Springplace Mission to the Cherokees, Volume 1: 1805–1813
The Moravian Springplace Mission to the Cherokees, Volume 2: 1814–1821
Edited and introduced by Rowena McClinton

The Moravian Springplace Mission to the Cherokees, Abridged Edition
Edited and with an introduction by Rowena McClinton

Keeping the Circle: American Indian Identity in Eastern North Carolina, 1885–2004
By Christopher Arris Oakley

Choctaws in a Revolutionary Age, 1750–1830
By Greg O'Brien

Choctaw Resurgence in Mississippi: Race, Class, and Nation Building in the Jim Crow South, 1830–1977
By Katherine M. B. Osburn

Cherokee Women: Gender and Culture Change, 1700–1835
By Theda Perdue

The Brainerd Journal: A Mission to the Cherokees, 1817–1823
Edited and introduced by Joyce B. Phillips and Paul Gary Phillips

Seminole Voices: Reflections on Their Changing Society, 1970–2000
By Julian M. Pleasants and Harry A. Kersey Jr.

The Yamasee War: A Study of Culture, Economy, and Conflict in the Colonial South
By William L. Ramsey

The Cherokees: A Population History
By Russell Thornton

Buffalo Tiger: A Life in the Everglades
By Buffalo Tiger and Harry A. Kersey Jr.

American Indians in the Lower Mississippi Valley: Social and Economic Histories
By Daniel H. Usner Jr.

William Bartram on the Southeastern Indians
Edited and annotated by Gregory A. Waselkov and Kathryn E. Holland Braund

Powhatan's Mantle: Indians in the Colonial Southeast
Edited by Peter H. Wood, Gregory A. Waselkov, and M. Thomas Hatley

Creeks and Seminoles: The Destruction and Regeneration of the Muscogulge People
By J. Leitch Wright Jr.

To order or obtain more information on these or other University of Nebraska Press titles, visit nebraskapress.unl.edu.

www.ingramcontent.com/pod-product-compliance
Lightning Source LLC
Chambersburg PA
CBHW021824220426
43663CB00005B/124